Utilizing Emotional Experience for Best Learning Design Practices

Sarah Sniderman
Learning Codes Inc., Canada

Published in the United States of America by
IGI Global
701 E. Chocolate Avenue
Hershey PA, USA 17033
Tel: 717-533-8845
Fax: 717-533-8661
E-mail: cust@igi-global.com
Web site: https://www.igi-global.com

Copyright © 2025 by IGI Global. All rights reserved. No part of this publication may be reproduced, stored or distributed in any form or by any means, electronic or mechanical, including photocopying, without written permission from the publisher.
Product or company names used in this set are for identification purposes only. Inclusion of the names of the products or companies does not indicate a claim of ownership by IGI Global of the trademark or registered trademark.

Library of Congress Cataloging-in-Publication Data

CIP PENDING

ISBN13: 9798369326633
EISBN13: 9798369326640

Vice President of Editorial: Melissa Wagner
Managing Editor of Acquisitions: Mikaela Felty
Managing Editor of Book Development: Jocelynn Hessler
Production Manager: Mike Brehm
Cover Design: Phillip Shickler

British Cataloguing in Publication Data
A Cataloguing in Publication record for this book is available from the British Library.

All work contributed to this book is new, previously-unpublished material.
The views expressed in this book are those of the authors, but not necessarily of the publisher.

Table of Contents

Foreword xvii

Acknowledgement xxiii

Preface xxiv

Chapter 1
A Tale of Two Occupational Health and Safety Programs 1
Lynda Jane Williams, University of Northern BC, Canada
Corrie Pitzer, SAFEMap International, Canada

Section 1
Theoretical Foundations: Broad Strokes

Chapter 2
The Interplay of Emotion and Cognition in Adult Learning: Learning Engages Emotion Alongside Cognition 17
Islam Asim Ismail, The English and Foreign Languages University, India
Fahad Saleh Aljabr, University of Ha'il, Saudi Arabia

Chapter 3
Heutagogy Weds Emotional Experience to Breed New Learning Design Practices 45
Urmila R. Menon, LEAD College of Management, Palakkad, India

Chapter 4
Emotional Learning Analytics in Education: Current Status, Trends, and Challenges 71
Kyriaki A. Tychola, MLV Research Group, Department of Informatics, Democritus University of Thrace, Kavala, Greece
Eleni Vrochidou, MLV Research Group, Department of Informatics, Democritus University of Thrace, Kavala, Greece
George A. Papakostas, MLV Research Group, Department of Informatics, Democritus University of Thrace, Kavala, Greece

Section 2
Theoretical Foundations: Narrowing the Focus

Chapter 5
Enhancing Online Adult Learning Through Emotional Social Intelligence
Instructional Competencies 119
    Carrie M. Grimes, Vanderbilt University, USA

Chapter 6
Examining the Role and Effect of Emotions in Adults' Online Learning 155
    J. B. Oleet, Mississippi State University, USA
    Chien Yu, Mississippi State University, USA

Chapter 7
Enhancing Adult Lifelong Learning: A Study of Social-Emotional Learning
Theory 205
    Jerine Jain Mathew, Christ University, India
    Sridevi Nair, Christ University, India

Chapter 8
Into It, Out of It: Emotions Can Prepare Us for and Prevent Us From
Performance 223
    Ian Gaither, Instructio Educational Services, Canada

Section 3
Putting Theory to the Test

Chapter 9
Fiction as Reflective Praxis for Affective Domain Learning in Medicine and
Healthcare Education: A Case Study From Pedagogic Practice 253
    Catherine Hayes, University of Sunderland, UK

Chapter 10
Kudumbashree Women Back to School in Kerala: Navigating Classroom
Emotions and Optimizing Instructor-Student Rapport for Enhanced Learning
Design 289
    Vishnu Achutha Menon, Institute for Educational and Developmental
        Studies, Noida, India

Chapter 11
Tiptoeing Through Interweaving Hero and Collective Journey Elements
in Course Design Practices: Motivation in Designing the Hero's Journey
Departure 317
    Caroline M. Crawford, University of Houston-Clear Lake, USA
    James L. Dillard, University of Calgary, Canada

Chapter 12
An Investigation of Students' Emotions, Emotion Regulation Strategies, and
Motives for Emotion Regulation 355
    Eda Bakır-Yalçın, Recep Tayyip Erdoğan University, Turkey
    Yasin Yalçın, Recep Tayyip Erdoğan University, Turkey

Chapter 13
Underlying Workplace Emotional Impacts upon a Professor's Experiential
Approach 379
    Caroline M. Crawford, University of Houston-Clear Lake, USA

Section 4
Focus on Educator Preparation

Chapter 14
Educator Preparation Design Practices That Encourage Candidate Social-
Emotional and Affective Competencies as Needed Dispositions for Teaching 419
    Billi L. Bromer, Independent Researcher, USA

Chapter 15
Promoting Pre-Service ESOL Teachers' Understanding of English Learners'
Social-Emotional Learning 449
    Brian Hibbs, Dalton State College, USA

Section 5
Learner Perspectives

Chapter 16
Arcie Mallari 479
    Arcie Mallari, Silid Aralan, Inc., Philippines

Chapter 17
Linda Alexanian 485
    Linda Alexanian, Organic Weave, Canada

Chapter 18
Mary Ann Becker 491
    Mary Ann Becker, Independent Researcher, USA

Chapter 19
Xuan-Vinh Nguyen 505
   Xuan-Vinh Nguyen, Independent Researcher, Canada

Conclusion 513

Compilation of References 515

About the Contributors 597

Index 605

Detailed Table of Contents

Foreword xvii

Acknowledgement xxiii

Preface xxiv

Chapter 1
A Tale of Two Occupational Health and Safety Programs 1
    Lynda Jane Williams, University of Northern BC, Canada
    Corrie Pitzer, SAFEMap International, Canada

This is an experience-based examination of the contrast between cognitive and affective outcomes in two programs within the same field. Both programs are delivered online without explicit instructional leadership, making them comparable with respect to delivery methodology. Conclusions drawn from the instructional design perspective expose the intrinsic difference between these two different types of outcomes, reflected not just in the delivery of training but also in appropriate methods of evaluation.

Section 1
Theoretical Foundations: Broad Strokes

Chapter 2
The Interplay of Emotion and Cognition in Adult Learning: Learning
Engages Emotion Alongside Cognition... 17
    Islam Asim Ismail, The English and Foreign Languages University,
       India
    Fahad Saleh Aljabr, University of Ha'il, Saudi Arabia

Learning holistically engages emotion and cognition, yet education often overlooks affective processes. This chapter explores their dynamic interplay through a comprehensive literature review examining theories on how emotions shape learning. The aims are to establish an evidence-based framework emphasizing the intentional integration of factors like motivation, curiosity, and self-efficacy with cognitive objectives in instructional design. The methodology includes synthesizing foundational theories and empirical studies, then exemplifying transformative potential through case studies demonstrating enhanced engagement and holistic development when addressing emotions. Results reveal that emotions can enable adults to take risks, overcome barriers, and achieve meaningful change through learning. Also, emotion and cognition are fundamentally intertwined; practical pedagogical approaches must integrate intellectual to unlock human potential. The chapter proposes an Emotional Learning Design framework for an impactful education through person-centered humanistic instructional practices.

Chapter 3
Heutagogy Weds Emotional Experience to Breed New Learning Design
Practices 45
    Urmila R. Menon, LEAD College of Management, Palakkad, India

This chapter explores the intersection of heutagogy and emotional experience in the evolution of learning design practices. Through a historical lens, it scrutinises the transition of learning methodologies, highlighting the pivotal role of technology and societal shifts. Furthermore, it scrutinises the future landscape of learning design, forecasting trends and emerging paradigms. Central to this exploration is the significance of emotional experience in the learning process. By synthesising heutagogical principles with emotional intelligence, novel learning design practices emerge, tailored to individual needs and preferences. Drawing on psychological insights, this section explores the complex connection between hormones and self-directed learning, revealing the physiological foundations of effective learning. Finally, it offers practical recommendations for educators and instructional designers, advocating for the integration of emotional engagement and self-directed learning strategies in the development of innovative learning models.

Chapter 4
Emotional Learning Analytics in Education: Current Status, Trends, and
Challenges.. 71
    Kyriaki A. Tychola, MLV Research Group, Department of Informatics,
        Democritus University of Thrace, Kavala, Greece
    Eleni Vrochidou, MLV Research Group, Department of Informatics,
        Democritus University of Thrace, Kavala, Greece
    George A. Papakostas, MLV Research Group, Department of
        Informatics, Democritus University of Thrace, Kavala, Greece

Learning Analytics (LA) are constantly evolving in the analysis and representation of data related to learners and educators to improve the learning and education process. Data obtained by sensors or questionnaires are processed employing new technologies. The emotional experiences of learners constitute a significant factor in the assimilation of knowledge about the learning process. The emerging technology of Emotional Learning Analytics (ELA) is increasingly being considered in educational settings. In this work, the significance and contribution of ELA in educational data processing are discussed as an integral part of designing and implementing computational models reflecting the learning process. In addition, a comprehensive overview of different methods and techniques for both LA and ELA is provided, while a conceptual model of ELA is proposed in parallel. Moreover, advantages, disadvantages, and challenges are highlighted. The final focus of the chapter is on ethical issues and future research directions.

Section 2
Theoretical Foundations: Narrowing the Focus

Chapter 5
Enhancing Online Adult Learning Through Emotional Social Intelligence
Instructional Competencies 119
    Carrie M. Grimes, Vanderbilt University, USA

The shift from traditional in-person classroom learning to legitimized programs of online learning for adult degree-seeking professionals has opened significant access and opportunity for institutions of higher education, as well as for the adult learners they serve. However, this increase in online graduate degree offerings has posed challenges to educators and the students they serve. Some of the most significant challenges for instructors are building and maintaining interpersonal connections and a socio-emotionally rewarding climate for learners. This chapter provides an analysis of how instructors can leverage emotional social intellligence (ESI) competencies in order to design and deliver learning experiences which support the unique needs of professional degree-seeking adult online learners in emotionally impactful ways. This chapter will specifically describe how online instructors may strategically use an ESI instructional framework to guide adult learners through beneficial socio-emotional learning experiences, in order to positively impact learning outcomes.

Chapter 6
Examining the Role and Effect of Emotions in Adults' Online Learning 155
    J. B. Oleet, Mississippi State University, USA
    Chien Yu, Mississippi State University, USA

For an online learning environment, educators can use the power of emotion to affect learning; therefore, it is essential to consider the emotional aspects of online learning when designing a learning environment. The purpose of this chapter is to examine current studies of learners' emotions during the online learning process and provide an up-to-date understanding of the issues as well as challenges pertinent to online teaching and learning. In addition to highlighting the dual role of emotions, the chapter illustrates how both positive and negative emotions can impact cognitive processes such as memory, attention, and problem-solving. It emphasizes the importance of fostering emotional awareness and self-regulation among learners, using strategies like reflective journaling and emotional logging. The chapter also provides practical recommendations for instructional designers and aims to create a compelling and emotionally supportive online learning environment, addressing the unique challenges posed by the pandemic and preparing learners for future disruptions.

Chapter 7
Enhancing Adult Lifelong Learning: A Study of Social-Emotional Learning
Theory 205
Jerine Jain Mathew, Christ University, India
Sridevi Nair, Christ University, India

This chapter explores the possibility of applying social-emotional learning theory to adult learning experiences and creating lifelong learners. Social-emotional learning (SEL) theory is a framework that emphasizes the use of tools and techniques focused on the development of social and emotional skills to improve overall well-being and success in life. It is based on the belief that individuals who possess these skills are better equipped to manage their emotions, build positive relationships, and make responsible decisions. In educational settings, SEL theory is often applied to help students develop these skills, which are seen as critical for academic success and personal well-being. It is implemented through explicit instruction, modeling, and practice, as well as through the creation of supportive learning environments. In recent years, there has been a growing interest in applying SEL theory to adult learners.

Chapter 8
Into It, Out of It: Emotions Can Prepare Us for and Prevent Us From
Performance 223
Ian Gaither, Instructio Educational Services, Canada

Emotional states can have a profound influence on learning and performance by facilitating or obstructing access to skills and knowledge. At one end of the emotional spectrum, Ideal Performance States (IPS) – achieved through optimal physiological and psychological arousal and self-efficacy – enable performers to fully access their innate and trained skills. At the opposite end, startling or surprising events can trigger "mental upset," that is, cognitive paralysis, loss of situational awareness, and ultimately loss of judgment. Domains such as sports psychology, aviation, and medicine have developed various tools and techniques to help performers attain and maintain the mental and emotional state they need to perform, supporting self-efficacy, resilience, and adaptability. Increasingly available immersive technologies such as virtual reality offer unprecedented access to opportunities to develop these and many other emotional skills, such as the ability to increase or decrease emotional responses to events in the outside world or even change how one experiences physical pain.

Section 3
Putting Theory to the Test

Chapter 9
Fiction as Reflective Praxis for Affective Domain Learning in Medicine and
Healthcare Education: A Case Study From Pedagogic Practice........................ 253
    Catherine Hayes, University of Sunderland, UK

Being able to effectively teach for affective learning domain delivery is now pivotal in instances of medical and healthcare education where numbers of older adults are rising exponentially in the United Kingdom (UK) as a direct demographic consequence of the baby boom generation. As a healthcare professional discipline, podiatric medicine has a key role in the maintenance of ambulatory health and wellbeing for older adults, so these statistics have clear implications for the education and training of graduates within this academic discipline. In the context of allied health professional practice, future practitioners need to be equipped and prepared not only to provide functional podiatric management but also to understand and integrate the greater sociological implications of an ageing population into practice. This chapter uses an illustrative case study from teaching practice to engage readers in the use of televised fiction to stimulate critical reflective practice when working with vulnerable older people and their families and carers.

Chapter 10
Kudumbashree Women Back to School in Kerala: Navigating Classroom
Emotions and Optimizing Instructor-Student Rapport for Enhanced Learning
Design 289
    Vishnu Achutha Menon, Institute for Educational and Developmental
       Studies, Noida, India

Kudumbashree is preparing to launch "Thirike Schoolil" or "Back to School," an ambitious campaign aimed at its 46 lakh members. This seeks to strengthen the organization's three-tier system and empower its women members to explore new opportunities. "Thirike Schoolil" aims to bolster the micro-economic livelihood activities of Neighbourhood Groups, raise awareness about digital technology, and foster a vision that elevates the status of women in society. In line with these efforts, the objective of this study is to investigate the impact of instructor-student rapport on the emotional support, emotion work, and emotional valence experienced by Kudumbashree women in school classrooms across Kerala. To achieve this goal, the study utilizes the Classroom Emotion Scale and Instructor-Student Rapport Scale as primary instruments for data collection. These instruments are carefully selected to assess both the emotional experiences of participants and the rapport dynamics between instructors and students within the classroom environment.

Chapter 11
Tiptoeing Through Interweaving Hero and Collective Journey Elements
in Course Design Practices: Motivation in Designing the Hero's Journey
Departure 317
    Caroline M. Crawford, University of Houston-Clear Lake, USA
    James L. Dillard, University of Calgary, Canada

Two participant case studies associated with online course design practices were framed through a basic qualitative analysis, including one instructor participant and one collegial learner participant. The lens through which online course design is framed are the motivational aspects of learning, paralleling the hero's journey and the associated collective journey within course design and considering the implementation of a course experience, through noting the elements of emotional engagement and experiential learning as necessary recognitions. After a thorough analysis the articulated ten themes are: Progressive Learner Engagement of Pedagogy, Andragogy, and Heutagogy; Communities of Practice and Landscapes of Practice Approaches; Collective Unconscious/Cognitive Dissonance; Interactive Activities; and, Philosophical Understanding/Differentiated Perceptions.

Chapter 12
An Investigation of Students' Emotions, Emotion Regulation Strategies, and
Motives for Emotion Regulation 355
    Eda Bakır-Yalçın, Recep Tayyip Erdoğan University, Turkey
    Yasin Yalçın, Recep Tayyip Erdoğan University, Turkey

This study aimed to identify the emotions experienced by students engaged in a project assignment for the Instructional Technologies course, the emotion regulation strategies they employed, and the motives behind their use of these strategies. The sample comprised 20 undergraduate students enrolled in the Instructional Technologies course at a state university in Turkey. Conducted as an explanatory case study, the research revealed that students commonly felt anxiety and excitement during the project preparation phase, excitement during the presentation phase, and relief post-presentation. Situation modification strategies were the most frequently used emotion regulation techniques, primarily for instrumental reasons to enhance performance. Furthermore, students often experienced multiple emotions and utilized various strategies to regulate these emotions. In this chapter, we discuss our findings in light of the related literature and make recommendations for emotional processes in the educational context.

Chapter 13
Underlying Workplace Emotional Impacts upon a Professor's Experiential
Approach 379
    Caroline M. Crawford, University of Houston-Clear Lake, USA

This autoethnographic case study focuses upon a university professor's experiences within a workplace environment, that impacted learning design approaches and practices. The strengths, weaknesses, opportunities, and threats within the workplace environment supported the creatively engaging and critically analytic approach to embracing areas of control and positive impact within the work environment. Through the storytelling narrative approach that progresses through a Currere Method of engagement, complex conversations may occur. Through these complex and difficult conversations, recognitions and outcomes that the case study participant would not have proactively engaged in learning design practices that were ultimately positive, impactful, and deeply meaningful to the learning outcomes of students progressing through degree-focused coursework. The sense of "becoming" within this case study is strengthened and on display throughout the Currere Method's journey.

Section 4
Focus on Educator Preparation

Chapter 14
Educator Preparation Design Practices That Encourage Candidate Social-
Emotional and Affective Competencies as Needed Dispositions for Teaching 419
    Billi L. Bromer, Independent Researcher, USA

University based educator preparation practices within onsite and online formats provide the practical knowledge and skills required for effective teaching but do not adequately provide a self-discovery experience where the needed social emotional growth of teacher candidates and the affective aspects of teaching are nurtured and encouraged. Enhanced self-awareness of the emotions experienced by teachers in daily encounters with students can be a component of educator preparation and its inclusion may minimize the stressors that lead to compassion fatigue and teacher burnout.

Chapter 15
Promoting Pre-Service ESOL Teachers' Understanding of English Learners'
Social-Emotional Learning 449
    Brian Hibbs, Dalton State College, USA

This chapter explores a research study intended to document and understand ESOL (English to Speakers of Other Languages) teacher candidates' experiences regarding a course unit on social-emotional learning for English learners. The chapter begins with an overview of social-emotional learning and its relevancy for multilingual learners of English. Next, the chapter reviews several studies that have investigated the role of the approach in (language) teacher education. The chapter then outlines the logistics of multimodule course unit on social-emotional learning embedded within a language teaching methodology course. Finally, the chapter summarizes the results of an exploratory study designed to document and understand teacher candidates' perspectives regarding the strengths and weaknesses of the course unit.

Section 5
Learner Perspectives

Chapter 16
Arcie Mallari 479
    Arcie Mallari, Silid Aralan, Inc., Philippines

Arcie shares his insights into empowerment and resilience through self-directed learning. He is currently exploring the benefits and applications of project-based learning. He wishes to become proficient in using these methodologies and tools to create curricula for students of Silid Aralan, the non-governmental organization he founded in 2007 to help low-performing, underprivileged learners in the Philippines and Indonesia. Arcie advocates that the classroom is the world. We cannot contain learning in a box; learning is everywhere.

Chapter 17
Linda Alexanian 485
    Linda Alexanian, Organic Weave, Canada

Linda describes her approach to personal and professional growth as both an entrepreneur and a mother of entrepreneurs. She learns for understanding and discovery, rather than mastery. When she first started her business five years ago, she made mistakes. Now not only is she learning from them, but she has taken a whole new approach to gaining the skills and knowledge she needs to become successful. She's moving beyond previous experiences and assumptions, asking the right questions, and exploring many paths to find answers.

Chapter 18
Mary Ann Becker 491
    Mary Ann Becker, Independent Researcher, USA

Mary Ann is pursuing ongoing creative development as a photographer, walking the streets of Paris and forests beyond the city. She hopes that she can provide others with social and historical information regarding what she has experienced, the places and the people she has visited and photographed. In this chapter, she strives to make others feel that they are not alone in the ways they process information, perceive the world, and learn. Every learner is unique and has something special to offer.

Chapter 19
Xuan-Vinh Nguyen 505
    Xuan-Vinh Nguyen, Independent Researcher, Canada

Xuan-Vinh solves business problems by continuing to develop as a curious generalist who is able to apply methodologies and tools acquired through past experiences to each new situation. He currently works as a project manager in the Information Technology space, which continues to evolve at a fast pace. He believes training can be pursued for several different reasons: to improve performance, to explore what we're curious about, and to understand more about the broader context in which we work. He is especially passionate about the Why. Why are we doing this as an organization? Why is this important?

Conclusion 513

Compilation of References 515

About the Contributors 597

Index 605

Foreword

When Sarah first approached me with the idea of a book on emotions and learning, focused on practical applications in professional contexts with adults, I was immediately hooked. I have four decades of experience in training and development, adult education (formal and informal), professional education (medicine, law, engineering), and higher education, as well as both the technological and human or organizational sides of learning technology development and adoption. I have worked in the trenches, developing programs and curriculum, as a consultant, project lead, and learning industry executive. I also have 35 years of experience training learning professionals in graduate programs. Across a broad range of experiences, I have observed how the affective side of things often gets ignored. And, at the same time, I am also familiar with the history of research on the affective domain and its limited place in the curriculum for students studying in subfields such as instructional design and development. So, an edited book of contributions concerning how researchers and practitioners are addressing the affective domain in current practice and thought seemed topical and a real contribution to the field.

Sarah, with her long-time interests in allied topics such as creativity, vulnerability, imagination, and complex problem-solving, with her wealth of professional experience – over twenty-five years – developing curriculum and training programs and working as a consultant in strategic human resources management, and with her willingness to approach messy problems, seemed an ideal person to put together a book that would address how the affective domain is conceptualized and accounted for in the development and delivery of professional and adult training programs out 'in the wild,' in the second decade of the new millennium. In those early discussions in coffee shops in the Fall of 2023, a decision was made to cast a wide net, so that the book might capture aspects of conceptualization, of theory, models or frameworks, and also examples of real practice on the ground. This is reflected in the organization of the contributions into the five subsections that comprise the book.

Drawing on my own experience, I recall that in early work I was involved with in the financial and transport industries I had to argue vigorously (not always successfully) to include motivational components in new training programs. If we expect people to change their behaviours and adopt new ways of working, then we have to have a broad outlook. We need, of course, to align the expected changes carefully with messaging and with performance measurement and management but, crucially, we also have to show workers 'what is in it for them' and the real impact on other stakeholders – colleagues, the organization, their customers. In short, we have to give them reasons to care.

It would seem obvious that addressing the motivation to learn new things and to transfer that learning, and identifying and promoting the learning and internalization of appropriate attitudes and values, are key to real and effective change. But too often the focus in L&D is on the cognitive element – knowledge and skills – to the utter exclusion of considerations of affect, motivation, attitude, values, and certainly of 'emotion.' We pay little attention to how affect will influence learning, and we ignore elements that we should be striving to teach or inculcate that constitute some form of affect – attitudes, values, motivations. Oddly, the resistance I encountered in addressing the affective dimension often came not from the line of business concerned or from executives, but from L&D. The focus on, and accountability for, delivering on time and on budget, or restrictions on hours of training, often mitigated against a more expansive approach that would incorporate affective components.

This is true even when competence-based approaches, which explicitly reference the place of affect in learning and performance, are involved. Competence-based programs, as the reader likely knows, are based on defining bundles of knowledge, skills *and attitudes*, or KSAs, that underpin performance on the job. Yet, even here, where attitudes figure so explicitly, there is often little attention given to the 'A's.

A notable exception and a good illustration of the critical importance of attitudes and dispositions in my own experience comes from my work over five years helping the International Civil Aviation Organization (ICAO) develop the competence-based approach and standards recently introduced for ICAO-accredited training and certifications across the Aviation industry worldwide. A key element in the aviation industry competency models is 'situational awareness.' This is, generally speaking, the ability of, say, a pilot, to observe and understand their current context, to project this understanding into the future to anticipate threats to operations and safety, and to formulate strategies to avoid or to respond to potential threats. It could equally be critical to the work of ground crew, pilots, flight crew, cabin crew, or airport management staff. Situational awareness requires skills and knowledge of operational contexts and systems, but it is fundamentally a *dispositional* competency and an attitude (perhaps even with underlying values). It speaks to the performer's attitude of vigilance, her ability to imagine possible scenarios, and her willingness to invest the effort to apply knowledge in a particular, imaginative way. The emergence of the central importance of situational awareness – in many forms and circumstances – is, I would say, a direct consequence of creating a model of developing competencies. Pursuing a competence-based approach to training is admittedly an effortful endeavour, but one can hope that the evolution towards competence-based models and approaches will still favour greater consideration of attitudes and the affective side of things

Leaving aside competence-based approaches, increasingly, today, there seems to be a recognition that addressing emotions and affect in the curriculum is important. This is clearly evident in, say, the curriculum of medical schools, nursing, and health sciences programs, and even generally in primary, secondary, and tertiary education, with e.g., the current emphasis on developing qualities such as 'empathy.' The research, though, on how best actually to promote the aim of inculcating empathic attitudes and behaviours, is still quite new. And less is known about how different educational or training programs *transfer* to the specific, often challenging operational contexts in which medical practitioners or primary school children must function, than we would like.

Building on the comments above, the issue of measurement, carried out in work contexts rather than laboratories, and the difficulties of measuring and understanding the mechanisms and conditions of transfer, have played some significant role in dictating the minimal attention to affect we observe in the history of training design, development, and delivery. The problem of measurement has probably played a role also in the secondary interest in academic research afforded to affect in general (and similarly to narrower constructs related to emotion and motivation), as compared with the study of aspects of perception and cognitive information-processing.

Pick up a textbook from the 80s with "Learning Theories" prominent in the title and you will find only a small proportion of content related to motivation and affect. Possibly there is some discussion of self-efficacy or an account of Keller's ARCS model (Keller, 1983, Keller & Kopp, 1987). Most of the readers who are in the field of learning and development will know of the ARCS Attention-model. Arguably, the ARCS model serves as a broad framework that can integrate research on constructs such as attention, boredom, self-efficacy, curiosity, flow, intrinsic and extrinsic motivation, attribution, and more. But in the end, it is simply that, a compendium of theories and ideas, and a template indicating the factors or dimensions that must be addressed in the design of effective instruction that takes the affective side into consideration. There is little in the way of specific prescriptions; the model is really a shorthand way of referencing a wide variety of theories and constructs.

One can also find, even from this time frame, approaches that are more specifically informative, and not simply a framework that organizes other sources of knowledge – theories, if you like, rather than simply a 'model.' A good example is Thomas Malone's (1981) *theory of intrinsically motivating instruction.* Malone carried out controlled experiments to identify what makes video games ("Pong," in that era!) so compelling and addictive. He questioned whether an understanding of those features that drive us to engage with such games could be generalized to features we should build into the design of instruction to ensure it is similarly intrinsically motivating. By manipulating the characteristics of the game and observing players' responses, specifically their engagement levels, he identified key elements – "challenge," "fantasy," and "curiosity" – that must be present and how they can be incorporated and manipulated.

While a lovely example of experimental research in the field, and a compelling one, Malone's theory, like the ARCS model and so much other work of previous decades, focuses on constructs that have a strong cognitive or information-processing dimension, and it also assumes an individualistic perspective. That is, the affective domain is addressed and interpreted from the standpoint of an individual learner and their internal states and processes. A general criticism of this might be developed from the circumstance that increasingly we also try to view learning through a socio-cultural lens that emphasizes the role of material culture, cultural context, and social processes. Learning does not merely occur in isolation (with a book, or hunched over a computer that delivers 'adaptive or personalized learning'…); our motivational states, emotions, and values obviously are a function of social engagement and the human and material contexts in which we find ourselves.

Even restricting ourselves to the individual perspective, it is now very clear – both from neurological or brain sciences studies and psychological studies – that affect and cognition are separate only as artificial abstractions from what is a far more integral reality. The evidence is now clear that memory, attention, focus, and reasoning are all conditioned by, and fundamentally dependent on, mood, emotional arousal, and other affective states. This is reflected in influential concepts and theories such as 'hot vs cold cognition' (Brand, 1986) and 'motivated reasoning' (Kunda, 1987; 1990) which emphasize the role of emotions and emotion-related brain subsystems in our thinking, reasoning, and behaviour. Fortunately, such developments have made their way into the current generation of typical "Learning Theories" textbooks.

More and more, emotion, motivation, and affect are coming to the fore among both our academic (or scientific) and popular ideas concerning learning. It is not hard to discern the larger landscape of this. In both academic research and the popular imagination, the notions of creativity, boredom, trauma, grit, empathy, self-esteem, identity, self-efficacy and self-concept, and well-being and emotional intelligence (to mention those that come to mind first) have assumed a large presence. Some of this is, of course, controversial, and some of these constructs (consider the vast 'wellness' industry) have even been essentially hijacked for commercial gain. But that the role of affect – whether in respect to how we learn, or what we should learn

– has taken on greater prominence is a welcome development both in the study of learning and in the education and practices of learning professionals.

Not surprisingly, we move forward in fits and starts, and along multiple trajectories – studies of brain function by neuropsychologists alongside studies of 'transformative learning experiences' in adults by sociologists. There is no way to neatly organize and categorize the emerging bodies of knowledge and practice, and in fact, there will never be any unifying theory of the role of affect in learning. There are diverse methods and paradigms of research, too many phenomena, too many contexts.

Given this reality, I would be happy to approach a book like this as an eclectic mix of different perspectives and experiences whose contributions can, I think, be connected in multiple ways to our own experiences and understanding. I would also urge the reader to pay attention to the perspective and role of the learners themselves. This is one of the interesting, recurrent themes that emerges from the various chapters: the role or contribution of the learners themselves, as distinct from the impact of the specific design of an instructional or educational program. Throughout the chapters, we encounter the pivotal role of e.g., self-direction, motivation, and self-awareness on the part of the learner, and the significance of the commitment of the learner to actually apply what they are learning in their work or profession.

I encourage the reader to make different connections and to extract and apply in their own practices what may be relevant practical lessons and learnings from the wide range of topics and contexts explored by the contributing authors. I hope this book can inspire you to advance your own reflection and practice, and thereby help learners achieve their goals while also enriching your own professional lives.

Steven Shaw
Concordia University, Canada

REFERENCES

Brand, A. G. (1985–1986). Hot cognition: Emotions and writing behavior. *Journal of Advanced Composition*, 6, 5–15.

Keller, J., & Kopp, T. (1987). An Application of the ARCS Model of Motivational Design. In Reigeluth, C. (Ed.), *Instructional design theories and models* (pp. 289–320). Erlbaum.

Keller, J. M. (1983). Motivational design of instruction. In Reigeluth, C. M. (Ed.), *Instructional-design theories and models: an overview of their current status* (pp. 386–434). Lawrence Erlbaum Associates.

Kunda, Z. (1987). Motivation and inference: Self-serving generation and evaluation of evidence. *Journal of Personality and Social Psychology*, 53(4), 636–647. DOI: 10.1037/0022-3514.53.4.636

Kunda, Z. (1990, November). The case for motivated reasoning. *Psychological Bulletin*, 108(3), 480–498. DOI: 10.1037/0033-2909.108.3.480 PMID: 2270237

Malone, T. W. (1981). Toward a theory of intrinsically motivating instruction. *Cognitive Science*, 5(4), 333–369.

Steven Shaw is a professor in the Department of Education, Concordia University, in Montreal. His research and professional work focus on the design, development, and implementation of technology to support learning and knowledge sharing, in particular at the enterprise scale. He co-founded the corporation that developed the first learning content management system, and served as the CLO of Eedo Knowledgeware, employed by Fortune 500 organizations such as Xerox, Dell, Eli Lily, Boeing, and the largest public sector organizations in the US and UK. Recently, he has been involved in a multi-year project to transform training and accreditation in aviation adhering to a competency-based approach, beginning with the development and acceptance of new standards mandated by ICAO and continuing with working groups that have developed concrete implementation models across the different air services disciplines. His areas of expertise include software development, systems implementation, content management, taxonomy and ontology development, design and evaluation of training programs and curricula in professional education, and psychometrics.

Acknowledgement

My family as always deserves my gratitude and appreciation, particularly my son Joshua, followed closely by friends who accept me for who I am.

I owe a very special debt to Professor Steven Shaw, as mentor, friend, and virtual family.

Preface

neither the one, the transformation of knowledge into emotion, nor the other, the release of an independently accumulated emotion through knowledge, is completely correct. there must be something between the two.
- Anselm Kiefer, Notebooks Volume 1: 1998-1999

What lies at the heart of learning? One of the most impactful experiences in my development as a learning professional was reading *Lying about the Wolf*, published in the late 1990s by David Solway. His forceful and so deeply argued critique of the current state of education shook me. As learning professionals, we had lost the plot. We didn't understand or feel the true depth and culture of learning, what it means to each of us as learners, citizens, and human beings. But at that point in my career, I wasn't ready to grapple with the implications for my own practice.

A quarter century later, I've finally been able to bring concerns about meaningful learning to the forefront of what I do, with a particular focus on the emotional aspects of learning.

Learning is a natural, shared human experience. It's about moving from who we are to who we want to become. The greater the gap, the greater the risk and more transformative the journey.

Academics, practitioners, and learners themselves tend to consider this transformation almost exclusively in cognitive terms, as knowledge and skills to be mastered. But real change requires learners to risk, practice, succeed, experiment, fail, and risk again.

Emotions are key to driving change. Learners must be willing, motivated, confident, committed, and determined to achieve goals, especially challenging ones.

What is our responsibility as learning designers? How can we set objectives, produce materials, and create conditions that will best support learners? We need to anticipate those moments when they may stumble, miss opportunities to learn, or even learn to avoid the risk of learning itself.

This book explores insights gained from decades of work in this field and describes best practices essential to understanding the emotional aspects of learning. The following chapters are written from the perspectives of academics, practitioners, and learners from a broad variety of contexts. We must all consider and care about what it means to provide the right support and resources through meaningful moments of change and growth.

I greatly appreciate the faith and effort of the people who contributed theoretical perspectives and practical insights to this book, which is organized as follows:

- *Theoretical Foundations: Broad Strokes:* The authors in this section of the book explore a diversity of theories – including transformative learning, heutagogy, and social constructivism among others – to establish a clear foundation for appreciating the influence of emotions on learning. It concludes with a review of emotional learning analytics, as measuring learners' emotions is fundamental to investigating their impact.
- *Theoretical Foundations: Narrowing the Focus:* These authors focus particularly on the theoretical implications for learners in more specific contexts, such as online and workplace environments, as well as the link from learning to performance on the job.
- *Putting Theory to the Test:* In this section, the authors share the results of putting conceptual ideas into practice in a series of studies exploring a wide range of content and contexts.
- *Focus on Educator Preparation:* A critical factor in changing how we approach learning is to ensure teachers are prepared to support learners in their social-emotional development. These authors share insights from both academic and practical standpoints.
- *Learner Perspectives:* This final section is devoted to sharing insights from learners. They are the ones most impacted by our decisions and actions. We must engage them in the effort to deliver the best possible learning and development experiences.

Finally, I will conclude with a brief summary of where this book has brought us and questions about next steps. But first, before moving on to the next section, please take a moment to read "A Tale of Two Occupational Health & Safety Programs," which sets the stage for the real-life challenges faced by practitioners in our field.

Chapter 1
A Tale of Two Occupational Health and Safety Programs

Lynda Jane Williams
University of Northern BC, Canada

Corrie Pitzer
https://orcid.org/0009-0003-3172-0414
SAFEMap International, Canada

ABSTRACT

This is an experience-based examination of the contrast between cognitive and affective outcomes in two programs within the same field. Both programs are delivered online without explicit instructional leadership, making them comparable with respect to delivery methodology. Conclusions drawn from the instructional design perspective expose the intrinsic difference between these two different types of outcomes, reflected not just in the delivery of training but also in appropriate methods of evaluation.

INTRODUCTION

I hadn't thought much about affective outcomes before encountering Sarah Sniderman's call for chapters. Most of my work as an instructor and designer of instructional programs has taken place within the realm of applied technology, where outcomes are things like mastering iterative loops. The student's emotional disposition with respect to loops is not at issue on the final exam, only whether they possess the required skill.

Then it struck me how two Occupational Health & Safety (OH&S) programs I had recently worked on as instructional designer exemplify the distinction between affective outcomes and the cognitive ones, I was more familiar with. At that point I knew I had a story to tell. It surprised me how deep the story turned out to be.

Given my previous experience as both facilitator and instructional designer, I was especially challenged to consider how one might evaluate an affective outcome, as assessment is obviously critical in the context of ensuring health and safety in the workplace.

However, I also realized even fact-based learning is never wholly devoid of affective intentions; at the same time, it is hard to influence attitudes without teaching any knowledge or skills. Grappling with the differences between a dominantly affective program and a dominantly cognitive one proved complex, until I realized there are qualitative differences that shift the emphasis from performance testing for achievement of outcomes to the proper integration of goals with instructional methods and the nature of the students themselves.

Let me lay the groundwork by describing the two programs concerned, both of which relate to OH&S, a discipline committed to the mitigation of risk to employees in the workplace.

UNBC's OH&S Certificate

The *Occupational Health and Safety Certificate* offered by Continuing Studies at UNBC (Continuing Studies, University of Northern BC, n.d.) is a popular, ten-course program that fulfills the educational requirement of the Canadian Registered Safety Technician (CRST) certification offered by the Board of Canadian Registered Safety Professionals. It is also accepted for laddering into the University of New Brunswick's diploma in Occupational Health and Safety.

Students are typically looking for a first job in occupational health and safety, with no prior experience, or sometimes transitioning into an OH&S role with their employer after working for many years. The only prerequisites are a grade 12 reading level and computer literacy skills, which the student is advised to assess for themselves before enrolling in the program.

To satisfy the roles required of it, the certificate delivers on learning outcomes of a concrete and practical nature within the regulatory framework of Canada. It is pitched at an introductory level of awareness and competence. For example, the course *Occupational Health & Safety Fundamentals* includes the outcome that a student will "recognize where Canada's privacy laws might apply in the workplace."

In addition to a high-stakes final quiz, students do pass/fail assignments to ensure they have recognized how to act in specific circumstances. The assignment for the fundamentals course, for example, includes a situation in which a student must recognize an obligation to secure exposed employee records and cite a justification based on lessons in the course.

The ten courses in the OH&S certificate are:

OH&S 01 – Occupational Health & Safety Fundamentals
OH&S 02 – Legislation: Acts & Regulations
OH&S 03 – Hazard Analysis, Risk Assessment & Control
OH&S 04 – Ergonomics for Injury Prevention & Accommodation
OH&S 05 – Hazardous Materials & Occupational Hygiene
OH&S 06 – Fire Safety Planning & Systems
OH&S 07 – Safety Inspections
OH&S 08 – Accident Investigation & Reporting
OH&S 09 – Emergency Preparedness & Response
OH&S 10 – Safety Program Design & Analysis

Examples of key content components of the certificate appear below.

Figure 1. A typical declaration of learning outcomes for a lesson in the certificate

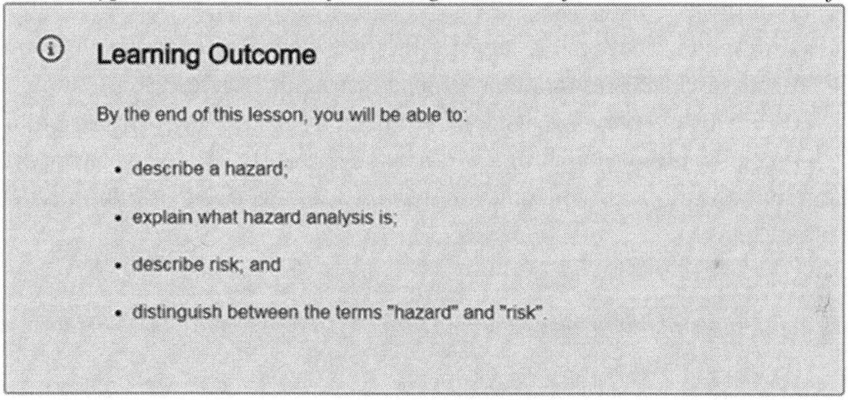

Learning Outcome

By the end of this lesson, you will be able to:

- describe a hazard;
- explain what hazard analysis is;
- describe risk; and
- distinguish between the terms "hazard" and "risk".

Figure 2. A typical evaluation question addressing one of the competency-based outcomes

__________ is the chance of a negative consequence, such as injury, loss, or damage.

- ○ risk
- ○ hazard
- ○ incident
- ○ accident

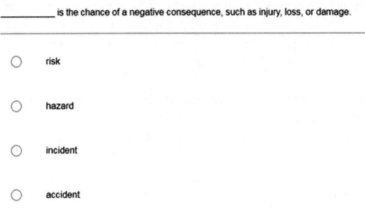

The answer is risk (a hazard is something that causes risk, not the chance of an accident occurring). The question is clearly addressing the learning outcome of distinguishing between hazard and risk.

Management Development Program (UNBC and SAFEMap)

I also did the instructional design for the *Management Development Program* (MDP) based on video presentations by lead instructor Corrie Pitzer.

Pitzer's videos feature experiences from his long history of management in industry, especially mining, and his goal is to inspire a proactive and positive approach to safety in the workplace. Students are expected to be leaders or future leaders in their organization.

Figure 3. Example of a learning outcome for an early lesson in the SAFEMap MDP

ⓘ **Learning Outcomes:**

- connect Pitzer's experience with how to lead, authentically; and
- engage with each of Pitzer's six (6) principles.

Pitzer narrates his experience working as a Human Resources manager in a South African mine, where he had to start by gaining the respect of miners who did dangerous jobs, working deep underground with hazardous chemicals in confined spaces.

One really needs to see the images involved to get a sense of the intensity.

Figure 4. Example of emotionally impactful content from Pitzer's presentation

"Everything I know in my career of safety, for 30 years, came from my experience in this extremely high risk environment."

Assignments in the MDP are based on engagement. Students are asked to discuss how the subject matter applies to their own management or work experience, either as a personal reflection or in small groups. They are asked to journal the results.

See the assignment for digesting Pitzer's six principles, below.

Figure 5. Content screen for review of Pitzer's principles

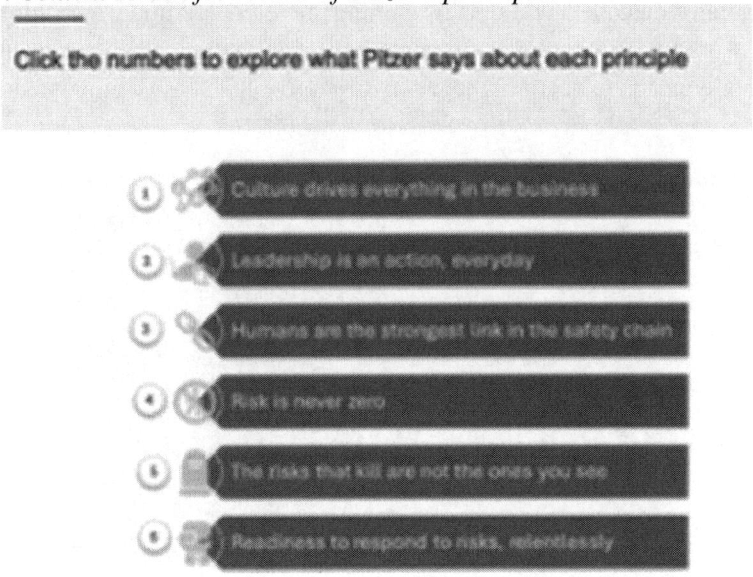

Click the numbers to explore what Pitzer says about each principle

(1) Culture drives everything in the business
(2) Leadership is an action, everyday
(3) Humans are the strongest link in the safety chain
(4) Risk is never zero
(5) The risks that kill are not the ones you see
(6) Readiness to respond to risks, relentlessly

As you can see below, evaluation questions also require students to apply the principles to their own experiences.

Figure 6. Content screen introducing activity for reflection

It is worth noting that there are formative quizzes along the way that students can use to test themselves on whether they've understood the concepts presented to them, but these are not intended for high-stakes evaluation; they are formative in intent.

Cognitive vs Affective Outcomes

My assessment of the two programs is that the certificate is focused on cognitive outcomes (demonstrated acquisition and application of key facts and skills), while the MDP outcomes are primarily affective. To put it another way, the OH&S certificate seeks to turn out students who can prove, via taking quizzes and doing assignments, that they have mastered material presented to them, while the MDP aims to move the needle on the attitude students have towards OH&S, as well as empowering them with tools for expressing their beliefs. It is less concerned with how regulations must be met or how to do a risk assessment, for example, and focuses instead on leadership.

Affective Outcomes

Iris Lim of Bond University, Australia, defines affective outcomes as "a subcategory of learning outcomes that focuses on the moods, feelings, or attitudes that result from an educational experience" (Bond, 2023).

Andreev says of the kind of outcome identified as attitude, "This is the internal state that reflects in the learner's behavior. It is complex to quantify but can be shown in the learner's response to people or situations" (Andreev, 2022).

The concept of affective outcomes isn't new. Even Bloom, who worked on his famous *Taxonomy of Educational Objectives* as far back as the 1950s, made reference to an affective, or emotion-based, domain in learning (Bloom's taxonomy, 2024).

When I started teaching in the 1990s, I could have told you the topics students would be covering in my introductory computer science courses, but I wouldn't even have referred to them as outcomes, let alone distinguished between cognitive and affective outcomes. I simply taught the curriculum.

By the time I retired from my job as Learning Technology Analyst and Manager at Simon Fraser University in 2017, I had lived through over a year of the disruption outcomes were imposing on the academy. Some departments embraced the idea of summing up the benefits of defined outcomes with transferrable skills, while others resisted the idea of granulizing the holistic experience of spending four years immersed in their discipline. And while outcomes of the concrete, cognitive kind were gaining ground everywhere, affective outcomes were far less evident.

Outcomes in the OH&S Certificate and MDP Program

In thinking about affective outcomes, in contrast to cognitive-based ones, I discovered there is always going to be a bit of yin in the yang. For example, while the OH&S certificate is focused on basic introductory knowledge and skills for progressing with aspirations to work as an OH&S technician in Canada, at the same time it is quietly instilling a respect for regulations and due process as it stresses the importance of compliance with the former and due diligence in following the latter. I view these as implicit and perhaps even unconscious affective outcomes, since it would be hard to emerge from the certificate without a healthy respect for regulatory authority in Canada.

In certain places, the content and textbook for the certificate touch on leadership and the need to be proactive about continuous improvement. For example, one of the outcomes for *Occupational Health & Safety Fundamentals* is to "explain why transformational leadership is needed to address the more challenging aspects of safety culture." Arguably, there is an implicit notion bound up in such an outcome that transformational leadership is a good thing. But the outcome is still largely focused on explaining or describing, rather than becoming a transformational leader motivated by personal conviction and belief.

The MDP, on the other hand, actively seeks to inspire students to be leaders in the mold of Corrie Pitzer. The outcomes are clearly affective. But even the MDP sometimes catches its breath along the way to introducing factual information. For example, it covers aspects of the history of OH&S and how theories have evolved over time, even though the emphasis remains on encouraging students to view themselves as change agents.

In short, while no course of education may be either purely cognitive or exclusively affective in its goals, it is perfectly possible to be predominantly one or the other. And in the case of the two OH&S programs, it is the OH&S certificate that is primarily cognitive-based and the MDP that leans heavily in the affective direction.

As a sidenote, it is also worth pointing out no instructor or instructional designer can ever ensure students achieve the intended outcomes or engage with the course as designed. A student taking the OH&S certificate to get ideas about developing a comparable certificate for his own country is an example of an unanticipated engagement. And it is beyond the control of the MDP to prevent a student from merely giving lip service to its goals to impress a mentor without internalizing its mission.

One can test for demonstration of targeted skills and knowledge. But how does one test beliefs and attitudes? The answer lies in a significant shift of emphasis away from the high-stakes evaluation focus of a final exam, towards more productive ways of evaluating the outcomes of programs with a predominantly affective focus.

Evaluating Affective Outcomes

It isn't hard to test whether a student has grasped how to apply a risk assessment treatment to a particular scenario via an assignment. But assignments can't prove you've convinced a business executive to regard occupational health and safety as a positive contributor to the bottom-line instead of a pesky expense. One way to approach meaningful assessment might be to connect the course, as a causative agent, with the executive's behavior over the course of several years, tracking their decisions and actions that impact occupational health and safety within their organization. The cost involved in such a longitudinal study would be a challenge, although it might be feasible if the scope were not too ambitious, and the program concerned ran long enough to make it possible. However, even supposing all this, future performance wouldn't prove the student had actually been convinced of the thesis taught in the MDP, for example, but only that they acted as if they did.

Cognitive outcomes are simple promises of what students can be expected to know and do after taking a course. From the point of view of the student, the outcomes also reflect clear expectations in terms of how they will be evaluated. But affective outcomes are different at a qualitative level, reflecting who the students are and who they want to become, the value of shared experience, and the validation or shaping of existing tendencies. This directly impacts how they can be evaluated.

Key Aspects of a Dominantly Affective Program

In her paper, *Learning through Vulnerability: Applying the Principle of Prospect-Refuge to Create Emotionally Resonant Learning Experiences*, Sniderman (n.d.) develops the idea of building emotional refuge into a course that confronts students with uncomfortable truths or the need to make themselves vulnerable. Perhaps math teachers should have done more of this for centuries, but overall, I think it's safe to say this kind of vulnerability is much more likely to be critical in an affective context.

The idea of refuge can be as straightforward as providing opportunities for self-reflection (safe spaces for ideas and feelings one may not want to share with others) or involve more insight into individual and group dynamics, such as making sure students are grouped in a manner that respects their underlying experiences or personalities. Activities are set according to the outcomes sought, but the circumstances in which those outcomes are pursued allow for intricacies such as gaining trust and accommodating temporary respites or variance among individuals.

As previously mentioned, there is always a bit of yin in the yang, and the math teacher mentioned in passing might do well to consider her students' emotions in designing her lessons should she, for example, be in the habit of calling on them to solve sums aloud. But being able to do those sums is still the outcome to be measured, in the end, by a test.

In the examples Sniderman shared in her paper (n.d.), one of the outcomes is to improve one's coaching skills. In another it's to reflect on and confront personal behavioral patterns that lead to recurring problems in one's life. In the MDP, the main outcome is for students to buy into proactive advocacy for OH&S as a win-win for employees and the businesses they lead. What all these examples have in common is (1) the outcome can't be measured effectively with standard knowledge/skill tests, and (2) the students concerned are being asked to make themselves vulnerable in order to change. Or perhaps, in the case of the MDP, to gain the conviction through shared experience to be willing to put oneself in a vulnerable position in the future, to promote ideas that might affect the bottom-line in the short run but grow the business more effectively over time.

I found it interesting that in both Sniderman's case of designing for a coaching course and Pitzer's MDP, the assignments involve engaging students in sharing experiences and meaningful discussion. In both cases, the students had to be drawn out and encouraged to explore the concepts concerned among themselves. There were no multiple-choice tests or equations to solve with well-defined answers. Instead, while guidance is provided to encourage the direction of progress, participants had a potentially infinite number of ways to progress.

The focus on who the students are and how to draw them into engagement with outcomes, without prescribing exactly how they achieve those outcomes, illustrates the qualitative differences at work for affective outcomes versus cognitive-based learning. I was curious to know if this insight into the nature of affective outcomes would resonate with Corrie Pitzer, creator of the MDP. Below are his responses to the questions I shared with him.

It is clear the MDP is imbued with a strong sense of personal conviction. Is it fair to say the goal is to pass on your experiences to a new generation of managers who can benefit from them? What challenges do you see in achieving the goal?

Corrie Pitzer (C.P.): The 'strong sense of personal conviction' evolved through a number of real-life experiences that shaped my views about leadership and about the difference that a leader can make in his/her engagement with others. In the same way that other leaders shared their life experiences with me, and their successes and failures meshed with my own successes and failures, I want to affect the emotions of others through this program. The difference between managing and leading is explored, and that difference is essentially about the competence to manage (the setting up of a plan, goals, execution, organizing work, and rewarding results – as a transaction between people) and the practice to lead (sharing passion, inspiring, daring, empowering, touching hearts, and caring – as a covenant between people).

The challenges will be tough:

- To make the sharing and the experiences real and meaningful. My choice was to use the medium of videos and to record myself – not using actors, voiceovers etc. – to ensure authenticity.
- To ensure that the 'students' *enact* the practices of leaders, not learn them or recite them. *Leadership is an action* is one of the principles and is also the only way in which leadership can be 'learned.' The students will be required to do real-life engagements in their worlds and ideally, we would want those people who they engaged with to be the verifiers and examiners.
- We will need to come up with creative ways to assess the *authenticity* and *longevity* of the learning.

Who do you envision taking the MDP courses? What kind of students?

C.P.: The target population is front-line and mid-level managers, with some experience, but still early in their careers. Students who have a genuine interest in making a difference to their careers, who might realize that the work they do, as a manager, has less to do with the skills of managing, than with the art of leading and inspiring people.

How would they gain entry to the course or decide to take it?

C.P.: Ideally, they will be willing to pay for the education themselves, but I can see that many companies will want to make the investment in their leader groups.

What knowledge and attitudes would you anticipate them bringing to the experience?

C.P.: I anticipate that they will have little knowledge about the concepts they will be exposed to, but will be drawn in by the fact that it is about 'safety leadership' in which most managers in organizations have a 'vested' interest… Safety is about people, and modern safety approaches are acknowledging that.

Assignments in the MDP ask students to apply course concepts to their own experience. Can you elaborate on how this helps them buy into the course goals?

C.P.: I see this essentially as applying the principle of 'cognitive dissonance,' which I have used many times and have found very valuable. If well-designed and executed, it shifts cognition to affect.

Evaluation of educational experiences that seek to change attitudes and instill convictions is always more challenging than testing for straightforward cognitive-based knowledge and skills. How do you view success for any student who completes the program?

C.P.: I envisage that each module will have the approach of requiring them to engage with people or processes in their own worlds, and that those engagements must show impact and durability. The final module will be planned such that students must design a 'change process' for their own environment, department, or team, etc., and utilize the learnings from the various modules (which sequentially is effectively a transformational process) to deploy this process. We will measure the *impact* they made through this process in various ways as a measure of success.

CONCLUSION

Corrie Pitzer clearly recognizes the value of affective outcomes and how they can contribute – through the efforts and initiatives of his students – to meaningful and lasting impacts on the organizations in which they work. Challenges in handling affective outcomes arise from the failure to appreciate how they differ from cognitive-based ones. Once the intrinsic differences are exposed, the urge to approach and assess affective outcomes in the 'usual way' falls away, leaving the field clear for discovering more meaningful approaches to instructional design and evaluation, such as proceeding from a holistic understanding of the students as individuals as well as the scope of the desired outcomes, including shifts in perspective that may play out over the entirety of a student's career.

REFERENCES

Andreev, A. (2022, Jul 26). *Learning* Outcomes. https://www.valamis.com/hub/learning-outcomes

Bloom's taxonomy. (2024, Apr 10). In *Wikipedia*. https://en.wikipedia.org/w/index.php?title=Bloom%27s_taxonomy&oldid=1218203352

Bond, L. (2023). Unlocking the Potential of Educational Escape Rooms in Higher Education: Theoretical Frameworks and Pathways Ahead. p. 27. *In Fostering Pedagogy Through Micro and Adaptive Learning in Higher Education: Trends, Tools,and Applications*. DOI: DOI: 10.4018/978-1-6684-8656-6.ch007

Sniderman, S. (n.d.). Learning through Vulnerability: Applying the Principle of Prospect-Refuge to Create Emotionally Resonant Learning Experiences.

Studies, C. University of Northern BC (n.d.). *OH&S - Occupational Health & Safety Online Certificate*. https://www2.unbc.ca/continuing-studies/courses/ohs-occupational-health-safety-online-certificate

Section 1
Theoretical Foundations: Broad Strokes

Chapter 2
The Interplay of Emotion and Cognition in Adult Learning:
Learning Engages Emotion Alongside Cognition

Islam Asim Ismail
https://orcid.org/0000-0001-5115-3005
The English and Foreign Languages University, India

Fahad Saleh Aljabr
https://orcid.org/0000-0003-4395-1060
University of Ha'il, Saudi Arabia

ABSTRACT

Learning holistically engages emotion and cognition, yet education often overlooks affective processes. This chapter explores their dynamic interplay through a comprehensive literature review examining theories on how emotions shape learning. The aims are to establish an evidence-based framework emphasizing the intentional integration of factors like motivation, curiosity, and self-efficacy with cognitive objectives in instructional design. The methodology includes synthesizing foundational theories and empirical studies, then exemplifying transformative potential through case studies demonstrating enhanced engagement and holistic development when addressing emotions. Results reveal that emotions can enable adults to take risks, overcome barriers, and achieve meaningful change through learning. Also, emotion and cognition are fundamentally intertwined; practical pedagogical approaches must integrate intellectual to unlock human potential. The chapter proposes an Emotional Learning Design framework for an impactful education through person-centered

DOI: 10.4018/979-8-3693-2663-3.ch002

humanistic instructional practices.

INTRODUCTION

Adult learning is a critical driver of development and change in the modern workforce. Organizations invest heavily in adult education and training programs as employees seek to gain new skills and adapt to emerging roles (Carliner, 2021). However, truly impactful learning requires more than just acquiring knowledge. It engages the whole person in a transformational experience (Dirkx, 2008). While cognitive aspects have traditionally been the focus, the emotional dimensions of learning are equally important. This chapter explores the dynamic relationship between emotion and cognition in adult learning. Our focus on adult learners is particularly relevant as this group faces unique challenges and opportunities in their learning journeys, often balancing education with work and personal responsibilities. Established theories have highlighted the role of motivation, confidence, and related affective issues that enable adults to take risks and achieve meaningful change (Knowles et al., 2005; Mezirow, 2000). However, the intersections between heart and mind are intricate and continue to warrant investigation. By examining emotions and integrating them into the learning process, designers can create holistic experiences that support adults through uncertainty on their developmental journeys.

Learning that goes beyond the surface level involves profound personal transformation rather than just acquiring information. According to Mezirow (2003), transformative learning changes our worldviews, beliefs, and ways of thinking, making them more inclusive, open-minded, reflective, and emotionally intelligent. This fundamental cognitive and emotional change process leads to comprehensive understanding (Dirkx, 2006).

Transformative education takes a comprehensive approach that involves the whole person in the learning experience. It includes the person's mind, heart, spirit, and body. Core values, a sense of purpose, and identity are central to this approach (Taylor, 2017). They develop curiosity, creativity, and compassion. The effect of transformative learning goes beyond academic achievement or job-related abilities. Students can gain a more profound comprehension of themselves and others, which helps them have greater empathy (Cranton, 2006).

The process of transformative learning involves a significant change in our perception and engagement with the world, which is accompanied by the acquisition of new knowledge and the cultivation of wisdom. Learning is fundamentally about growth, discovery, and the seemingly unlimited potential of humanity. When we approach education with care, it opens the doors to our best selves and allows us to unlock our full potential.

Many approaches to learning have historically focused solely on the cognitive aspect. These approaches prioritize the gathering and interpreting of information within the mind (Egan, 1997). However, this narrow perspective ignores the essential roles that emotion and the body play in the learning process.

Learning is well known as a comprehensive process encompassing the cognitive aspects as well as the learner's emotional, motivational, and physical dimensions. According to contemporary research, emotions significantly shape our attention, interpretation, memory, and motivation. Furthermore, our body's sensorimotor experiences provide a basis for encoding information into motor representations and metaphors (Immordino-Yang, 2011; Pekrun & Stephens, 2012; Lindgren & Johnson-Glenberg, 2013). Thus, it can be understood that educators can create effective instructional strategies catering to all learner aspects by recognizing the holistic nature of learning.

Without considering the emotional and physical context of learners' lives, excessive focus on cognition can limit our understanding of how people learn and may lead to less effective educational approaches (Durlak et al., 2011). To truly engage in meaningful learning, we must align our cognitive, emotional, and sensory-motor systems (Tokuhama-Espinosa, 2011). This requires an integrated perspective recognizing learning as an embodied, emotional, and cognitive experience.

Although there is a large body of research on emotions in learning for children and adolescents, the purpose here is to specifically focus on studies relevant to adult learning contexts - which includes higher education as well as professional development (in the workplace), lifelong learning, etc. Based on the preceding, this chapter explores the central question: What is the responsibility of learning designers in fostering emotional experiences during the learning process for adult learners? To investigate this, we conducted an illustrative review of key case studies on the interplay between emotion, cognition, and learning. Rather than providing an exhaustive account of all literature on the topic, we focus on select case studies that illustrate key aspects of this relationship.

The case studies in this chapter were selected based on their relevance to adult learning contexts, their focus on different aspects of emotional engagement in learning, and their potential to inform instructional design practices. These examples, while not exhaustive, provide a cross-section of research that highlights the multifaceted nature of emotion in learning processes.

The methodology involves an integrative review of contemporary research on embodied emotion theories of learning. AbuHamda et al. (2021, p. 71) stated, "Quantitative and qualitative methods are the engine behind evidence-based outcomes."

We systematically searched major databases such as but not limited to IGI Global, ERIC, PsycINFO, and Google Scholar using a combination of keywords such as "embodied cognition," "embodied emotions," "affective learning," and "instructional design." We included empirical studies, theoretical papers, and review articles published in peer-reviewed journals and edited books in the past ten years.

Our initial search returned approximately forty-nine articles published between 1964 and 2022. From these, we selected a subset of case studies that specifically illustrate the role of emotions in adult learning contexts and their implications for instructional design. These cases were chosen to represent a range of learning environments and emotional factors. In addition, the chosen case studies provide insights relevant to our central question.

Our methodology adheres to best practices for evidence-based scholarship (Torraco, 2005; Whittemore & Knafl, 2005;). The review helps us to produce the findings on learning as an embodied emotional experience, not just a cognitive process.

LITERATURE REVIEW

Research by Immordino-Yang and Damasio (2007) has shown that emotions play a crucial role in learning and memory. Traditional cognitive learning theories have tended to minimize the importance of affective and motivational influences, instead emphasizing the role of cold information processing (Mayer et al., 2001). However, research has highlighted the interplay of emotion, motivation, and cognition in learning, as Pekrun and Linnenbrink-Garcia (2014) noted.

It is no secret that emotions play a vital role in our cognitive processes. They can direct our attention, influence our motivation, and impact our memory formation and retrieval. Research has shown positive emotions can broaden our thought-action repertoires, sparking creativity, enhancing relationships, and encouraging conceptual processing. Negative emotions, on the other hand, tend to narrow our focus, encouraging analytical and detail-oriented thinking. However, it is worth noting that both positive and negative emotions can improve our memory encoding and retrieval under specific circumstances.

Self-regulated learning is a complex process that involves not just cognitive abilities but also motivational and affective factors. According to Boekaerts (2016) and Mega et al. (2014), students' emotions and appraisals of learning tasks can significantly impact their self-regulated learning. They influence students' choice of learning strategies, their persistence in learning, and the way they use cognitive strategies.

Moreover, students' goals and implicit beliefs about their abilities shape their emotional reactions to challenges they encounter during the learning process. These reactions can either promote or undermine their motivation and performance (Dweck, 2006). Therefore, it is important for educators to understand the role of motivational and affective factors in self-regulated learning and to help students develop their emotional regulation skills to achieve better academic outcomes.

Motivation in Adult Learning

Motivation is an important pillar for engagement and persistence in adult learning contexts. While external motivators such as employer expectations or incentives may initially induce participation, research indicates that internal motivation is key to sustaining learners' engagement through challenges (Barkley, 2020). Studies show that adults driven by intrinsic motivations demonstrate greater perseverance, enthusiasm, and self-efficacy than those driven solely by extrinsic rewards like bonuses or promotions (Deci & Ryan, 2008). This aligns with Malcolm Knowles' (1984) adult learning theory, which pointed to internal needs for competence and self-actualization. Fostering intrinsic motivation by making material personally meaningful, sparking curiosity, and tapping into passions sustains deeper commitment than short-term external carrots and sticks.

Intrinsic motivation stems from emotions compelling adults to seek out new challenges and continuously enrich their knowledge. As Malcolm Knowles' (1984) adult learning theory proposed, adults are often driven by internal needs for self-esteem, life satisfaction, and self-actualization. Facilitating opportunities for adults to pursue topics intrinsically meaningful to their identities and values can nurture what Knowles termed "a deep psychological need to be generally competent" (p. 12). Strategies like providing choices, sparking curiosity, and ensuring personal relevance are key to leveraging intrinsic motivation (Alderman, 1999). When learning experiences tap into adults' passions and sense of purpose, they ignite greater mastery orientation, engagement, and persistence. In contrast to externally mandated learning, intrinsic motivations aligned with adults' internal aspirations and interests sustain a deeper commitment to growth and discovery.

While still useful, extrinsic motivations are often less sustainable over time unless paired with intrinsic rewards. As adults experience achievement and satisfaction from learning itself, extrinsic motivators become less necessary (Alderman, 1999). However, extrinsic factors can encourage initial participation, so a holistic approach uses both intrinsic and extrinsic motivational levers. The emotions that drive adults to expand their horizons must come from within. By tapping into internal motivations, learning designers can help adults persist through the uncertainty inherent in transformation.

Traditionally, education has focused on developing cognitive skills, as seen in Benjamin Bloom's famous 1956 taxonomy, organizing learning objectives into cognitive, affective, and psychomotor domains (Forehand, 2010) The cognitive domain – receiving the most attention – involves knowledge, comprehension, application, analysis, synthesis, and evaluation. Bloom categorized emotions, attitudes, and values in the affective domain, but this area was often overlooked in favour of cold cognition (Hosek, 2021).

As Beard et al. (2007) noted, traditional behaviourist perspectives emphasized cognition as rational and affect as irrational. Emotions were deemed unstable and capable of distorting cognition, leading to reluctance to address them in education directly. However, contemporary research indicates that emotions are vital in attention, memory, motivation, and thinking (Immordino-Yang, 2016). Integrating emotional and cognitive aspects into learning can improve the learning experience and provide a more comprehensive understanding of human development. In addition, motivation is a critical point in adult learning because adult learners often have competing demands on their time and energy.

Although research on emotions in education has increased, there are still significant gaps in our understanding. Most studies focus on childhood or adolescent learning contexts, with less exploration in adult, workplace, or online settings (Dirkx, 2008; You & Kang, 2014). Additionally, few validated instructional frameworks integrate emotional skills training alongside cognitive development. More research is needed on how different emotions like curiosity, confusion, anxiety, flow, or boredom impact learning for different individuals. While progress has been made, the literature would benefit from more research across diverse learning environments, populations, and emotive states. Integrating affective dimensions in education remains an area ripe for multidisciplinary contributions (Pekrun & Stephens, 2012).

Confidence and Self-Efficacy

Confidence and belief in one's abilities are integral to adults navigating through learning challenges. According to Albert Bandura's social cognitive theory, an individual's self-efficacy level determines their willingness to put in the effort to overcome obstacles or to give up when faced with difficulties (1993). Individuals with higher self-efficacy set more challenging goals, put in greater effort when encountering obstacles, and demonstrate increased persistence in finding solutions (Pajares, 1996).

Learning designers can bolster the self-efficacy of adult learners by instilling confidence through small victories and mastery experiences (Hart, 2012). When adults increase their confidence, they can be motivated to undertake more advanced cognitive tasks and expand their knowledge base (Zimmerman, 2000). Positive outcomes can lead to further success, and it is important to frame failures as opportunities for growth rather than defeats to maintain self-efficacy.

Self-efficacy is crucial to cognitive performance and involves more than just motivation. Research has demonstrated that individuals with higher levels of self-efficacy show greater cognitive engagement and use efficient learning strategies such as critical thinking (Komarraju & Nadler, 2013). Adults who believe in their abilities are more likely to process information comprehensively and persist through complex tasks (Pintrich & De Groot, 1990). Thus, it becomes imperative to boost self-confidence in individuals to foster their cognitive development. By attending to the affective dimension of self-efficacy, learning designers can enable adults to unlock their maximum cognitive potential.

The Role of Learning Designers

In the context of corporate training, there is often an excessive focus on cognitive and technical skills, while the emotional aspect of learning is neglected (Dirkx, 2008). The learning objectives typically revolve around comprehending concepts, executing procedures, or using technology, with little consideration for how these activities might impact the learners' emotions. Such an approach assumes that acquiring knowledge and skills automatically elicits positive emotional responses, which is a limited perspective.

Research has found that emotions directly affect learning, memory, and motivation. Positive emotions, like interest and enjoyment, can lead to deeper and more meaningful learning, whereas negative emotions, such as anxiety, boredom, or frustration, can hinder encoding and retrieval. It is not sufficient to simply present information to elicit optimal emotional experiences (Immordino-Yang & Damasio, 2007; Pekrun & Stephens, 2012).

Therefore, to create impactful learning experiences, designers should intentionally design for emotional outcomes, not just cognitive goals. This involves identifying desired emotional states and creating activities that evoke them rather than relying on chance. Immersive scenarios can generate interest, scaffolding and low-stakes practice can build confidence, and social collaboration can foster enjoyment. For instance, Plass and Kaplan (2016) suggest these approaches in their research.

To create truly impactful learning experiences, it's important to incorporate instructional interventions that address both technical and emotional skills. Educators can cultivate a more holistic approach to learning by considering both cognitive and affective processes. Prioritizing emotional goals empowers learners to improve how they understand and regulate their learning states.

The interplay between emotion and learning can be seen clearly in examples from educational research. Specific studies help illustrate how emotional experiences shape student engagement, memory, and performance. For instance, research in online courses reveals how emotions like boredom, frustration, and anxiety influence satisfaction, task motivation, and information processing.

Learning designers and instructors often work closely together in adult and online learning contexts. However, this chapter primarily focuses on the design aspects of learning experiences. The author acknowledges that in some settings, these roles may overlap or be performed by the same individual, but our recommendations are primarily aimed at those responsible for the initial design and structure of learning experiences.

Results and Discussion

The following case studies and examples provide evidence of how intentionally targeting emotional states through instructional design enhances outcomes. Instructors can deeply impact the learning process by inducing curiosity, minimizing negative feelings, and promoting positive emotions like interest. The real-world examples give a glimpse into the power of aligning emotional and cognitive factors in the learning environment.

Case Study 1: Emotions in Online Learning

Consideration of the online learning environment's design and its effect on the learning outcomes is crucial. As per the 2009 study by Artino and Stephens, negative emotions such as boredom, frustration, and anxiety can adversely impact the learning experience. However, incorporating specific design elements can help alleviate these negative emotions. For instance, asking intriguing questions to stimulate curiosity can help counteract boredom, while providing learners with control over the lesson pace can help diminish anxiety. Furthermore, providing feedback and clear expectations can minimize frustration. By targeting emotional states through instructional design, we can enhance the overall learning experience and facilitate the achievement of desired outcomes.

Case Study 2: Interest in Science Classes

Lin et al.'s 2012 research shows that promoting interest can boost engagement and recall in science classes. The study observed that students who took part in practical experiments displayed more interest and performed better on tests than passive control groups. Active participation created curiosity and enjoyment, leading to more profound learning. This highlights how hands-on activities that generate interest can enhance memory and academic achievement. Instructors can cultivate better educational outcomes by intentionally designing for emotions like interest.

Case Study 3: Reducing Statistics Anxiety

Onwuegbuzie (2004) implemented an intervention to reduce library anxiety and statistics anxiety among graduate students. The design incorporated role-playing, humor, and small group activities to make learning statistics more relaxed and enjoyable. Students reported significantly lower anxiety levels and greater motivation to learn compared to the control group. The study concluded that reducing the negative emotional barriers enabled deeper engagement with challenging material.

Case Study 4: Foster Caring in Nursing Students

Sitzman (2007) advocated for nursing education to cultivate caring, empathy, and compassion alongside clinical skills. Interventions included reflective writing, discussing moral dilemmas, and role-modeling humanistic care. Students demonstrated increased caring self-efficacy, emotional intelligence, and ability to connect with patients. The study revealed that intentionally addressing emotional competencies can develop more holistic, ethical practitioners.

Case Study 5: Demonstrating successful integration of emotional elements in a learning program

The following case studies draw from both K-12 and adult learning environments. This diverse range of examples illustrates how emotional engagement in learning is important across different age groups and educational contexts. We examine these various scenarios to gain insights into the universal importance of integrating emotional issues in learning design and note any age-specific considerations.

At Yale Center for Emotional Intelligence, Marc Brackett and colleagues developed RULER, an evidence-based social and emotional learning (SEL) program for K-12 schools (Brackett, 2019). RULER teaches students to Recognize, Understand, Label, Express, and Regulate emotions in themselves and others. Studies show RULER schools see improvements in academic performance, behaviour, leadership skills, and well-being compared to control schools without SEL (Castillo et al., 2013). Their study concluded that students are better equipped to handle challenging situations socially and academically by developing emotional intelligence.

Another example is mindfulness training incorporated into higher education curriculums. Levy et al. (2019) found medical students who received mindfulness instruction demonstrated increased resilience, empathy, and responsiveness to psychosocial issues compared to peers. The results show that teaching learners mindfulness and emotion regulation skills enables them to manage stress and build critical capacities that benefit lifelong learning.

Targeted SEL and mindfulness training demonstrate how evidence-based emotional learning initiatives in K-12 and higher education settings provide diverse benefits for mental health, social skills, and academic achievement.

Case Study 6: Showcasing positive learning outcomes from addressing affective and psychomotor domains

At Stanford University, designing entrepreneurship education to engage students' passions and identities beyond cognitive skills led to increased creativity, personal growth, and humanitarian pursuits (Korn, 2022). Students created ventures like AI-optimized prosthetics that walk more naturally, machines to mass-produce vaccines quickly, and a startup providing solar power across Africa. Students' entrepreneurial inventions aimed to solve pressing world issues by tapping into purpose and emotion.

In health professions education, Gutsell and Inzlicht (2012) found that training reduced student anxiety and increased self-efficacy, enhancing the learning of surgical skills compared to technical training alone. Psychomotor skills flourished when paired with emotional support.

In the corporate world, leadership training that builds empathy, relationship skills, and self-awareness leads to more collaborative and ethical organizational behaviour (Kirkpatrick & Kirkpatrick, 2016).

Learning design engages emotions and the body, alongside cognition, to unlock creativity, ethical orientation, self-efficacy, and humanitarian purpose. Affective and psychomotor factors prove critical for meaningful education.

Case Study 7: The Influence of Motivation, Emotions, Cognition, and Metacognition on Students' Learning Performance

At a university in Mexico (Acosta-Gonzaga & Ramirez-Arellano, 2021), researchers explored the influence of emotions, cognition, and motivation on student performance in both face-to-face and blended learning environments. The study involved students enrolled in management and industrial engineering degree programs for face-to-face courses and a chemical biology degree program for a blended course in applied computing in biological sciences. The study employed structural equation modelling (SEM) to analyze the relationships between motivation, emotions, cognition, and metacognition. In the face-to-face learning context, data were collected from 222 students, while in the blended learning context, 116 students participated. The blended course used the Moodle platform to deliver content and track student interactions. In both settings, researchers measured students' emotions using the Student Engagement and Disaffection in School (SED) questionnaire and their motivational and cognitive strategies using the Motivated Strategies for Learning Questionnaire (MSLQ). Positive emotions like enjoyment and pride were encouraged through course design, while cognitive and metacognitive strategies were monitored to understand their impact on learning outcomes. The results showed that positive emotions significantly enhanced student engagement and academic performance in the blended learning environment. The blended course's design, which integrated multimedia principles and allowed for repeated review of content, helped foster a positive emotional state, leading to better use of cognitive and metacognitive strategies. In the face-to-face context, students' motivation and cognitive strategies were strongly linked to their academic success, highlighting the different dynamics at play in each learning environment.

Case Study 8: Fostering Empathy in Medical Students

Researchers at the University of Massachusetts implemented an intervention to build empathy skills in medical students (Nashine et al., 2019). Activities included role-playing patient interactions, self-reflection exercises, and discussions on emotional intelligence. Compared to a control group, students in the empathy curriculum demonstrated greater compassion, perspective-taking ability, and connectedness with patients (Nashine et al., 2019). Cultivating emotional capacities alongside clinical expertise can shape more caring, humanistic healthcare practitioners.

Case Study 9: Promoting Growth Mindset in Mathematics

A study at Stanford examined the impact of a growth mindset intervention on college math students (Rennie Center, 2015). Students learned about neuroplasticity – how the brain grows with effort. They practised replacing fixed mindset self-talk with a malleable view of intelligence. The intervention group displayed higher math motivation and achievement than the control group (Rennie Center, 2015). Fostering emotional beliefs that ability is expandable can combat negative stereotypes and boost STEM engagement.

Trends Emerging from the Case Studies

These case studies demonstrate that targeting emotional elements in instructional design can enhance learning outcomes. While each example focuses on a unique intervention and population, some common themes emerge. The examples demonstrate how thoughtfully addressing affective factors in tandem with building knowledge and competencies shapes more holistic, resilient, and ethically oriented learners and practitioners able to thrive in educational and professional environments.

The studies indicate that humanizing positive emotional states like curiosity, engagement, interest, and enjoyment through interactive, experiential learning activities stimulates deeper cognitive processing, enhances motivation, and improves achievement metrics such as memory retention and assessment performance.

Conversely, intentionally alleviating negative emotional barriers such as anxiety, boredom, and frustration through strategies like clear communication of expectations, ongoing feedback, and learner autonomy facilitates immersive focus and persistence with challenging concepts and skills and can promote deeper cognitive processing. Research on empathy and nursing care has also demonstrated that deliberately developing emotional intelligence skills and technical expertise can shape more compassionate and ethical practitioners.

Two approaches that prioritize the emotional aspect of holistic education are contemplation and self-awareness through mindfulness training and developing relational and communicative skills through role-playing, discussions, and narrative-based methods.

One of the key points to take away from this is that emotions profoundly impact our cognition, including our thoughts, beliefs, behaviours, and learning. Insights from neuroscience on neuroplasticity and the mind-body connection further support the idea of educating the whole person. By incorporating social-emotional learning, empathy training, emotional storytelling, and other approaches that prioritize emotions, we can create opportunities for significant personal growth.

The case study findings illustrate that emotions are not peripheral but profoundly intertwined drivers of cognition – influencing our beliefs, behaviours, creativity, and ability to grow. This aligns with insights from neuroscience and psychology emphasizing the mind-body connection and learning as an integrative, socioemotional process. The studies offer a compelling educational vision that embraces the whole person and recognizes emotional engagement as catalytic for unlocking purpose and human potential.

Although more research is required to establish best practices, studies have shown that emotional design factors play a crucial role in enhancing personal and professional growth and development. Education that prioritizes care, purpose, and creativity can have a transformative impact on both individuals and society. These cases provide a compelling argument for the importance of emotional engagement in promoting meaningful and humanistic teaching and learning.

Challenges in Current Approaches

Traditional education has often focused narrowly on cognitive learning objectives related to knowledge and skills acquisition. However, this exclusive emphasis on the cognitive domain is limited in several key ways (Dirkx, 2008; Immordino-Yang, 2015). First, it ignores the research showing emotions are intrinsically tied to attention, encoding, retrieval, and willingness to learn (Pekrun & Stephens, 2012; Tyng et al., 2017). Positive emotions like enjoyment or interest optimize learning, while negative emotions like boredom or anxiety interfere with processing and memory. Second, cognition-focused learning design disconnects content from personal meaning and relevance in learners' lives (Ambrose et al., 2010). Without an emotional hook, information often goes in one ear and out the other. People learn deeply when material engages their passions and interests at a personal level. A conceptual understanding devoid of emotion tends to be shallow and inert. Finally, cognitive goals alone develop only one area of the whole person. Holistic education also means nurturing ethical, social, emotional, physical, and aesthetic potentials (Zins et al., 2004). Exclusive intellectual development creates lopsided human capacities. The most impactful learning engages the head, heart, and body.

In summary, the traditional narrow focus on cognition fails to leverage the power of emotion, overlooks personal relevance, and inhibits holistic human development. An integrated approach that targets emotional and cognitive learning processes is essential for transformative education.

If emotional and physical aspects are not taken into account in learning design, and the sole focus is cognitive information transfer, there can be significant adverse effects on students' motivation, engagement, and depth of learning (Durlak et al., 2011; Lindgren & Johnson-Glenberg, 2013).

First, lack of emotional support risks increased anxiety, boredom, frustration, and other negative feelings that impair encoding and retrieval (Pekrun & Stephens, 2012). Learning environments devoid of positive emotional experiences fail to leverage enjoyment, interest, and curiosity to optimize cognitive processes.

Second, passive learning with minimal real-world action or physical involvement often fails to encode concepts into learners' embodied metaphorical frameworks. This can result in shallow learning (Lindgren & Johnson-Glenberg, 2013). Active, experiential learning that engages the senses and body strengthens memory and transfers skills into students' lives.

Third, emotionless cognitive learning can feel meaningless or irrelevant to students' passions and identities, reducing personal connection to the material (Immordino-Yang, 2015). Content disconnected from emotional value and significance is quickly forgotten.

In summary, failing to integrate emotion and physicality into learning design actively limits student motivation, embodied encoding, personal relevance, and holistic growth. For impactful, transformative learning, instructional approaches must align cognitive, affective, and psychomotor processes to educate the whole person.

Proposed Framework for Emotional Learning Design

This framework is specifically tailored to address adult learners' unique needs and characteristics. It also considers their life experiences, self-direction, and practical orientation to learning.

To enhance learning experiences, instructional design should intentionally integrate emotional dimensions with cognitive and psychomotor factors. A proposed framework, Emotional Learning Design (ELD), systematically incorporates affective processes.

The concept of ELD is based on the scientific study of emotional intelligence, which involves the ability to perceive, use, understand, and manage emotions (as described by Mayer, Salovey, & Caruso in 2008). This aligns with the embodiment theories that emphasize how our thinking is grounded in our bodily sensations and metaphorical conceptual systems (as discussed by Lakoff & Johnson in 1999).

The ELD framework guides learning designers through four key steps:

1. Identifying target emotional states conducive to learning, such as interest, enjoyment, confidence, and low anxiety. This could involve using pre-assessment surveys to understand learners' current emotional states and goals. For example, designers might ask learners to rate their confidence, interest, and anxiety levels related to the subject matter.
2. Engineering activities and environments to induce those emotional states through immersion, social involvement, challenge optimization, emotion regulation skills, and leveraging learner passions. This might include creating immersive scenarios that spark curiosity, incorporating storytelling elements to increase engagement, or designing collaborative activities to foster social connection and enjoyment.
3. Explicitly teaching emotional skills for metacognition, self-regulation, and building self-efficacy. This could involve incorporating mindfulness exercises to enhance self-awareness, teaching cognitive reframing techniques for emotion regulation, or using reflective journaling to build metacognitive skills. For instance, a module on presentation skills might include exercises on managing public speaking anxiety.

4. Assessing emotional outcomes alongside cognitive ones using techniques like surveys, observation, and self-reports. This could involve using post-activity surveys, observational checklists, or learner self-reports. For example, after a challenging problem-solving task, learners might be asked to rate their frustration levels and describe how they managed their emotions during the process.

For instance, in designing a professional development course on conflict resolution:

1. We might identify 'empathy' and 'emotional regulation' as target emotional states.
2. We could employ role-playing activities that simulate challenging workplace scenarios to induce these states.
3. We would explicitly teach techniques like active listening and 'pause-breathe-respond' for emotional regulation.
4. We could assess outcomes through peer feedback forms and self-reflection essays on emotional growth.

This integrated approach develops cognitive and emotional capabilities to keep learners engaged and integrate cognitive and emotional capabilities to foster lifelong learning.

In order to create meaningful emotional learning goals, it's necessary to carefully analyze the learners, the desired outcomes, and evidence-based strategies. According to Mayer et al. (2004), the first step is to identify which emotional skills to focus on, such as self-awareness, self-regulation, motivation, empathy, or social skills. There are helpful frameworks for classifying these skills, such as Bloom's affective taxonomy (Krathwohl et al., 1964) or Goleman's emotional intelligence model (Goleman, 2005).

Next, it is important to create objectives that clearly outline observable and measurable outcomes related to emotional competence (Dirkx, 2008). For example, objectives such as "Learners will report an increase in interest and confidence related to the subject matter" or "Learners will demonstrate focused attention and controlled frustration while completing challenging exercises" can be used. Objectives should be well-written, using active emotional verbs and avoiding vague language.

It is also key to align cognitive and emotional goals so they logically reinforce each other (Plass & Kaplan, 2016) – for example, pairing content retention objectives with curiosity or enjoyment goals. Objectives may scaffold in tiers from basic to more advanced skills. As Newman (2012) explains, frequent re-evaluation based on learner evidence fine-tunes objectives over time.

Recommendations for Learning Designers

The following recommendations apply to all professionals involved in designing learning experiences. These individuals are mainly learning designers and curriculum developers. It is worth mentioning that the specific job titles may vary across institutions; hence, these guidelines are relevant for anyone responsible for creating educational content and structures. The following is actionable advice for readers willing to implement the ELD framework.

When implementing the ELD framework:

- Start small by focusing on one or two key emotional skills per learning module.
- Use a variety of assessment methods to capture different aspects of emotional learning.
- Regularly solicit feedback from learners about their emotional experiences during the learning process.
- Collaborate with subject matter experts to identify emotionally challenging aspects of the content and design appropriate support strategies.

Learning designers should use empathy mapping and learner persona exercises to understand their target audience's emotional needs better. When planning lessons or modules, designers should also identify emotional learning objectives alongside cognitive goals. This will help them determine what feelings they want to evoke and how emotions can enhance or hinder desired outcomes. Designers should use strategies such as interactive storytelling, rich multimedia, relatable humour, relevant topics, and opportunities for creativity to cultivate positive states like curiosity, joy, and intrinsic motivation. They should also aim to minimize anxiety, frustration, and boredom by employing clear expectations, feedback loops, chunked material, variable pacing, and breaks. Incorporating techniques like role-play, artistic expression, narrative sharing, reflective writing, virtual field trips, and immersive experiences can make lessons more meaningful. Building interpersonal emotional intelligence, perspective-taking abilities, and supportive learning communities through empathy activities and discussion prompts is also essential. Mindfulness practices like breathing exercises and contemplative pauses can enhance focus, self-regulation, and resilience. Designers can collect emotional analytics via pulse surveys and engagement metrics to iterate based on qualitative and quantitative emotional data. Connecting learning to purpose, values, and real-world application can promote deeper psychological investment. The goal is to design intentionally for the whole person, crafting transformative experiences that honour the learner's intellect, inner world, and humanity.

Closing Remark

As designers of learning experiences, it's important to acknowledge that learning is more than just a cognitive process that deals only with the mind. It involves emotions, physical experiences, relationships, and identities in deep and meaningful ways. Using these emotional factors thoughtfully, we can spark curiosity, motivate learners, connect ideas with what's important, and make knowledge memorable. Our goal is to create learning experiences that engage both the mind and the heart, nourishing the whole person. When education recognizes our emotional selves, it becomes a transformative journey of self-discovery and unlimited potential for personal and societal growth. Let's have the courage to design such learning experiences.

CONCLUSION

This chapter has explored the integral yet complex interplay between emotion and cognition in adult learning. It also highlights the unique considerations necessary when designing learning experiences for mature students and professionals. Traditional perspectives emphasized cognition while neglecting affective and psychomotor factors. However, contemporary research demonstrates emotions fundamentally shape attention, engagement, encoding, retrieval, and willingness to learn. Positive emotions like interest and enjoyment optimize cognition, while negative emotions like anxiety and boredom impair it. While further research is warranted, key findings reveal that affective elements such as motivation, confidence, and environmental support profoundly shape adults' capability and willingness to learn. Emotions drive global learning processes; positive emotions like interest and joy enable deeper information processing, critical thinking, and mastery goal orientation. Negative emotions can also produce meaningful experiences when transformed through self-reflection. Beyond the acquisition of knowledge itself, emotions transform our subjective relation to what we learn.

Therefore, learning designers must move beyond a narrow cognitive focus to integrate emotional dimensions intentionally. This requires setting objectives to target emotional outcomes alongside content goals, engineering activities to induce supportive affective states, explicitly teaching emotional skill development, and assessing affective competencies. Frameworks like Emotional Learning Design provide models to incorporate emotional intelligence training alongside cognitive growth.

Examples illustrate the benefits of addressing emotions in domains ranging from entrepreneurship to health professions education. Holistic training builds empathy, creativity, self-awareness, and purpose. However, gaps remain in research and practice regarding adult learners, workplace contexts, diverse emotions, and longitudinal outcomes.

The case studies presented here provide an important elaboration of emotions' role in learning, but it is far from representing a full review. While there appears to be some overlap in the skills most often highlighted by educators across age levels and countries that are consistent with this framework for 21st-century learning, our proposed structure was also found insufficient in delivering a complete model of what 21st-century learning may or should entail. Future research would benefit from broader sampling coverage across different specific education domains impacting learner outcomes.

Overall, the evidence clearly indicates that emotion and cognition are fundamentally intertwined. Learning is not just an academic exercise but a meaningful experience engaging the whole person. To create impactful learning, we must explicitly design experiences addressing both heart and mind. While integrating affective dimensions is challenging, doing so allows us to nurture development in its fullest sense. Our emotions give meaning to knowledge and learning. By valuing the emotional side of the learning journey, we can empower transformative and human-centred educational experiences. The heart will always guide the mind.

In conclusion, learning engages our whole selves as human beings, not just our intellects. To deliver transformative experiences, education must nurture growth in emotional domains alongside cognitive ones. When learning designers leverage the power of emotion and the science of affective processes, they can unlock deeper, more meaningful educational experiences that inspire purpose and unlimited human potential. Our charge is to teach both minds and hearts.

ACKNOWLEDGMENT

The authors acknowledge that AI was used in this chapter for organization and clarity. However, they critically reviewed and refined the content to ensure the final outcomes reflect their own analytical skills. The use of AI demonstrates a responsible and ethical approach to integrating technology in academia, while ensuring the authors maintained full control over the intellectual depth and originality of the work.

REFERENCES

AbuHamda, E., Islam, A. I., & Bsharat, T. (2021). Understanding quantitative and qualitative research methods: A theoretical perspective for young researchers. *International Journal of Research*, 8(2), 71–79.

Acosta-Gonzaga, E., & Ramirez-Arellano, A. (2021). The influence of motivation, emotions, cognition, and metacognition on students' learning performance: A comparative study in higher education in blended and traditional contexts. *SAGE Open*, 11(2), 215824402110275. DOI: 10.1177/21582440211027561

Alderman, M. K. (2007). *Motivation for Achievement: Possibilities for Teaching and Learning* (3rd ed.). Routledge., DOI: 10.4324/9780203823132

Ambrose, S. A., Bridges, M. W., DiPietro, M., Lovett, M. C., & Norman, M. K. (2010). *How learning works: Seven research-based principles for smart teaching*. John Wiley & Sons.

Artino, A. R.Jr, & Stephens, J. M. (2009). Academic motivation and self-regulation: A comparative analysis of undergraduate and graduate students learning online. *The Internet and Higher Education*, 12(3), 146–151. DOI: 10.1016/j.iheduc.2009.02.001

Bandura, A. (1993). Perceived self-efficacy in cognitive development and functioning. *Educational Psychologist*, 28(2), 117–148. DOI: 10.1207/s15326985ep2802_3

Barkley, A. P. (2020). *Student engagement techniques: A handbook for college faculty*. John Wiley & Sons.

Beard, C., Clegg, S., & Smith, K. (2007). Acknowledging the affective in higher education. *British Educational Research Journal*, 33(2), 235–252. DOI: 10.1080/01411920701208415

Boekaerts, M. (2016). Engagement as an inherent aspect of the learning process. *Learning and Instruction*, 43, 76–83. DOI: 10.1016/j.learninstruc.2016.02.001

Brackett, M. (2019). *Permission to feel: Unlocking the power of emotions to help ourselves, our kids, and our society thrive.* Celadon Books.

Carliner, S. (2021). *Training design in the corporate world.* Routledge.

Castillo, R., Salguero, J. M., Fernández-Berrocal, P., & Balluerka, N. (2013). Effects of an emotional intelligence intervention on aggression and empathy among adolescents. *Journal of Adolescence*, 36(5), 883–892. DOI: 10.1016/j.adolescence.2013.07.001 PMID: 24011104

Cranton, P. (2006). *Understanding and promoting transformative learning: A guide for educators of adults.* Jossey-Bass.

Deci, E. L., & Ryan, R. M. (2008). Self-determination theory: A macrotheory of human motivation, development, and health. *Canadian Psychology*, 49(3), 182–185. DOI: 10.1037/a0012801

Dirkx, J. M. (2006). Engaging emotions in adult learning: A Jungian perspective on emotion and transformative learning. *New Directions for Adult and Continuing Education*, 2006(109), 15–26. DOI: 10.1002/ace.204

Dirkx, J. M. (2008). The meaning and role of emotions in adult learning. *New Directions for Adult and Continuing Education*, 2008(120), 7–18. DOI: 10.1002/ace.311

Durlak, J. A., Weissberg, R. P., Dymnicki, A. B., Taylor, R. D., & Schellinger, K. B. (2011). The impact of enhancing students' social and emotional learning: A meta-analysis of school-based universal interventions. *Child Development*, 82(1), 405–432. DOI: 10.1111/j.1467-8624.2010.01564.x PMID: 21291449

Dweck, C. S. (2006). *Mindset: The new psychology of success.* Random House.

Egan, K. (1997). *The educated mind: How cognitive tools shape our understanding.* University of Chicago Press. DOI: 10.7208/chicago/9780226190402.001.0001

Forehand, M. (2010). Bloom's taxonomy. In Orey, M. (Ed.), *Emerging perspectives on learning, teaching, and technology* (pp. 41–47). Jacobs Foundation.

Fredrickson, B. L. (2013). Positive emotions broaden and build. In *Advances in experimental social psychology* (Vol. 47, pp. 1–53). Academic Press.

Goleman, D. (2005). *Emotional intelligence.* Bantam.

Gutsell, J. N., & Inzlicht, M. (2012). Intergroup differences in the sharing of emotive states: Neural evidence of an empathy gap. *Social Cognitive and Affective Neuroscience*, 7(5), 596–603. DOI: 10.1093/scan/nsr035 PMID: 21705345

Hagelskamp, C., Brackett, M. A., Rivers, S. E., & Salovey, P. (2013). Improving classroom quality with the RULER approach to social and emotional learning. *School Psychology Review*, 42, 193–204. PMID: 23444004

Hart, J. W. (2012). Adult learning in the workplace. In Kasworm, C. E., Rose, A. D., & Ross-Gordon, J. M. (Eds.), *Handbook of adult and continuing education* (2010 ed., pp. 371–380). Sage.

Hosek, A. M. (2021). Cognitive vs. Affective: Reconsidering Bloom's Taxonomy. *Psychology Teacher Network*, 31(3), 9–13.

Immordino-Yang, M. H. (2011). Implications of affective and social neuroscience for educational theory. *Educational Philosophy and Theory*, 43(1), 98–103. DOI: 10.1111/j.1469-5812.2010.00713.x

Kirkpatrick, J. D., & Kirkpatrick, W. K. (2016). *Kirkpatrick's four levels of training evaluation*. ATD Press.

Knowles, M. S. (1984). *Andragogy in Action*. Jossey-Bass.

Knowles, M. S., Holton, E. F.III, & Swanson, R. A. (2005). *The adult learner* (6th ed.). Routledge. DOI: 10.4324/9780080481913

Komarraju, M., & Nadler, D. (2013). Self-efficacy and academic achievement: Why do implicit beliefs, goals, and effort regulation matter? *Learning and Individual Differences*, 25, 67–72. DOI: 10.1016/j.lindif.2013.01.005

Korn, M. (2022). Stanford course for entrepreneurs puts passion before business plans. Wall Street Journal. https://www.wsj.com/articles/stanford-course-for-entrepreneurs-puts-passion-before-business-plans-11641263201

Krathwohl, D. R., Bloom, B. S., & Masia, B. B. (1964). *Taxonomy of educational objectives, the classification of educational goals*. Handbook II: Affective domain. David McKay Company.

Lakoff, G., & Johnson, M. (1999). *Philosophy in the flesh: The embodied mind and its challenge to western thought*. Basic books.

Levy, D., Duffey, T., Yumiko, A., Cohen, S., Frye, A., & Weissman, G. (2019). The effect of mindfulness meditation training on medical student well-being, empathy, and suicidality. *Medical Science Educator*, 29(3), 905–911.

Lin, T. J., Liang, J. C., Tsai, C. C., & Chang, H. W. (2012). Science learning outcomes in alignment with learning environment preferences. *Journal of Science Education and Technology*, 21(6), 643–650.

Lindgren, R., & Johnson-Glenberg, M. (2013). Emboldened by embodiment: Six precepts for research on embodied learning and mixed reality. *Educational Researcher*, 42(8), 445–452. DOI: 10.3102/0013189X13511661

Mayer, J. D., Salovey, P., & Caruso, D. R. (2008). Emotional intelligence: New ability or eclectic traits? *The American Psychologist*, 63(6), 503–517. DOI: 10.1037/0003-066X.63.6.503 PMID: 18793038

Mayer, J. D., Salovey, P., Caruso, D. R., & Sitarenios, G. (2001). Emotional intelligence as a standard intelligence. *Emotion (Washington, D.C.)*, 1(3), 232–242. DOI: 10.1037/1528-3542.1.3.232 PMID: 12934682

Mega, C., Ronconi, L., & De Beni, R. (2014). What makes a good student? How emotions, self-regulated learning, and motivation contribute to academic achievement. *Journal of Educational Psychology*, 106(1), 121–131. DOI: 10.1037/a0033546

Mezirow, J. (2000). Learning to think like an adult: Core concepts of transformation theory. In Mezirow, J. (Eds.), *Learning as transformation: Critical perspectives on a theory in progress* (pp. 3–34). Jossey Bass.

Mezirow, J. (2003). Transformative learning as discourse. *Journal of Transformative Education*, 1(1), 58–63. DOI: 10.1177/1541344603252172

Murty, V. P., LaBar, K. S., & Adcock, R. A. (2016). Threat of punishment motivates memory encoding via amygdala, not midbrain, interactions with the medial temporal lobe. *The Journal of Neuroscience : The Official Journal of the Society for Neuroscience*, 36(26), 6969–6976. PMID: 22745496

Nashine, M. A., Becker, B. W., & Ranalli, L. A.. (2019). Impact of a Longitudinal Empathy Curriculum on Medical Students' Attitudes Towards Physician-Patient Communication. *Journal of General Internal Medicine*, 34, 2595. DOI: 10.1007/s11606-019-05395-6

Onwuegbuzie, A. J. (2004). Academic procrastination and statistics anxiety. *Assessment & Evaluation in Higher Education*, 29(1), 3–19. DOI: 10.1080/0260293042000160384

Pajares, F. (1996). Self-efficacy beliefs in academic settings. *Review of Educational Research*, 66(4), 543–578. DOI: 10.3102/00346543066004543

Pekrun, R., & Linnenbrink-Garcia, L. (Eds.). (2014). *International handbook of emotions in education*. Routledge. DOI: 10.4324/9780203148211

Pekrun, R., & Stephens, E. J. (2012). Academic emotions. In Harris, K. R., Graham, S., Urdan, T., Graham, S., Royer, J. M., & Zeidner, M. (Eds.), APA educational psychology handbook: Vol. 2. *Individual differences and cultural and contextual factors* (pp. 3–31). American Psychological Association.

Pintrich, P. R., & De Groot, E. V. (1990). Motivational and self-regulated learning components of classroom academic performance. *Journal of Educational Psychology*, 82(1), 33–40. DOI: 10.1037/0022-0663.82.1.33

Plass, J. L., & Kaplan, U. (2016). Emotional design in digital media for learning. In *Emotions, technology, design, and learning* (pp. 131–161). Academic Press. DOI: 10.1016/B978-0-12-801856-9.00007-4

Rennie Center. (2015). Stanford research shows promoting a growth mindset improves student grades. Rennie Center. https://www.renniecenter.org/news/stanford-research-shows-promoting-growth-mindset-improves-student-grades

Sitzman, K. L. (2007). Teaching-learning professional caring based on Jean Watson's theory of human caring. *International Journal for Human Caring*, 11(4), 8–15. DOI: 10.20467/1091-5710.11.4.8

Taylor, E. W. (2017). Transformative learning theory. In *Transformative learning meets Bildung* (pp. 17–29). Brill Sense. DOI: 10.1007/978-94-6300-797-9_2

Tokuhama-Espinosa, T. (2011). *Mind, brain, and education science: A comprehensive guide to the new brain-based teaching*. WW Norton & Company.

Tyng, C. M., Amin, H. U., Saad, M. N., & Malik, A. S. (2017). The influences of emotion on learning and memory. *Frontiers in Psychology*, 8, 1454. DOI: 10.3389/fpsyg.2017.01454 PMID: 28883804

Zimmerman, B. J. (2000). Self-efficacy: An essential motive to learn. *Contemporary Educational Psychology*, 25(1), 82–91. DOI: 10.1006/ceps.1999.1016 PMID: 10620383

Zins, J. E., Weissberg, R. P., Wang, M. C., & Walberg, H. J. (Eds.). (2004). *Building academic success on social and emotional learning: What does the research say?* Teachers College Press.

ADDITIONAL READING

Barkley, E. F. (2019). *Student engagement techniques: A handbook for college faculty*. John Wiley & Sons.

Belenky, D. M., & Nokes-Malach, T. J. (2012). Motivation and transfer: The role of mastery-approach goals in preparation for future learning. *Journal of the Learning Sciences*, 21(3), 399–432. DOI: 10.1080/10508406.2011.651232

D'Mello, S., & Graesser, A. (2012). Dynamics of affective states during complex learning. *Learning and Instruction*, 22(2), 145–157. DOI: 10.1016/j.learninstruc.2011.10.001

Immordino-Yang, M. H., & Faeth, M. (2010). The role of emotion and skilled intuition in learning. In Mind, Brain, and Education (pp. 69-83). Academic Press.

Kahu, E., Nelson, K., & Picton, C. (2017). Student interest as a key driver of engagement for first year students. *Student Success*, 8(2), 55–66. DOI: 10.5204/ssj.v8i2.379

Linnenbrink-Garcia, L., Patall, E. A., & Pekrun, R. (2016). Adaptive motivation and emotion in education: Research and principles for instructional design. *Policy Insights from the Behavioral and Brain Sciences*, 3(2), 228–236. DOI: 10.1177/2372732216644450

Lowe, T., & Molnar, B. (2021). Affect and cognition in the digital age. *Journal of Interactive Media in Education*, 1, 1–13.

Pekrun, R. (2006). The control-value theory of achievement emotions: Assumptions, corollaries, and implications for educational research and practice. *Educational Psychology Review*, 18(4), 315–341. DOI: 10.1007/s10648-006-9029-9

Pessoa, L. (2008). On the relationship between emotion and cognition. *Nature Reviews. Neuroscience*, 9(2), 148–158. DOI: 10.1038/nrn2317 PMID: 18209732

Schutz, P. A., & Lanehart, S. L. (2002). Introduction: Emotions in education. *Educational Psychologist*, 37(2), 67–68. DOI: 10.1207/S15326985EP3702_1

Tyng, C. M., Amin, H. U., Saad, M. N., & Malik, A. S. (2017). The influences of emotion on learning and memory. *Frontiers in Psychology*, 8, 1454. DOI: 10.3389/fpsyg.2017.01454 PMID: 28883804

Vanloffeld, J., & McGrenere, J. (2022). Case study: Designing an emotion-aware online learning system. In *Design Computing and Cognition'22* (pp. 243–260). Springer.

Zembylas, M., Bozalek, V., & Shefer, T. (2014). Tronto's notion of privileged irresponsibility and the reconceptualization of higher education: Implications for social justice. *Teaching in Higher Education*, 19(2), 107–118.

KEY TERMS AND DEFINITIONS

Affective domain: The aspects of learning related to emotions, attitudes, motivations, values, and social/emotional skills.

Affective outcomes: Measurable results related to emotions, attitudes, motivation, or other affective dimensions like enjoyment, engagement, confidence, interest, or connection to values.

Embodied cognition: The theory that cognitive processes like thinking and memory are shaped by and intertwined with our bodily sensations and sensorimotor experiences.

Emotional intelligence: The capacity to recognize, understand, express, and regulate emotions in oneself and others. Includes skills like self-awareness, empathy, and managing relationships.

Emotional design: The process of intentionally engineering environments, technologies, and activities to induce positive emotional experiences and outcomes.

Holistic education: Educational philosophy focused on nurturing the whole person including intellectual, emotional, physical, social, aesthetic, and spiritual dimensions.

Learning designer: A professional responsible for creating and structuring educational experiences, including developing learning objectives, planning instructional strategies, and designing assessments. In the context of this chapter, we focus on the learning designers' role in incorporating emotional elements into the learning process.

Transformative learning: Learning that expands worldviews and habits of mind to be more inclusive, self-reflective, and ethically responsible. Results in deep shifts in perspectives, values and identity.

APPENDIX

Teaching Note

This supplementary document expands on the key themes and insights presented in the main case study on integrating emotions into adult learning design. We explore together the challenges, factors, and potential solutions discussed in these cases through questions and answers. The epilogue and lessons learned section offers you, as a reader, a closer perspective on the long-term implications of emotion-aware learning design, along with key takeaways for practitioners. Finally, the list of additional sources provides you with valuable resources for further exploration of this critical topic in adult education and instructional design.

Questions and Answers:

1. What is the overall problem presented in these cases?
    The overall problem is how to effectively integrate emotions and affective factors into the design of adult learning experiences. Traditional approaches have focused narrowly on cognitive aspects while neglecting the crucial role of emotions in learning processes.
2. What are the key factors affecting emotional engagement in adult learning?
    The key factors that affect emotional learning are learner motivation, self-efficacy, anxiety levels, personal relevance of material, social/collaborative elements, challenge level, and instructional design choices that target emotional states. It is important to realize that adult learners' life experiences and competing responsibilities also impact emotional engagement.
3. What role do learning designers play in addressing the affective dimensions of adult education?
    Learning designers are responsible for intentionally engineering activities, environments, and assessments to induce positive emotional states that are conducive to learning. They identify target emotional outcomes, create relevant experiences, teach emotional skills, and measure affective results alongside cognitive ones.
4. What are some emerging technologies that could enhance emotional engagement in adult learning?
    Potential technologies that could enhance emotional engagement in adult learning are virtual/augmented reality for immersive experiences, AI-powered adaptive learning systems, biofeedback tools to measure

emotional states, and social learning platforms to foster connection. Mindfulness/meditation apps could also support emotional regulation.
5. What is a recommended framework for integrating emotions into adult learning design?

The Emotional Learning Design (ELD) framework is recommended. It involves: 1) identifying target emotional states, 2) implementing activities to induce those states, 3) explicitly teaching emotional skills, and 4) assessing emotional outcomes. This provides a systematic approach to address affective factors.

Epilogue and Lessons Learned:

Epilogue: As learning designers increasingly adopt emotion-aware approaches, we may see a shift towards more holistic, transformative educational experiences for adults. This could lead to improved learner engagement, retention, and transfer of knowledge to real-world contexts. However, challenges in measuring emotional outcomes and personalizing experiences at scale may persist.

Lessons learned:

1. Emotions are integral to learning, not peripheral – cognitive and affective processes are deeply intertwined.
2. Adult learners have unique emotional needs that must be considered in design.
3. Intentional design for emotional engagement can significantly enhance learning outcomes.
4. A systematic framework like ELD helps integrate affective elements effectively.
5. Ongoing research and experimentation are needed to refine emotion-aware learning design practices.

List of Additional Sources:

1. "Metaphors We Live By" by George Lakoff & Mark Johnson.
2. "Handbook of Emotions in Education" by Pekrun & Linnenbrink-Garcia.
3. "Design for How People Learn" by Julie Dirksen.
4. "Emotional Design" by Don Norman.
5. eLearning Industry website (https://elearningindustry.com/)

Relevant industries: Corporate training, higher education, professional development, online learning platforms, educational technology.

Chapter 3
Heutagogy Weds Emotional Experience to Breed New Learning Design Practices

Urmila R. Menon
https://orcid.org/0009-0008-9650-0339
LEAD College of Management, Palakkad, India

ABSTRACT

This chapter explores the intersection of heutagogy and emotional experience in the evolution of learning design practices. Through a historical lens, it scrutinises the transition of learning methodologies, highlighting the pivotal role of technology and societal shifts. Furthermore, it scrutinises the future landscape of learning design, forecasting trends and emerging paradigms. Central to this exploration is the significance of emotional experience in the learning process. By synthesising heutagogical principles with emotional intelligence, novel learning design practices emerge, tailored to individual needs and preferences. Drawing on psychological insights, this section explores the complex connection between hormones and self-directed learning, revealing the physiological foundations of effective learning. Finally, it offers practical recommendations for educators and instructional designers, advocating for the integration of emotional engagement and self-directed learning strategies in the development of innovative learning models.

DOI: 10.4018/979-8-3693-2663-3.ch003

Copyright © 2025, IGI Global. Copying or distributing in print or electronic forms without written permission of IGI Global is prohibited.

INTRODUCTION

In contemporary education, the fusion of heutagogy, or self-determined learning, with emotional experiences represents a significant evolution in learning design. The chapter aims to explore this integration, emphasizing how these concepts can address the dynamic needs of modern learners and enhance educational outcomes. Teachers can design more comprehensive and successful learning environments by coordinating learning procedures with each learner's autonomy and emotional engagement.

The concepts of andragogy are expanded upon by heutagogy, which was first proposed by Hase and Kenyon (2000). It emphasizes the development of learners' capabilities and self-direction. Heutagogy, which fosters a higher degree of autonomy and self-efficacy, places an emphasis on the learner's involvement in choosing what and how they learn, in contrast to traditional pedagogy and andragogy. This method is especially pertinent in the 21st century, when students must be flexible and self-motivated due to the speed at which technology is developing and the abundance of knowledge is available (Hase & Kenyon, 2000; Blaschke, 2012).

The learning process heavily relies on emotional experiences. Motivation, engagement, and memory recall can all be strongly impacted by emotions (Pekrun, 2006). Positive emotional experiences have the power to increase students' intrinsic motivation, increasing their propensity to connect deeply with the subject matter and persevere in the face of difficulties. On the other hand, worry and disengagement brought on by unpleasant emotions can hinder learning (Immordino-Yang & Damasio, 2007).

Integrating heutagogy with emotional experience can create a synergistic effect, leading to more profound and meaningful learning. By empowering learners to take charge of their learning journeys and creating emotionally supportive learning environments, educators can enhance both cognitive and emotional development. This holistic approach aligns with the goals of modern education, which seeks not only to impart knowledge but also to develop learners' critical thinking, problem-solving skills, and emotional intelligence (Chamo, Biberman-Shalev, & Broza, 2023).

In today's educational landscape, characterized by diversity and rapid change, the integration of heutagogy and emotional experience is crucial. Traditional educational models often fail to address the individualized needs of learners or to engage them on an emotional level. With its emphasis on self-determined learning, heutagogy promotes student participation in the classroom and develops a sense of accountability and ownership (Blaschke, 2012). When combined with strategies that promote positive emotional experiences, this approach can lead to higher levels of engagement, motivation, and ultimately, better learning outcomes (Immordino-Yang & Damasio, 2007).

This chapter will delve into the theoretical foundations and practical applications of integrating heutagogy with emotional experiences in learning design. Through an analysis of the advantages and difficulties associated with this methodology, the researchers hope to offer a thorough grasp of how these ideas might revolutionize contemporary education.

The subsequent sections will offer detailed insights into the principles of heutagogy, the role of emotions in learning, and practical strategies for creating heutagogic learning environments that are emotionally supportive and engaging.

Learning

Learning occurs through various modes, each offering distinct advantages and opportunities for the application of heutagogic principles. The primary modes of learning include formal, informal, and non-formal education. Understanding these modes and how heutagogy can be applied to them provides a comprehensive view of modern educational practices.

a. Formal Education: Formal education is structured and occurs within established institutions such as schools, colleges, and universities. This mode is characterized by a defined curriculum, standardized assessments, and certification upon completion. Traditionally, formal education follows pedagogical or andragogical approaches but can be enriched through heutagogy by promoting learner autonomy and capability development (Hase & Kenyon, 2007).

In formal education, heutagogy can be implemented by providing students with greater control over their learning paths. For example, students can choose projects, research topics, and assessment methods, which encourages a deeper engagement with the material and the development of critical thinking and problem-solving skills (Blaschke, 2012). Digital tools and resources further support this approach by offering a wide range of learning materials, facilitating self-directed exploration and study (Moore, 2020).

b. Informal Education: Informal education occurs outside formal institutions and is typically unstructured. It includes learning through daily activities, social interactions, media consumption, and personal experiences. Informal education is often self-directed, promoting lifelong learning and personal development (Livingstone, 2001).

Heutagogy naturally aligns with informal education due to its emphasis on learner autonomy and self-determination. Individuals engage in informal learning based on their interests and needs, often seeking out information and experiences that are immediately relevant and applicable to their lives. For instance, learning new skills through online tutorials, participating in community projects, or exploring hobbies are all forms of informal education (Hager & Halliday, 2009). Recognizing and valuing informal learning experiences can lead to more holistic and inclusive educational environments.

c. Non-formal Education: Workshops, professional development courses, and community education programs are examples of structured learning experiences that happen outside of traditional educational settings. The phrase "non-formal education" refers to these types of programs. According to Coombs and Ahmed (1974), non-formal education is adaptable and may be customized to meet the unique requirements and circumstances of students.

Heutagogy enhances non-formal education by fostering a learner-centered approach. Learners can set their own goals, choose how to achieve them, and reflect on their progress. This flexibility allows for the creation of learning experiences that are highly relevant and practical (Blaschke & Hase, 2016). For example, professional development programs can incorporate heutagogic principles by allowing participants to select training modules that align with their career goals and personal interests, thereby increasing motivation and engagement.

Applying heutagogy across different learning modes involves creating environments that support learner autonomy, encourage self-reflection, and provide opportunities for experiential learning. In formal education, this might include project-based learning, flipped classrooms, and digital learning platforms that offer personalized experiences (Blaschke, 2012). Informal education can be supported by providing access to diverse resources and communities of practice where learners can share knowledge and experiences (Livingstone, 2001). Non-formal education can benefit from designing flexible programs that allow learners to pursue their interests and develop their capabilities meaningfully (Coombs & Ahmed, 1974).

HEUTAGOGY

Heutagogy, which is another name for self-determined learning, is a learner-centered methodology that places an emphasis on helping students improve their capacity, potential, and autonomy. Its alignment with the objectives of the 21st-century educational landscape—which necessitates flexibility, adaptability, and lifetime learning skills—makes it crucial to modern learning design. By giving students the ability to take charge of their own learning, heutagogy empowers them. The development of flexibility and lifelong learning—two essential traits in the quickly evolving world of today—depend on this autonomy. As to Hase and Kenyon (2000), heutagogy is based on the ideas of andragogy but emphasizes that learners must be able to steer their own learning experiences in order to acquire motivation and self-efficacy.

The necessity for adaptive learning approaches has been brought to light by the Covid-19 epidemic. Heutagogy supports blended learning environments, combining face-to-face and online learning modalities to create adaptable educational experiences. Chamo, Biberman-Shalev & Broza (2023) found that heutagogic principles integrated into blended learning models enhance student engagement and capability development, making learning more effective and relevant to current educational needs. Heutagogy focuses on developing learners' capabilities rather than just competencies. This means developing the ability to think critically, solve problems, and learn in a range of contexts. Gardner et al. (2008) emphasize that heutagogic practices in nursing education, for instance, lead to more capable and adaptable practitioners who can handle complex and unpredictable situations in clinical settings.

An important factor in enthusing and inspiring students is their emotional experiences. Positive emotional experiences have the power to increase students' engagement and enthusiasm in their academic endeavours. According to Dweck (2006), fostering a growth mindset through positive emotional reinforcement encourages persistence and resilience in learning. Emotional engagement supports deep learning, where learners connect emotionally with the material, leading to better understanding and retention. Freire (1970) highlighted the significance of emotional connections in his work on critical pedagogy, where the emotional and social contexts of learning are integral to the educational process.

Incorporating emotional experiences in learning helps address the holistic development of learners. This includes their mental and emotional health, which is critical to establishing a welcoming and productive learning environment. Research by Chamo et al. (2023) indicates that heutagogy, when combined with emotional engagement strategies, can lead to more fulfilling and effective learning experiences. The integration of heutagogy and emotional experiences in modern learning design creates a more holistic, adaptable, and effective educational framework. By empowering learners, fostering deep engagement, and supporting personal growth, heutagogy and emotional experiences address the demands of contemporary education and prepare learners for the complexities of the modern world.

Origin of Heutagogy

Stewart Hase and Chris Kenyon established the concept of heutagogy, or self-determined learning, for the first time in 2000. The term itself is derived from the Greek word 'heut', meaning self, emphasizing the learner's role in determining their learning path. The concept emerged from Hase and Kenyon's dissatisfaction with traditional, didactic teaching methods prevalent in universities, which they felt did not adequately prepare learners for the complexities and unpredictability of the real world (Hase & Kenyon, 2000; Hase, 2013).

The initial introduction of heutagogy was aimed at creating a learning framework that went beyond andragogy (the method and practice of teaching adult learners) by focusing not just on the acquisition of knowledge but also on the development of capabilities- enabling learners to learn how to learn. This approach was particularly relevant given the rapid advancements in technology and the subsequent shifts in the educational landscape (Eberle, 2013).

Since its beginnings, heutagogy has become more and more relevant and useful, particularly with the introduction of Web 2.0 and the increased usage of social media, which offer platforms that encourage learner autonomy and the production of material created by learners themselves. This has fostered environments where learners can take charge of their educational journeys, making heutagogy a critical framework for lifelong learning in the 21st century (Moore, 2020).

As educational paradigms continue to evolve, heutagogy's emphasis on self-determination, capability development, and learner autonomy aligns well with the needs of modern learners and the demands of contemporary society. It encourages a shift from teacher-centered to learner-centered education, fostering skills that are essential for personal and professional growth in an increasingly complex world (Blaschke, 2012; Moore, 2020).

Proponents of Heutagogy and their Key Contributions

Stewart Hase and Chris Kenyon are the pioneering figures behind the concept of heutagogy. Their introduction of this learner-centered approach has significantly influenced modern educational practices by emphasizing self-determined learning, capability development, and learner autonomy. Their emphasis on learner autonomy and capability development has had a considerable impact on contemporary educational practices, and they have made substantial contributions to the discipline of heutagogy. Australian psychologist and educationalist Stewart Hase has concentrated on strengthening the theoretical foundations of heutagogy. He has written extensively about the importance of capability development over mere competence, arguing that in an ever-changing world, the ability to learn, adapt, and apply knowledge is more critical than the knowledge itself. Hase emphasizes the non-linear nature of learning and the crucial role of reflection in enhancing learning outcomes (Hase, 2014). His advocacy for capability development as a core principle of heutagogy underscores the need for learners to be equipped with skills that enable them to navigate and adapt to various life situations (Hase & Kenyon, 2007).

In addition to these theoretical contributions, Hase has explored the practical applications of heutagogy in workplace learning and professional development. He argues for creating learning environments that encourage self-directed learning and adaptability, which are essential in professional settings (Blaschke & Hase, 2016). Hase's work in digital learning environments highlights how online platforms can facilitate heutagogical practices by providing learners with access to resources, tools, and networks that support autonomous learning journeys. This strategy is in line with the growing emphasis on lifelong learning and the requirement that people constantly advance their knowledge and abilities in a world that is changing quickly (Moore, 2020).

Chris Kenyon has also played a vital role in integrating heutagogy with other educational frameworks such as andragogy and pedagogy. His work aims to provide a comprehensive approach to education that accommodates learners' needs across different stages of their educational journeys. Kenyon's efforts in integrating these frameworks highlight the importance of creating cohesive educational strategies that support learner autonomy and self-determination (Kenyon & Hase, 2010). Moreover, Kenyon has contributed to the practical implementation of heutagogical principles in various education and vocational training programs. His work emphasizes the creation of learning environments that encourage exploration, critical thinking, and self-reflection, essential components of a heutagogical approach (Kenyon, 2012).

The contributions of Hase and Kenyon have established heutagogy as a vital framework in modern education, particularly in fostering lifelong learning and adaptability in an increasingly complex world. Their work continues to influence educational research and practice, with ongoing studies exploring new applications and implications of self-determined learning. By advocating for learner-centered approaches and emphasizing the development of capabilities, Hase and Kenyon have significantly impacted how educators and institutions approach teaching and learning in the 21st century.

Core Principles of Heutagogy

Heutagogy is grounded in the belief that learners are capable of not only determining what they need to learn but also how they should learn it, thus fostering a deeper sense of ownership and responsibility (Blaschke, 2012; Hase & Kenyon, 2013). The core principles of heutagogy revolve around the following concepts:

a. Learner autonomy: Learners take charge of their learning experiences, deciding on the objectives, methods, and evaluation of their learning process (Hase & Kenyon, 2000; Blaschke, 2012).
b. Capability development: According to Eberle (2013) and Gardner et al. (2008), heutagogy places a strong emphasis on the development of students' capacities, which include qualities like critical thinking, problem-solving, and situational adaptation.
c. Non-linear learning: Unlike traditional learning methods that often follow a linear path, heutagogy supports a more flexible and iterative learning process where learners can revisit and reassess their learning needs and strategies (Blaschke, 2012; Hase & Kenyon, 2007).
d. Self-reflection and metacognition: In order to comprehend and enhance their learning processes, learners are urged to reflect on their experiences and cultivate metacognitive abilities (Blaschke, 2012; Hase & Kenyon, 2013).

Andragogy versus Heutagogy

Pedagogy is teacher-centered, with the teacher directing the learning process and content. In contrast, heutagogy is learner-centered, giving learners control over their learning (Hase & Kenyon, 2000). While andragogy, the method of teaching adult learners, emphasizes self-directed learning, it still often involves a structured approach guided by the educator. Heutagogy takes one step further by empowering students to autonomously choose their own learning paths and objectives, which promotes a greater degree of self-determination (Blaschke, 2012; Eberle & Childress, 2009).

Andragogy and heutagogy are two distinct approaches to learning, each having its own definitions and tenets. The phrase "andragogy," which refers to the method and practice of teaching adult learners, gained popularity thanks to Malcolm Knowles. According to Knowles, Holton, and Swanson (2015), it is predicated on a number of crucial ideas, including the need for knowledge, the learners' self-concept, the significance of the learners' experiences, the learners' willingness to learn, orientation to learning, and motivation. According to andragogy, adults are self-directed and anticipate having autonomy over their decisions. Adult learning programs ought to leverage participants' experiences and prioritize problem-solving and the prompt application of acquired knowledge.

Heutagogy, on the other hand, goes beyond andragogy by placing more of an emphasis on autonomous learning. Heutagogy, the term coined by Stewart Hase and Chris Kenyon, puts the student at the center of the learning process and gives them autonomy over their own educational path (Hase & Kenyon, 2000). The foundation of heutagogy is the idea that students should be able to identify their own learning requirements, create their own learning objectives, and assess their own development in addition to being self-directed. It places a strong emphasis on the growth of learners' capacities and double-loop learning, in which students consider and challenge their presumptions and the process of learning (Blaschke, 2012).

The learning approaches in andragogy and heutagogy differ significantly, particularly in methods and learner engagement. Andragogy employs structured learning environments where the role of the educator is to facilitate rather than direct learning. Educators provide resources, guide discussions, and support learners in applying knowledge to real-world situations. The learning process in andragogy is collaborative, leveraging the collective experiences of adult learners to enhance understanding and problem-solving skills (Knowles et al., 2015). Methods commonly used in andragogical settings include case studies, simulations, and problem-based learning, where learners engage in active learning through practical application and reflection.

On the other hand, heutagogy embraces a more autonomous and flexible learning approach. Learners in heutagogical environments have significant control over what, how, and when they learn. With this method, students pick and pursue projects according to their needs and interests, encouraging them to take charge of their own education. Technology is essential to heutagogy because it makes a wide range of resources accessible and allows for individualized learning (Blaschke, 2012).

The engagement of learners also differs between the two approaches. In andragogy, learners are expected to be self-directed but within a framework provided by the educator. This means that while learners have some control, the overall structure and objectives are often predetermined. In heutagogy, learners are not only self-directed but also self-determined, meaning they set their own learning goals and determine their own learning paths. This level of autonomy requires learners to be more proactive, reflective, and capable of managing their own learning processes (Hase & Kenyon, 2007).

To summarise, while both andragogy and heutagogy stress the value of learner autonomy and experience, heutagogy goes a step further by encouraging a self-determined, learner-centered method of instruction. While heutagogy gives learners complete control over their learning process and promotes flexibility and lifelong learning, andragogy offers adult learners a structured framework with an emphasis on immediate application and problem-solving.

Additionally, recent research underscores the relevance and application of heutagogy in various educational settings, particularly in the context of lifelong learning and digital education. For instance, heutagogical practices have been shown to be effective in promoting lifelong learning skills, which are essential in today's rapidly changing world (Chamo, Biberman-Shalev, & Broza, 2023). Additionally, the integration of digital technologies has further facilitated the implementation of heutagogical approaches by providing learners with tools to control their learning experiences (Blaschke, 2012; Eberle, 2013).

Heutagogical Framework

The heutagogical framework involves steps that emphasize learner autonomy, double-loop learning, and capability development. The goal of this framework is to establish an educational setting where students take charge of their education, think critically about it, reflect on their experiences, and acquire the skills required for lifelong learning. Below is an outline of the process, including practical applications and examples.

Step 1: Establishing Learner Autonomy: Heutagogy is based on the principle of learner autonomy, which holds students accountable for their own learning goals and routes. Teachers need to build environments that are student-centered to foster learner autonomy. These settings, which promote self-directed learning, can be both real and virtual. For instance, learners can select materials that best fit their interests using online platforms, which offer access to a vast variety of resources (Blaschke, 2012; Eberle, 2013). Promoting introspection and self-evaluation is another essential component. Learners can track their progress, reflect on their experiences, and pinpoint areas for growth with the aid of tools and activities like e-portfolios and reflective journals (Blaschke & Hase, 2016).

Step 2: Facilitating Double-loop Learning: In order to achieve deeper comprehension and transformative learning, double-loop learning entails challenging underlying assumptions and beliefs. Critical thinking should be encouraged by educators to support double-loop learning. It is crucial to incorporate activities that push students to challenge their presumptions and engage in critical thinking about what they have learned. In this sense, techniques like case studies, problem-based learning, and Socratic questioning work well (Argyris & Schon, 1996). Giving constructive criticism is also crucial. Fostering an environment rich in feedback, where students get helpful criticism from teachers and peers, allows them to improve their comprehension and pedagogical style (Moore, 2020).

Step 3: Fostering Capability Development: Capability development focuses on equipping learners with the skills and attributes necessary to navigate and adapt to complex, real-world situations. Designing real-world learning experiences is vital for fostering capability development. Incorporating real-world problems and scenarios into the curriculum can enhance learning. For example, project-based learning that involves community projects or internships provides practical experience and develops capabilities (Hase & Kenyon, 2007). Encouraging lifelong learning is another important aspect. Promoting lifelong learning involves encouraging learners to set long-term learning goals and pursue continuous professional development opportunities. Online courses and workshops can support this aim (Eberle, 2013).

In higher education, universities can implement heutagogical principles by offering flexible learning pathways, such as personalized degree programs where students can choose courses that align with their career goals and interests. Additionally, incorporating capstone projects that require students to solve real-world problems can enhance capability development (Blaschke & Hase, 2016). In corporate training, organizations can apply heutagogy in their training programs by encouraging employees to take charge of their professional development. Providing access to online learning platforms, facilitating peer-to-peer learning, and supporting mentorship programs can create a self-directed learning culture (Blaschke, 2012). Even in K-12 education, elements of heutagogy can be incorporated. For example, allowing students to choose topics for projects, engage in inquiry-based learning, and reflect on their learning processes can foster autonomy and critical thinking from an early age (Moore, 2020).

Developing a heutagogic framework involves creating an educational environment that prioritizes learner autonomy, promotes double-loop learning, and fosters capability development. By integrating these principles into various educational settings, educators can prepare learners to thrive in an ever-changing world, equipped with the skills and mindset necessary for lifelong learning.

Integrating Heutagogy across Modes of Learning

Integrating heutagogy across different modes of learning – formal, informal, and non-formal – enhances the adaptability and effectiveness of educational practices. By leveraging the principles of self-determined learning, educators can create a more flexible and personalized learning experience that caters to diverse learner needs and preferences.

In formal learning environments, such as schools and universities, heutagogy can be integrated to promote greater learner autonomy and engagement. Traditional curriculum-driven instruction can be augmented with opportunities for self-directed projects, inquiry-based learning, and reflective practices. Heutagogical approaches in formal settings can transform the role of educators from knowledge dispensers to facilitators of learning (Blaschke, 2012). This shift empowers students to take charge of their learning paths, thereby fostering critical thinking, problem-solving skills, and lifelong learning habits. Additionally, the integration of technology, such as learning management systems and digital portfolios, supports heutagogical practices by providing tools for learners to set goals, track progress, and reflect on their learning (Eberle, 2013).

Informal learning occurs outside of structured educational settings and includes activities such as reading, social interactions, and participation in online communities. Heutagogy aligns naturally with informal learning due to its emphasis on self-directed learning. According to Livingstone (2001), informal learning is driven by the learner's intrinsic motivation and personal interests, which align well with the principles of heutagogy. Integrating heutagogical practices in informal learning can involve using digital tools and social media platforms to create personal learning networks where learners can share resources, collaborate, and receive feedback. This approach not only supports knowledge acquisition but also fosters the development of critical soft skills such as communication, collaboration, and self-regulation.

Non-formal learning encompasses structured learning experiences outside traditional educational institutions, such as community education programs, professional development workshops, and online courses. Heutagogy can enhance non-formal learning by emphasizing learner autonomy and flexibility. For instance, Eberle (2013) suggests that heutagogical practices in non-formal settings enable learners to tailor their learning experiences to their specific needs and contexts, leading to more meaningful and sustained learning outcomes. Practical applications include designing modular courses that allow learners to choose topics of interest, incorporating reflective activities to facilitate deeper understanding, and using peer-to-peer learning to leverage the collective knowledge and experience of the learner group (Blaschke & Hase, 2016).

The holistic integration of heutagogy across formal, informal, and non-formal learning models creates a cohesive and adaptable educational ecosystem. By promoting self-determined learning, heutagogy helps learners develop the skills and mindset necessary for continuous learning and adaptation in a rapidly changing world. This approach is particularly relevant in the context of lifelong learning, where individuals must continually acquire new knowledge and skills to stay competitive and relevant (Eberle & Childress, 2009). Additionally, heutagogy's emphasis on double-loop learning, which involves reflecting on and challenging underlying assumptions and beliefs, supports the development of higher-order thinking skills and emotional intelligence (Argyris & Schon, 1996).

Practical examples of integrating heutagogy across learning modes include the use of project-based learning in formal education, where students design and execute projects based on their interests and goals. In informal learning, digital storytelling and social media engagement can facilitate self-directed exploration and expression. Non-formal learning can benefit from blended learning approaches that combine online modules with in-person workshops, allowing learners to engage with content at their own pace and apply their learning in real-world contexts (Hager & Halliday, 2009).

Emotional Experience in Learning

Integrating cognitive and emotional learning involves creating a learning environment where both intellectual and affective components are considered essential for effective education. This balanced approach acknowledges that emotions significantly influence cognitive processes such as attention, memory, and problem-solving.

Techniques for integrating cognitive and emotional aspects of learning:

a. Emotionally engaging content: Designing curriculum content that evokes emotions can enhance memory retention and understanding. For example, storytelling and real-world problem scenarios can make learning more relatable and engaging (Immordino-Yang & Damasio, 2007).
b. Reflective practices: Encouraging learners to reflect on their emotional responses to learning experiences can deepen understanding and promote self-awareness. Journals, discussion forums, and self-assessment tools can facilitate this process (Moon, 2004).
c. Social and collaborative learning: Creating a safe and supportive learning environment where learners feel comfortable expressing their emotions can lead to better engagement and outcomes. This includes providing timely feedback, encouraging open communication, and showing empathy (Noddings, 2005).

It has been demonstrated that achieving a balance between cognitive and emotional learning improves student engagement and learning results. Studies show that satisfying students' emotional needs boosts their drive to learn, which enhances both academic achievement and personal development. Motivated and involved students are more likely to find emotional connection in their academics. Pekrun et al. (2002), for example, discovered that whilst negative feelings like boredom and fear might impede motivation, positive emotions like pride and enjoyment can boost it. Research indicates that combining cognitive and emotional learning can improve students' academic performance. Social-emotional learning (SEL) programs in schools have been shown to enhance students' academic achievement, social behaviors, and attitudes toward learning, according to a meta-analysis conducted in 2011 by Durlak et al.

Development of critical soft skills like empathy, emotional control, and interpersonal communication is aided by an emphasis on emotional learning. More and more people are realizing how important these abilities are to success in both personal and professional settings (Goleman, 1995). Learning that involves emotional engagement provides long-term advantages in addition to immediate effects on academic performance. A passion for learning and a commitment to lifelong learning are more likely to emerge among emotionally invested learners, which are important in a world that is changing quickly (Jarvis, 2006).

Emotional Experience and Heutagogy

Emotional experiences are integral to enhancing self-determined learning, which is central to heutagogical principles. Heutagogy emphasizes learner autonomy, capability development, and the learners' ability to adapt and self-direct their educational journey. Integrating emotional experiences into this framework can significantly enhance the effectiveness and engagement of the learning process. Emotions play a critical role in motivation and engagement, as positive emotional experiences, such as feelings of enjoyment and satisfaction, can increase a learner's intrinsic motivation and engagement in the learning process (Pekrun et al., 2011). When learners feel emotionally connected to the content, they are more likely to persist through challenges and invest effort in their learning. Additionally, emotional states influence cognitive processes such as attention, memory, and problem-solving. Positive emotions can enhance these cognitive functions, leading to better retention and understanding of information. Conversely, negative emotions can hinder cognitive performance, making it essential to create a learning environment that fosters positive emotional experiences (Immordino-Yang & Damasio, 2007). Heutagogy encourages learners to engage in self-reflection and metacognition, assessing their learning strategies and outcomes. Emotional experiences can deepen this reflective process. For instance, reflecting on how certain content made them feel can help learners understand their preferences and motivations, leading to more effective self-directed strategies (Moon, 2013). Moreover, emotional experiences are integral to social interactions and collaboration, which are essential components of heutagogy. Positive social interactions and a supportive learning community can enhance emotional well-being and facilitate cooperative learning, where learners share knowledge and support each other's growth (Vygotsky, 1978).

Practical implementation of integrating emotions into learning can be achieved through various techniques and tools designed to foster positive emotional experiences. One effective technique is the use of interactive and engaging content. Multimedia resources, gamified learning activities, and interactive simulations can create engaging and emotionally stimulating content, making learning more enjoyable and memorable (Lee & Hammer, 2011). Reflective practices also play a crucial role. Incorporating reflective exercises such as journaling, discussion forums, and self-assessment tools encourages learners to reflect on their emotional responses to learning experiences, which can deepen understanding and promote self-awareness (Moon, 2013).

Additionally, creating a supportive learning environment is essential. This involves providing a safe space where learners feel comfortable expressing their emotions. Timely feedback, fostering open communication, and showing empathy towards learners' experiences and challenges can significantly enhance emotional well-being (Noddings, 2013). Collaborative learning opportunities also contribute to fostering positive emotional experiences. Group projects, peer reviews, and collaborative discussions promote positive social interactions and a sense of community, enhancing both emotional well-being and the development of social and emotional skills (Johnson & Johnson, 1999). Furthermore, personalized learning paths are vital. Allowing learners to personalize their learning paths based on their interests and emotional responses to content increases motivation and engagement (Blaschke, 2012). For instance, learners might choose their projects and then research topics and assessment methods, encouraging deeper engagement with the material and the development of critical thinking and problem-solving skills (Blaschke, 2012). Digital tools and resources further support this approach by offering a wide range of learning materials, facilitating self-directed exploration and study (Moore, 2020).

Connection between Fabula and Sjuzhet to Emotions and Learning

Gerard Genette's contributions to narratology have provided profound insights into how stories are structured and how these structures influence emotions and learning. His concepts of "fabula" and "sjuzhet" are crucial in understanding the relationship between narrative form and the emotional and cognitive engagement of learners.

Fabula refers to the chronological sequence of events in a story- the raw, unstructured timeline of occurrences. In contrast, sjuzhet pertains to the way these events are organized and presented to the audience, often manipulating time, perspective, and emphasis to enhance the storytelling experience (Bal, 2017). These narrative structures are not only pivotal in storytelling but also highly relevant in the context of learning, where they can be utilized to create engaging and emotionally resonant educational experiences.

The way a story is told (sjuzhet) can significantly affect the emotional responses of the audience. For example, by starting a narrative in the middle of things, a story can create immediate intrigue and emotional investment, compelling the audience to become more engaged (Abbott, 2008). Genette's analysis of temporal manipulations, such as analepsis (flashbacks) and prolepsis (flashforwards), show how altering the sequence of events can create suspense and evoke emotional responses that would not be as powerful if the story were told in straightforward chronological order (Genette, 1980). Applying Genette's principles of fabula and sjuzhet in educational contexts can enhance learning by leveraging the emotional power of narratives. When educational content is presented as a story, it can make the material more relatable and memorable.

Applying the principles of fabula and sjuzhet in learning design can significantly enhance emotional engagement and deepen learning. By structuring educational content as compelling narratives, educators can create immersive learning experiences that resonate emotionally with learners, thus promoting better engagement, retention, and understanding.

Using fabula, educators can craft realistic scenarios that follow a logical progression. These scenarios help learners see the relevance of the content to their own lives, fostering an emotional connection and deeper engagement. Presenting a learner with a story about a professional's career progression that mirrors their own aspirations can create a powerful emotional impact (Oatley, 2016).

Employing sjuzhet allows educators to manipulate the presentation of events to build suspense, highlight critical learning moments, and maintain learner interest. For example, starting a lesson with a surprising outcome and then backtracking to explore how it was reached can hook learners and sustain their engagement throughout the lesson (Abbott, 2008).

Reflective learning experiences, in which learners recount and analyse their learning journeys, can be structured using fabula and sjuzhet to emphasize key moments of learning and emotional growth. This not only reinforces the content but also helps learners develop self-awareness and critical thinking skills (Bruner, 1991).

Heutagogy, with its emphasis on self-determined learning, benefits significantly from the integration of narratives structures like fabula and sjuzhet. By leveraging these narrative techniques, heutagogical practices can create more engaging and emotionally resonant learning experiences.

In a heutagogical framework, learners are encouraged to take control of their learning paths. Allowing learners to create their own narratives (fabula) and present them in their own way (sjuzhet) can empower them and enhance their emotional engagement. This process promotes a deeper connection with the material as learners are more invested in a story they have crafted themselves (Blaschke, 2012).

Heutagogy promotes double-loop learning, where learners question underlying assumptions and values. Narratives structured using fabula and sjuzhet can facilitate this deeper level of reflection, as learners not only review what they have learned but also how they have learned it and the emotional journey they experienced (Argyris, 1991).

By incorporating narrative elements that evoke emotions, educators can create learning experiences that are memorable and impactful. For instance, a medical training program might use a patient's story (fabula) told from different perspectives (sjuzhet) to highlight the emotional aspects of patient care and empathy (Robin, 2008).

In business education, presenting a case study (fabula) in a non-linear fashion (sjuzhet) can heighten engagement. Starting with a surprising diagnosis or business outcome and then exploring the sequence of decisions and actions that led to it can make the learning process more engaging and memorable (Boehrer & Linsky, 1990).

In problem-based learning, presenting a complex problem (fabula) and allowing students to uncover the sequence of events and solutions (sjuzhet) themselves can enhance critical thinking and emotional investment. The process of discovery and the emotional highs and lows of problem-solving can make the learning experience more impactful (Hmelo-Silver, 2004).

Digital tools allow educators to create interactive narratives where learners can explore different paths and outcomes. By structuring these narratives using fabula and sjuzhet, educators can create emotionally engaging and personalized learning experiences that cater to diverse learning preferences (Robin, 2008).

Blending Heutagogy, Emotional Experience, and Narrative Structures

In the evolving landscape of education, integrating heutagogical principles with emotional experiences and narrative structures presents a compelling approach to enhance learning design. Heutagogy, or self-determined learning, emphasizes learner autonomy and capability development, which is crucial in fostering lifelong learning skills. Emotional experiences, integral to human learning, drive motivation, focus attention, and enhance memory retention. Narrative techniques, such as sjuzhet and fabula, offer a powerful framework for presenting learning materials in a compelling structure. This synthesis can create more engaging and effective learning environments (Blaschke & Hase, 2016; Genette, 1980; Immordino-Yang & Damasio, 2007).

Heutagogy builds on andragogy but extends its principles by emphasizing the learners' ability to set their own goals, manage their own learning processes, and reflect critically on their experiences. This approach is particularly relevant in today's rapidly changing world, where adaptability and continuous learning are essential (Hase & Kenyon, 2013). Research indicates that heutagogical practices enhance learner autonomy, critical thinking, and motivation, as learners engage deeply with material they have chosen and structured themselves (Blaschke, 2012). This self-directed learning aligns well with the needs of modern learners who must navigate complex and ever-changing information landscapes.

Emotions play a crucial role in learning by driving motivation, focusing attention, and enhancing memory. Positive emotions, such as curiosity and excitement, can significantly boost engagement and learning outcomes. Conversely, negative emotions like anxiety and boredom can impede learning (Pekrun et al, 2002). Emotional experiences in learning can be fostered through a supportive environment that encourages exploration, collaboration, and self-expression (Durlak et al., 2011). Techniques such as personalized feedback, interactive activities, and reflective practices help in creating a positive emotional climate that enhances learning (Noddings, 2005).

Gerard Genette's concept of sjuzhet and fabula provides a valuable framework for enhancing emotional engagement in learning, utilizing these narrative structures in educational contexts can make learning materials more engaging and memorable. For example, structuring information in a way that creates suspense, surprise, or a coherent storyline can capture learners' attention and evoke emotional responses, thereby facilitating deeper learning (Bruner, 1991).

To develop effective learning design practices that blend heutagogy, emotional experience, and narrative structures, educators and instructional designers can adopt several strategies:

a. Personalized Learning Paths: Allowing learners to create their own learning paths based on their interests and goals aligns with heutagogical principles and can be enhanced by incorporating narrative elements. Learners can construct their own "stories" by choosing the sequence and context in which they engage with the material (Blaschke, 2012).
b. Story-driven Learning Modules: Designing learning modules that follow a narrative structure can significantly enhance engagement. Using fabula to outline key concepts and events and sjuzhet to present these in a compelling way can include case studies, simulations, or project-based learning where learners follow a storyline that evolves based on their decisions (Robin, 2008).
c. Reflective Practices: Encouraging learners to reflect on their learning experiences and emotions through reflective journals, discussion forums, and peer reviews can help them articulate their thoughts and feelings, fostering deeper understanding and emotional engagement (Moon, 2004).
d. Emotional Scaffolding: Providing emotional support through positive feedback, encouragement, and a supportive learning community helps build a positive emotional climate that enhances learning (Noddings, 2005).
e. Technology Integration: Leveraging technology to support personalized and emotionally engaging learning experiences is essential. Adaptive learning platforms, digital storytelling tools, and virtual reality environments can create immersive and interactive learning experiences that evoke strong emotional responses (Siemens, 2013).

Integrating heutagogy with emotional experience and narrative structures like sjuzhet and fabula offers a holistic approach to learning design. By fostering learner autonomy, creating emotionally engaging experiences, and using compelling narratives, educators can enhance both the cognitive and emotional aspects of learning. This blended approach not only prepares learners for the complexities of the modern world but can also cultivate a lifelong love for learning.

Recommendations for Educators and Policy Makers

In the evolving landscape of education, integrating heutagogy with emotional experience can lead to more effective and personalized learning practices. This approach fosters autonomy, critical thinking, and emotional intelligence, which are essential for lifelong learning. The following recommendations offer strategies for educators and policymakers to integrate these principles into new learning design practices.

Promoting learner autonomy is crucial in heutagogical practices. Educators should develop curricula and policies that prioritize learner autonomy and self-directed learning. A flexible curriculum design allows students to choose their learning paths, select projects that interest them, and set their own learning goals, which can increase engagement and motivation (Blaschke, 2012). Self-assessment tools, such as reflective journals and peer reviews, encourage students to assess their own progress and reflect on their learning experiences, promoting deeper understanding (Eberle, 2013). Additionally, supporting students in creating personalized learning plans that outline their goals, strategies, and timelines encourages ownership and accountability in the learning process (Blaschke & Hase, 2016).

Fostering emotional engagement in the classroom can significantly enhance learning outcomes. Implementing emotional literacy programs can improve students' emotional intelligence and create a supportive learning environment (Goleman, 1995). Storytelling and narrative techniques, like fabula and sjuzhet, create emotionally engaging content that helps students better understand and remember complex concepts (Genette, 1980; Bruner, 1991). Incorporating social-emotional learning (SEL) into the curriculum can also help students develop essential skills such as empathy, cooperation, and conflict resolution, which are shown to improve social and academic outcomes (Durlak et al., 2011).

Leveraging technology to support heutagogical and emotional learning practices is essential in modern education. Online learning platforms that offer personalized learning experiences, such as adaptive learning systems and e-portfolios, can help track progress, provide feedback, and support self-directed learning (Siemens, 2013). Digital storytelling tools allow students to create and share their own stories, enhancing creativity, communication skills, and emotional engagement (Robin, 2008). Additionally, utilizing virtual reality and augmented reality to create immersive learning experiences can evoke strong emotional responses and make abstract concepts more tangible (Lee & Hammer, 2011).

Designing reflective and experiential learning opportunities is another effective strategy. Implementing experiential learning projects that require students to apply their knowledge in real-world contexts can enhance their practical skills and deepen understanding (Hmelo-Silver, 2004). Encouraging students to engage in reflective practices, such as journaling and discussions, helps connect emotional experiences with learning and fosters critical thinking (Moon, 2004). Promoting double-loop learning, where students question and revise their underlying assumptions and beliefs, further enhances critical thinking and adaptability (Argyris & Schon, 1996).

Professional development is crucial for implementing heutagogical and emotional learning practices. Workshops on heutagogical principles, emotional intelligence, and technology integration equip educators with effective strategies (Eberle & Childress, 2009). Collaborative learning communities and mentorship programs further support innovation and continuous improvement by enabling educators to share experiences and receive guidance (Johnson & Johnson, 1999; Hager & Halliday, 2009).

Developing supportive policies and frameworks at institutional and governmental levels is necessary to integrate heutagogy and emotional learning effectively into practice. Inclusive education policies should ensure that all students have access to flexible and personalized learning opportunities, accommodating diverse learning needs (Freire, 1970). Allocating funding for the development and implementation of heutagogical and emotional learning programs supports the necessary resources for technology integration, training, and curriculum development (Kenyon & Hase, 2010). Designing assessment frameworks that evaluate both cognitive and emotional learning outcomes is also crucial. Traditional testing methods should be complemented with assessments that measure emotional intelligence, creativity, and problem-solving skills (Pekrun, 2006).

Encouraging research and innovation in heutagogy and emotional learning is key for progress. Research grants for exploring these practices inform policy (Moore, 2020). Pilot programs test new designs and gather data for scaling successful models (Blaschke & Hase, 2016). Interdisciplinary collaboration among educators, psychologists, and technologists fosters comprehensive and effective educational practices (Noddings, 2005).

CONCLUSION

This chapter explored the integration of heutagogy and emotional experiences in modern learning design, emphasizing the importance of a learner-centered approach that fosters autonomy, self-direction, and emotional engagement. The researcher began with a comprehensive definition of heutagogy, highlighting its core principles of learner autonomy, capability development, and double-loop learning. This approach contrasts with traditional pedagogical and andragogical methods by emphasizing the learners' active role in shaping their academic journey (Blaschke, 2012).

The researcher traced the historical context of heutagogy, introduced by Stewart Hase and Chris Kenyon in the early 2000s, and discussed its evolution and growing relevance in response to the dynamic needs of contemporary education (Hase & Kenyon, 2000). Their contributions have significantly influenced modern educational practices, advocating for a shift towards more flexible, self-determined learning environments.

A step-by-step framework for implementing heutagogical principles was outlined, emphasizing practical applications such as reflective practices, personalized learning paths, and the use of digital tools to support self-directed learning.

The chapter also examined the different modes of learning – formal, informal, and non-formal – and discussed how heutagogy can be applied across these modes to create a holistic and effective learning experience. Emotional experience was given equal importance, with a focus on balancing cognitive and emotional learning to improve engagement and outcomes (Immordino-Yang & Damasio, 2007).

Furthermore, the researcher explored the connection between narrative structures, such as fabula and sjuzhet, and learning design. These narrative techniques were shown to enhance emotional engagement and deepen learning by creating compelling and emotionally resonant educational experiences (Bal, 2017; Bruner, 1991).

FUTURE DIRECTIONS

The integration of heutagogy and emotional experience in learning design is a promising area for future research and development. As educational environments continue to evolve, several key areas warrant further exploration:

a. Technology-enhanced learning: With the rise of digital learning platforms and artificial intelligence, there is a significant potential to develop adaptive learning systems that provide personalized learning experiences tailored to individual emotional and cognitive needs. Future research could focus on how these technologies can support heutagogical principles and enhance emotional engagement (Siemens, 2013).
b. Emotional analytics: The use of emotional analytics to assess and respond to learners' emotional states in real-time is an emerging field. Understanding how emotional data can be effectively integrated into learning design to improve outcomes and support self-directed learning is a critical area for further investigation (Woolf, 2010).

c. Cross-cultural studies: Examining how heutagogical practices and emotional learning designs can be adapted and applied in diverse cultural contexts will provide insights into creating more inclusive and effective educational practices globally. Cross-cultural research can help identify universal principles and culturally specific strategies for implementing these approaches (Marginson & Rhoades, 2002).

By continuing to explore and innovate in these areas, educators and researchers can develop more effective and engaging learning environments that meet the diverse needs of modern leaders, fostering lifelong learning and personal growth.

REFERENCES

Abbott, H. P. (2008). *The Cambridge introduction to narrative* (2nd ed.). Cambridge University Press. DOI: 10.1017/CBO9780511816932

Argyris, C. (1991). Teaching smart people how to learn. *Harvard Business Review*, 69(3), 99–109.

Argyris, C., & Schön, D. A. (1996). *Organizational learning II: Theory, method, and practice*. Addison-Wesley.

Bal, M. (2017). *Narratology: Introduction to the theory of narrative* (4th ed.). University of Toronto Press.

Blaschke, L. M. (2012). Heutagogy and lifelong learning: A review of heutagogical practice and self-determined learning. *International Review of Research in Open and Distance Learning*, 13(1), 56–71. DOI: 10.19173/irrodl.v13i1.1076

Blaschke, L. M., & Hase, S. (2016). Heutagogy: A holistic framework for creating twenty-first-century self-determined learners. In B. Gros, Kinshuk, & M. Maina (Eds.), *The future of ubiquitous learning: Learning designs for emerging pedagogies* (pp. 25-40). Springer. https://doi.org/DOI: 10.1007/978-3-662-47724-3_2

Boehrer, J., & Linsky, M. (1990). Teaching with cases: Learning to question. *New Directions for Teaching and Learning*, 1990(42), 41–57. DOI: 10.1002/tl.37219904206

Bruner, J. (1991). The narrative construction of reality. *Critical Inquiry*, 18(1), 1–21. DOI: 10.1086/448619

Chamo, N., Biberman-Shalev, L., & Broza, O. (2023). 'Nice to Meet You Again': When Heutagogy Met Blended Learning in Teacher Education, Post-Pandemic Era. *Education Sciences*, 13(6), 536. DOI: 10.3390/educsci13060536

Coombs, P. H., & Ahmed, M. (1974). *Attacking rural poverty: How non-formal education can help*. Johns Hopkins University Press.

Durlak, J. A., Weissberg, R. P., Dymnicki, A. B., Taylor, R. D., & Schellinger, K. B. (2011). The impact of enhancing students' social and emotional learning: A meta-analysis of school-based universal interventions. *Child Development*, 82(1), 405–432. DOI: 10.1111/j.1467-8624.2010.01564.x PMID: 21291449

Dweck, C. S. (2006). *Mindset: The New Psychology of Success*. Ballantine Books.

Eberle, J. (2013). Lifelong learning. In Hase, S., & Kenyon, C. (Eds.), *Self-determined learning: Heutagogy in action*. Bloomsbury Academic.

Eberle, J., & Childress, M. (2009). Using heutagogy to address the needs of online learners. In Rogers, P., Berg, G. A., Boettecher, J. V., & Justice, L. (Eds.), *Encyclopedia of distance learning* (2nd ed.). Idea Group Inc. DOI: 10.4018/978-1-60566-198-8.ch331

Freire, P. (1970). *Pedagogy of the Oppressed*. Penguin Books.

Gardner, A., Hase, S., Gardner, G., Dunn, S. V., & Carryer, J. (2008). From competence to capability: A study of nurse practitioners in clinical practice. *Journal of Clinical Nursing*, 17(2), 250–258. DOI: 10.1111/j.1365-2702.2006.01880.x PMID: 17419787

Genette, G. (1980). *Narrative Discourse: An Essay in Method* (Lewin, J. E., Trans.). Cornell University Press.

Goleman, D. (1995). *Emotional intelligence: Why it can matter more than IQ*. Bantam Books.

Hager, P., & Halliday, J. (2009). *Recovering informal learning: Wisdom, judgement and community*. Springer.

Hase, S. (2014). Capability and learning: Beyond competence. In Harteis, C., Rausch, A., & Seifried, J. (Eds.), *Discourses on professional learning: On the boundary between learning and working* (pp. 45–59). Springer., DOI: 10.1007/978-94-007-7012-6_4

Hase, S., & Kenyon, C. (2000). From andragogy to heutagogy. *UltiBase*. Retrieved from http://ultibase.rmit.edu.au/Articles/dec00/hase2.htm

Hase, S., & Kenyon, C. (2007). Heutagogy: A child of complexity theory. *Complicity: An International Journal of Complexity and Education*, 4(1), 111–119. DOI: 10.29173/cmplct8766

Hase, S., & Kenyon, C. (2013). *Self-determined learning: Heutagogy in action*. Bloomsbury Academic.

Hawk, T. F., & Shah, A. J. (2007). Using learning style instruments to enhance student learning. *Decision Sciences Journal of Innovative Education*, 5(1), 1–19. DOI: 10.1111/j.1540-4609.2007.00125.x

Hmelo-Silver, C. E. (2004). Problem-based learning: What and how do students learn? *Educational Psychology Review*, 16(3), 235–266. DOI: 10.1023/B:EDPR.0000034022.16470.f3

Immordino-Yang, M. H., & Damasio, A. (2007). We feel, therefore we learn: The relevance of affective and social neuroscience to education. *Mind, Brain and Education : the Official Journal of the International Mind, Brain, and Education Society*, 1(1), 3–10. DOI: 10.1111/j.1751-228X.2007.00004.x

Jarvis, P. (2006). *Towards a comprehensive theory of human learning*. Routledge.

Johnson, D. W., & Johnson, R. T. (1999). *Learning together and alone: Cooperative, competitive, and individualistic learning*. Allyn & Bacon.

Kenyon, C. (2012). Teaching and learning for adult capability: Becoming capable. In Hase, S., & Kenyon, C. (Eds.), *Self-determined learning: Heutagogy in action* (pp. 83–100). Bloomsbury Academic.

Kenyon, C., & Hase, S. (2010). Andragogy and heutagogy: A review of the literature and a presentation of an integrated educational framework. In Hase, S., & Kenyon, C. (Eds.), *Self-determined learning: Heutagogy in action* (pp. 13–35). Bloomsbury Academic.

Knowles, M. S., Holton, E. F., & Swanson, R. A. (2015). *The adult learner: The definitive classic in adult education and human resource development* (8th ed.). Routledge.

Lee, J. J., & Hammer, J. (2011). Gamification in education: What, how, why bother? *Academic Exchange Quarterly*, 15(2), 1–5.

Livingstone, D. W. (2001). Adults' informal learning: Definitions, findings, gaps and future research. *NALL Working Paper No. 21*. Retrieved from https://nall.oise.utoronto.ca/res/21adultsifnormal.htm

Marginson, S., & Rhoades, G. (2002). Beyond national states, markets, and systems of higher education: A glonacal agency heuristic. *Higher Education*, 43(3), 281–309. DOI: 10.1023/A:1014699605875

Moon, J. A. (2004). *A handbook of reflective and experiential learning: Theory and practice*. Routledge.

Moore, R. L. (2020). Developing lifelong learning with heutagogy: Contexts, critiques, and challenges. *Distance Education*, 41(3), 381–401. DOI: 10.1080/01587919.2020.1766949

Noddings, N. (2005). *The challenge to care in schools: An alternative approach to education*. Teachers College Press.

Noddings, N. (2013). *Caring: A relational approach to ethics and moral education*. University of California Press.

Oatley, K. (2016). Fiction: Simulation of social worlds. *Trends in Cognitive Sciences*, 20(8), 618–628. DOI: 10.1016/j.tics.2016.06.002 PMID: 27449184

Pekrun, R. (2006). The control-value theory of achievement emotions: Assumptions, corollaries, and implications for educational research and practice. *Educational Psychology Review*, 18(4), 315–341. DOI: 10.1007/s10648-006-9029-9

Pekrun, R., Goetz, T., Titz, W., & Perry, R. P. (2002). Academic emotions in students' self-regulated learning and achievement: A program of qualitative and quantitative research. *Educational Psychologist*, 37(2), 91–105. DOI: 10.1207/S15326985EP3702_4

Robin, B. R. (2008). Digital storytelling: A powerful technology tool for the 21st century classroom. *Theory into Practice*, 47(3), 220–228. DOI: 10.1080/00405840802153916

Siemens, G. (2013). Learning analytics: The emergence of a discipline. *The American Behavioral Scientist*, 57(10), 1380–1400. DOI: 10.1177/0002764213498851

Vygotsky, L. S. (1978). *Mind in society: The development of higher psychological processes*. Harvard University Press.

Woolf, B. P. (2010). *Building intelligent interactive tutors: Student-centered strategies for revolutionizing e-learning*. Morgan Kaufmann.

Chapter 4
Emotional Learning Analytics in Education:
Current Status, Trends, and Challenges

Kyriaki A. Tychola
 https://orcid.org/0000-0002-2528-4295
MLV Research Group, Department of Informatics, Democritus University of Thrace, Kavala, Greece

Eleni Vrochidou
MLV Research Group, Department of Informatics, Democritus University of Thrace, Kavala, Greece

George A. Papakostas
 https://orcid.org/0000-0001-5545-1499
MLV Research Group, Department of Informatics, Democritus University of Thrace, Kavala, Greece

ABSTRACT

Learning Analytics (LA) are constantly evolving in the analysis and representation of data related to learners and educators to improve the learning and education process. Data obtained by sensors or questionnaires are processed employing new technologies. The emotional experiences of learners constitute a significant factor in the assimilation of knowledge about the learning process. The emerging technology of Emotional Learning Analytics (ELA) is increasingly being considered in educational settings. In this work, the significance and contribution of ELA in educational data processing are discussed as an integral part of designing and implementing computational models reflecting the learning process. In addition, a comprehensive overview of different methods and techniques for both LA and ELA

DOI: 10.4018/979-8-3693-2663-3.ch004

is provided, while a conceptual model of ELA is proposed in parallel. Moreover, advantages, disadvantages, and challenges are highlighted. The final focus of the chapter is on ethical issues and future research directions.

INTRODUCTION

Learning Analytics (LA) can inform the learning process through the analysis of learner interactions during a course. LA seek to generate "actionable intelligence" through the cyclical process of learning (Campbell, DeBlois & Oblinger, 2007), aiming to improve teaching and learning quality (Clow, 2013). Although LA have been an active field since 1979, when "The Open University" analyzed ten years of progress of their thousands of students (Ferguson, 2012), it is only since 2008 that the concept of analytics has been applied in education, focusing on understanding and optimizing learning (Atkisson & Wiley, 2011). In 2010, the concept of LA was isolated from the field of analytics and emerged as an independent area (Ferguson, 2012). LA were conceptually clarified in 2011 (Atkisson & Wiley, 2011); since then, they have been employed in a wide range of applications.

LA are related to the manipulation of big data collected by various educational institutions and scientific fields to improve the learning experience (Crick, 2017). Generated data can be complex, heterogeneous, and difficult to understand. With the aid of LA methods, users can comprehend the data and turn it into knowledge that is crucial for making decisions (Vieira, Parsons & Byrd, 2018). Big data methods have several uses in LA (Cantabella, Martínez-España, Ayuso, Yáñez, & Muñoz, 2019), such as: (a) performance prediction, assessing how well students engage with peers and teachers in a virtual classroom; (b) risk identification, using behavior analysis of students to identify the likelihood that a student may drop a course; (c) data visualization; (d) intelligent feedback, improving the interactions and performance of learners; (e) course recommendations based on learners' interests which arise from their activities; and (f) estimation of learners' acquired skills.

Data processing and analysis are achieved by leveraging various new technologies (Banihashem et al., 2018) including social network analysis, user profiling, adaptive learning, and predictive modeling to make recommendations for improving education as well as suggesting novel approaches to instruction and learning. A globally implemented and commonly accepted model does not currently exist (Aristovnik et al., 2020). Thus, the educational sector has been challenged to determine the importance and significance of LA towards enhancing learning (Axelsen et al., 2020; Hernández-de-Menéndez et al., 2022).

Traditional teaching methods focus on the cognitive profile of the learners, evaluating knowledge acquired in the context of courses (Letteri, 1980). This approach should be considered incomplete, due to the lack of a human-centered model. During data collection, psychological and emotional factors should also be considered (Larradet et al., 2020). On this basis, a new scientific field has been developed, known as Emotional Learning Analytics (ELA). ELA refer to the analysis of learning through processing emotionally-based data of students using several techniques and computational methods. While the focus of LA is on the cognitive outcomes of students, ELA integrate emotional cues as well, with a goal to enhancing student well-being alongside academic and behavioral results.

Emotions have been shown to affect cognition (Öhman & Soares, 1994). While an educator may not be able to access the type and range of a learner's emotions directly, they can gather relevant information through observed behaviors and performance. Further, emotions can be ranked based on the purposes they serve. For instance, a learner may feel satisfaction, anxiety, or frustration during a project's presentation or pride, shame, or jealousy when the social context, in term of social identities and relationships with others, as well as community involvement, influences emotions experienced. Other emotions can be derived from the cognitive status of the learner. In general, emotions can range from joy to fear of the unknown, and they are not always easy to handle (Piniel & Albert, 2018). However, there are techniques and methods for managing them.

Although it is difficult to disambiguate emotions based on common assumptions in ELA investigations, nevertheless there is evidence of their impact on the cognitive process of learners (Febriantoro, Gauthier & Cukurova, 2023). Here lies the potential contribution of ELA: making better decisions through the processing and analysis of appropriate and representative data and parameters, to optimize teaching methods and knowledge gain.

ELA reflect an interdisciplinary approach, leveraging the sciences of psychology and cognitive learning. Substantially, the impact of psychology on the learners is investigated. The presented research is based on experiments and observations that reflect students' emotions via body language and facial expressions. For instance, beginner learners (Bosch & D'Mello, 2017) were taught a difficult subject in Computer Science and experienced fear and confusion due to its complexity, whereas in another case (Arroyo et al., 2009), various sensors were used in the classroom to record body actions during the teaching of mathematics, revealing that anxiety was evident in the order of 60%. In addition, Wang et al. (2013) used voice recognition recorders to help educators limit speaker time and encourage the active participation of learners. The results were spectacular as increased interactivity was observed among learners and educators.

This chapter aims to provide an exhaustive overview of the current status of ELA. This work covers a wide range of aspects, summarized in the following distinct points: (1) the contribution of ELA to teaching and learning; (2) a holistic review of different techniques, highlighting their impact during the learning process; (3) related advantages and disadvantages from various perspectives; (4) emerging challenges using different models in education; (5) ethical issues; and (6) future research directions. This review was motivated by the potential of complementing the current state of learning analytics in consideration of the emotional aspect of learning.

MOTIVATION AND CONTRIBUTION

The ELA field has developed over the last decade, allowing computer scientists to manipulate, explore, and analyze various data identifying potential issues and leading to better decisions. However, since these data are big and complex, more robust and efficient design methods are required. Nowadays, ELA in combination with LA have been established as a powerful tool for the process of gathering, measuring, analyzing, and reporting information on students, courses, and learning initiatives to better comprehend and enhance learning. Researchers are turning to the investigation of robust and efficient methods to resolve complex issues accurately and in a short time. Several review articles on the subject can be found in the recent literature; however, a complete investigation of ELA is lacking (although most reviews that refer to LA can apply indirectly to ELA, as a subset of LA).

Hernández-de-Menéndez et al. (2022) provide a bibliographic review analyzing various projects concerning LA in education and the experiences of the learners, including applications, results, and opportunities of LA in education. The authors found that most initiatives use LA to improve retention of students, while only a few are focused on improving teaching/learning procedures or addressing academic issues, concluding that LA could be a valuable method for helping the educational community become more familiar with new forms of educational delivery, such as those imposed by the COVID-19 pandemic.

In Banihashem et al. (2018), the authors present Cooper's systematic literature review to analyze, evaluate, and interpret the appropriateness of data collected, including benefits and challenges. Results indicated that with respect to LA in education, the greatest challenges concern ethics and privacy, while they can bring notable benefits for education through the provision of real-time feedback and personalized learning.

Results in a similar vein are presented in Dietz-Uhler & Hurn (2013), Lytras et al. (2018), Siemens (2013), and Spikol et al. (2017), while others, such as Drachsler & Greller (2016), Gašević et al. (2016), and Wintrup (2017) focus on the ethical issues involved in the process. Joksimovic et al. (2019) and Marzouk et al. (2016) address the necessity and value of LA as a useful evaluation tool, and Shen et al. (2018) analyze and explore the results of pedagogical strategies using Educational Data Mining (EDM)/LA techniques, highlighting the different impacts of policies on particular types of students.

Regarding other previous reviews of ELA, Hooda (2020), Mu, Cui & Huang (2020), P. Ordóñez de Pablos et al. (2019) and Romero & Ventura (2013) focus on the current state-of-the-art in this field, including specific tools, benchmarks, and methods applied in the educational context. In Williamson (2021), ELA is investigated from social, emotional, and economic points of view, bringing new statistical knowledge to conclude with a better understanding of how education is perceived and how policies are designed. In Du Boulay et al. (2010), the authors study the emotions of learners during the learning process to present a conceptual framework that takes into account – in addition to cognition – the motivation, metacognition, and affect of learners. In Noroozi et al. (2019), various tools are proposed to collect and analyze data related to the interaction and emotions of learners during various forms of teaching. In Suero Montero & Suhonen (2014), the authors discuss the impact of unpleasant feelings on learning and highlight potential analyses of emotions, including ethical issues, emotional data, and challenges due to the reliability of technology, specifically in online learning settings. In Bosch & D'Mello (2017), the focus is on the importance and impact of emotions during the learning process, concluding that "engagement and confusion" and "confusion and frustration" are the two most frequently occurring pairs of affective states.

Most of the aforementioned works propose the implementation of different techniques and analyze various data for educational purposes focusing on the outcome of successful learning. However, none of them provides a thorough study presenting and analyzing in detail the significance of ELA in the teaching and learning process, highlighting at the same time advantages and drawbacks, as well as challenges and ethical issues. This encouraged us to carry out a thorough investigation, approaching the ELA topic holistically. Hence, the contribution of our work lies in the detailed analysis of ELA, including all related aspects such as advantages, limitations, challenges, and ethical issues as well as responses to predefined key research questions.

RESEARCH METHODOLOGY

Within the context of this work, a literature review was conducted using the Kitchenham approach (Kitchenham, 2004) to identify the status of research in ELA, based on four basic research questions:

RQ1: To what extent are LA associated with emotions?
RQ2: What challenges do ELA techniques face with respect to learning?
RQ3: What benefits do ELA provide to learners and educators?
RQ4: What supplementing modern technologies are combined with traditional teaching methods?

We performed a search of peer-reviewed journal publications in the Scopus database using the query "(TITLE-ABS-KEY (learning analytics) AND (education) AND (emotions)) AND (LIMIT-TO (DOCTYPE, "ar") OR LIMIT-TO (DOCTYPE, "cp") OR LIMIT-TO (DOCTYPE, "ch")) AND (LIMIT-TO (LANGUAGE, "English")) AND PUBYEAR > 2012 AND PUBYEAR < 2024". The process before limitations returned 80 documents, and limiting document types (articles, conference papers, and book chapters) and language (English), 69 documents were returned. Figure 1 indicates the number of publications on the subject by year, from 2013 to 2023, i.e., for ten complete years. Although ELA methods have only been applied to education within the last decade, the ever-increasing number of publications shows an overall upward trend, indicating the significance of this research topic. Figure 2 illustrates highly frequently used keyword terms in ELA-related literature based on their occurrence. The font size indicates the frequency of the term given the keywords of the papers. As can be observed, most of the literature focuses on students, followed by learning analytics and systems, computer-aided instruction, educational computing, and sentiment analysis. In addition, teaching, curricula, motivation, and academic performance are the most commonly used terms related to outcomes and evaluation.

The scope of this work is to unravel the potential of ELA in education by presenting related advantages and disadvantages, emerging challenges, ethical issues, and future research directions. Therefore, in this work, a narrative review is conducted (Ferrari, 2015) to describe and synthesize the available literature on the topic, providing valuable conclusions, interpretations, and critiques from the gathered evidence. From the 69 retrieved papers, only 52 were specifically oriented to ELA in education, and thus relevant to our study and used in this work.

Figure 1. Number of relevant publications per year on the subject of ELA (Statistics July 2024)

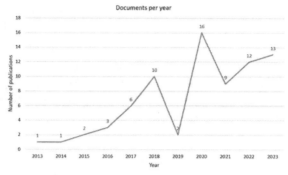

Figure 2. Cloud map of high-frequency terms used in emotional learning analytics based on paper keywords

LEARNING ANALYTICS (LA)

Various definitions have been provided for LA (Axelsen et al., 2020; Banihashem et al., 2018; Charitopoulos, Rangoussi, & Koulouriotis, 2020; Ifenthaler & Yau, 2022). Based on all definitions, we conclude with an overall definition of LA as *"collection of various educational data including static or dynamic information on an ongoing basis, measurements, visualization, analysis and reporting, and application of different techniques, tools, and modules to generate models for the interpretation of outcomes aiming to understand and improve learning environments, educational process, and experience from the perspective of efficient teaching and learning, while providing simultaneous evaluation and feedback."*

Data processing is achieved by various methods and techniques based on artificial intelligence (AI) and machine learning, including conventional methods of data analysis as well as statistics to address important educational questions (descriptive, diagnostic, predictive, and prescriptive) and thus to make decisions. This field is called Educational Data Mining (EDM) and includes data acquisition, analysis, and action (Bakhshinategh et al., 2018). LA provide powerful tools for teaching and learning, aiming to optimize data in terms of structure, accuracy, and visualization. Thus, feedback is an essential parameter. Nowadays, LA are an innovative form of educational process evaluation because, through the obtained results, teaching approaches are reformed to define a learning model which is more attractive to learners. Many representations of the analytical process have been developed over time in a variety of disciplines. However, a common model does not exist.

LA consist of three crucial components of concern to learners, educators, and developers: (1) high-quality data, (2) current pedagogical theory, and (3) human innovation. Theories of learning- appropriate data as well as rational and impartial planning should be taken into account in the stage of data processing. The relevance of data and the corresponding design depend on the type of measurements and the teaching/learning based on gnoseology (Knight & Buckingham Shum, 2017). It is understood that the development of approaches to analytics in learning also helps decision-making related to the selection of teaching/learning methods for the educator to promote knowledge optimally. At this point lies the difficulty of designing a uniform model containing non-measurable parameters and standardized curricula based on prior knowledge. Another difficult issue is the analysis. For instance, if the analysis is addressed to all groups of learners, they may not perceive concepts and procedures in the same way. Hence, the learning approach is multilayer including various groupings/isolating of learners. This problem is increasing since it also depends on the available supervisory tools (Crick, 2017).

LA TECHNIQUES

LA employ a variety of methods, including machine learning (decision trees, random forests, support vector machines, and genetic algorithms), artificial intelligence, data mining, and data visualization (Charitopoulos et al., 2020), including fuzzy logic, learning sciences, psychology, e-learning, and social aspects (Ranjeeth, Latchoumi, & Paul, 2020), as well as techniques such as Bayesian modeling, natural language processing (NLP), and predictive modeling. Prediction, clustering, connection mining, model discovery, and data separation for human judgment are among the most widely used Educational Data Mining (EDM) approaches (Nunn et al., 2016). According to Aldowah et al. (2019), data mining techniques can be ranked as: (a) Computer-Supported Learning Analytics (CSLA) that use data mining algorithms to develop the interaction of learners identifying learning opportunities; (b) Computer-Supported Predictive Analytics (CSPA) for learners' performance prediction, such as participation, engagement, and grades; (c) Computer-Supported Behavioral Analytics (CSBA) which are based on the behavior, preferences, and motivations of learners related to the learning environment; and (d) Computer-Supported Visualization Analytics (CSVA), providing visualization of learners' behavior during a learning activity.

LA focus on the cognitive profile of the students, assessing their knowledge solely via the course material. However, cognitive profiling by itself is not enough when obstacles created by emotions must be faced, significantly influencing learners' progress.

With respect to the LA process, there is no consensus related to the phases and requirements of the inserted data. There are different and contradictory opinions: some researchers assert that an action must be a part of the process, while some don't and others believe it is crucial that the outcomes be measured to determine the improvements due to interventions, as well as having a leader who can bargain for the resources required for deployment, such as effective LA tools (Tsai et al., 2020). LA experts or information technology (IT) departments create and use LA tools (Lee, Chang, & Chen, 2007). Practical and effective LA tools shorten the time between analysis and action (Chatti & Muslim, 2019). Many technologies for various educational goals have been developed by universities, e-learning companies, and collaborative ventures, such as predicting the success of learners and their needs for the content of a course.

EMOTIONAL LEARNING ANALYTICS (ELA)

ELA measure emotions within the context of the learning process. Teaching/learning methods adopt human-centered models, focusing on learners. Humans are entities and do not act in isolated fashion. On the contrary, they are affected by experiences and emotions. The acquisition and evaluation of knowledge at a given time can cause a plethora of emotions, from the thrill of success and satisfaction to the fear of failure or inflow of new information to gain knowledge. However, specific definitions for the concept of ELA are scarce, despite the major impact of emotions on the process of education.

A global definition based on the referenced literature can be formulated as follows (D'Mello & Jensen, 2022; Ulutaş, 2023): *"Emotional Learning Analytics (ELA) is a term referring to learning analysis through the processing of emotionally-based data to improve students' learning experiences by using several techniques and computational methods."*

Unlike traditional LA which focus on cognitive and behavioral data, ELA additionally integrate emotional cues towards providing an overall assessment of students' engagement and performance. The main difference between ELA and traditional LA is that LA are more oriented to the academic and behavioral outcomes of students (cognitive outcomes), while ELA also examines the emotional states of students and their impact on learning (well-being). Therefore, alongside traditional metrics of LA such as questionnaires, ELA introduce physiological and psychological metrics as well.

There are multiple ways emotions have been operationalized for ELA. There are models for categorizing emotions into distinct classes. Six basic emotions are identified: anger, happiness, sadness, fear, surprise, and disgust. *Discrete Emotion Models* such as the model introduced by Hoemann et al. (2022) are used for the latter purpose. Different approaches use *Dimensional Models*, such as the Circumplex Model of Affect (Zhaoxia Wang, Ho & Cambria, 2020), that represent emotions on continuous dimensions, e.g., positive to negative, high to low. *Appraisal Models* also consider the evaluation of students on triggering events, leading to their emotional responses (Hess, 2017). Other models split emotions into components, such as physiological responses, subjective feelings, and expressive behavior, and then analyze them to conclude the effects on learning over time. Such models are referred to as *Component Process Models* (Hoemann et al., 2022). *Machine Learning and AI Models* use sophisticated algorithms to detect and classify emotions from multiple sensory data sources such as text, speech, facial expressions, and body posture, by using NPL, computer vision, and deep learning algorithms. However, a *Multimodal Emotion Recognition Model* that can combine all these different sensory data could provide more accurate emotion detection results. Each type of model offers different insights and poses its own challenges for ELA. Selecting one, however, is based on the scope of each application and the available data types.

ELA integrate aspects of multiple separate scientific fields, such as affective sciences, educational sciences, and Emotional Data Mining (EDM) to understand how emotions influence learning outcomes with a view to improving them. Therefore, ELA aim to foster better academic performance and emotional well-being for students by determining, and thus, addressing all emotional aspects involved in the learning process. ELA are closely related to educational settings where the understanding of the emotional states of students is essential for delivering more effective teaching strategies, resulting in improved student engagement.

The term emotion data (ED) refers to data that reflect the learners' affective state during a particular time and are mined to discover the emotional patterns of a learner or group of learners. ED can be divided into (a) the causes of emotions and the identification of the learner's state, (b) consequences such as the impact of emotions during the learning activity or intervention by educators, and (c) actions, i.e., measures to influence the learner's current emotional state to a more desired state. ED can be especially helpful for the evaluation of progress made by students in both blended and online learning contexts.

ELA aim to draw conclusions considering all the components of educational parameters such as pedagogical practices, curricula, educators, and evaluation, in light of emerging technologies. Through new technologies, a holistic approach to learning can be adopted, including healthy interpersonal relationships and cognitive learning. By applying innovative methods, education can be radically changed. Emotions play a crucial role in the teaching/learning process since they affect the motivation, confidence, and academic progress of learners. Consequently, emotions are integral parts of learning and must be investigated in combination with cognitive factors. In addition, although the ELA field is in its infancy, the model's design based on the emotions of learners seems directly relevant to the fields of EDM and LA, promising to respond to various queries of educators (Febriantoro et al., 2023).

ELA TECHNIQUES

Different modern techniques, combined with traditional ones, have been applied to evaluate learners and educators during the educational process. These techniques employ different practices to improve the learning experience. Each practice needs to contain basic knowledge to be exploited, either individually or globally. The development of software for the analysis of emotions requires a huge amount of labeled data which is then processed leveraging the potential of machine learning algorithms and natural language processing (NLP) (Berehil, Roubi & Arrhioui, 2020; Dyulicheva & Bilashova, 2022). In general, the ELA approach aims to identify and measure learners' emotions through their behavior, while the impact of experienced emotions is evaluated by traditional methods such as questionnaires and/or technologies such as Augmented Reality (AR). However, traditional methods suffer from lack of objectivity (Rodríguez et al., 2020). Other novel technologies, such as ClassDojo for example (Williamson, 2017), are being applied to establish an emerging government "psychopolitical" approach for measuring socio-emotional learning. This is achieved through gamification techniques (Daineko et al., 2023) creating new notions about "character development," "development mentalities," and "personal properties." These technologies can act effectively to encourage and reward learners (Barahona Mora, 2020).

Affective computing's debut in advanced learning systems might define them as intelligent systems, which is a revolutionary approach to evaluating a learner's pedagogical welfare and leads to a realistic understanding of the learner's progress throughout the learning experience in diverse learning environments. At the same time, emotional feedback or interventions to the learning process are also provided. In learning systems, the emotion data are inserted either implicitly or explicitly, i.e., via an information-system approach to detect the emotions through supporting users to communicate them. Data analysis is completed through questionnaires and surveys using computational linguistic techniques (Munezero et al., 2013), or through sensors or wearable devices placed on the learner's body.

There are several different ways emotion has been operationalized for the purpose of ELA. Traditionally, *questionnaires and self-report surveys* are employed to directly record students' emotions. The latter is the most straightforward method, yet its reliability can be affected by the self-consciousness of students.

Behavioral observation is another traditional method, referring to the observation of students to detect changes in emotional states. This method could be reliable particularly for experienced observers (since it can be affected by observer bias), yet it is costly and time-consuming because a trained expert needs to be present for all educational activities.

Physiological measures refer to metrics captured by sensors, such as heart rate and brain activity. The captured data can be very objective. However, the latter is an invasive method that presupposes wearable sensors for the students, which could be stressful (which would then influence the measurements). The use of sensors may not always be feasible, since sensors are costly. Moreover, measurements can be influenced by the quality of sensors, their correct placement, the environmental conditions, and more. Emerging technologies are prominent in delivering results of high accuracy, both non-invasively and at lower cost, in real-time.

Natural language processing (NLP), computer vision, signal processing, and artificial intelligence (AI) can be employed for *facial expression analysis*, *voice analysis*, and *text analysis* to provide real-time emotion detection. Their reliability could be influenced by the quality of the captured data, by cultural differences resulting in differences of expression, and by variations in speech patterns and environmental noise.

Reliability refers to the consistency of measurements. All methods involving sensory measurements could potentially be more reliable (provided the algorithms and sensors are accurate), while self-reports and observations may vary in reliability among different or even the same individuals and observers over time. *Validity* in this case refers to how well measurements capture the nature and scale of emotions. In this case, physiological measures or voice analysis could be more valid, yet they may fail to identify different emotions correctly. In general, multimodal approaches that combine several different methods could provide results that are both more reliable and more valid.

Many systems have been developed for these purposes (Feidakis et al., 2013). For example, AutoTutor (Du Boulay et al., 2010) was designed to recognize the learner's affective state through the detection of conversational cues, facial features, and posture, attempting to move learners towards (or keep them in) a positive learning state like "engaged" and move them away from negative learning states like "bored." Gaze Tutor (Rus et al., 2013) is a biology learning environment that tracks eye movements to determine when students are fading out or distracted and then initiates gaze-reactive conversations to get them interested again. Emot-control (Conver, 2020) is a cross-platform online application designed to gather emotional self-reports and offer fuzzy rule-based emotional feedback. It also has a virtual animated assistant that employs facial expressions and synthesized speech to provide empathetic feedback. Caring Agent Maggie (Lee et al., 2007) is a pedagogic agent leveraging body language, hand gestures, facial expressions, and social discourse to demonstrate empathy and attentive listening in interaction with learners. In addition, this technology aims to address the negative emotions of learners, to demonstrate care by providing appropriate advice, and help them overcome their academic problems.

Due to constant technological evolution, various applications are designed in a collaborative manner, combining a range of features and characteristics and supplementing utilized technologies to provide additional benefits of different types during learning. Thus, technologies such as artificial intelligence (AI) and virtual/augmented reality (VR/AR) are used to enable ELA in education frameworks.

AI has transformative potential in STEM education to enhance students' learning experiences by using technologies like NLP, sentiment analysis, and facial expression recognition (Xu & Ouyang, 2022). AI algorithms can provide personalized feedback to students during argumentation and reasoning activities, improving science teaching and learning. AI models can analyze text or speech to detect emotions, sentiments, and affective states. Applications include assessing student engagement, identifying emotional distress, and monitoring well-being. AI algorithms analyze facial features to recognize emotions (e.g., happiness, sadness, anger) to assess student reactions during online learning or in virtual classrooms. In addition, AI can process physiological data (heart rate, skin conductance, etc.) to infer emotions (Vidal, 2023).

VR/AR technologies overlay digital content onto the real world and create entirely digital environments to provide immersive learning experiences. Immersive environments can evoke emotions and simulate real-world scenarios (Lampropoulos et al., 2022). VR/AR applications enhance empathy, social skills, and emotional regulation. In addition, VR/AR can simulate complex scenarios, enhance understanding of abstract concepts, and engage students in interactive learning. Moreover, wearable devices or sensors in educational settings can provide real-time feedback while using adaptive learning systems to personalize learning experiences based on students' emotional responses. Adjusting content, difficulty, or pacing can enhance engagement and motivation. Additionally, AI-driven chatbots can provide emotional support, answer questions, and offer resources. They create a safe space for students to express feelings and seek guidance. Early identification of at-risk students allows timely interventions (Chng, Tan & Tan, 2023; Cukurova & Luckin, 2018).

CONCEPTUAL MODEL OF ELA FOR EDUCATIONAL DATA PROCESSING

Despite all the developed techniques in the ELA field, nowadays a complete prediction model capable of making generalized decisions to be applied in all cases does not exist. ELA modelling is oriented to the configuration of different characteristics of learners, such as behavior, learning performance, evaluation, support, and feedback, as well as to learning features, such as curriculum, cognitive level, and support of learners by educators. In this context, corresponding collected data could be used to develop a representative model. Various techniques for data processing and analysis to identify those factors that contribute to the configuration of attitudes have been developed. The ultimate goal is to improve the educational process and for learners to acquire knowledge, based on individual capabilities and interests.

Based on the above, we propose a conceptual model for educational data processing, including emotions. Figure 3 shows the general stages of the proposed conceptual model for decision-making.

Figure 3. Conceptual design of the proposed model

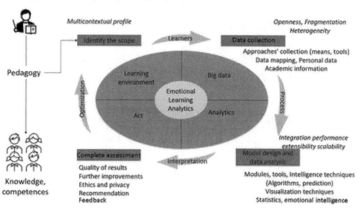

According to the above framework, initially the purpose of the investigation is defined. Then, collected data based on different techniques such as clustering and classification are mapped. Various indicators and parameters are also defined and visualized in charts to facilitate interpretations. In the next stage, the model is designed and developed including cognitive and psychometric information using corresponding modules and tools, respectively. This stage is significant since a bad initial design would lead to the redesign and reidentification of parameters. Finally, the assessment stage offers quality results and suggestions for model optimization (Kazanidis, Pellas & Christopoulos, 2021). Various devices are used for data mining such as Intelligent Tutoring Systems (ITS) (Alkhatlan & Kalita, 2019) and Virtual Learning Environments (VLE) (Alves, Miranda & Morais, 2017), aiming to capture the emotions of learners during the learning process and evaluate them through the observation of actions, such as body language, facial expressions, or voice timbre.

It should be noted that the proposed framework is general and abstract, allowing it to be adaptable and applicable across various contexts and situations; thus, it constitutes a broader structure that could be tailored to any specific needs. In general, no one-size-fits-all model for ELA exists. Context, learner demographics, and educational settings significantly impact the effectiveness of the model.

RESULTS

In this section, the selected articles are presented in tabular form (Table 1). Table 1 includes information on the results of studies where applicable, the measures, the proposed approach, supporting data, and the field of application. Insights from these works were synthesized to support the discussion and future directions presented in the following section. Review articles were also included in this work and therefore are mentioned in Table 1; however, details such as data, approaches, measures, and results could not be provided due to the nature of these articles.

DISCUSSION AND FUTURE DIRECTIONS

Emotions pervade the learning process, even unconsciously, and affect memory, engagement, decision-making, and other cognitive functions. Students experience several emotions during courses, namely "academic emotions" (Pekrun & Stephens, 2012) which are categorized into four main groups: achievement, topic, social, and epistemic emotions. Emotions are not accidental; they happen for a reason. Not all students will experience the same emotions during a course.

Emotions are experienced as conceptual entities resulting from interactions among the environment, body, and brain. They can be characterized in physiological, behavioral, neurobiological, and subjective terms (D'Mello & Jensen, 2022). Moreover, the same emotion can range from minor to intense and can be manifested differently, across different people and different triggering events. Therefore, emotions cannot be strictly defined; they are complex, adaptive, and dynamic, characterized by ambiguity and variability. The latter is the main challenge for ELA, which aims to study the emotions of students during learning and provide beneficial data-driven insights.

Therefore, a critical appraisal of underlying assumptions that characterize ELA is necessary. One assumption is the *universal experience of emotions*, i.e., that all emotions experienced are expressed in the same way. Another assumption is that of *static emotion categories*, meaning that emotions belong only to a category of a predetermined basic list.

The relationship of affect with cognition and learning is a study area of psychology (Isen, 2003). Basic principles concerning this link include *interconnection*, since affect, cognition, and learning are interrelated. One affects the other: emotions influence cognition, which involves the mental steps of acquiring, processing, and understanding information, and then learning occurs as a result. *Social cognition* should also be considered to affect this link, since it can subjectively shape interactions and judgements, as well as *metacognition* (Winne, 2021), which refers to how learners understand their own cognition and its properties. *Learning and motivation* are also basic principles since emotions can impact motivation, which is essential for acquiring new knowledge.

Table 1. Summary of selected works

Ref.	Application	Data	Approach/Method	Measures	Results
(Nguyen, 2023)	Climate change education	Hashtags from TikTok	Youth express emotions to relate to viewers and situate their content	Analytical approach	Utility of ELA to explore youth's perspectives and provide insights to frame climate change education
(Kasliwal, Gunjan & Shete, 2023)	E-learning platform evaluation	E-Learners Academic Reviews (ELAR) dataset	Machine learning models (Multilayer Perceptron (MLP), Logistic Regression (LR), Random Forest (RF), Decision Tree (DT))	Precision Accuracy	90% accuracy in all academic emotion categories of excitement, happy, satisfied, not satisfied, and frustration
(Bittencourt et al., 2023)	Review article	Roadmap for positive psychology and artificial intelligence in education			
(Kivimäki, Ketonen & Lindblom-Ylänne, 2023)	Evaluation of structured learning diaries	Interviews with students	Rank- and median-based statistical tests	Analytical approach	Differences in how changes in difficulty and emotion ratings were made
(Plintz & Ifenthaler, 2023)	Review article	Current state of research on emotion measurement in online learning environments			
(Ulutaş, 2023)	Review article	Rethinking learning engagement through ELA in K-12 classrooms through social-emotional learning and mindfulness			
(Xu, Wu & Ouyang, 2023)	Evaluation of collaborative pattern	Audio data of verbal communication, computer screen data of click stream, video data of facial expressions, pair programming task data	Multimodal learning analytics (k-clustering, quantitative content analysis, click stream analysis, video, statistical analysis, epistemic network analysis, process mining	Clusters of collaborative types	Four collaborative patterns associated with different levels of process and summative performances
(Li & Yao, 2023)	Student facial expression recognition in classroom	Public dataset RAF-DB, Sefl-collected real classroom teaching video data	Improved Deep Neural Network Model with Mixed Attention Mechanism	Accuracy	88.71% on RAF-DB 86.14% on self-data
(Hasnine et al., 2023)	Online learners' affective states	Real-time facial video capture	Multimodal learning analytics (Multi-Task Cascaded Convolutional Neural Networks for face detection, Mini Xception for emotions extraction, HaarCascade and PNP for eye detection and gaze estimation)	Classification into 5 scales of engagement and 2 types of concentration	
(Giannakos & Cukurova, 2023)	Review article	The role of learning theory in multimodal learning analytics (MMLA) research			

continued on following page

Table 1. Continued

Ref.	Application	Data	Approach/Method	Measures	Results
(Febriantoro et al., 2023)	Review article	The contribution of physiological data to collaborative learning			
(Zheng, Zhong & Niu, 2022)	A learning analytics-based personalized feedback approach	Discussion transcripts in online collaborative learning, questionnaires, interviews	Bidirectional encoder representations from transformers (BERT) to classify texts with respect to behaviors and emotions	Analytical approach, self-report measures	Improved collaborative knowledge-building level and emotions, students had better co-regulated behavioral patterns
(Singh, Bangay & Sajjanhar, 2022)	A platform using AR to enhance learning analytics	Accelerometer, gyroscope, and magnetometer data, facial expressions, voice semantics	-	Analytical approach	Identify and classify the sources of data, generate metrics relevant to learning outcomes, use AR to visualize analytics, ensure data is used to dynamically adapt the learning process
(Shukla & Garg, 2022)	Review article	Exploration of the unstructured data in terms of sentiments of online learners regarding their perceived learning			
(Daoudi, 2022)	Review article	Current state of the art related to the application of learning analytics to serious educational games			
(Singh, Bangay & Sajjanhar, 2022)	A platform using AR to enhance learning analytics	Audio and video recordings, acceleration, user interface control, heart rate, respiratory rate, body and ambient temperature, longitude/latitude	AI and Machine Learning algorithms for AR-based Learning Analytics (emotion, interaction, learning, sensory, spatial)	Analytical approach	Identify and classify the sources of data, generate metrics relevant to learning outcomes, use AR to visualize analytics, ensure data is used to dynamically adapt the learning process
(Shu, Zhao, Liu, Li & Huang, 2022)	The impact of synchronous live class on online course learning behavior	Online course student logs, forum texts, and instant messaging program Tencent QQ group text	NLP emotional tendency analysis Interface of Baidu AI Open Platform	Descriptive statistics	Overall, positive emotional tendencies towards live class
(Kim, Lee & Kim, 2021)	LA for longitudinally learning-related emotions, learner participation level, and cognitive effort of students	Asynchronous online discussion text	IBM tone analyzer to detect emotions, multilevel ordered logit models, multilevel Poisson regression models	Descriptive analyses	Positive or negative expressed emotions led to higher participation in ongoing discussions and participation level predicted the rate of change in textual revision
(Namoun & Alshanqiti, 2020)	Review article	Synthesis of intelligent models and paradigms applied in education to predict the attainment of student learning outcomes			

continued on following page

Table 1. Continued

Ref.	Application	Data	Approach/Method	Measures	Results
(Cebral-Loureda & Torres-Huitzil, 2021)	Neural Deep Learning Model for Learning Analytics	Text, images, sound, movement	Deep learning neural models (RetinaFace for face detection, RF for action unit detection, ResMaskNet for facial expression recognition)	Classification to 7 emotional states	-
(Joseph-Richard, Uhomoibhi & Jaffrey, 2021)	Affective responses of students viewing their own predictive LA dashboard	Reflective responses (verbalize 8 predefined emotions)	Content analysis	Percentage of affect responses	-
(Zheng et al., 2021)	Case study of instructor interaction with an LA dashboard	Transcripts	Sequential mining techniques	Probability of most likely co-occurrence between activities and 5 emotions	Determination of co-occurrence patterns
(Crescenzi-Lanna, 2020)	Review article	Practices in recent Multimodal Learning Analytics and Learning Analytics research literature to identify tools and strategies for the assessment of progress and behavior of children under 6 years old in respect of their learning			
(Gkontzis, Kotsiantis, Kalles, Panagiotakopoulos & Verykios, 2020)	Analysis of activity, polarity and emotions of tutors and students to predict students' grades	Course logins, threads, messages from an academic platform	NLP for analysis of polarity (3 classes) and emotions (8 classes), regression algorithms (RF, additive Regression (AR), KNN, SMOreg)	Predictive precision (maximum error)	Models' comparison ranked first the AR model for the objectives of written assignments and final examinations grades, and SMOreg for the average grade
(Antoniou et al., 2020)	Real-time affective analytics data while experiencing virtual patient and mixed reality scenarios	Heart Rate, electrodermal activity, electroencephalography (EEG)	-	Descriptive statistics	Increased attention/concentration state, usage of bio-sensors assist in the detection of the emotional state and could provide real-time ELA
(PraveenKumar, Manorselvi & Soundarapandiyan, 2020)	Sentimental analysis of students' feelings and emotions towards online teaching	Text of students' feedback	Lexicon-based sentimental analysis	Sentiment scores and emotional variance, emotions classification in 8 classes	Positive sentiments/emotions towards online teaching and emotions vary concerning the online class timing
(Hsieh et al., 2020)	Design of interactive robot-assisted teaching to help overcome academic difficulties	Big data emotional dataset (the Google facial expression comparison dataset)	Anticipatory computing to robots, based on AI, statistical analysis of students' achievements and motivation questionnaire	Attention, relevance, confidence, and satisfaction scores	The robot interacts with the students, which improves their learning motivation

continued on following page

Table 1. Continued

Ref.	Application	Data	Approach/Method	Measures	Results
(P. E. Antoniou et al., 2020)	Efficacy of wearable biosensors for affect detection in a learning process involving a serious game in a VR/MR platform	Heart rate, electrodermal activity, and EEG	Variations of statistical metrics have been correlated with existing theoretical interpretations regarding educationally relevant affective analytics, such as engagement and educational focus	Average signal ratios	This sensor configuration can lead to credible affective state detection
(Sun, Ouyang, Li & Chen, 2020)	Minecraft's effect on secondary students' creativity, emotion, and collaborative behaviors	Creativity questionnaire	-	Self-report measures	Students' creativity was increased, emotions of enjoyment, hope, and pride towards programming were improved, anxiety was decreased
(Zaki, Zain, Noor & Hashim, 2020)	Development of a conceptual model of learning analytics in serious games for STEM education	Group interviews with students	-	Learning profiles, student profiling, serious games characteristics, curriculum profiles, key stakeholders	Experts are satisfied with all the LA themes for serious games for STEM learning provided in the instrument
(Tempelaar, Rienties & Nguyen, 2020)	Design of predictive models of academic performance based on computer-generated trace data and survey data	Trace data from technology-enhanced learning systems, computer log data of a static nature, questionnaires, and course performance data	Multiverse statistical analysis	Regression-based predictions, confidence measures, course performance measures	Bias present in surveys adds predictive power in the explanation of performance data and other questionnaire data
(Russell, Smith & Larsen, 2020)	Supporting at-risk student resilience through learning analytics	Performance scores and platform trace data, survey questionnaire	Cox proportional hazards Regression model	Descriptive statistics (mean and standard deviations of key variables)	At-risk students using an LA platform is associated with a final passing grade
(Srimadhaven et al., 2020)	Analyze the effectiveness of VR for under-graduate students of higher education	Tests, assessments, challenging tasks, multiple-choice questions, debugging, and evaluations	Reinforcement learning and learning analytics analysis	Cognitive behavior and competency skills by using the rubrics metrics	-

continued on following page

Table 1. Continued

Ref.	Application	Data	Approach/Method	Measures	Results
(Vidhya & Vadivu, 2019)	Inspect student performance using emotional state on learning analytics	Questionnaire	Logistic Regression and SVM, to predict learning capacity of students	Classification of emotions, learning, and intelligence	-
(Pham & Wang, 2018)	Prediction of learners' emotions in mobile online learning	Photoplethysmography (PPG) signals and facial expressions videos	Feature extraction, feature fusion, and prediction models (SVM with RBF-kernel)	Average accuracy of classification, R^2 prediction of learning outcome	84.4% accuracy 50.6% R^2
(Berman & Artino, 2018)	Development of an online engagement metric using virtual patients	Time on page, multiple-choice question answer accuracy, use of clinical reasoning tool, and scoring of written summary statements	Statistical analysis (confirmatory factor analysis, consistency reliability analysis with Cronbach's alpha, calculation of descriptive statistics, correlation analysis)	Self-report measure of motivational, emotional, and cognitive engagement	Correlation of engagement score with self-report measure was statistically significant
(Staudt, Grushetskaya, Rangelov, Domanska & Pinkwart, 2018)	Identify emotions by measuring heart rate, electrodermal activity, and skin temperature during the learning process	Heart rate (HR), electrodermal activity (EDA), skin temperature (TEMP)	Statistical evaluation of HR and signal analysis of EDA and TEMP for differentiation in 5 emotions	Measure of the arousal dimension, descriptive statistics	-
(Dafoulas, Maia, Clarke, Ali & Augusto, 2018)	Sensor-generated data in a number of collaborative learning scenarios	Heartbeat, emotion detection, sweat levels, voice fluctuations, and duration and pattern of contribution via voice recognition	Learning analytics of sensor-generated biometrics through a platform, expression of 6 basic emotions	Classification of participants' contributions	-
(Pereira, Souza & Menezes, 2018)	Digital game to classify facial expressions and identify emotional states of players	Facial images, log records of players' actions, events or states of game, questionnaire	VGG Face CNN to identify the facial expressions	Percentage of learning assessment (3 classes)	Computational architecture of Learning Analytics was superior to the manual process, by the questionnaire

continued on following page

Table 1. Continued

Ref.	Application	Data	Approach/Method	Measures	Results
(Moreno-Marcos, Alario-Hoyos, Munoz-Merino, Estevez-Ayres & Kloos, 2018)	Sentiment Analysis in forum messages of online courses	Forum messages and characteristics of the discussion interactions (e.g. votes, number of replies, timestamps, etc.)	Supervised (Logistic regression, SVM, DT, RF, Naïve Bayes) and unsupervised (lexicon-based: Dictionaries, SentiWorldNet) Algorithms for sentiment analysis	AUC, Kappa (sentiment classification in 3 classes)	AUC between 0.71 and 0.85 Kappa between 0.38 and 0.61 Most reliable approach was RF
(San Pedro, Baker & Heffernan, 2017)	Prediction model of college attendance, engagement, and learning in digital environments	Student knowledge, academic emotions, disengaged behaviors, and other information on student usage	Logistic regression model, computational models, mining/learning analytics methodologies	Descriptive statistics, cross-validated AUC ROC and cross-validated Kappa	AUC ROC of 0.687 Kappa value of 0.266 Educational data assess cognitive constructs (learning, academic emotions, behavior)
(Liu et al., 2016)	Emotion and topic detection for comments in online course platform	Student text comments	Multi-view emotion recognition model (2 classes), deterministic emotional information-based topic mining	Predictive and real support rates, probability distribution of words	81.4% positive emotion prediction rate 79.81% real positive emotions
(Voigt, Kieslinger & Schäfer, 2017)	User experiences around sentiment analyses for workplace learning	Words, sentences, postings	Sentiment analysis (dictionary-based, machine learning)	Sentiment polarity (percentage of positive and negative words)	-
(D. T. Tempelaar, Rienties & Nguyen, 2017)	Learning analytics using dispositions, self-regulation, and emotions	Demographic, trace data, course performance measures, dispositional attitudes, motivation, engagement, goal setting, self-regulated learning, learning emotions, epistemic emotions data	Linear, multivariate models for hierarchical regression analysis, student clustering based on K-Means, cluster analysis of the LMS trace data solely	Descriptive statistics of performance	Outcome of 4 clusters
(Bannert, Molenaar, Azevedo, Järvelä & Gašević, 2017)	Develop an understanding of multimodal data that capture cognitive, meta-cognitive, affective, and motivational states of learners over time	Multimodality online trace data (log-files, eye gaze behaviours, transpiration, facial expressions of emotions, heart rate, and electro-dermal activity)	Poster work discussing the relevance of LA to measure and support students' learning in adaptive educational technologies, with no implementation	-	-

continued on following page

Table 1. Continued

Ref.	Application	Data	Approach/Method	Measures	Results
(Sedrakyan, Leony, Muñoz-Merino, Kloos & Verbert, 2017)	Visualizations of affective states of students in computer-based learning environments	-	Visualization techniques to show the frequency of each affective state for each activity, the accumulated amount of time dedicated and frequency of affective dimension, emotions, relation between emotion frequency and work dedication	-	Exploratory analysis of the developed visualizations with a small number of students
(Pereira, De Souza & De Menezes, 2016)	Computational architecture for LA in game-based learning	Records with evidence of game-based learning, gameplay video recording	Data mining (WEKA) to extract patterns from data records, Computer vision (VGG ANN) to extract behavior and emotion data	-	The program is just being developed
(Westera, van der Vegt, Bahreini, Dascalu & van Lankveld, 2016)	Software components for the development of serious games	Recordings of facial expressions, interaction data	Emotion Detection, Performance Statistics, text language processing	-	Presentation of a set of software components
(Bosch et al., 2016)	Detect students' affect in the real-world environment of a school computer lab	Observation data (affect labels), videos for head and body movements	Computer vision learning analytics and machine learning (C4.5 trees and Bayesian classifiers)	AUC Classification accuracy	Efficient automatic detection of boredom, confusion, delight, engagement, and frustration
(Tamura & Murakami, 2015)	Heartbeat feedback for learners' emotional self-control	Heartbeat, video data	Descriptive statistics	-	Effective for self-regulated learning
(Suero Montero & Suhonen, 2014)	Review article	Discussing the fusion of emotional data and learning analytics in online learning settings			
(Leony, Muñoz-Merino, Pardo & Delgado Kloos, 2013)	Visualizations embedded in intelligent systems for emotional awareness	Students' logs	Hidden Markov Models (5 states, 4 emotions)	-	10 types of visualizations (time-based, context-based, of change in emotion, of accumulated information)

A deeper understanding of these principles could help strengthen the relationships among affect, cognition, and learning, since emotions influence the processing of information, and the new knowledge is the result of such processing.

Specifically, ELA provide many benefits for choosing the most efficient teaching methods and evaluating the progress of both learners and educators, using innovative techniques and practices. Benefits can be ranked based on the improvement of the learning environment, the level of individual learning, and the automatic feedback received by learners or educators. Another category of benefits focuses on learners' skills and competencies, leading to improved academic performance and reduced gaps between learners (which may be due to varying socioeconomic conditions). Furthermore, through data analysis, the status of the educational system is also evaluated. Courses are assessed based on their potential to fit with learners' interests and preferences; collected data allow for the improvement or re-identification of curricula. Thus, it can be feasible to customize the educational experience for each individual. The teaching performance of professors can also be improved as the institution is able to analyze their behavior. Moreover, the use of big data could allow the identification of post-education employment opportunities and permit the alignment of education with market needs.

Based on the up-to-date adaptation of LA and ELA in education, the following conclusions can be drawn regarding the potential advantages for three different target groups: learners, educators/instructors, and institutions/schools.

Target Group A: Learners

I. Development of stronger social/emotional skills improving student academic performance
II. Enhanced engagement leading to fewer behavioral problems
III. Enriched, personalized learning environment
IV. Increased self-awareness, self-confidence, and self-reflection
V. Optimization of learning outcomes
VI. Optimization of adaptivity
VII. Reduction/elimination of negative emotions
VIII. Provision for individual learning
IX. Reduced emotional distress

Target Group B: Educators/Instructors

I. Enhanced assessment services
II. Direct feedback and insight
III. Ability to modify teaching content according to learners' desire
IV. Optimization of teachers' performance
V. Better understanding of teaching and learning
VI. Improvement of teaching strategies
VII. Apt recommendations of sources for study
VIII. Prediction of learner performance
IX. Reduction/prevention of learner dropout

Target Group C: Institutions/Schools

I. Target course identification
II. Learning design improvement
III. Improved educational decision-making
IV. Increased learner success
V. Increased eligibility for grants, funding, and other financial support to implement/sustain ELA-based learning initiatives
VI. Curriculum optimization
VII. Improvement of accountability
VIII. Reduction/prevention of attrition from courses/programs
IX. Analysis of standard assessment techniques and instruments

However, the potential benefits are not assured as ELA also come with challenges. The foremost challenge relates to privacy. Steps of the process related to data collection and data distribution require careful consideration regarding learners' privacy. Variations of privacy laws in different jurisdictions, guidelines for handling data, and ensuring privacy laws are observed can become quite complex.

Beyond privacy concerns, issues surrounding the scope and analysis of data are another challenge that ELA need to overcome. Truly accurate models require high-quality data for a broad scope. Institutions may not have the capacity to collect, store, clean, analyze, and visualize the necessary data to develop accurate models. Additionally, the data required for analysis cannot be approached in a universally applicable manner. Deployment of different learning activities and analytics of these activities must be tailored for each specific context.

A main obstacle obstructing the further evolution of ELA is related to the lack of a standardized methodology framework and theory that the research community could adopt. Other limiting factors concern the lack of modern data acquisition smart devices and the different types of information and data processing methods, particularly related costs and execution time (West, Heath & Huijser, 2015). In addition, the idea of personalized learning, which is supported in the LA field, is restricted because external factors affecting learners' performance cannot be taken into account (Cleveland-Innes & Campbell, 2012). Ultimately, LA and ELA are predictive, not psychic. They can predict learner outcomes, but cannot foresee situations like future training needs or future courses of action based on learners' performance.

Regarding the challenges that emerge from LA and ELA, the following aspects are critical:

I. Lack of common frameworks, theories, and strategies to model design and implementation
II. Concerns about data collecting, storage, analysis, and privacy
III. Lack of a holistic study (available data do not include external parameters that affect learners)
IV. Scarcity of data, limiting the ability to predict future needs of learners
V. Data processing issues due to limited integration, analysis, and visualization of data as a result of lacking qualified staff, resources, or funds
VI. Lack of common-sense understanding and nuanced awareness of educational contexts
VII. Potential for use as a means of surveillance instead of support
VIII. Benefits accruing to certain groups of learners and educators more than others
IX. Applications of LA/ELA primarily to benefit the needs of institutions rather than those of individuals
X. Unquantifiable information
XI. Inadvertent promotion of Techno-Idealism (belief that technology is a panacea and can solve all problems)
XII. Learners/educators feeling threatened, knowing their actions are being monitored

Data leveraging is one of the many issues facing ELA (Bodily et al., 2018). Researchers strive to solve two primary challenges: interpretability and data accuracy. Teachers and students do not actively participate in the development of ELA systems; they only have an observational role. IT departments and LA specialists have primary responsibility for the design and deployment of ELA solutions. It's unclear the degree of beneficial impact that ELA have on learning, as a result of educational institutions' greater focus on non-completion indicators, perseverance, and grades than on the motivation, engagement, and satisfaction of its students. The quality and application of data is crucial for ELA to enhance the learning process and forecast students' progress, because more formative learning assessment figures are insufficient (Guzmán-Valenzuela et al., 2021).

Moreover, it is important to extract relevant information from big data sets. Only the relevant subset of available data should be evaluated pedagogically and used to provide real learning outcomes (Guenaga & Garaizar, 2016). ELA are too big to suit all learners. ELA models are not able to gather general data or provide generalization. They ought to concentrate on a certain scope by using specific high-quality data to provide true insights for learning and teaching.

To this end, the concerns related to data, systems, and integration of emerging technologies can be summarized in the following points:

- The scope and quality of data concern the amount and variety of data, including data that can be used for evaluation. In particular, ELA rely on data from various sources (e.g., learning management systems, student interactions, and assessments); thus it involves analyzing diverse data types (e.g., text, clickstream, sensor data). Choosing appropriate algorithms and models can be complex.
- The primary determinant of an individual's performance is the platform being utilized for data tracking.
- Accurate systems for timely data tracking are lacking.
- Technical resources are required to manage big data.
- Acceptance and implementation of LA/ELA systems are impacted by ethical and privacy concerns around information management.
- Lack of theoretical and educational foundations can lead to false assumptions.
- Effective practices focusing on learners and educators is lacking (i.e., a complete methodology which could guarantee the success of passing from theory to practice is needed).
- There is an absence of real-time feedback systems, that is, systems that provide information while the learning process is in progress.
- From organizational and institutional perspectives, educators, administrators, and students may resist ELA adoption due to fear of job displacement or concerns about privacy. Providing adequate training could emphasize benefits (e.g., personalized learning, early intervention) and address misconceptions. ELA implementation requires infrastructure (hardware, software), skilled personnel, and ongoing maintenance.

It is obvious that there are several issues to be addressed. First, the role of pedagogy in data analytics plays an important role. Pedagogy should drive LA, and not the converse. The data cannot take a truly holistic perspective, without manipulating for example the interpersonal relationships among students. Data without transparency and the use of ineffective algorithms lead to insufficient information and evaluation of students and instructors who already have expectations – the issue is that LA might add a set of data-driven expectations. Data privacy and the use of data are also strong concerns for the use of LA. Legal and ethical issues are implicated. Once the data have been warehoused, access must be strictly controlled. Last, there is the issue of whether data are really measuring student learning or are just being used to boost student retention and course completion. Researchers need to be clear about what the data are measuring and predicting, and why.

Based on the above, future research in the ELA field can be directed towards the following four key areas: data, technology, evaluation, and ethical issues.

Data:

- Data analysis should be based on pedagogical and epistemological practices.
- Data needs to be action-oriented.
- The problem under study must be defined accurately.
- The decision analysis approach to the data must be articulated.
- A detailed plan must be put in place and insignificant data rejected.
- Real-time insights must be gathered and interpreted.
- Educational data can be gathered using AI and Soft Computing approaches, but the quality of the supplied data will determine the outcomes.
- Data validation checks, data cleaning, and integration protocols must be implemented.
- Data formats and metadata must be standardized.
- Hybrid models that combine machine learning, natural language processing, and statistical techniques must be developed.
- Collaboration with domain experts is needed to interpret results, since ELA bridge education, data science, and psychology.

Technology:

- Foundations must be established related to the accuracy of technologies and means.
- More accurate and faster systems for data processing must be developed.
- Outliers for early intervention must be identified.
- Potential predictions will allow all learners to achieve optimal goals.
- Standard assessment techniques and instruments must be analyzed.
- Platforms supporting big data must be developed.
- Methods can be enhanced by introducing alternative instructional and assessment approaches.
- Secured funding, collaboration with IT departments, and exploration of cloud-based solutions can mitigate resource limitations.
- Collaboration among educators, data scientists, and policymakers can be fostered to create an interdisciplinary research team.
- Integrating AI, VR/AR, and ELA into existing educational systems requires careful planning, teacher training, and infrastructure devel-

opment. Effective integration requires professional development for teachers to understand how to use these tools effectively. By investing in comprehensive training programs for educators including workshops, courses, and ongoing support to build their confidence and competence in using AI, VR/AR, and ELA effectively is a future direction. These frameworks must be reviewed and updated regularly to stay aligned with evolving technologies.

- Schools and institutions may face challenges in adopting these technologies due to budget constraints and lack of technical expertise. Schools can collaborate with technology companies, universities, and research institutions. Partnerships can provide access to resources, expertise, and funding.
- AI and ELA systems rely on student data for personalized learning experiences. VR/AR applications may collect sensitive information, raising concerns about data security. Ensuring data privacy, consent, and protection against breaches is crucial.
- Disparities in device availability, internet connectivity, and digital literacy can exacerbate educational inequalities as not all students have equal access to technology. Hence, addressing digital inequities by providing devices, internet access, and technical support to all students is a solution to eliminate inequalities.
- Educators need to align technology use with learning objectives. Simply adopting new tools without considering their impact on teaching and learning can be counterproductive.
- VR/AR hardware and software can be expensive. Schools must weigh the benefits against the costs. Sustainable funding models are essential for maintaining and updating technology infrastructure. Securing allocation funds or sponsorships specifically for technology integration including sustainability and maintenance costs is another direction.
- Sophisticated algorithms and sensors for the accurate collection and interpretation of emotional states are required.
- ELA in already existing educational platforms and systems must be incorporated.
- Computational resources and efficient algorithms for real-time processing of emotional cues must be leveraged.

Evaluation:

- Institutes must be aligned with the point of view of educators and learners.
- Supporting teaching and learning strategies must be developed.
- Individual student performance must be monitored.
- Curricula must be tested and evaluated.
- Methods which guarantee the correct interpretation of outcomes must be developed.
- Contributions from instructors is always necessary, especially concerning guidance and assessment processes.
- Ensemble methods, transfer of learning, and personalized models must be explored, while continuously adapting them based on the evolving educational contexts.

Ethical issues:

- Learners' emotional profiles will be created based on collected emotional data to which only those in charge will have access, thus ensuring the confidentiality of the data.
- Collected data is only to be used by learners/educators for the duration of the course and it should not be used by third parties or for any reason beyond educational purposes.
- The kind of data that will be collected and used should be made known to educators and learners alike.
- Data must be anonymized.
- Learners can self-control and self-observe their information; they must have access to the data and processing principles and know the duration for which data and outcomes will be stored.
- Balancing data utility with privacy protection is crucial. It is necessary to develop clear privacy policies, obtain informed consent, anonymize data, and comply with regulations (e.g., GDPR, FERPA).

Ethical considerations such as privacy and consent lead to the need for robust algorithms to accurately assess emotions, because AI algorithms may perpetuate biases present in training data. Educators must be aware of potential bias and work to mitigate it. Emerging technologies need to be integrated into the entire process.

CONCLUSIONS

Due to the importance of its tools and techniques for enhancing the teaching-learning process, ELA is a developing topic that is gaining the attention of the learning community. Enhancing student achievement and retention is the goal of ELA. Teachers will be able to monitor their pupils' development and keep an eye on the learning approaches that have the best chance of working. Additionally, students may assess their progress, identify their advantages and disadvantages, and advance their education. Institutes leveraging ELA can improve learner satisfaction and retention with good results. However, there is not enough research done from the perspectives of the students. Privacy and ethical issues, lack of appropriate data, and thus incorrect interpretation and decision-making can severely impact ELA application. It's essential to customize learning settings and provide students the freedom to choose their own education. ELA can be a beneficial strategy used to explore how different people learn and assist them in customizing the process to meet their requirements. Giving them control over their learning experience is the ultimate aim. Appropriate training of professionals and academics is essential to assist in creating and implementing dynamic and captivating educational experiences. However, ELA integration does raise a number of ethical and privacy-related concerns, such as seeking informed permission from trainees with diverse socio-cognitive backgrounds, health issues, or intellectual impairments since this is especially crucial for them.

ELA are powerful tools for awareness, reflection, and engagement of participants in education and learning, aiming to provide a rich educational environment, while facilitating and enhancing the process with the active participation of both teachers and learners. Today, the concept of learning encompasses a human-centric model (Casalino, Castellano, Mitri, Kaczmarek-Majer, & Zaza, 2024), meaning that human beings, i.e., students, are the central and most significant entities in the learning process. The actions and interactions of humans reflect their emotional states and their experiences. Hence, complex emotions with multiple components, which may dynamically unfold over the course of the learning process, must be taken into account. Despite great strides in the fields of emotional science and neuroscience, there is still a lot more to be understood regarding emotions. The process of modelling a system should include a variety of parameters, emphasizing both the science of learning and the science of emotion. Learning design is a complex process and representative data should be selected on a case-by-case basis to produce results that are as unbiased as possible. Open issues such as the reliability level, the types of data and correlations taken into account when designing models, learners' rating criteria, relationships, and patterns used by algorithms must all be considered.

As the area of ELA develops, it will be crucial to handle technological issues, negotiate ethical dilemmas, and guarantee that the advantages of emotional insights are achieved while upholding the privacy and liberty of the individual.

ACKNOWLEDGMENT

This work was supported by the MPhil program "Advanced Technologies in Informatics and Computers," hosted by the Department of Informatics, Democritus University of Thrace, Greece.

REFERENCES

Aldowah, H., Al-Samarraie, H., & Fauzy, W. M. (2019). Educational data mining and learning analytics for 21st century higher education: A review and synthesis. *Telematics and Informatics*, 37, 13–49. DOI: 10.1016/j.tele.2019.01.007

Alkhatlan, A., & Kalita, J. (2019). Intelligent Tutoring Systems: A Comprehensive Historical Survey with Recent Developments. *International Journal of Computer Applications*, 181(43), 1–20. DOI: 10.5120/ijca2019918451

Alves, P., Miranda, L., & Morais, C. (2017). The Influence of Virtual Learning Environments in Students' Performance. *Universal Journal of Educational Research*, 5(3), 517–527. DOI: 10.13189/ujer.2017.050325

Antoniou, P., Arfaras, G., Pandria, N., Ntakakis, G., Bambatsikos, E., & Athanasiou, A. (2020). Real-Time Affective Measurements in Medical Education, Using Virtual and Mixed Reality. In *Lecture Notes in Computer Science (including subseries Lecture Notes in Artificial Intelligence and Lecture Notes in Bioinformatics)* (pp. 87–95). DOI: 10.1007/978-3-030-60735-7_9

Antoniou, P. E., Arfaras, G., Pandria, N., Athanasiou, A., Ntakakis, G., Babatsikos, E., Nigdelis, V., & Bamidis, P. (2020). Biosensor Real-Time Affective Analytics in Virtual and Mixed Reality Medical Education Serious Games: Cohort Study. *JMIR Serious Games*, 8(3), e17823. DOI: 10.2196/17823 PMID: 32876575

Aristovnik, A., Keržič, D., Ravšelj, D., Tomaževič, N., & Umek, L. (2020). Impacts of the COVID-19 Pandemic on Life of Higher Education Students: A Global Perspective. *Sustainability (Basel)*, 12(20), 8438. DOI: 10.3390/su12208438

Arroyo, I., Cooper, D. G., Burleson, W., Woolf, B. P., Muldner, K., & Christopherson, R. (2009). Emotion sensors go to school. *Frontiers in Artificial Intelligence and Applications*, 17–24. DOI: 10.3233/978-1-60750-028-5-17

Atkisson, M., & Wiley, D. (2011). Learning analytics as interpretive practice. *Proceedings of the 1st International Conference on Learning Analytics and Knowledge*, 117–121. New York, NY, USA: ACM. DOI: 10.1145/2090116.2090133

Axelsen, M., Redmond, P., Heinrich, E., & Henderson, M. (2020). The evolving field of learning analytics research in higher education. *Australasian Journal of Educational Technology*, 36(2), 1–7. DOI: 10.14742/ajet.6266

Bakhshinategh, B., Zaiane, O. R., ElAtia, S., & Ipperciel, D. (2018). Educational data mining applications and tasks: A survey of the last 10 years. *Education and Information Technologies*, 23(1), 537–553. DOI: 10.1007/s10639-017-9616-z

Banihashem, S. K., Aliabadi, K., Pourroostaei Ardakani, S., Delaver, A., & Nili Ahmadabadi, M. (2018). Learning Analytics: A Systematic Literature Review. *Interdisciplinary Journal of Virtual Learning in Medical Sciences*, 9(2). Advance online publication. DOI: 10.5812/ijvlms.63024

Bannert, M., Molenaar, I., Azevedo, R., Järvelä, S., & Gašević, D. (2017). Relevance of learning analytics to measure and support students' learning in adaptive educational technologies. *Proceedings of the Seventh International Learning Analytics & Knowledge Conference*, 568–569. New York, NY, USA: ACM. DOI: 10.1145/3027385.3029463

Barahona Mora, A. (2020). Gamification for Classroom Management: An Implementation Using ClassDojo. *Sustainability (Basel)*, 12(22), 9371. DOI: 10.3390/su12229371

Berehil, M., Roubi, S., & Arrhioui, K. (2020). Towards a model for an emotionally intelligent learning environment using NLP tools. *Proceedings of the European Conference on E-Learning, ECEL*. https://doi.org/DOI: 10.34190/EEL.20.096

Berman, N. B., & Artino, A. R.Jr. (2018). Development and initial validation of an online engagement metric using virtual patients. *BMC Medical Education*, 18(1), 213. DOI: 10.1186/s12909-018-1322-z PMID: 30223825

Bittencourt, I. I., Chalco, G., Santos, J., Fernandes, S., Silva, J., Batista, N., Hutz, C., & Isotani, S. (2023). Positive Artificial Intelligence in Education (P-AIED): A Roadmap. *International Journal of Artificial Intelligence in Education*. Advance online publication. DOI: 10.1007/s40593-023-00357-y

Bodily, R., Kay, J., Aleven, V., Jivet, I., Davis, D., Xhakaj, F., & Verbert, K. (2018). Open learner models and learning analytics dashboards. *Proceedings of the 8th International Conference on Learning Analytics and Knowledge*, 41–50. New York, NY, USA: ACM. DOI: 10.1145/3170358.3170409

Bosch, N., & D'Mello, S. (2017). The Affective Experience of Novice Computer Programmers. *International Journal of Artificial Intelligence in Education*, 27(1), 181–206. DOI: 10.1007/s40593-015-0069-5

Bosch, N., D'Mello, S. K., Baker, R. S., Ocumpaugh, J., Shute, V., Ventura, M., & Zhao, W. (2016). Detecting student emotions in computer-enabled classrooms. *IJCAI International Joint Conference on Artificial Intelligence*, 4125–4129.

Campbell, J. P., DeBlois, P. B., & Oblinger, D. G. (2007). Academic Analytics: A New Tool for a New Era. *EDUCAUSE Review*, 42(4), 40.

Cantabella, M., Martínez-España, R., Ayuso, B., Yáñez, J. A., & Muñoz, A. (2019). Analysis of student behavior in learning management systems through a Big Data framework. *Future Generation Computer Systems*, 90, 262–272. DOI: 10.1016/j.future.2018.08.003

Casalino, G., Castellano, G., Di Mitri, D., Kaczmarek-Majer, K., & Zaza, G. (2024). A Human-centric Approach to Explain Evolving Data: A Case Study on Education. *2024 IEEE International Conference on Evolving and Adaptive Intelligent Systems (EAIS)*, 1–8. IEEE. DOI: 10.1109/EAIS58494.2024.10569098

Cebral-Loureda, M., & Torres-Huitzil, C. (2021). Neural Deep Learning Models for Learning Analytics in a Digital Humanities Laboratory. *2021 Machine Learning-Driven Digital Technologies for Educational Innovation Workshop*, 1–8. IEEE. DOI: 10.1109/IEEECONF53024.2021.9733775

Charitopoulos, A., Rangoussi, M., & Koulouriotis, D. (2020). On the Use of Soft Computing Methods in Educational Data Mining and Learning Analytics Research: A Review of Years 2010–2018. *International Journal of Artificial Intelligence in Education*, 30(3), 371–430. DOI: 10.1007/s40593-020-00200-8

Chatti, M. A., & Muslim, A. (2019). The PERLA Framework: Blending Personalization and Learning Analytics. *International Review of Research in Open and Distance Learning*, 20(1). Advance online publication. DOI: 10.19173/irrodl.v20i1.3936

Chng, E., Tan, A. L., & Tan, S. C. (2023). Examining the Use of Emerging Technologies in Schools: A Review of Artificial Intelligence and Immersive Technologies in STEM Education. *Journal for STEM Education Research*, 6(3), 385–407. DOI: 10.1007/s41979-023-00092-y

Cleveland-Innes, M., & Campbell, P. (2012). Emotional presence, learning, and the online learning environment. *International Review of Research in Open and Distance Learning*, 13(4), 269. DOI: 10.19173/irrodl.v13i4.1234

Clow, D. (2013). An overview of learning analytics. *Teaching in Higher Education*, 18(6), 683–695. DOI: 10.1080/13562517.2013.827653

Conver, S. (2020). Investing in Education: The Ideas Behind Venture Philanthropy and the Marketized Practice of Educational Improvement. *Proceedings of the 2020 AERA Annual Meeting*. Washington DC: AERA. DOI: 10.3102/1577229

Crescenzi-Lanna, L. (2020). Multimodal Learning Analytics research with young children: A systematic review. *British Journal of Educational Technology*, 51(5), 1485–1504. DOI: 10.1111/bjet.12959

Crick, R. (2017). Learning Analytics: Layers, Loops and Processes in a Virtual Learning Infrastructure. In *Handbook of Learning Analytics* (pp. 291–307). Society for Learning Analytics Research (SoLAR). DOI: 10.18608/hla17.025

Cukurova, M., & Luckin, R. (2018). *Measuring the Impact of Emerging Technologies in Education: A Pragmatic Approach*. DOI: 10.1007/978-3-319-71054-9_81

D'Mello, S. K., & Jensen, E. (2022). Emotional Learning Analytics. In *The Handbook of Learning Analytics* (pp. 120–129). SOLAR., DOI: 10.18608/hla22.012

Dafoulas, G. A., Maia, C. C., Clarke, J. S., Ali, A., & Augusto, J. (2018). Investigating the role of biometrics in education – The use of sensor data in collaborative learning. *MCCSIS 2018 - Multi Conference on Computer Science and Information Systems;Proceedings of the International Conferences on e-Learning 2018*.

Daineko, L. V., Goncharova, N. V., Zaitseva, E. V., Larionova, V. A., & Dyachkova, I. A. (2023). Gamification in Education: A Literature Review. In *Lecture Notes in Networks and Systems* (pp. 319–343). DOI: 10.1007/978-3-031-48020-1_25

Daoudi, I. (2022). Learning analytics for enhancing the usability of serious games in formal education: A systematic literature review and research agenda. *Education and Information Technologies*, 27(8), 11237–11266. DOI: 10.1007/s10639-022-11087-4 PMID: 35528757

Dietz-Uhler, B., & Hurn, J. E. (2013). Using learning analytics to predict (and improve) student success: A faculty perspective. *Journal of Interactive Online Learning*, 12(1), 17–26.

Drachsler, H., & Greller, W. (2016). Privacy and analytics. *Proceedings of the Sixth International Conference on Learning Analytics & Knowledge - LAK '16*, 89–98. New York, New York, USA: ACM Press. DOI: 10.1145/2883851.2883893

Du Boulay, B., Avramides, K., Luckin, R., Martínez-Mirón, E., Méndez, G. R., & Carr, A. (2010). Towards systems that care: A Conceptual Framework based on motivation, metacognition and affect. *International Journal of Artificial Intelligence in Education*, 20(3), 1997–229. DOI: 10.3233/JAI-2010-0007

Dyulicheva, Y. Y., & Bilashova, E. A. (2022). Learning analytics of MOOCs based on natural language processing. *CEUR Workshop Proceedings*.

Febriantoro, W., Gauthier, A., & Cukurova, M. (2023). The Promise of Physiological Data in Collaborative Learning: A Systematic Literature Review. In *Lecture Notes in Computer Science (including subseries Lecture Notes in Artificial Intelligence and Lecture Notes in Bioinformatics)* (pp. 75–88). DOI: 10.1007/978-3-031-42682-7_6

Feidakis, M., Daradoumis, T., Caballe, S., & Conesa, J. (2013). Measuring the Impact of Emotion Awareness on e-learning Situations. *2013 Seventh International Conference on Complex, Intelligent, and Software Intensive Systems*, 391–396. IEEE. DOI: 10.1109/CISIS.2013.71

Ferguson, R. (2012). Learning analytics: Drivers, developments and challenges. *International Journal of Technology Enhanced Learning*, 4(5/6), 304. DOI: 10.1504/IJTEL.2012.051816

Ferrari, R. (2015). Writing narrative style literature reviews. *Medical Writing*, 24(4), 230–235. DOI: 10.1179/2047480615Z.000000000329

Gašević, D., Dawson, S., Rogers, T., & Gasevic, D. (2016). Learning analytics should not promote one size fits all: The effects of instructional conditions in predicting academic success. *The Internet and Higher Education*, 28, 68–84. DOI: 10.1016/j.iheduc.2015.10.002

Giannakos, M., & Cukurova, M. (2023). The role of learning theory in multimodal learning analytics. *British Journal of Educational Technology*, 54(5), 1246–1267. DOI: 10.1111/bjet.13320

Gkontzis, A. F., Kotsiantis, S., Kalles, D., Panagiotakopoulos, C. T., & Verykios, V. S. (2020). Polarity, emotions and online activity of students and tutors as features in predicting grades. *Intelligent Decision Technologies*, 14(3), 409–436. DOI: 10.3233/IDT-190137

Guenaga, M., & Garaizar, P. (2016). From Analysis to Improvement: Challenges and Opportunities for Learning Analytics. *IEEE Revista Iberoamericana de Technologias del Aprendizaje*, 11(3), 146–147. DOI: 10.1109/RITA.2016.2589481

Guzmán-Valenzuela, C., Gómez-González, C., Rojas-Murphy Tagle, A., & Lorca-Vyhmeister, A. (2021). Learning analytics in higher education: A preponderance of analytics but very little learning? *International Journal of Educational Technology in Higher Education*, 18(1), 23. DOI: 10.1186/s41239-021-00258-x PMID: 34778523

Hasnine, M. N., Nguyen, H. T., Tran, T. T. T., Bui, H. T. T., Akçapınar, G., & Ueda, H. (2023). A Real-Time Learning Analytics Dashboard for Automatic Detection of Online Learners' Affective States. *Sensors (Basel)*, 23(9), 4243. DOI: 10.3390/s23094243 PMID: 37177447

Hernández-de-Menéndez, M., Morales-Menendez, R., Escobar, C. A., & Ramírez Mendoza, R. A. (2022). Learning analytics: State of the art. [IJIDeM]. *International Journal on Interactive Design and Manufacturing*, 16(3), 1209–1230. DOI: 10.1007/s12008-022-00930-0

Hess, U. (2017). Emotion Categorization. In *Handbook of Categorization in Cognitive Science* (pp. 107–126). Elsevier., DOI: 10.1016/B978-0-08-101107-2.00005-1

Hoemann, K., Gendron, M., & Barrett, L. F. (2022). Assessing the Power of Words to Facilitate Emotion Category Learning. *Affective Science*, 3(1), 69–80. DOI: 10.1007/s42761-021-00084-4 PMID: 36046100

Hooda, M. (2020). Learning Analytics Lens: Improving Quality of Higher Education. *International Journal of Emerging Trends in Engineering Research*, 8(5), 1626–1646. DOI: 10.30534/ijeter/2020/24852020

Hsieh, Y.-Z., Lin, S.-S., Luo, Y.-C., Jeng, Y.-L., Tan, S.-W., Chen, C.-R., & Chiang, P.-Y. (2020). ARCS-Assisted Teaching Robots Based on Anticipatory Computing and Emotional Big Data for Improving Sustainable Learning Efficiency and Motivation. *Sustainability (Basel)*, 12(14), 5605. DOI: 10.3390/su12145605

Ifenthaler, D., & Yau, J. Y.-K. (2022). Higher Education Stakeholders' Views on Guiding the Implementation of Learning Analytics for Study Success. *ASCILITE Publications*, 453–457, 453–457. Advance online publication. DOI: 10.14742/apubs.2019.311

Isen, A. M. (2003). Positive affect as a source of human strength. In *A psychology of human strengths: Fundamental questions and future directions for a positive psychology* (pp. 179–195). American Psychological Association., DOI: 10.1037/10566-013

Joksimovic, S., Kovanovic, V., Joksimović, S., Kovanović, V., & Dawson, S. (2019). The Journey of Learning Analytics. In *HERDSA Review of Higher Education*.

Joseph-Richard, P., Uhomoibhi, J., & Jaffrey, A. (2021). Predictive learning analytics and the creation of emotionally adaptive learning environments in higher education institutions: A study of students' affect responses. *The International Journal of Information and Learning Technology*, 38(2), 243–257. DOI: 10.1108/IJILT-05-2020-0077

Kasliwal, P. S., Gunjan, R., & Shete, V. (2023). Computation of E-learners Textual Emotion to Enhance learning Experience. *International Journal of Intelligent Systems and Applications in Engineering*, 11(10s), 849–858.

Kazanidis, I., Pellas, N., & Christopoulos, A. (2021). A Learning Analytics Conceptual Framework for Augmented Reality-Supported Educational Case Studies. *Multimodal Technologies and Interaction*, 5(3), 9. DOI: 10.3390/mti5030009

Kim, M. K., Lee, I. H., & Kim, S. M. (2021). A longitudinal examination of temporal and iterative relationships among learner engagement dimensions during online discussion. *Journal of Computers in Education*, 8(1), 63–86. DOI: 10.1007/s40692-020-00171-8

Kitchenham, B. (2004). Procedures for performing systematic reviews. In *UK, Keele University*. UK, Keele University: Keele. https://doi.org/DOI: 10.1.1.122.3308

Kivimäki, V., Ketonen, E. E., & Lindblom-Ylänne, S. (2023). Engineering students' justifications for their selections in structured learning diaries. *Frontiers in Education*, 8, 1223732. Advance online publication. DOI: 10.3389/feduc.2023.1223732

Knight, S., & Buckingham Shum, S. (2017). Theory and Learning Analytics. In *Handbook of Learning Analytics* (pp. 17–22). Society for Learning Analytics Research (SoLAR). DOI: 10.18608/hla17.001

Lampropoulos, G., Keramopoulos, E., Diamantaras, K., & Evangelidis, G. (2022). Augmented Reality and Virtual Reality in Education: Public Perspectives, Sentiments, Attitudes, and Discourses. *Education Sciences*, 12(11), 798. DOI: 10.3390/educsci12110798

Larradet, F., Niewiadomski, R., Barresi, G., Caldwell, D. G., & Mattos, L. S. (2020). Toward Emotion Recognition From Physiological Signals in the Wild: Approaching the Methodological Issues in Real-Life Data Collection. *Frontiers in Psychology*, 11, 1111. Advance online publication. DOI: 10.3389/fpsyg.2020.01111 PMID: 32760305

Lee, T.-Y., Chang, C.-W., & Chen, G.-D. (2007). Building an Interactive Caring Agent for Students in Computer-based Learning Environments. *Seventh IEEE International Conference on Advanced Learning Technologies (ICALT 2007)*, 300–304. IEEE. DOI: 10.1109/ICALT.2007.87

Leony, D., Muñoz-Merino, P. J., Pardo, A., & Delgado Kloos, C. (2013). Provision of awareness of learners' emotions through visualizations in a computer interaction-based environment. *Expert Systems with Applications*, 40(13), 5093–5100. DOI: 10.1016/j.eswa.2013.03.030

Letteri, C. A. (1980). Cognitive Profile: Basic Determinant of Academic Achievement. *The Journal of Educational Research*, 73(4), 195–199. DOI: 10.1080/00220671.1980.10885234

Li, L., & Yao, D. (2023). Emotion Recognition in Complex Classroom Scenes Based on Improved Convolutional Block Attention Module Algorithm. *IEEE Access : Practical Innovations, Open Solutions*, 11, 143050–143059. DOI: 10.1109/ACCESS.2023.3340510

Liu, Z., Zhang, W., Sun, J., Cheng, H. N. H., Peng, X., & Liu, S. (2016). Emotion and Associated Topic Detection for Course Comments in a MOOC Platform. *2016 International Conference on Educational Innovation through Technology (EITT)*, 15–19. IEEE. DOI: 10.1109/EITT.2016.11

Lytras, M. D., Aljohani, N. R., Visvizi, A., Ordonez De Pablos, P., & Gasevic, D. (2018). Advanced decision-making in higher education: Learning analytics research and key performance indicators. *Behaviour & Information Technology*, 37(10–11), 937–940. DOI: 10.1080/0144929X.2018.1512940

Marzouk, Z., Rakovic, M., Liaqat, A., Vytasek, J., Samadi, D., Stewart-Alonso, J., Ram, I., Woloshen, S., Winne, P. H., & Nesbit, J. C. (2016). What if learning analytics were based on learning science? *Australasian Journal of Educational Technology*, 32(6). Advance online publication. DOI: 10.14742/ajet.3058

Moreno-Marcos, P. M., Alario-Hoyos, C., Munoz-Merino, P. J., Estevez-Ayres, I., & Kloos, C. D. (2018). Sentiment analysis in MOOCs: A case study. *2018 IEEE Global Engineering Education Conference (EDUCON)*, 1489–1496. IEEE. DOI: 10.1109/EDUCON.2018.8363409

Mu, S., Cui, M., & Huang, X. (2020). Multimodal Data Fusion in Learning Analytics: A Systematic Review. *Sensors (Basel)*, 20(23), 6856. DOI: 10.3390/s20236856 PMID: 33266131

Munezero, M., Montero, C. S., Mozgovoy, M., & Sutinen, E. (2013). Exploiting sentiment analysis to track emotions in students' learning diaries. *Proceedings of the 13th Koli Calling International Conference on Computing Education Research*, 145–152. New York, NY, USA: ACM. DOI: 10.1145/2526968.2526984

Namoun, A., & Alshanqiti, A. (2020). Predicting Student Performance Using Data Mining and Learning Analytics Techniques: A Systematic Literature Review. *Applied Sciences (Basel, Switzerland)*, 11(1), 237. DOI: 10.3390/app11010237

Nguyen, H. (2023). TikTok as Learning Analytics Data: Framing Climate Change and Data Practices. *LAK23: 13th International Learning Analytics and Knowledge Conference*, 33–43. New York, NY, USA: ACM. DOI: 10.1145/3576050.3576055

Noroozi, O., Alikhani, I., Järvelä, S., Kirschner, P. A., Juuso, I., & Seppänen, T. (2019). Multimodal data to design visual learning analytics for understanding regulation of learning. *Computers in Human Behavior*, 100, 298–304. DOI: 10.1016/j.chb.2018.12.019

Nunn, S., Avella, J. T., Kanai, T., & Kebritchi, M. (2016). Learning Analytics Methods, Benefits, and Challenges in Higher Education: A Systematic Literature Review. *Online Learning : the Official Journal of the Online Learning Consortium*, 20(2). Advance online publication. DOI: 10.24059/olj.v20i2.790

Öhman, A., & Soares, J. J. F. (1994). "Unconscious anxiety": Phobic responses to masked stimuli. *Journal of Abnormal Psychology*, 103(2), 231–240. DOI: 10.1037/0021-843X.103.2.231 PMID: 8040492

Ordóñez de Pablos, P., Lytras, M. D., Zhang, X., & Chui, K. T. (2019). *Opening Up Education for Inclusivity Across Digital Economies and Societies (Patricia Ordóñez de Pablos* (Lytras, M. D., Zhang, X., & Chui, K. T., Eds.). IGI Global., DOI: 10.4018/978-1-5225-7473-6

Pekrun, R., & Stephens, E. J. (2012). Academic emotions. In. APA educational psychology handbook: Vol. 2. *Individual differences and cultural and contextual factors* (pp. 3–31). American Psychological Association., DOI: 10.1037/13274-001

Pereira, H. A., De Souza, A. F., & De Menezes, C. S. (2016). A Computational Architecture for Learning Analytics in Game-Based Learning. *2016 IEEE 16th International Conference on Advanced Learning Technologies (ICALT)*, 191–193. IEEE. DOI: 10.1109/ICALT.2016.3

Pereira, H. A., De Souza, A. F., & De Menezes, C. S. (2018). Obtaining evidence of learning in digital games through a deep learning neural network to classify facial expressions of the players. *2018 IEEE Frontiers in Education Conference (FIE)*, 1–8. IEEE. DOI: 10.1109/FIE.2018.8659216

Pham, P., & Wang, J. (2018). Predicting Learners' Emotions in Mobile MOOC Learning via a Multimodal Intelligent Tutor. In *Lecture Notes in Computer Science (including subseries Lecture Notes in Artificial Intelligence and Lecture Notes in Bioinformatics)* (pp. 150–159). DOI: 10.1007/978-3-319-91464-0_15

Piniel, K., & Albert, Á. (2018). Advanced learners' foreign language-related emotions across the four skills. *Studies in Second Language Learning and Teaching*, 8(1), 127–147. DOI: 10.14746/ssllt.2018.8.1.6

Plintz, N., & Ifenthaler, D. (2023). LEVERAGING EMOTIONS TO ENHANCE LEARNING SUCCESS IN ONLINE EDUCATION: A SYSTEMATIC REVIEW. *20th International Conference on Cognition and Exploratory Learning in Digital Age, CELDA 2023*.

PraveenKumar., T., Manorselvi, A., & Soundarapandiyan, K. (2020). Exploring the students feelings and emotion towards online teaching: sentimental analysis approach. In Re-imagining Diffusion and Adoption of Information Technology and Systems: A Continuing Conversation: IFIP WG 8.6 International Conference on Transfer and Diffusion of IT, TDIT 2020, Tiruchirappalli, India, December 18–19, 2020, Proceedings, Part I (pp. 137-146). Springer International Publishing.

Ranjeeth, S., Latchoumi, T. P., & Paul, P. V. (2020). A Survey on Predictive Models of Learning Analytics. *Procedia Computer Science*, 167, 37–46. DOI: 10.1016/j.procs.2020.03.180

Rodríguez, A. O. R., Riaño, M. A., García, P. A. G., Marín, C. E. M., Crespo, R. G., & Wu, X. (2020). Emotional characterization of children through a learning environment using learning analytics and AR-Sandbox. *Journal of Ambient Intelligence and Humanized Computing*, 11(11), 5353–5367. DOI: 10.1007/s12652-020-01887-2

Romero, C., & Ventura, S. (2013). Data mining in education. *Wiley Interdisciplinary Reviews. Data Mining and Knowledge Discovery*, 3(1), 12–27. DOI: 10.1002/widm.1075

Rus, V., D'Mello, S., Hu, X., & Graesser, A. C. (2013). Recent Advances in Conversational Intelligent Tutoring Systems. *AI Magazine*, 34(3), 42–54. DOI: 10.1609/aimag.v34i3.2485

Russell, J.-E., Smith, A., & Larsen, R. (2020). Elements of Success: Supporting at-risk student resilience through learning analytics. *Computers & Education*, 152, 103890. DOI: 10.1016/j.compedu.2020.103890

San Pedro, M. O. Z., Baker, R. S., & Heffernan, N. T. (2017). An Integrated Look at Middle School Engagement and Learning in Digital Environments as Precursors to College Attendance. *Technology. Knowledge and Learning*, 22(3), 243–270. DOI: 10.1007/s10758-017-9318-z

Sedrakyan, G., Leony, D., Muñoz-Merino, P. J., Kloos, C. D., & Verbert, K. (2017). Evaluating Student-Facing Learning Dashboards of Affective States. In *Lecture Notes in Computer Science (including subseries Lecture Notes in Artificial Intelligence and Lecture Notes in Bioinformatics)* (pp. 224–237). DOI: 10.1007/978-3-319-66610-5_17

Shen, S., Mostafavi, B., Barnes, T., & Chi, M. (2018). Exploring Induced Pedagogical Strategies Through a Markov Decision Process Frame-work: Lessons Learned. *Journal of Educational Data Mining*, 10(3).

Shu, F., Zhao, C., Liu, Q., Li, H., & Huang, Y. (2022). Enhancing Adults' Online Course Learning Behavior Performance through Live Class in Distance and Open Education. *Proceedings of the 6th International Conference on Education and Multimedia Technology*, 65–69. New York, NY, USA: ACM. DOI: 10.1145/3551708.3556205

Shukla, P., & Garg, A. (2022). Sentiment Analysis of Online Learners in Higher Education: A Learning Perspective through Unstructured Data. In *Intelligent System Algorithms and Applications in Science and Technology* (pp. 157–170). Apple Academic Press., DOI: 10.1201/9781003187059-15

Siemens, G. (2013). Learning Analytics. *The American Behavioral Scientist*, 57(10), 1380–1400. DOI: 10.1177/0002764213498851

SINGH., M., BANGAY, S., & SAJJANHAR, A. (2022). An Architecture for Capturing and Presenting Learning Outcomes using Augmented Reality Enhanced Analytics. *2022 IEEE International Symposium on Mixed and Augmented Reality Adjunct (ISMAR-Adjunct)*, 611–612. IEEE. DOI: 10.1109/ISMAR-Adjunct57072.2022.00126

Singh, M., Bangay, S., & Sajjanhar, A. (2022). Augmented Reality Enhanced Analytics to Measure and Mitigate Disengagement in Teaching Young Children. *2022 IEEE International Symposium on Mixed and Augmented Reality Adjunct (ISMAR-Adjunct)*, 782–785. IEEE. DOI: 10.1109/ISMAR-Adjunct57072.2022.00166

Spikol, D., Prieto, L. P., Rodríguez-Triana, M. J., Worsley, M., Ochoa, X., Cukurova, M., & Ringtved, U. L. (2017). Current and future multimodal learning analytics data challenges. *Proceedings of the Seventh International Learning Analytics & Knowledge Conference*, 518–519. New York, NY, USA: ACM. DOI: 10.1145/3027385.3029437

Srimadhaven, T., Chris Junni, A., & Naga Harshith, J. (2020). Learning Analytics: Virtual Reality for Programming Course in Higher Education. *Procedia Computer Science*, 172, 433–437. DOI: 10.1016/j.procs.2020.05.095

Staudt, K., Grushetskaya, Y., Rangelov, G., Domanska, M., & Pinkwart, N. (2018). Heart rate, electrodermal activity and skin conductance as new sources for Learning Analytics. *CEUR Workshop Proceedings*.

Suero Montero, C., & Suhonen, J. (2014). Emotion analysis meets learning analytics. *Proceedings of the 14th Koli Calling International Conference on Computing Education Research*, 165–169. New York, NY, USA: ACM. DOI: 10.1145/2674683.2674699

Sun, D., Ouyang, F., Li, Y., & Chen, H. (2020). Exploring creativity, emotion and collaborative behavior in programming for two contrasting groups. *Proceedings of International Conference on Computational Thinking Education*, 36–37.

Tamura, Y., & Murakami, K. (2015). Heartbeat feedback for learners' emotional self control. *Workshop Proceedings of the 23rd International Conference on Computers in Education, ICCE 2015*.

Tempelaar, D., Rienties, B., & Nguyen, Q. (2020). Subjective data, objective data and the role of bias in predictive modelling: Lessons from a dispositional learning analytics application. *PLoS One*, 15(6), e0233977. DOI: 10.1371/journal.pone.0233977 PMID: 32530954

Tempelaar, D. T., Rienties, B., & Nguyen, Q. (2017). Towards Actionable Learning Analytics Using Dispositions. *IEEE Transactions on Learning Technologies*, 10(1), 6–16. DOI: 10.1109/TLT.2017.2662679

Tsai, Y.-S., Rates, D., Moreno-Marcos, P. M., Muñoz-Merino, P. J., Jivet, I., Scheffel, M., Drachsler, H., Delgado Kloos, C., & Gašević, D. (2020). Learning analytics in European higher education—Trends and barriers. *Computers & Education*, 155, 103933. DOI: 10.1016/j.compedu.2020.103933

Ulutaş, N. K. (2023). *Rethinking Learning Engagement Through Emotional Learning Analytics in K-12 Classrooms Through Social-Emotional Learning and Mindfulness*. DOI: 10.4018/979-8-3693-0066-4.ch009

Vidal, J. (2023). Emerging Technologies: The Birth of Artificial Intelligence (AI) in Education. SSRN *Electronic Journal*. DOI: 10.2139/ssrn.4512063

Vidhya, R., & Vadivu, G. (2019). Smart Way to Inspect Student Performance using Emotional State on Learning Analytics. [IJRTE]. *International Journal of Recent Technology and Engineering*, 8(3), 5352–5357. DOI: 10.35940/ijrte.C6882.098319

Voigt, C., Kieslinger, B., & Schäfer, T. (2017). User Experiences Around Sentiment Analyses, Facilitating Workplace Learning. In *Lecture Notes in Computer Science (including subseries Lecture Notes in Artificial Intelligence and Lecture Notes in Bioinformatics)* (pp. 312–324). DOI: 10.1007/978-3-319-58562-8_24

Wang, Zuowei, Miller, K., & Cortina, K. (2013). Using the LENA in teacher training: Promoting student involvement through automated feedback. *Unterrichtswissenschaft*, ●●●, 4.

Wang, Z., Ho, S.-B., & Cambria, E. (2020). A review of emotion sensing: Categorization models and algorithms. *Multimedia Tools and Applications*, 79(47–48), 35553–35582. DOI: 10.1007/s11042-019-08328-z

West, D., Heath, D., & Huijser, H. (2015). Let's Talk Learning Analytics: A Framework for Implementation in Relation to Student Retention. *Online Learning : the Official Journal of the Online Learning Consortium*, 20(2). Advance online publication. DOI: 10.24059/olj.v20i2.792

Westera, W., van der Vegt, W., Bahreini, K., Dascalu, M., & van Lankveld, G. (2016). Software components for serious game development. *Proceedings of the European Conference on Games-Based Learning*.

Williamson, B. (2017). Decoding ClassDojo: Psycho-policy, social-emotional learning and persuasive educational technologies. *Learning, Media and Technology*, 42(4), 440–453. DOI: 10.1080/17439884.2017.1278020

Williamson, B. (2021). Psychodata: Disassembling the psychological, economic, and statistical infrastructure of 'social-emotional learning.'. *Journal of Education Policy*, 36(1), 129–154. DOI: 10.1080/02680939.2019.1672895

Winne, P. H. (2021). Cognition, Metacognition, and Self-Regulated Learning. In *Oxford Research Encyclopedia of Education*. Oxford University Press., DOI: 10.1093/acrefore/9780190264093.013.1528

Wintrup, J. (2017). Higher Education's Panopticon? Learning Analytics, Ethics and Student Engagement. *Higher Education Policy*, 30(1), 87–103. DOI: 10.1057/s41307-016-0030-8

Xu, W., Wu, Y., & Ouyang, F. (2023). Multimodal learning analytics of collaborative patterns during pair programming in higher education. *International Journal of Educational Technology in Higher Education*, 20(1), 8. DOI: 10.1186/s41239-022-00377-z

Zaki, N. A. A., Zain, N. Z. M., Noor, N. A. Z. M., & Hashim, H. (2020). Developing a Conceptual Model of Learning Analytics in Serious Games for STEM Education. *Jurnal Pendidikan IPA Indonesia*, 9(3), 330–339. DOI: 10.15294/jpii.v9i3.24466

Zheng, J., Huang, L., Li, S., Lajoie, S. P., Chen, Y., & Hmelo-Silver, C. E. (2021). Self-regulation and emotion matter: A case study of instructor interactions with a learning analytics dashboard. *Computers & Education*, 161, 104061. DOI: 10.1016/j.compedu.2020.104061

Zheng, L., Zhong, L., & Niu, J. (2022). Effects of personalised feedback approach on knowledge building, emotions, co-regulated behavioural patterns and cognitive load in online collaborative learning. *Assessment & Evaluation in Higher Education*, 47(1), 109–125. DOI: 10.1080/02602938.2021.1883549

Section 2
Theoretical Foundations: Narrowing the Focus

Chapter 5
Enhancing Online Adult Learning Through Emotional Social Intelligence Instructional Competencies

Carrie M. Grimes
https://orcid.org/0009-0007-5937-0048
Vanderbilt University, USA

ABSTRACT

The shift from traditional in-person classroom learning to legitimized programs of online learning for adult degree-seeking professionals has opened significant access and opportunity for institutions of higher education, as well as for the adult learners they serve. However, this increase in online graduate degree offerings has posed challenges to educators and the students they serve. Some of the most significant challenges for instructors are building and maintaining interpersonal connections and a socio-emotionally rewarding climate for learners. This chapter provides an analysis of how instructors can leverage emotional social intellligence (ESI) competencies in order to design and deliver learning experiences which support the unique needs of professional degree-seeking adult online learners in emotionally impactful ways. This chapter will specifically describe how online instructors may strategically use an ESI instructional framework to guide adult learners through beneficial socio-emotional learning experiences, in order to positively impact learning outcomes.

DOI: 10.4018/979-8-3693-2663-3.ch005

Copyright © 2025, IGI Global. Copying or distributing in print or electronic forms without written permission of IGI Global is prohibited.

REVIEW OF RELATED LITERATURE

In order to best conceptualize the complexity and breadth of the landscape of the issues encompassing the prospective impact of ESI competencies on adult online learning experiences, an examination of the relevant scholarship is essential. Source materials of this literature review include peer reviewed journal articles and chapters, along with research study reports generated by think tanks and non-profit agencies. Constructs of emotional intelligence, social intelligence, the ESI instructional environment, ESI instructor competencies, adult learning, online learning, and the benefits of ESI instructional practices for learners are examined. This synthesis of the literature empowers us to better understand the relevant applications of ESI theory to the phenomenon of promoting a positive emotional classroom climate and enhanced learning experience for adults enrolled in online professional degree programs.

Emotional Intelligence (EI) Theory

The exploration of emotional intelligence (EI) has garnered considerable scholarly attention over the past few decades, highlighting its significance in shaping individuals' personal and professional experiences. The foundational work of Mayer and Salovey (1993, 1997) conceptualized EI as a form of intelligence distinct from traditional cognitive abilities, involving the capacity to recognize, understand, manage, and utilize emotions effectively. This early research provided a robust theoretical framework that served as a foundation for subsequent studies examining the impact of EI across various domains (Ding et al., 2024). Mayer and Salovey (1997) proposed that emotional intelligence comprises four key components: perceiving emotions, facilitating thought through emotions, understanding emotions, and managing emotions. These components encompass the ability to accurately identify emotions in oneself and others, utilize emotional information to enhance cognitive processing, comprehend the nuances of emotional experiences, and regulate emotions effectively.

Goleman (1995; 2000) advanced Salovey and Mayer's framework by identifying five key competencies of emotional intelligence: self-awareness, self-regulation, motivation, empathy, and social skills. Each competency encompasses distinct facets, such as recognizing and comprehending one's emotions, managing impulses, cultivating a drive towards achievement, understanding others' emotions empathetically, and adeptly navigating social interactions. This framework has been influential in shaping contemporary discussions on EI and its practical applications. A significant body of research has since emerged to support the validity and utility of emotional intelligence as a construct. For instance, Boyatzis, Goleman, and Rhee (2000) developed the Emotional Competence Inventory (ECI), a tool for assessing

EI competencies across various domains. This instrument has provided insights into the clustering of competencies and their predictive role in personal and professional success (Boyatzis, 2021).

Lopes, Salovey, and Straus (2003) explored the relationship between EI, personality, and the perceived quality of social relationships. Their findings suggest that individuals with higher EI tend to perceive their social relationships as more positive and satisfying. This highlights the importance of EI in navigating complex social interactions and fostering meaningful connections. Joseph and Newman's (2010) integrative meta-analysis of EI furthered the work of Lopes, Salovey and Straus (2003) underscoring that EI significantly predicts job performance, life satisfaction, and mental health. They proposed a cascading model in which EI influences outcomes through cognitive, emotional, and motivational processes. This model reinforces the interconnectedness of emotional and cognitive processes in shaping individuals' experiences. Fernandez-Berrocal and Extremera (2006) provided a comprehensive review of the first 15 years of EI research, noting its applications in education, health, and workplace settings. Their review highlights the growing recognition of EI as a critical factor in enhancing well-being and interpersonal relationships. In 2017, Zhoc, Li, and Webster introduced new reliability and validity evidence for the Emotional Intelligence Scale (EIS), a measure that captures the multifaceted nature of EI. This scale provides a valuable tool for researchers and practitioners seeking to assess EI and its impact on various outcomes.

Since its genesis in 1993, emotional intelligence theory has evolved from its initial conceptualization as a distinct form of intelligence into a comprehensive framework encompassing a range of competencies. Its impact spans multiple domains, including education, health, and professional settings. The evidence suggests that EI contributes to enhanced interpersonal relationships, professional success, and overall well-being. Moreover, the development and validation of assessment tools such as the ECI and EIS have facilitated further research into the practical applications of EI.

Emotional Social Intelligence (ESI) Theory

It was Bar-On (1985) who is credited with establishing a link between the twin theories of social intelligence (SI) (Thorndike, 1920; McClelland, 1973; Gardner, 1983) and emotional intelligence (Salovey & Mayer, 1990; Goleman, 1995) to establish ESI theory. Kihlstrom and Cantor (2000) define social intelligence as the ability to understand and navigate complex social environments. This includes skills such as interpreting social cues, anticipating others' reactions, and adjusting behavior accordingly. By incorporating elements of emotional intelligence, such as empathy and self-awareness, ESI enables individuals to manage their own emotions and influence those of others, fostering positive social interactions. Goleman, Boyatzis, and McKee (2002) developed a theoretical framework comprised of four clusters of ESI competencies (two social, two emotional):

Figure 1. ESI competency model (Goleman, Boyatzis, and McKee, 2002)

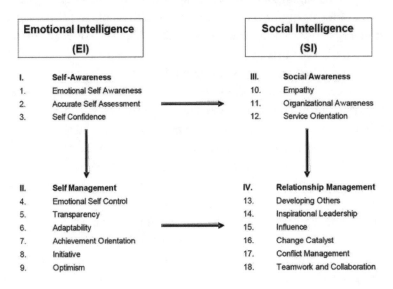

The competency model portrays ESI as an integrative concept that combines emotional intelligence and social intelligence to navigate complex interpersonal dynamics effectively. This nuanced interplay has garnered significant attention due to its potential impact on personal and professional relationships, communication, and overall well-being.

In their research, Bar-On, Tranel, Denburg, and Bechara (2003) also explored the neurological substrate of ESI, identifying brain regions associated with emotional and social processing. Their research indicates that the prefrontal cortex plays a pivotal role in modulating emotional responses and navigating social interactions. This neurological foundation supports the interconnectedness of emotional and social intelligence, highlighting the importance of effective emotional regulation in achieving successful social outcomes. Lopes, Brackett, Nezlek, Schutz, Sellin, and Salovey (2004) furthered the scholarship through their examination of the relationship between emotional intelligence and social interaction. They found that individuals with higher emotional intelligence experienced more positive social interactions, suggesting that emotional competencies contribute to successful social exchanges.

This aligns with the concept of ESI, where emotional understanding informs and enhances social relationships.

Boyatzis, Gaskin, and Wei (2015) went on to explore the impact of ESI on behavior, suggesting that individuals with higher ESI are more likely to exhibit prosocial behavior and adaptability. These behavioral tendencies contribute to stronger interpersonal relationships and enhanced group dynamics, emphasizing the practical benefits of cultivating ESI in various contexts. Kumar et al. (2008) emphasize the interconnected nature of emotional, social, and cognitive intelligence. They argue that these forms of intelligence work synergistically to enable individuals to navigate complex environments effectively. For instance, emotional awareness can inform social decisions, while cognitive abilities can guide emotional regulation in social situations. ESI theory represents a powerful confluence of emotional and social competencies that enable individuals to navigate complex interpersonal dynamics effectively by fostering positive relationships, successful social interactions, and adaptive behavior.

ESI and Teaching and Learning

The integration of emotional social intelligence (ESI) into teaching and learning environments has demonstrated the potential to transform both the process and outcomes of education. By understanding and leveraging the emotional and social aspects of instruction, educators can create more effective, engaging, and supportive learning experiences for students (Brackett & Katulak, 2013; Christison & Murray, 2023). Several studies have highlighted the positive impact of ESI on teaching competence and effectiveness. Poulou et al. (2019) found that B.Ed. teacher trainees with higher emotional intelligence demonstrated greater teaching competence, suggesting that ESI plays a significant role in shaping educators' instructional practices. Valente et al. (2020) and Ramana (2013) further support this notion, revealing a positive correlation between emotional intelligence and teacher effectiveness. This emphasizes the importance of ESI in fostering successful teaching outcomes.

Incorporating ESI into classroom practices can enhance educators' ability to understand and respond to students' emotional and social needs. Seema (2012) discusses the critical role of emotional intelligence in classroom settings, highlighting its potential to improve student engagement and learning outcomes. Similarly, Syiem (2012) underscores the significance of emotional intelligence in teaching, emphasizing its impact on students' academic and emotional development. Anand and Kerketta (2016) postulate that modeling emotional intelligence serves as a foundation for "better living;" by equipping students with ESI skills, educators can foster resilience, empathy, and self-awareness, contributing to students' holistic development. Chechi (2012) also explores the connection between emotional intelligence and teaching, suggesting that educators who cultivate ESI are better equipped to address diverse classroom dynamics and student needs. The interplay between teachers' approaches to teaching, students' approaches to learning, and learning outcomes has also been examined by Uiboleht, Karm, and Postareff (2018). Their qualitative multi-case study underscores the significance of teachers' ESI capacity in shaping students' approaches to learning and, consequently, their learning outcomes. This dynamic relationship affirms that educators who prioritize ESI can positively influence students' educational experiences.

The role of ESI in adult education and self-directed learning is also notable. Muller (2008) examined the interrelationships between self-directed learning and emotional intelligence, highlighting the importance of ESI in facilitating change and problem-solving in adult learners. Rager (2009) further emphasizes the role of emotion in self-directed learning, suggesting that educators who understand and address adult learners' emotional experiences and motivations to exercise independence can enhance learning outcomes. The scholarship roundly asserts that educators who cultivate their own ESI competencies can create environments that support students' academic and emotional growth, fostering more adaptive and engaged learners.

ESI Instructional Competency

The integration of emotional social intelligence (ESI) into instructional practices has become increasingly recognized as a key component of effective teaching. ESI competencies enable educators to navigate the emotional and social dynamics of the classroom, fostering a supportive learning environment conducive to student engagement and achievement (Alam & Ahmad, 2018). Mamat and Ismail (2021) highlight the importance of integrating emotional intelligence into teaching practices among university teachers in higher education. This integration not only improves educators' ability to manage classroom dynamics but also supports their capacity to engage students on a deeper emotional level. By incorporating ESI into instructional practices, educators can create a more inclusive and effective learning experience. Jennings et al. (2020) discuss the impact of teachers' social and emotional competence on student and classroom outcomes. Their research suggests that educators with higher ESI competency contribute to more positive classroom environments, characterized by better student-teacher relationships and improved academic and social-emotional outcomes. This underscores the potential of ESI in promoting prosocial classroom dynamics. Research has also explored the relationship between teachers' ESI and their approaches to conflict management (Asrar-ul-Haq et al., 2017), revealing that educators with ESI skills tend to navigate interactions adeptly by favoring cooperative and avoidance styles (Aliasgari & Farzadnia, 2012; Valente & Lourenço, 2020). This suggests that higher ESI competency empowers teachers to handle conflicts constructively, promoting positive relationships within the educational environment.

Brackett and Caruso are leading scholars in their (2007) examination of the role of emotionally intelligent teachers in creating supportive learning environments. They emphasize the need for teachers to develop skills in emotional awareness, self-regulation, and empathy to effectively address students' diverse needs. This skills-based approach to ESI training can enhance instructional practices and foster student success. Kaur, Shri, and Mital (2019) further explore the role of emotional intelligence competencies in effective teaching and teacher performance in higher education settings. Their findings suggest that educators with higher ESI demonstrate greater teaching effectiveness and adaptability. This aligns with prior research on the importance of ESI in shaping successful teaching outcomes.

Sharma and Arora (2012) and Mortiboys (2005) emphasize the importance of teaching with emotional intelligence in higher education settings. Their work supports the notion that faculty members with higher ESI are better equipped to address the challenges of diverse learning environments and to foster meaningful connections with university students through the application of practical ESI teaching strategies.

Classroom Climate and Student Well-being

According to well-being theory (Seligman, 2011), several elements contribute to students' well-being, including positive emotions, engagement, relationships, meaning, and accomplishments. Research pertaining to the social climate of learning communities demonstrates that the socio-emotional characteristics of a learning setting influence factors such as students' optimistic acceptance of life, their psychological and physiological well-being, and academic success (Ruus et al., 2007). Research by Rania et al. (2013) reinforces the existence of a strong correlation between well-being and climate in their study of how classroom environments impact undergraduate nursing students' well-being. While these studies focused on in-person learning communities, the work of Mustika et al. (2021) specifically investigated how the atmosphere of an online learning environment is connected to graduate students' well-being and found that almost all aspects of the online learning climate were significantly predictive of students' well-being. Climate inputs in the online setting such as peer-to-peer communication, the quality of instructors' communication, the personal relevance of content, and the opportunity to receive feedback were all important predictors of students' well-being (Rakow et al., 2023; Mustika et al., 2021).

Adult Learners & Adult Learning Online

Recent studies indicate that adult online learners identify the top benefits of online education as access to a more diverse community of learners, access to more institutions and degree programs, an increased sense of agency/independence, the ability to work at one's own pace, and flexibility and convenience (Castro & Tumibay, 2021; Paudel, 2021; Tareen & Haand, 2020). When considering how to best serve adult learners in professional graduate degree online programs, it is important to recognize that they are a distinct category of learners with unique needs and motivations, which has important implications for the design and facilitation of online learning environments. Cercone (2008) asserts that adult learners have significant personal and professional responsibilities (childcare, work) that interfere with and/or influence their learning experiences. Typically, adults electively enroll in graduate educational programs and juggle their classes and coursework around these responsibilities. Due in part to the fact that they are self-selecting into professional degree studies, adult learners are also more likely to be highly motivated and focused (Merriam & Caffarella, 1999). For adults, the learning process involves self-discovery, and transforming not just what one learns, but also the way in which one learns (Cercone, 2008). Understanding these distinctive features is essential for designing effective learning experiences for adults. Key conceptual frameworks, including transformative learning theory (Mezirow, 1993; 1997), self-directed learning, and Knowles' theory of andragogy (1984), shed light on the specific needs and motivations of adult learners in context.

Andragogy provides a useful window into better understanding the specific characteristics and learning preferences of adult learners (Knowles, 1984). A fundamental aspect of andragogy is the concept of self-directed learning. Adult learners are typically intrinsically motivated and have a strong desire to take ownership of their learning journey, engaging in learning that is relevant and applicable to their personal and professional lives (Merriam & Caffarella, 1999). Providing clear learning objectives and guidance, while still allowing flexibility for learners to pursue their specific interests and goals, promotes a self-directed learning process for adults. Transformative learning theory complements andragogy by emphasizing the transformative process that adult learners undergo as they engage in the learning process (Mezirow, 1997). Adult learners in professional graduate programs are often seeking opportunities for critical reflection, in order to challenge their existing assumptions and beliefs. Adult learners are more likely to feel as if their needs are being effectively met if learning experiences incorporate reflection, dialogue, and the exploration of diverse points of view which contribute to a sense of transformation for the learner.

Another key principle of andragogy is the emphasis on the learners' prior experiences. Adult learners bring their life experiences and pre-existing knowledge into the learning process, which shapes their perspectives and contributes to their understanding of the course material. Andragogy also emphasizes the importance of practical application; adult learners are motivated by the immediate relevance and applicability of what they learn (Cercone, 2008; Knowles, 1984). By integrating practical, job-related applications into the learning experience such as case studies, simulations, and authentic assessments that bridge the gap between theory and praxis, educators can enhance the motivation and engagement of adult learners. In the specific context of professional graduate degree programs, adult learners have a strong appetite for the application of newly acquired knowledge and skills directly to their professional lives, fostering deeper learning and skills transfer to the work environment.

Merriam (2001) asserts that self-directed learning theory is tightly coupled with andragogy in its aim to enable adults to achieve autonomy and develop a lifelong learning mindset by establishing learner-centered environments that foster opportunities for individual discovery. Candy's (1991) research identifies four key elements of self-directed learning: preparedness for learning, existence of learning initiatives, efficient learning techniques, and a conducive learning atmosphere. Self-directed learning interventions such as goal setting, self-monitoring, and reflective practice have beneficial effects on adult learners, including favorable impacts on their knowledge, skills, and attitudes (Loeng, 2020). Du Toit-Brits' (2019) study on self-directed learning underscores the significant role that educators play in transforming learning environments into spaces that foster individuals' empowerment and provide them with opportunities to learn socio-emotionally and cooperatively. Additional strategies for enhancing self-directed learning for adults include allowing classroom discourse to unfold in flexible accordance with learners' expressed needs and interests, granting options for assessments, and providing ongoing feedback (Merriam et al., 2007; Cho & Heron, 2015).

Online learning contexts are particularly promising as complementary environments for principles of self-directed learning and andragogy. Recent studies indicate that adult online learners identify an increased sense of agency/independence and the ability to work at one's own pace as top benefits of online education (Castro & Tumibay, 2021; Paudel, 2021; Tareen & Haand, 2020). Online students need to proficiently navigate digital environments, efficiently manage their time, and proactively seek out resources and assistance. Online learning provides adults with opportunities to customize their learning experiences, study asynchronously at their own pace, and explore personal interests (Cho & Heron, 2015). Online environments also offer various digital resources, interactive tools, and collaborative platforms that support self-directed learning. Studies indicate a positive correlation between these kinds of self-directed learning activities and learner autonomy, motivation, and satisfaction in online settings (Zhu et al., 2020). When empowered with self-direction, adult learners are more likely to actively engage and persist in their online studies. Self-regulatory skills, perceived control, self-efficacy, a sense of comfort online, and course design are crucial factors affecting self-directed learning in online settings (du Toit-Brits, 2019; Futch et al., 2016; Song, 2005). Instructors can facilitate the success of adult learners in online education by promoting self-directed learning, which enables learners to take an active and independent approach to their learning process.

ESI Instructor Competencies & Benefits Within Adult Online Learning Settings

ESI competencies are skills which empower individuals to identify, comprehend, and leverage social emotional data about themselves and other people in order to positively impact interpersonal and personal outcomes (Goleman, Boyatzis & McKee, 2002). While the current scholarship pertaining to ESI instructional applications to adult online learning settings is scarce, one can imagine how the application of these competencies might empower an instructor to design, facilitate, and co-create online classroom environments which foster positive emotional experiences for adult learners. ESI theory has the capacity to be particularly relevant in online learning environments (Bonesso et al., 2020), where the absence of a physical in-person presence makes it all the more challenging to navigate complex interpersonal dynamics effectively. The use of an ESI framework as an instructional tool for promoting positive adult online learning experiences is necessarily grounded in a constructivist perspective in which learning is viewed as an active, social enterprise of ongoing, collective meaning-making (Bada & Olusegun, 2015; Tam, 2000).

Scholars agree that instructors who possess a heightened level of ESI competency are equipped to effectively share knowledge and cater to the unique needs of professional learners with empathy and understanding (Kaur et al., 2019). This deeper connection can foster trust and care, creating a more supportive and engaging learning environment; Ramana's meta-analysis (2013) further suggests that an emotionally intelligent instructor can effectively manage negative emotions, maintain optimism, and motivate both themselves and their students. One noted form of management in online learning settings is through explicit modeling; instructors may demonstrate high ESI capacity through their own instructional design and facilitation choices, which support adult learners' skill development through observation and subsequent emulation (Shabani, Khatib & Ebadi, 2010; Majeski et al., 2017). This requires instructors to be highly intentional in their efforts to foster a positive emotional climate that supports adult online learners for impact.

Emotional social intelligence (ESI) theory further suggests that individuals with elevated ESI competencies are more likely to exhibit prosocial behaviors and adaptability (Jennings & Greenburg, 2009). These behavioral tendencies contribute to stronger interpersonal relationships and enhanced group dynamics, emphasizing the practical benefits of cultivating ESI in contexts such as online learning environments. In addition, individuals with higher ESI skills (Lievens & Chan, 2017) can better apply their emotional and social knowledge to real-world situations, increasing the probability of positive outcomes related to communication, conflict resolution, and relationship building.

There is significant evidence to support that the socio-emotional characteristics of a learning environment, whether online or in-person, are closely linked to the emotional experiences individuals have within a learning community. According to Rovai (2002) and Derakhshandeh et al. (2023), adult learners online seek feelings of affiliation, partnership, and engagement with their peers and instructors. Garrison, Anderson, and Archer (2001) claim that an atmosphere of emotional support within a learning community has the potential to enhance the overall perceptions of the learning environment, boost students' motivation, and minimize disengagement. Rovai's research (Lowenthal et al., 2023) also discovered when online instructors created conditions where students could express themselves openly and present alternative viewpoints, students were more likely to feel a sense of emotional connection. Online instructors who invite social presence with adult learners in these ways have also reported an increase in the emotional expression and socio-emotional support across the learning community (Rovai, 2007). Jézégou (2012, p.11) describes these conditions as fundamental to the sense of "presence" that must be established in distance learning environments, in order to promote the aforementioned self-direction strongly favored by adult learners. When empowered in these ways, adult learners are more likely to actively engage and persist in their online studies. Majeski, Stover, Valais, and Ronch (2017) advanced this work through their investigation of the fostering of emotional intelligence in online higher education courses. Their research affirms that integrating ESI into online teaching practices can enhance students' learning experiences and outcomes.

Applications of ESI Competencies to Online Instructional Practices

Given the scholarship's strongly established positive correlations between learners' socio-emotional experiences and a wide array of beneficial outcomes, equipping online instructors with evidence-based tools to build their ESI instructional capacity is paramount. Boyatzis et al. (2019) defines emotional social intelligence competencies relative to project managers overseeing work teams as:

> the pillars of cognitive readiness…frequently involved in enhancing the cognitive readiness of teams. They are extremely useful for reducing tension and increasing cooperation among team members by identifying and assessing their feelings, anticipating their actions, acknowledging their concerns, and following up on their issues (PMI, 2013). They also help in acquiring flexibility in order to react promptly to challenges and threats. Emotional and social intelligence competencies are related to the understanding and management of the self and of interpersonal relationships (p.148).

In light of the fact that cognitive readiness is an antecedent to learning and that this definition is centered around adult actors, it serves as a thought-provoking scaffolding for a consideration of the benefits of an ESI-competent instructional strategy, with the "project manager" as "instructor" and the "team" as the "adult learners". While multiple scholars have expanded Goleman (1995; 2002), Salovey and Mayer (1990), and Bar-On's (1985) seminal scholarship into the landscape of learning environments, the four domains and eighteen competencies outlined in Goleman, Boyatzis, and McKee's (2002) *Emotional Social Intelligence Competency Model* (Figure 1) provide an appropriate dominant framework for further informing evidence-based ESI instructional strategies. Finally, an integration of what is understood about the needs of adult learners (Knowles, 1984; Lewis & Bryan, 2021) and the affordances and constraints of online learning environments (Zamecnik et al., 2022; Lowenthal et al., 2023) offer additional essential context to inform a strategy for manifesting a positive social emotional experience for adult online learners. The following representation (Figure 2) of an ESI-competency based framework for online adult learners which synthesizes key research is proposed to inform evidence-based instructional practices. The framework incorporates practices that apply to both synchronous and asynchronous learning experiences.

Figure 2. Conceptual frame of ESI competency-based instruction for online adult learners (Grimes, 2024)

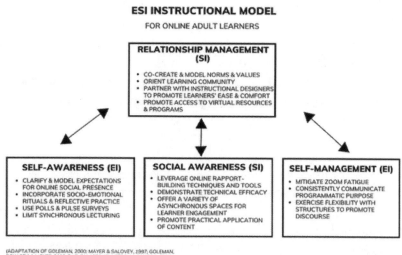

This conceptual framework illustrates the forces which contribute to the formation of an ESI-based instructional environment within an online adult learning community. Relationship management is the primary dimension, with the other three dimensions serving as both antecedents of and reinforcements for this competency. A consideration of each factor follows, along with recommended instructional practices. Instructional practices are inclusive of efforts led by the faculty member tasked with teaching the course both synchronously and asynchronously, as well as some contributions from institutional colleagues in roles related to overall degree program administration and instructional design. An optimization of social emotional experiences for online adult learning communities is realized when these individuals work in concert, with a shared understanding of the driving ESI forces at play.

Self-awareness (EI)

Like the captain of a ship, the instructor has an outsized influence on successfully developing an online learning atmosphere and its conjoined collective sense of emotional well-being for participants. This begins with the intentional cultivation of self-awareness for the instructor and is complemented by practices which promote a halo effect of self-awareness across the learning community. Seal, Boyatzis, and Bailey (2006, p. 204) characterize self-awareness in organizational settings as a kind of intrapersonal insight, which serves as "the link between [one's] thoughts, feelings and actions." When teaching adult professionals online, an instructor's comprehension of their needs and preferences is critical to the genesis of a positive socio-emotional climate, as are instructional behaviors which establish a sense of presence for all participants (Jézégou, 2012; Whiteside et al., 2023). Each instructor brings a unique set of beliefs and values into the learning community with them; the ways in which these are communicated to students through an instructor's persona, behavior, and dialogue in asynchronous and synchronous settings serves to establish an overall presence and socio-emotional atmosphere for learning, particularly in the early weeks of a course, when students are more impressionable to an instructor's style.

An instructional style which is characterized by centering the learner is most effective in adult online learning communities. Exercising self-awareness as the instructor involves focusing on the learners' experiences, interests, perspectives, and needs, as opposed to primarily lecturing about course material like a "sage on the stage" (King, 2010, p.30). As a "guide on the side" (King, 2010, p.30), the instructor is modeling a balanced and self-confident presence which fosters mutual respect and promotes class participation (Dallimore et al., 2004). This facilitation approach aligns with andragogical principles (Knowles, 1984; Lewis & Bryan, 2021) and is proven to foster positive student-instructor relationships, positive student perceptions of the class, and a generative learning climate (Katsarou & Chatzipanagiotou, 2021). Intentional facilitation of a dynamic learner-centered environment is essential in online learning spaces, which are bidimensional in nature, and therefore inherently predisposed to feeling more flat. With the above in mind, the following key instructional recommendations are offered to optimize the ESI dimension of self-awareness within adult online learning environments.

Model and Clarify Expectations for Social Presence at the Onset

This includes explicitly articulating an expectation for students to leave their cameras on; promoting active utilization of the chat space and emojis for parallel discourse, inquiry, and expressions of support; articulating the preferred means of signaling a desire to participate (virtual or manual hand raising); modeling active and appropriate participation through instructor facial expression, nodding, listening and other forms of verbal and non-verbal communication; and eliciting participation from members of the community who are less vocal in the learning environment to promote inclusion and illumination of a variety of perspectives.

Incorporate Socio-emotional Rituals and Reflective Practice

One ritual that promotes collective emotional self-awareness and social presence is opening each class with a "two-word check-in" during which each student has the opportunity to share how they are feeling or share something personal about themselves with the larger group (Berry, 2019; Brackett, 2019). This valuable socio-emotional technique, which can be facilitated in a round-robin manner or through a chat waterfall (if time is limited), not only promotes rapport and interpersonal connection, but softens the sometimes abrupt transitions adults make from their personal and professional lives into the synchronous online environment.

Additionally, class time dedicated to quiet intrapersonal reflective practice can serve as a powerful centering mechanism for adult learners, who often have significant personal and professional responsibilities (childcare, work) that interfere with and/or influence their learning experiences (Cercone, 2008) and increase their cognitive load. Evidence demonstrates that adult learners in professional graduate programs are often seeking opportunities for critical reflection, in order to challenge their existing assumptions and beliefs (Mezirow, 1997). By holding space for reflective work, instructors bolster collective self-awareness and provide a bridge between personal experiences and the acquisition of new knowledge that is characteristic of experiential learning (Kolb, 1984). Opening synchronous and/or asynchronous learning sessions with a reflective prompt (a question about students' experiences, a quote from the readings, a video clip, a piece of music or poetry) and an invitation to engage in quiet introspection about the prompt can both be meaningful and inspire valuable metacognition about one's identity and greater purpose. A subsequent sharing of individual reflections in the larger group may escalate collective meaning-making and socio-emotional bonds.

Use Polls and Pulse Surveys

Soliciting feedback from students is a useful technique to give instructors information on how the course is going and what might be done to make it a better learning environment (Lewis, 2002). Wlodkowski and Ginsberg (2017) and Lyn and Broderick (2023) specifically examined the impact of iterative course feedback on adult online learners and found that the opportunity to offer feedback on instruction has a direct impact on adults' motivation to learn. To promote instructor self-awareness and enhance teaching methods and learning outcomes, instructors can use virtual tools to curate feedback in real time, in order to interrogate instructional choices, check for understanding, and promote continuous improvement processes (Yen et al., 2017). Nimble online platforms such as PollEverywhere©, Slido©, and Mentimeter© allow instructors to quickly curate formative feedback.

Limit Synchronous Lecturing

When lecturing in synchronous sessions, instructors should limit it to spans of under five minutes, strategically using their voice as a means of clarifying the agenda and objectives, providing meaningful feedback and affirmation to students, facilitating discussion amongst students, and synthesizing collective learnings. Instructors should actively exercise self-awareness by being mindful of their social presence in the learning environment by making room for many voices to be shared outside of their own. Asynchronous learning spaces may be leveraged for more lecture-style content delivery. Utilizing a flipped curriculum, in which asynchronous content is taken up by learners in advance of synchronous gatherings, and synchronous gatherings provide time to explore material, aids in this endeavor. In this model learners encounter information before class, and synchronous class time is dedicated to interactive activities that involve higher order thinking and investigation of relevant themes, knowledge, and practical applications (Brame, 2013).

Social Awareness (SI)

Boyatzis et al. (2019, p. 151) describe social awareness as "understand[ing] what people experience, to be able to see their point of view, and to cultivate relationships in tune with a large number of different people;" this includes considering the motivations and emotions of others and "the meaning of what they do and say" (Basu & Mermillod, 2011, p. 183). This complex ESI competency also animates organizational awareness, which consists of the ability to "identify social and power networks as well as the underlying values that drive the functioning of groups" (Boyatzis et al., 2019, p. 151). When considered within the context of adult online learning settings, the instructor must capitalize upon the unique attributes of these spaces in order to promote an ESI climate for participants.

While the absence of in-person engagement in online programs is observed by some as an impediment to fostering a salient socio-emotional environment, distance learning offers pathways for involvement that are distinct from in-person instruction and additive in nature, including private and public chat features and discussion tools, synchronous and asynchronous locations for interaction, access to recordings of learning sessions, and the improvisational implementation of randomized and coordinated small groups. For socially aware instructors, this means designing engagement opportunities which allow students to go "deeper and further" into the material through their interactions with others (Palloff & Pratt, 2007, p.111) in order to enhance both the level of participation and the capacity for emotional connection. Given that students in online programs express a desire to avoid isolation and feel a sense of connection with fellow students and instructors (Thomas et al., 2014;

Song et al., 2016), it follows that they would opt to participate in synchronous and asynchronous experiences which have the capacity to fulfill that need.

With the above in mind, the following key instructional recommendations are offered to optimize the ESI dimension of social awareness within adult online learning environments.

Leverage Rapport-building Techniques and Tools

Self-disclosure, expressions of warmth, openness, concern, encouragement for students to share personal life stories and identities, and the playful incorporation of humor and levity are recommended socially aware instructional strategies. Both humor and self-disclosure are proven to contribute to group cohesion, task motivation, and learning outcomes for adult learners (Brookfield, 1987; Garrison, 2009). In online settings, performing confirming behaviors such as always leaving one's camera on, overtly nodding, adding affirmative words and emojis to the chat, and inviting social conversation in the online environment should be socially aware priorities for online instructors of adult learners. One technique for identifying group dynamics is visiting breakout rooms while they are in session and modeling active listening. Zooming into student discussions, observing interactions, and engaging with nods and facial expressions are instructor behaviors which signal that breakout rooms are valuable student-centered learning spaces, and also allow instructors to collect data about students' peer-to-peer interactions which may usefully inform future instructional choices. Socially aware instructors should also exercise intentionality in their use of breakout rooms by including purposeful diversification and rearrangement of groupings of students, which afford online learners with opportunities to interact with multiple classmates over time.

Demonstrate Technical Efficacy

An instructor's awareness of, belief in, and positive communication about the benefits of online learning for adult degree-seeking professionals will have a cascade effect across the learning community, promoting shared buy-in regarding the learning modality. To demonstrate social awareness and uphold their endorsement, online instructors should possess technical competency with tools and platforms, along with some fluency regarding current evidence which supports the key benefits of online learning for adults. If training is required to achieve efficacy, instructors should seek out training resources at their institution.

Offer a Variety of Asynchronous Spaces for Learner Engagement

This includes spaces and activities such as video-based discussions (VoiceThread©, Flip©), collaborative documents (Google Docs©), mind maps (LucidChart©, Miro©, MindMeister©), and white/post-it boards (Padlet©, Mural©, Kami©). By facilitating these kinds of ecosystems for learners, instructors create opportunities to observe and gain insight into group dynamics, and to promote valuable interpersonal connections across the learning community beyond the bounds of synchronous sessions.

Promote Practical Application of Content

Adult learners are motivated by the immediate relevance and applicability of what they learn (Cercone, 2008; Knowles, 1984) which shapes their perspectives and contributes to their understanding of the course material. Understanding this perspective empowers instructors to adopt socially aware methodologies into their teaching strategies. Practical application can be achieved through the use of role plays, case studies (provided and self-generated), participatory action research, and authentic assessments that bridge the gap between theory and practice and amplify learner agency. Simulation-based virtual experiential learning tools such as SchoolSims© "offer 6-8 decision points in a choose-your-own-adventure format, where a mix of live actor scenes and artificial intelligence allows learners to experience the consequences of their decisions while bridging the gap between theory and practice" (SchoolSims, 2024). Given that enhanced diversity of participants is a benefit of online learning communities (Paudel, 2021; Tareen & Haand, 2020), engagement in practical application with others provides adult learners with important chances to participate in dialogue which allows for the exploration of diverse points of view and cultivates empathy for alternative experiences. Therefore, socially aware instructors should pay particular attention to practical application enterprises that enable group work and teaming and be aware of emerging technologies in this arena.

Self-management (EI)

Boyatzis et al. (2019) characterize the ESI dimension of self-management as a:

positive outlook, which is the ability to see the positive side of things; drive to achieve, which concerns the ability to set personal challenging standards and continuously find a way to improve; and adaptability, which is useful in volatile and unstable environments because it helps to quickly metabolize change. In the organizational context, but also in everyday personal life, self-management competencies matter a lot because the person's mental state and moods end up influencing the mood of others through an emotional contagion (Goleman, 2011, p. 151)

The instructor's capacity for effective self-management cannot be understated, as established by the conceptual frame (Figure 2). In particular, the instructor serves as an ongoing navigational beacon of purpose throughout the online adult learning experience and is tasked with repeatedly reminding adult learners of the essential "why" of their participation in their studies in order to promote a rewarding emotional experience and sense of drive to accomplish challenging graduate work (Mezirow, 1993; Sinek, 2011). This reification of purpose is particularly significant in the landscape of online professional graduate degree programs, where the investment of resources is typically substantial and the geographic location distal. In addition, the rapidly evolutive nature of online learning tools and platforms necessitates that instructors have the capacity to grow in their skills and strategies to keep pace with instructional innovations.

With the above in mind, the following key instructional recommendations are offered to optimize the ESI dimension of self-management within adult online learning environments.

Mitigate Zoom Fatigue

While overly rigid lesson planning is not in alignment with principles of self-directed learning and andragogy, instructors are still encouraged to be mindful of the resource of time and the phenomenon of "Zoom fatigue" in planning their teaching online methods (Toney et al., 2021). In synchronous meetings this includes incorporating self-management instructional strategies such as bookending focal small group activities with large group discourse; a large group introduction of the activity and clarifications of objectives at the onset; and a large group share out and synthesis of small group learnings at the conclusion. In asynchronous meetings this includes the thoughtful integration of a variety of learner inputs such as recorded lectures, reflection prompts, collaboration boards, readings, and external media.

The influence of the instructor's affect is significant in shaping the socio-emotional atmosphere of the learning community. Mirror neurons will facilitate emotional contagion (Winkleman & Harmon-Jones, 2006; Barsade, 2002; Goleman, 2006) from instructor to students; therefore, in as much as possible, instructors should self-manage a positive affect throughout their teaching practice, given its outsized impact across the learning community and capacity to energize the bidimensional learning space.

Consistently Communicate Programmatic Purpose

In order to fulfill the need for autonomy and self-direction that adult learners typically crave, providing students with clarity regarding the fundamental goals of learning and the rationale for selected course materials and activities are valuable self-management practices for instructors. These adult learning needs may be complicated by feelings of distance and inaccessibility online students experience as a result of their geographic dislocation from the physical campus. Therefore, instructors with high self-management skills should bridge this gap by ensuring that programmatic communications, digital interfaces (LMS), syllabi, and learning activities and assignments reflect a cohesive quality of purpose and shared mission that serves to motivate learners' appetite for ongoing learning and achievement, even amidst setbacks or perceived limitations.

Exercise Flexibility with Structures to Promote Discourse

Instructors who are able to self-manage by making room for iteration, innovation, and deviation from rigid structures and lesson plans contribute to a more positive socio-emotional climate for adult online learners, who prefer a learning experience rooted in autonomy, practicality, and collective needs. The instructor's primary role is to facilitate communication by continuously fostering and encouraging effective interaction among students (Bostock, 2018). In turn, adult learners need to recognize their responsibility in maintaining the communication space between themselves, the instructor, and their classmates.

Relationship Management (SI)

The relationship management dimension of ESI for learning settings encompasses both student-to-student, student-to-instructor, and instructor-to-institution partnerships and is elemental to the existence of a beneficial socio-emotional learning environment. As an ESI competency, relationship management is interdependent with the domains of self-awareness, social awareness, and self-management. That is to say, the instructor's competency across the other three domains has an impact on their capacity for relationship management, and relationship management, in turn, shapes the instructor's other ESI competencies. This dynamic is illustrative of the conceptualization of ESI competency as the outcome of a kind of alchemy of interactive forces between the self, others, systems, and environments. Once relationships are initiated, specific activities and behaviors within the learning environment enable their development, including student involvement. Involvement describes a learner's participation in the environment, both behaviorally, emotionally, and cognitively, as well as the provision of such an environment by the instructor and the system (Paas et al., 2005). Interest in peers and subject matter facilitates involvement and inspires a sense of motivation, morale, and self-efficacy amongst learners that contributes to the building of relationships and the instructor's capacity to effectively engage in ongoing relationship management efforts.

When an instructor possesses high competency in the relationship management domain of ESI, this serves as the foundation for generating a positive socio-emotional online learning environment for adults. Effective relationship management "includes all competencies used to persuade and guide, negotiate, resolve conflicts, and achieve collaboration, such as influenc[ing], coach[ing] and mentor[ing], inspirational leadership, teamwork, and conflict management" (Boyatzis et al., 2019). Of all the ESI domains, relationship management is the one most closely coupled with leadership.

With the above in mind, the following key instructional recommendations are offered to optimize the ESI dimension of relationship management within adult online learning environments, keeping in mind that these efforts may overlap with other ESI dimensions, and may vary in accordance with the kind of online learning model (cohort-based, program-based, self-paced).

Co-create and Model Values and/or Norms of Engagement

Co-creating and periodically referencing shared core values and/or norms of engagement across learning environments and experiences, as appropriate, reifies and promotes suprapersonal connections and a collective sense of identity. It also serves to guide expectations for engagement and provide a compass for any future conflict management. When considering the constraints of a lack of physical proximity for adult online professional degree learners, the ongoing pursuit and articulation of a shared purpose and collective values is beneficial to upholding the dimension of relationship management. While traditional face-to-face environments possess more universally agreed upon expectations and norms that signal a high-quality learning environment, the benchmarks of excellence within the virtual landscape of adult learning are still relatively novel, ambiguous, and uncodified. Therefore, any and all adaptive activities which promote the illumination of shared goals and ideals and empower program participants with a sense of self-direction and practical orientation, are beneficial to the enterprise of supporting a positive socio-emotional experience for all. Instructors are encouraged to actively model the agreed-upon norms and values in their facilitation practices and interactions with students.

Orient Learners to Their New Learning Community

Materials such as a shared collection of student biographies (provided by students and assembled and disseminated by administration), which highlight both personal and professional identities, are recommended. Adult online learners can also be acclimated to their new degree program community by hosting a welcoming online orientation. This should occur outside of class time, where students meet and learn about one another as individuals prior to onset of studies, and a shared group identity is introduced. These efforts are illustrative of providing guidance and leadership to the learning community, which will contribute to future relationship management efforts. In addition, these efforts aid in offsetting transactional distance which is defined as "a psychological and communications gap, a space of potential misunderstanding between the inputs of lecturer and those of the student" created in part by the "physical distance inherent to online learning" (Moore, 1991, p. 2; Bostock, 2018, p.12).

Partner with Instructional Designers to Promote Learners' Ease and Comfort

The LMS (learning management system) of an online course serves as the primary systemic interface for online adult learners, and is where courses are typically introduced, organized, engaged with, and delivered. Common current learning management platforms such as Blackboard©, Brightspace©, and Canvas© offer particular integrations and student-facing structures which may or may not contribute to a learner's sense of clarity and comfort, depending upon how they are structured. In many ways, the LMS functions as the opening act for a course or degree program, overtly signaling the brand of the institution, the personality of a course environment, the overall level of organization, and the quality of the design of the learning experience for current and future courses (Moos, 1987; Balkaya & Akkucuk, 2021). In order to build and maintain a high quality LMS, instructors must typically exercise relationship management skills across their institution, leveraging the expertise of partners in information technology and instructional design to contribute to the establishment of a low-friction virtual learning experience which reduces cognitive load for adult learners (Costley, 2020), who are often juggling significant personal and professional responsibilities in addition to their obligations as a student (Cercone, 2008).

For adult online learners, who are often busy with competing personal and professional obligations and typically paying a premium for a degree, an LMS interface which is aesthetic, low-friction, and institutionally branded offers a more welcoming, comfortable, and predictable online learning experience that contributes to positive perceptions of the learning experience and reduces technology-induced distress. Easy-to-access online course materials, nimble interactive asynchronous content, and seamless integration of external engagement platforms contribute to clarity and comfort. Student digital comfort-level is defined as a reduction of students' vulnerabilities, brought about by high-quality instructional design and teaching strategies, so that students are more likely to succeed in their online courses (Futch et al., 2016). When instructors exercise leadership in these collaborative efforts at the onset, it contributes to the mitigation of unnecessary frustrations for distance learners over time.

Promote Access to Virtual Resources and Programs

Instructors are encouraged to provide invitations and opportunities for adult online learners to engage with the broader institution through ongoing communication, programming, and resources such as career services offerings, digital newsletters, student engagement and wellness online events, university-sponsored webinars and colloquiums, and regional in-person gatherings. Faculty may serve as institutional advocates for the expansion of engagement/programming opportunities for remote learners. By fostering connection to the broader institution, instructors build capacity for furthering students' relationships across the university and contribute to fortifying the alumni network.

Long-Term Benefits of Applying ESI Competencies to Online Instructional Practices

As the aforementioned ESI instructional strategies are leveraged over time, students may experience a sense of increased investment in the learning experience, which further motivates ongoing behaviors that serve to reinforce interpersonal relationships and learning outcomes. Interpersonal connections which are forged generate other benefits which are foundational to students' overall socio-emotional experience. These include mutual support, trust, and social cohesion. Social cohesion (Friedkin, 2004), a suprapersonal phenomenon that reflects students' and instructor's knowledge of one another, and their interest in getting to know each other more, is further characterized by supportive and friendly intra-group behaviors which promote harmony and belonging (Dwyer et al., 2004; Fraser & Treagust, 1996; Thomas et al., 2014). The ability for online adult learners to develop prosocial bonds (student-to-student and student-to-instructor) which are characterized by mutual trust and support is fundamental to bridging the divide that may be felt in the absence of physical in-person presence and proximity. When amalgamated, an instructor's ESI practices of self-awareness, social awareness, self-management, and relationship management advance the establishment of a relational and psychologically safe online learning experience (Edmondson et al., 2004; 2018; Edmondson & Roloff, 2008).

CONCLUSION

Emotional Social Intelligence theory (Bar-On, 1985; Salovey & Mayer, 1990; Goleman, 1995) provides a useful theoretical framework for considering optimal instructional design practices for adult online learning communities; when synthesized with the broader scholarship pertaining to online learning, adult learning, and socio-emotional constructs such as well-being, the conceptual lens for investigating these phenomena is sharpened. The benefits of a perceived favorable socio-emotional climate for adult online learners are irrefutable and include increased academic achievement and motivation; lasting positive perceptions of academic experience; increased sense of belonging, well-being, and self-efficacy; and enhanced affiliation with and loyalty towards the institution (Hong et al., 2021; Rania et al., 2014; Shea et al., 2005; Tafjel & Turner, 2004; Thomas et al., 2014; Wang et al., 2020). Therefore, as online professional degree programs for adults continue to advance in their ubiquity, it behooves institutions of higher education to be equipped to compete in the marketplace by offering high-quality online learning experiences for adults. It follows that the instructors and university personnel responsible for these programs must be provided with the necessary training, resources, evidence-based tools, and practices to effectively design and facilitate online learning experiences which contribute to a positive socio-emotional climate.

REFERENCES

Alam, A., & Ahmad, M. (2018). The role of teachers' emotional intelligence in enhancing student achievement. *Journal of Asia Business Studies*, 12(1), 31–43. DOI: 10.1108/JABS-08-2015-0134

Aliasgari, M. A. J. I. D., & Farzadnia, F. (2012). The relationship between emotional intelligence and conflict management styles among teachers. *Interdisciplinary Journal of Contemporary Research in Business*, 4(8), 555–562.

Anand, S., & Kerketta, E. (2016). Teaching emotional intelligence: A foundation for better living. *International Journal of Applied Research*, 2(5), 967–969.

Arghode, V. (2013). Emotional and social intelligence competence: Implications for instruction. *International Journal of Peagogies and Learning*, 8(2), 66–77. DOI: 10.5172/ijpl.2013.8.2.66

Asrar-ul-Haq, M., Anwar, S., & Hassan, M. (2017). Impact of emotional intelligence on teacher s performance in higher education institutions of Pakistan. *Future Business Journal*, 3(2), 87–97. DOI: 10.1016/j.fbj.2017.05.003

Bada, S. O., & Olusegun, S. (2015). Constructivism learning theory: A paradigm for teaching and learning. *Journal of Research & Method in Education*, 5(6), 66–70.

Balkaya, S., & Akkucuk, U. (2021). Adoption and use of learning management systems in education: The role of playfulness and self-management. *Sustainability (Basel)*, 13(3), 1127. DOI: 10.3390/su13031127

Bar-On, R. (1985). The development of an operational concept of psychological wellbeing. Unpublished doctoral dissertation, Rhodes University, South Africa.

Bar-On, R., Tranel, D., Denburg, N. L., & Bechara, A. (2003). Exploring the neurological substrate of emotional and social intelligence. *Brain*, 126(8), 1790–1800. DOI: 10.1093/brain/awg177 PMID: 12805102

Barsade, S. (2002). The ripple effect: Emotional contagion and its influence on group behavior. *Administrative Science Quarterly*, 47(4), 644–675. DOI: 10.2307/3094912

Basu, A., & Mermillod, M. (2011). Emotional intelligence and social-emotional learning: An overview. *Online Submission*, 1(3), 182–185.

Berry, S. (2019). Teaching to connect: Community-building strategies for the virtual classroom. *Online Learning : the Official Journal of the Online Learning Consortium*, 23(1), 164–183. DOI: 10.24059/olj.v23i1.1425

Bonesso, S., Bruni, E., Gerli, F., Bonesso, S., Bruni, E., & Gerli, F. (2020). Emotional and social intelligence competencies in the digital era. *Behavioral competencies of digital professionals: Understanding the role of emotional intelligence*, 41-62.

Bostock, J. R. (2018). A model of flexible learning: Exploring interdependent relationships between students, lecturers, resources and contexts in virtual spaces. *Journal of Perspectives in Applied Academic Practice*, 6(1), 12–18. DOI: 10.14297/jpaap.v6i1.298

Boyatzis, R. (2021). Learning life skills of emotional and social intelligence competencies. In M. London (Ed.), *The Oxford handbook of lifelong learning* (2nd ed., pp. 131–145). Oxford University Press.

Boyatzis, R., Goleman, D., & Rhee, K. (2000). Clustering competence in emotional intelligence: Insights from the emotional competence inventory (ECI). In Bar-On, R., & Parker, J. D. A. (Eds.), *Handbook of emotional intelligence*. Jossey-Bass.

Boyatzis, R. E. (1982). *The competent manager: A model for effective performance*. John Wiley & Sons.

Boyatzis, R. E., Gaskin, J., & Wei, H. (2015). Emotional and social intelligence and behavior. Handbook of intelligence: Evolutionary theory, historical perspective, and current concepts, 243-262. DOI: 10.1007/978-1-4939-1562-0_17

Boyatzis, R. E., Goleman, D., Gerli, F., Bonesso, S., & Cortellazzo, L. (2019). Emotional and social intelligence competencies and the intentional change process. In *Cognitive Readiness in Project Teams* (pp. 147–169). Productivity Press. DOI: 10.4324/9780429490057-7

Brackett, M. (2019). *Permission to feel: Unlocking the power of emotions to help our kids, ourselves, and our society thrive*. Celadon Books.

Brackett, M. A., & Caruso, D. R. (2007) Emotional literacy for educators. Cary, NC: SELMedia.

Brackett, M. A., & Katulak, N. A. (2013). Emotional intelligence in the classroom: Skill-based training for teachers and students. In *Applying emotional intelligence* (pp. 1–27). Psychology Press.

Brame, C. (2013). *Flipping the classroom*. Vanderbilt University Center for Teaching.

Brookfield, S. D. (1987). *Developing critical thinkers: Challenging adults to explore alternative ways of thinking and acting*. Jossey-Bass.

Candy, P. C. (1991). *Self-Direction for Lifelong Learning*. Jossey-Bass.

Castro, M. D. B., & Tumibay, G. M. (2021). A literature review: Efficacy of online learning courses for higher education institutions using meta-analysis. *Education and Information Technologies*, 26(2), 1367–1385. DOI: 10.1007/s10639-019-10027-z

Cercone, K. (2008). Characteristics of adult learners with implications for online learning design. AACE review (formerly. *AACE Journal*, 16(2), 137–159.

Chechi, K. V. (2012). Emotional intelligence and teaching. *International Journal of Research in Economics & Social Sciences*, 2(2), 297–304.

Cho, M. H., & Heron, M. L. (2015). Self-regulated learning: The role of motivation, emotion, and use of learning strategies in students' learning experiences in a self-paced online mathematics course. *Distance Education*, 36(1), 80–99. DOI: 10.1080/01587919.2015.1019963

Christison, M., & Murray, D. E. (2023). THE IMPORTANCE OF EI COMPETENCE FOR TEACHERS AND LEADERS IN DIVERSE ELT CONTEXTS. *European Journal of Applied Linguistics & TEFL*, 12(2).

Costley, J. (2020). Using cognitive strategies overcomes cognitive load in online learning environments. *Interactive Technology and Smart Education*, 17(2), 215–228. DOI: 10.1108/ITSE-09-2019-0053

Dallimore, E. J., Hertenstein, J. H., & Platt, M. B. (2004). Classroom participation and discussion effectiveness: Student-generated strategies. *Communication Education*, 53(1), 103–115. DOI: 10.1080/0363452032000135805

Derakhshandeh, Z., Vora, V., Swaminathan, A., & Esmaeili, B. (2023, March). On the importance and facilitation of learner-learner interaction in online education: a review of the literature. In *Society for Information Technology & Teacher Education International Conference* (pp. 207-215). Association for the Advancement of Computing in Education (AACE).

Ding, C., Ramdas, M., & Mortillaro, M. (2024). Emotional intelligence in applied settings: Approaches to its theoretical model, measurement, and application. *Frontiers in Psychology*, 15, 1387152. DOI: 10.3389/fpsyg.2024.1387152 PMID: 38515968

Du Toit-Brits, C. (2019). A focus on self-directed learning: The role that educators' expectations play in the enhancement of students' self-directedness. *South African Journal of Education*, 39(2), 1–11. DOI: 10.15700/saje.v39n2a1645

Dwyer, K. K., Bingham, S. G., Carlson, R. E., Prisbell, M., Cruz, A. M., & Fus, D. A. (2004). Communication and connectedness in the classroom: Development of the connected classroom climate inventory. *Communication Research Reports*, 21(3), 264–272. DOI: 10.1080/08824090409359988

Edmondson, A. C., Kramer, R. M., & Cook, K. S. (2004). Psychological safety, trust, and learning in organizations: A group-level lens. Trust and distrust in organizations: Dilemmas and approaches, 12(2004), 239-272.

Edmondson, A. C., & Roloff, K. S. (2008). Overcoming barriers to collaboration: Psychological safety and learning in diverse teams. In *Team effectiveness in complex organizations* (pp. 217–242). Routledge.

Fernández-Berrocal, P., & Extremera, N. (2006). Emotional intelligence: A theoretical and empirical review of its first 15 years of history. *Psicothema*, 18, 7–12. PMID: 17295952

Fraser, B. J., & Treagust, D. F. (1986). Validity and use of an instrument for assessing classroom psychological environment in higher education. *Higher Education*, 15(1-2), 37–57. DOI: 10.1007/BF00138091

Friedkin, N. E. (2004). Social cohesion. *Annual Review of Sociology*, 30(1), 409–425. DOI: 10.1146/annurev.soc.30.012703.110625

Fuhrmann, B. S., & Grasha, A. F. (1983). *A practical handbook for college teachers*. No Title.

Futch, L. S., DeNoyelles, A., Thompson, K., & Howard, W. (2016). Comfort" as a Critical Success Factor in Blended Learning Courses. *Online Learning : the Official Journal of the Online Learning Consortium*, 20(3), 140–158. DOI: 10.24059/olj.v20i3.978

Gardner, H. (1993). Multiple intelligences.

Garrison, D. R. (2009). Communities of inquiry in online learning. In *Encyclopedia of distance learning* (2nd ed., pp. 352–355). IGI Global. DOI: 10.4018/978-1-60566-198-8.ch052

Garrison, D. R., Anderson, T., & Archer, W. (2001). Critical thinking, cognitive presence, and computer conferencing in distance education. *American Journal of Distance Education*, 15(1), 7–23. DOI: 10.1080/08923640109527071

Goleman, D. (1995). *Emotional intelligence*. Bantam Books.

Goleman, D. (2000a). Emotional intelligence. In Sadock, B., & Sadock, V. (Eds.), *Comprehensive textbook of psychiatry* (7th ed.). Lippincott Williams & Wilkins.

Goleman, D. (2011). Emotional mastery. *Leadership Excellence*, 28(6), 12–13.

Goleman, D., Boyatzis, R. E., & McKee, A. (2002). *Reawakening your passion for work*. Harvard Business School Publishing Corporation.

Hong, F.-Y., Shao-I., C., Huang, D.-H., & Chiu, S.-L. (2021). Correlations among classroom emotional climate, social self-efficacy, and psychological health of university students in Taiwan. *Education and Urban Society*, 53(4), 446–468. DOI: 10.1177/0013124520931458

Jennings, P., Frank, J., & Montgomery, M. (2020). Social and emotional learning for educators. *Rethinking learning: A review of social and emotional learning for education systems*, 127-153.

Jézégou, A. (2012). Towards a distance learning environment that supports learner self-direction: The model of presence. *International Journal of Self-Directed Learning*, 9(1), 11–23.

Joseph, D. L., & Newman, D. A. (2010). Emotional intelligence: An integrative meta-analysis and cascading model. *The Journal of Applied Psychology*, 95(1), 54–78. DOI: 10.1037/a0017286 PMID: 20085406

Katsarou, E., & Chatzipanagiotou, P. (2021). A critical review of selected literature on learner-centered interactions in online learning. *Electronic Journal of e-Learning*, 19(5), 349–362. DOI: 10.34190/ejel.19.5.2469

Kaur, I., Shri, C., & Mital, K. M. (2019). The role of emotional intelligence competencies in effective teaching and teacher's performance in higher education. *Higher Education for the Future*, 6(2), 188–206. DOI: 10.1177/2347631119840542

Kihlstrom, J. F., & Cantor, N. (2000). Social intelligence. Handbook of intelligence, 2, 359-379.King, A. (1993). From sage on the stage to guide on the side. *College Teaching*, 41(1), 30–35.

Knowles, M. S. (1984). Andragogy in action.

Kolb, D. A. (1984). *Experiential Learning: Experiences as a source of learning and development*. Prentice-Hall.

Kumar, N., Rose, R. C., & Subramaniam, . (2008). The bond between intelligences: Cultural, emotional, and social. *Performance Improvement*, 47(10), 42–48. DOI: 10.1002/pfi.20039

Lewis, C. (2002). *Lesson study: A handbook of teacher-led instructional change*. Research for Better Schools.

Lewis, N., & Bryan, V. (2021). Andragogy and teaching techniques to enhance adult learners' experience. *Journal of Nursing Education and Practice*, 11(11), 31–40. DOI: 10.5430/jnep.v11n11p31

Loeng, S. "Self-Directed Learning: A Core Concept in Adult Education", Education Research International, vol. 2020, Article ID 3816132, 12 pages, 2020. https://doi.org/DOI: 10.1155/2020/3816132

Lopes, P. N., Brackett, M. A., Nezlek, J. B., Schütz, A., Sellin, I., & Salovey, P. (2004). Emotional intelligence and social interaction. *Personality and Social Psychology Bulletin*, 30(8), 1018–1034. DOI: 10.1177/0146167204264762 PMID: 15257786

Lopes, P. N., Salovey, P., & Straus, R. (2003). Emotional intelligence, personality, and the perceived quality of social relationships. *Personality and Individual Differences*, 35(3), 641–658. DOI: 10.1016/S0191-8869(02)00242-8

Lowenthal, P. R., Horan, A., DeArmond, M. C., Lomellini, A., Egan, D., Johnson, M., Moeller, K. N., Keldgord, F., Kuohn, J., Jensen, S., Stamm, A., & Pounds, D. (2023). Classroom Community and Online Learning: A Synthesis of Alfred Rovai's Research. *TechTrends*, 67(6), 931–944. DOI: 10.1007/s11528-023-00904-3

Lyn, A. E., Broderick, M., & Spranger, E. (2023). Student well-being and empowerment: SEL in online graduate education. In *Exploring Social Emotional Learning in Diverse Academic Settings* (pp. 312–336). IGI Global. DOI: 10.4018/978-1-6684-7227-9.ch016

Majeski, R. A., Stover, M., Valais, T., & Ronch, J. (2017). Fostering emotional intelligence in online higher education courses. *Adult Learning*, 28(4), 135–143. DOI: 10.1177/1045159517726873

Mamat, N. H., & Ismail, N. A. H. (2021). Integration of emotional intelligence in teaching practice among university teachers in higher education. *Malaysian Journal of Learning and Instruction*, 18(2), 69–102.

Mandermach, B. J., Gonzales, R. M., & Garrett, A. L. (2006). An examination of online instructor presence via threaded discussion participation. *Journal of Online Learning and Teaching*, 2, 248–260.

McClelland, D. C. (1973). Testing for competence rather than for" intelligence. *The American Psychologist*, 28(1), 1–14. DOI: 10.1037/h0034092 PMID: 4684069

McCombs, B. L. (1997). Self-assessment and reflection: Tools for promoting teacher changes toward learner-centered practices. *NASSP Bulletin*, 81(587), 1–14. DOI: 10.1177/019263659708158702

Mega, C., Ronconi, L., & De Beni, R. (2014). What makes a good student? How emotions, self-regulated learning, and motivation contribute to academic achievement. *Journal of Educational Psychology*, 106(1), 121–131. DOI: 10.1037/a0033546

Merriam, S. B. (2001). Andragogy and self-directed learning: Pillars of adult learning theory. *New Directions for Adult and Continuing Education*, 2001(89), 3–14. DOI: 10.1002/ace.3

Merriam, S. B., & Caffarella, R. S. (1999). *Learning in Adulthood* (2nd ed.). Jossey-Bass.

Merriam, S. B., Cafferella, R. C., & Baumgartner, L. M. (2007). *Learning in adulthood* (3rd ed.). Jossey-Bass.

Mezirow, J. (1993). A transformation theory of adult learning. In *Adult Education Research Annual Conference Proceedings* (Vol. 31, pp. 141-146).

Mezirow, J. (1997). Transformative learning. *New Directions for Adult and Continuing Education*, 74(74), 5–12. DOI: 10.1002/ace.7401

Moos, R. H. (1987). Person-environment congruence in work, school, and health care settings. *Journal of Vocational Behavior*, 31(3), 231–247. DOI: 10.1016/0001-8791(87)90041-8

Mortiboys, A. (2013). *Teaching with emotional intelligence: A step-by-step guide for higher and further education professionals*. Routledge. DOI: 10.4324/9780203806463

Muller, K. E. (2008). Self-directed learning and emotional intelligence: Interrelationships between the two constructs, change, and problem solving. *International Journal of Self-Directed Learning*, 5(2), 11–22.

Murphy, E., & Rodriguez, A. M. (2012). Rapport in distance education. *International Review of Research in Open and Distance Learning*, 13(1), 167–190. DOI: 10.19173/irrodl.v13i1.1057

Mustika, R., Yo, E.C., Faruqi, M., & Zhuhra, R.T. (2021). Evaluating the Relationship Between Online Learning Environment and Medical Students' Wellbeing During COVID-19 Pandemic.

Paas, F., Tuovinen, J. E., Van Merrienboer, J. J., & Aubteen Darabi, A. (2005). A motivational perspective on the relation between mental effort and performance: Optimizing learner involvement in instruction. *Educational Technology Research and Development*, 53(3), 25–34. DOI: 10.1007/BF02504795

Palloff, R. M., & Pratt, K. (2007). *Building online learning communities: Effective strategies for the virtual classroom*. John Wiley Sons.

Paudel, P. (2021). Online education: Benefits, challenges and strategies during and after COVID-19 in higher education. *International Journal on Studies in Education*, 3(2), 70–85. DOI: 10.46328/ijonse.32

Pekrun, R., Goetz, T., Frenzel, A. C., Barchfeld, P., & Perry, R. P. (2011). Measuring emotions in students' learning and performance: The Achievement Emotions Questionnaire (AEQ). *Contemporary Educational Psychology*, 36(1), 36–48. DOI: 10.1016/j.cedpsych.2010.10.002

PMI (Project Management Institute). (2013). 5th ed.). Guide to the Project Management Body of Knowledge/PMBOK.

Poulou, M. S., Reddy, L. A., & Dudek, C. M. (2019). Relation of teacher self-efficacy and classroom practices: A preliminary investigation. *School Psychology International*, 40(1), 25–48. DOI: 10.1177/0143034318798045

Rager, K. B. (2009). I feel, therefore, I learn: The role of emotion in self-directed learning. *New Horizons in Adult Education and Human Resource Development*, 23(2), 22–33. DOI: 10.1002/nha3.10336

Rakow, K. E., Upsher, R. J., Foster, J. L., Byrom, N. C., & Dommett, E. J. (2023). "It Ain't What You Use, It's the Way That You Use It": How Virtual Learning Environments May Impact Student Mental Wellbeing. *Education Sciences*, 13(7), 749. DOI: 10.3390/educsci13070749

Ramana, T. V. (2013). Emotional intelligence and teacher effectiveness: An analysis. Voice of research, 2(2), 18-22.

Rania, N., Siri, A., Bagnasco, A., Aleo, G., & Sasso, L. (2014). Academic climate, well-being and academic performance in a university degree course. *Journal of Nursing Management*, 22(6), 751–760. DOI: 10.1111/j.1365-2834.2012.01471.x PMID: 23617787

Rosier, R. H. (Ed.), *(1994-1997). The competency model handbook* (Vol. 1-4). Linkage.

Rovai, A. (2002). Building Sense of Community at a Distance. *International Review of Research in Open and Distance Learning*, 3(1), 1–16. DOI: 10.19173/irrodl.v3i1.79

Rovai, A. (2007). Facilitating online discussions effectively. *The Internet and Higher Education*, 1(1), 77–88. DOI: 10.1016/j.iheduc.2006.10.001

Ruus, V. R., Veisson, M., Leino, M., Ots, L., Pallas, L., Sarv, E. S., & Veisson, A. (2007). STUDENTS WELL-BEING, COPING, ACADEMIC SUCCESS, AND SCHOOL CLIMATE. *Social Behavior and Personality*, 35(7), 919–936. DOI: 10.2224/sbp.2007.35.7.919

Salovey, P., & Mayer, J. D. (1990). Emotional intelligence. *Imagination, Cognition and Personality*, 9(3), 185–211. DOI: 10.2190/DUGG-P24E-52WK-6CDG

Salovey, P., & Mayer, J. D. (1995). Emotional intelligence and the construction and regulation of feelings. *Applied & Preventive Psychology*, 4(3), 197–208. DOI: 10.1016/S0962-1849(05)80058-7

Scherer, K. R. (2009). The dynamic architecture of emotion: Evidence for the component process model. *Cognition and Emotion*, 23(7), 1307–1351. DOI: 10.1080/02699930902928969

SchoolSims. (2024, May 28). Simulations for school leaders & teachers. https://schoolsims.com/

Seal, C. R., Boyatzis, R. E., & Bailey, J. R. (2006). Fostering emotional and social intelligence in organizations. *Organizational Management Journal*, 3(3), 190–209. DOI: 10.1057/omj.2006.19

Seema, G. (2012). *Emotional intelligence in classroom*. Advances in Management.

Seligman, M. E. (2011). *Flourish: A visionary new understanding of happiness and well-being*. Simon and Schuster.

Shabani, K., Khatib, M., & Ebadi, S. (2010). Vygotsky's zone of proximal development: Instructional implications and teachers' professional development. *English Language Teaching*, 3(4), 237–248. DOI: 10.5539/elt.v3n4p237

Sharma, S., & Arora, S. (2012). Teaching with emotional intelligence in higher education. Opinion. *International Journal of Management*, 2(1), 52–58.

Shea, P., Li, C. S., Swan, K., & Pickett, A. (2005). Developing learning community in online asynchronous college courses: The role of teaching presence. *Journal of Asynchronous Learning Networks*, 9(4), 59–82.

Sinek, S. (2011). *Start with why: How great leaders inspire everyone to take action*. Penguin.

Song, D., & Bonk, C. J. (2016). Motivational factors in self-directed informal learning from online learning resources. *Cogent Education*, 3(1), 1205838. DOI: 10.1080/2331186X.2016.1205838

Song, L. (2005). Adult learners' self-directed learning in online environments: Process, personal attribute, and context. Unpublished Dissertation, The University of Georgia, Athens, GA.

Song, L., & Hill, J. R. (2007). A conceptual model for understanding self-directed learning in online environments. *Journal of Interactive Online Learning*, 6(1), 27–42.

Syiem, I. (2012). Emotional intelligence: Why it matters in teaching. IOSR Journal of Humanities and Social Science [Internet]. *IOSR Journals*, 2(2), 42–43.

Tajfel, H., & Turner, J. C. (2004). The social identity theory of intergroup behavior. In *Political psychology* (pp. 276–293). Psychology Press. DOI: 10.4324/9780203505984-16

Tam, M. (2000). Constructivism, instructional design, and technology: Implications for transforming distance learning. *Journal of Educational Technology & Society*, 3(2), 50–60.

Tareen, H., & Haand, M. T. (2020). A case study of UiTM post-graduate students' perceptions on online learning: Benefits challenges. *International Journal of Advanced Research and Publications*, 4(6), 86–94.

Thomas, L., Herbert, J., & Teras, M. (2014). A sense of belonging to enhance participation, success and retention in online programs. The International Journal of the First Year Thorndike, E. L. (1920). Intelligence and its use. Harper's Magazine, 140, 227-235.

Toney, S., Light, J., & Urbaczewski, A. (2021). Fighting Zoom fatigue: Keeping the zoombies at bay. *Communications of the Association for Information Systems*, 48(1), 10. DOI: 10.17705/1CAIS.04806

Uiboleht, K., Karm, M., & Postareff, L. (2018). The interplay between teachers' approaches to teaching, students' approaches to learning and learning outcomes: A qualitative multi-case study. *Learning Environments Research*, 21(3), 321–347. DOI: 10.1007/s10984-018-9257-1

Valente, S., & Lourenço, A. A. (2020, February). Conflict in the classroom: How teachers' emotional intelligence influences conflict management. [). Frontiers Media SA.]. *Frontiers in Education*, 5, 5. DOI: 10.3389/feduc.2020.00005

Valente, S., Veiga-Branco, A., Rebelo, H., Lourenço, A. A., & Cristóvão, A. M. (2020). The relationship between emotional intelligence ability and teacher efficacy.

Wang, M. T., Degol, J. L., Amemiya, J., Parr, A., & Guo, J. (2020). Classroom climate and children's academic and psychological well being: A systematic review and meta-analysis. *Developmental Review*, 57, 100912. DOI: 10.1016/j.dr.2020.100912

Whiteside, A. L., Dikkers, A. G., & Swan, K. (Eds.). (2023). *Social presence in online learning: Multiple perspectives on practice and research*. Taylor & Francis.

Winkleman, P., & Harmon-Jones, E. (2006). *Social neuroscience*. Oxford University Press.

Wlodkowski, R. J., & Ginsberg, M. B. (2017). *Enhancing adult motivation to learn: A comprehensive guide for teaching all adults*. John Wiley & Sons.

Yen, Y. C. G., Dow, S. P., Gerber, E., & Bailey, B. P. (2017, June). Listen to others, listen to yourself: Combining feedback review and reflection to improve iterative design. In *Proceedings of the 2017 ACM SIGCHI Conference on Creativity and Cognition* (pp. 158-170). DOI: 10.1145/3059454.3059468

Zhoc, K. C., King, R. B., Chung, T. S., & Chen, J. (2020). Emotionally intelligent students are more engaged and successful: Examining the role of emotional intelligence in higher education. *European Journal of Psychology of Education*, 35(4), 839–863. DOI: 10.1007/s10212-019-00458-0

Zhoc, K. C., Li, J. C., & Webster, B. J. (2017). New reliability and validity evidence of the Emotional Intelligence Scale. *Journal of Psychoeducational Assessment*, 35(6), 599–614. DOI: 10.1177/0734282916653901

Zhu, M., Bonk, C. J., & Doo, M. Y. (2020). Self-directed learning in MOOCs: Exploring the relationships among motivation, self-monitoring, and self-management. *Educational Technology Research and Development*, 68(5), 2073–2093. DOI: 10.1007/s11423-020-09747-8

Chapter 6
Examining the Role and Effect of Emotions in Adults' Online Learning

J. B. Oleet
 https://orcid.org/0009-0001-1262-7500
Mississippi State University, USA

Chien Yu
Mississippi State University, USA

ABSTRACT

For an online learning environment, educators can use the power of emotion to affect learning; therefore, it is essential to consider the emotional aspects of online learning when designing a learning environment. The purpose of this chapter is to examine current studies of learners' emotions during the online learning process and provide an up-to-date understanding of the issues as well as challenges pertinent to online teaching and learning. In addition to highlighting the dual role of emotions, the chapter illustrates how both positive and negative emotions can impact cognitive processes such as memory, attention, and problem-solving. It emphasizes the importance of fostering emotional awareness and self-regulation among learners, using strategies like reflective journaling and emotional logging. The chapter also provides practical recommendations for instructional designers and aims to create a compelling and emotionally supportive online learning environment, addressing the unique challenges posed by the pandemic and preparing learners for future disruptions.

DOI: 10.4018/979-8-3693-2663-3.ch006

Copyright © 2025, IGI Global. Copying or distributing in print or electronic forms without written permission of IGI Global is prohibited.

INTRODUCTION

The role of emotions in adult online learning has become increasingly critical. According to Dirkx (2001), "Emotions are important in adult learning because they can either impede or motivate learning" (p. 63). Similarly, Wlodkowski (1999) emphasized that emotions are crucial in influencing learning motivation; therefore, instructional designers must understand how to manage emotional expression and integration during teaching. Dirkx's and Wlodkowski's insights highlight the foundational role of emotions in learning, setting the stage for deeper exploration into how emotions affect online learning environments. Emotions are integral to the learning environment, significantly impacting students' learning experiences (Cleveland-Innes & Campbell, 2006). These foundational perspectives establish instructional designers' need to understand and harness the power of emotions to optimize learning outcomes in adult learners.

As online learning has gained popularity, understanding the emotional experiences of adult online learners has become essential. Lee and Chei (2020) noted that online learners might experience emotions more frequently than in traditional face-to-face settings. Emotions significantly influence learners' problem-solving abilities (Lee & Chei, 2020), learning persistence (Tang et al., 2021), engagement (Luo & Luo, 2022), motivation (Feraco et al., 2022), satisfaction (Wu et al., 2021b), and achievement (Putwain et al., 2022). Furthermore, emotions are necessary for student adjustment to the online learning role (Cleveland-Innes et al., 2007), the choice of instructional format (Artino, 2010), and perception, expression, and self-management (Kang et al., 2007). These studies underscore the multifaceted impact of emotions on various aspects of online learning for adults, emphasizing the need for instructional designers to adopt strategies that cater to the emotional well-being of learners.

Research on online learning emphasizes the importance of learners' feelings in creating a sense of community and developing online communities (Hara & Kling, 2003; Rovai & Wighting, 2005; Perry & Edwards, 2005). Numerous studies have acknowledged the role of emotion in online learning. For instance, Goldsworthy (2000) and Spitzer (2001) highlighted the importance of affective dimensions in online learning, suggesting that emotions significantly influence how adults engage with and absorb learning materials. Emotions are recognized for impacting adult learning thought patterns (Opengart, 2005). Different definitions and perspectives on emotions offer various approaches to studying them (Plutchik, 2001).

Psychological perspectives conceptualize emotions as private components of an individual's personality structure, while sociological perspectives view emotions as socially or culturally constructed (Barbalet, 1998; Lupton, 1998). These insights highlight the critical role of emotions in fostering a sense of community and belonging in online learning environments, which is essential for creating supportive and engaging learning experiences for adult learners. Although research on emotions in online learning environments has increased, understanding how students experience online learning from an emotional perspective and how technology mediates these emotions remains underexplored.

This chapter examines current studies on adult learners' emotions during online learning and provides an updated understanding of the relevant issues and challenges. Practical insights and strategies for online instructional designers to better manage and facilitate emotional expression follow a comprehensive mix-focused literature review. We have selected literature based on three criteria: our exposure, expertise, and experience (Kraus et al., 2022). This methodology ensures that we include studies that provide comprehensive insights into the role of emotions in adult online learning theories and methods. By understanding the dynamics of emotions in online learning, instructional designers can improve instructional design practices and create more effective and engaging learning environments for adults.

DEFINING EMOTIONS IN LEARNING

Evolutionary and Behavioral Perspectives

Emotions have been categorized and understood from various perspectives over time. Darwin considered emotions as mechanisms for the adaptation and survival of species, with individual survival contributing to this broader evolutionary significance (O'Regan, 2003). This foundational view underscores how emotions help individuals respond to environmental challenges, enhancing survival. In adult online learning, this perspective can help instructional designers understand how to create environments that stimulate positive emotional responses, thereby enhancing engagement and retention.

Another significant perspective is the behaviorist view, which considers emotions as responses to stimuli involving the delivery, omission, or termination of rewards and punishments (O'Regan, 2003). In this view, emotions are motivators of behavior and transformations of dispositions to act (Barbalet, 1998), influencing choices made in response to specific stimuli (Lerner & Keltner, 2000). For instructional designers, this means designing learning activities that incorporate immediate feedback and rewards to elicit positive emotions and motivate learners.

Physiological, Psychological, and Socio-cultural Perspectives

Emotion can also be regarded as a combination of physiological, psychological, and psychomotor components. For example, James (1952) defined emotions as feelings that follow the perception of exciting facts. Understanding this can help instructional designers create stimulating content that evokes positive emotional responses, enhancing learning outcomes. While Rolls (2018) describes emotions as states elicited by the presentation, termination, or omission of rewards and punishers, a viewpoint often associated with the behaviorist theory discussed above, his work also integrates psychological processes related to emotion regulation, making it relevant to this broader discussion. From a socio-cultural perspective, Denzin (1984) described emotions as social interactions involving oneself and others. This perspective is crucial for online learning environments where social interaction is mediated through technology.

Complexity and the Multifaceted Nature of Emotions

The diverse definitions of emotions highlight their complexity, making studying their relationship with learning challenging. This complexity necessitates a comprehensive approach to studying emotions, incorporating psychological and sociological perspectives to grasp their multifaceted impact on learning thoroughly (LeDoux, 1999). Bowlby (1969) added that emotions are phases of an individual's intuitive appraisals of their internal states and responses to a sequence of environmental situations. Therefore, emotions cannot be separated from the learning environment (Lehman, 2006). Cleveland-Innes and Campbell (2012) described emotional presence as the outward expression of emotion, affect, and feeling by individuals within a learning community as they interact with learning technology, course content, students, and instructors. Instructional designers should note the importance of creating emotionally supportive learning environments that cater to the holistic needs of adult learners.

Categorizing Emotions in E-learning

To better understand the range of emotions that learners experience during e-learning, Loderer, Pekrun, and Lester (2018) built on Pekrun's (1992) affective processing model, which categorizes emotions into four distinct types: positive activating emotions, negative activating emotions, positive deactivating emotions, and negative deactivating emotions.

Positive activating emotions, such as enjoyment, play a crucial role in e-learning by energizing and motivating learners encouraging active engagement with the material. These emotions foster a productive learning environment where students feel enthusiastic and involved. Conversely, negative activating emotions, like anxiety, also generate energy but in a way that introduces tension or stress. While these emotions can be detrimental if they become overwhelming, they can also serve as powerful motivators when managed effectively, driving learners to focus and persevere through challenges.

On the other hand, positive deactivating emotions, such as relief, emerge after a learner has overcome a difficult task. These emotions help reduce stress and create a sense of accomplishment, allowing learners to feel ready to move forward. However, if learners become overly reliant on these feelings of relief, they may become complacent, reducing their overall engagement with the course material. Negative deactivating emotions, such as boredom, have the most significant potential to harm the learning process. These emotions reduce energy and motivation, often leading to disengagement and a lack of participation in learning activities. Addressing and managing these emotions is critical to maintaining learner involvement and ensuring the learning experience is effective. The duality of how emotions can support and hinder learning will be discussed in more detail later in this chapter.

Duffy et al. (2018) similarly found that enjoyment and anxiety are the most strongly experienced emotions in e-learning. Furthermore, recognizing these categories allows instructional designers to develop strategies that foster positive activating emotions and appropriately manage activating and deactivating emotions, ensuring they support rather than hinder the learning process. Harley et al. (2018) reported that enjoyment and curiosity were the highest-intensity emotional states in their experimental study involving learning in augmented reality. These findings highlight the importance of creating engaging and enjoyable learning experiences that capture learners' curiosity, sustain their interest, and help reduce anxiety, making the learning process more accessible and practical.

Emotional Impact on Online Learning Behaviors

In online learning environments, emotions significantly influence specific behaviors. Negative emotions such as confusion, frustration, discouragement, anxiety, and anger can negatively impact learners' engagement and motivation. Conversely, positive emotions like joy can lead to increased dedication, participation, motivation, and interest in the course (Zembylas et al., 2008). For instructional designers, this means incorporating elements that reduce negative and enhance positive emotions to improve engagement and motivation.

D'Errico et al. (2016) found that students' positive emotions across online learning activities were more common than negative ones, particularly during synchronous activities with teachers and peers. This finding suggests incorporating synchronous activities to foster positive emotions and enhance the learning experience. They further revealed that experiencing positive emotions during exam preparation strongly correlates with students' motivation, supporting their learning process and outcomes. Lee and Chei (2020) also found that learners' emotions could be crucial in online learning outcomes. These insights are essential for instructional designers aiming to create learning experiences that foster positive emotional responses to improve learning outcomes.

According to Pan et al. (2022), positive emotions could be conducive to online learning outcomes, while negative emotions could be detrimental. Wu et al. (2021) noted that positively-motivated learners had higher online learning satisfaction. However, Hilliard et al. (2020) found positive effects of negative emotions on online learning outcomes, while Liu et al. (2021) reported that positive emotions negatively influenced online learners' outcomes. These seemingly paradoxical findings highlight the complex and multifaceted nature of emotions' role in instructional design for online learning. Both positive and negative emotions can play significant roles, but their effects are not universally predictable and depend heavily on various affective, cognitive, and contextual factors (Artino & Jones, 2012; Marchand & Gutierrez, 2012). Understanding these nuances is crucial for instructional designers aiming to create positive emotional learning environments. By recognizing that emotions can support and encumber learning in different contexts, instructional designers can develop strategies that harness the positive aspects of emotions while mitigating their potential drawbacks, ultimately leading to more effective online learning experiences.

Impact of COVID-19 on Emotions in Adult Online Learning

The COVID-19 pandemic brought unprecedented changes to the educational landscape, significantly impacting adult online learning. As traditional face-to-face instruction transitioned to remote and online formats, the emotional experiences of adult learners became more pronounced and complex than ever.

Increased Anxiety and Stress

The sudden shift to online learning due to the COVID-19 pandemic heightened anxiety and stress among adult learners. Many faced technological challenges, such as adapting to new learning platforms, troubleshooting technical issues, and ensuring reliable internet access. The abrupt transition also disrupted the work-life-study balance, increasing stress as learners juggled professional responsibilities, family commitments, and academic requirements. The pervasive uncertainty about the future added to this anxiety, making it difficult for learners to focus and stay motivated. This ambiguity aligns with earlier discussions on negative emotions leading to avoidance behaviors and the need for self-efficacy support (Lin & Muenks, 2022).

Isolation and Loneliness

One of the most significant emotional impacts of the COVID-19 pandemic on adult learners was the feeling of isolation and loneliness. The lack of physical interaction with peers and instructors exacerbated feelings of disconnection. For many adult learners, the social aspect of education plays a crucial role in their motivation and engagement. The shift to online learning removed these opportunities for in-person interaction, leaving many feeling alone and unsupported. This shift highlights the importance of social presence and community building, as Sogunro (2015) and Jian and Koo (2020) emphasize.

Adaptation and Resilience

Despite the challenges, the COVID-19 pandemic fostered adaptation and resilience among adult learners. The necessity to navigate new technologies and online learning environments pushed learners to develop new skills and coping mechanisms. Many adult learners demonstrated remarkable resilience, adapting to new learning modalities and finding innovative ways to stay engaged and motivated. This resilience highlights the importance of designing online courses that support the development of self-efficacy and adaptability, helping learners build confidence in their ability to succeed online. The enhanced ability to adapt and persevere connects with the role of positive emotions in fostering self-regulation and persistence, as discussed by Yang et al. (2024).

Impact on Motivation and Engagement

The pandemic had a mixed impact on motivation and engagement among adult learners. For some, the flexibility of online learning provided a conducive environment for continuing their education amidst the pandemic's constraints. However, the lack of structured learning environments and face-to-face interaction decreased motivation and engagement for others. Various factors, including online instruction quality, technology access, and individual learner characteristics, influenced the motivation to learn during the pandemic. This finding reinforces the importance of intrinsic and extrinsic motivation discussed by Ryan and Deci (2000) and the role of positive emotions in enhancing cognitive engagement (Chi & Wylie, 2014). As discussed earlier, the relationship between emotions and learning outcomes is not always straightforward. While positive emotions often enhance cognitive engagement, they can also introduce complexities that depend on the context, individual differences, and the relationship of various factors. Therefore, understanding and managing these emotional dynamics is crucial for creating effective online learning environments.

Emergence of New Emotional Dynamics

The pandemic also led to the emergence of new emotional dynamics in online learning. Blending home, work, and study environments blurred personal, professional, and academic life boundaries, creating unique emotional challenges. Adult learners had to manage competing demands and stressors, often impacting their emotional well-being and academic performance. The constant presence of family members, the need to assist children with online learning, and the lack of a dedicated study space were common issues. These dynamics highlight the need for flexible and supportive learning environments, as emphasized in earlier discussions on emotional engagement and cognitive impact (Tzafilkou et al., 2021; Schwabe et al., 2023).

Support Systems and Resources

The COVID-19 pandemic highlighted the critical role of support systems and resources in online learning. The availability of mental health resources, academic support, and technological assistance became increasingly important for helping adult learners navigate the challenges of online education. Institutions with robust support systems could better maintain student engagement and success during the pandemic. As previously discussed, this ability underscores the importance of providing comprehensive support services in fostering a supportive learning environment (Travis et al., 2020).

The COVID-19 pandemic has underscored the importance of understanding and addressing the emotional experiences of adult learners in online education. Building on the insights gained from examining the emotional impacts of the COVID-19 pandemic, the challenges of increased anxiety and isolation, and the need for adaptation have highlighted the critical role of emotional studies for online teaching and learning.

Emotion Studies for Adult Online Teaching and Learning: Trends, Issues, and Challenges

Many researchers have indicated that emotions are integral to learning and everyday experiences (Dirkx, 2006; Wolfe, 2006). Emotions create purpose and shape the context of learning experiences (Merriam & Caffarella, 1999), and they play a critical role in constructing meaning and knowledge of the self in the adult learning process (Dirkx, 2001). O'Regan (2003) reported that students express their emotions about various aspects of an online course, such as design and organizational issues (e.g., lack of clear instructions), cognitive issues (e.g., learning materials, success), social issues (e.g., during communication), time management, or technology. Additionally, Cleveland-Innes et al. (2007) noted that students disclose emotions concerning social, teaching, and cognitive presence in online courses. These insights underline the multifaceted nature of emotions in online learning environments and the diverse ways they can influence learner experiences.

Understanding the Role of Positive Emotions in Adult Online Learning

Positive emotions are pivotal in adult learning, particularly in online environments. According to Dirkx (2001) and supported by Fredrickson's (2001) broaden-and-build theory, emotions such as excitement, curiosity, joy, and interest not only enrich the learning experience but are fundamental in motivating adult learners to engage more thoroughly with the content. Fredrickson's theory posits that positive emotions expand individuals' thought-action repertoires, thereby fostering the development of their enduring personal resources, including physical, intellectual, social, and psychological assets. This theoretical framework highlights the essential role of positive emotions in promoting deeper engagement and resilience among adult learners.

However, it is essential to note that the relationship between positive emotions and learning outcomes is complex and not always as straightforward as it might appear. While positive emotions generally enhance engagement and motivation, their effects can vary depending on several factors. Acknowledging these nuances is vital for a more comprehensive understanding of how emotions influence online learning.

The correlation between positive emotions and increased motivation among adult learners is a pivotal topic of discourse. Motivation is a crucial variable in online learning that stimulates and maintains online learning behaviors (Yu, 2022). Generally, motivation can be divided into extrinsic and intrinsic motivation. While extrinsic motivation refers to individuals' desire to pursue an activity to obtain some external outcome, intrinsic motivation refers to individuals' desire to pursue the activity to gain a sense of inherent satisfaction (Ryan & Deci, 2000).

Ryan and Deci's (2000) Self-Determination Theory (SDT) provides a critical framework for comprehending this phenomenon. According to SDT, positive emotion-driven intrinsic motivation is crucial for sustained engagement and learning. Adults who are interested in a subject and derive enjoyment from the process are more inclined to invest the required time and effort to enhance their knowledge and proficiency. This intrinsic motivation is particularly significant in the self-directed nature of online learning environments, where students must independently engage thoroughly with the material. Understanding intrinsic motivation is essential for designing online courses that foster a supportive and engaging learning atmosphere for adult learners.

Positive emotions and cognitive engagement in online learning are inextricably linked. Deep cognitive strategies are used more frequently by adult learners experiencing positive emotions (Chi & Wylie, 2014). These strategies incorporate meaningful learning and critical thinking instead of surface learning or rote memorization. This view supports Park and Yun (2017), who note that positive affective states motivate adult learners to engage with the material more deeply, enhancing information retention and comprehension. Additionally, engagement in collaborative activities and discussions is enhanced by positive emotions (Croft et al., 2015; Lucardie, 2015). This increased engagement is advantageous for the comprehension of the individual learner and the collective knowledge of the learning community. By fostering positive emotions, instructional designers can create an environment that promotes active participation and collaborative learning, which is cardinal for building a cohesive learning community among adults.

Self-regulation and Persistence in Adult Online Learning

Self-regulation stands as a cornerstone of effective learning, embodying the capacity of adult learners to manage their thoughts, feelings, and actions in pursuit of long-term goals. Wong et al. (2021) outlined the essence of self-regulation, which encompasses goal setting, progress monitoring, motivation maintenance, and the strategic adjustment of approaches to learning. Within this framework, the role of emotional experiences is pivotal, significantly influencing learners' self-regulation capacity. Wong et al. (2021) provided a comprehensive analysis that underscores how emotional states interact with self-regulatory processes, making their work indispensable for understanding adult online learning dynamics.

Emotional State, Self-regulation, and Resilience. Positive emotional states play a crucial role in enhancing self-regulation. Lu et al. (2022) demonstrated that joy, interest, or pride in accomplishments can significantly bolster adult learners' motivation and confidence, which is vital in pursuing learning objectives. As such, instructional designers should create emotionally engaging content that promotes positive feelings because these emotions link to improved self-regulation. Positive emotions are not merely fleeting states but are instrumental in encouraging adult learners to set more ambitious goals and adopt deep learning strategies. The influence of positive emotions on self-regulation emphasizes the importance of fostering an emotionally supportive learning environment that catalyzes learner motivation and engagement.

Beyond enhancing self-regulation, positive emotions foster resilience in adult learners. Yang et al. (2024) highlighted that successes and positive feedback can cultivate a resilient attitude toward challenges. Instructors can learn from this by providing timely and constructive feedback, which boosts learners' confidence and helps them develop resilience, a critical trait for overcoming setbacks and maintaining long-term engagement. This resilience is crucial for overcoming obstacles, allowing adult learners to maintain focus and continue striving toward their goals despite difficulties. Developing resilience through positive emotional experiences is critical in sustaining motivation and perseverance over the long term and is essential for successful learning outcomes.

While positive emotions bolster self-regulation and facilitate learning, negative emotions often hinder effective educational self-management (Yang et al., 2024). Research highlights the intricate ways in which feelings such as anxiety, frustration, and boredom can undermine self-regulation, leading adult learners toward procrastination, avoidance behaviors, and reliance on superficial learning strategies (Huang & Wang, 2024). As online educators, it is crucial to identify and mitigate these negative emotional triggers by incorporating strategies that promote emotional regulation and reduce stress, such as clear instructions, supportive feedback, and a manageable workload.

Persistence in Adult Online Learning. Persistence in the context of learning is fundamentally about maintaining a steady effort toward achieving educational goals, even when faced with difficulties. Emotional experiences play a significant role in shaping a learner's persistence, with positive emotions being particularly influential in reinforcing the determination to continue learning despite obstacles. Positive emotions may impact adult learners' persistence, influencing their engagement, mindset, and overall satisfaction with the learning process. Park and Yun's (2018; 2020) research highlighted how positive emotional states, such as confidence and enjoyment, can significantly boost persistence. Instructional designers can create a positive and engaging learning environment where learners feel supported and valued, greatly enhancing their persistence and drive to achieve their educational goals. For example, an instructional designer might create an online course that includes frequent opportunities for positive reinforcement, such as personalized feedback, recognition of milestones, and interactive and gamified elements that reward progress. These strategies help to create a learning atmosphere where students feel motivated and encouraged to keep pushing forward, even when they encounter challenges.

These emotions contribute to persistence by enhancing engagement, increasing adult learners' involvement and interest in learning, and making them more likely to stay committed to their goals. The experience of positive emotions can also encourage a growth-oriented mindset, where challenges become opportunities for growth rather than insurmountable obstacles. Fueled by positive emotions, enjoyment and satisfaction with the learning process can motivate adult online learners to continue their educational journey, even when faced with difficulties.

Negative emotions such as frustration, anxiety, and disappointment can significantly challenge adult online learners' persistence. Ajjawi et al. (2019) highlighted that negative emotional experiences, especially those stemming from repeated frustrations or failures, can erode adult learners' confidence and motivation. Recognizing these emotional states allows instructional designers to create more resilient learning pathways, integrating elements like peer support, mentoring, and frequent, encouraging feedback to help learners navigate and overcome these emotional barriers.

Acknowledging the Role of Negative Emotions in Adult Online Learning

While the positive impacts of emotions on learning have been well-documented, it is equally important to acknowledge the role of negative emotions in the educational process, especially within the context of adult learning in online environments. Negative emotions such as frustration, anxiety, boredom, and confusion can significantly undermine the learning experience, negatively impacting motivation and engagement (Rowe & Fitness, 2018). These emotions can create substantial barriers to learning, making it crucial for instructional designers to develop strategies to mitigate their effects.

Negative emotions from various aspects of the learning environment can significantly impact adult learners' motivation and engagement. Technical difficulties, challenging course materials, and a lack of explicit instruction can lead to frustration and confusion, causing adult learners to disengage from the course (Rowe & Fitness, 2018). These emotional responses are not merely transient states but can affect adult learners' engagement with the material and their overall educational journey. Recognizing and addressing these negative emotions is vital for maintaining learner engagement and promoting a positive educational experience for adults.

Negative emotions have a profound effect on adult learners' motivation. Birmingham et al. (2021) highlighted that anxiety over performance or frustration due to a lack of understanding can significantly reduce a learner's desire to continue a course. This demotivation can be particularly damaging in online learning environments where adult learners rely heavily on self-motivation to progress through materials and complete assignments. The absence of immediate, in-person feedback and support can sometimes exacerbate these feelings, leading to a downward spiral of motivation and engagement. Moreover, Tzafilkou et al. (2023) discussed how boredom or confusion can lead to decreased engagement with the learning material. Not fully engaged adult learners may skip through materials without thoroughly understanding them or withdraw from participating in discussions and assignments. This lack of engagement affects the individual's learning outcomes and can diminish the overall learning experience for the entire cohort, as the collaborative aspects of learning are compromised.

Influence of Emotional Engagement

Engagement can be deemed as the continuing efforts learners make to achieve goals in academic learning (Jung & Lee, 2018). It is a multidimensional structure consisting of behavioral, cognitive, and emotional aspects. Behavioral engagement refers to an individual's participation in learning activities. Cognitive engagement is considered an individual's willingness to perform complex tasks. Emotional engagement includes an individual's emotional reactions to learning (Fredricks et al., 2004). Engagement is a significant indicator of the quality of online education (Xu et al., 2020). Understanding these dimensions of engagement helps instructional designers design strategies that enhance overall student involvement and success.

Research indicates that emotional engagement enhances the immediate learning experience and significantly affects the long-term retention of information. The relationship between emotion and memory is a critical area of study within educational psychology. Tyng (2017) asserts that emotionally engaging content is inherently more memorable. Their contention is rooted in the idea that emotional arousal can enhance the consolidation of memories, making them more robust and more accessible to retrieve later. This principle suggests that when adult learners engage with content that evokes positive emotions, they are more likely to remember it over time.

Further supporting this notion, Mayer (2020) and Elmi (2020) highlighted how positive emotions can enhance memory formation. According to these studies, positive emotional experiences during learning can improve information encoding, facilitating easier recall of learned material. This effect correlates to positive emotions stimulating cognitive processes conducive to memory formation and retention.

Understanding and leveraging the role of emotions in adult online learning is paramount for creating compelling educational experiences. Knowing the potential impact of positive and negative emotions, instructional designers can craft strategies that enhance engagement, motivation, and learning outcomes. They, therefore, ensure that adult learners are supported emotionally and cognitively, leading to more successful and fulfilling educational journeys.

Negative Emotions Leading to Avoidance Behaviors and Reduced Self-efficacy

In addition to draining motivation and reducing engagement, negative emotions in the learning environment can lead to avoidance behaviors and negatively impact adult learners' self-efficacy. These aspects of the emotional experience in education, particularly online, offer further insight into the complex relationship between emotions and learning outcomes. Lin and Muenks (2022) discussed how these emotional states could lead adult learners to procrastinate, skip study sessions, or even drop out of courses to escape the discomfort associated with these emotions. Again, note the importance of instructional designers creating a supportive and responsive learning environment where adult learners feel comfortable addressing their emotional struggles. For example, stress management workshops or one-on-one virtual counseling sessions can help learners manage their emotions constructively. By acknowledging and addressing these emotional struggles, instructional designers can plan for and reduce avoidance behaviors, thus helping learners maintain their self-efficacy.

Analogously, Fang et al. (2022) emphasized that negative emotions can significantly influence adult learners' decisions to avoid challenging tasks, hindering their learning progress and growth opportunities. Such behaviors impede knowledge acquisition and limit the development of resilience and coping strategies crucial for lifelong learning. Providing timely support and clear instructions can mitigate these negative emotions and help maintain learners' engagement and persistence. Instructional designers can incorporate regular check-ins and adaptive feedback systems to help identify and address these negative emotions early on.

Negative emotional experiences can severely undermine adult learners' belief in their abilities, known as self-efficacy. Travis et al. (2020) highlighted that low self-efficacy can initiate a vicious cycle of avoidance, decreased effort, and poorer performance, reinforcing negative emotions. For instructional designers, this means implementing strategies such as scaffolded learning, where complex tasks are broken into manageable steps, helping learners build confidence as they progress. This cycle can be particularly detrimental in adult online learning environments where learners may already face challenges related to isolation and lack of immediate feedback. Without the necessary interventions, these negative emotions can persist, leading to long-term disengagement and a decline in educational aspirations. Addressing these negative emotional experiences is crucial to fostering a supportive learning environment that promotes confidence and persistence.

Fostering Social Presence and Community Building in Adult Online Learning

The concept of social presence, or the sense of being with others in a learning environment, plays a pivotal role in the efficacy of adult online courses. In settings where physical presence is inherently absent, fostering a sense of connection and community among adult learners becomes both a challenge and an opportunity for instructional designers. Chaudhry et al. (2024) emphasized that emotional experiences directly impact adult learners' perception of social presence, suggesting that the emotional climate of an online course can significantly influence the overall learning experience. This finding suggests that instructional designers should prioritize creating emotionally rich interactions to foster a strong sense of community. For example, they might incorporate synchronous video discussions where learners can engage in real-time conversations, allowing them to see and hear their peers and strengthening their sense of presence. Additionally, creating dedicated online spaces such as discussion forums or group projects where learners can collaborate and share their experiences can further enhance the feeling of being part of a learning community. Implementing these strategies can enable instructional designers to cultivate a learning environment where learners feel connected, supported, and engaged.

Social Presence

Positive emotional experiences can significantly enhance social presence in adult online learning environments. When adult learners feel understood, respected, and valued, these positive emotions can cultivate a stronger sense of social presence. Sogunro (2015) highlighted the importance of empathetic and supportive interactions in fostering a sense of community and belonging among adult learners. Instructional designers can incorporate activities that promote peer-to-peer interaction and empathy, such as collaborative projects and discussion forums. This emotional connectivity enriches the learning experience and encourages more active participation, deeper discussions, and a more substantial commitment to group activities. These findings underscore the importance of fostering positive emotional experiences to build a strong sense of community and social presence in online courses.

While positive emotional experiences enhance social presence in adult online learning environments, it is crucial to acknowledge that negative emotions can have the opposite effect, significantly diminishing this sense of connection and community. Jian and Koo (2020) explained how feelings of isolation, being misunderstood, or being overlooked can significantly reduce the sense of social presence in online courses. The absence of physical cues and interactions inherent in online learning settings can exacerbate feelings of disconnection among adult learners, leading to a decline in participation and overall engagement. Instructional designers should strive to create an inclusive and engaging online environment that actively works to mitigate these feelings of isolation. For example, they might incorporate regular small-group discussions or peer-review activities, encouraging learners to interact closely with their peers.

Additionally, offering virtual office hours or discussion boards where learners can easily reach out to instructors for guidance and support can help reduce isolation by making learners feel more connected and supported. This dichotomy between the impact of positive and negative emotions highlights the critical role of emotional experiences in educational outcomes. Further mitigation strategies are recommended later in this chapter.

Community Building

Creating a learning community, particularly in online environments, is a nuanced process that significantly depends on the emotional experiences of its members. As adult learners navigate the complexities of acquiring new knowledge and skills, the emotional climate within the learning community can either function as a catalyst for growth and connection or become a barrier to collaboration and engagement. The research underscores the significance of positive emotional experiences in cultivating strong bonds between adult learners, thereby establishing a robust and engaged learning community. For example, Abedini et al. (2023) and Ke (2010) emphasized the power of positive emotions in fostering a robust learning community using methods from constructivist learning theory.

The Role of Positive Emotional Experiences. Shared positive emotional experiences play a pivotal role in strengthening the bonds between adult learners. Research in this area primarily focuses on how learners' feelings of respect, value, and understanding contribute to a sense of community. Celebrating achievements, collaboratively overcoming challenges, and sharing moments of joy and satisfaction can significantly enhance the sense of belonging among adult learners (Abedini et al., 2023). Instructional designers should design activities that celebrate achievements and create opportunities for adult learners to share their successes and challenges. This sense of belonging, in turn, boosts their motivation, engagement, and satisfaction with the learning experience. For example, positive emotions enhance the individual's learning experience and encourage active participation and contribution to the community (Ke, 2010). As such, positive emotions serve as the glue that binds the learning group together, creating an environment where adult learners feel connected and supported.

Addressing Negative Emotional Experiences. Conversely, negative emotional experiences can significantly disrupt community building. Lee (2022) highlighted how feelings of exclusion, competition, or conflict within the learning community can undermine collaboration and support, creating divisions and reducing the learning environment's effectiveness. Instructional designers must actively work to identify and address sources of negative emotions within the learning community, promoting inclusive and supportive interactions. If not adequately addressed, such negative emotions can lead to divisions among adult learners, eroding the sense of belonging and mutual support essential for a thriving learning community. Addressing these negative emotions promptly and effectively is crucial to maintaining a healthy and supportive learning community.

Implications of a Strong Sense of Belonging. The sense of belonging that emerges from shared positive experiences can have profound implications for adult learners. Feeling part of a supportive and connected community can significantly boost their motivation and engagement (Cao et al., 2023). This is because they are more likely to participate actively and contribute to a community where their feelings are valued and understood. The supportive environment of a learning community can facilitate deeper learning and understanding and create a culture that reinforces self-regulation and persistence, as discussed earlier in the chapter. These skills are critical for adult online learners and contribute to their long-term success and satisfaction with learning.

Improving Learning Outcomes in Adult Online Learning

According to Baumeister et al. (2007), emotions can significantly influence learning outcomes; the impeding effect of negative emotions, such as stress, anger, and embarrassment, can influence decision-making and lead people to take inappropriate risks. Understanding these dynamics is critical for designing learning experiences that minimize stress and foster positive emotional engagement, enhancing decision-making and overall learning outcomes. However, it is critical to acknowledge that the relationship between emotions and learning is complex. While positive emotions generally lead to positive outcomes and negative emotions to negative outcomes (Cleveland-Innes & Campbell, 2012), this is not always the case. Emotions can play dual roles depending on context, intensity, and the learner's ability to manage them. Recognizing and leveraging this complexity allows instructional designers to create more nuanced and effectual learning experiences.

Cognitive Impact of Emotions in Adult Online Learning

The cognitive impact of emotions on adult learning, particularly within online environments, has garnered increasing attention in educational research. Emotions significantly influence crucial cognitive processes such as attention, memory, and problem-solving. These skills are vital for successful learning outcomes in adult online education. Shuck et al. (2013) and Hookka et al. (2019) provide insights into how emotional experiences can shape these cognitive functions, highlighting both emotions' facilitative and inhibitory effects on learning. These studies are pivotal for instructional designers seeking to understand how to leverage positive emotions to enhance cognitive engagement and mitigate the negative impacts of stress and anxiety.

Facilitative Role of Positive Emotions. Positive emotions play a crucial role in facilitating cognitive functions essential for learning, particularly within the context of adult online education. While emotions are focal in all learning contexts, *their impact can be particularly significant in online education* due to its unique challenges. Positive emotions not only help to overcome the lack of social presence and immediate feedback but also enhance cognitive engagement, self-regulation, and persistence in a more autonomous and sometimes isolating environment, as previously discussed. Research has demonstrated that emotions significantly mediate students' learning behaviors and success in online environments, profoundly impacting learning outcomes and cognitive processes, with both positive and negative emotional experiences playing a critical role, especially during the pandemic (Seow et al., 2023; Kaiqi & Kutuk, 2024; Wu & Yu, 2022). Finally, Endres et al. (2020) provide valuable insights into how emotions such as joy, interest, and curiosity can significantly enhance cognitive processes among adult online learners. These findings collectively suggest that the facilitative role of positive emotions might indeed be more critical in online learning than in traditional face-to-face or other instructional contexts. By incorporating engaging and interactive content that stimulates curiosity and joy, instructional designers can significantly improve learners' cognitive engagement and retention.

Inhibitory Effects of Negative Emotions. Negative emotions such as anxiety, stress, and frustration can significantly impact the cognitive processes critical to learning, particularly in the context of adult online education. Tzafilkou et al. (2021) explored how these emotional states can impede learners' cognitive functions, highlighting the challenges that negative emotions pose to the learning process. Designing interventions that include stress reduction techniques, such as mindfulness activities or clear and structured learning materials, can help mitigate these negative impacts and support better cognitive performance.

Impact of Anxiety and Stress. Schwabe et al. (2023) further explained how anxiety can monopolize cognitive resources, hindering the ability to concentrate and retain information, while chronic stress can negatively affect brain function, thereby impairing memory and learning efficiency. Instructional designers must incorporate elements that reduce cognitive load and stress, such as providing clear instructions, segmenting information, and offering regular breaks during intense learning sessions. Despite these challenges, it is critical to recognize that negative emotions are not universally detrimental within the learning process; moderate levels of such emotions may serve as motivators, spurring learners to confront challenges and enhance their performance.

Thus, understanding the cognitive impact of emotions is essential for educators aiming to create effective and supportive online learning environments. By leveraging positive emotions and mitigating the negative effects of stress and anxiety, educators can enhance cognitive engagement and improve learning outcomes for adult learners. This balanced approach ensures learners are challenged and supported, fostering a more resilient and productive learning experience.

Emotional Experiences and Feedback Reception in Adult Online Learning

Learners' emotional states significantly influence receptiveness to feedback in adult online learning. Feedback in the educational context serves as a tool for informing learners of their progress and areas for improvement, and it also serves as a significant emotional trigger (Say et al., 2024). Depending on the learners' emotional state, feedback can either motivate and encourage them or lead to frustration, anxiety, or demotivation. Say et al. (2024) offer a critical perspective on how feedback can be optimized to support emotional well-being, emphasizing the need for instructional designers to craft supportive and constructive feedback.

Positive emotional states enhance the likelihood of learners perceiving feedback as a constructive tool for improvement rather than criticism. Research from Hill et al. (2021) and Spooner et al. (2022) highlighted the importance of emotional context in how adult learners receive and act upon feedback. Hill et al. (2021) and Spooner et al. (2022) underline the necessity of emotionally intelligent feedback mechanisms that consider the learners' emotional responses, promoting resilience and ongoing engagement.

Hill et al. (2021) examined how adult learners respond to different types of feedback, highlighting the nuanced emotional and motivational dynamics at play. Their findings suggest that while positive feedback can evoke strong, positive emotions, its impact on motivation can be transient. On the other hand, negative feedback, when managed well, can foster resilience and engagement in learners.

Say et al. (2024) introduced an intriguing perspective on the role of feedback in learning, suggesting that minimizing feedback and allowing learners to experience extended states of uncertainty can enhance their ability to self-regulate their learning. This approach challenges conventional feedback practices by proposing that a degree of uncertainty encourages learners to engage more deeply with the material, develop critical thinking skills, and rely on their judgment rather than external validation. By navigating uncertainty, adult learners are prompted to reflect on their understanding, make decisions independently, and build confidence in their problem-solving abilities.

Building on the insights provided by Say et al. (2024), it becomes essential to explore strategies that can further enhance the emotional experiences of adult online learners, mainly through the integration of targeted and constructive feedback. Given the unique challenges and dynamics of online learning environments, it is crucial to identify and implement methods that support academic success and foster emotional well-being and resilience. Effective instructional design should, therefore, integrate continuous emotional support and strategically structured feedback to maintain a productive learning environment.

Embracing the Importance of a Growth Mindset in Adult Online Learning

The "growth mindset" concept is the belief that one's abilities and intelligence can be developed with effort, learning, and persistence (Dweck, 2016). This mindset contrasts with a fixed mindset, where individuals believe their abilities and intelligence are static and unchangeable. Embracing a growth mindset is crucial for adult online learners for several reasons.

Encouraging Lifelong Learning

A growth mindset fosters an attitude of lifelong learning, which is particularly important for adult learners who often need to continuously update their skills and knowledge to remain relevant in their careers. Instructional designers can help learners foster this mindset, so they can stay adaptable and open to new information and challenges, aligning with the necessity of self-regulation and persistence in adult online learning environments. These outcomes support continuous learning by mitigating the fear of failure and encouraging persistence (Wong et al., 2021).

Increasing Resilience

Learners with a growth mindset are more likely to view challenges and failures as opportunities to learn and grow than indicators of their limitations. This resilience helps them persist in the face of difficulties, which is essential for success in online learning environments where self-motivation is critical. Resilience, bolstered by a growth mindset, enables learners to tackle complex tasks and recover from setbacks more effectively (Dweck, 2016). As previously discussed, there is a close relationship to the strategies that support resilience and adaptability, where emotional fortitude transforms stress and anxiety into motivational tools (Rowe & Fitness, 2018; Lin & Muenks, 2022).

Promoting Self-efficacy

Believing in improving through effort and learning increases self-efficacy, i.e., the belief in one's ability to succeed. This self-belief empowers learners to take on new challenges and persist through obstacles. High self-efficacy is linked to better learning outcomes and increased persistence in academic endeavors (Bandura, 1997). Self-efficacy is emphasized in the emotional impact on learning behaviors and outcomes, highlighting the role of emotions in shaping learners' self-perceptions and engagement (Travis et al., 2020). Instructional designers can foster self-efficacy by designing progressively challenging tasks that build confidence and competence.

Enhancing Problem-solving Skills

A growth mindset encourages an exploratory approach to problem-solving, where learners experiment with different strategies and learn from their mistakes. This adaptability is crucial in dynamic online learning environments. Learners who view problems as solvable through effort are more likely to develop innovative solutions and improve their critical thinking skills (Dweck, 2016). This approach aligns with cognitive engagement and problem-solving discussions, where positive emotions enhance cognitive processes and creative thinking (Chi & Wylie, 2014). Emotional resilience fostered by a growth mindset enables learners to approach complex problems with curiosity and determination.

Supporting Emotional Well-being

Embracing a growth mindset helps learners manage negative emotions such as frustration and anxiety, as they are more likely to see these emotions as temporary and surmountable. This positive emotional regulation contributes to well-being and sustained motivation (Dweck, 2016). By promoting a growth mindset, instructional designers can help learners maintain a positive attitude toward learning and manage stress more effectively. For example, instructional designers might incorporate reflective activities where learners are encouraged to identify challenges they have overcome and apply those strategies to current situations. Stress management workshops or mindfulness exercises can also equip learners with practical tools to handle stress in real-time. The strategies for managing negative emotions and promoting resilience, highlighting the importance of emotional regulation in online learning, overlap but remain vital (Birmingham et al., 2021). Shifting the focus from immediate success to long-term growth can reduce pressure and improve emotional well-being.

Measuring Emotions in Online Learning

Research studies on the role of emotions in online learning have used various methods to collect data on learners' emotions. Although most of these methods have been used to examine cognitive dimensions of the learning process, they have also been applied to study emotions in online learning (Woznitza & Volet, 2005). These methods include snapshot-type measures, categorical scale questionnaires, stimulated recall measures, qualitative approaches such as interviews, observations (e.g., facial movements during communication), and content analysis based on texts and emotional transcription (as cited in Zembylas et al., 2008). This diversity in methodological approaches highlights the complexity and multifaceted nature of studying emotions in online learning environments.

Quantitative Measures

Most studies have used different combinations of quantitative methods and focused on individual or group aspects of online learning. For example, Duffy et al. (2018) constructed and validated a scale for measuring emotions experienced by students engaged in medical learning environments. Learners used a 5-point scale (from "not at all" to "very strong") to rate their level of experiencing each of 22 emotions, based on single words representing positive activating emotions (e.g., enjoyment), negative activating emotions (e.g., anxiety), positive deactivating emotions (e.g., relaxation), or negative deactivating emotions (e.g., boredom). Using Pekrun's (2006) control-value model, this scale provides a nuanced understanding of the range and intensity of emotions experienced by learners, offering valuable insights for instructional designers seeking to create emotionally supportive learning environments.

Moreover, Duffy et al. (2018) reported that the Achievement Emotions Questionnaire (AEQ) (Pekrun et al., 2011) is the most commonly used emotion survey in educational settings. The AEQ measures a wide range of emotions related to academic achievement, such as enjoyment, hope, pride, anger, anxiety, shame, hopelessness, and boredom. Its comprehensive nature makes it a valuable tool for understanding how different emotions affect learning processes and outcomes.

Qualitative Measures

Qualitative approaches to measuring emotions in online learning include interviews, observations, and content analysis. For instance, qualitative studies often involve detailed interviews with learners to gain insights into their emotional experiences and the factors influencing these emotions. Interviews can provide a rich, contextualized understanding of how learners' emotions evolve and respond to specific instructional strategies or learning activities. Observations of facial expressions and other non-verbal cues during online interactions can also provide valuable data on learners' emotional states. Content analysis of discussion forum posts, chat transcripts, and other textual data can reveal patterns in emotional expression and highlight areas where learners may be experiencing emotional challenges. For example, Zembylas (2008) applied qualitative methodology to investigate emotional presence using learners' monthly emotion journals and interviews. This study's analysis resulted in two broad themes: positive and negative learning-related emotions. Using journals and interviews allows for a deeper exploration of learners' emotional experiences, providing rich, qualitative data that can complement quantitative findings by offering more profound insights into the context and nuances of learners' emotional experiences.

Biometric Measures

According to Mayer (2020), a potential complementary direction for future research is to explore the role of biometric measures of emotion during learning, such as electro-dermal activity (EDA) or heart rate variability (HRV). Biometric measures offer objective data on physiological responses associated with emotional states, providing an additional layer of understanding that can enhance the interpretation of self-reported and observational data.

For example, EDA measures the skin's electrical conductance, which varies with sweat gland activity and can indicate emotional arousal. HRV measures the variation in time between heartbeats, which can reflect stress and relaxation levels.

These biometric measures can provide real-time, continuous data on learners' emotional states, offering valuable insights into how emotions fluctuate during learning activities and in response to different instructional strategies.

Integrating Multiple Methods

Researchers and instructional designers should consider integrating multiple methods to understand emotions experienced during online learning comprehensively. Combining quantitative measures, qualitative approaches, and biometric data can provide a holistic view of learners' emotional experiences. This multimethod approach allows for triangulation, where findings from different methods can corroborate and enrich each other, leading to more robust and nuanced insights.

For instance, self-report scales can quantify the intensity and frequency of emotions, while interviews and observations can explore the underlying causes and contextual factors. Biometric measures can provide objective data on physiological responses, adding another dimension to understanding emotional experiences. By understanding and leveraging these various approaches, instructional designers can gain valuable insights into learners' emotional experiences and develop strategies to create more supportive and effective online learning environments. This comprehensive approach provides the necessary information and tools to help instructional designers address the emotional dimensions of learning, leading to improved engagement, motivation, and achievement of learning outcomes for adult learners.

Leveraging the Dual Role of Emotions in Adult Online Learning

Emotions deeply affect various facets of the learning journey, from cognitive engagement and memory retention to motivation and the capacity for persistence. In addition to building on the insights gained from examining the emotional impacts of the COVID-19 pandemic on adult online learning, it is crucial to delve deeper into the dual role of emotions in this context. Understanding and leveraging these dynamics effectively can significantly enhance learning outcomes.

Enhancing Traditionally Positive Emotions

Emotions typically classified as positive, such as joy, interest, and curiosity, enhance cognitive functions, boost motivation, and improve problem-solving abilities. Positive emotions foster an environment where attention is heightened, information processing is more efficient, and creativity is unlocked. However, it is essential to recognize that excessive positivity can also have drawbacks. For instance, overemphasizing positivity might lead to complacency, where learners feel overly confident and do not engage deeply with challenging material. Additionally, it can create an unrealistic expectation that learning should always be enjoyable, potentially discouraging learners when they inevitably encounter challenging or less engaging content.

Understanding the balance between fostering positive emotions and ensuring critical engagement is crucial for working with adult learners. To address these issues, instructional designers might integrate reflective activities where learners assess not only their successes but also areas where they struggled or encountered difficulties. Encouraging discussions about challenges faced during learning and how they were overcome can help maintain a balanced perspective. Furthermore, instructional designers can introduce varied tasks that include enjoyable activities and those requiring more sustained effort and concentration, helping learners build resilience and persistence alongside positivity.

Recognizing Traditionally Negative Emotions

Conversely, emotions often labeled as negative, such as anxiety, stress, and frustration, are generally seen as impediments to learning. However, these emotions can also catalyze growth and deeper engagement. For example, anxiety can heighten focus and drive when learners are faced with challenging tasks, motivating them to put in the extra effort needed to succeed. When managed correctly, stress can stimulate problem-solving and creative thinking by pushing learners to explore new approaches. Frustration can lead to persistence and resilience as learners work through difficulties and ultimately experience the satisfaction of overcoming obstacles. Recognizing the potential positive aspects of negative emotions can help instructional designers create learning environments that harness these emotions to support learning rather than mitigate them.

Instead of merely managing anxiety, instructional designers can frame it as an essential part of the learning process that signals the importance of the task. By encouraging learners to view anxiety as a motivator rather than a barrier, they can channel this emotion into focused energy for tackling complex problems. Similarly, stress can be leveraged to promote time management and prioritization skills, teaching learners to thrive under pressure. Frustration can be positioned as a natural part of the learning journey, prompting learners to develop persistence and a problem-solving mindset. By integrating activities that acknowledge and harness these emotions, such as challenging problem-based learning tasks, reflection exercises on managing difficult emotions, and group discussions about shared experiences with stress and frustration, educators can help learners build their resilience and a growth mindset. As discussed, this approach mitigates the negative impacts of these emotions and transforms them into opportunities for deeper learning and personal growth (Birmingham et al., 2021; Rowe and Fitness, 2018).

For example, creating a safe environment for risk-taking by implementing a growth mindset culture can motivate learners to view challenges as opportunities for growth. Including reflection prompts in assignments that ask learners to describe a challenge they faced and how they overcame it helps normalize struggle and resilience. For example, learners could reflect on a challenging project and discuss their strategies to manage their stress and complete the task.

Introducing stress management techniques as part of the curriculum can also be beneficial. Beginning each online session with a five-minute mindfulness exercise using guided meditation apps like Headspace can help learners manage stress and build resilience. Utilizing time management tools and techniques, such as the Pomodoro Technique, which involves working in focused bursts with short breaks in between, can help learners manage anxiety and improve productivity. These strategies not only help mitigate the negative impacts of stress and anxiety but also promote a culture of resilience and adaptability. This change is significant for maintaining motivation and engagement in facing challenges, as Lin and Muenks (2022) and Fang et al. (2022) noted.

Rethinking the Emotional Spectrum

This nuanced understanding of emotional impacts suggests a need to rethink the binary classification of emotions. Instead of categorizing emotions as positive or negative, we should consider their dynamic and context-dependent nature. Recognizing that emotions can have beneficial and detrimental impacts depending on the situation is crucial for developing effective instructional strategies. As such, mild anxiety can drive focus and determination in learners when appropriately harnessed, but if left unchecked, it can escalate into overwhelming stress that hinders performance. Using scaffolded assignments that gradually increase in difficulty can motivate learners to develop their skills progressively without feeling overwhelmed. Similarly, joy can enhance engagement and creativity, but excessive positivity may lead to complacency or superficial engagement with the material.

To illustrate, after a successful collaborative project that fosters joy and satisfaction, a debrief session where learners reflect on what went well and where improvements can be made ensures that they remain engaged and critically assess their work. This balances emotional engagement with critical thinking and mitigates the risk of learners becoming overly complacent or disengaged. These strategies highlight the importance of understanding the dual nature of emotions and how they can both support and hinder learning outcomes. By recognizing and addressing these dualities, instructional designers can create learning environments that effectively leverage the full spectrum of emotional experiences, as discussed in earlier sections on emotional engagement and cognitive impact (Schwabe et al., 2023; Tzafilkou et al., 2021).

Comprehensive Recommendations and Strategies for Instructional Designers

The COVID-19 pandemic has reshaped the educational landscape, compelling a rapid shift from traditional face-to-face learning to online environments. This sudden change has brought to light the significant emotional challenges faced by post-pandemic adult learners in the online learning context. Understanding and addressing these emotional experiences is crucial for instructional designers to create supportive and effective learning environments.

Fostering Emotional Awareness and Self-regulation

Emotional awareness and self-regulation are foundational to effective learning. As instructional designers, integrating activities and tools that help learners recognize and manage their emotions is essential. Instructional designers can promote more dynamic and participatory learning experiences by cultivating an atmosphere that supports learning through curiosity, interest, and pleasure.

Emotional Self-awareness

Reflective activities can play a significant role in helping learners become more attuned to their emotional states, fostering self-awareness and regulation. For instance, incorporating weekly reflective journals into the course structure allows learners to document and reflect on their emotional experiences. This practice can help learners identify stress patterns and manage their emotional responses more effectively (Tyng et al., 2017). For example, John, an adult learner balancing work and family responsibilities, uses weekly reflective journals to recognize his stress patterns. By reflecting on his emotional experiences, John learns to manage his time better and seek help when needed, improving his overall engagement in the course.

Tracking Emotional State

Implementing digital tools like MoodScope or Google Forms for daily emotional logging can also help learners track their emotional states. Instructional designers should set up these tools and provide clear instructions, enabling learners to identify patterns and triggers that affect their learning (Zembylas, 2008). For example, an adult learner, Maria, uses a Google Form to log her daily emotions. Over time, she notices that her motivation dips on days with back-to-back work meetings. Maria improves her engagement and performance by adjusting her schedule to include short breaks.

Building a Sense of Community

Creating dedicated discussion forums for sharing emotional experiences and coping strategies can foster a supportive community. Diep et al. (2019) highlighted the importance of encouraging learners to share personal stories, experiences, and interests, especially relating to the course content. Instructional designers should ensure these forums are well-integrated into the course and moderated to maintain a positive environment (Cleveland-Innes & Campbell, 2012). For instance, learners share their emotional experiences in an online course in a dedicated forum. Lisa, a student dealing with anxiety, shares a breathing technique that helps her stay calm. Other students try the technique and report feeling more relaxed, creating a supportive peer network.

Designing for Emotional Engagement

Creating emotionally engaging content is essential for maintaining motivation and improving learning outcomes. Instructional designers should focus on interactive and multimedia content to enhance engagement. These strategies make the learning experience more enjoyable and contribute to a deeper and more meaningful engagement with the content.

Utilizing Interactive Elements

Interactive elements such as quizzes, simulations, and games can significantly enhance the adult online learning experience, making it more engaging and enjoyable for learners. Rincon-Flores and Santos-Guevara (2021) emphasized that such aspects stimulate interest and curiosity, leading to positive emotional experiences promoting active participation and deeper learning. Alamri et al. (2020) highlighted the significance of relevant and relatable content in sparking curiosity and interest among learners, which are critical components of intrinsic motivation. Therefore, utilizing material that resonates with adult learners' interests and goals is another powerful strategy for eliciting positive emotions and enhancing motivation and engagement in learning.

Incorporating Interactive Video Lectures

Interactive video lectures with embedded quizzes and polls can significantly enhance engagement. Using platforms like EdPuzzle, instructional designers can create content that keeps learners actively thinking about the material (Chi & Wylie, 2014). For example, in a history course, instructional designers use EdPuzzle to embed quizzes within video lectures on the Civil War. This interactive element engages students and helps them retain important information through active participation.

Implementing Spaced Repetition Techniques

Spaced repetition techniques, using flashcard apps like Anki, help learners review material at increasing intervals to support long-term retention of information. Instructional designers should integrate these tools into the curriculum and provide training materials on effectively using spaced repetition apps and techniques when necessary (Mayer, 2020). For example, instructional designers can incorporate Anki flashcards with gamified elements in a medical terminology course. This method helps students review complex medical terms effectively, making learning enjoyable and rewarding.

Encouraging Intrinsic Motivation Through Personalized Projects

Incorporating projects where learners choose topics of personal interest can boost intrinsic motivation. Instructional designers should ensure these projects are well-integrated into the course objectives and aligned with learning outcomes (Ryan & Deci, 2000). For example, in a business administration course, learners develop a business plan for an idea they are passionate about pursuing. Maria, a student interested in sustainable agriculture, creates a plan for a local organic farm. Her passion for the topic keeps her motivated and engaged, leading to a high-quality project and deeper learning.

Balancing Emotional Engagement

Balancing positive and negative emotions is crucial for maintaining optimal learning conditions. Instructional designers should design assignments and activities that manage this balance effectively.

Fostering Social Interaction and Collaboration

Kryshko et al. (2020) emphasized the role of social interaction in creating a sense of community and belonging, which can enhance learners' emotional well-being and contribute to a more engaging and supportive learning experience. Encouraging interaction and collaboration in the learning process is also vital for fostering emotional connections among learners. Trespalacios and Uribe-Florez (2020) highlighted the significance of designing activities that promote collaborative engagement, such as group projects, peer reviews, and participation in discussion forums. These activities facilitate knowledge and skills acquisition and enhance the emotional and social aspects of learning.

Utilizing Scaffolded Assignments

Scaffolded assignments gradually increase in difficulty and can help manage anxiety and boost confidence. Instructional designers should ensure that the difficulty progression is manageable for learners (Wu et al., 2021). For instance, in a programming course, instructional designers start with simple coding exercises and progressively increase the complexity of the activities. This approach helps learners build confidence and competence without feeling overwhelmed.

Incorporating a Mix of Individual and Group Activities

A mix of individual and group activities can prevent monotony and maintain engagement. Instructional designers should create diverse activities that stimulate emotions by catering to introspective and social learning experiences (Park & Yun, 2017). For example, in a literature course, individual analytical essays might evoke curiosity, reflection, and personal satisfaction as learners explore ideas independently. In contrast, group discussions and presentations can stimulate excitement, collaboration, and a sense of belonging as learners engage with their peers. This variety keeps learners engaged and ensures they experience a range of emotions that contribute to both independent and collaborative learning.

Implementing Debrief Sessions

Debrief sessions after collaborative projects help learners reflect on their experiences and maintain critical engagement. Instructional designers should plan these sessions to ensure learners process their emotions and learn from their experiences (Fredrickson, 2001). For example, instructional designers schedule a debrief session after a group project on environmental science. Learners discuss what went well, the challenges they faced, and how they overcame them. This reflection helps learners critically engage with the material and their emotional responses.

Providing Constructive Feedback

Feedback is crucial in guiding learners' efforts and maintaining their motivation. Instructional designers should develop feedback mechanisms that emphasize effort and improvement.

Promoting Growth and Learning

Fong and Shallert (2023) emphasized the importance of delivering feedback that promotes growth and learning rather than causing anxiety or frustration. This approach to feedback is critical in creating a learning environment where students feel supported and encouraged to develop their skills and knowledge. However, Say et al. (2024) established that limiting feedback in specific adult online learning environments can increase engagement and promote higher critical thinking. Facilitating social interaction in learning environments further enhances this process by providing opportunities for peer feedback and collaborative problem-solving, which are essential for fostering positive emotions and reinforcing instructor feedback. These social interactions allow learners to share experiences, discuss challenges, and celebrate successes, contributing to a supportive learning community that encourages continuous growth and learning.

Highlighting Progress and Offering Specific Suggestions

Feedback should highlight progress and offer specific suggestions for improvement. Instructional designers should ensure that feedback mechanisms focus on outcomes and the learning process (Hill et al., 2021). For example, in a statistics course, instructional designers develop a feedback system that emphasizes students' efforts and provides constructive suggestions for improvement. Sarah, a student struggling with data analysis, feels supported and motivated to improve her skills through this feedback.

Recognizing Achievements

Recognizing achievements through virtual certificates or badges can boost morale and motivation. Instructional designers should incorporate gamification elements to celebrate learner milestones (Birmingham et al., 2021). For example, instructional designers gamify achievements using Classcraft in a language course. Students earn virtual badges and certificates for completing language milestones, motivating them through recognition and positive reinforcement.

Offering Empathetic Support

Feedback should acknowledge learners' challenges and offer support. Instructional designers should ensure that feedback mechanisms are empathetic and supportive (Lin & Muenks, 2022). For instance, Vihn, an adult learner in a management course, feels frustrated with a challenging assignment. Instructional designers incorporate empathetic feedback, acknowledging his struggles and offering one-on-one support, helping Vihn feel understood and supported.

Creating a Supportive Learning Environment

A supportive environment is essential for fostering confidence and persistence among adult learners. Instructional designers should ensure that all materials and interactions promote inclusivity and support.

Ensuring Accessibility Through Universal Design for Learning (UDL) Principles

All course materials should follow Universal Design for Learning (UDL) principles, promoting accessibility. Instructional designers should provide closed captions, transcripts, and alternative formats for content (Sogunro, 2015). For example, instructional designers ensure that all videos in a course include closed captions and transcripts. This inclusive design approach helps students with hearing impairments fully participate in the course.

Incorporating Regular Check-ins with Learners

Regular check-ins with learners provide opportunities to discuss challenges and seek advice. Incorporating synchronous communication tools in online learning environments can significantly enhance learners' social presence and emotional engagement. Lu et al. (2022) showed the effectiveness of live video sessions, real-time chats, and webinars in simulating the immediacy and intimacy of face-to-face interactions, which are crucial for fostering a sense of connection and community among learners. Instructional designers should incorporate these check-ins into the course structure (Abedini et al., 2023). Establishing a regular schedule for live sessions can create a routine that learners can look forward to, enhancing their engagement and commitment to the course. For instance, in an online nursing program, instructional designers schedule regular virtual office hours using Zoom. Nayra, a student juggling coursework and clinical hours, uses these check-ins to get guidance, helping her stay on track and reducing her stress.

While synchronous communication is valuable for building a social presence, it should be balanced with asynchronous elements to accommodate different time zones, schedules, and learning preferences. This balance ensures that all learners have equal opportunities to engage and participate.

Recognizing and Celebrating Learner Achievements

Recognizing and celebrating learner achievements fosters a sense of community and recognition. Instructional designers should plan virtual award ceremonies and highlight learner accomplishments (Ke, 2010). At the end of a semester, instructional designers organize a virtual award ceremony to celebrate student achievements. Awards are given for various accomplishments, such as best project, most improved, and peer support, fostering a sense of community and recognition.

Promoting Inclusivity and Emotional Support

Promoting inclusivity and emotional support in learning environments is essential for fostering positive emotional experiences and enhancing learner engagement. Majeski et al. (2018) emphasized the importance of creating an inclusive environment supporting emotional well-being, ensuring that all learners feel valued, respected, and supported, regardless of their backgrounds or circumstances. Instructional designers can promote inclusivity by incorporating diverse perspectives and materials into the curriculum, confirming that content is representative of various cultures, experiences, and viewpoints. Additionally, they can create opportunities for all learners to express themselves through anonymous feedback channels or discussion forums where diverse opinions are encouraged and respected.

Providing Robust Technological Support

Ensuring learners have the necessary technological support is crucial for a smooth learning experience. Instructional designers should develop and implement robust technological support systems.

Offering Training Sessions and Resources

Offering live and recorded training sessions on using the learning management system (LMS) and other necessary tools helps learners navigate technology confidently. Instructional designers should create comprehensive training resources (Cleveland-Innes et al., 2007). For instance, instructional designers provide live and recorded LMS training sessions in a digital marketing course. Step-by-step guides and video tutorials are available on the course homepage, ensuring learners are comfortable with the technology.

Establishing a Dedicated Help Desk

A dedicated help desk available via email, chat, and phone ensures learners can resolve technical issues promptly. While establishing and managing a help desk is typically the responsibility of the IT department or other support services, instructional designers can play a key role by coordinating with these departments to ensure that support is aligned with the learning schedule (Tzafilkou et al., 2023). For example, an instructional designer might work with IT to plan for extended support during peak times, such as assignment deadlines, to assist students more effectively. This collaboration helps ensure that technical issues are quickly resolved, minimizing disruptions to their learning.

Soliciting and Acting on Learner Feedback

Regularly soliciting learner feedback about tools ensures a smooth learning experience. Instructional designers should use feedback to continuously improve (Pekrun et al., 2011). While instructional designers may not directly implement changes to technical tools, they can play a crucial role in evaluating and sharing this feedback with the appropriate departments to drive improvements. For instance, after the first month of an online psychology course, instructional designers solicit student feedback about the LMS and other tools. Based on these insights, they can identify patterns and areas needing improvement and collaborate with IT or other relevant departments to suggest adjustments that enhance the user experience, such as simplifying navigation or providing additional resources for commonly used tools.

Fostering a Growth Mindset

Encouraging a growth mindset among learners promotes resilience, self-efficacy, and a positive attitude towards learning. Instructional designers should integrate activities and messages to reinforce a growth mindset (Dweck, 2006). For instructional designers, fostering a growth mindset among adult learners involves several key strategies.

Creating a Culture of Learning from Mistakes

Creating a culture where mistakes are seen as learning opportunities can help learners develop a growth mindset. Instructional designers should incorporate this message into course communications and activities. For example, in an online creative writing course, instructional designers can emphasize that mistakes are a natural part of learning. They might share stories of famous authors who faced numerous rejections before achieving success, highlighting the setbacks and what these authors learned from their experiences. These authors would have used rejection to refine their work, improve their storytelling, and build resilience. Instructional designers can encourage students to view setbacks as valuable opportunities for growth, fostering a mindset that embraces learning through challenges. Such strategies, which include reflection and stress management techniques, can help students build resilience and embrace challenges without fear of judgment (Lin & Muenks, 2022). This approach encourages learners to take risks, learn from their experiences, and ultimately develop a mindset that values persistence and growth through adversity.

Emphasizing Effort and Perseverance

Emphasizing effort and perseverance rather than innate talent reinforces the idea that abilities can be developed through dedication and hard work. Instructional designers should ensure that course materials and feedback highlight the importance of effort and perseverance (Bandura, 1997). For instance, in a math course, instructional designers might include stories of mathematicians who overcame significant challenges through persistent effort, encouraging students to persist despite difficulties. While related, resilience is equally important but distinct, as discussed in this chapter. Instructional designers can incorporate both concepts by creating an environment where learners are encouraged to persevere through challenges and develop the resilience to recover from setbacks and maintain their commitment to learning.

Integrating Growth Mindset Activities

Instructional designers should integrate activities that reinforce a growth mindset. Activities could include reflective journals where learners document their challenges and how they overcame them, peer reviews that provide constructive feedback on effort and improvement, and discussions about personal growth experiences. These activities encourage learners to adopt a growth mindset by highlighting the learning and development process. In addition to these specific growth mindset activities, fostering emotional awareness, designing for emotional engagement, and balancing emotional responses are equally important. Providing constructive feedback, creating a supportive learning environment, and offering robust technological support also contribute to a comprehensive strategy for developing a growth mindset. Together, these approaches create an emotionally supportive and effective online learning environment. Such strategies are particularly crucial in addressing the challenges brought on by the pandemic and preparing learners for future disruptions, ensuring they can thrive in the online learning environment.

Providing Challenging Yet Achievable Tasks

Design tasks that stretch learners' abilities but are achievable with effort. Scaffold assignments gradually increase in difficulty, allowing learners to build confidence as they progress. For instance, in a coding course, starting with simple programming exercises and gradually introducing more complex projects that require integrating multiple skills learned throughout the course can help maintain engagement and build competence. This approach aligns with setting challenging yet achievable goals to leverage mild anxiety for positive outcomes (Wu et al., 2021). Creating a balance between challenge and skill level keeps learners in optimal engagement, where they can experience growth without being overwhelmed.

Emphasizing the Learning Process

Shift the focus from grades and outcomes to the learning process. Encourage learners to reflect on their progress, strategies, and lessons from each task. Using reflective journals where learners document their learning experiences, challenges faced, and how they overcame them can highlight the value of the learning process over the final result. This practice enhances emotional awareness and supports self-regulation (Tyng, 2017). Reflection helps learners connect their emotional experiences with learning outcomes, fostering a deeper understanding of their growth.

Tailoring Feedback to Foster a Growth Mindset

While constructive feedback was discussed earlier, it is important to expand on how tailored feedback specifically fosters a growth mindset. To cultivate a growth mindset effectively, ensure instructors can provide holistic feedback on effort, strategies, and specific improvement methods rather than solely on the outcome. This approach aids learners in recognizing challenges as opportunities to develop their skills and resiliency. For example, rather than providing generic criticism, feedback should be framed in a way that emphasizes specific strategies for improvement. Instead of saying, "Your analysis is weak," an instructor might say, "Your analysis shows potential and would be even stronger if you incorporated more evidence from the text. Consider exploring these specific areas." This type of feedback addresses the immediate task and encourages learners to think about how they can apply these strategies in future work, fortifying the idea that abilities can be developed over time through effort and learning. (Hill et al., 2021; Spooner et al., 2022). By utilizing tailored feedback, instructional designers can help learners internalize the belief that their abilities can be expanded through dedication and perseverance. This targeted approach helps build a mindset that values learning from mistakes and views setbacks as stepping stones to more significant achievement.

Encouraging Persistence and Effort

Praise effort, perseverance, and improvement rather than innate talent or intelligence. Reinforce the idea that abilities can be acquired through hard work and dedication. Recognize and celebrate incremental progress in learners' work, such as improved grades on successive assignments, and encourage them to continue putting in effort. This strategy promotes persistence and resilience through emotional support and recognition of effort (Park & Yun, 2018). Focusing on effort and improvement motivates learners to continue striving towards their goals, even when faced with challenges.

Promoting a Supportive Learning Environment

Foster a supportive and collaborative learning environment where learners feel comfortable taking risks and seeking help. Encourage peer support and create opportunities for group work and discussions. Organizing study groups or peer tutoring sessions where learners can collaborate and support each other can enhance the learning experience and reinforce the growth mindset. This approach aligns with creating a supportive learning environment to enhance social presence and community building (Sogunro, 2015; Abedini et al., 2023). A supportive environment ensures learners feel valued and understood, which is crucial for maintaining motivation and engagement.

Adopting a growth mindset is essential for adult learners in online environments. It promotes resilience, self-efficacy, and a positive attitude toward learning, which are crucial for success in self-directed online learning settings. By implementing strategies that foster a growth mindset, instructional designers and educators can create learning experiences that enhance learners' academic achievements and support their personal and professional growth. Emphasizing the importance of effort, persistence, and continuous learning helps learners navigate the complexities of online education and prepares them for lifelong learning and adaptation in an ever-changing world.

Supporting Mental Health and Well-being

Supporting learners' mental health and well-being is crucial, especially during heightened stress like the COVID-19 pandemic. Instructional designers should prioritize mental health resources and well-being activities to help learners manage their emotional health effectively.

Providing Access to Mental Health Resources

Providing access to mental health resources, such as counseling services, stress management workshops, and mental health hotlines, can help learners manage their emotional health. Instructional designers should ensure that information about these resources is readily available and communicated to learners. For instance, in an online course, the homepage could include links to virtual counseling services, stress management webinars, and contact information for mental health hotlines.

Integrating Well-being Activities into the Course

Incorporating well-being activities into the course can also be beneficial. Mindfulness exercises, virtual wellness breaks, and stress-relief techniques can be integrated into the course structure to promote well-being. For example, instructional designers might schedule short mindfulness sessions at the beginning or end of live classes or provide guided meditation videos that learners can access. Additionally, offering virtual wellness breaks during long sessions can help learners recharge and reduce stress.

Conducting Regular Check-ins with Learners

Regular check-ins with learners through surveys, polls, or one-on-one meetings can help educators assess their well-being and offer support as needed. These check-ins can also provide valuable insights into learners' experiences and needs, allowing instructional designers to adjust their strategies accordingly. For example, a weekly anonymous survey could be used to gauge learners' stress levels and identify common concerns, which can then be addressed in course adjustments or through additional support resources. By implementing these strategies, instructional designers can support learners' mental health and well-being, creating a more supportive and effective online learning environment.

CONCLUSION

Research on emotions in online learning environments has widely increased and emerged with the expansion of online learning. Educators and instructional designers should carefully consider the types of learning environments they create and focus on creating emotionally safe environments where learners can freely construct their knowledge. Settings low in emotional awareness that can fail to produce a sense of engagement do not fully develop the student's potential. Therefore, underestimating the role and effect of emotions in online learning environments is ill-advised.

Furthermore, while the emphasis has often been on creating positive emotional environments, it is equally important to recognize and explore the complexity of emotions, including the dual impacts of positive and negative emotions. Understanding how emotions like anxiety and stress can serve both as obstacles and as motivators is vital for today's adult online learners. Future research should delve deeper into this complexity, examining how different emotional experiences influence learning outcomes and how these can be effectively managed to support diverse learner needs. A nuanced understanding of emotions will inform more effective educational practices, helping learners thrive in increasingly digital and emotionally complex learning landscapes.

Finally, research on the effects of emotions and learning would also benefit the discipline by concentrating on creating positive learning environments and emotional teaching strategies. Although the current body of research has yet to provide conclusive answers, the ongoing exploration of how students experience online learning emotionally remains a critical area of inquiry. So, to develop new theories and conduct empirical studies to provide further guidance for the successful design and delivery of online courses, a closer look at the measurement of emotions in online learning, both qualitatively and quantitatively, would greatly enhance how adult educators understand emotion and learning, as well as their effects.

REFERENCES

Abedini, A., Abedin, B., & Zowghi, D. (2023). A framework of environmental, personal, and behavioral factors of adult learning in online communities of practice. *Information Systems Frontiers*. Advance online publication. DOI: 10.1007/s10796-023-10417-2

Ajjawi, R., Dracup, M., Zacharias, N., Bennett, S., & Boud, D. (2020). Persisting students' explanations of and emotional responses to academic failure. *Higher Education Research & Development*, 39(2), 185–199. DOI: 10.1080/07294360.2019.1664999

Alamri, H., Lowell, V., Watson, W., & Watson, S. L. (2020). Using personalized learning as an instructional approach to motivate learners in online higher education: Learner self-determination and intrinsic motivation. *Journal of Research on Technology in Education*, 52(3), 322–352. DOI: 10.1080/15391523.2020.1728449

Amabile, T. M. (1996). *Creativity in context: Update to The Social Psychology of Creativity*. Westview Press.

Artino, A. R.Jr. (2010). Online or face-to-face learning? Exploring the personal factors that predict students' choice of instructional format. *The Internet and Higher Education*, 13(4), 272–276. DOI: 10.1016/j.iheduc.2010.07.005

Artino, A. R.Jr, & Jones, K. D.II. (2012). Exploring the complex relations between achievement emotions and self-regulated learning behaviors in online learning. *The Internet and Higher Education*, 15(3), 170–175. DOI: 10.1016/j.iheduc.2012.01.006

Bandura, A. (1997). *Self-Efficacy: The Exercise of Control*. W.H. Freeman and Company.

Barbalet, J. (1998). *Emotion, social theory and social structure*. Cambridge University Press. DOI: 10.1017/CBO9780511488740

Baumeister, R. F., DeWall, C. N., & Zhang, L. (2007). Do emotions improve or hinder the decision-making process? In K. D. Vohs, R. F. Baumeister, R. F. & G. Loewenstein (Eds.), *Do emotions help or hurt decision making? A hedgefoxian perspective* (pp. 11–31). New York: Russell Sage.

Birmingham, W. C., Wadsworth, L. L., Lassetter, J. H., Graff, T. C., Lauren, E., & Hung, M. (2023). COVID-19 lockdown: Impact on college students' lives. *Journal of American College Health*, 71(3), 879–893. DOI: 10.1080/07448481.2021.1909041 PMID: 34292141

Bowlby, J. (1969). *Attachment and loss* (Vol. I). Basic Books.

Cao, W., & Yu, Z. (2023). Exploring learning outcomes, communication, anxiety, and motivation in learning communities: A systematic review. *Humanities & Social Sciences Communications*, 10(1), 866. DOI: 10.1057/s41599-023-02325-2

Chaudhry, S., Tandon, A., Shinde, S., & Bhattacharya, A. (2024). Student psychological well-being in higher education: The role of internal team environment, institutional, friends and family support and academic engagement. *PLoS One*, 19(1), e0297508. DOI: 10.1371/journal.pone.0297508 PMID: 38271390

Chi, M. T. H., & Wylie, R. (2014). The ICAP Framework: Linking cognitive engagement to active learning outcomes. *Educational Psychologist*, 49(4), 219–243. DOI: 10.1080/00461520.2014.965823

Cleveland-Innes, M., & Campbell, P. (2006, November). *Understanding emotional presence in an online community of inquiry*. Paper presented at the 12th Annual SLOAN-C ALN Conference, Orlando, Florida.

Cleveland-Innes, M., & Campbell, P. (2012). Emotional presence, learning, and the online learning environment. *International Review of Research in Open and Distance Learning*, 13(4), 269–292. DOI: 10.19173/irrodl.v13i4.1234

Cleveland-Innes, M., Garrison, R., & Kinsel, E. (2007). Role adjustment for learners in an online community of inquiry: Identifying the needs of novice online learners. *International Journal of Web-Based Learning and Teaching Technologies*, 2(1), 1–16. DOI: 10.4018/jwltt.2007010101

Croft, N., Dalton, A., & Grant, M. (2010). Overcoming isolation in distance learning: Building a learning community through time and space. *The Journal for Education in the Built Environment*, 5(1), 27–64. DOI: 10.11120/jebe.2010.05010027

D'Errico, F., Paciello, M. & Cerniglia, L. (2016). When emotions enhance students' engagement in e-learning processes. *Journal of e-Learning and Knowledge Society*, *12*(4).

Denzin, N. (1984). *On understanding emotion*. Jossey-Bass.

Diep, A. N., Zhu, C., Cocquyt, C., De Greef, M., Vo, M. H., & Vanwing, T. (2019). Adult learners' needs in online and blended learning. *Australian Journal of Adult Learning*, 59(2), 223–253. DOI: 10.22459/AJAL.2019.18

Dirkx, J. M. (2001). The Power of feelings: Emotion, imagination, and the construction of meaning in adult learning. *New Directions for Adult and Continuing Education*, 2001(89), 63–72. DOI: 10.1002/ace.9

Duffy, M. C., Lajoie, S. P., Pekrun, R., & Lachapelle, K. (2018). Emotions in medical education: Examining the validity of the Medical Emotion Scale (MES) across authentic medical learning environments. *Learning and Instruction*.

Dweck, C. (2016). *Mindset: The new psychology of success*. Ballantine Books.

Elmi, C. (2020). Integrating social emotional learning strategies in higher education. *European Journal of Investigation in Health, Psychology and Education*, 10(3), 848–858. DOI: 10.3390/ejihpe10030061 PMID: 34542515

Endres, T., Weyreter, S., Renkl, A., & Eitel, A. (2020). When and why does emotional design foster learning? Evidence for situational interest as a mediator of increased persistence. *Journal of Computer Assisted Learning*, 36(4), 514–525. Advance online publication. DOI: 10.1111/jcal.12418

Fang, C. M., McMahon, K., Miller, M. L., & Rosenthal, M. Z. (2021). A pilot study investigating the efficacy of brief, phone-based behavioral interventions for burnout in graduate students. *Journal of Clinical Psychology*, 77(12), 2725–2745. DOI: 10.1002/jclp.23245 PMID: 34517431

Fensie, A. (2023). Toward a science of adult learning. https://doi.org/DOI: 10.13140/RG.2.2.13966.95043

Feraco, T., Resnati, D., Fregonese, D., Spoto, A., & Meneghetti, C. (2022). An integrated model of school students' academic achievement and life satisfaction linking soft skills, extracurricular activities, self-regulated learning, motivation, and emotions. *European Journal of Psychology of Education*, •••, 1–22. DOI: 10.1007/s10212-022-00601-4

Fong, C. J., & Schallert, D. L. (2023). Feedback to the future: Advancing motivational and emotional perspectives in feedback research. *Educational Psychologist*, 58(3), 146–161. DOI: 10.1080/00461520.2022.2134135

Fredrickson, B. L. (2001). The role of positive emotions in positive psychology: The broaden-and-build theory of positive emotions. *The American Psychologist*, 56(3), 218–226. DOI: 10.1037/0003-066X.56.3.218 PMID: 11315248

Goldsworthy, R. (2000). Designing instruction for emotional intelligence. *Educational Technology*, 40(5), 43–58.

Hara, N., & Kling, R. (2003). Students' distress with a web-based distance education course: An ethnographic study of participants' experiences. *Turkish Online Journal of Distance Education*, 4(2).

Hill, J., Berlin, K., Choate, J., Cravens-Brown, L., McKendrick-Calder, L., & Smith, S. (2021). Exploring the emotional responses of undergraduate students to assessment feedback: Implications for instructors. *Teaching & Learning Inquiry*, 9(1), 294–316. DOI: 10.20343/teachlearninqu.9.1.20

Hilliard, J., Kear, K., Donelan, H., & Heaney, C. (2020). Students' experiences of anxiety in an assessed, online, collaborative project. *Computers & Education*, 143, 103675. DOI: 10.1016/j.compedu.2019.103675

Hökkä, P., Vähäsantanen, K., & Paloniemi, S. (2020). Emotions in learning at work: A Literature review. *Vocations and Learning*, 13(1), 1–25. DOI: 10.1007/s12186-019-09226-z

Huang, T., & Wang, W. (2024). Relationship between fear of evaluation, ambivalence over emotional expression, and self-compassion among university students. *BMC Psychology*, 12(1), 128. DOI: 10.1186/s40359-024-01629-5 PMID: 38449046

James, W. (1952). *The principles of psychology*. Encyclopedia Britannica.

Jiang, M., & Koo, K. (2020). Emotional presence in building an online learning community among non-traditional graduate students. *Online Learning : the Official Journal of the Online Learning Consortium*, 24(4), 93–111. DOI: 10.24059/olj.v24i4.2307

Kaiqi, S., & Kutuk, G. (2024). Exploring the impact of online teaching factors on international students' control-value appraisals and achievement emotions in a foreign language context. *The Asia-Pacific Education Researcher*, 33(4), 943–955. DOI: 10.1007/s40299-024-00831-8

Kang, M., Kim, S., & Park, S. (2007). Developing emotional presence scale for measuring students' involvement during e-Learning process. In Montgomerie, C., & Seale, J. (Eds.), *Proceedings of World Conference on Educational Multimedia, Hypermedia and Telecommunications 2007* (pp. 2829–2832). Chesapeake, VA: AACE.

Ke, F. (2010). Examining online teaching, cognitive, and social presence for adult students. *Computers & Education*, 55(2), 808–820. DOI: 10.1016/j.compedu.2010.03.013

Kryshko, O., Fleischer, J., Waldeyer, J., Wirth, J., & Leutner, D. (2020). Do motivational regulation strategies contribute to university students' academic success? *Learning and Individual Differences*, 82, 101912. DOI: 10.1016/j.lindif.2020.101912

LeDoux, J. (1999). *The emotional brain: The mysterious underpinnings of emotional life*. Phoenix.

Lee, J. Y., & Chei, M. J. (2020). Latent profile analysis of Korean undergraduates' academic emotions in e-learning environment. *Educational Technology Research and Development*, 68(3), 1521–1546. DOI: 10.1007/s11423-019-09715-x

Lee, K. (2021). Embracing authenticity and vulnerability in online PhD studies: The self and a community. In Fawns, T., Aitken, G., & Jones, D. (Eds.), *Online Postgraduate Education in a Postdigital World. Postdigital Science and Education*. Springer., DOI: 10.1007/978-3-030-77673-2_4

Lehman, R. (2006). The role of emotion in creating instructor and learner presence in the distance education experience. *Journal of Cognitive Affective Learning*, 2(2), 12–26.

Lerner, J., & Keltner, D. (2000). Beyond valence: Toward a model of emotion-specific influences on judgment and choice. *Cognition and Emotion*, 14(4), 473–503. DOI: 10.1080/026999300402763

Lin, S., & Muenks, K. (2022). Perfectionism profiles among college students: A person-centered approach to motivation, behavior, and emotion. *Contemporary Educational Psychology*, 71, 102110. Advance online publication. DOI: 10.1016/j.cedpsych.2022.102110

Liu, B., Xing, W., Zeng, Y., & Wu, Y. (2021). Quantifying the influence of achievement emotions for student learning in MOOCs. *Journal of Educational Computing Research*, 59(3), 429–452. DOI: 10.1177/0735633120967318

Lu, Y., Hong, X., & Xiao, L. (2022). Toward high-quality adult online learning: A systematic review of empirical studies. *Sustainability (Basel)*, 14(4), 2257. DOI: 10.3390/su14042257

Lucardie, D. (2014). The impact of fun and enjoyment on adult's learning. *Procedia: Social and Behavioral Sciences*, 142, 439–446. DOI: 10.1016/j.sbspro.2014.07.696

Luo, Z., & Luo, W. (2022). Discrete achievement emotions as mediators between achievement goals and academic engagement of Singapore students. *Educational Psychology*, 44(6), 749–766. DOI: 10.1080/01443410.2022.2048795

Lupton, D. (1998). *The emotional self: A socio-cultural exploration*. Sage. DOI: 10.4135/9781446217719

Majeski, R. A., Stover, M., & Valais, T. (2018). The community of inquiry and emotional presence. *Adult Learning*, 29(2), 53–61. DOI: 10.1177/1045159518758696

Marchand, G. C., & Gutierrez, A. P. (2012). The role of emotion in the learning process: Comparisons between online and face-to-face learning settings. *The Internet and Higher Education*, 15(3), 150–160. DOI: 10.1016/j.iheduc.2011.10.001

Mayer, R. E. (2020). Searching for the role of emotions in e-learning. *Learning and Instruction*, 7, 1–3. DOI: 10.1016/j.learninstruc.2019.05.010

Merriam, S. B., & Caffarella, R. S. (1999). *Learning in adulthood*. Jossey-Bass.

O'Regan, K. (2003). Emotion and e-learning. *JALN*, 7(3), 78–92.

Opengart, R. (2005). Emotional intelligence and emotion work: Examining constructs from an interdisciplinary framework. *Human Resource Development Review*, 4(1), 49–62. DOI: 10.1177/1534484304273817

Pan, X., Hu, B., Zhou, Z., & Feng, X. (2022). Are students happier the more they learn? Research on the influence of course progress on academic emotion in online learning. *Interactive Learning Environments*, •••, 1–21. DOI: 10.1080/10494820.2022.2052110

Park, S., & Yun, H. (2017). Relationships between motivational strategies and cognitive learning in distance education courses. *Distance Education*, 38(3), 302–320. DOI: 10.1080/01587919.2017.1369007

Pekrun, R., Goetz, T., Frenzel, A. C., Barchfeld, P., & Perry, R. P. (2011). Measuring emotions in students' learning and performance: The Achievement Emotions Questionnaire (AEQ). *Contemporary Educational Psychology*, 36(1), 36–48. DOI: 10.1016/j.cedpsych.2010.10.002

Perry, B., & Edwards, M. (2005). Exemplary online educators: Creating a community of inquiry. *Turkish Online Journal of Distance Education*, 6(2), 46–54.

Plutchik, R. (2001). The nature of emotions. *American Scientist*, 89(4), 344–350. DOI: 10.1511/2001.28.344

Putwain, D. W., Wood, P., & Pekrun, R. (2022). Achievement emotions and academic achievement: Reciprocal relations and the moderating influence of academic buoyancy. *Journal of Educational Psychology*, 114(1), 108–126. DOI: 10.1037/edu0000637

Rincon-Flores, E. G., & Santos-Guevara, B. N. (2021). Gamification during Covid-19: Promoting active learning and motivation in higher education. *Australasian Journal of Educational Technology*, 37(5), 43–60. DOI: 10.14742/ajet.7157

Rovai, A., & Wighting, M. (2005). Feelings of alienation and community among higher education students in a virtual classroom. *The Internet and Higher Education*, 8(2), 97–110. DOI: 10.1016/j.iheduc.2005.03.001

Rowe, A. D., & Fitness, J. (2018). Understanding the role of negative emotions in adult learning and achievement: A social functional perspective. *Behavioral Sciences (Basel, Switzerland)*, 8(2), 27. DOI: 10.3390/bs8020027 PMID: 29461487

Ryan, R. M., & Deci, E. L. (2000). Self-determination theory and the facilitation of intrinsic motivation, social development, and well-being. *The American Psychologist*, 55(1), 68–78. DOI: 10.1037/0003-066X.55.1.68 PMID: 11392867

Say, R., Visentin, D., Saunders, A., Atherton, I., Carr, A., & King, C. (2024). Where less is more: Limited feedback in formative online multiple-choice tests improves student self-regulation. *Journal of Computer Assisted Learning*, 40(1), 89–103. DOI: 10.1111/jcal.12868

Schwabe, L., Hermans, E. J., Joëls, M., & Roozendaal, B. (2022). Mechanisms of memory under stress. *Neuron*, 110(9), 1450–1467. DOI: 10.1016/j.neuron.2022.02.020 PMID: 35316661

Seow, A. N., Lam, S. Y., Choong, Y. O., & Choong, C. K. (2024). Online learning effectiveness in private higher education institutions: The mediating roles of emotions and students' learning behaviour. *Quality Assurance in Education*, 32(2), 180–196. DOI: 10.1108/QAE-07-2022-0128

Shuck, B., Albornoz, C., & Winberg, M. (2013). *Emotions and their effect on adult learning: A constructivist perspective*. https://digitalcommons.fiu.edu/sferc/2007/2007_suie/4/

Sogunro, O. A. (2015). Motivating factors for adult learners in higher education. *International Journal of Higher Education*, 4(1), 22–37.

Spitzer, D. R. (2001). Don't forget the high touch with the high tech in distance learning. *Educational Technology*, 41(2), 51–55.

Spooner, M., Duane, C., Uygur, J., Smyth, E., Marron, B., Murphy, P. J., & Pawlikowska, T. (2022). Self-regulatory learning theory as a lens on how undergraduate and postgraduate learners respond to feedback: A BEME scoping review: BEME Guide No. 66. *Medical Teacher*, 44(1), 3–18. DOI: 10.1080/0142159X.2021.1970732 PMID: 34666584

Tang, D., Fan, W., Zou, Y., George, R. A., Arbona, C., & Olvera, N. E. (2021). Self-efficacy and achievement emotions as mediators between learning climate and learning persistence in college calculus: A sequential mediation analysis. *Learning and Individual Differences*, 92, 102094. DOI: 10.1016/j.lindif.2021.102094

Travis, J., Kaszycki, A., Geden, M., & Bunde, J. (2020). Some stress is good stress: The challenge-hindrance framework, academic self-efficacy, and academic outcomes. *Journal of Educational Psychology*, 112(8), 1632–1643. DOI: 10.1037/edu0000478

Trespalacios, J., & Uribe-Florez, L. J. (2020). Developing online sense of community: Graduate students' experiences and perceptions. *Turkish Online Journal of Distance Education*, 21(1), 57–72. DOI: 10.17718/tojde.690340

Tyng, C. M., Amin, H. U., Saad, M. N. M., & Malik, A. S. (2017). The influences of emotion on learning and memory. *Frontiers in Psychology*, 8, 1454. DOI: 10.3389/fpsyg.2017.01454 PMID: 28883804

Tzafilkou, K., Perifanou, M., & Economides, A. A. (2021). Negative emotions, cognitive load, acceptance, and self-perceived learning outcome in emergency remote education during COVID-19. *Journal of Educational Technology & Society*, 26(4), 7497–7521. DOI: 10.1007/s10639-021-10604-1 PMID: 34149299

Wlodkowski, R. (1999). *Enhancing adult motivation to learn*. Jossey-Bass.

Wolfe, P. (2006). The role of meaning and emotion in learning. *New Directions for Adult and Continuing Education*, 110(110), 35–41. DOI: 10.1002/ace.217

Wong, J., Baars, M., He, M., de Koning, B. B., & Paas, F. (2021). Facilitating goal setting and planning to enhance online self-regulation of learning. *Computers in Human Behavior*, 124, 106913. Advance online publication. DOI: 10.1016/j.chb.2021.106913

Wosnitza, M., & Volet, S. (2005). Origin, direction and impact of emotions in social online learning. *Learning and Instruction*, 15(5), 449–464. DOI: 10.1016/j.learninstruc.2005.07.009

Wu, C., Gong, X., Luo, L., Zhao, Q., Hu, S., Mou, Y., & Jing, B. (2021). Applying control-value theory and unified theory of acceptance and use of technology to explore pre-service teachers' academic emotions and learning satisfaction. *Frontiers in Psychology*, 12, 738959. DOI: 10.3389/fpsyg.2021.738959 PMID: 34819895

Wu, C., Jing, B., Gong, X., Mou, Y., & Li, J. (2021b). Student's learning strategies and academic emotions: Their influence on learning satisfaction during the COVID-19 pandemic. *Frontiers in Psychology*, 12, 717683. DOI: 10.3389/fpsyg.2021.717683 PMID: 34630228

Wu, R., & Yu, Z. (2022). Exploring the effects of achievement emotions on online learning outcomes: A systematic review. *Frontiers in Psychology*, 13, 977931. DOI: 10.3389/fpsyg.2022.977931 PMID: 36160514

Yang, Y. D., Zhou, C. L., & Wang, Z. Q. (2024). The relationship between self-control and learning engagement among Chinese college students: The chain mediating roles of resilience and positive emotions. *Frontiers in Psychology*, 15, 1331691. DOI: 10.3389/fpsyg.2024.1331691 PMID: 38445063

Yun, H., & Park, S. (2020). Building a structural model of motivational regulation and learning engagement for undergraduate and graduate students in higher education. *Studies in Higher Education*, 45(2), 271–285. DOI: 10.1080/03075079.2018.1510910

Zembylas, M. (2008). Adult learners' emotions in online learning. *Distance Education*, 29(1), 71–87. DOI: 10.1080/01587910802004852

Zembylas, M., Theodorou, M., & Pavlakis, A. (2008). The role of emotions in the experience of online learning: Challenges and opportunities. *Educational Media International*, 45(2), 107–117. DOI: 10.1080/09523980802107237

KEY TERMS AND DEFINITIONS

Constructive Feedback: Constructive feedback emphasizes learners' efforts and improvements rather than just the results. This type of feedback helps maintain motivation and fosters a growth mindset, encouraging continuous learning and development.

Growth Mindset: A growth mindset is the belief that abilities and intelligence can be developed through effort, learning, and persistence. Instructional designers can promote a growth mindset by designing challenging yet achievable tasks, emphasizing the learning process, normalizing mistakes, and offering constructive feedback.

Intrinsic Motivation: Intrinsic motivation refers to learners' internal drive to engage in activities because they find them inherently enjoyable and satisfying. Instructional designers can foster intrinsic motivation by incorporating personalized projects and activities that align with learners' interests and goals.

Negative Emotion: refers to unpleasant and disruptive feelings that can make people feel miserable and sad. Some examples of negative emotions include anger, fear, sadness, resentment, frustration, anxiety, and loneliness.

Positive Emotion: refers to pleasant or desirable responses to our environment or internal dialogue. Examples of positive emotions include happiness, joy, interest-excitement, amusement, gratitude, and inspiration.

Scaffolded Assignments: Scaffolded assignments are designed to gradually increase in complexity, helping learners build skills and confidence incrementally. This approach helps manage anxiety and fosters a sense of achievement, contributing to positive emotional engagement.

Self-Efficacy: is a person's belief in their ability to achieve a goal or complete a task. It is also a reflection of confidence in one's ability to control their behavior, motivation, and social environment.

Self-Regulation: Self-regulation is the ability of learners to manage their thoughts, emotions, and behaviors to achieve their learning goals. Instructional designers support self-regulation by including goal-setting, progress tracking, and reflective activities within the course design.

Supportive Learning Community: A supportive learning community is an online environment where learners feel connected and supported by their peers and instructors. This sense of community is created through interactive activities, discussions, and collaborative projects, enhancing emotional well-being and engagement.

Chapter 7
Enhancing Adult Lifelong Learning:
A Study of Social-Emotional Learning Theory

Jerine Jain Mathew
https://orcid.org/0009-0007-8215-8854
Christ University, India

Sridevi Nair
https://orcid.org/0000-0002-1529-4297
Christ University, India

ABSTRACT

This chapter explores the possibility of applying social-emotional learning theory to adult learning experiences and creating lifelong learners. Social-emotional learning (SEL) theory is a framework that emphasizes the use of tools and techniques focused on the development of social and emotional skills to improve overall well-being and success in life. It is based on the belief that individuals who possess these skills are better equipped to manage their emotions, build positive relationships, and make responsible decisions. In educational settings, SEL theory is often applied to help students develop these skills, which are seen as critical for academic success and personal well-being. It is implemented through explicit instruction, modeling, and practice, as well as through the creation of supportive learning environments. In recent years, there has been a growing interest in applying SEL theory to adult learners.

INTRODUCTION

Social-emotional learning (SEL) is an educational approach to improving the social and emotional skills of the learner. Sometimes referred to as social-emotional literacy or social and emotional learning, SEL proposes that in school curricula, social and emotional skills be granted the same level of importance as other commonly taught subjects like mathematics, science, and languages (Rosanbalm, 2021).

SEL focuses on teaching skills such as self-awareness, self-management, social awareness, relationship skills, and responsible decision-making (CASEL, 2023). These skills help students build positive relationships, make responsible decisions, manage their emotions effectively, and navigate social situations. One of the key principles of SEL is that these skills are teachable and can be developed over time. By integrating SEL into the curriculum, educators can create a supportive and inclusive learning environment that promotes the holistic development of students. SEL programs often include activities and lessons that help students identify and understand their emotions, develop empathy and perspective-taking skills, and learn effective communication and conflict resolution strategies.

Research has shown that SEL can have a positive impact on academic performance, behavior, and overall well-being (Durlak et al., 2011). Students who participate in SEL programs often show improved social skills and increased motivation. SEL also contributes to creating a positive climate, where students feel safe, supported, and engaged in their learning.

History of SEL

SEL as a theory originated in the 1960s and has undergone significant evolution since then. It began as an intervention at the Yale Child Study Center's Comer School Development Program (Close et al., 2023). The program addressed the pressing social and emotional needs of students in low-income African American communities, particularly those struggling in New Haven's elementary schools. The program's success, likely due in part to its proximity to Yale University, led to its expansion within the New Haven public school system (Elias et al., 1997).

Realizing the potential of the technique, researchers then proceeded to formalize the theory and develop a framework, defining core competencies and key concepts. The establishment of the Collaborative for Academic, Social, and Emotional Learning (CASEL) in 1994 and the publication of "Promoting Social and Emotional Learning: Guidelines for Educators" (Elias et al., 1997) served as landmark contributions, providing a framework for educators to integrate SEL practices into their classrooms. As of today, CASEL continues to be the leading voice on research and practice in the area of SEL.

SEL-related Competencies

As discussed in the previous section, social-emotional learning (SEL) is an educational approach that focuses on developing individuals' emotional intelligence, self-awareness, and interpersonal skills. The core components of SEL were defined in the CASEL 5 framework (CASEL, 2023), which suggests that any SEL technique will target the development of the five key competencies. The framework is presented in Figure 1:

Figure 1. CASEL 5 framework

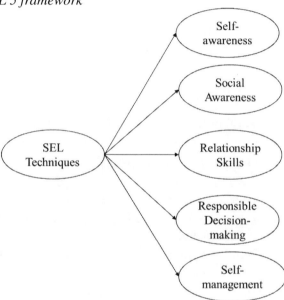

1. Self-awareness: The ability to accurately recognize one's emotions and thoughts and their influence on behavior. This includes recognizing strengths and limitations, having confidence, and possessing a growth mindset.
2. Social Awareness: The ability to understand the perspectives of and empathize with others, including those from diverse backgrounds and cultures. This also involves recognizing social cues and adapting to different social contexts.
3. Relationship Skills: The ability to establish and maintain healthy and rewarding relationships with diverse individuals and groups. This includes communicating clearly, listening actively, cooperating, resisting inappropriate social pressure, negotiating conflict constructively, and seeking help when needed.

4. Responsible Decision-making: The ability to make constructive choices about personal and social behavior based on ethical standards, safety concerns, and social norms. This includes considering the well-being of oneself and others, and recognizing when help is needed.
5. Self-management: The ability to regulate emotions, thoughts, and behaviors effectively in different situations. This includes managing stress, controlling impulses, motivating oneself, and setting and achieving goals.

The CASEL 5 framework provides a holistic approach to SEL, emphasizing the interconnected nature of these competencies and their importance in fostering positive social interactions, academic achievement, and overall well-being. It serves as a guide for educators, policymakers, and researchers to incorporate SEL into educational settings effectively.

SEL and Adult Learning

Social-emotional learning (SEL) is typically associated with K-12 education, but its principles are also highly relevant in adult learning contexts. SEL in adult learning refers to the process of developing social and emotional skills in adults to enhance their well-being, relationships, and effectiveness in various contexts (Zins et al., 2004). SEL in adult learning emphasizes skills such as self-awareness, self-management, social awareness, relationship skills, and responsible decision-making, similar to its focus in K-12 education.

SEL could have a significant impact on adult learning in many ways. Firstly, it would help adults develop the skills needed to navigate complex social and emotional situations in both personal and professional settings. Secondly, it would promote a positive learning environment by fostering empathy, understanding, and respect among adult learners. Finally, SEL in adult learning can lead to improved mental health, stress management, and overall well-being among adult learners (Schonert-Reichl et al., 2015).

Research has shown that SEL can have a positive impact on adult learners. For example, SEL programs for adult learners have been found to improve communication skills, conflict resolution abilities, and overall emotional intelligence (Paolini, 2020). These skills are particularly valuable in the workplace, where effective communication and relationship-building are essential.

Grossman (2019) also found that SEL techniques were effective in driving learning in adults. Improved self-awareness and self-regulation skills allows them to manage their emotions and behaviors more effectively, which in turn can lead to improved focus, concentration, and overall learning engagement.

Thus, given the theoretical basis and the research in the area of SEL, in this chapter the researchers explore the possibility of developing learners in organizations through the application of SEL techniques. To do so, the researchers first provide a definition and description of lifelong learners and their characteristics.

Lifelong Learners

Creating a culture of lifelong learning within organizations is crucial for their long-term success and competitiveness. Lifelong learners are primarily individuals committed to continuous personal and professional development and they bring several key benefits to organizations. Firstly, they are more adaptable to change, which is essential in today's rapidly evolving business landscape. Lifelong learners embrace new technologies, trends, and ways of working, helping organizations stay agile and responsive to market shifts (McGowan, 2020).

Secondly, lifelong learners are more innovative. Their curiosity and commitment to learning lead them to think creatively and generate fresh ideas. This innovative mindset can drive organizational growth and competitiveness by fostering a culture of innovation and continuous improvement (Tucker, 2002).

Moreover, lifelong learners tend to be more engaged and motivated in their work (Crow, 2006). They see learning as a way to grow and develop, which enhances their job satisfaction and commitment to the organization. This, in turn, can lead to higher employee retention rates and a more positive work environment (Kyndt et al., 2008).

Additionally, promoting lifelong learning can help organizations develop future leaders (Taşçı, 2019). Lifelong learners are more likely to take on leadership roles and excel in them. They have the skills and mindset to inspire and motivate others, driving positive change within the organization.

Overall, fostering a culture of lifelong learning is essential for organizations that want to thrive in today's dynamic business environment. It not only helps them stay competitive and innovative but also enhances employee engagement and retention. By investing in lifelong learning initiatives, organizations can cultivate a workforce that is agile, innovative, and committed to driving success.

In order to create lifelong learners, one must first understand the key characteristics of lifelong learners. Lifelong learning is a concept that has gained increasing importance in the context of today's rapidly changing world. Lifelong learners are individuals who engage in continuous learning and personal development throughout their lives. Lifelong learning refers to the ongoing, voluntary, and self-motivated pursuit of knowledge for personal or professional development. It is characterized by a commitment to learning as a lifelong process, rather than a discrete event or phase of life (Aspin & Chapman, 2007).

Several theoretical frameworks help explain the characteristics of lifelong learners. Andragogy, or adult learning theory, was proposed by Malcolm Knowles in 1980. Unlike pedagogy, which focuses on the teaching of children, andragogy is concerned with the education of adults. Knowles emphasized the self-directed nature of adult learning, suggesting that adults are motivated to learn by internal factors such as personal growth and fulfillment, rather than external rewards or pressures. Andragogy also emphasizes the importance of engaging learners as active participants in the learning process, recognizing that adults bring a wealth of life experiences and prior knowledge to their learning (Knowles, 1980). As such, adult learners benefit from learning activities that are relevant, experiential, and problem-centered, allowing them to apply new knowledge and skills to real-world situations.

Transformative learning theory, proposed by Jack Mezirow in 1991, suggests that learning is not just the acquisition of new information or skills, but a process of perspective transformation. According to Mezirow, transformative learning occurs when individuals critically reflect on their assumptions, beliefs, and ways of thinking, and are able to revise these perspectives based on new experiences (Mezirow, 1991). This process often involves a disorienting dilemma, where individuals encounter information or experiences that challenge their existing beliefs, leading to a period of reflection and reassessment. Through this process, individuals are able to develop more complex, nuanced, and inclusive perspectives, leading to personal growth and development.

Both andragogy and transformative learning theory have significant implications for the characteristics of lifelong learners. Lifelong learners, by nature, are self-directed and motivated by personal growth and development. They are open to new ideas and perspectives, and they are willing to critically reflect on their assumptions and beliefs. Lifelong learners also value experiential learning and problem-solving, seeking out opportunities to apply their learning to real-world situations. In this way, transformative learning theory and andragogy provide theoretical frameworks that help explain the key characteristics of lifelong learners and underscore the importance of lifelong learning in personal and professional development.

Given this theoretical base, the top five characteristics of lifelong learners are often considered to be:

- Curiosity: Lifelong learners possess a strong desire to learn and understand the world around them. They ask questions, seek out new information, and remain open-minded. Curiosity is often defined as a desire to know or learn something new. It is characterized by a sense of wonder, interest, and exploration (Loewenstein, 1994). Curiosity motivates individuals to seek out new experiences, ask questions, and engage with the world around them (Kashdan et al., 2009). According to the information gap theory, curiosity arises when there is a gap between what we want to know and what we do know (Loewenstein, 1994). The optimal arousal theory suggests that curiosity arises from a need to maintain an optimal level of stimulation or arousal (Berlyne, 1960).

Curiosity plays a crucial role in learning and development. It is a driving force behind exploration and discovery, leading to the acquisition of new knowledge and skills (Litman et al., 2005). In the workplace, curiosity is increasingly recognized as a valuable trait. Curious individuals are more likely to seek out new opportunities, take on challenges, and adapt to change (Kashdan et al., 2009). They are also more innovative, coming up with new ideas and solutions to problems (Litman et al., 2005).

- Self-motivation: Motivation plays a crucial role in learning, influencing the extent to which individuals engage with educational activities and persist in the face of challenges. They are driven by an internal desire to learn and grow, often setting goals and taking the initiative to achieve them. They are proactive in seeking out learning opportunities. Learner motivation refers to the internal processes that energize, direct, and sustain learning behavior (Pintrich, 2003). It is influenced by a variety of factors, including individual characteristics, social context, and task characteristics (Ryan & Deci, 2000). Motivation can be intrinsic, arising from within the individual, or extrinsic, arising from external rewards or pressures. According to Ryan and Deci (2000), intrinsic motivation is far stronger and longer lasting than motivation arising from extrinsic factors.
- Persistence: Lifelong learners are committed to their learning journey, even in the face of challenges or setbacks. They understand that learning is a process that requires effort and dedication. Persistence refers to the ability to continue striving towards a goal despite obstacles and challenges (Duckworth et al., 2007). It involves a combination of motivation, effort, and resilience, allowing individuals to sustain their efforts over time (Dweck, 2010). Persistence is often seen as a key predictor of academic success and achievement (Duckworth & Quinn, 2009).

One prominent theory in the area of persistence was developed by Carol Dweck (2006). The theory distinguishes between a growth mindset, where individuals believe their abilities can be developed through effort and perseverance, and a fixed mindset, where individuals believe their abilities are innate and unchangeable. Research has shown that individuals with a growth mindset are more likely to persist in the face of challenges (Dweck, 2006).

- Adaptability: Adaptability is the ability to adjust to new conditions and environments (Martin & Rubin, 1995). It involves being flexible, open-minded, and able to learn from experience (DeRue & Ashford, 2010). Adaptability allows individuals to thrive in unpredictable and changing circumstances, making it a valuable skill in both personal and professional contexts.

According to the dynamic skill theory, adaptability is a dynamic process that involves continuously updating one's skills and knowledge to meet the demands of a changing environment (Ritter & Schooler, 2001). Another theory, the cognitive-affective personality system (CAPS), suggests that adaptability is influenced by individuals' cognitive and affective processes, such as their beliefs, attitudes, and emotions (Mischel & Shoda, 1995). According to this theory, individuals who are able to regulate their thoughts and emotions are better able to adapt to new situations.

- Reflectiveness: Lifelong learners take time to reflect on their learning experiences, understanding what has been learned and how it can be applied in the future. They use this reflection to continually improve their learning process. Reflectiveness involves the ability to critically examine one's thoughts, feelings, and actions, and to learn from past experiences (Moon, 1999). It is characterized by a willingness to engage in self-reflection and self-examination, leading to greater self-awareness and personal growth (Schön, 1983). Reflectiveness is important in both academic and professional settings, as it allows individuals to learn from their experiences and improve their performance.

Several theories have been proposed to explain the nature of reflectiveness. Schön (1983) introduced the concepts of "reflection-in-action" and "reflection-on-action," suggesting that individuals can reflect both in the moment (while engaging in an activity) and after the fact (upon completion of an activity). Another theory, the dual-process theory of reflection, suggests that reflection involves two processes: reflection-on-experience, which involves thinking about past experiences and their implications, and reflection-in-experience, which involves thinking about current experiences and how they relate to past experiences (Kolb, 1984). According to this theory, both forms of reflection are important for learning and development.

The above given list reflects only some key characteristics of lifelong learners. The presence and development of these competencies and abilities will enable individuals to be open to learning and remain constantly in learning mode. These characteristics work together to create a mindset that values learning as a lifelong pursuit and enables individuals to adapt and thrive in an ever-changing world. In the next section, the researchers will explore the link between the CASEL 5 framework for SEL and the learner characteristics discussed in this section.

Relationship Between the CASEL 5 Framework and Lifelong Learners

The objective of this chapter was to explore if the application of SEL techniques could help create and support lifelong learners. Given an exploration of the concept of SEL, the history and evolution of the theory, an understanding of the SEL model proposed by CASEL (CASEL 5 framework), and a review of the concept and characteristics of lifelong learners, the last step is to understand how the CASEL 5 characteristics link to the characteristics of lifelong learners.

The five dimensions of the CASEL 5 framework are self-awareness, social awareness, relationship skills, responsible decision-making, and self-management. The five key characteristics of lifelong learners, as proposed by transformative learning theory and andragogy (or adult learning theory), include curiosity, self-motivation or learner motivation, persistence, adaptability, and reflectiveness. This chapter will now explore how each of the CASEL competencies can be harnessed to develop corresponding learner characteristics.

Firstly, the development of curiosity. Enhanced self-awareness will increase an individual's understanding of their interests and motivations. Additionally, drawing from information gap theory, curiosity arises from the gap in the knowledge we have and the knowledge we want (Loewenstein, 1994). Understanding and identifying this gap requires a strong sense of self-awareness.

Another way to promote or increase curiosity is through the development of empathy and the ability to understand another person's perspective. This can be achieved through increased social awareness. Encouraging collaboration and active listening can also expose individuals to new ideas and interests. Collaborations will be successful only through improved relationship skills that create a supportive environment nurturing curiosity (Rubin, 2009).

Additionally, encouraging learners to explore their interests, values, and goals can help them understand what motivates them. Self-awareness activities, such as reflecting on past successes and identifying personal strengths, can help learners connect their learning goals to their intrinsic motivations. Enhanced self-management skills, such as goal setting, time management, and perseverance, can help learners stay motivated in the face of challenges. Providing strategies for setting achievable goals and breaking them down into manageable tasks can increase motivation.

Another way that learner motivation can be improved is by developing better decision-making skills. Teaching responsible decision-making skills, such as weighing the risks and benefits of different options, can help learners make choices that align with their goals and values. Encouraging learners to take ownership of their learning and make choices that support their motivation can enhance their sense of agency and engagement. This also aligns with adult learning theory; adult learners are more motivated when they are able to take control of the learning process and allowed to make decisions regarding what, when, and how to learn (Knowles, 1980).

A concept closely linked to motivation is persistence. SEL can help individuals become more persistent by helping them understand their strengths and areas for growth, thereby enhancing their ability to persevere in the face of challenges. Self-awareness activities, such as reflection on past successes and setbacks, can help individuals develop a growth mindset and recognize that effort leads to improvement. Self-management skills help individuals regulate their emotions and maintain a positive attitude, enabling them to persevere in the face of challenges. Providing strategies for breaking tasks into smaller, more manageable steps can help individuals stay motivated and focused on their goals, while teaching effective communication and problem-solving skills can help individuals navigate challenges and maintain relationships that support their goals.

The fourth characteristic to explore is adaptability. Adaptability is a critical skill in navigating the complexities of the modern world. Self-awareness is foundational to adaptability, as it involves understanding one's emotions, thoughts, and behaviors. By developing self-awareness, individuals can recognize when they need to adapt and understand how their actions impact others and the situation (Durlak et al., 2011). Self-management skills, such as emotional regulation and impulse control, are also crucial for adaptability. These skills help individuals respond effectively to change and manage stress and challenges (Brackett et al., 2019). Similarly, social awareness allows individuals to navigate social situations efficiently and effectively, as well as understand and empathize with others, fostering adaptability in different social and learning environments.

Lastly is the learner characteristic of reflectiveness. According to Kolb (1984), reflectiveness is a crucial stage of any learning experience. Adults learn by reflecting on past experiences, thoughts, knowledge, and feelings. Like all the other characteristics, reflectiveness stems from a heightened level of self-awareness. By developing self-awareness, individuals can reflect on their actions and experiences, leading to greater self-understanding and personal growth (Roeser et al., 2012). Relationship skills help individuals communicate effectively, listen actively, and collaborate with others, enhancing their ability to reflect on their learning experiences and incorporate feedback for continuous improvement. Self-management skills help individuals regulate their emotions and behaviors, allowing them to pause and reflect before reacting impulsively. Additionally, responsible decision-making involves considering the consequences of one's actions on oneself and others. By developing this skill, individuals can make thoughtful and reflective decisions that align with their values and goals (Weissberg et al., 2015).

These competencies can be developed as a part of any training program. For instance, when aiming to cultivate curiosity in learners, you might integrate Inquiry-Based Learning (IBL) into a Project Management training module. Here, learners could be presented with a complex project scenario that lacks a straightforward solution. By encouraging them to ask probing questions, explore various approaches, and seek out additional information, you foster their sense of curiosity. This process not only engages learners in deeper thinking but also promotes a proactive exploration of innovative solutions beyond the information initially provided.

For developing collaborative skills, you could implement group problem-solving sessions within a Strategic Thinking program. In this context, small groups of learners might be tasked with addressing a strategic challenge, such as devising a market entry strategy for a new region. Each group member could assume a different organizational role—such as marketing, finance, or operations—requiring them to collaborate and integrate diverse perspectives into a cohesive strategy. This activity encourages active listening, negotiation, and teamwork, as participants must consider and harmonize various viewpoints to achieve a common goal.

The CASEL competencies provide a framework for developing the social and emotional skills that are essential for fostering a mindset of lifelong learning. By cultivating these competencies, individuals can enhance their curiosity, self-motivation, persistence, adaptability, and reflectiveness, leading to a more enriching and fulfilling lifelong learning journey. Figure 2 summarizes the proposed relationships between the CASEL5 framework and the learner characteristics.

Figure 2. Proposed conceptual model

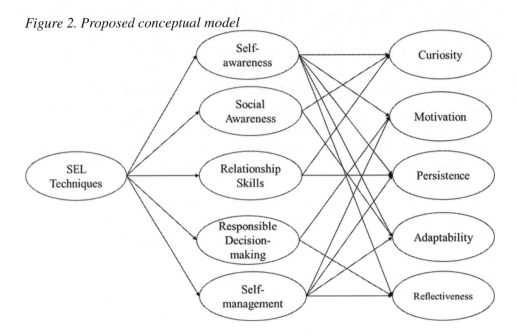

Scope for Future Research

Future research on social-emotional learning (SEL) and lifelong learners is vast and multifaceted, inviting exploration into various dimensions and impacts of SEL in adult education. Future studies could delve into the longitudinal effects of SEL programs on lifelong learning habits, investigating how SEL principles influence adult learners' continuous personal and professional development. Additionally, research could empirically examine the integration of SEL into various adult education contexts, such as workplace training, higher education, and community programs, to understand its effectiveness across different environments and populations. Comparative studies could also be conducted to assess the differential impacts of SEL on diverse demographic groups, including variations by age, gender, cultural background, and socio-economic status, to tailor interventions more effectively. Moreover, exploring the role of technology and digital platforms in delivering SEL to adult learners could provide insights into innovative methods for broader dissemination and engagement.

Implications

The current study explores the application of social-emotional learning (SEL) theory in the context of adult lifelong learning, particularly in the workplace. Traditionally, SEL has been primarily associated with academic and school education, focusing on the development of social and emotional skills in children and adolescents. However, the changing dynamics of the modern workplace, characterized by rapid technological advancements and increasing complexity, highlight the importance of emotional intelligence and social skills in adults as well, setting the ground for exploring SEL in the context of adult learning.

In today's business environment, where change is constant and upskilling is essential, organizations are recognizing the need to invest in the development of their employees' social and emotional competencies. While formal training sessions remain valuable, they can be resource-intensive and may not always be able to address the evolving needs of the workforce. Therefore, redesigning the training interventions to also focus on SEL competencies would greatly enhance the ability of the employees to continue their learning journey.

By fostering a culture of lifelong learning, organizations can empower their employees to adapt to change, collaborate effectively, and navigate complex challenges. This not only enhances individual performance and well-being but also contributes to the overall agility and productivity of the organization. One avenue to create lifelong learners, as per theory, is the use of social-emotional learning techniques. These techniques will develop key competencies in individuals, which will in turn facilitate the development of characteristics like curiosity, persistence, reflectiveness, adaptability, and motivation, i.e., the key characteristics of lifelong learners. Thus, based on the theoretical analysis, organizations must incorporate key SEL techniques and practices into their training and thereby facilitate the creation of lifelong learners, rather than focus on training on specific skills (CASEL, 2023).

Social-emotional learning (SEL) techniques are diverse and adaptable to various settings. One popular technique is mindfulness, which helps individuals develop self-awareness and emotional regulation by focusing on the present moment. Another technique is the use of social-emotional skill-building activities, such as role-playing and group discussions, to enhance social awareness and relationship skills. Additionally, incorporating reflective practices, like journaling or group reflections, can promote self-awareness and responsible decision-making. These techniques are often integrated into workplace activities to create a supportive learning environment that fosters SEL competencies, benefiting overall employee well-being and organization success.

CONCLUSION

In the current chapter, the researchers discussed social-emotional learning theory and its history, then covered the competencies associated with social-emotional learning theory, or SEL. These competencies were covered in the context of adult learners. The researchers aimed to understand whether SEL can be used to develop competencies that contribute to creating lifelong learners. This analysis is based on theoretical input and forms a basis for future research in the area. Hence, the propositions of this chapter need to be empirically tested to establish their validity.

Theoretically, SEL competencies – self-awareness, self-management, social awareness, relationship skills, and responsible decision-making – are crucial for adult learners in navigating the complexities of the modern workplace. By fostering these competencies, SEL can help adults become more adaptable, resilient, and self-driven in their learning journey.

The literature reviewed in the chapter suggests that incorporating SEL into adult learning can be highly effective. It can help create a culture of continuous learning and self-improvement, where individuals are motivated to seek out new knowledge and skills. This, in turn, can lead to a more agile and productive workforce, better equipped to meet the challenges of today's rapidly changing business landscape. Incorporating SEL into adult learning in the workplace is a promising approach to enhancing the capabilities of employees in a rapidly changing business landscape. By recognizing the value of emotional intelligence and social skills, organizations can create a more resilient and adaptable workforce, better equipped to thrive in today's dynamic work environment.

REFERENCES

Aspin, D. N., & Chapman, J. D. (Eds.). (2007). *Values education and lifelong learning: Principles, policies, programmes* (Vol. 10). Springer Science & Business Media. DOI: 10.1007/978-1-4020-6184-4_1

Berlyne, D. E. (1960). Conflict, arousal, and curiosity.

Brackett, M. A., Bailey, C. S., Hoffmann, J. D., & Simmons, D. N. (2019). RULER: A theory-driven, systemic approach to social, emotional, and academic learning. *Educational Psychologist*, 54(3), 144–161. DOI: 10.1080/00461520.2019.1614447

CASEL. (2023, March 3). What is the Casel Framework? CASEL. https://casel.org/fundamentals-of-sel/what-is-the-casel-framework/

Close, M., Killingly, C., Gaumer-Erickson, A. S., & Noonan, P. M. (2023). SEL and Its Origins. Inclusive Education for the 21st Century: Theory. *Policy & Practice*.

Crow, S. (2006). What motivates a lifelong learner? *School Libraries Worldwide*, 12(1), 22–34.

DeRue, D. S., & Ashford, S. J. (2010). Who will lead and who will follow? A social process of leadership identity construction in organizations. *Academy of Management Review*, 35(4), 627–647.

Duckworth, A. L., Peterson, C., Matthews, M. D., & Kelly, D. R. (2007). Grit: Perseverance and passion for long-term goals. *Journal of Personality and Social Psychology*, 92(6), 1087–1101. DOI: 10.1037/0022-3514.92.6.1087 PMID: 17547490

Duckworth, A. L., Quinn, P. D., & Seligman, M. E. (2009). Positive predictors of teacher effectiveness. *The Journal of Positive Psychology*, 4(6), 540–547. DOI: 10.1080/17439760903157232

Durlak, J. A., Weissberg, R. P., Dymnicki, A. B., Taylor, R. D., & Schellinger, K. B. (2011). The impact of enhancing students' social and emotional learning: A meta-analysis of school-based universal interventions. *Child Development*, 82(1), 405–432. DOI: 10.1111/j.1467-8624.2010.01564.x PMID: 21291449

Dweck, C. S. (2010). Mind-sets. *Principal Leadership*, 10(5), 26–29.

Elias, M., Zins, J. E., & Weissberg, R. P. (1997). *Promoting social and emotional learning: Guidelines for educators*. Ascd.

Grossman, J. (2021). Social-emotional learning and educator implementation.

Kashdan, T. B., Gallagher, M. W., Silvia, P. J., Winterstein, B. P., Breen, W. E., Terhar, D., & Steger, M. F. (2009). The curiosity and exploration inventory-II: Development, factor structure, and psychometrics. *Journal of Research in Personality*, 43(6), 987–998. DOI: 10.1016/j.jrp.2009.04.011 PMID: 20160913

Knowles, M. S. (1980). From pedagogy to andragogy. *Religious Education (Chicago, Ill.)*.

Kolb, D. A. (1984). *Experiential learning: Experience as the source of learning and development*. Prentice-Hall.

Kyndt, E., Dochy, F., Michielsen, M., & Moeyaert, B. (2009). Employee retention: Organisational and personal perspectives. *Vocations and Learning*, 2(3), 195–215. DOI: 10.1007/s12186-009-9024-7

Litman, J. (2005). Curiosity and the pleasures of learning: Wanting and liking new information. *Cognition and Emotion*, 19(6), 793–814. DOI: 10.1080/02699930541000101

Loewenstein, G. (1994). The psychology of curiosity: A review and reinterpretation. *Psychological Bulletin*, 116(1), 75–98. DOI: 10.1037/0033-2909.116.1.75

Martin, A. J., & Rubin, R. S. (1995). A new model of career success: A longitudinal study of U.S. Army officers. *Personnel Psychology*, 48(2), 397–421.

McGowan, H. E., & Shipley, C. (2020). *The adaptation advantage: Let go, learn fast, and thrive in the future of work*. John Wiley & Sons.

Mezirow, J. (1991). Transformative dimensions of adult learning. Jossey-Bass, 350 Sansome Street, San Francisco, CA 94104-1310.

Moon, J. A. (1999). *Reflection in learning and professional development: Theory and practice*. Routledge.

Paolini, A. C. (2020). Social Emotional Learning: Key to Career Readiness. *Anatolian Journal of Education*, 5(1), 125–134. DOI: 10.29333/aje.2020.5112a

Pintrich, P. R. (2003). A motivational science perspective on the role of student motivation in learning and teaching contexts. *Journal of Educational Psychology*, 95(4), 667–686. DOI: 10.1037/0022-0663.95.4.667

Ritter, F. E., & Schooler, L. J. (2001). The learning curve. International encyclopedia of the social and behavioral sciences, 13, 8602-8605.

Roeser, R. W., Skinner, E., Beers, J., & Jennings, P. A. (2012). Mindfulness training and teachers' professional development: An emerging area of research and practice. *Child Development Perspectives*, 6(2), 167–173. DOI: 10.1111/j.1750-8606.2012.00238.x

Rosanbalm, K. (2021). *Social and Emotional Learning during COVID-19 and Beyond: Why It Matters and How to Support It*. Hunt Institute.

Rubin, H. (2009). *Collaborative leadership: Developing effective partnerships for communities and schools*. Corwin Press.

Ryan, R. M., & Deci, E. L. (2000). Intrinsic and extrinsic motivations: Classic definitions and new directions. *Contemporary Educational Psychology*, 25(1), 54–67. DOI: 10.1006/ceps.1999.1020 PMID: 10620381

Schön, D. A. (1983). *The reflective practitioner: How professionals think in action*. Basic Books.

Schonert-Reichl, K. A., Oberle, E., Lawlor, M. S., Abbott, D., Thomson, K., Oberlander, T. F., & Diamond, A. (2015). Enhancing cognitive and social–emotional development through a simple-to-administer mindfulness-based school program for elementary school children: A randomized controlled trial. *Developmental Psychology*, 51(1), 52–66. DOI: 10.1037/a0038454 PMID: 25546595

Taşçı, G., & Titrek, O. (2019). Evaluation of lifelong learning centers in higher education: A sustainable leadership perspective. *Sustainability (Basel)*, 12(1), 22. DOI: 10.3390/su12010022

Tucker, R. B. (2002). *Driving growth through innovation: How leading firms are transforming their futures*. Berrett-Koehler Publishers.

Weissberg, R. P., Durlak, J. A., Domitrovich, C. E., & Gullotta, T. P. (2015). Social and emotional learning: Past, present, and future.

Zins, J. E. (Ed.). (2004). *Building academic success on social and emotional learning: What does the research say?* Teachers College Press.

Chapter 8
Into It, Out of It:
Emotions Can Prepare Us for and Prevent Us From Performance

Ian Gaither
https://orcid.org/0009-0004-7739-9408
Instructio Educational Services, Canada

ABSTRACT

Emotional states can have a profound influence on learning and performance by facilitating or obstructing access to skills and knowledge. At one end of the emotional spectrum, Ideal Performance States (IPS) – achieved through optimal physiological and psychological arousal and self-efficacy – enable performers to fully access their innate and trained skills. At the opposite end, startling or surprising events can trigger "mental upset," that is, cognitive paralysis, loss of situational awareness, and ultimately loss of judgment. Domains such as sports psychology, aviation, and medicine have developed various tools and techniques to help performers attain and maintain the mental and emotional state they need to perform, supporting self-efficacy, resilience, and adaptability. Increasingly available immersive technologies such as virtual reality offer unprecedented access to opportunities to develop these and many other emotional skills, such as the ability to increase or decrease emotional responses to events in the outside world or even change how one experiences physical pain.

INTRODUCTION

"I'm just not in the zone" said the astronaut after catastrophically crashing the 15-meter Canadarm robot into the International Space Station. As a young instructional designer monitoring a simulated training session at the Canadian Space Agency,

DOI: 10.4018/979-8-3693-2663-3.ch008

this was the first time I had heard about this "zone." In school, we'd learned about SKAs – skills, knowledge and attitudes – as the essential ingredients of performance. However, as the astronaut, an ex-fighter pilot, later explained, these ingredients alone could not predict great performance. Rather, how a performer feels as they perform – their "affect" – is as important as the other factors. My notebook from that period reads "SKA+A?"

Throughout a career in simulation-based training, I've come to realize that while simulations attempt to recreate a realistic external task environment, they are most powerful when they can also allow learners to experience and practice regulation of their internal, emotional state, and in doing so, be better able to apply their skills, knowledge, and attitudes.

This chapter examines the deep connection between emotional states, learning, and performance. While there is substantial research in this area, it is not always obvious to practitioners how to incorporate emotions into instructional design projects. As such, this chapter attempts to explore how various high-stakes domains such as sport, aviation, and medicine are currently moving beyond the classic SKAs, and incorporating affective states into their training programs to optimize performance.

This chapter is divided into three sections:

- **"Into it"** explores how emotions can be used to prepare us for performance as well as techniques that help performers discover and get into what is called an "Ideal Performance State."
- **"Out of it"** reviews states of emotional and mental upset caused by the "fight or flight" response and elements of curricula that aim to overcome this dysfunctional state.
- **"Real feelings virtually generated"** describes ways in which immersive technologies are being used to develop appropriate emotional responses that can be applied to the real world.

Into It: The Ideal Performance State

"When I'm in the zone, everything just flows. I'm not thinking. My mind and body are doing what I've trained them to do. Every stroke and every lap has been rehearsed, not only in the pool but during the dozens of times I have visualized the race. I have already rehearsed working through all the feelings I might have during the race, and this mental preparation gives me great confidence before I hit the water." (M. Brown, personal communication, 2024).

Before the 1980's an athlete's state of mind was considered to be, at best, a distraction from their physical readiness to perform (Smith & Thelen, 2003). Since then, elite athletes have become aware of and, increasingly, trained to get "in the zone" before competition. This "Ideal Performance State" (Loehr, 1983) is characterized by:

- Focused attention
- Absence of fear
- Confidence
- A sense of control
- An enhanced sense of enjoyment and immersion in the activity at hand.

This state, which overlaps with the popular concept of being in a "flow" state (Csikszentmihalyi, 1990) occurs when the individual is sufficiently alert and engaged to maximize focus, energy, and motivation for the task at hand.

Ideal Performance State as Optimal Level of Arousal

The Ideal Performance State is found on a spectrum of physiological and psychological arousal (Yerkes, et al., 1908). It occurs within 30 and 60 percent of maximum, about half-way between sleep and panic.

Figure 1. Optimal level of arousal and task performance

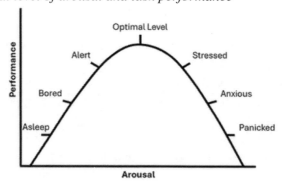

Performance on either side of the *optimal level* drops off, into ever-lower levels of engagement on the left side and decreasing levels of self-control and awareness on the right side.

Anyone who has learned to drive knows this spectrum of feelings, starting with high anxiety the first time you accelerate and mounting to near-panic while merging onto a busy highway. With exposure and practice, skill becomes more automatic, diminishing the level of attention needed to drive. Eventually, during long-uneventful drives or traffic jams, alertness drops and we even risk falling asleep at the wheel. Of course, the safest state is a range in the middle of the chart: the optimal level.

This level of excitement relates to how well someone can handle the task they are performing or the environment they are managing. Beyond the skills and knowledge, they bring to the task at hand, their attitudes and beliefs about themselves play a critical role that can either multiply or divide their capability.

Ideal Performance State as Exercise of Perceived Self-efficacy

The concept of *perceived self-efficacy* (Bandura, 1977) provides another lens on the Ideal Performance State. Perceived self-efficacy is the expectation individuals have that their efforts will produce the desired outcomes. When coupled with appropriate skills and knowledge, this "I can and will do it" attitude has been correlated with higher levels of performance.

The behaviors and characteristics of people with high self-efficacy read like a recipe for the Ideal Performance State.

Generally, people with high self-efficacy are:

- **Achievement-oriented**: They set high goals for themselves and commit to achieving them, resulting in higher levels of achievement.
- **Motivated**: Their sense of purpose motivates them to take on challenging tasks.
- **Confident**: They believe that they have or can develop the ability to complete tasks and achieve goals.
- **Resilient**: They persist or even increase effort in the face of difficulties or obstacles. Setbacks are viewed as opportunities for learning rather than insurmountable barriers.
- **Able to manage stress:** They experience lower levels of stress and anxiety and feel more capable of handling demanding situations.

Some amount of an individual's self-efficacy may be innate and genetically based (Cloninger et al., 2019). However, it seems to be mostly formed through interactions with a person's environment, that is, social modeling, life-experiences, and education (Bandura, 1977). The results of this natural development process are reflected in a person's core character – how they see themselves and interact with the world. Self-efficacy can also be developed deliberately, just as physical skills are – through practice. When developed, the cognitive behaviors related to self-efficacy can be invoked during learning or performance as part of a pre-performance warm up, be it for sport, surgery, piloting an airliner, or teaching a class. Indeed, almost any performance can be enhanced when the performer has learned how to get "in the zone."

Getting Into the Zone

Bandura's ingredients for this "recipe for success'" are presented below, mapped to techniques that sports psychologists, coaches, mentors, and athletes use to help a performer learn to get in the zone reliably:

Table 1. Exercising self-efficacy

Ingredients of Self-efficacy	Techniques Employed to Get Into the Zone
Vicarious Experiences Seeing others (especially people similar to us) achieve things helps us believe that we can accomplish similar things.	Observe and model techniques and strategies from experienced performers, role models, peers. Examples: goalies watching highlight reels of their favorite goalies.
Verbal Persuasion Encouragement from others can convince us to put in more effort than we might otherwise do.	Provide motivational feedback. Having people that we trust believe in us can provide great feelings of support. Examples: recalling reasons why one wanted to do the sport or activity and past successes.
Self-talk Inner dialogue before and during performance expresses and confirms beliefs.	Become aware of default inner dialogue. Example: discovering and using messages that elicit the desired emotional response.
Emotional and Physical States Positive mood states enhance efficacy. Excessive stress diminishes performance.	Monitor and manage stress and distractions with stress management techniques. Examples: breathing, self-monitoring, removing distractions.

continued on following page

Table 1. Continued

Ingredients of Self-efficacy	Techniques Employed to Get Into the Zone
Mastery Experiences Past successes provide proof in our ability to be successful. This is especially true when past successes were the result of perseverance and overcoming obstacles. "If I can do that, I can probably do this too."	Recall/visualize aspects of past successes and the related feelings and mindsets before performance. Build a history of success. Examples: providing opportunities for success during an activity like batting practice can help build more resilience as the level of challenge increases. Gradual challenge-ramps build confidence.
Imagined Experiences Visualizing successful task performance and recounting positive messages to oneself can increase confidence.	Visualize successful outcomes and work through various situations and strategies to enhance mental preparation. Examples: a swimmer mentally rehearsing a race in real time, applying motivational and affirmational self-talk to boost confidence and focus.

Many of the practices listed above are reflected in the previous quote from Canadian Olympic swimmer Michael Brown. Just as Mike spent hours in the pool exercising physical skills, he also engaged in deliberate affective exercise – simulating and rehearsing the feelings he wanted to experience during performance. This practice aligns with the neuroplasticity principle that "neurons that fire together, wire together." (Bebb, 1949) That is, by repeatedly inducing specific emotional states during training, Brown strengthened the neural pathways associated with those emotions, enhancing his ability to access optimal emotional states during actual performance.

Like a physical skill, the Ideal Performance State can be developed through training and rehearsal. But is that state the same for everyone?

IZOF: Individual Zone of Optimal Functioning

To reliably get in the zone, one must first know where to find it. Building on the Ideal Performance State concept, the Individual Zone of Optimal Functioning theory (Hanin, 1994) zooms in on the "optimal level" of arousal and affirms that individuals find their zone between 30-60% of the maximum level of physical and emotional anxiety.

Figure 2. Individual zone of optimal functioning

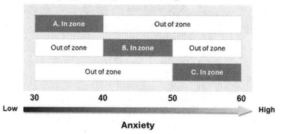

Further research (Hanin, 2000) found that a variety of factors can influence where individuals find the zone. For instance:

- Novice performers benefit from lower levels of arousal while they build confidence.
- Intermediate performers develop better coping mechanisms when exposed to progressively higher levels of arousal.
- Experts often find their focus, energy, and motivation are maximized under higher levels of arousal.
- Simple tasks are more easily performed at higher levels of arousal than complex decision-making tasks.

Individual preferences can also play a significant role in where the zone is found. Michael Jordan was renowned for trying to be as relaxed as possible before a game, chatting and joking around with people right before stepping on the court (Zone A). By contrast, Canadian Olympic swimmer Michael Brown speaks of a 3-hour pre-race ritual that involved an increasing narrowing of vision and thoughts, using headphones to block out the world as he prepared his mind and body to race (Zone B).

To discover what works for them, athletes can be taught to document factors that support or detract from their best state, such as rest and recovery, nutrition and hydration, physical preparation, and mental preparation (Wesch, 2022).

Table 2. Adapted from "Identify Your Ideal Performance State"

IPS FACTORS	What works	What doesn't work
Rest and Recovery		
Nutrition and Hydration		
Physical Preparation		
Mental Preparation		
Other Factors		

(Wesch, 2022)

This self-reflective practice encourages athletes to take responsibility for their physical, mental, and emotional readiness. Through experimentation and collaboration during training, they discover and begin to craft personalized recipes or warm-up routines that will help them achieve their most ready and able state on game day.

Imagining into Reality

This chapter started with a quote from an Olympic athlete describing his vivid visualization and how it allowed him to race on a kind of autopilot, where there were no surprising feelings or sensations. It turns out the practice of creating a mental simulation of a situation triggers the same parts of the brain to light up as when the actual activity is being performed (Jeannerod, 1994). A groundbreaking study in neuroplasticity (Christakou et al., 2019) showed that after ceasing physical practice of a piece of complex music, pianists slowly lost their ability to perform it at a professional level. Surprisingly, repeated, vivid, real-time mental rehearsal was shown to revive the skill and even result in the player having a higher level of skill than when they stopped playing. Canadian virtuoso pianist Glenn Gould reported that he spent more time rehearsing pieces in his mind. This approach allowed him to deeply internalize the music, resulting in the high precision and unique emotional depth in his performances (Mesaros, 2008).

These studies and anecdotes explain why visualization techniques have been an integral part of sports training, as they indicate that practice and rehearsal are not limited only to real world constraints but can be accessed by closing the eyes and immersing oneself in a simulated experience.

Canadian Olympic swimmer Michael Brown recalls practicing for his 200-meter swim using mental simulation that recreated every aspect of the race: hearing the starting gun, diving in, breathing and counting strokes just as he would in a real race, all the time maintaining the mindset and emotional posture that he found to be his "zone." These visualizations also allow athletes to play out different scenarios to develop a set of adaptive strategies that can be employed under different circumstances.

Representative affective learning practice design (Hedrick et al., 2015) suggests that practice and rehearsal are incomplete if they only recreate the application of knowledge and skills but not the affective dimension of the real tasks. That is, to make performance reliable, one needs to practice getting into the affective state that one wants to have on game day.

Of all of the techniques employed by athletes to evoke feelings, few are as seemingly universal and powerful as music.

Soundtrack for Success

We all intuitively know how music can set or alter a mood, whether it is relaxing dinner music or party music intended to get people dancing. Research in sports physiology/psychology has shown that music can manipulate psychological and psychophysical states in ways that can have significant impact on performance in competitive sport (Bishop et al., 2009). Here are some examples:

- MRI studies showed that stimulating music with upbeat tempos can create aroused emotional states and can even decrease reaction time. (Bishop et al., 2009). When the rhythm of the music is in time with the activity, the music has performance enhancing effects such as reducing the perceived effort and reducing energy expenditure (Terry et al., 2012). This effect is theorized to work by shifting mental focus away from internal physical signals of exertion, creating an external attentional focus and increased efficiency of movement, as might happen when one is dancing to music with a strong beat.
- Lyrical content of songs has been found to direct attention to the activity and skill by affirming the situation at hand in ways that create positive mental imagery and self-talk (Mesagno, et al., 2009). For instance, "Lose Yourself" by Eminem is often cited as a perfect "pump-up tune" as it conveys a message about giving yourself over to the effort required to succeed. This potential for "semantic resonance" between song and activity can enhance the sense of commitment to an activity.
- Melody and harmony have been shown to be able to evoke strong emotional responses (Juslin, et. al., 2008). Consider how, for certain people, the rousing melody of "Chariots of Fire" may evoke sentiments of honor, pride, and resilience.

Despite these findings, the wide variety of preferences for music ensure that no one piece can reliably create the same response in everyone who listens to it. Sports psychologists expend effort to match individuals or teams with music that will create the appropriate psychophysical states required to modify energy and focus.

Hockey Canada goal-tender coach Chris Chisamore would produce pre-game pump-up music videos for teams, combining highlights of past games with humor, images of camaraderie, and upbeat rock music. Eventually, various goalies would approach Chris with requests to substitute the music with music they had chosen to personalize and amplify the effect of these pre-game packaged visualizations.

Sports psychologist Costas Karageorghis went so far as to work with a music producer to craft a bespoke piece of music to support Dai Green's training for the 400-meter hurdle in the 2020 Olympics (Gray, 2016). By listening to and discussing music that moved Dai, Karageorghis and the producer teased out the elements such as melodic themes, sound textures, and short lyrical content that they thought would evoke a strong response. Then, with Dai's participation, the producer created a custom piece of music that Dai was able to use as a powerful stimulant for his pre-game warm-up, bolstering many personal-best times leading up to the Olympics. While injuries kept Dai from the Olympic podium, the strategic use of personalized music to enhance mood, attention, and performance was established as a powerful performance enhancing tool – essentially, a soundtrack for success.

The Ideal Performance State is as powerful as it is personal. While some common foundations exist (i.e., exercising self-efficacy), each individual will find their zone and the path to get there is as unique as they are.

Thinking Out Loud: Integrating the Ideal Performance State

These concepts have proven to have impact in the domain of sports training and performance but have great applicability far beyond sport. One could imagine that enhanced performance states could increase the quality of task execution across a wide variety of domains, both personal and professional.

The following questions could be asked to explore how these concepts might be applied in a learning and performance context:

Table 3. Questions to explore application of concepts

What is the typical affective state of an expert performer during performance?	During the analysis phase, it could be helpful to understand not only the skills, knowledge, and attitudes that experts apply, but also what they believe to be an ideal state for the task at hand, along with any tricks they may have developed to help them get there. These, in turn, may be used to provide learners with cues that help them attempt to reach similar states.
What types of feelings could a learner experience before and during learning and performance?	During the analysis phase, it could be helpful to discover what affective states learners typically experience as they acquire new skills and how these change over time. Does the topic instill terror? Boredom? Curiosity? This information might identify areas of performance that could benefit from self-efficacy support.
How can learning activities be scaffolded to help learners stay in the zone?	During design, ensure that the challenge curve allows new learners to progressively build mastery and confidence while pushing more experienced learners to stretch their skills. Self-efficacy measures, like those outlined in Figure 1, might help learners build beliefs and habits that support performance.
How can learners be encouraged to discover their own Ideal Performance State?	Figure 3 provided an example of a worksheet that can be used during training to help people discover the factors that helped them achieve their Ideal Performance State. Where appropriate, similar measures could be taken to help learners begin to attend to and take responsibility for managing their state.

Ideal states aren't always available

The Ideal Performance State has been shown to be a unique psychological state that supports peak performance. However, performance psychologists have observed athletes struggling to get into an emotional state and even experience anxiety about not being in a perfect state (Dymond, 2014). As such, they advocate for an approach which acknowledges the unpredictability of human emotions and emphasizes the importance of being able to manage less-than-ideal conditions to maintain or quickly regain performance levels in the face of adversity.

Out of It: Mental Upset

"The difference between theory and practice is that in theory, there is no difference." (Brewster, 1882)

I smelled the smoke a moment before the fire alarm went off. Running back to my office, I found that the dollar store candle I had burning on my desk had disintegrated and flames were consuming a pile of newspapers and threatening the curtains. Grabbing the fire extinguisher, I pointed and squeezed the handle, to no effect. I screamed for help. A neighbor, who had come to investigate, yelled over the alarm, "Did you pull out the pin?"

Later, while airing out the apartment, we reflected on the fact that in the heat of the moment, I – who theoretically knew how to use an extinguisher – could not recall one of the three simple steps required to use it in the face of a real fire. In essence, *I knew how to use it, just not how to use it in a panic.* Neuroscience can help us understand how panic can undermine performance.

Startle and Surprise

The well-known "fight or flight" response has helped all living creatures protect themselves from the dangers of the natural world. The neurological underpinning of this response is a testament to nature's genius. A sudden stimulus is processed via two independent brain pathways simultaneously (LeDoux, 1997). The first "quick and dirty" pathway relays the signal to the amygdala (the "emotion center" of the brain that sits atop of the brain stem), triggering a "danger" response in the autonomic nervous system. An involuntary "startle" reaction such as blinking, jerking, or jumping increases muscle tension and adrenaline secretion, kick-starting the body to fight or flee (Landis, Hunt, 1939). A second pathway directs the signal to the neocortex (new brain) for deeper processing and analysis to determine if the threat is real and if immediate response is required. For example, after hearing a loud sound, you might ask yourself, "Was that a balloon bursting or a gunshot?"

While a startle is an involuntary physiological response to a sudden stimulus, surprise is a state of cognitive dissonance arising from differences between expectations and perceptions (Horstmann, 2006). Surprises can be triggered by unexpected or contradictory information, such as a pilot noticing that the information on their flight displays does not agree. When accompanied with a fear response, surprise triggers many of the same physiological effects as startle, along with "attentional tunneling" as the neocortex tries to resolve the disparity between expected and actual reality.

A search of NASA's Aviation Safety Reporting System (NASA, 2024), which is a voluntary, anonymous database for pilots to report safety-related information, reveals that events that startle or surprise are not uncommon. Examples include:

- Impacts of birds on windscreen or engine
- Sudden turbulence
- Alarms or warning systems being triggered
- Spotting objects in front of aircraft
- Contradictory information on flight displays
- Uncommanded changes to the aircraft speed, pitch, or bank angle

While the circuitry of the startle and surprise response evolved to respond quickly to simple situations requiring fight or flight, the human environment requires more complex responses. This mismatch of biological programming to performance demands can collude to create maladaptive responses that impair performance when it is needed most.

Effects of Startle and Surprise

A study by the European Union Aviation Safety Agency (EASA, 2015) revealed that over 70% of aviation accidents were exacerbated by the results of startle and surprise. That is, if the effects of startle and surprise had been better managed, the impact of these accidents could have been reduced.

The negative effects include:

- When **startled**:
  - Disruption of fine-motor control due to the rapid engagement of the motor system causing jerking, jumping, blinking, or shouting. (Valls-Solé et al., 1999)
  - Inability to continue the physical or mental activity they were previously doing for 100ms to 10 seconds, depending on the severity of startle.
- When **surprised**:
  - Loss of situational awareness due to attentional tunneling: locking on to an aspect of the environment (such as a specific flight instrument) and locking out other information. (EASA, 2015)
- When **startled and/or surprised**:
  - Impairment of cognitive functions such as memory-retrieval and decision-making abilities (Hermans et al., 2014) due to sudden release of cortisol, causing stress, fear, or anger.
  - Negative self-talk ("I messed up") that can further degrade cognitive functions.
  - Cognitive paralysis, also known as "freezing," "choking," or unstructured hyper-vigilance, can occur when emotions overrule all cognitive processes in the face of perceived danger (EASA, 2015).

Obviously, none of these maladaptive reactions are desirable for someone performing a critical task and charged with safe-keeping other people's lives.

Self-efficacy Affects Response

"Surprise intensifies any emotion connected to the event that causes the surprise, whether positive or negative." (European Union Aviation Safety Agency, 2015)

The degree to which a particular startle or surprise can trigger emotional responses can be related to the individual's past associations and beliefs about the trigger (EASA, 2015). For instance, a pilot who struggled with recovery from aircraft "stalls" (unintentional loss of lift) in training may experience a more significant fear response when they hear the audible stall warning in flight, as they have come to associate this sound with a situation for which their self-efficacy is low. This, in turn, can increase their anxiety, increase negative self-talk ("I'm gonna blow it"), and enhance the negative cognitive effects (EASA, 2015). Looking back at Figure 1, which portrays the Ideal Performance State as an optimal level of arousal, one might imagine that a negative internal response adds to the level of excitement which pushes the person's state further to the right side of the graph where anxiety and panic occur.

Domain expertise doesn't always correlate to judgment

Flight simulation studies in which pilots were challenged to respond to surprising aeronautical events (Kochan, 2005) proved that high levels of knowledge and experience did not always correspond to high levels of judgment (i.e., the ability to choose the best course of action). In many cases, people with higher levels of judgment outperformed colleagues with much higher levels of experience.

The EASA report proposes that domain experts, who may feel pressure to be right, may have trouble accepting that there is something out of their control or understanding. As such, they may be delayed in taking appropriate actions.

While commercial aviation training systems incorporate realistic simulations, training for abnormal situations or emergencies is, to a great degree, determined by regulatory requirements, bounded by the economics of training schedules and costs, and, therefore, unlike reality, premeditated and predictable. As such, it remains challenging to recreate the authentic emotional states that might be felt, and need to be managed, after a real startle or surprise.

The EASA report suggests that this training gap should be addressed with training interventions that build meta-cognitive skills, emotional resilience, and adaptability so that pilots can continue to exercise good judgment in a crisis.

Recommendations for Training

"Between stimulus and response there is a space. In that space is our power to choose our response. In our response lies our growth and our freedom." (Frankl, 2006)

Figure 4. Adaptive skills separate stimulus and response

The stimuli that create startle and surprise cannot always be prevented. However, with training, the response to these stimuli can be managed. As such, EASA's experimental startle and surprise training program aims to help pilots apply stress management and meta-cognitive strategies to prevent negative psychological and physiological responses from clouding their judgment. By using the Relax>Observe>Confirm model, pilots are able to regain their composure and awareness under simulated adverse conditions.

Here is the routine that pilots are taught to follow immediately upon being startled and/or surprised:

- **Relax**: Upon recognition of a startle or surprise response, the pilots are trained to take some physical action, such as pushing themselves into the back of their seats, as a cue to use stress-management techniques such as structured breathing. In the multi-crew environment, pilots are encouraged to check on their co-pilot by saying their name or, if need be, touching the co-pilot to help them regain their composure.
- **Observe**: As attentional tunneling or "lock on/lock out" is a great threat during stressful events, this step reminds pilots to scan their environment so that they don't exclude important information that may be pertinent to the situation. Many accidents have occurred when attention was singularly focused on a single issue, to the exclusion of the basic operation of the aircraft.
- **Confirm**: As a mental model of the situation is created, pilots confirm their assumptions, actively avoid cognitive bias, and apply their critical thinking and problem-solving skills.

These steps are intended to help pilots create and maintain a space between stimulus and response, a space from which they can continue to operate the plane while applying other structured practices such as threat and error management and aeronautical decision-making, to ensure a safe outcome. Naturally, this model applies to situations that afford the crew some time to think, and may only be applicable after rapid, almost automated steps are carried out to prevent imminent disaster.

The experimental curriculum provides instruction on the startle and surprise phenomenon, along with key concepts such as meta-cognition and adaptive skills. Like an athlete learning to find their own Ideal Performance State, the pilots are instructed to track and evaluate their own responses to a number of simulated surprise events. By reflecting on their own responses, they begin to develop a repertoire of ways to enact the Relax>Observe>Confirm technique, adapted to the needs of the situation.

Another startle and surprise curriculum based on EASA's experiment (Oaster et al., 2022) emphasizes a mentorship relationship with trainees to:

- Normalize and destigmatize "freezing," so that learners are more willing to admit to themselves when they have been startled or surprised
- Support the learner's self-efficacy by showing they are invested in their success and reinforcing useful beliefs, opinions, and attitudes
- Offer modeling techniques that allow learners to adapt to an adverse situation
- Help learners develop mental models of how to respond to these situations

In both curricula, students practice adaptive techniques in simulated flight scenarios. Given the setting and time constraints, participants were expecting a startle or surprise during training, such as a bird strike or a loss of a major system. Despite this expectation, they were able to create a habit of applying these meta-cognitive techniques over and over, with the expectation that they would become part of the operational routine, just like pulling out an emergency checklist and, by doing so, allowing them to avoid cognitive paralysis or attentional tunneling.

Of course, simulations are expensive, time-consuming, time-limited, and, therefore, don't provide high realism in which people can experience the real, visceral panic that might happen in real life. A deeper level of immersion is required for that.

Knowing It (in the) Cold

"I must not fear. Fear is the mind-killer. Fear is the little-death that brings total obliteration. I will face my fear. I will permit it to pass over me and through me. And when it has gone past I will turn the inner eye to see its path. Where the fear has gone there will be nothing. Only I will remain." Herbert (1978)

The ability to respond under stress is useful across various aspects of life, both personal and professional. To test this response, physiological and psychological researchers use what is called a "cold pressor test." Participants submerge their hand or arm into ice-water, allowing researchers to measure the physical and mental pressure that subjects experience.

Everyone who has tried to swim in very cold water knows that it can trigger an autonomic response similar to panic as pulse spikes and hyperventilation and brain chemistry can create chaotic, fearful feelings. Along with some physiological aspects related to cold exposure, it seems to produce the "flight" part of the "fight or flight" response.

And yet, in recent years, "ice-plunges", once known mainly as a quirk of Scandinavian culture, have become a mainstream activity, popularized and celebrated for various health benefits, such as enhancing circulation and mood due to dopamine release. As an effective way to introduce stress, it also provides an effective way to learn about mental resilience. Cold water training has long been used in military training for members of elite units who need to have the mental and physical resilience to avoid panic in high-stress situations.

Studies using the induced stress of the "cold pressor test" have shown that after three exposures to icy water, the physiological markers of stress (blood pressure, heart rate, and perceived stress levels) begin to decrease and can even end up lower than a control group that wasn't exposed to the cold water (Minkley et al. 2014). In other words, an overwhelming, seemingly automatic stress response can, with exposure, be improved and even enhance a person's ability to self-regulate and modify their response to the attack on the senses. Further studies found a strong relationship between people who had experienced serious and stressful negative life events and their stress response to the cold pressor test, suggesting that exposure to adversity in one context might contribute to improved adaptive responses and resilience in other contexts (Seery et al. 2010). Indeed, cold-water swimmers often report that skills learned from cold-water exposure translate to better emotional resilience in the rest of their lives. Together, these studies suggest a kind of "do or die" mechanism, whereby people are forced, through experience, to create adaptive responses that lead them to have greater general adaptive skills.

How do these theories translate into practice when one is up to their neck in icy water? Cold-water dippers describe a wide array of personal habits or scripts that they use to push past the physical and psychological suffering. Examples include structured breathing, gaze fixing, imagining oneself from outside, counting, mantras, and other tricks borrowed from fields such as mindfulness and meditation.

By having a repertoire of ingrained, scripted habits, and a belief in one's ability to adapt to a stressful event, one can get beyond panic and regain their ability to think and act rationally.

Thinking Out Loud: Integrating Lessons from Startle and Surprise Research

Meta-cognitive adaptive skills are applicable to every domain which might involve performance under pressure. The following questions could be asked to explore how these concepts might be applied in a learning and performance context:

Table 4. Questions to explore applications of concepts

What types of surprises could interrupt a performer from being able to apply their skills and knowledge?	During the analysis phase, it could be valuable to understand what kinds of surprising events performers might encounter on the job and how these can detract from their application of their skills and knowledge.
	This may provide ideas for scenarios and techniques that can be used to help learners adapt to unforeseen circumstances.
How is the performer likely to respond to a surprise?	During analysis and evaluation, it could be valuable to understand what typical maladaptive responses to surprises look like. Do learners typically over-fixate on small details? Do they flail around? Do they acknowledge problems? Understanding these potential responses may help prepare the learners to mitigate them.
How can the learning environment allow for realistic practice that incorporates the feelings that might be experienced during performance?	During analysis and design, discovering and incorporating factors that increase the opportunity to experience realistic emotions will increase the chance of adaptive responses being developed during training.
How can we normalize being destabilized?	During conduct of training, de-stigmatizing maladaptive responses may help prevent learners and performers from hiding their state.
What kind of stress-management, meta-cognitive skills, or adaptive strategies would help learners be able to apply their knowledge and skill in adverse situations?	When appropriate, including strategies to overcome stressful situations can help ensure performers can access their knowledge and skill under adverse conditions.

The world of modeling and simulation have traditionally striven to recreate reality, or enough of it to enable authentic practice, allowing practitioners to work through and learn to react to various scenarios. Aircraft simulators provide learners with a real cockpit surrounded by a 180-degree movie theater on top of a set of hydraulic jacks that recreate the feelings of pitch, yaw, roll, and acceleration. While this represents the high-end of the simulation spectrum, the spectrum has remained expensive to create, operate and, therefore, hard to access. As such, access to opportunities for authentic practice in realistic conditions has remained limited. Until now.

REAL FEELINGS, VIRTUALLY GENERATED

"Learning is experience. Everything else is just information." (Attributed to Einstein, n.d.)

The Royal Canadian Navy officer pulls the VR headset off her face and proclaims: "I am so angry at the crew. Someone should have spoken up earlier…and louder!". She has just spent 10 minutes aboard a large ship, monitoring instruments and listening to crew-dialogue while speeding towards a fatal collision with a freight ship. As the co-designer of this historical re-creation, I was relieved that the exercise achieved the desired result: an emotional gut-punch. Several sailors noted that while they had studied this nautical disaster in government reports and videos, they had never *felt* it before. In this case, the feelings evoked were awe at the failures of decision-making and communication. Our working assumption was that by immersing sailors in the experience of the accident, strong emotions would bolster attitudes about maintaining safe practices.

Outside Looking In vs. Inside Looking Around

Movies, videos, and books are essentially all rectangles that we, usually seated, look into in order to have an experience. As such, we are always outside these experiences, which are framed by the theater, living room, or office we are in. Full immersion in a virtual environment such as a virtual reality (VR) headset means being surrounded by that environment rather than looking into it. It means being completely isolated from the sights and sounds of the real world.

Figure 5. Looking into experiences vs. immersion inside experiences

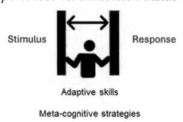

Like Star Trek's Holodeck, immersive scenarios envelop consciousness with simulations that the brain perceives as real experiences. Once the realm of science fiction, these technologies are now widely accessible through affordable portable headsets and have a proven track record for training routine skills. Increasingly VR is being used to teach attitudes and emotional regulation skills.

VR as an Empathy Machine

"It's a machine, but through this machine we become more compassionate, we become more empathetic, and we become more connected." (Milk, 2015)

I'm standing in a homeless woman's tent home – virtually, but not uninvited, as the "We Live Here" VR app (Alfrobel, 2020) had shown up in the catalog of experiences to try on my Oculus Quest headset. I had just met Rocky as she is being beckoned to leave before police arrive to clear out the tent city, and her home.

Once she is gone, the 360-degree video of her tent home turns into an interactive 3D model that I am invited to explore. Her phone buzzes and I pick it up and listen to a message from a friend hoping she is safe. A tiny model of a house glows and picking it up, it becomes an animation depicting her past, her previous life with her husband in the home they once owned. A box of photos glows for a moment. I pick it up and examine her old photos, turning each one over to read the writing on the back, piecing together her story. Dropping a photo, I swear at myself, and lean over to pick it up and look to see that I haven't damaged it. It goes back in the box, and I set it carefully back on the table. This is when I realize that my belief has been suspended. I'm behaving not like someone remotely exploring information on a screen, but rather as myself, a visitor in Rocky's home. By exploring and discovering (rather than just being shown) the events leading to her living in a tent, I become a witness, which feels like so much more than being an observer.

I'm not alone in feeling the emotional impact of some of these kinds of experiences. VR has been employed as a highly effective tool to increase empathy in several ways:

- Front-line mental health practitioners in the UK have been using VR to experience the world through the perspective of their patients (Riches et al., 2022). By experiencing different simulated mental conditions, they can develop a more compassionate approach to care, leading to increased ability to de-escalate situations and reduce the use of restrictive practices (such as constraints or seclusion).
- The United Nations is currently developing a series of VR experiences that allow participants to join various populations such as migrants in vignettes of their daily lives (Milk, 2015). They report that this type of immersive engagement deepens people's understanding and empathy for the plight of these populations.

While VR can be used to help people increase their emotional response to situations, it can also be used to down-regulate it when needed.

VR as Exposure Therapy

"The first time a doctor or nurse sees a critically wounded child, emotions inevitably run high. It's a natural human response, but these emotions can be so strong that care slows down and mistakes can be made. So, while most medical training focuses on diagnostics and treatment protocols, we need opportunities to have simulated experiences that help us learn to cope with the situation and manage our own emotions." (D. Poenaru, personal communication, 2024)

The pediatric trauma team at Montreal Children's Hospital has recently started using a VR tool called PetitVR (CBC News, 2023), which provides medical caregivers with a set of virtual reality scenarios in which they respond to pediatric emergencies, including rare, severe injuries or illnesses. These acute-care simulations require the close collaboration of a team of caregivers who apply diagnostic and treatment protocols to help a young patient.

While training scenarios with medical mannequins have traditionally been used to practice procedural skills, Dr. Poenaru believes that the deep immersion available in VR provides a unique opportunity for caregivers to practice managing their own and others' emotional reactions. For instance, a simulated, upset parent can be included in scenarios and their level of anxiety can be dynamically "dialed up" to increase the emotional tenor of the situation.

Naturally, these events can be upsetting for the medical team as well. Traditional medical education has relied on post-event debriefings to review what happened, discuss how it was handled, and address the emotional impacts that may have been experienced. This group process, which can include a social worker, provides an opportunity to learn from the experience – whether simulated or real – and provide mutual support as needed. By combining immersive, simulated scenarios with real debriefings, programs like this, as well as the aforementioned startle and surprise training, can act as a kind of preventative exposure therapy with aims to inoculate performers from mental upset when it matters most.

VR as Immersive Therapeutic

Psychological therapies such as psychosynthesis have used mental imagery techniques to help surgery patients manage stress, regain a sense of control, and improve clinical outcomes (Bresler, 2005). A new class of immersive therapeutics (ITx) are increasingly being used to manage physical ailments, acknowledging the role that mental states play in physical well-being. For instance, RelievERx (RelievERx, 2022) is an FDA-approved, doctor-prescribed daily program that participants follow six minutes a day for 56 days to reduce chronic back pain. It includes breathing techniques and vivid visualizations aimed to help someone alter their interpretation of and reaction to pain, finding a space between stimulus and response. Studies using this technology showed results that were as good or better than pharmacological treatments. With healthcare systems under increasing stress, immersive therapeutic experiences promise to be an increasingly important tool in the doctor's bag.

With low-cost headsets and the rapid advances in production technologies (i.e., no-code platforms, artificial intelligence), immersive therapeutics and interactive experiences provide opportunities to develop stress-management, meta-cognitive, and adaptive skills that have, until now, been difficult to achieve in training.

Thinking Out Loud

Easy access to immersive simulations has opened up exciting possibilities, not only for high performance domains such as sport, aviation, and medicine, but for any field in which emotional engagement with a subject is beneficial.

The following questions could be asked to explore how immersive simulation might be applied in a learning and performance context:

Table 5. Questions to explore application of simulation

What type of affective objectives could be exercised within a virtual learning experience?	During the analysis phase, consider how the affective components of performance can be addressed, along with skills and knowledge.
What kinds of scenarios and stories would you like your learners to experience?	During the analysis and design phases, consider how learning objectives can exist within a narrative structure that learners can experience.
What aspects of the experiences could help recreate these emotional responses?	During the design phase, think like a movie director and search for events or features of the experience that can evoke the desired emotions.
What other design elements would increase the impact of the simulated experiences (e.g., journalling, discussion, etc.)?	During the design phase, be sure to allow for opportunities for reflection and debriefing to help learners make sense of the emotional experience, and, by doing so, give it the opportunity to make a long-term impression.

SUMMARY

The Ideal Performance State describes a perfect match between a situation, challenge, or task and a performer's ability to deal with it. It is experienced as a "flow state" in which one is focused, confident, and fully able to apply one's skills and knowledge. Everyone may find their own "zone" for a given situation, on a range of excitation between sleep and panic.

The Ideal Performance State is far from being a random phenomenon. It can be:

- Discovered through trial and error and reflection,
- Supported with exercises that support self-efficacy, and
- Deliberately triggered through habits, routines, and performance rituals.

Startles and surprises can push performers out of an ideal state and closer to panic. In these states of "mental upset" or "freeze," attention can be overly narrowed or scattered, creating a loss of situational awareness and judgment. This phenomenon increases the chance of an adverse event leading to a negative outcome. However, like the Ideal Performance State, adaptive responses can be developed by learning about and practicing:

- Stress management routines to overcome panic or freeze,
- Meta-cognitive techniques to build awareness of what is happening, and
- Other practices that may need to be invoked to manage the situation at hand.

Whether learning to get into an ideal state, or out of an un-ideal one, visualization – either by mental imagery or technical simulation – provides a unique method for the brain to practice changing itself. Increasingly low-cost simulations suggest a future in which people will have unprecedented opportunities to develop both routine skills and emotional regulation habits to help them succeed in reality.

REFERENCES

Alfrobel Inc. (2020). *We Live Here* [VR experience]. Meta. https://www.meta.com/experiences/2537261906377373/

Attributed to Einstein. A. (n.d.). Learning is experience. Everything else is just information. [Quote]. Retrieved from https://www.brainyquote.com/authors/albert-einstein-quotes

Bandura, A. (1977). Self-efficacy: Toward a unifying theory of behavioral change. *Psychological Review*, 84(2), 191–215. DOI: 10.1037/0033-295X.84.2.191 PMID: 847061

Bishop, D. T., Karageorghis, C. I., & Kinrade, N. P. (2009). Effects of musically-induced emotions on choice reaction time performance. *The Sport Psychologist*, 23(1), 59–76. DOI: 10.1123/tsp.23.1.59

Bishop, D. T., Karageorghis, C. I., & Loizou, G. (2007). A grounded theory of young tennis players' use of music to manipulate emotional state. *Journal of Sport & Exercise Psychology*, 29(5), 584–607. DOI: 10.1123/jsep.29.5.584 PMID: 18089894

Bresler, D. (2005). Physiological consequences of guided imagery. *Practical Pain Management*, 5(6).

Brewster, B. (1882). Theory and practice. [Retrieved from Google Books.]. *The Yale Literary Magazine*, 47(5), 202.

CBC News. (2023, June 16). Montreal Children's Hospital uses VR tool for pediatric trauma. *CBC News*. https://www.cbc.ca/player/play/1.7138766

Christakou, A., Vasileiadis, G., & Kapreli, E. (2021). Motor imagery as a method of maintaining performance in pianists during forced non-practice: A single case study. *Physiotherapy Theory and Practice*, 37(4), 540–548. DOI: 10.1080/09593985.2019.1636917 PMID: 31267825

Cloninger, C. R., Cloninger, K. M., Zwir, I., & Keltikangas-Järvinen, L. (2019). The complex genetics and biology of human temperament: A review of traditional concepts in relation to new molecular findings. *Translational Psychiatry*, 9(1), 290. DOI: 10.1038/s41398-019-0621-4 PMID: 31712636

Craske, M., Liao, B., Brown, L., & Vervliet, B. (2012). Role of inhibition in exposure therapy. *Journal of Experimental Psychopathology*, 3(3), 322–345. DOI: 10.5127/jep.026511

Csikszentmihalyi, M. (1990). *Flow: The psychology of optimal experience*. Harper & Row.

Dymond, D. (2014, August 14). Ideal performance state? How about ideal performance no matter what state? [LinkedIn post].

European Union Aviation Safety Agency. (2015). *Startle effect management* (Final report EASA_REP_RESEA_2015_3).

Frankl, V. E. (2006). *Man's Search for Meaning*. Beacon Press.

Garfield, C. A., & Bennett, H. Z. (1984). *Peak performance: Mental training techniques of the world's greatest athletes*. Tarcher.

Gray, R. (Host). (2016, September 22). Applying music in sport [Audio podcast episode]. In *The Perception Action Podcast*. Retrieved from https://perceptionaction.com/36c/

Hanin, Y. L. (2003). Performance related emotional states in sport: A qualitative analysis. *Forum Qualitative Sozialforschung / Forum: Qualitative. Social Research*, 4(1).

Headrick, J., Renshaw, I., Davids, K., Pinder, R., & Araújo, D. (2015). The dynamics of expertise acquisition in sport: The role of affective learning design. *Psychology of Sport and Exercise*, 16(1), 83–90. DOI: 10.1016/j.psychsport.2014.08.006

Herbert, F. (1965). *Dune*. Chilton Books.

Hermans, E. J., Henckens, M. J., Joëls, M., & Fernández, G. (2014). Dynamic adaptation of large-scale brain networks in response to acute stressors. *Trends in Neurosciences*, 37(6), 304–314. DOI: 10.1016/j.tins.2014.03.006 PMID: 24766931

Horstmann, G. (2006). Latency and duration of the action interruption in surprise. *Cognition and Emotion*, 20(2), 242–273. DOI: 10.1080/02699930500262878

Jeannerod, M. (1994). The representing brain: Neural correlates of motor intention and imagery. *Behavioral and Brain Sciences*, 17(2), 187–202. DOI: 10.1017/S0140525X00034026

Juslin, P. N. (2009). Emotion in music performance. In Hallam, S., Cross, I., & Thaut, M. (Eds.), *The Oxford handbook of music psychology* (pp. 377–389). Oxford University Press.

Koch, M. (1999). The neurobiology of startle. *Progress in Neurobiology*, 59(2), 107–128. DOI: 10.1016/S0301-0082(98)00098-7 PMID: 10463792

Kochan, J., Breiter, E., & Jentsch, F. (2005). Surprise and unexpectedness in flying: Factors and features. *13th International Symposium on Aviation Psychology*, 398-403.

Landis, C., & Hunt, W. A. (1939). *The Startle Pattern*. Farrar & Rinehart.

Lang, P. J., Bradley, M. M., & Cuthbert, B. N. (1990). Emotion, attention, and the startle reflex. *Psychological Review*, 97(3), 377–395. DOI: 10.1037/0033-295X.97.3.377 PMID: 2200076

LeDoux, J. (1997). Emotion, memory and the brain. *Scientific American*, 7(1), 68–75. PMID: 8023118

Loehr, J. E. (1983). The ideal performance state. *Science Periodical on Research and Technology in Sport*, 1, 1–7.

Maddox, T., Sparks, C. Y., Oldstone, L., Chibbaro, M., Sackman, J., Judge, E., Maddox, R., Bonakdar, R., & Darnall, B. D. (2024). Perspective: The promise of virtual reality as an immersive therapeutic. *Journal of Medical Extended Reality*, 1(1), 27–34. DOI: 10.1089/jmxr.2023.0003

Majid, A., & Mohammad, R. (2021). The impact of music on sports activities: A scoping review. *Journal of New Studies in Sport Management*, 2(4), 274–285.

Mesagno, C., Marchant, D., & Morris, T. (2009). Alleviating choking: The sounds of distraction. *Journal of Applied Sport Psychology*, 21(2), 131–147. DOI: 10.1080/10413200902795091

Mesaros, H. (2008). *Bravo Fortissimo Glenn Gould: The Mind of a Canadian Virtuoso*. American Literary Press.

Milk, C. (2015, March). How virtual reality can create the ultimate empathy machine [Video]. TED Conferences. https://www.ted.com/talks/chris_milk_how_virtual_reality_can_create_the_ultimate_empathy_machine/transcript?language=en

Minkley, N., Schröder, T. P., Wolf, O. T., & Kirchner, W. H. (2014). The socially evaluated cold-pressor test (SECPT) for groups: Effects of repeated administration of a combined physiological and psychological stressor. *Psychoneuroendocrinology*, 45, 119–127. DOI: 10.1016/j.psyneuen.2014.03.022 PMID: 24845183

National Aeronautics and Space Administration. (2024). *Aviation Safety Reporting System (ASRS)*. NASA. https://asrs.arc.nasa.gov/

Nideffer, R. M. (2002). *Getting into the optimal performance state*. Enhanced Performance Systems.

North, A. C., & Hargreaves, D. J. (2008). Music and taste. In North, A. C., & Hargreaves, D. J. (Eds.), *The social and applied psychology of music* (pp. 75–142). Oxford University Press. DOI: 10.1093/acprof:oso/9780198567424.003.0003

Oaster, B. D., Peck, G. D., Scott, R. A., & Feith, G. A. (2022). The E-Factor—The importance of self-efficacy and adaptive skills surrounding startle & surprise events in the cockpits of modern jet airliners. Unpublished manuscript, London, United Kingdom.

RelievERx Inc. (2022). *RelievERx* [Virtual reality tool for pain management]. https://www.relieveRx.com

Riches, S., Iannelli, H., Reynolds, L., & Hamilton, L. (2022). Virtual reality-based training for mental health staff: A novel approach to increase empathy, compassion, and subjective understanding of service user experience. *Advances in Simulation (London, England)*, 7(1), 19. DOI: 10.1186/s41077-022-00217-0 PMID: 35854343

Seery, M. D., Leo, R. J., Lupien, S. P., Kondrak, C. L., & Almonte, J. L. (2013). An upside to adversity? Moderate cumulative lifetime adversity is associated with resilient responses in the face of controlled stressors. *Psychological Science*, 24(7), 1181–1189. DOI: 10.1177/0956797612469210 PMID: 23673992

Smith, L. B., & Thelen, E. (2003). Development as a dynamic system. *Trends in Cognitive Sciences*, 7(8), 343–348. DOI: 10.1016/S1364-6613(03)00156-6 PMID: 12907229

Terry, P. C., Karageorghis, C. I., Mecozzi Saha, A., & D'Auria, S. (2012). Effects of synchronous music on treadmill running among elite triathletes. *Journal of Science and Medicine in Sport*, 15(1), 52–57. DOI: 10.1016/j.jsams.2011.06.003 PMID: 21803652

Usher, E. L., & Pajares, F. (2008). Self-efficacy for self-regulated learning: A validation study. *Educational and Psychological Measurement*, 68(3), 443–463. DOI: 10.1177/0013164407308475

Wesch, N. (2022). Identify Your IPS. Special Olympics. https://soctraining.ca/sites/default/files/2022-10/Ideal-Performance-State_WORKSHEET_EN.pdf

Wickens, C. D. (2001). Keynote address: Attention to safety and the psychology of surprise. In *11th International Symposium on Aviation Psychology* (pp. 1-11). The Ohio State University.

Yerkes, R. M., & Dodson, J. D. (1908). The relation of strength of stimulus to rapidity of habit-formation. *The Journal of Comparative Neurology and Psychology*, 18(5), 459–482. DOI: 10.1002/cne.920180503

Section 3
Putting Theory to the Test

Chapter 9
Fiction as Reflective Praxis for Affective Domain Learning in Medicine and Healthcare Education:
A Case Study From Pedagogic Practice

Catherine Hayes
University of Sunderland, UK

ABSTRACT

Being able to effectively teach for affective learning domain delivery is now pivotal in instances of medical and healthcare education where numbers of older adults are rising exponentially in the United Kingdom (UK) as a direct demographic consequence of the baby boom generation. As a healthcare professional discipline, podiatric medicine has a key role in the maintenance of ambulatory health and well-being for older adults, so these statistics have clear implications for the education and training of graduates within this academic discipline. In the context of allied health professional practice, future practitioners need to be equipped and prepared not only to provide functional podiatric management but also to understand and integrate the greater sociological implications of an ageing population into practice. This chapter uses an illustrative case study from teaching practice to engage readers in the use of televised fiction to stimulate critical reflective practice when working with vulnerable older people and their families and carers.

DOI: 10.4018/979-8-3693-2663-3.ch009

Copyright © 2025, IGI Global. Copying or distributing in print or electronic forms without written permission of IGI Global is prohibited.

INTRODUCTION

The multiple British Academy Film and Television awards that the British sit-com, 'The Royle Family,' won between 1998 and 2012 bear testimony to its popularity with public viewers across the United Kingdom (UK). The Manchester-based comedy was one of the most basic examples of media production ever seen in television and was intentionally focused on working class life at the turn of the 21st century. Typifying intergenerational relationships, the members of the family were the central characters and at this stage of the chapter, it is worth introducing them to readers who may not be familiar with the programme. Jim Royle was the father of the family, a stereotypical misogynistic epitome of Northern working-class paternalism. Jim was married to his long-suffering wife Barbara, who worked part-time in a cake shop and was the only person to take any degree of responsibility for the domestic chores. Together they had two children: Denise, the very epitome of laziness, and her younger brother Antony (also known as Lurkio), whose sole reason for existence appears to be making endless cups of tea upon demand for the TV-centric family. Alongside this nuclear family were Barbara's mother, the Nana of the family (Norma Jean Speakman), and Denise's fiancé, Dave Best, alongside a host of the family's equally working class (or in some instances criminal) friends, such as Twiggy, Darren, and their next-door neighbours Joe, Mary, and Cheryl Carrol. All characters provide insight into a specific dimension of reality and the harshness of existence in a very specific lifeworld, examined through the lens of the camera by the audience, who either based their personal assumptions of characters directly on what they saw as representative of elements in their own lives, or perceived as a direct representation of something they had never experienced in the context of their own lives in very different social circles.

Nana Speakman was a central character in the 'The Royle Family,' mum to Barbara and mother-in-law to 'Jim.' The first episode of the series typifies media portrayal of a grandmother in British working-class society with all the pathos of vulnerability and widowhood, as the gran of Antony and Denise arrives for Sunday lunch with the Royles. The portrayal of the acceptance of Nana as outspoken, hypocritical, deaf, and loud during that initial episode provides all the evidence we need to challenge our assumptions of her portrayal. We compare the sociological 'isms' of prejudice, with racism and sexism, to illuminate the social norm that permits us to laugh at someone because of their age and the behaviours associated with it. A source of derision and hilarity in the family – they usually laugh at her, rather than with her – she is often portrayed as being perceived as an irritation to her son-in-law and demonstrates behaviour such as talking over the top of the TV, being outspoken, and promulgating the level of her wisdom due to age. Her physical appearance is representative of the media portrayal of an older woman, in a dress, cardigan set, and pearls, all of which typify Sunday appearances for the 'Nana' of the family.

This chapter provides an insight into how the Nana of the Royle Family was used as a character to drive affective domain learning around the key sociological concept of ageism and how this was achieved in the context of pedagogic praxis. For those unfamiliar with the impact of ageism in healthcare professional practice, the chapter also incorporates insight into this phenomenon. In order for readers to understand the intergenerational dynamics among the Royle Family's illustrious characters, a brief precis of each, as provided above, was necessary. Wherever possible, though, it will be advantageous for readers to access the array of free online clips available from the British Broadcasting Corporation (BBC), if the 'Royle Family' does happen to be an area of unfamiliar viewing territory.

THE DEMOGRAPHY OF AGEING

In the UK there currently are ten million people aged over sixty-five years, and over the next twenty years the number of older adults will rise exponentially as a consequence of the baby boom generation (Sultana et al., 2018; Shlisky, 2017). As a healthcare professional discipline, podiatry has a key role in the maintenance of ambulatory health and wellbeing for older adults, so these statistics have clear implications for the education and training of podiatry graduates. In the context of allied health professional practice, future practitioners need to be equipped and prepared not only to provide functional podiatric management, but also to understand and integrate the greater sociological implications of an ageing population into practice (Kemp et al., 2018).

DEMOGRAPHIC IMPACT ON PODIATRIC EDUCATIONAL PROVISION NEED

Demographically, the number of older people who present with foot pain and dysfunction is high. By the age of 65 years, 98% of people have one or more foot complaints impacting on their ambulatory wellbeing (Menz, 2016). In the wider context of public health and wellbeing, remaining ambulatory is an essential part of the capacity of older people to socialise, integrate, and remain an engaged part of our society. This capacity is linked to the concept of functional independence and, where unaddressed, leads to premature morbidity and an enforced sedentary lifestyle as an older person (Adogwa et al., 2017).

Podiatrists, as allied healthcare professionals, are ideally situationally placed to actively engage with older adults during the course of their lower limb assessment, diagnosis, and management regimen in clinical practice (Nancarrow & Borthwick, 2016). Independent variables in the relationship of the podiatrist to the patient can impact on potential levels of ageism in practice, whether these are intentional or not (Kagan, 2017). Their perceptions, along with the rest of society's, are often shaped by previous experience, or where this is not something that has been part of their lives, their cultural acclimatisation to older people through their portrayal in the media (Phillips & Waugh, 2018).

Each of these issues has a strategic implication for podiatric undergraduate curricula across the globe. Few studies to date have addressed the need for social gerontology to become an integral part of the curriculum both clinically and academically, despite the fact that older adults represent a significant part of overall patient caseloads in everyday podiatric practice (McGarry, 2015).

THE AGENCY OF AGE

In society, older people are often wrongly labelled as being less competent than their younger counterparts, by sole virtue of their evident physical signs of ageing. Research indicates that in general, people across all generations are also statistically more likely to wrongly associate elderly names with the characteristics of incompetence (North & Fiske, 2015). These associations are inherently linked to the desirability of certain traits above others by younger generations. The alleged incompetence of the elderly is a social construct and whilst physical senescence is an inevitable part of the ageing process for us all, diminished capacity demonstrates the broad gap between perceived and actual reality in relation to the maintenance of physical fitness and aesthetic appearance.

CHALLENGING PERCEPTIONS OF AGEING IN PRACTICE

Cuddy, Norton, and Fiske (2016) advocate the view that age and our perceptions of its chronology predicate the basis of the relationships we build with older adults and the interactions we have with them. These perceptions belie assumptions about the political stance, employability, social interactional capacity, and communication abilities of those we interact with on a daily basis; they are an implicit part of our capacity to subconsciously, rightly or wrongly, presuppose things about others. Part of seeing the media portrayal of the elderly on popular TV and media contributes to being able to relate or attune thinking to these typically presented stereotypes and can either serve to legitimise or challenge the way people interact with one another across intergenerational boundaries. In turn this can lead to intergenerational division or intergenerational solidarity (Park & Lee, 2017). Combined with other embedded social stances, such as gender, faith perspectives, sexuality, and our different racial and ethnic backgrounds, age has the potential to act as a vehicle for society to reflect on how it interacts with all people, not just older ones, on the attributions of individualism.

TEMPORAL CONTINUUM OF AGEING

What delineates age as an attribution is that it involves no active choice or option – if we live long enough, we will become by virtue of our senescence, old. It is therefore a dynamic that changes based on our relative standing on a temporal continuum which provides a window into the physical and mental processes of senescence that eventually lead to the ultimate destination from life – death. As such, age is perceived by the majority of populations, whether consciously or unconsciously, as a stage in life relative to, and with greater relevance to, impending death. In The Canterbury Tales, an historical example from English Literature, as Chaucer (c.1380) writes in the Pardoner's Tale, an old man metaphorically knocks at the door of death, with his staff,

> 'Ne deeth, allas! ne wol nat han my lyf;
> Thus walke I, lyk a restelees caityf,
> And on the ground, which is my modres gate,
> I knokke with my staf, bothe erly and late,
> And seye, "leve moder, leet me in!
> Lo, how I vanish, flesh, and blood, and skin!
> Allas! whan shul my bones been at reste?'
> (Chaucer, circa 1380; from a published version, 1835)

Natural processes of senescence across society are often deemed and treated as sociological problems, which are only exacerbated and exaggerated by the media portrayal of older adults. Only relatively low proportions of the older population are seen regularly on television, and they are often characterised by the negatively ageist and stereotypical features of the media's portrayal of ageing such as confusion, depression, eccentricity, or the extremes of severe functional senescence, which are themselves often exacerbated by the portrayal of co-morbidity. Ageing ultimately removes the perceived capacity of older people to participate in aspects of life that have been associated with enjoyment and fulfilment: physical and cognitive abilities, sexuality, and what Zebrowitz and Montepare (2000) term, in the context of living, 'effectiveness.'

PODIATRIC MEDICINE AS A DISTINCTIVE SIGNATURE PEDAGOGY

Podiatric Medicine is the healthcare profession dealing with lower limb pathologies and the impact of systemic conditions which limit physical capacity for ambulation and, as a consequence, socialisation and a sense of general wellbeing as well. The responsibility of podiatrists as an integral part of the allied healthcare workforce is the assessment, diagnosis, and management of lower limb pathology. Over the last twenty-five years, the role of the podiatrist has expanded almost beyond recognition; disciplinary expertise stretches across the fields of human biomechanics and kinesiology, rheumatology, diabetology, and podopaediatrics, to name just a few. It is worth reflecting, though, that podogerontology has been a less attractive source of career progression and development, with focus on caring for the foot problems of older adults, largely being designated to the preserve of those who wish to work over prolonged timespans in community clinics. This is also a reflection of both the capacity of education to change perceptions of specialism in the care of older people and the regard podiatry has as a collective of those we most often serve in clinical practice. Thankfully the majority of UK Higher Education Institutes with responsibility for the delivery of undergraduate podiatric curricula have reflected on this need and have incorporated a gerontological focus into their respective podiatry curricula.

OVERVIEW OF THE PEDAGOGIC DESIGN AND IMPLEMENTATION OF LEARNING

The pedagogic process of delivery was designed to facilitate students in reflecting on the sociological concept of ageism and to illustrate the everyday realities of being an older adult in 21st century Britain. This addressed issues such as capacity for intergenerational relationality and solidarity between younger and older adults; challenged assumptions about the processes of senescence, death, and dying; and considered the sociocultural norms that pervade UK society. Embedded within it was the impact of media on the widely held perceptions of older adults in society and how, if ageism is to be avoided in practice (Kagan, 2017), the imperative not to homogenise them into an ambiguous group.

There were around twenty students in each session of the teaching I undertook on podiatric gerontology. Sessions were scheduled at weekly intervals and lasted three hours between 9.00am and midday. In total, I had six sessions with the students at the beginning of Semester 2, Level 6 (Stage 3) of the academic calendar year. Alongside challenging stereotypical perceptions of ageing in practice, I also had to cover the physical, functional processes of ageing in some relatively less sociological and more cognitive sessions on physiological senescence. The need to embed sociological perspectives within podiatric curricula is now a widely accepted norm in the context of podiatric medical education. This session was designed with a double purpose – to make students critically introspective of their own practice of working in the context of podiatry with older adults and to integrate this capacity for reflexivity with a sound underpinning comprehension of what the physical and psychosocial implications of senescence could mean in practice.

Benchmarking relevant entry behaviour was a challenge and also a huge benefit to how sessions were conducted. The cohort was largely constituted of students aged around 21 and was complemented by a number of mid-life career changers. I had to challenge my own assumptions of their experiences to date and consolidated this with a brainstorming session when introducing the module, so that they could also benchmark themselves against others and learn through their experiences or acknowledge a lack of genuine address of the stereotyping of old age in the real world.

I began the session with a certain degree of disclosure about myself. My active interest in the sociology of ageing ultimately stemmed from being raised by my grandparents and the relationship that I was thus able to cultivate with them. I was acutely aware of the concept of intergenerational solidarity and how this had impacted my perception of other older people. My own level of disclosure represented a window into my processes of critical introspection; I kept this professional by relating it back to how it had impacted on the assumptions I held (sometimes rightly and sometimes wrongly) about the older adults I met in my own podiatric practice. This diffused the power balance between the students and me. Traditionally, clinical settings permit a degree of familiarity, but the seriousness of wielding a scalpel blade and ensuring the valid and reliable diagnosis of foot pathologies in practice leaves little scope for overt pleasantries or personal engagement. Highlighting the notion of 'personhood' and how the personal underpins the professional in podiatric practice became a key opening discussion for the students as I introduced the concepts of cognition, metacognition, epistemic cognition, and their interrelationships; their integral roles in professional practice, and the capacity for critical reflexivity.

My pedagogic design was underpinned by Social Constructivist approaches to learning (Wadsworth, 1996). The purpose was not to dictate new attitudes and behaviours but to promote reflexive praxis in action as a by-product, acknowledging the presupposition and need to challenge long-held assumptions about older adults in practice. At the end of the previous week's session and in preparation for their study of social gerontology, students were asked to pick an older person portrayed by the media and to write down all of their characteristics. They came back with ideas about older people they thought were atypical, like Miss Marple, comedic characters such as Del and Rodney's Uncle Albert, and the pitiful Dot Cotton (who at the time was being poisoned by her son and characters from the Last of the Summer Wine), all characters they believed epitomised the oldest generations of society.

I then led discussion to a series of newspaper clippings I had collected, some on Hugh Hefner from the Playboy mansion, some on a couple who had a trial separation after sixty four years of marriage, one about a man who had murdered his wife at the age of eighty-six, and a series of birthday cards, all of which focused on ageing as a somewhat derogatory experience, where it was acceptable to make fun of senescence. This was undertaken firstly by anonymising names and ages and then asking students to see how and more importantly why their opinions differed when they knew the actual ages and identities of the people in question.

I then explained that, for the purposes of driving critical introspection on the stereotyping of ageism, we would be using Nana Speakman's character to inform group learning, discourse analysis, and reflective and reflexive praxis of relevance to podiatric practice. A key example \ was when we explored the concept of intergenerational solidarity between Barbara and her mother (Nana), in the episode where Barbara is doing her mother's hair and contemplating her mother's hints for her to do more by means of washing her nightie. Without doubt this is an emotive episode; the decline in Nana's health provides a foreboding warning of decline that ultimately leads to her death in the next episode.

DECONSTRUCTING KNOWLEDGE AND EXPERIENCE

Students were asked to consider any aspect of the interaction which might be socially deconstructed. Some came back with context of care provision, the gender balance between mother and daughter, the intergenerational expectations that people place on one another, and the overlooked or unanticipated elements of working with older adults. Sexuality was raised as an issue; physical appearance and the need to conform to the stereotypical appearance of an older person was another. Helplessness, hopelessness, and fear were others. Some students cried, and one student left the room, which we later learned was because of the close relationship she had with her own grandparents. It also raised issues for me in terms of the ethical obligations I had as an educator and facilitator to follow up and make sure that students had not been unduly upset by the sessions.

Each session was run as a 'coffee morning,' which was unusual. I wanted to promulgate an air of informality about learning that would break down boundaries. The classroom was set up in a large block of tables as opposed to classroom style. I brought in a kettle, milk, coffee, and tea and started the initial session with chocolate biscuits, which week on week were replaced by the communal contributions of other various unwanted Christmas leftovers. Having the kettle in the room provided a means of ensuring a grounding in emotive wellbeing, the sense that we were human; we were discussing challenging issues, yet we could do this in a non-threatening manner.

The sociability of the module did as much to drive it as the content. An area of reflection for me at the end as an educator and facilitator was the impact of social interactivity on learning, and whether I could actually know or feel how much students had taken away from the sessions in terms of their learning before I actually received their formative and summative assessments. Of course, I assumed I couldn't claim undue credit for inspiring the motivation of the class one hundred percent. I also presumed (wrongly) that my student cohort was skewed by the inevitability of people choosing the module because they were genuinely interested in working or studying podogerontology. In fact, the majority of people there were not – they had opted to take my module so that they could avoid the mathematics of an optional biomechanics module and thought it might be an easier 'fix,' rather than anticipating they might learn anything majorly worthwhile. One notable factor was class attendance. I had 100% attendance throughout these sessions, despite there being a relatively heavy preparatory workload for each session in terms of watching Nana Speakman in online clips and needing to contribute to class discussions.

THE RELEVANCE OF METACOGNITIVE AND EPISTEMIC KNOWLEDGE

The use of metacognitive knowledge and the capacity of podiatrists to challenge their implicitly held assumptions were both important considerations in the contemplation of current and future professional interactions with patients in the context of professional practice. This also provided an ideal platform for the consideration of tacit and implicit knowledge alongside values in the context of affective domain learning. Values-based learning is, by its subjective nature, complex and multi-dimensional (Kennedy et al., 2015). Empathic learning in practice meant that audio-visual mechanisms of engaging with the sociology of care provision extended my reach as a learning facilitator and gave a clear focus to drive discussion; students were given the freedom to internalise and make meaning of a fictional story, relate to or refute the stance of characters, and posit opinions on the reality of subjective experience in practice. This also pivoted on their capacity to recall memorable aspects from experiential learning in podiatric practice as well as their previous experiences and was dependent on the dynamic nature of formal and informal learning and its application to podiatric assessment, diagnosis, and management.

STUDENT ENGAGEMENT AND PROACTIVE LEARNING OPPORTUNITIES

In the context of values-based learning, the opportunity to reflect on societal values and benchmark them against our own is an invaluable source for initiating processes of reflection and critical introspection. Critical introspection, when translated into a responsive behavioural characteristic or attribution in the context of patient care, can have a lasting impact on patients and their families and carers, which otherwise may have gone unnoticed or unrecognised in healthcare practice.

Proactive, student-centred learning, with a deliberate move away from learner passivity, formed the basis of the now much popularised Problem-based and Inquiry-based learning of 21st century pedagogic practice. It was annotated in historical pedagogical approaches over a century ago, and it ensured a move towards criticality and reflexivity in health professions educations that now characterises provision across national, international, and global centres of learning excellence. The repricocity between learner and teacher, rather than a distinct power base in favour of the teacher, meant that individualised and personalised reflection in affective domain learning became possible in the context of deep rather than surface approaches to learning. A switch to learner autonomy and a sense of owning learning as a process that is facilitated by others, rather than the acquisitioned transfer of knowledge from one mind to another, became key drivers in this process. The relative synergy between engaged learners and their facilitator is a key aspect of pedagogic practice that matters in this learning process. This procedural change underpins the concept of authentic transformative learning, which is truly authentic and can become an embedded part of learners' critical reflection and reflexivity as a consequence of critical introspection.

This has great significance for the concept of empowered learning and accountability for behavioural responses to learning. In relation to Nana Speakman, this was of direct relevance to the contemplation of the stereotypical presentation of older adults in the media in relation to ageism, gender, and the notion of intergenerational solidarity, all of which are directly relevant to the development of metacognitive processing and enhanced skills of critical engagement using their socially constructivist origins of knowledge around podogerontology.

Student-centred learning is broadly based on constructivism as a theory of learning, which is built on the idea that learners must deconstruct and subsequently reconstruct knowledge in the light of new meanings in order to learn effectively, with learning being most effective when, as part of an activity, the learner constructs a meaningful product. As previously outlined, student-centred learning is closely aligned with processes of transformative learning, which result in ongoing qualitative change over time. The focus is on enhancing and empowering the learner and developing their critical ability.

EMBEDDING THE ROYLES INTO PEDAGOGIC DESIGN

The Royle Family members were deliberately targeted in the process of pedagogic design for their capacity to promulgate the notion of lived human experience and to highlight how the process of story-making for storytelling can be driven by case study methodology. The programme has been lauded by contemporary sociologists for being one of the first TV programmes to present a window into the lives of others in the form of a 'fly on the wall' documentary. Its context and setting provide a means of challenging assumptions that are both epistemically- and societally-based and which combine across a collective society to inform social responsiveness to people, their lives, and their contributions to a civic community. Although this pedagogic intervention focuses on 'Nana' (Nana Speakman), it would equally have been possibly to explore the sociology of old age via the ontological lenses of other members of the family – Jim, Barbara, Denise, Antony, and Dave.

Considering Nana Speakman in the context of a case-based scenario also provides a means of identifying and revealing issues for exploration in a classroom setting which otherwise might remain unspoken or unaddressed. This is important not only in introducing the mechanisms by which students make meaning of given situations, but also how they internalise and project their experience of individuals onto others, with whom they may subconsciously categorise or align them. The process also provides a context which potentiates the synergy of both inductive and deductive processes to exist side by side in the pragmatic questioning of the meaning of ageism on individual, collective, and global stages. The outcome is the framing of new questions for empirical research and, perhaps most importantly for the context of podiatric gerontology, critical reflection and reflexivity on the processes of clinical praxis.

In making meaning of evidence-based approaches to professional practice, context is everything – again, what made the 'Royle Family' an ideal choice for framing a particular focus of meaning-making was the relative consistency of its context. Yin (2013) defined the clear relationship between the phenomenon under scrutiny (in this instance, ageism) and the contextual significance within which it is constructed (the Royles' living room).

The specific language and discourse of the programme underpin the articulation of ageism as a phenomenon, how it can be interpreted in the context of the meaning of student lives, and what concepts such as intergenerational solidarity might mean to them and how they approach podiatric practice.

FUNDAMENTALS OF CASE STUDY ANALYSIS

Within this chapter, the concept of ageism has been framed in a case study of podogerontology in Higher Education. In this respect, it is the manifestation of a social phenomenon that can be used to illustrate the evidence base of teaching in the affective domain. Like all case studies, we have to acknowledge the transcendence of subject disciplinarity; throughout the chapter, we will draw on theories of education, psychology, sociology, and anthropology to illustrate the relative ambiguity, purpose, and complexity of teaching to facilitate this domain of learning. Yin (2013) rooted this particular type of case study in the context of empirical enquiry, with several defining features which serve this illustration of Higher Education well:

- The focus of teaching reflecting the practicality of real-life interaction rather than the constraint of a hypothesis
- The complexity of real life, which serves to provide a degree of ambiguity and acknowledges that the boundaries of affective domain learning are often blurred
- The acknowledgment of the diverse array of literature and resources available, which can consolidate and triangulate alternative findings in research of affective domain learning
- The capacity to challenge assumptions about the everyday social and cultural norms of ageism that pervade 21st century Britain, via deliberate and considered theoretical explanation

This approach ensures the definitive delineation between the testifiability of knowledge and the questions posed of it (Yin, 2013). Where this is of particular relevance in relation to affective domain learning is the level of implicit or tacit knowledge that accompanies reflective contemplation and a call to acknowledge and address social norms.

An explanatory approach to social and behavioural sciences frames the underpinning of attitudes and behaviours in clinical practice. Socialisation prior to experiential learning frame these both theoretically and in practice. Facilitating affective domain learning necessitates driving critical reflection on practice in an effort to bridge the praxis gap between the two.

FRAMING NANA SPEAKMAN AS AN INDIVIDUAL CASE STUDY OF AGEISM

Framing the parameter of the case (in this case the concept of ageism) on the character of Nana Speakman is a pivotal part of being able to frame her contribution and the impact she has on students at a specific point in time. Both were identified by Stake (2013) in terms of definition and context. As such, Nana Speakman is used as an instrumental case study of ageism in practice where it becomes possible to examine her, broadly speaking, as an ethnographic case study. Temporality is an issue if we consider the longevity of her contribution to the programme (which also increases the likelihood of most students being familiar with her character in its stereotypical presentation across TV media). This was outlined as a key issue by Simons (2009), who posited that such a simplistic overview provided an ideal opportunity to implement a specific case study.

In the context of pedagogic practice in Higher Education, this approach means that in the context of facilitating students in their affective domain learning, it is possible to iteratively develop the session in the light of student engagement. This raises questions of how measuring parity and consistency among sessions might be formally reported in relation to the quality and perception of the student experience.

THE SOCIAL CONSTRUCTION OF NANA SPEAKMAN'S REPRESENTATIVE REALITY

It can be academically debated that central to all human capacity for interpretation is the social construction of reality. This capacity to socially construct reality provided a degree of synergy between the students and Nana Speakman, transcending the concept of ageism. This transcendence is wholly reliant on the projection of meaning by Nana Speakman's character and the innate capacity of the students to interpret, translate, and articulate this meaning-making into a pragmatic interpretation. As a consequence, using Nana Speakman's character to generate more questions about ageism enables them to answer not just the 'how' questions of who she is and how she might represent society's perception of an older woman, but also the 'why.' The process of social constructivism as an underpinning educational philosophy provides a truth in this context that is fundamentally relative and entirely dependent on the interpreter's own stance or perspective. This is something that will be discussed later in the chapter when we consider the notion of intergenerational solidarity. It is here that we can also place emphasis on the subjective nature of meaning-making in education, and also raise debates about how we can impact transformative learning via specific affective domain learning strategies. Since affective domain learning affects how students recognise and acknowledge the influence of their own epistemic cognition, it can be argued that the knowledge gained becomes an embedded part of the knower, rather than something that exists in abstraction separate from them.

MEANING-MAKING AND THE CONCEPT OF EPISTEMIC COGNITION

The cohort's interpretation of Nana Speakman's character is as much embedded in epistemic cognition as in interpretation of the real world. Specific experiential learning from life and practice means that specific information can be retrieved from memory, related, and then articulated relative to Nana Speakman's fictional world. This process has been deemed as a combinatorial impact (Kelly, 2017). From a social constructivist perspective, memory depends on the process of transformative learning, which then becomes an embedded part of the knower (in this case the students, who have not necessarily contemplated Nana Speakman as representative of the embodiment of ageism before).

By using a pedagogical case study such as Nana Speakman, it is possible to inform wider issues of direct relevance to professional practice and evidence-informed decision-making within the context of wider societal decision-making and contemplation. Nana Speakman provides student cohorts with a mechanism for providing a holistic overview of exemplary ageism as a societal and family norm. This in turn can be used to drive critical reflection and reflexivity of it. As part of the process, students can also draw on a range of evidence sources, such as published literature from the field of ageism and podogerontology, which permits multiple facets of the phenomena of ageism to be explored through a wide variety of theoretical lenses.

CASE STUDY AS METHODOLOGY AND METHOD

Philosophically, Case Study as a methodological approach is based on a tradition founded in both positivism and constructivism. Whilst positivism was established as the predominant of the two epistemological approaches, it was not until the mid-sixties that transcending the need for pure objectification was first posited as an accepted norm in the context of social science research. In moving beyond what is empirically measurable and observable to constructing reality, the potential for case studies to illuminate and generate questions about the 'why' of human experience was recognized. From an epistemological perspective, constructivism provides a truth that is fundamentally relative and entirely dependent on the interpreter's own epistemic stance or epistemic positionality. Emphasis could then be placed equally on the subjective nature of meaning-making and the place that this epistemological approach occupies when object and subject need to be operationally defined and delineated (Kelly, 2016).

An Intrinsic Case Study design permitted the identification of the pedagogical case study in terms of its extent and range (Stake, 1995). This entailed the identification that a specific situation (i.e., pedagogical intervention) would be studied using a new approach to facilitating an affective domain learning opportunity. The complex ambiguity of being able to initiate a degree of conscious reflection and critical reflexivity surrounding the concept of potential ageism within clinical podiatric practice became the focus of the Case Study. Here, the author utilised the approach adopted by Simons (2009) to construct a typology for the purpose of an Evaluative Case Study, where a pedagogical innovation or element of creative praxis in teaching was introduced. In this sense, the Evaluative Case Study became a mechanism of translating experiential and tacit knowledge into practice, and it offered the potential to provide new insights as a key part of how practitioners generate new and valuable 'professional knowledge' (Burgess & Wellington, 2010). For this work to have a strategic relevance and influence in professional circles, the pedagogical intervention was acknowledged as needing a robust evidence base, which undertaking such an evaluation could effectively fulfil. It is important to acknowledge here that this resultant evidence base may indeed stem from the collation of narratives and discourses around practice development, or where there may be elements of dissonance, they can then serve to form the basis of further pedagogical research.

Multiple permutations of building a theory with Evaluative Case Study research data are possible and the author had to discern and justify the best adaptation of a recognised model possible to provide a clear framework of research execution. Eisenhardt's (1989) Process of Building Theory from Case Study Research was used for this stage, as outlined below in Table 1:

Table 1. Adaptation of 'Process of Building Theory from Case Study Research'

STAGES	PROCESSES	RATIONALE FOR IMPLEMENTATION
Stage 1. Initiation	• Clear framing and operational definition of research phenomenon	✓ Reduces ambiguity and provides methodological focus
	• Acknowledging the existence of a priori construct	✓ Enables constructs to be grounded in the published or acknowledged extant evidence base
	• Considering how an existing theory or hypotheses could impact on the focus of inquiry	✓ Maintains and develops theoretical flexibility
Stage 2. Case Selection and Sampling Technique	• Defining a specific research population	✓ Enhances the external validity of the findings
	• Operationalising a theoretical sampling technique	✓ Provides a focused emphasis on those specific phenomena that can prove, extend, or develop further an existing evidence base
Stage 3. Developing the Specifics of Research Design and Methodology	• Implementing multiple data collection methods/mixed methods approaches	✓ Provides a mechanism of triangulating data so that theoretical emergence can be clearly grounded in theory
	• Establishing the combined impact of qualitative and quantitative data	✓ Strengthens grounding of theory by triangulation of evidence
	• Including multiple investigators	✓ Facilitates combined and synergistic perspectives in relation to the collated evidence base
		✓ Facilitates the notion of divergent perspectives and strengthens the methodological process of grounding
Stage 4. Initial Data Collection	• Synergising data collection, transcription, and analysis	✓ Enables data enrichment via a focused thematic adjustment to interview schedules / data collection
	• Implementing potentially flexible and opportunistic data collection methods	✓ Enhances the analysis phase speed and provides purposeful adjustments to the data collection process
		✓ Allows investigators to exploit emergent themes and fundamentally unique characteristics of the specific case under investigation

continued on following page

Table 1. Continued

STAGES	PROCESSES	RATIONALE FOR IMPLEMENTATION
Stage 5. Data Analysis	• Analysing the case (phenomena-specific)	✓ Gains familiarity with data and preliminary theory generation
	• Identifying emergent theory from the potential crossover of methodological approaches	✓ Moves beyond superficial thematic analysis to deep conceptual explanation of theoretical emergence
Stage 6. Framing and Establishing Testable Hypotheses	• Attempting repeatability rather than the sampling of cases and applying systematic logic across the process of framing and establishing testable hypotheses	✓ Provides conclusive confirmation, extends knowledge, and provides a strategic focus for theoretical postulation
	• Examining specific causation factors in relationships and interactions (i.e., the 'why' rather than the 'how' of the specific case)	✓ Provides enhanced levels of internal validity to the case study
Stage 7. Embedding Extant literature	• Iteratively comparing opposing and contested viewpoints from the extant literature and affirming consistency with that which is in the same field	✓ Enhances the degree of apparent internal validity
		✓ Highlights and extends the claim of external validity
Stage 8. Theoretical Saturation and Case Completion	• Stating completion of theoretical saturation where possible	✓ Provides closure to the case at the point at which no more can be added

Eisenhardt's (1989)

Stage 1: Initiation

Eisenhardt's seminal work established that there are three fundamental aspects of initiating a Case Study; these are a) Clear framing and operational definition of research phenomenon b) Acknowledging the existence of a priori construct and c) Considering how an existing theory or hypotheses could impact on the focus of inquiry (Eisenhardt, 1989).

Clear Framing and Operational Definition of Research Phenomenon

Operationally defining the research phenomenon is fundamental to the establishment of a case not shrouded in ambiguity. Yin highlighted that, because of the sheer volume of data it is possible to collect, the process of analysis can become simply overwhelming without clear focus (Yin, 2011).

The pragmatic integration of knowledge into practice necessitated challenging the legitimacy of academic findings from traditional research into learning domains, in this instance the affective domain. In the context of pedagogical research discourse, 'research' has generally required no differentiation of practice-based versus theoretical research; for the first time, this has become a focal point of debate around the value of pedagogical research to applied practice. This has important ramifications for the research-contingent areas of academic curricula and the programmes that podiatry undergraduates seek to access. It focuses on the holistic, societal, civic, and corporate worth of education beyond individual benefit alone. An Evaluative Case Study was therefore confirmed to have the potential to serve in the capacity of illuminating and illustrating key aspects of the epistemic positionality underpinning attitudes and behaviours towards the elderly in clinical practice settings and practical life, and as such are inherently valued in terms of how this can be achieved in practice.

This Evaluative Case Study emphasised the need for podiatry students to reflect on and apply critical reflexivity to the concept of ageism in podiatric practice and to contemplate the potential impact that this could have on the high proportions of older adults occupying the demographic profile of podiatry intervention in the Western world.

The specific intent of this study was to provide a depth of understanding of how the use of the character of Nana Speakman from the situational comedy 'The Royle Family' could be used as a means of driving and then capturing the epistemic cognition of podiatry students in their formative stages of learning. It was posited as a mechanism by which processes of critical reflexivity could be used to facilitate students in their wider thinking of what it means to be old, and how their interactions with older adults have the capacity to impact on them beyond the context of a functional podiatric clinical intervention. This was achieved by researching a mechanism of completely different affective domain teaching, learning, and assessment than any other previously used. My own contribution to ascertaining this level of understanding was directed at being able to identify an explanation of the 'how' and 'why' of podiatry students engaging or not engaging with processes of reflection and reflexivity. To achieve this objective, I stated two highly interrelated research questions: *"What are the metacognitive processes that frame how podiatry students perceive older adults?"* and *"How and why do podiatry students react to the integration of media portrayal of the elderly within pedagogical practice?"* As explained below, these research questions provided a well-defined focus to the Evaluative Case Study research and specified the nature of data to be gathered.

ACKNOWLEDGEMENT OF THE EXISTENCE OF A PRIORI CONSTRUCT

In determining the use of extant theoretical constructs to guide my approach in theory-building research, I had to consider two individual potential approaches that I could adopt (Moore et al., 2015).

It is useful to examine each in turn to see the impact of each approach.

The Provision of a Specific and Explicit Conceptual Framework

There was the option to use a conceptual analytical framework to make explicit theoretical statements in relation to the notion of using media portrayal of the elderly as part of podogeriatric curricula with podiatry students (Miles & Huberman, 1994). This would have provided a means of visibly 'mapping' major concepts simultaneously so that the interrelationships in the phenomena could be clearly seen and articulated (Saldaña, 2015).

Not Being Constrained by the Existence of Prior Theory

This is where the iterative development of theoretical emergence and hypothetical understanding underpin and provide purposefulness to the Evaluative Case Study research. The second option was to attempt not to be constrained by the existence of prior theory. Instead, I needed to regard the development of theoretical emergence, potential hypotheses, and conceptual possibilities in a topic area that already had been the focus of much pedagogical research (Cohen, Manion & Morrison, 2013)

There were evident parallels in Grounded Theory approaches to research and the development of Constructivist Grounded Theory (Charmaz, 2014). I combined both approaches since the intention of my study was to provide a new perspective in an already established research field (i.e., my focus was on theory building rather than theory testing). This provided reassurance that I did not overlook significant issues, that I could make meaning of occurrences, and that I could clearly define established priorities within affective domain learning. Doing so subsequently provided a clear set of constructs for investigation and ultimately guided and facilitated a sense of focus for the research.

Using established research questions as a guide, this conceptual framework was used to comprehensively group constructs comprehensively related to the contextual conditions, influencing the implementation of the media-based intervention (e.g., the resources necessary, context of the feedback, supplementary annotation on formative work, metric data). As a researcher, the author paid attention to the context and interaction between herself and the podiatry students, within which human action was one of the most significant factors. Eisenhardt (1989) posited that the identification of constructs is tentative in theory-building research, something found to be accurate in the context of this research when new contributing factors were revealed during iterative data collection, which consequently needed to be added to the process of data analysis.

EXISTING THEORY/ HYPOTHESES AND IMPACT ON THE FOCUS OF INQUIRY

Eisenhardt (1989) proposed that research detailing theoretical emergence must start with a 'tabula rasa' and allude to the ideal of no former theoretical consideration, since any pre-contemplated phenomena may skew the interpretation of a fresh data set and potentially limit the findings. I followed this to a certain extent by not explicitly identifying specific relationships among the constructs identified in my conceptual framework, where I adopted the teleological view advocated by Knobe and Samuels (2013). It was here that this teleological theory reflected my basic assumptions regarding the phenomena under scrutiny (i.e., the concept of ageism) and what was known in the extant literature. The adoption of this teleological view of the implementation of media usage in pedagogical practice enhanced my capacity as a researcher to understand how a specific intervention could be used to gain insight into processes of student learning and engagement.

CASE SELECTION AND SAMPLING TECHNIQUE

Theoretical sampling lies at the heart of purist Case Study research (Yin, 2013). This was a means of collecting data with the specific purpose of generating theory via the concurrent collection and analysis of data. The researcher moved to the most purposive area for data collection in the light of what initial analysis revealed. This enriched the theory as it was developed from one data set to the next. The unit of analysis in the study was related to the way the research questions were operationally defined and the generalisations needed at the end of the study (Yin, 2011). The unit of analysis in the study could be defined as the intervention with media, or to be even more specific, the procedural steps taken during the implementation.

DEVELOPING THE SPECIFICS OF RESEARCH DESIGN AND METHODOLOGY

The potential to triangulate the process of data collection was important to the study. It permitted a much more robust formulation of constructs and hypotheses. It has also been posited that the collection of data via a variety of means ensured a fuller picture of the phenomena under scrutiny could be achieved. The primary goal of data collection was via a semi-structured questionnaire and a series of short interviews, for which interview guides were developed for use with the podiatry students. I adopted the stance of Joukes et al. (2016), ensuring that the primary goal of my interviews was to elicit the respondent's views and experiences in my own terms, rather than to collect data sets designed to collate responses from specific pre-established response categories. The initial stage of the research process was interviewing the doctoral students on a one-to-one basis. The interview provided a context for explanation and discussion of the purpose of the inquiry and was designed to engage podiatry students and to motivate their interest in the processes of assessment and feedback across the whole podiatric medicine programme. Bias was minimised by providing limited insight into the conceptual framework underpinning the study.

The qualitative data sets were used only to suggest theoretical arguments which could then be strengthened (or weakened) by quantitative support. A survey instrument in the form of a questionnaire was developed to collect data that would either confirm or refute the interpretation of the data. Respondents were the same podiatry students who had taken part in the initial interviews. Collating both quantitative and qualitative evidence aided the research process in illuminating the level of interpretive consistency between the researcher and the podiatry students in relation to the author's capacity as an authentic researcher and student capacity to articulate their experiences.

INITIAL DATA COLLECTION

Eisenhardt (1989) originally noted the increasing degree of overlap in instances where data collection and data analysis take place concurrently. The author implemented Ritchie and Spencer's qualitative Framework Analysis (2002), which is outlined below. This was a pragmatic means of ensuring the researcher could become familiar with the data collected and identify thematic sufficiency to the point where the researcher could move to the next interview, adapting the schedule as necessary. It facilitated the process of actively exploring the similarities and differences in the data, and the overall relationships within and between them (Duff and Anderson, 2015). This gap was bridged through the use of memos and field notes as advocated by Charmaz (2003), which permitted the author to maintain a record of what Van Maanen (2011) would later term the 'streaming consciousness' of key significance to the research process. This process also enhanced my capacity to make meaning of the data sets collected, since they were contextualised and framed in the memos and field notes (Fink, 2013). The net outcome of this stage was the active enrichment of collected data.

DATA ANALYSIS

Ritchie and Spencer's Framework Analysis (2002) was used as a mechanism of data analysis in this study for purely pragmatic reasons:

Table 2. Framework analysis

Step 1: Familiarisation with the Data Set   **Through immersion in the raw data, it is possible to manually become familiar with each data set (termed familiarisation). It is a combinatorial process of re-listening to audio recording files and the extensive reading and re-reading of transcripts and field notes.**
Step 2: Identifying a Thematic Framework   Following familiarisation with the data, the key issues and themes that have been identified form the basis of a thematic framework. This is carried out through a deductive process drawing on a priori issues that form the aims of the study as well as issues raised by the participants that recur in the data. At a result, a detailed index of the data is developed, thus allowing data to be labelled and explored.
Step 3: Indexing   The thematic framework is applied, and all data contained in the transcripts indexed against the codes. This allows for the identification of portions or sections of the data that correspond to a particular theme or concept in the thematic framework.
Step 4: Charting   The data that has been indexed is then rearranged to form charts of the themes. Charts are produced for key themes with entries from the data, linked to individual participants.
Step 5: Testing of emergent themes   The emergent theory is then used to devise the questionnaires, which form an integral part of data triangulation for the study.

Ritchie and Spencer (2002)

In keeping with Yin's recommendation that all case studies should have an embedded analytical strategy to guide the process of deciding what ought to be analysed, the data was sorted pragmatically in conjunction with the process of familiarisation (Yin, 2011). Whereas Yin presents three definitive analytic strategies:

pattern-matching, explanation-building, and time-series analysis, the author made the decision to remain faithful to Ritchie and Spencer's Framework Analysis to make the data collected highly accessible. To understand the 'how' and 'why' associated with the media intervention project, with the intention of providing direct answers to initial and established research hypotheses and research statements, the author implemented an approach which allowed the co-construction of answers within a framework that supported the analytical process. This was a decision based on the pragmatics of prioritising and categorising the most salient findings of the study from the initial data sets.

FRAMING AND ESTABLISHING TESTABLE HYPOTHESES

The next stage of the iterative process in the Evaluative Case Study research was to establish the degree of alignment or refutability between the existing evidence bases and to see whether there was any degree of strategic fit with the most salient findings of my own study. The focus here was to ensure that theoretical findings could be coherently aligned to the data set, in accordance with the seminal work of Eisenhardt (1989). This raises important considerations in how the quality of my Evaluative Case Study is assessed by any outsider and is best articulated in the following table.

Table 3. Criteria of quality evaluation in case study design

Research Quality Criterion	Description	Implementation Process
Criterion 1: Construct Validity	• Providing clear operational definitions at the initial introduction of the Case Study research	• Triangulation of several sources of evidence • Review of data (Check of content validity) interpretation by participants • Engagement of both qualitative and quantitative methods in a mixed methods design

continued on following page

Table 3. Continued

Research Quality Criterion	Description	Implementation Process
Criterion 2: Internal Validity	• Ensuring and validating causal relationships through active comparison, rather than creating unlinked relationships in the data sets	• Analytical approach to co-constructing meaning within an established framework of logic • Content validity check repeated by research participants • Articulation of contextual significance of case findings • Integration of several illustrative citations in the final case study research report • Formulation of a database of findings to act as a checklist • Iterative linkage of theoretical propositions to the extant literature as they emerge
Criterion 3: External validity	• Clearly identifying the parameters of research to which the findings of the study can be generalised	• Analytical generalisation of findings within an established methodological framework • Explicit linkage of theoretical propositions/ emergence to the extant literature
Criterion 4: Reliability	• Ensuring repeatability of the procedural elements of the study (When working with spoken discourse, this can be replaced by the concepts of 'Trustworthiness' and 'Authenticity' since the case study will provide snapshots at any given time, which are essentially non-repeatable due to the dynamic and everchanging features of human opinion)	• Validation of the systematic Framework Analysis tool • Case Study research design and methodology as expressed by a stipulated protocol

EMBEDDING EXTANT LITERATURE

In order to build theoretical propositions, it is necessary to make an active comparison of the most salient conceptual or hypothetical findings with the extant published evidence base (Eisenhardt, 1989). Within the context of my own study, I needed to ask fundamental questions about what knowledge my findings consolidated, refuted, and in some cases bore no relevance to whatsoever.

THEORETICAL SATURATION AND CASE COMPLETION

Reaching the point of closure in the emergence of new themes was outlined by Eisenhardt (1989) as the point to end the study and draw together the most salient findings. The possibility of further incremental or iterative learning at this stage is minimal since all notable phenomena have been identified and examined already (Glaser & Strauss, 1967). Within my own study, as with many others conducted in practice, there was a pragmatic decision of when to end case collection. This was another reason why I adopted theoretical sampling technique; I could account for how many cases I would have even before data collection began.

BENCHMARKING STUDENT ENTRY BEHAVIOUR

Benchmarking the entry behaviour of students is usually undertaken with regard for formalised learning. Teaching gerontology necessitates a level of pre-professionalisation that encompasses both childhood and adolescent socialisation prior to the study of the subject. Childhood and adolescent socialisation theory points towards the potential influence that students' gender, ethnic background, socio-economic status, political affiliation, political ideology, and bonds between respondents and their grandparents (as an integral part of intergenerational solidarity) have on stereotypes towards older people and the attitudes they display towards elderly patients. The family as a socialising agent has been seminally recognised as being responsible for the initial transmission of culture to the child (Parsons, Bales & Family, 1955) Moreover the family can also socialise children into certain gender or sex roles. It cannot be taken for granted that all members of a student cohort will have had a stereotypical relationship with their grandparents, any more than their grandparents can be believed to be stereotypical. This is rooted in the concept of social constructivist approaches to learning, where learning necessitates drawing on a pre-existing body of knowledge or lived experience.

CLASSROOM DISCUSSIONS

Embedding discussions such as these into classroom time with students in the facilitation of their learning has become a formal mechanism or methodology for addressing the universal truths of human experience across the life trajectory of all members of society. This has the potential to humanise podiatric medical curricula, some of which has been traditionally functionally focused. The role of storytelling and narrative in conveying concepts in the affective domain is a key mechanism of promoting reflection and reflexivity in practice (Fitzpatrick, 2018); it provides a rich generation of perspectives and responses and also values divergent discussion as a driver of academic debate. Whilst not undertaken every day in the context of inquiry-based learning approaches, using television media clips to immerse students in the audio-visual elements of learning affords them the opportunity to consider three-dimensional versions of older people and their portrayal in the media (Marris, 2018).

The case specificity that this provides through a central character means that the motivation and commitment to learn is hinged around a specific case, which is uniquely positioned to drive discussion and debate of sociological and biomedical importance to their applied clinical practice. Alongside this, it gives scope to contextualise this particular element of the curriculum relative to others such as evidence-based practice, the socio-economic implications of healthcare provision, and the wider implications of each for behavioural health. From a strategic standpoint of education providers, it also provides a rationale for contemplating Higher Education's sustainability in practice, in relation to affective domain learning outcomes (Stough et al., 2018).

DRIVING ASSESSMENT WITH TEACHING AND LEARNING

To ensure that students had the opportunity of individualising their learning from the module, I set a negotiated generic assessment topic where they could choose any aspect of the sociology of ageing and develop it into a written report. They then had to accompany this by a fifteen-minute teaching session about the implications of what they had learned that was of relevance to clinical podiatric practice, presenting this to their peers as an educational tool for practice. Some students presented posters, others used Powerpoint slides as a backdrop to driving discussions, and still others used other media portrayals of the elderly to extend issues that, due to our specific focus on Nana Speakman, had been subtly missed. Formative assessment mechanisms ensured students had significant feedback to move forward into the summative elements of their assessment. In comparison to other optional modules that year, the group had a 100% pass rate and 100% attendance. Their marks were on average 15% higher than their counterparts, following independent marking and moderation of all optional module assessments as a collective. Students who had undertaken the module also had grades of an average of 12% higher in clinical practice examinations, regardless of their levels of performance in other modules.

STUDENT-REPORTED IMPACT OF PEDAGOGIC INTERVENTION

As a TV programme, 'The Royle Family' can be unashamedly categorised as a fictional yet realistic vehicle for consideration of the ethnographic paradigm, where there is a multiplicity of data which can be used to triangulate evidence around particular issues such as sociological norms in family life (Wolgemuth et al., 2015). Choosing Nana Speakman was deliberate in that she provided me, as an educator and facilitator, with the opportunity to use her character to illuminate the use of theoretical lenses in examining her character, as well as using her character as a tool for the development of critical reflection and reflexivity in podiatric practice.

Students reported key aspects of what can be termed transformative learning in these sessions. Their assumptions about their own perceptions and beliefs about things beyond old age surprised them. What surprised them most was their unconscious bias in relation to the negative stereotyping of older adults, which had until then been acted out in behavioural responses and which they consequently felt they could challenge via reflection and reflexivity on their practice.

MEDIA IMPACT

The media is a pivotal mechanism of socialisation for young people with the capacity to influence and shape negative portrayals of already marginalised sections of society (Cherry et al., 2015). Depictions of older adults often have negative connotations, and as podiatry academics are also educational gerontologists with core responsibilities to challenge assumptions and raise awareness, this has clear implications for their educational praxis (Ylänne, 2015).

ACTIVE PEDAGOGY: THE IMPACT OF NEGATIVE STEREOTYPING

Negative stereotyping is one of the fundamental origins of the often unintentional denial of access to specific healthcare services for older adults. A prime example of this in podiatric practice is the provision of community biomechanics services, where older adults are often simply labelled as being 'too old' for biomechanical intervention on the basis of age, prior to any functional assessment of their musculoskeletal status. This is important, as not all older people follow the same trajectory of functional senescence; individual consideration of functional capacity ought to be extended to all patients, regardless of their allocation to specific clinical caseloads.

By raising awareness of this often unintentional approach to categorising people, it will potentially be possible to reduce levels of active ageism in podiatric practice.

SEVEN LESSONS LEARNED FROM STUDENT FEEDBACK ON THE SESSIONS

Lesson 1

Negotiated assessment is an ideal opportunity to individualise learning, keep students focused and motivated, and reduce the likelihood of disengagement with assessment strategy, plagiarism, and surface learning.

Lesson 2

Student-centred learning can be tokenistic in operational practice. Remaining faithful to authentic student-centred learning requires ongoing commitment to the development of materials that stimulate student capacity to use epistemic and metacognitive processes to make meaning and internalise key concepts that will continue to mean something in their future practice.

Lesson 3

Students might have preferred learning styles but driving learning with principles of social interactivity works. We often forget education is a social science and the implications of operationalising this in practice.

Lesson 4

Teaching capacity for reflection and critical reflexivity is as important as overall module content and innovative pedagogic practice.

Lesson 5

The power balance between learner and facilitator can be pivotal in students having confidence to project their learning consolidation forward in a group setting. It also provides the student with a greater and more authentic approach to critical thinking which, in turn, contributes to their capacity for critical writing.

Lesson 6

What students bring to the classroom is an invaluable source of reflection and learning for others. Assessing people's entry behaviour on the basis of academic qualifications alone is exceptionally limited and ought to be complemented with a values-based approach to the assessment of relevant experience in practice.

Lesson 7

Learning within the classroom can be used to drive learning beyond the classroom so that education becomes an integrated part of life, not something that exists in abstraction from it.

CONCLUSION

UK and global societies need to prepare for an exponential increase in their constitution in relation to the rising numbers of older people. It is critical to address values-based learning relative to inadvertent or deliberate prejudice in response to the functional and psychosocial healthcare needs of older patients. Since these prejudicially negative attitudes and largely unfounded perceptions directly impact on the lives and self-regard of older people for themselves, healthcare curricula for professionals whose careers will have a significant degree of contact with older members of society must move beyond tokenism when they embed the teaching of sociological concepts such as ageism into their operational curricula. Being able to systematically evaluate the impact of these curricula via case study analysis provides just one mechanism, beyond informal student feedback of both impact and understanding of pedagogic research in the field. Using fictitious characters like Nana Speakman provides a means of driving affective domain learning with a three-dimensional approach to representation of the complex and diverse nature of ageism in 21st century societies. The universality of the process of ageing is one which transcends time, but is also one, perhaps most ironically, that we all will eventually face if we live long enough.

The need to address stereotyping is fundamental if we are to change the practice and perspectives of the ageist generations of staff that practice them, often inadvertently rather than out of deliberate intergenerational disrespect. Where ageism is at its most dangerous is in relation to the potential for negative prejudice. As humans we have an inbuilt predisposition to categorise and homogenise for ease of our own cognitive thinking processes; this is part of our capacity to comprehend, relate, and synthesise the information that bombards our visual and auditory senses with new meanings of what it is to 'be old.' It is in this sense that we ought not be surprised that the negative stereotyping of ageing is characterised by the same processes. Perceived contrasts between age groups and our relative perceptions of them are rooted in our evaluative capacities, which again alter with time and our own positions on a temporal continuum.

From the integration of the Evaluative Case Study approach, it was possible to make six key observations:

- Case study research emphasised the value of processes of self-regulation and reflexivity, on behalf of the researcher and the research participants, which can be mutually beneficial.
- Case study research provided a means of examining the functional dynamics of experience as well as providing a lens to identify the processes of active implementation of phenomena.
- Case study research provided a mechanism of making research data accessible to a wide audience and for reflection and adaptation to events.
- The co-construction of reality with participants meant knowledge and who controls it can be accounted for and readily established. Epistemologically this is significant in the establishment and development of core knowledge of a specific case, such as the potential for ageism in applied podiatric clinical practice.
- The use of case study research enabled the in-depth systematic interpretation of policy, experience, and context.
- The temporality of case study research meant it was not dependent on time or constrained by methodological approach and method, which was responsive to a shift in focus and unanticipated developmental progression.

In the context of podiatric medicine specifically and allied health generally, it is pivotal that we amplify collective and individual understanding of this assumptive potential, so that it can be acknowledged as something often unconsciously behaviourally expressed in everyday interactions with older people. This is not merely an issue of raising awareness. It ought to be an address of conscience for podiatry as a clinical and academic discipline working predominantly with older adults in clinical practice, research, and education and who are, by virtue of this, often the focus of teaching and learning facilitation with the next generation of healthcare workers.

REFERENCES

Adogwa, O., Elsamadicy, A. A., Sergesketter, A. R., Black, C., Tarnasky, A., Ongele, M. O., & Karikari, I. O. (2017). Relationship Among Koenig Depression Scale and Postoperative Outcomes, Ambulation, and Perception of Pain in Elderly Patients (≥ 65 Years) Undergoing Elective Spinal Surgery for Adult Scoliosis. *World Neurosurgery*, 107, 471–476. DOI: 10.1016/j.wneu.2017.07.165 PMID: 28826716

Burgess, H. & Wellington, J. (2010) "Exploring the impact of the professional doctorate on students' professional practice and personal development: early indications" in Work Based Learning E-journal Vol.1, No.1, pp. 160-176.

Charmaz, K. (2003). *Grounded theory. Qualitative psychology: A practical guide to research methods*. Sage.

Charmaz, K. (2014). Constructing grounded theory. *Sage (Atlanta, Ga.)*.

Chaucer, G. (1835). *The Pardoner's Tale*. Clarendon Press.

Cherry, C., Hopfe, C., MacGillivray, B., & Pidgeon, N. (2015). Media discourses of low carbon housing: The marginalisation of social and behavioural dimensions within the British broadsheet press. *Public Understanding of Science (Bristol, England)*, 24(3), 302–310. DOI: 10.1177/0963662513512442 PMID: 24336448

Clarke, A. (2005). Situational analysis: Grounded theory after the postmodern turn. *Sage (Atlanta, Ga.)*.

Cohen, L., Manion, L., & Morrison, K. (2013). *Research methods in education*. Routledge. DOI: 10.4324/9780203720967

Cuddy, A. J., Norton, M. I., & Fiske, S. T. (2016). Corrigendum to "This Old Stereotype: The Pervasiveness and Persistence of the Elderly Stereotype". *The Journal of Social Issues*, 72(3), 614–614. DOI: 10.1111/josi.12185

Duff, P. A., & Anderson, T. (2015). Case-study Research. *The Cambridge Guide to Research in Language Teaching and Learning*, 112.

Eisenhardt, K. M. (1989). Building theories from case study research. *Academy of Management Review*, 14(4), 532–550. DOI: 10.2307/258557

Fink, C. K. (2013). Consciousness as Presence: An Exploration of the Illusion of Self. *Buddhist Studies Review*, 30(1), 113–128. DOI: 10.1558/bsrv.v30i1.113

Fitzpatrick, J. J. (2018). Teaching Through Storytelling: Narrative Nursing. *Nursing Education Perspectives*, 39(2), 60. DOI: 10.1097/01.NEP.0000000000000298 PMID: 29461432

Glaser, B., & Strauss, A. (1967). *The discovery of grounded theory: Strategies of qualitative research*. Wiedenfeld and Nicholson.

Joukes, E., Cornet, R., de Bruijne, M. C., & de Keizer, N. F. (2016). Eliciting end-user expectations to guide the implementation process of a new electronic health record: A case study using concept mapping. *International Journal of Medical Informatics*, 87, 111–117. DOI: 10.1016/j.ijmedinf.2015.12.014 PMID: 26806718

Kagan, S. H. (2017). 6 Ageism and the Helping Professions. *Ageism: Stereotyping and Prejudice against Older Persons*, 165.

Kelly, D. M. (2017). Teaching for social justice. *Revista Intercambio*, (3), 26.

Kelly, G. (2016). Methodological considerations for the study of epistemic cognition in practice. *Handbook of Epistemic Cognition*, 393-408.

Kemp, C. L., Ball, M. M., Morgan, J. C., Doyle, P. J., Burgess, E. O., & Perkins, M. M. (2018). Maneuvering Together, Apart, and at Odds: Residents' Care Convoys in Assisted Living. *The Journals of Gerontology: Series B*.

Kennedy, M., Billett, S., Gherardi, S., & Grealish, L. (2015). Practice-based learning in higher education: jostling cultures. In *Practice-based Learning in Higher Education* (pp. 1–13). Springer. DOI: 10.1007/978-94-017-9502-9_1

Knobe, J., & Samuels, R. (2013). Thinking like a scientist: Innateness as a case study. *Cognition*, 126(1), 72–86. DOI: 10.1016/j.cognition.2012.09.003 PMID: 23063235

McGarry, A. (2015). Sample evaluation of caseload complexity in a community health-care NHS trust. *British Journal of Community Nursing*, 20(4), 174–180. DOI: 10.12968/bjcn.2015.20.4.174 PMID: 25839875

Menz, H. B. (2016). Chronic foot pain in older people. *Maturitas*, 91, 110–114. DOI: 10.1016/j.maturitas.2016.06.011 PMID: 27451329

Miles, M. B., & Huberman, A. M. (1994). *Qualitative data analysis: An expanded sourcebook*. Sage.

Moore, G. F., Audrey, S., Barker, M., Bond, L., Bonell, C., Hardeman, W., & Baird, J. (2015). Process evaluation of complex interventions: Medical Research Council guidance. *BMJ (Clinical Research Ed.)*, 350(mar19 6), h1258. DOI: 10.1136/bmj.h1258 PMID: 25791983

Nancarrow, S., & Borthwick, A. (2016). Interprofessional working for the health professions. *The Routledge companion to the professions and professionalism*, 343.

North, M. S., & Fiske, S. T. (2015). Modern attitudes toward older adults in the ageing world: A cross-cultural meta-analysis. *Psychological Bulletin*, 141(5), 993–1021. DOI: 10.1037/a0039469 PMID: 26191955

Park, H., & Lee, J. (2017). The influence of media, positive perception, and identification on survey-based measures of corruption. *Business Ethics (Oxford, England)*, 26(3), 312–320. DOI: 10.1111/beer.12143

Parsons, T., Bales, R. F., & Family, S. (1955). *Interaction Process*.

Phillips, R., & Waugh, F. (2018). Emancipatory social work with older people: challenging students to overcome the limitations of ageism and institutional oppression. *Social Work and Policy Studies: Social Justice, Practice and Theory, 1*(001).

Ritchie, J., & Spencer, L. (2002). Qualitative data analysis for applied policy research. *The qualitative researcher's companion, 573*, 305-329.

Saldaña, J. (2015). The coding manual for qualitative researchers. *Sage (Atlanta, Ga.)*.

Shlisky, J., Bloom, D. E., Beaudreault, A. R., Tucker, K. L., Keller, H. H., Freund-Levi, Y., Fielding, R. A., Cheng, F. W., Jensen, G. L., Wu, D., & Meydani, S. N. (2017). Nutritional Considerations for Healthy Ageing and Reduction in Age-Related Chronic Disease. *Advances in Nutrition*, 8(1), 17–26. DOI: 10.3945/an.116.013474 PMID: 28096124

Simons, H. (2009). *Case study research in practice*. SAGE publications. DOI: 10.4135/9781446268322

Stake, R. E. (1995). The art of case study research. *Sage (Atlanta, Ga.)*.

Stake, R. E. (2013). *Multiple case study analysis*. Guilford Press.

Stough, T., Ceulemans, K., Lambrechts, W., & Cappuyns, V. (2018). Assessing sustainability in higher education curricula: A critical reflection on validity issues. *Journal of Cleaner Production*, 172, 4456–4466. DOI: 10.1016/j.jclepro.2017.02.017

Sultana, J., Fontana, A., Giorgianni, F., Basile, G., Patorno, E., Pilotto, A., Molokhia, M., Stewart, R., Sturkenboom, M., & Trifirò, G. (2018). Can information on functional and cognitive status improve short-term mortality risk prediction among community-dwelling older people? A cohort study using a UK primary care database. *Clinical Epidemiology*, 10, 31–39. DOI: 10.2147/CLEP.S145530 PMID: 29296099

Van Maanen, J. (2011). *Tales of the field: On writing ethnography*. University of Chicago Press. DOI: 10.7208/chicago/9780226849638.001.0001

Wadsworth, B. J. (1996). *Piaget's theory of cognitive and affective development: Foundations of constructivism*. Longman Publishing.

Wolgemuth, J. R., Erdil-Moody, Z., Opsal, T., Cross, J. E., Kaanta, T., Dickmann, E. M., & Colomer, S. (2015). Participants' experiences of the qualitative interview: Considering the importance of research paradigms. *Qualitative Research*, 15(3), 351–372. DOI: 10.1177/1468794114524222

Yin, R. K. (2011). *Applications of case study research*. Sage.

Yin, R. K. (2013). *Case study research: Design and methods*. Sage.

Ylänne, V. (2015). Representations of ageing in the media. *Routledge handbook of cultural gerontology*, 369-376.

Zebrowitz, L. A., and Montepare, J. M. (2000). Too young, too old: Stigmatizing adolescents and elders. *The social psychology of stigma*, 334-373.

ADDITIONAL READING

Brown, L. G., & Wang, C. H. (2022). Dismantling ageism among nursing students. *Teaching and Learning in Nursing*, 17(2), 240–244. DOI: 10.1016/j.teln.2021.12.002

Burnes, D., Sheppard, C., Henderson, C. R.Jr, Wassel, M., Cope, R., Barber, C., & Pillemer, K. (2019). Interventions to reduce ageism against older adults: A systematic review and meta-analysis. *American Journal of Public Health*, 109(8), e1–e9. DOI: 10.2105/AJPH.2019.305123 PMID: 31219720

Chang, E. S., Kannoth, S., Levy, S., Wang, S. Y., Lee, J. E., & Levy, B. R. (2020). Global reach of ageism on older persons' health: A systematic review. *PLoS One*, 15(1), e0220857. DOI: 10.1371/journal.pone.0220857 PMID: 31940338

Donizzetti, A. R. (2019). Ageism in an aging society: The role of knowledge, anxiety about aging, and stereotypes in young people and adults. *International Journal of Environmental Research and Public Health*, 16(8), 1329. DOI: 10.3390/ijerph16081329 PMID: 31013873

Ertürk, N. O., & Karaçizmeli, A. (2021). Ageism and Continuous Education. *Voices from the Classroom: A Celebration of Learning*, 237.

Gordon, S. (2020). Ageism and age discrimination in the family: Applying an intergenerational critical consciousness approach. *Clinical Social Work Journal*, 48(2), 169–178. DOI: 10.1007/s10615-020-00753-0

Kruger, T. M. (2019). The role of educators and employers in reducing (or perpetuating) ageism. *Innovation in Aging*, 3(Supplement_1), S47–S47. DOI: 10.1093/geroni/igz038.183

Levy, S., & Apriceno, M. (2019). Ageing: The role of ageism. *OBM Geriatrics*, 3(4), 1–16. DOI: 10.21926/obm.geriatr.1904083

Marques, S., Mariano, J., Mendonça, J., De Tavernier, W., Hess, M., Naegele, L., Peixeiro, F., & Martins, D. (2020). Determinants of ageism against older adults: A systematic review. *International Journal of Environmental Research and Public Health*, 17(7), 2560. DOI: 10.3390/ijerph17072560 PMID: 32276489

Swift, H. J., & Chasteen, A. L. (2021). Ageism in the time of COVID-19. *Group Processes & Intergroup Relations*, 24(2), 246–252. DOI: 10.1177/1368430220983452 PMID: 33746563

KEY TERMS AND DEFINITIONS

Ageism: Is the term used to describe discrimination or prejudice against the age of a person.

Authenticity: Is the term used to describe being genuine or truthful.

Constructivism: Within the context of education Constructivism is built upon the theory of Jean Piaget which indicate that humans create knowledge via the interaction of their experiences and their consequent ideas.

Critical Reflection: Is the process of identifying, challenging, and acknowledging long held suppositions and pre-assumptions.

Epistemic Knowledge: Is the term used to describe the mind's relation to perceived and actual reality.

Learning Domains: Are defined and classified as Psychomotor, Cognitive and Affective.

Metacognition: Is the conscious awareness, acknowledgement, and understanding of one's own thought processes in the context of meaning making.

Prejudice: Is wrongful pre-supposition or belief about an issue before having evidence which makes it possible to substantiate them.

Reflexivity: Is the conscious capacity to examine and interrogate one's own experiences and reflections, which can be productively used to inform future actions.

Signature Pedagogies: Is the term used to describe the specific styles of teaching and instruction which characterise individual academic disciplines and/or professions.

Chapter 10
Kudumbashree Women Back to School in Kerala:
Navigating Classroom Emotions and Optimizing Instructor–Student Rapport for Enhanced Learning Design

Vishnu Achutha Menon
 https://orcid.org/0000-0003-4028-3685
Institute for Educational and Developmental Studies, Noida, India

ABSTRACT

Kudumbashree is preparing to launch "Thirike Schoolil" or "Back to School," an ambitious campaign aimed at its 46 lakh members. This seeks to strengthen the organization's three-tier system and empower its women members to explore new opportunities. "Thirike Schoolil" aims to bolster the micro-economic livelihood activities of Neighbourhood Groups, raise awareness about digital technology, and foster a vision that elevates the status of women in society. In line with these efforts, the objective of this study is to investigate the impact of instructor-student rapport on the emotional support, emotion work, and emotional valence experienced by Kudumbashree women in school classrooms across Kerala. To achieve this goal, the study utilizes the Classroom Emotion Scale and Instructor-Student Rapport Scale as primary instruments for data collection. These instruments are carefully selected to assess both the emotional experiences of participants and the rapport dynamics between instructors and students within the classroom environment.

DOI: 10.4018/979-8-3693-2663-3.ch010

Copyright © 2025, IGI Global. Copying or distributing in print or electronic forms without written permission of IGI Global is prohibited.

INTRODUCTION

The *Kudumbashree* program, initiated by the State Poverty Eradication Mission (SPEM) in Kerala, India, was launched in 1998 by then Prime Minister Atal Bihari Vajpayee. Named *Kudumbashree,* which translates to "prosperity of the family" in Malayalam, the program aims to empower women, elevate their socio-economic status, and promote their active involvement in local governance. At its core, *Kudumbashree* focuses on community development through grassroots-level neighborhood groups called "Ayalkoottams." These groups, comprising local women, collaborate on various initiatives to enhance socio-economic conditions. The program places significant emphasis on skill development, income-generating activities, and the promotion of micro-enterprises, making it a comprehensive platform for women's empowerment and community upliftment. One of *Kudumbashree*'s distinguishing features is its network of community-based groups, ensuring women's active participation in decision-making and developmental activities. Encouraging women to engage in micro-enterprises and income-generating activities is central to economic independence and sustainability. *Kudumbashree* aims to alleviate poverty by empowering women to take charge of their economic well-being, thereby contributing to overall family and community development. The program extends its impact to local governance by involving women in activities such as local self-government elections, reinforcing its holistic approach. Skill development and training are integral components of the program, equipping women with essential skills for diverse income opportunities and enhancing their capacity for self-reliance and socio-economic growth.

In a recent development, *Kudumbashree* is preparing to launch "Thirike Schoolil" or "Back to School," a pioneering campaign for its 4.6 million members. This initiative, possibly the largest organized by *Kudumbashree* in Kerala, aims to strengthen its three-tier system and empower women members to embark on new ventures. "Thirike Schoolil" seeks to bolster micro-economic livelihood activities of Neighborhood Groups, raise awareness about digital technology, and inspire a transformative vision for women's status. Classes reminiscent of school days will be conducted in over 2,000 government schools on holidays, involving the participation of 20,000 Area Development Societies, 1,070 Community Development Societies, 15,000 resource persons, and members of various training groups. The campaign, scheduled to conclude on December 10, 2024, underscores *Kudumbashree*'s commitment to education, women's empowerment, and community development. The objective of this study is to investigate the impact of instructor-student rapport on emotional support, emotion work, and emotional valence experienced by *Kudumbashree* women in school classrooms in Kerala.

This study was motivated by several key factors. Firstly, it seeks to align with *Kudumbashree*'s mission of empowering women and enhancing their socio-economic status through active participation and skill development. Understanding how rapport between instructors and students influences emotional support, emotion work, and emotional valence is crucial within educational settings that are pivotal to Kudumbashree's initiatives.

The choice to study emotional support, emotion work, and emotional valence among *Kudumbashree* women in school classrooms in Kerala is rooted in several interconnected reasons. Within the context of the *Kudumbashree* project, which focuses on empowering women through socio-economic initiatives and community development, understanding these emotional aspects is crucial.

Emotional support directly impacts women's engagement, satisfaction, and overall well-being within educational settings, aligning with Kudumbashree's goal of enhancing women's socio-economic status through education and skill development.

Emotion work, which involves the management and expression of emotions in educational contexts, is particularly relevant to Kudumbashree's approach to self-reliance and empowerment among its members.

Emotional valence, reflecting the positive or negative quality of emotions experienced in educational settings, directly influences women's perceptions of their educational experiences and their outcomes. Understanding the emotional valence among *Kudumbashree* women in classrooms can provide insights into their motivational levels, satisfaction with learning, and overall educational attainment, thereby informing strategies to enhance educational outcomes within the program.

The study aims to shed light on how educational environments can impact women's growth and development within the program, particularly through the ongoing "Thirike Schoolil" campaign aimed at strengthening members' skills and knowledge. Emphasizing emotional well-being, the research explores how positive instructor-student relationships can contribute to women's satisfaction and engagement in learning. Uncovering factors that enhance emotional support and positive emotional experiences in classrooms, the study aims to inform policies and strategies that can enhance the effectiveness of *Kudumbashree* and similar women empowerment programs. Addressing a gap in existing literature, this research aims to provide empirical evidence and practical insights into the dynamics of instructor-student rapport specific to marginalized and empowered women in community-based initiatives like Kudumbashree, contributing to broader efforts in women's socio-economic advancement and educational enhancement.

Personally, this study aligns with my interests in educational psychology, particularly in how socio-economic initiatives like *Kudumbashree* can influence educational experiences and outcomes through emotional dynamics. This research aims to contribute empirical evidence that can inform policies and practices to better support women's empowerment and educational success within community-based initiatives like *Kudumbashree*.

Review of the Literature

The connection between instructors and students significantly impacts various educational outcomes, including teaching satisfaction, affective commitment, and teaching efficacy (Frisby et al., 2016). Numerous studies highlight the importance of positive relationships in educational settings, emphasizing different facets of this interaction. Small (1982) identified a correlation between students' emotional states at the semester's end and their evaluations, suggesting that the emotional climate within a classroom plays a crucial role in students' academic experiences. This aligns with Wilson's (2008) advocacy for a relationship-oriented teaching approach, arguing that instructors who build positive connections with students experience heightened job satisfaction.

Similarly, Frisby and Martin (2010) assert that rapport between instructors and students, coupled with classroom connectedness, enhances student participation. Frisby (2019) supports this by establishing a positive link between emotional contagion and perceptions of rapport with instructors, indicating that emotional dynamics within the classroom significantly influence student engagement. Lee and van Vlack (2018) further demonstrate that deep acting, which involves genuine emotional expression, correlates with positive emotions, thereby improving classroom management self-efficacy. These findings underscore the benefits of positive emotional interactions in educational settings, as highlighted by Timoštšuk and Ugaste (2012), who observed that positive emotions have the most significant impact on personal teaching experiences.

The complexity of emotional dynamics in teaching is further illustrated by Mohammad (2019), who described the practicum as an emotionally positive experience, and Yin et al. (2013), who demonstrated that teachers' emotional intelligence significantly impacts teaching satisfaction and their use of emotional labor strategies. However, Becker et al. (2014) argue that teachers' emotions are as influential on students' emotions as their instructional behavior, suggesting a bidirectional influence.

Further complicating the picture, Trigwell et al. (2012) found that students adopting a deeper approach to learning report lower levels of positive emotions and higher levels of negative emotions, while Yin et al. (2017) showed that surface acting in teachers had a detrimental impact. Postareff and Lindblom-Ylänne (2011) noted that teachers with learning-focused profiles exhibited more positively charged emotions, suggesting that the alignment of teaching practices with personal values enhances emotional well-being. Yan et al. (2011) highlighted the benefits of developing emotional skills in elementary classrooms, which can lead to improved learning outcomes and prosocial behavior. This supports the idea that emotional skills are crucial for both teachers and students.

Studies such as Geertshuis (2019) and Zhang et al. (2019) highlight the fluctuating nature of emotional well-being and its predictive power on teaching styles through academic self-efficacy. Goetz et al. (2020) showed that appraisals of control and value mediate the effects of perceived teaching characteristics on academic emotions, emphasizing the importance of perception in emotional experiences. Timoštšuk et al. (2016) emphasized good preparation and constructivist methods in reducing negative experiences among student teachers, while Sharma et al. (2016) established a positive correlation between emotional intelligence and academic achievement among teacher trainees.

The connection between instructors and students significantly influences various educational outcomes, including teaching satisfaction, affective commitment, and teaching efficacy (Frisby et al., 2016). Multiple studies underscore the importance of these relationships, albeit with some nuances and contrasting findings. Wilson (2008) advocates for a relationship-oriented teaching approach, emphasizing the cultivation of positive connections between instructors and students. He argues that such relationships enhance job satisfaction among teachers. This is supported by Frisby and Martin (2010), who found that rapport and classroom connectedness increase student participation. Frisby (2019) extends this by establishing a positive association between emotional contagion and perceptions of rapport with instructors. Similarly, Lee and van Vlack (2018) demonstrate that deep acting, which involves genuinely expressing positive emotions, enhances classroom management self-efficacy. Timoštšuk and Ugaste (2012) observed that positive emotions have the most significant influence on personal teaching experiences, further highlighting the benefits of positive emotional dynamics in the classroom.

The structural model proposed by Sakiz (2012) underscores the direct and indirect relationships between perceived instructor affective support and various emotional and motivational variables, suggesting that emotional support from instructors is critical for student motivation and engagement. Jomon and John (2017) posit that higher emotional competence correlates with increased student engagement, indicating that instructors who can manage their emotions effectively create more engaging learning environments. Burić (2019) found that even the act of faking positive emotions contributes positively to class affect and intrinsic motivation. Lehman et al. (2008) underscore the effectiveness of one-to-one tutoring in achieving learning gains and nurturing positive attitudes towards learning.

Hosotani and Imai-Matsumura (2011) emphasize that high-quality teachers utilize emotional competence in their teaching practices, indicating that the ability to manage emotions is crucial but perhaps not sufficient on its own. Eren (2014) suggests that prospective teachers' emotions about teaching and their emotional styles must be considered to fully understand their future teaching plans. Mohammad (2019) describes the practicum as an emotionally positive experience, further supporting the notion that positive emotional experiences in teaching are beneficial. Yin et al. (2013) demonstrate that teachers' emotional intelligence significantly impacts teaching satisfaction and the use of emotional labor strategies, while Becker et al. (2014) argue that teachers' emotions are as influential on students' emotions as their instructional behavior. Goldman and Goodboy (2014) find that confirming behaviors by instructors heighten students' emotional interest and support, leading to a more positive emotional classroom environment. Conversely, Olson et al. (2019) note that female teachers who employ deep acting strategies often experience emotional exhaustion and unpleasant emotions, indicating potential emotional costs associated with emotional labor.

The relationship between learning approaches and emotions is also complex. Trigwell et al. (2012) find that students adopting a deeper learning approach report lower levels of positive emotions and higher levels of negative emotions, while H. Yin et al. (2017) show that surface acting in teachers has a detrimental impact. Postareff and Lindblom-Ylänne (2011) note that teachers with learning-focused profiles exhibit more positively charged emotions regarding their teaching experiences. Yan et al. (2011) highlight the benefits of developing emotional skills in elementary classrooms, which can improve learning outcomes, prosocial behavior, and positive emotional development among students.

Fluctuations in emotional well-being throughout the semester are noted by Geertshuis (2019), suggesting that emotional states are not static and can vary significantly. Soanes and Sungoh (2019) find that female science teachers tend to possess slightly higher levels of emotional intelligence compared to their male counterparts, indicating potential gender differences in emotional competencies. Zhang et al. (2019) demonstrate that academics' emotions in teaching can predict teaching styles, both directly and indirectly through academic self-efficacy. Goetz et al. (2020) show that appraisals of control and value mediate the effects of perceived teaching characteristics on academic emotions, emphasizing the importance of perception in emotional experiences. Timoštšuk et al. (2016) emphasize the importance of good preparation and a willingness to use constructivist, pupil-oriented methods in reducing negative experiences among student teachers and promoting effective teaching. Sharma et al. (2016) establish a positive and significant correlation between emotional intelligence and the academic achievement of teacher trainees.

Schutz (2014) illustrates the diverse emotional landscape within classrooms, highlighting the spectrum from joy during successful lessons to frustration with challenging students. This variability underscores the complexity of emotional experiences in educational settings. Quinlan (2016) further emphasizes the role of emotions in enriching social and relational experiences in college teaching, supporting student development. This aligns with Taxer et al. (2019), who argue that high-quality teacher-student relationships can reduce emotional exhaustion by increasing enjoyment and mitigating anger in the classroom. These findings suggest that positive emotional dynamics are integral to both teacher well-being and effective teaching.

Trigwell (2012) corroborates this by linking positive emotions to student-focused teaching approaches, suggesting that teachers' emotional states directly influence their pedagogical methods. Similarly, Hagenauer et al. (2015) stress the significance of interpersonal teacher-student relationships in shaping teachers' emotional experiences, indicating that the quality of these relationships is crucial for promoting a positive emotional climate in the classroom. Asrar-ul-Haq et al. (2017) further expand on this by demonstrating a positive relationship between emotional self-awareness, self-confidence, achievement, and teacher job performance. This suggests that teachers' emotional competencies are essential for their professional effectiveness.

The importance of emotional authenticity is highlighted by Keller and Becker (2021), who found that students highly value teachers' self-reported emotional authenticity. This is supported by H. Yin (2015), who suggests that deep acting and expressing naturally felt emotions are effective emotional labor strategies for teachers. Dewaele et al. (2018) advocate for training in emotional competencies to enhance classroom practices for both trainee and experienced teachers. Reyes et al. (2012) add that the positive relationship between classroom emotional climate and grades is mediated by student engagement, indicating that positive emotional environment can lead to better academic outcomes.

Mainhard et al. (2018) emphasize that the way teachers relate interpersonally to their students significantly predicts student emotions, supporting the notion that teacher-student rapport is critical. Frenzel et al. (2021) find that positive emotions are linked to desirable outcomes, while negative emotions lead to undesirable consequences, reinforcing the importance of maintaining a positive emotional atmosphere. Suleman et al. (2019) propose that improving the emotional intelligence of undergraduate students can further enhance their academic performance, suggesting that emotional intelligence training should be an integral part of educational programs.

Wang (2022) adds that teachers with high self-efficacy have a more significant positive impact on the relationship between teacher work engagement and student academic achievement compared to those with low self-efficacy. This highlights the importance of self-efficacy in enhancing the effectiveness of teacher-student interactions.

Goetz et al. (2021) reveal that higher relationship quality is associated with stronger positive emotions and weaker negative emotions over time, suggesting that the benefits of positive teacher-student relationships are sustained over the long term. Chen (2019) highlights that positive teacher emotions lead to student-centered approaches, while negative emotions have adverse consequences, further emphasizing the importance of emotional well-being for effective teaching. Demetriou et al. (2009) suggest that female teachers are better equipped to engage their students, indicating potential gender differences in emotional competencies. Hagenauer et al. (2016) find that Australian teacher educators exhibit higher and more intense expressions of positive emotions in their teaching practices, suggesting cultural variations in emotional expression.

Kang and Wu (2022) posit that positive emotional classroom rapport can mitigate or eliminate students' feelings of shame, highlighting the protective role of positive emotional climates. Valente et al. (2020) demonstrate that teachers adept at perceiving and managing emotions exhibit greater levels of teacher efficacy, reinforcing the importance of emotional intelligence in teaching. Titsworth et al. (2013) propose expanding emotional response theory to encompass both processes and discrete emotions, suggesting a need for a more nuanced understanding of emotions in educational settings. Wara et al. (2018) observe that increased emotional engagement among students correlates with improvements in academic achievement, indicating that emotional engagement can lead to better educational outcomes. Thakur (2016) suggests that teachers who receive training in emotional intelligence are expected to have higher levels of knowledge and performance, and that there is no significant difference between male and female teacher trainees regarding emotional competence, indicating the universal benefits of emotional intelligence training.

Direct instruction was associated with slightly lower levels of positive emotions and higher levels of boredom compared to the other two teaching methods (Bieg et al., 2017). The professional development of teachers necessitates a holistic, whole-school approach (Golby, 1996). Combining moment-to-moment data on teachers' interpersonal behavior with physiological arousal has the potential to elucidate differences in teachers' emotional outcomes (Donker et al., 2020). Teachers' management of emotions is considered a discretionary, voluntary-based element within their role structure (Oplatka, 2007). Stress among teachers may lead to negative consequences that undermine their ability to maintain personal health and positive relationships with students; gender also acts as a significant predictor for mental well-being scores in the group at baseline (Telles et al., 2019). When teachers feel the need to express anger, it is essential for them to address the issue with students (Jiang et al., 2019). Effective communication between learners and tutor-counselors has been shown to significantly enhance positive emotions, reduce negative emotions, and reinforce learners' participation in distance learning programs (Kalogiannakis & Touvlatzis, 2015). Work motivation does not influence the indirect relationship between spiritual intelligence and emotional intelligence on teacher performance (Jelińska & Paradowski, 2021). Emotional intelligence plays a critical role in teachers' satisfaction with their work (Arif et al., 2019). The activities in which pre-service teachers engage are significant to them (Rinchen et al., 2016). Deep acting positively predicts joy over time (Burić et al., 2019). A positive and significant correlation exists between emotional intelligence and academic performance among students at the higher secondary level (Rabha & Saikia, 2019). Teachers often experience positive emotions ranging from moderate to high intensity (Stephanou & Oikonomou, 2018). Positive emotions are positively related to job satisfaction (Parveen & Bano, 2019). Women, final year students, and those who volunteer with youth organizations tend to have higher emotional intelligence (Thulasingam et al., 2020). There is no significant difference between male and female job satisfaction and emotional intelligence (Roy, 2022). Evidence suggests that an increase in emotional intelligence levels leads to improved work productivity and effectiveness (Gill, 2017). The effect of teacher mindfulness on classroom emotions is partially mediated by work engagement (Tao, 2022). Early information about students' emotions can be beneficial for both teachers and students in improving classroom results and learning outcomes (Ruiz et al., 2016). Positive emotions are not only directly related to a student-oriented approach to teaching (Kordts-Freudinger, 2017). Empathetic behaviors exhibited by teachers impact students' self-reported success (Bozkurt & Ozden, 2010). Instructors should be adept at recognizing the role of non-verbal communication in classes and using it appropriately; the number of emotions reported by teachers decreases as the distance from the teachers increases (Chen, 2020)

Schutz (2014) illustrates the diverse emotional landscape within classrooms, highlighting the spectrum from joy during successful lessons to frustration with challenging students. This variability underscores the complexity of emotional experiences in educational settings. Quinlan (2016) emphasizes the role of emotions in enriching social and relational experiences in college teaching, supporting student development. Taxer et al. (2019) argue that high-quality teacher-student relationships can reduce emotional exhaustion by increasing enjoyment and mitigating anger in the classroom. These findings suggest that positive emotional dynamics are integral to both teacher well-being and effective teaching.

Trigwell (2012) corroborates this by linking positive emotions to student-focused teaching approaches, suggesting that teachers' emotional states directly influence their pedagogical methods. Similarly, Hagenauer et al. (2015) stress the significance of interpersonal teacher-student relationships in shaping teachers' emotional experiences, indicating that the quality of these relationships is crucial for cultivating a positive emotional climate in the classroom. Asrar-ul-Haq et al. (2017) expand on this by demonstrating a positive relationship between emotional self-awareness, self-confidence, achievement, and teacher job performance. This suggests that teachers' emotional competencies are essential for their professional effectiveness.

The importance of emotional authenticity is highlighted by Keller and Becker (2021), who found that students highly value teachers' self-reported emotional authenticity. This is supported by H. Yin (2015), who suggests that deep acting and expressing naturally felt emotions are effective emotional labor strategies for teachers. Dewaele et al. (2018) advocate for training in emotional competencies to enhance classroom practices for both trainee and experienced teachers. Reyes et al. (2012) add that the positive relationship between classroom emotional climate and grades is mediated by student engagement, indicating that creating a positive emotional environment can lead to better academic outcomes.

Mainhard et al. (2018) emphasize that the way teachers relate interpersonally to their students significantly predicts student emotions, supporting the notion that teacher-student rapport is critical. Frenzel et al. (2021) find that positive emotions are linked to desirable outcomes, while negative emotions lead to undesirable consequences, reinforcing the importance of maintaining a positive emotional atmosphere. Suleman et al. (2019) propose that improving the emotional intelligence of undergraduate students can further enhance their academic performance, suggesting that emotional intelligence training should be an integral part of educational programs.

Wang (2022) adds that teachers with high self-efficacy have a more significant positive impact on the relationship between teacher work engagement and student academic achievement compared to those with low self-efficacy. This highlights the importance of self-efficacy in enhancing the effectiveness of teacher-student interactions.

Goetz et al. (2021) reveal that higher relationship quality is associated with stronger positive emotions and weaker negative emotions over time, suggesting that the benefits of positive teacher-student relationships are sustained over the long term. Chen (2019) highlights that positive teacher emotions lead to student-centered approaches, while negative emotions have adverse consequences, further emphasizing the importance of emotional well-being for effective teaching. Demetriou et al. (2009) suggest that female teachers are better equipped to engage their students, indicating potential gender differences in emotional competencies. Hagenauer et al. (2016) find that Australian teacher educators exhibit higher and more intense expressions of positive emotions in their teaching practices, suggesting cultural variations in emotional expression.

Kang and Wu (2022) posit that positive emotional classroom rapport can mitigate or eliminate students' feelings of shame, highlighting the protective role of positive emotional climates. Valente et al. (2020) demonstrate that teachers adept at perceiving and managing emotions exhibit greater levels of teacher efficacy, reinforcing the importance of emotional intelligence in teaching. Titsworth et al. (2013) propose expanding emotional response theory to encompass both processes and discrete emotions, suggesting a need for a more nuanced understanding of emotions in educational settings. Wara et al. (2018) observe that increased emotional engagement among students correlates with improvements in academic achievement, indicating that creating emotional engagement can lead to better educational outcomes. Thakur (2016) suggests that teachers who receive training in emotional intelligence are expected to have higher levels of knowledge and performance, and that there is no significant difference between male and female teacher trainees regarding emotional competence, indicating the universal benefits of emotional intelligence training.

The literature consistently highlights the critical role of emotions in educational settings. Positive emotional dynamics between teachers and students enhance teaching satisfaction, affective commitment, and teaching efficacy. However, cultural and contextual factors can moderate these relationships, indicating a need for tailored approaches to emotional competence training in different educational contexts. The evidence suggests that cultivating positive emotional climates and enhancing emotional competencies among both teachers and students are essential for improving educational outcomes.

Hypotheses

1. There is no significant relationship between instructor-student rapport and emotional support.
2. There is no significant relationship between instructor-student rapport and emotion work.
3. There is no significant relationship between instructor-student rapport and emotional valence.

Methodology

The study employed the Classroom Emotion Scale and Instructor-Student Rapport Scale as primary tools for data collection, chosen specifically to assess emotional experiences and rapport dynamics between instructors and students in the classroom.

The Classroom Emotion Scale explores emotion work, including the emotional labor students engage in, such as managing or masking emotions. Recent research has expanded this scope to encompass a broader range of emotional processes. Analysis of behavioral outcomes such as compliance, challenging behavior, note-taking habits, and student engagement provides insights into how instructors can strategically influence student emotions to achieve positive behavioral outcomes (Frey, 2019).

The Instructor-Student Rapport Scale was instrumental in examining how instructors and students contribute to cultivating positive relationships in conducive learning environments (Frisby & Myers, 2008). This scale facilitated assessment of rapport dynamics, offering insights into interaction quality, mutual respect, and understanding within the educational context. By evaluating rapport dimensions, educators can pinpoint areas for improvement and implement targeted strategies to enhance communication, trust, and collaboration among all stakeholders. Effective application of the Instructor-Student Rapport Scale aims to establish a supportive and inclusive classroom climate conducive to academic success and student well-being.

The sample comprised 389 women actively engaged in school activities on Sundays from October 5th to December 5th, 2023. Participants were distributed across age groups: 18-38 years (7.2%), 38-58 years (9.2%), 58-78 years (79.5%), and over 78 years (3.8%). Purposive sampling was employed to ensure a diverse representation. Participants were drawn from government schools (39.5%), aided schools (54.1%), and unaided schools (6.2%), with 70% from rural areas, providing a balanced urban-rural perspective. Both online and offline questionnaires were utilized, and informed consent was obtained to uphold ethical standards. Data analysis employed a three-tiered approach integrating descriptive statistics, correlation coefficients, and linear regression to substantiate the relationships under investigation.

Here are operational definitions for the constructs under study:

1. *Instructor-student rapport:* This refers to the quality of the relationship between educators and students, characterized by mutual respect, trust, and understanding. It involves positive interactions that promote a conducive learning environment. This construct is measured by assessing the frequency and quality of supportive behaviors, communication, and the overall sense of connectedness between instructors and students.
2. *Emotional support:* It is defined as the provision of empathy, care, and encouragement by instructors to students within the educational setting. It includes actions that help students feel valued, understood, and motivated. This support can be measured through students' perceptions of their instructors' availability, responsiveness, and the emotional climate created in the classroom.
3. *Emotion work:* This refers to the management and regulation of emotions by individuals, particularly in professional settings. In the context of education, it involves the efforts of instructors and students to display appropriate emotions that align with educational goals and expectations. This can include strategies such as surface acting (altering outward expressions) and deep acting (changing internal feelings). Emotion work is measured by assessing the frequency and intensity of these strategies used by both instructors and students.
4. *Emotional valence:* This refers to the intrinsic attractiveness or aversiveness of an emotional experience. In educational settings, it indicates whether the emotions experienced by students are positive (e.g., joy, satisfaction) or negative (e.g., frustration, anxiety). Emotional valence is typically measured using self-report

scales that capture students' emotional responses to classroom experiences and interactions with instructors.

Results

Table 1. Descriptive statistics and correlation matrix

Variable	Mean	SD	(1)	(2)	(3)	(4)
Instructor student rapport	47.3856	3.03084	1	.351**	.215**	.744**
Emotional support	39.4267	1.91519		1	.373**	.382**
Emotion work	17.4344	1.60827			1	.235**
Emotional valence	9.1671	.57915				1

The table outlines the descriptive statistics and correlation matrix for various variables in the study. In terms of descriptive statistics, the mean and standard deviation for each variable are provided. Notably, the mean Instructor-Student Rapport score is 47.3856 with a standard deviation of 3.03084; the respective means and standard deviations of Emotional Support, Emotion Work, and Emotional Valence are also reported in the table above.

Moving to the correlation matrix, the relationships between variables are expressed through Pearson's correlation coefficients. A positive and moderate correlation is observed between Instructor-Student Rapport and Emotional Support ($r = .351$, $p < .01$). A positive and significant correlation exists between Instructor-Student Rapport and Emotion Work ($r = .215$, $p < .01$). Emotion Work and Emotional Support are positively correlated ($r = .373$, $p < .01$), and Emotional Valence shows significant positive correlations with Instructor-Student Rapport ($r = .744$, $p < .01$), Emotional Support ($r = .382$, $p < .01$), and Emotion Work ($r = .235$, $p < .01$).

Table 2. Linear regression predicting emotional support from instructor student rapport

Predictor	β	t	R^2	Adj. R^2	F	Sig.
Instructor student rapport	.351	7.379	.123	.121	54.452	<0.001

The findings from the linear regression analysis depicted in Table 2 reveal a meaningful relationship between instructor-student rapport and emotional support among *Kudumbashree* women in school classrooms in Kerala. The regression coefficient (β) of 0.351 signifies that for every one-unit increase in instructor-student rapport, there is a corresponding increase of 0.351 units in predicted emotional support. The high t-value of 7.379, with a significance level (Sig.) less than 0.001, underscores the statistical significance of this relationship. The model fit statistics indicate that approximately 12.3% of the variability in emotional support can be attributed to the variation in instructor-student rapport, as indicated by the R^2 value of 0.123. The adjusted R^2 of 0.121 accounts for the number of predictors in the model. The F-value of 54.452 is also statistically significant ($p < 0.001$), suggesting that the overall regression model is robust in predicting emotional support. While the R^2 value is relatively modest, it implies that instructor-student rapport plays a substantial role in explaining variability in emotional support.

Table 3. Linear regression predicting emotion work from instructor student rapport

Predictor	β	t	R^2	Adj. R^2	F	Sig.
Instructor student rapport	.215	4.333	.046	.044	18.776	<0.001

The outcomes of the linear regression analysis, as presented in Table 3, shed light on the relationship between instructor-student rapport and emotion work among *Kudumbashree* women in school classrooms in Kerala. The regression coefficient (β) of 0.215 signifies that for each one-unit increase in instructor-student rapport, there is a corresponding increase of 0.215 units in predicted emotion work. The high t-value of 4.333, coupled with a significance level (Sig.) less than 0.001, underscores the statistical significance of this relationship. Although the R^2 value of 0.046 is relatively modest, it implies that approximately 4.6% of the variability in emotion work can be attributed to the variation in instructor-student rapport. The adjusted R^2 of 0.044, accounting for the number of predictors in the model, corroborates this relationship. The statistically significant F-value of 18.776 indicates that the overall regression model is effective in predicting emotion work.

Table 4. Linear regression predicting emotional valence from instructor student rapport

Predictor	β	t	R^2	Adj. R^2	F	Sig.
Instructor student rapport	.744	21.927	.554	.553	480.793	<0.001

The findings from Table 4, which presents the results of a linear regression analysis predicting emotional valence based on instructor-student rapport, reveal a compelling and statistically significant relationship. The regression coefficient (β) of 0.744 signifies that for each one-unit increase in instructor-student rapport, there is an associated increase of 0.744 units in the predicted emotional valence. The remarkably high t-value of 21.927, coupled with a significance level (Sig.) less than 0.001, underscores the robust statistical significance of this relationship. The substantial R2 value of 0.554 indicates that approximately 55.4% of the variability in emotional valence can be explained by the variation in instructor-student rapport. The adjusted R2, at 0.553, reinforces this relationship, considering the number of predictors in the model. The highly significant F-value of 480.793 emphasizes the effectiveness of the overall regression model in predicting emotional valence.

Discussion

The assertion that there exists a significant relationship between instructor-student rapport and the emotional support of *Kudumbashree* women is intriguing and merits critical analysis. The positive β coefficient suggests a direct and positive association between these two variables, indicating that as instructor-student rapport increases, emotional support tends to increase as well. This finding aligns with established literature highlighting the importance of interpersonal relationships in educational settings, particularly in contexts where learners may face socio-economic challenges. The statistically significant t-value and F-value bolster confidence in the observed relationship between instructor-student rapport and emotional support. These statistical measures indicate that the relationship between these variables is unlikely to have occurred by chance, further underscoring the validity of the findings.

However, it's important to note that statistical significance does not necessarily imply causation. While the results provide evidence of an association between instructor-student rapport and emotional support, other factors may also contribute to the observed outcomes. Despite the relatively low R2 value, which suggests that instructor-student rapport accounts for only a modest portion of the variability in emotional support, it's essential to consider the broader context in which these relationships are situated. The complexity of human interactions, coupled with the multifaceted nature of emotional support, may contribute to the modest explanatory power of the model. Variables not accounted for in the analysis, such as individual differences in personality or external stressors, could also influence emotional support among *Kudumbashree* women.

The significant relationship between instructor-student rapport and emotional support of the *Kudumbashree* women can be attributed to several factors:

- *Trust and communication:* A strong rapport between instructors and students enhances trust and open communication. When *Kudumbashree* women feel comfortable and valued by their instructors, they are more likely to seek emotional support when needed. Trust and communication facilitate the exchange of emotional support between instructors and students, contributing to the significant relationship observed.

- *Sense of belonging:* Instructors who establish a positive rapport with *Kudumbashree* women create a sense of belonging within the educational environment. Feeling connected to their instructors and peers enhances the perception of emotional support among *Kudumbashree* women, as they perceive themselves as part of a supportive learning community where their emotional needs are acknowledged and addressed.
- *Validation and empowerment:* Emotional support from instructors validates the experiences and challenges faced by *Kudumbashree* women, empowering them to navigate their educational journey with confidence. Acknowledging their emotions and providing empathetic support, instructors help build resilience and self-efficacy among *Kudumbashree* women, contributing to their overall emotional well-being.
- *Role modeling and guidance:* Instructors who demonstrate empathy, compassion, and understanding serve as role models for *Kudumbashree* women, guiding them through both academic and personal challenges. Through their supportive actions and behaviors, instructors inspire and empower *Kudumbashree* women to seek help when needed and to offer support to their peers, thereby strengthening the emotional support network within the educational community.
- *Culturally sensitive approaches:* Instructors who are attuned to the cultural norms and values of *Kudumbashree* women are better equipped to provide culturally sensitive emotional support. Incorporating culturally relevant practices and perspectives into their teaching and support strategies, instructors demonstrate respect for the cultural identity and experiences of *Kudumbashree* women, leading to a deeper sense of emotional connection and support.

The assertion of a significant relationship between instructor-student rapport and emotion work among *Kudumbashree* women prompts a critical examination of the findings and their implications. The positive β coefficient indicates a direct and positive association between these variables, suggesting that as instructor-student rapport increases, so does the level of emotion work performed by *Kudumbashree* women. This finding appears counterintuitive at first glance, as one might expect a supportive rapport to alleviate rather than exacerbate the emotional labor experienced by individuals. However, it is plausible that in the context of *Kudumbashree* women, heightened rapport with instructors may lead to increased emotional investment in their educational pursuits, thereby necessitating greater emotion work to manage the associated challenges and expectations.

The statistically significant t-value and F-value lend robustness to the observed association between instructor-student rapport and emotion work, indicating that the relationship is unlikely to be a result of random chance. However, caution is warranted in interpreting these findings, as statistical significance does not imply causation. While the results suggest a meaningful connection between rapport and emotion work, it is essential to consider other potential factors that may influence the observed outcomes. Despite the relatively low R^2 value, which suggests that instructor-student rapport explains only a modest proportion of the variability in emotion work, the findings underscore the potential role of interpersonal dynamics in shaping emotional experiences among *Kudumbashree* women. It is important to recognize that emotion work is a complex and multifaceted phenomenon influenced by a myriad of individual, interpersonal, and contextual factors. Thus, while rapport with instructors may contribute to the explanation of variability in emotion work, it is likely that other unaccounted-for variables also play a significant role in shaping emotional experiences within this population. The interpretation of the findings should be tempered by the limitations of the study. The reliance on self-reported measures of rapport and emotion work introduces the possibility of response bias and social desirability effects, which may impact the accuracy of the results. The cross-sectional nature of the data limits the ability to draw causal inferences or establish temporal precedence between rapport and emotion work.

The claim of a significant relationship between instructor-student rapport and the emotional valence of *Kudumbashree* women warrants careful examination and critical analysis. The substantial β coefficient suggests a strong positive association between these variables, indicating that as rapport between instructors and students increases, so does the emotional valence experienced by *Kudumbashree* women. This finding suggests that positive interactions with instructors may contribute to a more positive emotional experience for these women within the educational context. The exceptionally high t-value and F-value provide compelling evidence of the association between instructor-student rapport and emotional valence, indicating that the relationship is unlikely to have occurred by random chance. These statistical measures lend robustness to the observed association and enhance confidence in the validity of the findings.

However, again it is essential to acknowledge that statistical significance does not imply causation, and other factors may also contribute to the observed outcomes. The high R^2 value, indicating that approximately 55.4% of the variability in emotional valence can be attributed to the variation in instructor-student rapport, underscores the importance of interpersonal relationships in shaping emotional experiences among *Kudumbashree* women. This substantial proportion of explained variance suggests that instructor-student rapport plays a significant role in influencing emotional valence within the educational context. The adjusted R^2 further reinforces this relationship, indicating that the observed association is unlikely to be spurious or a result of overfitting. Despite the strength of the statistical findings, it is essential to consider potential limitations of the study. The cross-sectional nature of the data may limit the ability to establish causal relationships between instructor-student rapport and emotional valence. The reliance on self-reported measures of rapport and emotional valence introduces the possibility of response bias and social desirability effects, which may impact the accuracy of the results.

CONCLUSION

This study offers a comprehensive analysis of the impact of instructor-student rapport on various emotional dimensions among *Kudumbashree* women in school classrooms in Kerala. Through a detailed examination of descriptive statistics, correlation coefficients, and linear regression results, significant insights into these relationships have been uncovered. The descriptive statistics reveal notable mean scores for instructor-student rapport and highlight the positive nature of these relationships within the sample. The correlation matrix demonstrates significant associations between instructor-student rapport and emotional support, emotion work, and emotional valence. Linear regression analysis further confirms the predictive relationships between instructor-student rapport and emotional outcomes, with rapport significantly predicting emotional support, emotion work, and emotional valence. These findings underscore the importance of positive relationships within educational settings to promote emotional well-being among *Kudumbashree* women. However, further research is warranted to explore additional factors contributing to emotional outcomes and to inform targeted interventions aimed at enhancing student well-being and academic success in similar contexts.

Implications

This study carries several implications for educational practices and policies. Educators should prioritize cultivating positive rapport with *Kudumbashree* women, emphasizing trust, open communication, and cultural sensitivity to establish supportive learning environments. Strengthening rapport not only enhances emotional support and well-being but also contributes to heightened engagement and satisfaction among students. Recognizing and supporting the emotional labor performed by *Kudumbashree* women is crucial for effectively managing emotions within educational contexts. Integrating culturally sensitive teaching approaches can further deepen emotional connections and support networks. Institutions should consider developing training programs for instructors on interpersonal skills and cultural competence to standardize practices that promote positive relationships and emotional support. Continued research using longitudinal and mixed-methods approaches can advance understanding of factors influencing emotional experiences among *Kudumbashree* women, guiding future policy and curriculum development. Emphasizing emotional intelligence and effective communication in professional development for educators can cultivate inclusive and supportive learning environments, complemented by community and peer support networks that enhance overall well-being and academic success. Advocating for policies that acknowledge the impact of interpersonal dynamics on educational outcomes can further advance equitable educational opportunities for marginalized groups within diverse cultural contexts.

REFERENCES

Arif, I., Umer, A., Kazmi, S. W., & Khalique, M. (2019). Exploring the relationship among university teachers' emotional intelligence, emotional labor strategies, and teaching satisfaction. *Abasyn Journal of Social Sciences*, 12(1). Advance online publication. DOI: 10.34091/AJSS.12.1.03

Asrar-ul-Haq, M., Anwar, S., & Hassan, M. (2017). Impact of emotional intelligence on teacher s performance in higher education institutions of Pakistan. *Future Business Journal*, 3(2), 87–97. DOI: 10.1016/j.fbj.2017.05.003

Becker, E. S., Goetz, T., Morger, V., & Ranellucci, J. (2014). The importance of teachers' emotions and instructional behavior for their students' emotions – An experience sampling analysis. *Teaching and Teacher Education*, 43, 15–26. DOI: 10.1016/j.tate.2014.05.002

Bieg, M., Goetz, T., Sticca, F., Brunner, E., Becker, E., Morger, V., & Hubbard, K. (2017). Teaching methods and their impact on students' emotions in mathematics: An experience-sampling approach. *ZDM Mathematics Education*, 49(3), 411–422. DOI: 10.1007/s11858-017-0840-1

Bozkurt, T., & Ozden, M. S. (2010). The relationship between empathetic classroom climate and students' success. *Procedia: Social and Behavioral Sciences*, 5, 231–234. DOI: 10.1016/j.sbspro.2010.07.078

Burić, I. (2019). The role of emotional labor in explaining teachers' enthusiasm and students' outcomes: A multilevel mediational analysis. *Learning and Individual Differences*, 70, 12–20. DOI: 10.1016/j.lindif.2019.01.002

Burić, I., & Frenzel, A. C. (2021). Teacher emotional labour, instructional strategies, and students' academic engagement: A multilevel analysis. *Teachers and Teaching*, 27(5), 335–352. DOI: 10.1080/13540602.2020.1740194

Burić, I., Slišković, A., & Penezić, Z. (2019). A two-wave panel study on teachers' emotions and emotional-labour strategies. *Stress and Health*, 35(1), 27–38. DOI: 10.1002/smi.2836 PMID: 30194896

Chen, J. (2019). Exploring the impact of teacher emotions on their approaches to teaching: A structural equation modelling approach. *The British Journal of Educational Psychology*, 89(1), 57–74. DOI: 10.1111/bjep.12220 PMID: 29603123

Chen, J. (2020). Teacher emotions in their professional lives: Implications for teacher development. *Asia-Pacific Journal of Teacher Education*, 48(5), 491–507. DOI: 10.1080/1359866X.2019.1669139

Demetriou, H., Wilson, E., & Winterbottom, M. (2009). The role of emotion in teaching: Are there differences between male and female newly qualified teachers' approaches to teaching? *Educational Studies*, 35(4), 449–473. DOI: 10.1080/03055690902876552

Dewaele, J.-M., Gkonou, C., & Mercer, S. (2018). Do ESL/EFL teachers' emotional intelligence, teaching experience, proficiency and gender affect their classroom practice? In *Emotions in Second Language Teaching* (pp. 125–141). Springer International Publishing. DOI: 10.1007/978-3-319-75438-3_8

Donker, M. H., van Gog, T., Goetz, T., Roos, A.-L., & Mainhard, T. (2020). Associations between teachers' interpersonal behavior, physiological arousal, and lesson-focused emotions. *Contemporary Educational Psychology*, 63(101906), 101906. https://doi.org/10.1016/j.cedpsych.2020.101906

Frenzel, A. C., Daniels, L., & Burić, I. (2021). Teacher emotions in the classroom and their implications for students. *Educational Psychologist*, 56(4), 250–264. DOI: 10.1080/00461520.2021.1985501

Frey, T. K. (2019). Classroom emotions scale. In *Communication Research Measures III* (pp. 195–201). Routledge. DOI: 10.4324/9780203730188-16

Frisby, B. N. (2019). The influence of emotional contagion on student perceptions of instructor rapport, emotional support, emotion work, valence, and cognitive learning. *Communication Studies*, 70(4), 492–506. DOI: 10.1080/10510974.2019.1622584

Frisby, B. N., Beck, A.-C., Smith Bachman, A., Byars, C., Lamberth, C., & Thompson, J. (2016). The influence of instructor-student rapport on instructors' professional and organizational outcomes. *Communication Research Reports*, 33(2), 103–110. DOI: 10.1080/08824096.2016.1154834

Frisby, B. N., & Martin, M. M. (2010). Instructor–student and student–student rapport in the classroom. *Communication Education*, 59(2), 146–164. DOI: 10.1080/03634520903564362

Frisby, B. N., & Myers, S. A. (2008). The Relationships among Perceived Instructor Rapport, Student Participation, and Student Learning Outcomes. *Texas Speech Communication Journal*, 33, 27–34.

Geertshuis, S. A. (2019). Slaves to our emotions: Examining the predictive relationship between emotional well-being and academic outcomes. *Active Learning in Higher Education*, 20(2), 153–166. DOI: 10.1177/1469787418808932

Goetz, T., Bieleke, M., Gogol, K., van Tartwijk, J., Mainhard, T., Lipnevich, A. A., & Pekrun, R. (2021). Getting along and feeling good: Reciprocal associations between student-teacher relationship quality and students' emotions. *Learning and Instruction*, 71(101349), 101349. DOI: 10.1016/j.learninstruc.2020.101349

Goetz, T., Keller, M. M., Lüdtke, O., Nett, U. E., & Lipnevich, A. A. (2020). The dynamics of real-time classroom emotions: Appraisals mediate the relation between students' perceptions of teaching and their emotions. *Journal of Educational Psychology*, 112(6), 1243–1260. DOI: 10.1037/edu0000415

Golby, M. (1996). Teachers' Emotions: An illustrated discussion. *Cambridge Journal of Education*, 26(3), 423–434. DOI: 10.1080/0305764960260310

Goldman, Z. W., & Goodboy, A. K. (2014). Making students feel better: Examining the relationships between teacher confirmation and college students' emotional outcomes. *Communication Education*, 63(3), 259–277. DOI: 10.1080/03634523.2014.920091

Hagenauer, G., Gläser-Zikuda, M., & Volet, S. (2016). University teachers' perceptions of appropriate emotion display and high-quality teacher-student relationship: Similarities and differences across cultural-educational contexts. *Frontline Learning Research*, 4(3), 44–74. DOI: 10.14786/flr.v4i3.236

Hagenauer, G., Hascher, T., & Volet, S. E. (2015). Teacher emotions in the classroom: Associations with students' engagement, classroom discipline and the interpersonal teacher-student relationship. *European Journal of Psychology of Education*, 30(4), 385–403. https://doi.org/10.1007/s10212-015-0250-0

Jelińska, M., & Paradowski, M. B. (2021). Teachers' engagement in and coping with emergency remote instruction during COVID-19-induced school closures: A multinational contextual perspective. *Online Learning : the Official Journal of the Online Learning Consortium*, 25(1). Advance online publication. DOI: 10.24059/olj.v25i1.2492

Jiang, J., Vauras, M., Volet, S., & Salo, A.-E. (2019). Teacher beliefs and emotion expression in light of support for student psychological needs: A qualitative study. *Education Sciences*, 9(2), 68. DOI: 10.3390/educsci9020068

Jomon, K. J., & Romate John Ph, D. (2017). Emotional competence and student engagement of the first year undergraduate students in Kerala. *International Journal of Indian Psychology*, 4(4). Advance online publication. DOI: 10.25215/0404.144

Kalogiannakis, M., & Touvlatzis, S. (2015). Emotions experienced by learners and their development through communication with the tutor-counsellor. *European Journal of Open Distance and E-Learning*, 18(2), 36–48. DOI: 10.1515/eurodl-2015-0012

Kang, C., & Wu, J. (2022). A theoretical review on the role of positive emotional classroom rapport in preventing EFL students' shame: A control-value theory perspective. *Frontiers in Psychology*, 13, 977240. Advance online publication. DOI: 10.3389/fpsyg.2022.977240 PMID: 36532974

Keller, M. M., & Becker, E. S. (2021). Teachers' emotions and emotional authenticity: Do they matter to students' emotional responses in the classroom? *Teachers and Teaching*, 27(5), 404–422. DOI: 10.1080/13540602.2020.1834380

Kordts-Freudinger, R. (2017). Feel, think, teach – Emotional Underpinnings of Approaches to Teaching in Higher Education. *International Journal of Higher Education*, 6(1), 217. https://doi.org/doi:10.5430/ijhe.v6n1p217

Lee, M., & van Vlack, S. (2018). Teachers' emotional labour, discrete emotions, and classroom management self-efficacy. *Educational Psychology*, 38(5), 669–686. DOI: 10.1080/01443410.2017.1399199

Lehman, B., Matthews, M., D'Mello, S., & Person, N. (2008). What are you feeling? Investigating student affective states during expert human tutoring sessions. In *Intelligent Tutoring Systems* (pp. 50–59). Springer Berlin Heidelberg. DOI: 10.1007/978-3-540-69132-7_10

Mainhard, T., Oudman, S., Hornstra, L., Bosker, R. J., & Goetz, T. (2018). Student emotions in class: The relative importance of teachers and their interpersonal relations with students. *Learning and Instruction*, 53, 109–119. DOI: 10.1016/j.learninstruc.2017.07.011

Mohammad, S. (2019). Investigation of EFL student teachers' emotional responses to affective situations during practicum. *European Journal of Educational Research*, 8(4), 1201–1215. DOI: 10.12973/eu-jer.8.4.1201

Olson, R. E., McKenzie, J., Mills, K. A., Patulny, R., Bellocchi, A., & Caristo, F. (2019). Gendered emotion management and teacher outcomes in secondary school teaching: A review. *Teaching and Teacher Education*, 80, 128–144. DOI: 10.1016/j.tate.2019.01.010

Oplatka, I. (2007). Managing emotions in teaching: Toward an understanding of emotion displays and caring as nonprescribed role elements. *Teachers College Record (1970)*, *109*(6), 1374–1400. DOI: 10.1177/016146810710900603

Parveen, H., & Bano, M. (2019). Relationship between teachers' stress and job satisfaction: Moderating role of teachers' emotions. *Pakistan Journal of Psychological Research*, 34(2), 353–366. DOI: 10.33824/PJPR.2019.34.2.19

Postareff, L., & Lindblom-Ylänne, S. (2011). Emotions and confidence within teaching in higher education. *Studies in Higher Education*, 36(7), 799–813. DOI: 10.1080/03075079.2010.483279

Quinlan, K. M. (2016). How emotion matters in four key relationships in teaching and learning in higher education. *College Teaching*, 64(3), 101–111. DOI: 10.1080/87567555.2015.1088818

Rabha, B., & Saikia, P. (2019). Emotional intelligence and academic performance of higher secondary school students: A study in Kamrup district, India. *The Clarion- International Multidisciplinary Journal,* 8(1), 34. DOI: 10.5958/2277-937X.2019.00005.4

Reyes, M. R., Brackett, M. A., Rivers, S. E., White, M., & Salovey, P. (2012). Classroom emotional climate, student engagement, and academic achievement. *Journal of Educational Psychology*, 104(3), 700–712. DOI: 10.1037/a0027268

Rinchen, S., Ritchie, S. M., & Bellocchi, A. (2016). Emotional climate of a pre-service science teacher education class in Bhutan. *Cultural Studies of Science Education*, 11(3), 603–628. https://doi.org/10.1007/s11422-014-9658-0

Roy, M. (2022). A study on emotional intelligence and job satisfaction level among male and female teachers of elementary level in Kolkata. Towards Excellence, 1138–1144. https://doi.org/DOI: 10.37867/te1404103

Ruiz, S., Charleer, S., Urretavizcaya, M., Klerkx, J., Fernández-Castro, I., & Duval, E. (2016). Supporting learning by considering emotions: Tracking and visualization a case study. *Proceedings of the Sixth International Conference on Learning Analytics & Knowledge - LAK '16*. DOI: 10.1145/2883851.2883888

Sakiz, G. (2012). Perceived instructor affective support in relation to academic emotions and motivation in college. *Educational Psychology*, 32(1), 63–79. DOI: 10.1080/01443410.2011.625611

Schutz, P. A. (2014). Inquiry on teachers' emotion. *Educational Psychologist*, 49(1), 1–12. DOI: 10.1080/00461520.2013.864955

Sharma, P., Mangal, S., & Nagar, P. (2016). To study the impact of Emotional Intelligence on Academic Achievement of teacher trainees. *IRA International Journal of Education and Multidisciplinary Studies*, 4(1). Advance online publication. DOI: 10.21013/jems.v4.n1.p6

Singh Gill, G. (2017). An exploration of emotional intelligence in teaching: Comparison between practitioners from the United Kingdom & India. *Journal of Psychology & Clinical Psychiatry*, 7(2). Advance online publication. DOI: 10.15406/jpcpy.2017.07.00430

Small, A. C. (1982). The effect of emotional state on student ratings of instructors. *Teaching of Psychology*, 9(4), 205–211. DOI: 10.1207/s15328023top0904_3

Soanes, D. G., & Sungoh, S. M. (2019). Influence of emotional intelligence on teacher effectiveness of science teachers. *Psychology (Irvine, Calif.)*, 10(13), 1819–1831. DOI: 10.4236/psych.2019.1013118

Stephanou, G., & Oikonomou, A. (2018). Teacher emotions in primary and secondary education: Effects of self-efficacy and collective-efficacy, and problem-solving appraisal as a moderating mechanism. *Psychology (Irvine, Calif.)*, 09(04), 820–875. DOI: 10.4236/psych.2018.94053

Suleman, Q., Hussain, I., Syed, M. A., Parveen, R., Lodhi, I. S., & Mahmood, Z. (2019). Association between emotional intelligence and academic success among undergraduates: A cross-sectional study in KUST, Pakistan. *PLoS One*, 14(7), e0219468. DOI: 10.1371/journal.pone.0219468 PMID: 31291333

Tao, W. (2022). Understanding the relationships between teacher mindfulness, work engagement, and classroom emotions. *Frontiers in Psychology*, 13, 993857. Advance online publication. DOI: 10.3389/fpsyg.2022.993857 PMID: 36248498

Taxer, J. L., Becker-Kurz, B., & Frenzel, A. C. (2019). Do quality teacher–student relationships protect teachers from emotional exhaustion? The mediating role of enjoyment and anger. *Social Psychology of Education*, 22(1), 209–226. DOI: 10.1007/s11218-018-9468-4

Telles, S., Sharma, S. K., Gupta, R. K., Pal, D. K., Gandharva, K., & Balkrishna, A. (2019). The impact of yoga on teachers' self-rated emotions. *BMC Research Notes*, 12(1), 680. Advance online publication. DOI: 10.1186/s13104-019-4737-7 PMID: 31640779

Thakur, S. (2016). Comparative study of emotional competence among teacher trainees in relation to gender. *International Journal of Science and Research (Raipur, India)*, 5(1), 956–959. DOI: 10.21275/v5i1.NOV152874

Thulasingam, M., Sen, A., Olickal, J., Sen, A., Kalaiselvy, A., & Kandasamy, P. (2020). Emotional intelligence and perceived stress among undergraduate students of arts and science colleges in Puducherry, India: A cross-sectional study. *Journal of Family Medicine and Primary Care*, 9(9), 4942. DOI: 10.4103/jfmpc.jfmpc_823_20 PMID: 33209826

Timoštšuk, I., Kikas, E., & Normak, M. (2016). Student teachers' emotional teaching experiences in relation to different teaching methods. *Educational Studies*, 42(3), 269–286. DOI: 10.1080/03055698.2016.1167674

Timoštšuk, I., & Ugaste, A.Timoštšuk. (2012). The role of emotions in student teachers' professional identity. *European Journal of Teacher Education*, 35(4), 421–433. DOI: 10.1080/02619768.2012.662637

Titsworth, S., McKenna, T. P., Mazer, J. P., & Quinlan, M. M. (2013). The bright side of emotion in the classroom: Do teachers' behaviors predict students' enjoyment, hope, and pride? *Communication Education*, 62(2), 191–209. DOI: 10.1080/03634523.2013.763997

Trigwell, K. (2012). Relations between teachers' emotions in teaching and their approaches to teaching in higher education. *Instructional Science*, 40(3), 607–621. DOI: 10.1007/s11251-011-9192-3

Trigwell, K., Ellis, R. A., & Han, F. (2012). Relations between students' approaches to learning, experienced emotions and outcomes of learning. *Studies in Higher Education*, 37(7), 811–824. DOI: 10.1080/03075079.2010.549220

Valente, S., Veiga-Branco, A., Rebelo, H., Lourenço, A. A., & Cristóvão, A. M. (2020). The relationship between emotional intelligence ability and teacher efficacy. *Universal Journal of Educational Research*, 8(3), 916–923. DOI: 10.13189/ujer.2020.080324

Wang, L. (2022). Exploring the relationship among teacher emotional intelligence, work engagement, teacher self-efficacy, and student academic achievement: A moderated mediation model. *Frontiers in Psychology*, 12, 810559. Advance online publication. DOI: 10.3389/fpsyg.2021.810559 PMID: 35046879

Wara, E., Aloka, P. J. O., & Odongo, B. C. (2018). Relationship between emotional engagement and academic achievement among Kenyan secondary school students. *Academic Journal of Interdisciplinary Studies*, 7(1), 107–118. DOI: 10.2478/ajis-2018-0011

Wilson, J. H. (2008). Instructor attitudes toward students: Job satisfaction and student outcomes. *College Teaching*, 56(4), 225–229. DOI: 10.3200/CTCH.56.4.225-229

Yan, E. M., Evans, I. M., & Harvey, S. T. (2011). Observing emotional interactions between teachers and students in elementary school classrooms. *Journal of Research in Childhood Education*, 25(1), 82–97. DOI: 10.1080/02568543.2011.533115

Yin, H. (2015). The effect of teachers' emotional labour on teaching satisfaction: Moderation of emotional intelligence. *Teachers and Teaching*, 21(7), 789–810. DOI: 10.1080/13540602.2014.995482

Yin, H., Huang, S., & Lee, J. C. K. (2017). Choose your strategy wisely: Examining the relationships between emotional labor in teaching and teacher efficacy in Hong Kong primary schools. *Teaching and Teacher Education*, 66, 127–136. DOI: 10.1016/j.tate.2017.04.006

Yin, H.-B., Lee, J. C. K., Zhang, Z.-H., & Jin, Y.-L. (2013). Exploring the relationship among teachers' emotional intelligence, emotional labor strategies and teaching satisfaction. *Teaching and Teacher Education*, 35, 137–145. DOI: 10.1016/j.tate.2013.06.006

Zhang, L.-F., Fu, M., Li, D. T., & He, Y. (2019). Emotions and teaching styles among academics: The mediating role of research and teaching efficacy. *Educational Psychology*, 39(3), 370–394. DOI: 10.1080/01443410.2018.1520970

Chapter 11
Tiptoeing Through Interweaving Hero and Collective Journey Elements in Course Design Practices:
Motivation in Designing the Hero's Journey Departure

Caroline M. Crawford
University of Houston-Clear Lake, USA

James L. Dillard
https://orcid.org/0000-0002-9136-2095
University of Calgary, Canada

ABSTRACT

Two participant case studies associated with online course design practices were framed through a basic qualitative analysis, including one instructor participant and one collegial learner participant. The lens through which online course design is framed are the motivational aspects of learning, paralleling the hero's journey and the associated collective journey within course design and considering the implementation of a course experience, through noting the elements of emotional engagement and experiential learning as necessary recognitions. After a thorough analysis the articulated ten themes are: Progressive Learner Engagement of Pedagogy, Andragogy, and Heutagogy; Communities of Practice and Landscapes of Practice Approaches; Collective Unconscious/Cognitive Dissonance; Interactive Activities;

DOI: 10.4018/979-8-3693-2663-3.ch011

and, Philosophical Understanding/Differentiated Perceptions.

INTRODUCTION

Taking the emotional experiences of both learners and instructors into account is imperative for the design of strong and supportive learning practices. Within online learning environments, such practices have significant potential to drive positive emotional experiences on the part of the learner. Equally, the emotional experiences of the instructor must be recognized as reflecting and supporting the learner's successful journey through the course experience. However, careful consideration should be given to the efforts towards supporting the cognitive-constructivist understandings around the learning process, when recognizing the precarious experiential learning efforts that occur within online learning environments. Using emotional experiences to help learners attain and retain information throughout the progressive learner engagement of pedagogy, andragogy, and heutagogy (Crawford et al., 2018; Crawford et al., 2019) equally embraces the nuances associated with successfully embedding learning within both communities of practice and landscapes of practice approaches (Wenger-Trayner et al., 2014; Wenger-Trayner & Wenger-Trayner, 2015; Wenger-Trayner & Wenger-Trayner, 2020).

Within this chapter, a qualitative autoethnographic participant case studies approach engages the discussion, towards an understanding of course design practices, through the lens of the online course instructor as well as the lens of the online course learner. The data were analyzed through hand coding, offering a deep, rich approach to the emerging codes, categories, and themes. Findings reflect ten overarching themes, including: progressive learner engagement of pedagogy, andragogy, and heutagogy; communities of practice and landscapes of practice approaches; collective unconscious, including cognitive dissonance; interactive activities; and, philosophical understandings as well as differentiated perceptions.

Joseph Campbell's work associated with the hero's journey, which may also be referred to as the hero's quest, may suggest an instructional design practice that leads to awakening the learner's subject matter understanding. The building blocks of knowledge attainment and informational understanding at differentiated levels of reach and achievement may suggest a learning journey with an emphasis upon experience.

Yet rethinking the hero's journey (Campbell 2004, 2008) and the collective journey (Gomez, 2017a, 2017b, 2017c, 2017d; Webster, 2020) results in the ability to intermix a more opaque understanding of the learner's process associated with learning, a narrative that equates to and attempts to potentially embed the journey within an online course design. This embedded experience may be considered a hero's journey that is articulated in the following manner:

The hero's journey is a common narrative archetype, or story template, that involves a hero who goes on an adventure, learns a lesson, wins a victory with that newfound knowledge, and then returns home transformed. The hero's journey can be boiled down to three essential stages:
- *The departure. The hero leaves the familiar world behind.*
- *The initiation. The hero learns to navigate the unfamiliar world.*
- *The return. The hero returns to the familiar world. (MasterClass, 2021, para. 4-5)*

Further, returning to Campbell (2008) as an expert in the hero's journey, the following description may be offered:

A hero ventures forth from the world of common day into a region of supernatural wonder: fabulous forces are there encountered and a decisive victory is won: the hero comes back from this mysterious adventure with the power to bestow boons on his fellow men. (p. 23)

However, after framing the hero's journey, Gomez's collective journey (Gomez, 2017a, 2017b, 2017c, 2017d; Webster, 2020) rethinks this journey as a differentiated and potentially supplementary model that offers a dynamic style of narrative and storytelling progression. As suggested by Gomez and shared by Webster (2020), each "argues that more than ever, modern storytelling relies on the ability for storytellers to listen, in order to effectively guide and redirect audiences to an understanding" (Webster, 2020, p. 4). The ability to motivate through story drivers as well as impactful elements that may be thematic in nature (Bernstein, 2013; Webster, 2020) is directly supportive of educational design, especially within an online course design. As suggested by Gomez (2017c), "Hero's Journey stories are about how the individual actualizes by achieving personal change, but Collective Journey stories are about how communities actualize in their attempt to achieve systemic change" (para. 18). As a digital age understanding of the narrative of storytelling within a learning environment, Gomez frames storytelling as a narrative style within a collective journey:

What is required is a new kind of storytelling, a narrative engine that lends itself to our nonlinear, networked, omni-perspective digital age. The kind of storytelling where any audience member can suddenly and at any point start commenting on, participating in, or redirecting the narrative.

It's a model of storytelling we call the Collective Journey. (2017b, para. 21-22)

The important take away from Gomez's work is the suggested elemental aspects of the collective journey: regenerative listening; superpositioning; social self-organization; and, change-making (2017d, para. 16). In direct alignment with online learning course design environments is the learner-centered nature of the engagement, with an intriguing motivational aspect associated with a differentiation from the hero's journey to the collective journey, noting that "The difference, from the standpoint of Collective Journey, is that we must now acknowledge that story has become porous. It is now participative. That friend of ours is now demanding to be genuinely heard" (Gomez, 2017d, para. 25). Suggesting the import and impact of the singularity of each person involved within a learning opportunity is deeply impactful and has the opportunity to heighten the experience through the quality of communications that occur. This leads into social self-organization, Gomez (2017f) reflects, as an experience that:

… represents how pervasive communications technologies enabled groups of people to generate a spontaneous self-organized social system.

In the social sciences, self-organization happens "when some form of overall order arises from local interactions between parts of an initially disordered system. The process can be spontaneous [happening suddenly and without centralized leadership] when sufficient energy is available." (para. 7-8)

The coming together of a group of people to collaborate and develop an experience into a heightened event of understanding is well reflected as a parallel understanding as embraced by Wenger-Trayner's community of learning and community of practice frameworks (Wenger-Trayner et al., 2014; Wenger-Trayner & Wenger-Trayner, 2015, 2020).

With a juxtaposition of the hero's journey with the evolving understanding of the collective journey, or the individual journey that is evolving through the collective coming together of like-minded colleagues, a shared verbiage may support alignments between the two journeys of understanding. Table 1 articulates an alignment of progressive journeys, resulting in a differentiated labeling system that supports the new verbiage of the journey initiation, the journey experience, and the journey outcome that also includes resulting change.

Table 1. Hero's journey versus collective journey

	Hero's Journey	**Collective Journey**
Journey Initiation	Departure	Regenerative Listening
Journey Experience	Initiation	Superpositioning Social Self-organization
Journey Outcome: Resulting Change	Return	Change-making

The focus of this discussion is upon the journey initiation, reflecting the online course design decisions that are motivational as progressive learner engagement, developing a sense of communities of practice within embedded real-world experiences, working within a community approach towards learner cognitive dissonance and understanding, as well as interactivities and philosophical understandings that may support differentiated perceptions of the learning process.

BACKGROUND

Personalizing the learning approach is necessary for supporting learner motivation. Reflecting upon this recognition, the ability to develop a sense of intrinsic motivation and the learner's sense of *choice and voice* within a course experience offer an engaging approach to the learner's online course experience (Alamri et al., 2020; Alqurashi, 2019; Diwakar et al., 2023; Dunn & Kennedy, 2019; Harrington & Thomas, 2023; Nafukho et al., 2023; Neelen & Kirschner, 2020; Nkomo et al., 2021; Schmitz & Hanke, 2023). Equally, the perception of instructor facilitative quality within online course experience directly impacts the learner experience, with equal consideration towards online course design (Achen & Rutledge, 2023; Asfahani et al., 2023; Calavia et al., 2023; Kilag et al., 2023; Mallarangan et al., 2024; Martin et al., 2023; McLean & Attardi, 2023; Salendab, 2023).

Impactful to the online course experience and the associated learner engagement, is an associated understanding within humanist environments wherein a natural desire to engage in interactive activities is a realistic expectation. Yet within an online environment, analysis and careful consideration of the different types and expectations associated with interactive activities must be considered. Since as early as 1989, Moore (1989) was analyzing the different types of interactive activities that might occur within instructional environments, beginning with the foundational learner-content, learner-instructor, and learner-learner (Moore, 1989) expectations; however, as further interest and intrigue associated with interactive activities within learning environments evolved, recognition of the nuanced depth and breadth of interactive activity occurring within a learning environment has been slowly realized. This is impactful work within online course design, due to the realization that motivational engagement and knowledge acquisition are carefully designed into online learning environments. The currently articulated interactive activities include the following:

- Learner-content (Moore, 1989)
- Learner-interface (Hillman, Willis & Gunawardena, 1994)
- Learner-instructor (Moore, 1989)
- Learner-learner (Moore, 1989)
- Learner-self (Crawford, 2001)
- Learner-community (Burnham & Walden, 1997)
- Instructor-community (Crawford, 2001)

- Instructor-content (Crawford, 2001)
- Instructor-interface (Crawford, 2001)
- Instructor-self (Crawford, 2001, 2003)
- Learner-Web of Things (Crawford et al, 2021)
- Instructor-Web of Things (Crawford et al, 2021)
- Instructor-instructor colleagues (Crawford et al, 2021)

This qualitative autoethnographic participant case studies approach was implemented, to more profoundly understanding the depth and breadth of experienced instructional designers who hold experiential roles as instructor and as learner colleague may offer insightful understandings that may support and enhance the current body of literature in this ever-evolving field of online learning course design practices. The strength of a self-study approach to this discussion supports a focus upon the lived experiences of persons who are at the center of the experience, bringing forward a qualitative approach that offers an autoethnographic understanding that emphasizes the participant's case study within a storytelling framework of understanding. Further, this storytelling is supported and reflected through a hero's journey that emphasizes elements of a larger community's a collective journey lens. This re-emphasis upon a hero's journey departure, towards a collective journey, highlights the motivation-driven approach towards designing course design practices within an online learning environment.

The discussion is framed in a distinctly focused manner. The major heading areas that offer a short introduction to the subject matter, immediately followed by the autoethnographic ruminations of the instructor and the collegial learner, as well as an alternate trope articulated as a culturally transcendent journey, are: learner motivation as an emotional experience; designing a hero's journey archetype in online courses; and, the departure, focused upon online course motivation. The autoethnographic text was qualitatively analyzed, resulting in findings that were articulated through the codes, then grouped into categories, then ultimately grouped into primary themes. The five themes qualitatively represented through a deep, rich understanding that embedded direct quotations from the participants, included: Progressive Learner Engagement of Pedagogy, Andragogy, and Heutagogy; Communities of Practice and Landscapes of Practice Approaches; Collective Unconscious/Cognitive Dissonance; Interactive Activities; and, Philosophical Understanding/Differentiated Perceptions. Solutions and recommendations coalesced around the thematic findings, while future research directions articulate that the qualitative study's thematic findings support the collegial learner as the central focus of the online learning experience, while responsibility for the interactive activities are held by both the instructor and the collegial learner. Yet, an important recognition towards online course design must be emphasized; namely, the online course design and nuanced expertise of the instructor as a facilitative guide must be realized.

LEARNER MOTIVATION AS AN EMOTIONAL EXPERIENCE

Learner motivation is an inherent expectation within learning environments, whether traditional face-to-face learning environments, blended or flipped learning environments, online learning environments, or the promulgated mix of instructionally relevant expectations that support the learner's formal as well as informal learning needs. What supports the learner while engaging in the learning environment, meaning engaging with knowledge to learn and frame their understanding in new and different ways? An equally impactful question is how do learners engage with others in the course environment, including colleague learners, the facilitative instructor, and others who may be embedded within the learning environment experience? A facilitative instructor is an amalgamation of a traditional instructor's role, as well as a traditional facilitator's role within a learning environment, wherein the online facilitative instructor not only guides the learner's understanding of the subject matter but equally facilitates the motivational engagement and community-building endeavors within and throughout the course experience. Motivating efforts that emphasize the hero's journey and the collective journey, highlighting both the individual learner's successful journey through the course learning experience while equally supporting the community-embedded and engaged constructivist understandings associated with conceptual frameworks of understanding and social engagement and associated social connectedness throughout the learning experience (Vygotsky, 1933/1966, 1934/1987, 1935, 1962, 1978 1981) directly supports the facilitative strengths of the instructor within course design experiences. More fully considering learner motivation and learning as an emotional experience, what is the extent to which the learning experience supports and potentially impacts the learner's real-world environment outside the bounds of the metaphoric four walls of the learning environment? This includes learner motivation related to the ability of the learner to self-regulate their own learning experience, as well as the learner's sense of self-efficacy and recognition of oneself that supports the conception of the interwoven hero's journey throughout the learning environment.

Instructor Ruminations

As a course facilitative instructor, my course design practices emphasize the importance of social learning and collegial engagement as an experiential journey, a cognitively experiential *becoming* that supports the learner's developing competencies as well as extended capabilities. There are a few elements that I continuously integrate into my online course design practices, that I initially learned through face-to-face course experiences as well as carefully listening to and learning from collegial learners. These elements include: the importance of collegial engagement as a social learning practice; publicly representing learned knowledge and associated achievements; deeply thoughtful and detailed interactions with collegial learners, including extensive feedback on all assignments; and, an emphasis upon student ownership of the course experience.

First, the importance of collegial engagement as a social learning practice is emphasized throughout all of my online course design practices. The desire to be seen and heard is important within human experience, yet within an online course experience it is an even deeper, richer need for the learners to feel a sense of belonging within the learning community. I design opportunities for learners to engage throughout the course in many different ways, including discussion board posts and video conference team assignments, that support the learners experiencing their colleagues throughout their learning journey in each course. Seeing, hearing, and communicating with colleagues in an online course experience is imperative, not only for a sense of socialization and belonging, but as means through which the learners check their understanding, develop a sense of collegiality amongst learners, and support each other in formal as well as informal ways. These efforts initiate a sense of community that is modeled and emphasized by the course instructor. An initial response to this level of interactive activity within an online course experience is regularly deemed uncomfortable and unusual when compared to past online course experiences, but the learners swiftly develop a comfort, a vulnerability, through this level of relational engagement. Course colleagues begin to know each other, trust each other, and depend upon each other within the course journey. This level of engagement emphasizes the motivational supports that are inherent within developing a sense of *belonging* in an online course, supporting not only a learner's sense of self-efficacy and self-regulatory efforts, but also student success associated with the successful completion of the course experience because learners want to ensure that their place and space in the course experience doesn't *let down* their course colleagues.

Second is publicly representing learned knowledge and associated achievements. Within online courses that I design, there is always a level of public presentation of assignments. This may occur within team video conference presentations that are primarily in-course experiences, or through an experience that I've labeled as a *collegial community* engagement that emphasizes reaching out beyond the metaphoric four walls of a classroom experience and requesting assignment reviews and feedback from each learner's larger and multiple communities within which each person experiences their life journey. The collegial community includes family, friends, co-workers, and work supervisors, as well as students and instructors outside of our course experience. The emphasis is upon developing each learner's sense of knowledge achievement and strength of standing within their own personal communities, while equally moving through the uncomfortable process of the formative evaluation and feedback loop. An unexpected yet desirable benefit of the implementation of the *collegial community* expectation associated with course assignments is that each learner's larger community communicates their respect for the work achieved and requests opportunities to learn more from the learners, so there is a real shift from learner to instructor; the emphasis upon this external engagement has resulted in expanded job opportunities, new job offers, and expansion of networking opportunities. From an instructor's consideration, the emphasis upon publicly representing learned knowledge as well as assignment deliverable products prior to submitting formal in-course assessment efforts resulted in a significantly enhanced quality of assignments that were noted easier to evaluate. The mandate to publicly display and represent the learner's course learning and associated course efforts within a public venue assured an enhanced emphasis upon assignment effort. The real world representation of each learner's professional self was a motivating factor that supported not only the instructor's ease of course evaluation efforts but equally an enjoyable movement from focused time on assessing the assignment deliverable product into enhanced and personalized reflections associated with assignment ideas, enhancement, and even *next steps* that reflect a more engaged instructor experience.

Third is deeply thoughtful and detailed interactions with collegial learners, including extensive feedback on all assignments. Online course design practices emphasize the development of learning communities through humanist social engagement opportunities. The emphasis upon modeling a supportive and engaged course experience is heavily modeled at the beginning of the course experience by the course instructor, emphasizing the expectation of quality course engagement and mutually respectful interest in all course colleagues. During the initial week or two of the course experience, the instructor models expectations for all learners while equally emphasizing a perception of continuous engagement within the course environment. I have learned that early emphasis upon modeling expectations in the course experience, through representing labels such as *colleagues* when referring to course learners and supporting my own natural style of comfortable communication through the use of terms such as *brilliant* and *outstanding* when referring to the great questions, ideas, information, and efforts shared by learners early in the course seems to *set the stage* for the remainder of the online course experience. The respectful engagement and styles of communication are displayed by the course instructor, with the learners slowly taking on similar ways of communicating and aligning with the course culture that the instructor has modeled and informally emphasized within the course experience. Through this initial depth and breadth of instructor engagement, the culture and tone of the course experience is set, with the learners following suit. From a motivational consideration, people want to be involved and included in an experience that is positive, professional, and respectful. The community is bound within explicit and implicit expectations, supporting a learning community that emphasizes respectful recognition and support of course colleagues. The social learning, the community, the emotional and cognitive vulnerability that may be comfortably embraced within this type of online course environment emphasizes not only striving towards attaining information competencies through a mutually supportive journey, but equally creating a potentially supportive environment within which learners have opportunities to expand further beyond the course objectives and into a more personalized emphasis upon creativity and expanded capabilities. Focusing upon the quality and the value of a course experience that is personally and professionally meaningful supports a motivational focus that shifts the online course design and learner efforts from meeting course expectations into a potentially long-term and impactful experience that extends far beyond the specific course experience.

Fourth and finally, an emphasis upon student ownership of the course experience is imperative. Shifting the consistent focus from the online course instructor into a more collegial and facilitative learning experience not only frees the instructor to offer deeper supports and guidance to potentially struggling students, but the personalized approach to student ownership as their own *choice and voice* supports a more personal learner journey that may offer a motivational support due to the understanding that the learner has a level of control over their learning experience. I attempt to integrate this concept of *choice and voice* into online course design practices at different levels of emphasis and engagement dependent upon the course subject matter and course objectives. One course design comes to mind, that well represents this concept. This course is considered a core degree plan course mandate; many of the students who enroll really do not want to be in the course, but they have no choice if they are going to complete their degree plan and graduate. Recognizing this, I wanted to emphasize the social learning aspect of this course in different ways; meaning, each learner needed to learn a specific element of the subject matter and be able to present and discuss the subject matter readings and video-embedded information in a coherent manner. Yet mandatory course readings can be so dry and boring. I wanted to recreate the expectation into something more engaging and viably impactful. For this reason, I created an assignment in each unit that was focused on mandatory readings. At the very beginning of the course, the students were assigned to review four or five distinctly separate yet similar reading topics in each unit and choose which one of the reading options that they would choose for that unit of instruction. This was a self-regulatory tool that the students would use throughout the rest of the course experience, so that they were not overwhelmed with choices as each new unit began. The students could choose a different reading, if desired, but at least each learner started a unit of instruction knowing that they'd already made their choice of mandatory readings. Associated with the mandatory readings was a team video conference discussion, so that a small group of students would come together and discuss the important elements of their reading topics, sharing and discussing interesting ideas and concepts. These team video conferences were recorded and then posted in each of the course's unit discussion boards, so that everyone else in the course could review the recorded presentation of information and associated discussions; this not only supported an extended understanding of information without reading all the articles, but students also learned more about course colleagues and deepened a sense of relational belonging within the course experience, because teams changed in each unit to ensure colleagues could create more personalized connections and relationships as the course progressed. From a motivational standpoint, the learners had to own their reading assignment, because their understanding of the information was on public display within our course experience, yet an equally impactful yet informal element to the reading assignments and associated team discussions was the development of stronger community engagement and sense of collegial course experience amongst our learners. They supported and cheered each other on by highlighting the great ideas and quality of work achieved by each team, as well as colleagues as individuals. The motivational aspects of this assignment were a surprise to the instructor, as the course design strengthened the quality of the learner experience and ownership of information throughout the course experience.

The effort of the instructor towards developing online course design practices that emphasized a high level of motivational engagement resulted in a course experience that emphasized the quality of learning that occurred, as well as emotional supports that supported learner vulnerability amongst colleagues, and even a level of self-efficacy around the learning that occurred through each collegial assignment engagement.

Collegial Learner Ruminations

As a student learner for more than 14 years, I have observed that learner motivation falls under three distinct categories: a learner is required to learn the material for a degree requirement, a learner has to learn the material for progression in their greater personal goals, and/or the learner wishes to learn the material for reasons of their own which may or may not be related to the previous motivations. Now we will examine these three sets of motivations and the results they have upon the student learning experience.

The first motivation, the learner engaging with the material as part of a degree requirement, is truthfully the most difficult and problematic motivation for a student learner to deal with if there is no inherent interest in the material, and it is merely being interacted with to satisfy a degree requirement. These learners are typically highly unmotivated because they have often times no real interest in the material. To these learners, this material is not relevant to their educational interest, merely being a requirement that must be satisfied for them to move forward into classes which actually interest them. Frequently, the students will decry these courses as "pointless" or "gatekeeping," viewing these courses as just one more method to keep them away from their true interest. This learner will typically have a low motivation when engaging with the material as they feel it is something being forced upon them and thus only wish to do the bare minimum to exit the course in a successful manner.

The second motivation, learning the material to move forward in personal goals, is closely related to the first but the question of willingness comes into play with this learner. This learner is engaging with this material willingly, as they see it as a stepping stone to a larger goal. This larger goal may be simply satisfying requirement for obtaining a degree, but what differentiates the second learner from the first is attitude. Typically, the first learner has a neutral to negative attitude regarding material, whereas the second learner has a neutral to positive attitude regarding the material as they see the course they are engaging with as a gateway to something better. This learner will generally have a medium to high motivation as they feel this material will help with the betterment of their future.

The third learner, someone who wishes to learn the information in this course, could be categorized as someone who is satisfying a degree requirement, or learning a new skill to help them in their current or future employment situation, or simply someone who enjoys learning. What really differentiates this learner from the previous two is eagerness to engage with the material being presented regardless of the purpose behind their engagement. This learner will typically have a positive outlook and a high motivation to engage with material. Of these three learners, the first is obviously the most difficult to reach and least likely to engage with the material outside the classroom. While the second and third types of learners will be actively attempting to utilize this material beyond the requirements of the course, the first learner will have to be motivated and strongly encouraged to move beyond the walls of the classroom and engage with the material in any context other than purely academic.

A solution to this issue is to help show that this material is not merely pointless academic busywork, but there is actually a valid application of this content outside the walls of the classroom. This is particularly relevant for the first type of learner as, from the moment they registered for the class, they saw little value beyond simply checking a box. By providing motivation for the first type of learner, the other two learner types will follow along in their wake.

Students in the learning environment engage in a variety of manners with others in the course context. Often times, and this is particularly true in younger less experienced students, there is a fear or awe of the instructor. Many of these students will hesitate to ask questions or dispute something with the instructor even if it is clearly in error. The students have been convinced to believe that the instructor is an all-knowing all-seeing vengeful God who will brook no dissent. Students with this frame of mind pose a particular problem as they will often times not bring personal issues which have bearing upon the class to the instructor until it is far too late for the instructor to help them. When I personally have encountered difficulties during my studies, I have not hesitated to inform instructors every time the situation changed to ensure that, should I need assistance, the instructor would not feel blindsided by my request.

Students interact with each other in a range of ways depending on their personalities and the situations within which they are required to interact. In group work settings, there will often be one or two strong personalities which will rise from the group, in the best case to lead, or in the worst case to dominate the group's efforts. These kinds of social interactions can also lead to resentment and negative feelings if the various group members are not all contributing in an equitable manner or if some of the group members feel that they are being marginalized or otherwise dismissed. During my educational experiences, particularly given my level of experience, I will often allow younger students to take the lead to provide them the experience I already possess. If the younger students fail to rise to the occasion, then I will fill the leadership void within the classroom social hierarchy in order to help guide the students through the tasks required by the course material. In several instances when I have been forced to take a leadership role, it was because the younger students were frightened of interacting with, or presenting a problem to, the instructor.

When students lack solid motivation, beyond the need to satisfy a degree requirement, many will have difficulty regulating their workloads in relation to the rest of their professional and personal lives. If a learner is not positively motivated, for whatever reason, their self-efficacy drops and engaging with the material becomes an unpleasant task. Personally, I have witnessed many students who are unhappy with whatever task they are given and they procrastinate and delay completion of said task as long as possible. This has reached even into the graduate education levels where, in some of my experiences, it is not uncommon for students to request deadline extensions in order to complete their work. As these students were my colleagues in these courses, I was aware of the course load involved. As I did not require the same deadline extensions as they did, I can only surmise that it was some form of procrastination or other delays which brought them to the point of requiring an extension to complete their assignments.

Alternate Trope: Culturally Transcendent Journey

While my advanced age and experience more than likely has provided me an edge over my learning colleagues, I suspect that there is a cultural difference which has contributed positively to my success in the academic arena. That cultural difference is the fact that I possess military experience. Particularly, I possess experience derived from my time as military journalist. At the time of my graduation, the military journalism school was the second most challenging in the entire Department of Defense, with the hardest being the Naval nuclear power program. Graduating from the Defense Information School (DINFOS) second in my class, I was prepared for high-pressure situations and unyielding deadlines.

After accepting my posting to a Coast Guard District Public Affairs Office for a four-year tour, responding to all manner of minor and major emergencies and crisis news events, I then opened a Public Affairs Detachment (PADET) and was part of a two-person staff responding to the same kinds of incidences for another four years before my medical retirement. Additionally, before I entered military service, I was a restaurant manager given tremendous responsibility before I even turned 18. All of this together served to instill high degrees of organization and resilience within an already strong work ethic.

When I arrived in higher education, I merely considered it another job. Each semester, my job was to excel in each course that I was registered for and to perform to the highest level of my abilities. I looked at my instructors as my superior officers; if I ran into an issue, it was contingent upon myself to not only present the issue to the instructor but, where possible, present a solution or solutions to the problem I was experiencing. Most of the students with whom I've had the privilege of learning seem to regard higher education as just a more advanced form of public schooling, as that is often their personal experience with education of any kind. The only instances I can recall of students having zero adjustment issues with course material are when the students in question are former military or have some form of management or other organizational experience in their backgrounds.

While there is really no way to bridge this cultural divide, short of forcibly inducting some of these students into military or management organizations, there are lessons from military and management organizations that instructors or student peers can pass to younger students to help them better manage their time and direct their efforts toward accomplishing their goals. While these organizational education efforts will never substitute for the total immersion that military life, or the life of a manager, will provide, quite frankly it is better than nothing. The difficulty that I have experienced when I attempt to pass along this wisdom to my peers is getting them to both listen to, and implement, the information I'm providing them. Unfortunately, all too often the students in question believe they know what is best as it's the way they've always done their classes. Even at the graduate level, there is a closed mindedness for new methods of time management and organization, while honestly, time management is among the top five skills I have learned in my 51 years.

DESIGNING A HERO'S JOURNEY ARCHETYPE IN ONLINE COURSES

How might one design a hero's journey into the learning environment? Especially within an online course experience, the semiotic and metaphoric journeys through the learning process equally reflect a collective journey understanding. Yet within the journey of the hero as well as the learning process, similarities arise that reflect the initiation, experience, outcome and potential resulting change after the journey concludes. From a social learning understanding, the hero's journey archetype parallels with the learning community or community of practice (Wenger, 1998) are clarified, emphasizing social interrelations and interactive activities to support knowledge acquisition as meaning-making, a social practice, and sense of identity within the community. This reflects a humanist understanding of the teaching and learning process. Social learning within the community suggests an initiation of the instructional journey and the experiential aspects of the instructional journey as instructor and collegial learners work together to learn, unlearn, relearn, and embed a vulnerability throughout the learning process, achieving learning and practical understandings. The result is the outcome as a conclusion of the instructional journey, with new and differentiated understandings as a result of a change in the people who are embedded in the community, as instructors and collegial learners, while expanding the outcome and potential impact into the larger real-world environment.

Instructor Ruminations

Integrating the concept of a hero's journey, as well as a collective journey, into an online course design is a complex effort that interweaves so many different aspects of *becoming* by each learner within the course experience. Equally impactful is that the course instructor must rethink their place in the course and their associated facilitative practices, due to the more personalized journey of each learner, while equally considering the collective course experience and outcomes. This dualistic approach to the course experience emphasizes natural aspects of a course flow, such as a course's learning community approach that highlights course initiation and coming together of colleagues, the majority of the course experience associated with learning goals and objectives, as well as the course outcome expectations and potential for the course to offer impactful changes in learner understanding. The hero's journey is a more personalized odyssey, while the collective journey is a larger social experience, with both the individual as well as collective community journeys equally viable and emphasized. The instructor must design an online course to guide the duality of the course experience, much like a metaphoric dance wherein the social learning experience of the learning community offers a holistic coming together of enhanced understanding, while the individual learner as a reflective learner moves into and out of the larger collective spaces while being equally cognizant of their own personal learning journey and associated experiences. Each learner is responsible for their own initiatives, moving through the assigned expectations and associated efforts, while coming together within a collegially social and supportive space with the intent to learn, unlearn, and relearn, within a respectful and vulnerably engaging community of colleagues who are sharing their personalized journeys within the larger collegial spaces.

Collegial Learner Ruminations

Designing a hero's journey in an online course can be properly done with a bit of forethought and student involvement. The departure portion of the hero's journey could be accomplished by having the students review the course modules and then simply answer a pre-course survey regarding whether or not they have ever done anything related to the content. For example, if one of the course modules presents a one-page training in an online format, the pre-course survey could prompt the students if they have ever prepared any sort of one-page piece of educational material. Examples could be provided such as a newsletter, a flyer, a brochure, or any other similar printed material. Comparisons could then be made between the printed and online media, highlighting the fact that the online version is merely a new iteration of previous techniques and technology.

The second part of the hero's journey, entering the unfamiliar world, would be where the student learners engage with technology they have never utilized before to accomplish a task, for example, using a web-based publishing software to create their one-page educational material. While the basic task of creating a page of text with the intent to inform might be familiar, the manner in which it is now created would be unfamiliar. Within an online course, the first two segments of the hero's journey would have to be repeated multiple times. Each module of the course would cover a familiar concept; single-page educational documents, brief informational pamphlets, and other common items. The second part of the hero's journey would take these familiar concepts and bring them forward into the realm of unfamiliar technology and techniques. For example, the single-page educational documents would become simple single-page websites. The brief informational pamphlets would become multipage websites. This would continue for all the various modules and lessons.

The hero's journey would come full circle to the return to the familiar by taking all of these concepts and unifying them under one single lesson. For example, if the overall course was teaching how to make a simple informative website, the individual modules would address single informational pages, linking single informational pages together, basic layout and design, and using images and graphic elements. The final stage of the hero's journey would be uniting all of these single lessons into one final example. What would make it familiar to the students is having the instructor point out that what the students created is an example of a simple website with multiple pages, something that the student learners very likely encounter multiple times every day as they navigate the informational sources of the modern world.

As a student learner I have engaged in such projects in the past where the beginning of the weekly module consisted of examining the task which needed to be completed by the end of the week, developing the product required to be submitted for evaluation over the course of week, and then returning to the familiar by presenting this material to a select portion of our learning cohort. This is familiar because simply discussing our experiences among colleagues, it could be argued, is one of the most familiar and comfortable things within which anyone can engage, associated with not only content and learned skill, but may also include the comfortability associated with instructional strategies that are implemented.

Alternate Trope: Culturally Transcendent Journey

Culturally speaking, the military is the epitome of the hero's journey. In order to arrive at recruit training, you generally enter one of the more familiar places: an airport. You're flown via commercial airline to your destination and then you board a bus and travel for several hours in the dark of night. When the bus arrives at its destination you immediately begin part two of the hero's journey; you leave everything familiar behind. Familiarity becomes just a memory as learning and change, whether welcome or not, await around every corner. Once graduated from your training, you return home for a period of leave (vacation) but your once-familiar surroundings have now forever been altered because you have forever been altered.

When you arrive at your new unit, the hero's journey begins anew. There is new learning to accomplish, new policies and procedures to understand; it takes a while for the alien to become familiar. This is a process that is repeated multiple times throughout a military career until, eventually, the military life itself becomes the familiar and the world of the civilian the unfamiliar. This juxtaposition is very common in military life and why the transition from military back to civilian is often times so difficult and painful. The hero's journey cannot be taken in reverse and there is never any opportunity to unlearn what you have learned. The order and discipline which was so much a part of the previous hero's journey is absent in your return to civilian familiarity and it creates a severe cognitive dissonance within the person experiencing it.

In the military, there are often opportunities for military members to be student learners. Their age, rank, or job status notwithstanding, all military members must continuously learn. The learning taking place in these sorts of hero's journey are rather abbreviated, as there is an urgency to exposing the military student learners to the new knowledge, ensuring they understand the new knowledge, testing their competence, and then releasing them back into the service to perform these tasks as part of their routine. Military learning is often times high-pressure learning, as in the military a mistake might cause injury or death, whereas in the classroom a mistake is simply mistake and might result in a poor grade.

Even as far removed from the military as I currently am, the cognitive dissonance still exists from time to time. I often find myself taking my assignments far more seriously than my colleagues, due to the high-pressure learning environment that I was exposed to when I was a very young adult. I often times have to remind myself, sometimes out loud to my classmates, that it's just an assignment and no one's going to die. While everyone else in the room gets a good chuckle, it's more serious in the back of my mind.

THE DEPARTURE: ONLINE COURSE MOTIVATION

The journey's initiation is referred to as the hero's journey departure. As a comparison to the collective journey as a digital age *next step* consideration, reflective of a culturally transcendent journey, one may consider the first week or two of a formal course experience wherein the instructor may attempt to create a sense of community and collegial engagement within the learning environment and amongst collegial learners. How is this designed into a course experience? To what extent might interactive activities mandate learner engagement and consideration associated with similarities and collaborative opportunities with course colleagues? Does the course instructor design these opportunities to initiate engagement or are the collegial learners left to their own devices to find their place and their space within the learning community? As the departure is the initial hero's journey impetus, it is important to recognize that the hero joins a new and unusual realm with people who may or may not have had previous connections betwixt and between the instructor and the learners who come together in this current learning community space. The familiar is left behind for many collegial learners, developing new customs and associated ways of learning, new levels of awareness, new potential acquaintances, and a level of conversant expectation associated with the new course instructor and subject matter.

Instructor Ruminations

The initiation of the hero's journey is considered the departure, while the collective course experience is considered to be a regenerative listening point in the course process. Initiating an online course experience emphasizes the design of practices that support an individual's experience and associated expectations, with an equal level of community representation of *place and space* that supports an individual learner's introduction into the larger collective community. This has the potential to be a precarious positioning, that therefore emphasizes the modeling and embedded guidance required of the instructor at this point in the course journey. The instructor must set the tone of the course experience as well as the level of quality and expectation that learners are expected to achieve throughout the course journey. Recognizing this complex initiation of the course journey, the online course design must carefully reflect upon and design into the initial several days of the course a participative engagement that not only emphasizes a carefully developing level of intimacy amongst course colleagues, but also a depth of understanding that reflects genuine engagement and relationally respectful collegial curiosity. Within my online course design practices, I initially start with several individual procedural expectations, sometimes referred to as *housekeeping* assignments, such as setting up different resource tool accounts and successfully attaining initial yet mandated plagiarism tutorial certificates of successful completion. Equally, while the individual learner is progressing through their individual assignment expectations, there is a discussion board expectation that requires a professional introduction of each course colleague. The instructor models this expectation by posting the first professional introduction post, emphasizing the professional background, including areas of subject matter expertise and experience, while also offering a bit of background information that lightly touches on a personal background of understanding. As soon as each learner posts their own professional introduction post, the instructor deeply engages with each learner's post, highlighting professional strengths and creative talents, while also extending questions and queries that attempt to more fully engage the learner. This is also a modeling attempt to guide other learners to engage in a similarly respectful manner with colleague posts. This experience ensures that learners recognize similarities and interesting differences among each other, recognizing themselves in others, reaching out to develop professional connections as well as respectfully highlighting impressive experiences, ideas, and life learnings, that begin to develop a collective community that emphasizes respect, support, and a developing vulnerability or intimacy that will slowly grow into a depth of understanding amongst course learners. The departure is the course journey's initiation, setting standards of expectation and engagement related to individual learners within the course, while equally modeling an underlying yet developing participatory expectation of professional supports that reflect a slowly recognized intimacy and understanding.

Collegial Learner Ruminations

The most effective methods for encouraging collegial interaction and cooperation within online learning environments is to mandate group activities. Online learning is inherently a solitary exercise, so in order to overcome the very nature of online learning, the instructor must force the students to come together. While the instructor can simply assign groups and make the grade for the exercise dependent on cooperation, that is not necessarily the best prescription for success. A better method is for the instructor to relate success stories of previous online classes and student groups working together.

Recommending a particular type of messaging application that was successful in previous classes and individual working groups is a very natural way for the instructor to guide the students in forming a temporary online community. I have personally experienced this several times, but in my case the instructor did not maneuver us to utilize a particular application. Instead, one of my fellow students had previously utilized a particular application to great success. All the members of the online class immediately formed a group chat on this application and our lives were made immeasurably easier in coordinating all of our group work efforts. When I took a subsequent class with the same instructor, on the first day the class modules were open, and to carry the learning forward in the spirit of my previous classmate, I suggested to the members of the class that we all form a group chat to allow for ease of communication for our online group activities using that same application.

Overall, trying to force online learners to cooperate is difficult without making their cooperation a part of their overall course assessment. If online cooperation is recommended and not required, then it's likely that the online students will remain within their comfort zone. I use the term comfort zone deliberately as many student learners, including myself, would prefer to work in a solitary manner and not in group projects. Any activities that could foster this kind of collegial and cooperative community in an online learning situation have to be mandated by the instructor to ensure they will be taken seriously and accomplished. Without that mandate, more often than not the online learning environment will remain a solitary one.

Alternate Trope: Culturally Transcendent Journey

Online learning in the military, as far as I know, remains a solitary endeavor. However, mandating cooperation and participation in the military is far simpler than in the civilian higher education setting. As military personnel are a part of a chain, or chains, of command, it is quite simple for someone above them in the chain to merely issue an order that this cooperation or that interactive activity is a job requirement. There is little doubt that this order will be carried out, as failure to obey an order can bring severe disciplinary action down upon the individual who refuses said order.

While my own experience of learning in the military is dated, to say the least, many of the training courses that I personally proctored were filled with individuals who were forced to be there. The desire to participate was abysmal, the assembled learners at best represented a hostile audience, and myself and my Lieutenant were presenting material that perhaps 10% of our "class" would ever need to utilize. Nonetheless, despite the unwillingness to participate and thinly veiled hostility, we were able to induce participation simply by the fact that our unit was higher on the food chain than theirs. By virtue of our job, and our ability to speak with the authority of a two-star Admiral, we were able to compel these individuals to participate in our training.

While not entirely the same thing, higher education in the military does share one common ground with higher education: if you want to advance along your chosen course, either toward higher military rank or higher academic degree, you must comply with the directives issued to you by those above you. In the case of the military, it is your superior officers; in the case of academia, it is your instructors. Everyone has the right, to varying degrees, to choose noncompliance. But with noncompliance comes consequences; disciplinary action in the military and poor academic marks and possible academic suspensions or expulsions in higher education.

How the instructor presents cooperation among student learners, whether in a face-to-face class or in an online setting, is critical. If you want the student learners to exit their comfort zones, then you have to provide some manner for them to do so in the least dramatic of ways. It's kind of like giving a dog a pill: if you merely try to give the dog a pill they will fight it, but if you wrap the pill in cheese the dog believes they're getting a treat and it makes everything easier. The instructor providing the students guidance on an easy way to form this cooperative community is the cheese around the pill of moving out of their comfort zone. As long as the cheese is there, the pill will be swallowed and everyone will do what's needed to accomplish the goals.

FINDINGS: CODES, CATEGORIES, AND THEMES

As previously articulated, a qualitative autoethnographic participant case studies approach engaged the discussion, towards an understanding of course design practices, through the lens of the online course instructor as well as the lens of the online course learner. The inclusion of the instructor participant ruminations, the collegial learner participant ruminations, and the addition of the alternate trope's culturally transcendent journey consideration, were presented in the topic areas offered within the headings: learner motivation as an emotional experience; designing a hero's journey archetype in online courses; and, the departure, focused upon online course motivation. The data was analyzed, resulting in codes, which were then collapsed into categories and then summarized in themes. Table 2 offers a visual analysis of the codes, categories, and themes through a progressive analysis and presentation of findings.

Table 2. Codes, categories, and themes

Codes	Categories	Themes
• Real-world Display of Learned Knowledge • Progressive Course Design	Progressive Display of Learning	Progressive Learner Engagement of Pedagogy, Andragogy, and Heutagogy
• Procrastination • Imperative Initial Assignment Success	Initial Success	
• Collegial Engagement • Temporary Parallel Online Communication • How Instructor Presents Cooperation • Presenting Work to Colleagues	Engaged Communications & Cooperation	Communities of Practice and Landscapes of Practice Approaches
• Student Ownership • Pay It Forward Wisdom/ • Closed Mindedness • Real World Environment	Personal Ownership of Course Experience	
• Familiarity -- Forever Altered • Nobody is Going to Die/ • Cognitive dissonance	Perspicacity	Collective Unconscious/ Cognitive Dissonance
• Hero's Journey Cannot Be Unlearned/Cognitive Dissonance	No Going Back	

continued on following page

Table 2. Continued

Codes	Categories	Themes
• Leadership Based Upon Colleagues	Leadership	Interactive Activities
• Force Group Activities • Pretest of Student Knowledge	Pre-engagement Course Design	
• Learner Similarities & Differences Recognitions • Collegial Experiences – Familiarity • Engagement/ Cooperation	Familiarity	
• Learning Impetus • Military Learning • High Pressure Learning • Hot Wash – Feedback to Instructors • Course Perception/Performance	Viability of Perceptions	Philosophical Understanding/ Differentiated Perceptions
• Comply with Directives	Guiding Instructions	
• Place and Space	Place and Space	

The data set was extensive, with the initial 290 codes offering an extensive initial understanding, resulting in 12 categories. The resulting five themes may be presented as:

- Progressive Learner Engagement of Pedagogy, Andragogy, and Heutagogy
- Communities of Practice and Landscapes of Practice Approaches
- Collective Unconscious/Cognitive Dissonance
- Interactive Activities
- Philosophical Understanding/Differentiated Perceptions

Each articulated theme is framed through viable quotations that represent deep and rich understandings of the codes, leading into categories and then ultimately the themes.

Theme One: Progressive Learner Engagement

Theme One, the Progressive Learner Engagement of Pedagogy, Andragogy, and Heutagogy, is represented through two articulated categories of Progressive Display of Learning and Initial Success. The codes represent four specific articulations overall. The Progressive Display of Learning articulates two codes. The first code is the Real-world Display of Learned Knowledge, described as, "Second is publicly representing learned knowledge and associated achievements" (Instructor Ruminations). The second code was Progressive Course Design that emphasizes course module design considerations:

"Each module of the course would cover a familiar concept; single-page educational documents, brief informational pamphlets, and other common items. The second part of the hero's journey would take these familiar concepts and bring them forward into the realm of unfamiliar technology and techniques. .... The hero's journey would come full circle to the return to the familiar by taking all of these concepts and unifying them under one single lesson." (Collegial Learner Ruminations)

The Initial Success category initiates the Procrastination code, reflected through, "If a learner is not positively motivated, for whatever reason, their self-efficacy drops and engaging with the material becomes an unpleasant task. Personally, I have witnessed many students who are unhappy with whatever task they are given and they procrastinate and delay completion of said task as long as possible" (Collegial Learner Ruminations). The emphasis is upon the learner's engagement, with a progressive understanding through the learning designs designated as pedagogy, andragogy, and heutagogy.

Theme Two: Communities of Practice and Landscapes of Practice Approaches

Theme Two is presented as Communities of Practice and Landscapes of Practice Approaches. Two categories were articulated: Engaged Communications and Cooperation; and, Personal Ownership of Course Experience. The Engaged Communications and Cooperation category is bound by four codes, with aligned quotations of influence. Code One is Collegial Engagement, reflected through, "First, the importance of collegial engagement as a social learning practice is emphasized throughout all of my online course design practices" (Instructor Ruminations). Code Two is Temporary Parallel Online Communication, articulated through:

"Recommending a particular type of messaging application that was successful in previous classes and individual working groups is a very natural way for the instructor to guide the students in forming a temporary online community." (Collegial Learner Ruminations)

Code Three highlights How Instructor Presents Cooperation, suggesting, "How the instructor presents cooperation among student learners, whether in a face-to-face class or in an online setting, is critical. If you want the student learners to exit their comfort zones then you have to provide some manner for them to do so in the least dramatic of ways" (Collegial Learner Ruminations).

The second category is Personal Ownership of Course Experience, within which three codes were realized. The first code is Student Ownership, noting that, "Fourth and finally, an emphasis upon student ownership of the course experience is imperative" (Instructor Ruminations). The second code is Pay It Forward Wisdom, Closed Mindedness, wherein is highlighted that,

"The difficulty that I have experienced when I attempt to pass along this wisdom to my peers is getting them to both listen to, and implement, the information I'm providing them. Unfortunately, all too often the students in question believe they know what is best as it's the way they've always done their classes. Even at the graduate level, there is a closed mindedness for new methods of time management and organization, while honestly, time management is among the top five skills I have learned in my 51 years." (Collegial Learner Ruminations)

A support associated with learner collegial engagement is a supportive understanding, within communities of practice as well as within landscapes of practice as a course design approach.

Theme Three: Collective Unconscious, Cognitive Dissonance

Theme Three is the Collective Unconscious, Cognitive Dissonance, with two categories: Perspicacity; and No Going Back. The first category offers two codes. The first code is Familiarity, Forever Altered, supported with the recognition that, "Once graduated from your training, you return home for a period of leave (vacation) but your once-familiar surroundings have now forever been altered because you have forever been altered." (Collegial Learner Ruminations). The second code is that Nobody is Going to Die, Cognitive Dissonance:

"Even as far removed from the military as I currently am, the cognitive dissonance still exists from time to time. I often find myself taking my assignments far more seriously than my colleagues, due to the high-pressure learning environment that I was exposed to when I was a very young adult. I often times have to remind myself, sometimes out loud to my classmates, that it's just an assignment and no one's going to die. While everyone else in the room gets a good chuckle, it's more serious in the back of my mind." (Collegial Learner Ruminations)

The second category is No Going Back, with the code designated as Hero's Journey Cannot be Unlearned, Cognitive Dissonance:

> *"The hero's journey cannot be taken in reverse and there is never any opportunity to unlearn what you have learned. The order and discipline which was so much a part of the previous hero's journey is absent in your return to civilian familiarity and it creates a severe cognitive dissonance within the person experiencing it." (Collegial Learner Ruminations)*

The collective unconscious within the course environment may be reflected as a level of cognitive dissonance, within which the learner is progressing through a reflective journey through knowledge acquisition and a sense of familiarity that is enhanced by a clarity of recognition associated with the viability of the knowledge's placement within the knowledge landscape.

Theme Four: Interactive Activities

Theme Four is Interactive Activities, with three designated categories: Leadership; Pre-Engagement Course Design; and, Familiarity. Leadership's code is Leadership Based upon Colleagues, described as:

> *"I will often allow younger students to take the lead to provide them the experience I already possess. If the younger students fail to rise to the occasion, then I will fill the leadership void within the classroom social hierarchy in order to help guide the students through the tasks required by the course material." (Collegial Learner Ruminations)*

The second category is Pre-Engagement Course Design, with the first code presented as Force Group Activities:

> *"The most effective methods for encouraging collegial interaction and cooperation within online learning environments is to mandate group activities. Online learning is inherently a solitary exercise, so in order to overcome the very nature of online learning, the instructor must force the students to come together." (Collegial Learner Ruminations)*

The second code is PreTest of Student Knowledge, reflected as the role of:

> *"Designing a hero's journey in an online course can be properly done with a bit of forethought and student involvement. The departure portion of the hero's journey could be accomplished by having the students review the course modules and then simply answer a pre-course survey regarding whether or not they have ever done anything related to the content." (Collegial Learner Ruminations)*

The third category is Familiarity, with the first code as Learning Similarities and Differences Recognitions:

"This is also a modeling attempt to guide other learners to engage in a similarly respectful manner with colleague posts. This experience ensures that learners recognize similarities and interesting differences among each other, recognizing themselves in others, reaching out to develop professional connections as well as respectfully highlighting impressive experiences, ideas, and life learnings, that begin to develop a collective community that emphasizes respect, support, and a developing vulnerability or intimacy that will slowly grow into a depth of understanding amongst course learners." (Instructor Ruminations)

The second code is Collegial Experiences, Familiarity, suggesting that, "This is familiar because simply discussing our experiences among colleagues, it could be argued, is one of the most familiar and comfortable things within which anyone can engage, associated with not only content and learned skill, but may also include the comfortability associated with instructional strategies that are implemented" (Collegial Learner Ruminations). The third and final code is Engagement, Cooperation, supporting that, "Overall, trying to force online learners to cooperate is difficult without making their cooperation a part of their overall course assessment. If online cooperation is recommended and not required, then it's likely that the online students will remain within their comfort zone" (Collegial Learner Ruminations). Interactive activities are supportive of the larger understanding of the hero's journey as well as the collective journey, noting the necessity to offer narratives and engagements between course colleagues.

Theme Five: Philosophical Understanding, Differentiated Perceptions

Theme Five is noted as Philosophical Understanding, Differentiated Perceptions, with three articulated categories: Viability of Perceptions; Guiding Instructions; and, Place and Space. The first category is Viability of Perceptions, with four codes. Learning Impetus code is suggested as:

"I have observed that learner motivation falls under three distinct categories: a learner is required to learn the material for a degree requirement, a learner has to learn the material for progression in their greater personal goals, and/or the learner wishes to learn the material for reasons of their own which may or may not be related to the previous motivations." (Collegial Learner Ruminations)

The second code is Military Learning, High Pressure Learning, emphasizing that:

"The learning taking place in these sorts of hero's journey are rather abbreviated, as there is an urgency to exposing the military student learners to the new knowledge, ensuring they understand the new knowledge, testing their competence, and then releasing them back into the service to perform these tasks as part of their routine. Military learning is often times high-pressure learning, as in the military a mistake might cause injury or death, whereas in the classroom a mistake is simply mistake and might result in a poor grade." (Collegial Learner Ruminations)

The third and final code is Course Perception, Performance:

"When I arrived in higher education, I merely considered it another job. Each semester, my job was to excel in each course that I was registered for and to perform to the highest level of my abilities. I looked at my instructors as my superior officers; if I ran into an issue, it was contingent upon myself to not only present the issue to the instructor but, where possible, present a solution or solutions to the problem I was experiencing." (Collegial Learner Ruminations)

The second category is Guiding Instructions, with the code articulated as Comply with Directives: "While not entirely the same thing, higher education in the military does share one common ground with higher education: if you want to advance along your chosen course, either toward higher military rank or higher academic degree, you must comply with the directives issued to you by those above you" (Collegial Learner Ruminations). The third category is Place and Space, emphasized as:

"Equally impactful is that the course instructor must rethink their place in the course and their associated facilitative practices, due to the more personalized journey of each learner, while equally considering the collective course experience and outcomes." (Instructor Ruminations)

Further, a well-rounded consideration is:

"Initiating an online course experience emphasizes the design of practices that support an individual's experience and associated expectations, with an equal level of community representation of place and space that supports an individual learner's introduction into the larger collective community." (Instructor Ruminations)

The differentiated perceptions in philosophical beliefs and understandings are brought forward as an interwoven engagement in effort as well as prior experiences.

SOLUTIONS AND RECOMMENDATIONS

The interwoven themes that resulted from the participant reflections were curiously aligned with the Collegial Learner Ruminations, reflecting a majority of codes within the themes: Progressive Learner Engagement of Pedagogy, Andragogy, and Heutagogy; Communities of Practice and Landscapes of Practice Approaches; Collective Unconscious/Cognitive Dissonance; Interactive Activities; and, Philosophical Understanding/Differentiated Perceptions. Equally intriguing, the Instructor Ruminations were not strongly reflected as thematic areas of focus beyond the parallel ruminations of Interactive Activities that were supported by both the Instructor and the Collegial Learner. Table 3 reflects a majority of codes within the themes:

Table 3. Alignment of themes to instructor and collegial learner ruminations

Ruminations	Theme
Collegial Learner	• Progressive Learner Engagement of Pedagogy, Andragogy, and Heutagogy • Communities of Practice and Landscapes of Practice Approaches • Collective Unconscious/Cognitive Dissonance • Philosophical Understanding/Differentiated Perceptions
Tie: Instructor and Collegial Learner	• Interactive Activities

The clear emphasis of analysis has been aligned with the strength of the Collegial Learner's impactful reflections and ruminations associated with the emotional engagement and experiential learning within online course design practices.

The practical implications of these solutions and recommendations suggest more explicit philosophical shifts and understandings to support online course instructional design, online course development, and online course implementation by facilitative instructors. Suggestions related to professional development, modeling, and mentoring of current and future online course instructors is necessary, with a focused interest upon clarification of instructional beliefs associated with the way that a course is designed for learners, as well as how an instructor facilitates a course experience. Crawford (2016) offers a framework related to an instructor's philosophical beliefs about the teaching and learning process, reflected through the articulated responses to questions that emphasize learning theory considerations:

- Learning Theories and The Impact Upon Instructional Success
- How the Instructor Believes that She Learns
- How the Instructor Designs Online Courses
- How the Instructor Instructs
- How the Instructor Believes that Other People Learn

- How the Instructor Believes the Subject is "Best" Taught (p. 23)

These are important questions to raise and that each instructor must analyze and carefully reflect upon, towards enhancing a critical analysis and critically pedagogic understanding of beliefs associated with how people learn knowledge, as well as how the instructor actually thinks about the instruction within a learning environment. As Driscoll (2004) articulated, related to learning theories:

A learning theory, therefore, comprises a set of constructs linking observed changes in performance with what is thought to bring about those changes. Constructs refer to the concepts theorists invent to identify psychological variables. Memory, for example, is a construct implicated in cognitive perspectives on learning. In other words, we look at the fact that people can demonstrate the same performance time after time and reason that they do so because they have remembered it. We have invented the concept of memory to explain this result. (p. 9)

The instructor facilitates the course experience based within an understanding of their own successful engagement with the subject matter; meaning having been a successful learner throughout their course experiences, the instructor may implement a model of the way that they were taught information while going to school. This is a natural expectation and experience, because many instructors teach the way that they were taught. In many situations, the assumption was that they were successful, so other learners would also be successful implementing similar styles of instructional engagement. Yet a deeper critical analysis of instructional prowess may be useful within an instructional environment, as not only do learning environments shift and change, as well as subject matter may shift and change over time, but the learners who are raised within different cultural and societal expectations and styles of engagement also shift and change over time and within different communities. Equally impactful is the differentiation associated with learning environments, as the traditional face to face instructional environment is maintained, while additional learning environmental experiences have been growing in interest and associated supports, including online learning, hybrid learning, flipped learning, field-based hands-on learning, and virtual learning environments.

The ways of prior generational and cultural learning may not support the current learner needs; however, the course must be designed to support multiple generations within one learning environment, so as to support all learners as well as towards the successful embedding of the learned knowledge within the current societal and cultural milieu needs and requirements of learned knowledge. This moves towards a recognition of the learner's needs within learning environments. As learning environments shift and change, a widening experiential understanding associated with learning environments is in the process of being realized. Yet with many different learners from innumerable generations, prior learning experiences, comfortableness within different learning environments, and outside-of-course-experience expectations, a sensitivity towards the learner's needs and comfortableness within the learning environment must be addressed. Recognizing this, microlearning events may be necessary, to help the learner to understand the course environment within which the learner is expected to engage with the subject matter, the instructor, as well as learning colleagues. Each course experience is different and, as such, each course may require differentiated microlearning events to explain the course experience and expectations to learners who are new to the course environment, the course instructor, as well as the course experience. Offering a conceptual framework of understanding (Vygotsky, 1933/1966, 1934/1987, 1935, 1962, 1978 1981) to the learner as early in the course experience as possible, may support the motivation and successful engagement of learners who are new to the experience or may develop a level of discomfort and potential anxiety associated with the initial learning experience.

FUTURE RESEARCH DIRECTIONS

The principles of Joseph Campbell's hero's journey (2004, 2008) and the work of Jeff Gomez in the area of a revised consideration that has been coined the Collective Journey (2017a, 2017b, 2017c, 2017d, 2017e, 2017f) are impactful to consider. A recognition of nuanced design practices emphasizes a requirement for better understanding approaches to online learning course development and implementation within a supportive online method of facilitation and engagement. The interwoven reality of online course design, the nuanced quality and understandings of the online instructor's facilitation practices and comfort within an online learning environment, as well as the collegial learner's prior and immediate learning experiences, do color the collective journey within an online course experience.

Online learning is a sustainable trend into the future. Equally trending is the need for higher education instructors to learn how to design engaging instructional environments within an online space. Further trending is the ability to instruct within online learning environments. Many instructors use their own previous classroom-based learning experiences to determine how to instruct within face-to-face settings; indeed, many instructors maintain similar instructional styles as their prior instructors due to the comfort, understanding, and success associated with that style of instruction for the then-learner-now-instructor; however, the novelty associated with online learning environments requires that instruction be differentiated from traditional face-to-face classroom instruction. Instructors must learn new ways of engaging the learner and new ways to facilitate the instructional process in order to be successful. Equally impactful is the necessary understanding of online course design, embedding motivational aspects that support the learner's progressive journey through the course learning experience.

CONCLUSION

Motivational engagement and associated considerations of the learner colleague must be thoughtfully designed into the course experience, while equally imperative are the supports related to training and subsequent experiential expertise of the facilitator within an online course environment. The clarity of the findings emphasizes the impact of online course design upon the collegial learner and, subsequently, the online community of learners. The lack of research that brings forward the voice of the online collegial learner must be remedied, addressing the current gap in the literature. Implementing the quality of metaphoric understanding associated with the hero's journey as well as the parallel collective journey may be implemented to enhance the online course structure and experiential engagement, as well as the quality of learning colleagues' experiences.

REFERENCES

Achen, K., & Rutledge, D. (2023). The transition from emergency remote teaching to quality online course design: Instructor perspectives of surprise, awakening, closing loops, and changing engagement. *Community College Journal of Research and Practice*, 47(6), 428–442. DOI: 10.1080/10668926.2022.2046207

Alamri, H., Lowell, V., Watson, W., & Watson, S. L. (2020). Using personalized learning as an instructional approach to motivate learners in online higher education: Learner self-determination and intrinsic motivation. *Journal of Research on Technology in Education*, 52(3), 322–352. DOI: 10.1080/15391523.2020.1728449

Alqurashi, E. (2019). Predicting student satisfaction and perceived learning within online learning environments. *Distance Education*, 40(1), 133–148. DOI: 10.1080/01587919.2018.1553562

Asfahani, A., El-Farra, S. A., & Iqbal, K. (2023). International Benchmarking of Teacher Training Programs: Lessons Learned from Diverse Education Systems. *EDUJAVARE: International Journal of Educational Research*, 1(2), 141–152.

Bernstein, P. (2013, December 13). The 3 rules of transmedia storytelling from transmedia guru Jeff Gomez. *IndieWire*. https://www.indiewire.com/2013/12/the-3-rules-of-transmedia-storytelling-from-transmedia-guru-jeff-gomez-32325

Burnham, B., & Walden, B. (1997). Interactions in distance education: A report from the other side. In *Proceedings of the Adult Education Research Conference*. Oklahoma State University. http://www.edst.educ.ubc.ca/aerc/1997/97burnham.html

Calavia, M. B., Blanco, T., Casas, R., & Dieste, B. (2023). Making design thinking for education sustainable: Training preservice teachers to address practice challenges. *Thinking Skills and Creativity*, 47, 101199. DOI: 10.1016/j.tsc.2022.101199

Campbell, J. (2004). *Pathways to bliss: Mythology and personal transformation* (Vol. 16). New World Library.

Campbell, J. (2008). *The hero with a thousand faces* (Vol. 17). New World Library.

Crawford, C. M. (2001). Developing webs of significance through communications: Appropriate interactive activities for distributed learning environments. *Campus-Wide Information Systems*, 18(2), 68–72. DOI: 10.1108/10650740110386675

Crawford, C. M. (2003). Emerging learning environments: Enhancing the online community. *Academic Exchange Quarterly*, 7(4), 131–135.

Crawford, C. M. (2016). Creating teacher immediacy in online learning environments. In S. D'Austino's (Ed.) *Teacher Immediacy in Online Learning Environments.* (pp. 15-36). IGI Global.

Crawford, C. M., Andrews, S., & Wallace, J. K. Y. (2021). Co-creative collegial communities of instructional engagement. [IJHIoT]. *International Journal of Hyperconnectivity and the Internet of Things*, 5(2), 38–56. DOI: 10.4018/IJHIoT.2021070103

Crawford, C. M., White, S. A., & Young Wallace, J. (2019). Rethinking pedagogy, andragogy and heutagogy. *Academic Exchange Quarterly*, 23(1), 4–10.

Crawford, C. M., Young, J., & White, S. A. (2018). Rethinking pedagogy, andragogy and heutagogy. *Academic Exchange Quarterly*, 22(4), 15–20.

Diwakar, S., Kolil, V. K., Francis, S. P., & Achuthan, K. (2023). Intrinsic and extrinsic motivation among students for laboratory courses-Assessing the impact of virtual laboratories. *Computers & Education*, 198, 104758. DOI: 10.1016/j.compedu.2023.104758

Driscoll, M. P. (2004). *Psychology of Learning for Instruction* (3rd ed.). Pearson Education.

Dunn, T. J., & Kennedy, M. (2019). Technology-enhanced learning in higher education; motivations, engagement, and academic achievement. *Computers & Education*, 137, 104–113. DOI: 10.1016/j.compedu.2019.04.004

Gomez, J. (2017a, February 6). Why is this happening? A new narrative model explains it. *Collective Journey* [blog]. https://blog.collectivejourney.com/why-is-this-happening-d1287d5ee4ee

Gomez, J. (2017b, February 7). The hero's journey is no longer serving us: classic storytelling models are faltering in the digital age. *Collective Journey* [blog]. https://blog.collectivejourney.com/the-heros-journey-is-no-longer-serving-us-85c6f8152a50#.psdwtk4kp

Gomez, J. (2017c, February 17). The collective journey comes to television: Game of Thrones, Walking Dead, Orange is the New Black & others are subverting the hero's journey. *Collective Journey* [blog]. https://blog.collectivejourney.com/the-collective-journey-story-model-comes-to-television-151bb4011ce2

Gomez, J. (2017d, March 8). Regenerative listening: Collective journey narratives require genuine engagement. *Collective Journey* [blog]. https://blog.collectivejourney.com/the-secret-to-new-storytelling-regenerative-listening-5250c65b6391

Gomez, J. (2017e, May 22). Superpositioning: each of us can now be in five places at once. *Collective Journey* [blog]. https://blog.collectivejourney.com/superpositioning-fef1e10ff24c

Gomez, J. (2017f, September 16). Social self-organization: story can take what we imagine and make it real. *Collective Journey* [blog]. https://blog.collectivejourney.com/social-self-organization-47a562cfb351

Hardt, M. (2010). Militant life. *New Left Review*, 64, 151–160.

Harrington, C., & Thomas, M. (2023). *Designing a motivational syllabus: Creating a learning path for student engagement.* Taylor & Francis.

Hillman, D., Willis, D. J., & Gunawardena, C. (1994). Learner-interface interaction in distance education: An extension of contemporary models and strategies for practitioners. *American Journal of Distance Education*, 8(2), 30–42. DOI: 10.1080/08923649409526853

Kilag, O. K., Marquita, J., & Laurente, J. (2023). Teacher-led curriculum development: Fostering innovation in education. *Excellencia: International Multi-disciplinary Journal of Education (2994-9521)*, *1*(4), 223-237.

Lorenz, E. (1963). The predictability of hydrodynamic flow. Transactions of the N. Y 387 Academy of Science, 25, 409 – 432.

Lorenz, E. (1994). *The essence of chaos.* University of Washington Press.

Lorenz, E. N. (1972). Predictability: does the flap of a butterfly's wings in Brazil set off a tornado in Texas? *139th Annual Meeting of the American Association for the Advancement of Science.*

Mallarangan, A. D. D., Rahman, A., Nur, S., Lathifah, Z. K., & Lubis, F. M. (2024). Analysis Of The Influence Of Continuous Training Development And Education On Professional Competence Of Teachers In Public Schools. *Journal of Education*, 6(2), 13449–13456.

Martin, F., Kumar, S., Ritzhaupt, A. D., & Polly, D. (2023). Bichronous online learning: Award-winning online instructor practices of blending asynchronous and synchronous online modalities. *The Internet and Higher Education*, 56, 100879. DOI: 10.1016/j.iheduc.2022.100879

MasterClass. (2021, September 3). *Writing 101: What is the Hero's Journey? 2 Hero's Journey Examples in Film.* Masterclass. https://www.masterclass.com/articles/writing-101-what-is-the-heros-journey

McLean, S., & Attardi, S. M. (2023). Sage or guide? Student perceptions of the role of the instructor in a flipped classroom. *Active Learning in Higher Education*, 24(1), 49–61. DOI: 10.1177/1469787418793725

Moore, M. (1989). Three types of interaction. *American Journal of Distance Education*, 3(2), 1–7. DOI: 10.1080/08923648909526659

Nafukho, F. M., Irby, B. J., Pashmforoosh, R., Lara-Alecio, R., Tong, F., Lockhart, M. E., El Mansour, W., Tang, S., Etchells, M., & Wang, Z. (2023). Training design in mediating the relationship of participants' motivation, work environment, and transfer of learning. *European Journal of Training and Development*, 47(10), 112–132. DOI: 10.1108/EJTD-06-2022-0070

Neelen, M., & Kirschner, P. A. (2020). *Evidence-informed learning design: Creating training to improve performance*. Kogan Page Publishers.

Nkomo, L. M., Daniel, B. K., & Butson, R. J. (2021). Synthesis of student engagement with digital technologies: A systematic review of the literature. *International Journal of Educational Technology in Higher Education*, 18, 1–26. PMID: 34778529

Salendab, F. (2023). Proposed instructional scheme in the new normal education: Basis for pedagogical strategies/practices. *Psychology and Education: A Multidisciplinary Journal*, 6(8), 712-719.

Schmitz, B., & Hanke, K. (2023). Engage me: Learners' expectancies and teachers' efforts in designing effective online classes. *Journal of Computer Assisted Learning*, 39(4), 1132–1140. DOI: 10.1111/jcal.12636

Vygotsky, L. S. (1933/1966). Play and its role in the mental development of the child. *Social Psychology*, 12(6), 62–76.

Vygotsky, L. S. (1934/1987). Thinking and speech. In R.W. Rieber & A.S. Carton (Eds.), *The collected works of L.S. Vygotsky, Volume 1: Problems of general psychology (pp. 39–285)*. Plenum Press.

Vygotsky, L. S. (1935). *Mental development of children during education*. Uchpedzig.

Vygotsky, L. S. (1962). *Thought and language*. MIT Press. DOI: 10.1037/11193-000

Vygotsky, L. S. (1978). *Mind in society: The development of higher psychological processes*. Harvard University Press.

Vygotsky, L. S. (1981). The genesis of higher mental functions. In Wertsch, J. V. (Ed.), *The concept of activity in Soviet psychology*. Sharpe.

Webster, L. (2020). Marvel, Star Wars and the risk of being a hero: Social responsibilities for transmedia storytellers in the age of collective journey. *Cultural Science Journal*, 12(1), 59–67. DOI: 10.5334/csci.138

Wenger, E. (1998). *Communities of practice: Learning, meaning, and identity*. Cambridge University Press., DOI: 10.1017/CBO9780511803932

Wenger-Trayner, E., Fenton-O'Creevy, M., Hutchison, S., Kubiak, C., & Wenger-Trayner, B. (2014). *Learning in Landscapes of Practice: Boundaries, Identity, and Knowledgeability in Practice-Based Learning*. Routledge., DOI: 10.4324/9781315777122

Wenger-Trayner, E., & Wenger-Trayner, B. (2015). Communities of practice: A brief introduction. Wemger-Taylor. https://wenger-trayner.com/introduction-to-communities-of-practice/

Wenger-Trayner, E., & Wenger-Trayner, B. (2020). *Learning to Make a Difference: Value Creation in Social Learning Spaces*. Cambridge University Press., DOI: 10.1017/9781108677431

KEY TERMS AND DEFINITIONS

Communication: The efforts associated with attempting to engage with others so as to share concepts, perceptions, and understandings.

Engagement: The effort to communicate and develop a relationship with others in an environment. Within an online course learning experience, this is an attempt towards attaining knowledge acquisition, achieving learning objectives, as well as developing supportive relational communications.

Experience: Within an online learning environment course, this is the requisite process associated with the learning experience.

Learning: The procedural journey that each student learner must progress through as an individual experience as well as within a larger community experience of recognition. Depending upon the learning theory and associated philosophical beliefs systems associated with the teaching and learning process, this may be an individual or a nuanced community experience.

Motivation: The efforts associated with engaging with an experience, which may offer a high level of interest or a low level of interest which is dependent upon the learner's sense of need and associated hierarchy of interest. Motivation may require self-regulatory efforts and may engage in a learner's sense of self-efficacy and associated success.

Online Course: This is a learning environment within which the learners and the instructor are engaged from a physical distance.

Perception: The view of an individual person, related to self or an external entity. Within a learning environment, this also includes a learner's understanding and beliefs associated with the subject matter, the learning environment, the sense of belonging within a learning space, as well as the learner's potential beliefs associated with successful attainment of knowledge while equally focused upon attaining articulated learning objectives.

Chapter 12
An Investigation of Students' Emotions, Emotion Regulation Strategies, and Motives for Emotion Regulation

Eda Bakır-Yalçın
https://orcid.org/0000-0001-5178-486X
Recep Tayyip Erdoğan University, Turkey

Yasin Yalçın
https://orcid.org/0000-0002-3877-9836
Recep Tayyip Erdoğan University, Turkey

ABSTRACT

This study aimed to identify the emotions experienced by students engaged in a project assignment for the Instructional Technologies course, the emotion regulation strategies they employed, and the motives behind their use of these strategies. The sample comprised 20 undergraduate students enrolled in the Instructional Technologies course at a state university in Turkey. Conducted as an explanatory case study, the research revealed that students commonly felt anxiety and excitement during the project preparation phase, excitement during the presentation phase, and relief post-presentation. Situation modification strategies were the most frequently used emotion regulation techniques, primarily for instrumental reasons to enhance performance. Furthermore, students often experienced multiple emotions and utilized various strategies to regulate these emotions. In this chapter, we discuss our findings in light of the related literature and make recommendations for emotional

DOI: 10.4018/979-8-3693-2663-3.ch012

Copyright © 2025, IGI Global. Copying or distributing in print or electronic forms without written permission of IGI Global is prohibited.

processes in the educational context.

INTRODUCTION

Emotions have attracted the attention of educational researchers due to their potential role in the educational context, especially in learning. It is important to investigate how students regulate negative and positive emotions, as emotions can both help and hinder performance and learning (Alonso-Tapia et al., 2020; Harley et al., 2019). Emotion regulation is characterized as a series of processes by which individuals manage their own emotions or direct the flow of their emotions; in many ways, it forms the basis of leading a healthy life (Koole, 2009; Pekrun & Stephens, 2010; Rottweiler et al., 2022). Kappas (2011) argued that individuals can regulate their emotions and reduce the effect of negative emotions on physiological and psychological states. Accordingly, the ability of students to intervene in and change the emotional reactions they experience is important for learning and academic success (Sorić et al., 2013). It has been suggested that positive emotions enable learners to use flexible, creative, and deep learning strategies (Pekrun, 2014). Students who experience positive emotions in the educational context can produce ideas and strategies to a greater extent, and this situation may help them develop more comprehensive and adaptive coping strategies (Sutton & Wheatley, 2003). Negative emotions, on the other hand, are described as disadvantageous because they can increase the frequency of avoidance behaviors in many performance-related situations (Vuorela & Nummenmaa, 2004). To minimize the effect of negative emotions, learners should use successful emotion regulation strategies (Burić et al., 2016). Successful emotion regulation is related to how well the psychological characteristics of the individual, the demands of the situation, and the strategies used match each other in a given context (Rottweiler et al., 2022). For this reason, adopting a more holistic perspective and examining all emotional processes, including emotions and emotion regulation, will contribute to our understanding of the role emotions play in educational settings. In this study, we took a holistic approach to investigating the emotions of higher education students, the emotion regulation strategies they use, and why they resort to emotion regulation.

Emotions and Emotion Regulation

Emotion is a multidimensional construct that reveals individuals' adaptations to the events they encounter in daily life, their reactions to them, and their individual personality (Smith & Lazarus, 1990). Recognizing the complexity of emotions, researchers have explored how individuals manage and regulate these emotions in various theories and models. According to Thompson (1994), emotion regulation "consists of the extrinsic and intrinsic processes responsible for monitoring, evaluating, and modifying emotional reactions, especially their intensive and temporal features, to accomplish one's goals" (p. 27). Furthermore, while Gross (1998a) describes emotion regulation as a process that includes all conscious and unconscious strategies used to increase, maintain, or decrease one or more components of the emotional response, Koole (2009) and Xu et al. (2019) describe emotion regulation as the processes by which people experience and manage their emotions.

There are different opinions regarding the relationship between emotion and emotion regulation as well. Some researchers claim that emotion generation and emotion regulation are separate but related processes, some researchers assert that they are two distinct processes, and others maintain that the distinction between emotion generation and emotion regulation is conceptually difficult and that the two are intertwined (Gross, 2015b; Gross & Feldman Barrett, 2011; Kappas, 2011). Kappas (2011) stated that it is difficult to conceptually separate emotion generation and emotion regulation from each other. Gross (2015a), on the other hand, emphasized that emotion regulation has a separate valuation process from emotion generation. By adopting the view that emotion generation and emotion regulation are different but related, he assumed that emotion regulation is carried out at five points in the emotion generation process in the Emotion Regulation Process Model (Gross, 1998a, 2015b). According to Gross (1998b), individuals regulate emotion by i) selecting a situation, ii) modifying the situation, iii) focusing or diverting attention, iv) altering the meaning of the situation, or v) modulating the response. Two main categories of emotion regulation are antecedent-focused and response-focused. Antecedent-focused emotion regulation involves strategies employed before the emotional response is activated, while response-focused emotion regulation involves strategies used after an emotional response has been triggered. Among the strategies Gross mentioned, selecting and modifying the situation, focusing or diverting attention, and cognitive reappraisal (i.e., altering the meaning) indicate antecedent-focused emotion regulation, while response modulation signifies response-focused emotion regulation (See Table 1).

Table 1. Categories and strategies of emotion regulation in emotion regulation process model

Model	Emotion Regulation Category	Emotion Regulation Strategy Family	Description
Gross's Emotion Regulation Process Model	Antecedent-focused	Situation selection	Choosing or avoiding situations.
		Situation modification	Changing a situation to alter its emotional effect.
		Attentional deployment	Redirecting attention away from the emotional stimulus.
		Cognitive change	Changing the way to think about a situation to alter its emotional significance.
	Response-focused	Response modulation	Influencing physiological, experiential, or behavioral responses to emotions (e.g., suppression)

Source: Gross (1998a, 2015b)

Individuals use various strategies for emotion regulation. Although not all are equally effective or applicable to the situation, individuals still employ these strategies to regulate their emotions (Harley et al., 2019). As noted above, emotion regulation strategies have been classified in various ways. While Gross (1998a, 2015b) made a distinction based on the temporal characteristics of emotion regulation (i.e., antecedent- vs. response-focused), proposing a series of strategies during the emotion generation process, Koole (2009), on the other hand, developed a classification based on the system that generates emotion and its psychological functions. His classification highlighted three major functions: need-oriented, goal-oriented, and person-oriented. Need-oriented functions aim to satisfy basic psychological needs, such as competence, relatedness, and autonomy. Goal-oriented functions focus on achieving specific goals. Finally, person-oriented functions relate to the maintenance and enhancement of one's self-concept and personal values.

Each of these classification systems approaches a given emotion regulation strategy differently. For example, while focusing one's attention in another direction is explained by the concentrating strategy according to Gross's (1998b) model, Koole (2009) indicates that it is a goal- or need-oriented strategy at the attention level. According to Koole (2009), if an individual uses this strategy for a personal goal, they are using a goal-oriented strategy and if they want to eliminate the negative effects of the situation, they are using a need-oriented strategy.

Garnefski and Kraaij (2006), on the other hand, emphasized the conscious and cognitive aspects of emotion regulation and created a different classification. Their classification includes nine specific strategies, divided into adaptive and maladaptive categories. Acceptance, positive refocusing, refocus on planning, positive reappraisal, and putting into perspective constitute the adaptive strategies; self-blame, rumination, catastrophizing, and blaming others are cited as the maladaptive strategies.

Aldao et al. (2010) organized the strategies based on their relationship with psychopathological symptoms (Cavicchioli et al., 2021) and also classified emotion regulation strategies as adaptive and maladaptive. Adaptive strategies are beneficial in preventing psychopathology and coping with stress in a healthy manner, while maladaptive strategies exacerbate emotional problems and show a positive relationship with psychopathology (Aldao & Nolen-Hoeksema, 2012; Naragon-Gainey et al., 2017).

The Control-Value Theory of achievement emotions is another primary theory developed to explain emotional processes in academic settings. It serves as an integrative framework for examining the precursors and impacts of emotions within academic and achievement contexts and suggests that evaluations of control and value are fundamental to the emergence of achievement-related emotions (Pekrun, 2006). Although Pekrun (2006) did not classify the strategies in the Control-Value Theory, he stated that learners engage in appraisal-, emotion-, and problem-oriented approaches during the emotion regulation process and adopt strategies accordingly. In appraisal-oriented regulation, learners use various strategies by focusing on the valuation process and cognitive factors, such as reappraising a situation or event. In emotion-oriented regulation, students target the affective factors of a situation or event to regulate their emotions, such as by using relaxation techniques. Finally, in problem-oriented regulation, students use strategies to increase their competencies or agency, such as consulting competence-based treatments. Research shows that some emotion regulation strategies are more effective than others (Kobylińska & Kusev, 2019); however, the use and effectiveness of these strategies depend on contextual, social, and individual factors (Kobylińska & Kusev, 2019; Rottweiler et al., 2022; Zhoc et al., 2022).

There are different models of emotion regulation in the literature and each of them offers unique perspectives on how individuals regulate their emotions. This study adopts Gross's Emotion Regulation Process Model as a theoretical framework (Gross, 1998a, 2015b) because it is particularly suited for analyzing both antecedent-focused and response-focused strategies. It also provides a structured framework to explore varied approaches used by students to regulate their emotions. By employing this model, the study aims to delve into how students navigate their emotional experiences in the context of a group project, offering deeper insights into their emotion regulation processes.

Motives for Emotion Regulation

For individuals to benefit from emotion regulation processes and strategies, it is important for them to understand why they use emotion regulation (Tamir, 2016). Motives for emotion regulation are effective in choosing and implementing a strategy (Jarrell & Lajoie, 2017). According to a taxonomy developed by Tamir (2016), individuals regulate their emotions for hedonic or instrumental reasons. The two types of hedonic motives are i) prohedonic and ii) contrahedonic. Prohedonic motives involve regulating emotions to increase the ratio of pleasure to pain, while contrahedonic motives aim to decrease pleasure to achieve a hedonic balance. On the other hand, the four categories of instrumental emotion regulation are i) performance, ii) epistemic, iii) social, and iv) eudaimonic. Performance motivation involves regulating an individual's emotions to improve cognition and behavior. Emotion regulation for epistemic reasons involves regulating emotions to obtain the desired information. Individuals who regulate emotions due to social motivation aim to shape their bilateral, group, or social relationships. Finally, eudaimonic motivation involves regulating emotions to reinforce one's sense of meaning in life. Individuals who regulate emotions for either hedonic or instrumental reasons develop strategies suitable for their goals. For this reason, the emotion regulation process should be able to answer questions such as which emotion is generated, why emotion regulation is used, and which strategy is adopted, and it should offer a holistic perspective.

Emotion Regulation in the Educational Context

Although cognitive structures are frequently examined and emotions are often neglected in studies in the educational context (Artino & Jones, 2012), there are claims that this trend is shifting (Titsworth et al., 2013). Nonetheless, some researchers assert that there are few studies on emotion regulation, especially in the academic context (Burić et al., 2016; Rottweiler et al., 2022). While emotion and emotion regulation processes affect students' academic performance, they are also very important for students' psychological well-being (Gross, 1998b; Jarrell et al., 2022; Pekrun, 2014). Research shows that emotion regulation plays a crucial role in psychological functionality and well-being (Rottweiler et al., 2022). Accordingly, knowing learners' emotions, their motives for emotion regulation, and the emotion regulation strategies they use will allow us to have a greater understanding of the emotional processes and their relationship with other contextual, social, and individual factors in learning environments.

Different strategies for emotion regulation have different psychological and cognitive effects, and these differences affect learning in various ways (Zhoc et al., 2022). For example, Jarrell et al. (2022) stated that while students' use of the reappraisal strategy during the exam preparation process had positive effects on their exam performance, using the suppression strategy during exam times had negative effects. Also, reappraisal had an indirect effect on learning strategies through emotions, but suppression had no effect on learning strategies. Zhoc et al. (2022), on the other hand, stated that the effects of the suppression and reappraisal strategies on student engagement in online environments are different. However, emotion regulation strategies play a mediating role between students' well-being and engagement. In a study with university students during the pre-exam period, Schmidt et al. (2010) found that the most important strategy was seeking social support, regardless of the emotions experienced and how the exam was evaluated, when a stressful situation such as an exam is taken into account. However, when students' typical academic context is considered, the emotion regulation strategies used by students emerged in relation to the type of emotion they experienced. These findings reveal the importance of specific aspects of the academic environment in studies. Without defining the specific aspects of the academic environment, a correct approach cannot be established as to whether emotion regulation strategies are successful, adaptive, or appropriate (Naragon-Gainey et al., 2017). Emotion regulation processes are important for an educational environment leading to positive outcomes such as academic success, effective teaching, and overall satisfaction (Hoffmann et al., 2020). For these reasons, findings from emotion regulation research will contribute to both the academic achievement and psychological well-being of students.

Purpose of the Study

Given the significant impact that emotions have on learning, motivation, and performance within educational contexts, it is essential to understand how students regulate these emotions to foster both academic success and positive psychological experiences. Since students' emotions can be destructive and impact achievement of their goals, it is important for students to use successful strategies to influence the formation, intensity, and duration of the emotions they experience (Burić et al., 2016). Although the relationship between emotion generation and emotion regulation is complex and controversial, some researchers argue that the processes of emotion generation and regulation are interlinked because the strategies employed for emotion regulation can influence the generation of emotions (Jarrell & Lajoie, 2017). Moreover, depending on the context in which emotion regulation is performed, strategies may either be effective and lead to success or be ineffective and result in failure. It is important to address which strategies are used in specific contexts and whether these strategies result in successful emotion regulation. Adopting a holistic approach to examining students' emotional processes is crucial for promoting both academic achievements and psychological well-being.

In this study, we explored the emotions experienced by higher education students and the emotion regulation strategies they employed while working on a group project for an Instructional Technologies course. Specifically, we aimed to investigate how students generate and regulate their emotions throughout the semester as they developed and presented their projects. The purpose of this study was to gain an in-depth understanding of the emotion generation and regulation processes in this academic context. The research questions guiding this study are:

1. What emotions do students experience before, during, and after the project presentations?
2. Why do students regulate emotions before, during, and after the project presentations?
3. What strategies do students use to regulate their emotions?

Method

In this study, we used the case study method. The case study method is an in-depth study or exploration of a phenomenon or situation in its natural environment (Crowe et al., 2011). More specifically, the exploratory case study method was used. Exploratory case studies allow the investigation of a theory by observing a phenomenon (Glaser & Strauss, 1967) and may entail adopting intuitive paths (Yin, 2003).

Participants

Participants consisted of 20 undergraduate students studying in the Social Sciences program at the Faculty of Education of a state university in Turkey. Students' emotional experiences (i.e., experienced emotions and emotion regulation processes) during a group project in the Instructional Technologies course were examined in depth. Participants' ages ranged between 20 and 27, with a mean of 21.25 and a standard deviation of 1.59. Participants consisted of three male and 17 female students. The study was approved by the Institutional Ethics Committee at the researchers' institution. Participants were informed about the study, and participation was voluntary.

Procedures and Materials

The study was carried out with undergraduate students enrolled in the Instructional Technologies course. The Instructional Technologies course is required for students in the second year of the Social Sciences program. During the course, students worked on and presented a semester project that they completed in groups of three or four between Week 7 and Week 14. Working on semester projects entailed forming groups and selecting a Web 2.0 tool as the topic of the project in Week 2. Students were expected to choose one of the given Web 2.0 tools (i.e., Kahoot, Easel.ly, Edpuzzle, Powtoon, Plickers, Bookwidgets, Prezi, and Emaze) and either introduce the selected Web 2.0 tool and its application areas or develop instructional material using the Web 2.0 tool based on an instructional objective. Both options included a presentation, and all group members contributed to the presentation of the projects. Students were asked to use message and visual design principles as they developed instructional materials and presentations. The project evaluation criteria differed based on the options students chose as a group. For the tool introduction option, information about the application (e.g., application login, sharing features, export options, etc.), the tool's use areas, and the presentation were considered evaluation criteria. Here, students were expected to provide information about the tool with a presentation and then demonstrate how the tool could be used in the educational context. For the instructional material development option, the evaluation criteria included developing an instructional objective that entailed the use of the Web 2.0 tool, developing sample instructional material aligned with the instructional objective, and applying the instructional material in a session with the whole class.

Data Collection

Data collection began in Week 7 and continued until Week 14 of the semester. Participants presented their semester projects between Week 7 and Week 14. During the process, an online document was created for each volunteer participant on Google Drive. Participants were instructed to document the emotions they experienced at least once during each of the following phases: project preparation, project presentation, and upon completion of the presentation. The document contained information about the emotions they experienced, whether they used emotion regulation, which strategy they used if they did, and why they regulated their emotions.

Before the onset of data collection, participants received a brief training about the theoretical background of the study, focusing on emotions, emotion regulation and its strategies, and other important points of the data collection web tool and instrument. Using the data collection instrument, they were allowed to write about their detailed emotional experiences as text as desired. The structure of the data collection instrument is presented in Table 2. Students were not supplied with a predefined list of emotions or emotion regulation strategies; instead, they were asked to describe the emotions they experienced and the strategies they employed in their own words. Although students worked on a group project, they were asked to describe the emotional processes they experienced individually, and group-level experiences were excluded from analysis.

Table 2. Data collection instrument

	Before the Presentation of the Project (Preparation)	**During the Presentation of the Project**	**After the Presentation of the Project**
Emotions that you experienced			
If you regulated your emotion:			
Why did you regulate your emotion?			
Which strategy did you use to regulate your emotion?			

Data Analysis

Data gathered using the instrument were examined according to Gross's Process Model of Emotion Regulation and Tamir's taxonomy of motives in emotion regulation.

The strategies of emotion regulation reported by students were categorized based on Gross's (1998a, 2015b) Process Model of Emotion Regulation. This classification aimed to determine whether the emotions were antecedent-focused or response-focused and to identify the specific category within each group.

Furthermore, the responses to the question of why emotions were regulated were analyzed according to Tamir's (2016) taxonomy of motives in emotion regulation.

Data analysis was completed with both authors reaching consensus on coding and classification. Participants were given an opportunity to review the reduced data before the analysis was finalized, ensuring accuracy and completeness.

Findings

Emotions Experienced

The frequencies of emotions experienced by students during the semester project are presented in Table 3. These emotions were categorized based on student responses as emotions experienced before, during, and after their project presentation. Each frequency indicates the number of students who reported experiencing the corresponding emotion. Since some students reported experiencing multiple emotions, the total number of emotions may exceed the sample size. Additionally, each percentage represents the proportion of emotions experienced in a particular phase of the semester project.

Table 3. The frequency and percentage of emotions experienced by students during the semester project

Emotion Experienced	Before the Presentation		During the Presentation		After the Presentation	
	f	%	f	%	f	%
Anger	1	3.7	-	-	-	-
Anxiety	6	22.2	-	-	-	-
Boredom	4	14.8	-	-	-	-
Curiosity	1	3.7	2	20.0	-	-
Disappointment	1	3.7	-	-	-	-
Excitement	6	22.2	4	40.0	1	10.0
Happiness	1	3.7	1	10.0	2	20.0
Overwhelm	1	3.7	-	-	-	-
Prejudice	1	3.7	-	-	-	-
Pride	-	-	-	-	2	20.0
Regret	-	-	-	-	1	10.0
Relief	-	-	-	-	4	40.0
Stress	5	18.5	1	10.0	-	-

According to Table 3, students most often experienced anxiety and excitement during the project preparation phase (n = 6, 22.2%), followed by stress (n = 5, 18.5%) and boredom (n = 4, 14.8%). During the presentation phase, excitement was expressed as the most frequently experienced emotion (n = 4, 40.0%). It is worth noting that anxiety was experienced only during the project preparation phase, before the presentation. Relief was the most frequently experienced emotion after the presentation (n = 4, 40.0%). Although the number of students who experienced each emotion is provided in the table, we observed that most students experienced more than one emotion, especially during the project preparation phase.

Emotion Regulation Strategies

Table 4 categorizes the different emotion regulation strategies used by students and presents the frequency and percentage of each strategy's use. This categorization helps to identify which strategies were most frequently employed by students, offering insights into the methods used for regulating emotions in an educational context.

Table 4. The frequency and percentage of emotion regulation strategies used by students during the semester project

Emotion Regulation Strategy Family	Emotion Regulation Strategy	f	%
Situation Selection	-	-	-
Situation Modification	Talking to friends	5	17.9
	Seeking social support	5	17.9
	Taking action (e.g., studying)	8	28.6
Attention Deployment	Distraction (e.g., drinking coffee, watching favorite cartoons or videos, listening to music)	5	17.9
	Mindfulness	1	3.6
	Focusing	1	3.6
Cognitive Change	Self-talk	2	7.1
	Acceptance (acceptance of emotions)	1	3.6
Response Modulation	-	-	-

According to the results in Table 4, students mostly used situation modification strategies (n = 18, 64.3%) during the project preparation phase. In particular, taking action to complete their project (n = 8, 28.6%), seeking social support (n = 5, 17.9%), and talking with their peers (n = 5, 17.9%) emerged as the most frequently used strategies. For example, Participant 3 shared the following about the strategies she used to modify the situation and regulate her emotions of stress and excitement: *"I did a little research to learn the material, repeated the presentation to cope with my excitement, and listened carefully to my peers who presented. The conversation I had with my teammates also made me feel better."* Participant 3 used the strategies of taking action (i.e., studying), seeking social support, and talking with friends.

In addition to situation modification strategies, attention deployment strategies were frequently used by participants (n = 7, 25.0%). Specifically, distraction strategies such as drinking coffee or watching popular videos on the Internet and social media were used by students in the process of attention deployment. Participant

16 shared the following about the emotion regulation strategy she used: *"I try to cope with the emotion of boredom while studying by taking a small coffee break."* Participant 9 stated that she regulated her excitement by listening to music she liked, which is another one of the attention deployment strategies.

We observed that most of the students used more than one strategy to regulate their emotions. It is notable that cognitive change strategies were minimally used. Students who used cognitive change strategies stated that they accepted their emotions or had internal conversations with themselves about how to complete the project. None of the students used strategies related to situation selection or response modulation. However, it is understandable that strategies related to situation selection cannot be used within the scope of a required course because students have no control over the mandatory nature of the course and cannot choose to avoid it.

The emotions and emotion regulation strategies used by students are presented in Table 5. The table also shows the emotions students experienced before (i.e., incoming) and after (i.e., outgoing) emotion regulation and the specific emotion regulation strategy they used. When the table is examined, it is evident that students tend to regulate their negative emotions. Only one student (i.e., Participant 11) stated that although she attempted to regulate her anxiety, she was not successful and, as a result, felt regret.

Table 5. Overview of emotion and emotion regulation processes of participants

Participant	Incoming Emotion	Strategy	Outgoing Emotion
Participant 1	Boredom	• Cognitive change: self-talk • Situation modification: talking to friends	Pride
Participant 2	Excitement	• Attention deployment: distraction • Situation modification: seeking social support and talking to friends	Relief
Participant 3	Stress	• Situation modification: taking action, seeking social support, and talking to friends • Attention deployment: focusing	Relief
Participant 4	Excitement	• Situation modification: taking action, seeking social support, and talking to friends	Unspecified
Participant 5	Boredom	• Attention deployment: distraction • Cognitive change: self-talk	Happiness
Participant 6	Excitement, stress, and anxiety	• Situation modification: seeking social support	Unspecified
Participant 7	Boredom, anger, and stress	• Attention deployment: mindfulness	Unspecified
Participant 8	Anxiety	• Situation modification: taking action	Relief and excitement

continued on following page

Table 5. Continued

Participant	Incoming Emotion	Strategy	Outgoing Emotion
Participant 9	Excitement	• Attention deployment: distraction	Unspecified
Participant 10	Stress	• Unspecified	Unspecified
Participant 11	Anxiety	• Situation modification: taking action	Regret
Participant 12	Anxiety	• Situation modification: seeking social support, talking to friends, and taking action	Unspecified
Participant 13	Disappointment	• Situation modification: taking action	Pride and relief
Participant 14	Anxiety	• Situation modification: taking action	Unspecified
Participant 15	Prejudice and curiosity	• Attention deployment: distraction	Unspecified
Participant 16	Excitement and happiness	• No emotion regulation	Unspecified
Participant 17	Excitement and anxiety	• Situation modification: taking action	Happiness
Participant 18	Stress	• Attention deployment: distraction	Unspecified
Participant 19	Boredom	• Unspecified	Unspecified
Participant 20	Being overwhelmed	• Cognitive change: acceptance	Unspecified

Motives for Emotion Regulation

When the responses to the question of what motivates students to regulate emotions were analyzed, it was revealed that performance motivation, mostly for instrumental reasons, was the primary reason. Instrumental reasons were followed by hedonic and social motivations. These results are presented in Table 6. According to the table, students who regulate emotions for hedonic reasons resort to emotion regulation especially because they want to eliminate the effects of negative emotions. We observed that most of the students used emotion regulation for both instrumental and hedonic reasons.

Table 6. Motives for emotion regulation

Emotion Regulation Motives	f
Hedonic	
Prohedonic	6
Contrahedonic	0
Instrumental	
Performance	10
Epistemic	0
Social	2
Eudaimonic	0

In examining the motives behind students' emotion regulation, various reasons emerged. Participant 20, who regulated emotions for hedonic reasons, responded that she regulated the feeling of being overwhelmed. Regarding her specific reason for regulating this feeling, she said: *"Because this emotion would increase my anxiety and affect me negatively."* She resorted to emotion regulation because she did not want to experience the negativity caused by the feeling of being overwhelmed and anxiety. Participant 6, who stated that she employed emotion regulation for instrumental reasons, shared the following statement regarding the reason for emotion regulation: *"The anxiety, excitement, and stress I felt could distract me from doing my homework, delay doing it, and cause me to make mistakes in things I was otherwise going to do right."* Participant 3, who was determined to regulate emotions for social reasons, said: *"Fulfilling my duty without putting my groupmates in a bad situation gave me relief."* In the educational context, it is possible to claim that students generally regulate emotions for instrumental reasons. Performance-based emotion regulation was the most frequently cited reason among instrumental reasons.

DISCUSSION

In this study, we investigated the emotions experienced by students, the emotion regulation strategies they employed, and their motives for resorting to emotion regulation while working on a group project in a required Instructional Technologies course. In the process of emotion regulation, describing certain strategies as good and adaptive, or bad and non-adaptive, is not the best approach (Naragon-Gainey et al., 2017). It is critically important to understand the contextual characteristics, emotion regulation goals, individual characteristics, and the situational demands.

Findings from this study align with the existing literature, as students reported experiencing a wide variety of emotions in academic settings (Bakır-Yalçın & Usluel, 2024; D'Mello & Graesser, 2012; Dever et al., 2022; Kahu et al., 2015; Karamarkovich & Rutherford, 2021; Lee & Chei, 2020; Pekrun, 2006; Pekrun et al., 2002). The findings revealed that students frequently experienced excitement and anxiety, particularly during the process of working on the project. Considering the adverse effects of negative emotions on learning outcomes, it is crucial for instructors to adopt approaches or implement learning activities that enhance students' positive emotions and mitigate negative emotions (Ganotice et al., 2016).

We observed that the negative emotions experienced during the project preparation and presentation phases were regulated and replaced by neutral and positive emotions such as relaxation and pride. In fact, only one student expressed regret over his inability to regulate his emotions and use appropriate strategies. From this perspective, it can be argued that successful emotion regulation reduces negative emotional experiences. This finding, which aligns with the existing literature, underscores the importance of emotion regulation in academic environments (Harley et al., 2019). Successful emotion regulation involves an individual's recognition of their emotions and the selection of appropriate strategies to manage them (Pekrun, 2014).

Emotion regulation is implemented through various strategies. When we examined the emotion regulation strategies employed by students, we found that they predominantly used strategies to modify the situation. Specifically, students chose to regulate their emotions by studying, which can be considered a 'taking action' strategy. We also found that students employed strategies to modify the situation and direct attention during the process of completing the project assignment. An examination of the relevant literature reveals that reappraisal and suppression strategies are predominantly investigated in studies, with findings generally discussed in the context of these two strategies (Rottweiler et al., 2022). For example, in their study with university students, Jarrell et al. (2022) found that the reappraisal strategy used by students was beneficial, while the suppression strategy was detrimental during exams. The researchers emphasized the importance of encouraging students to adopt more effective strategies. Conversely, Rottweiler et al. (2022) revealed that speaking with friends or upper-grade students is a more effective emotion regulation strategy in an academic context compared to a non-academic context.

In this study, we observed that students did not prefer distraction strategies; instead, they actively tried to cope with their emotions. Moreover, Schmidt et al. (2010) stated that seeking social support is the most important strategy for students in stressful situations. Based on these studies, the context in which emotion regulation occurs significantly affects emotion regulation and the strategies used (Zhoc et al., 2022). This study also revealed that many students employed multiple strategies in the process of emotion regulation. This finding is consistent with the literature (Rottweiler et al., 2022). Upon examining the incoming emotions, we found that students generally regulated their negative emotions, indicating that they engaged in coping. A similar finding was reported by Burić et al. (2016) in their study. According to the researchers, students generally regulate their negative emotions and use appropriate strategies for the situation, believing that negative emotions adversely affect their academic success. However, they are either unaware of or overlook strategies that can enhance or maintain positive emotions. Therefore, it is crucial for students to be aware of and capable of implementing a broad repertoire of emotion regulation strategies to engage in successful emotion regulation.

In this study, when examining the motives that prompted students to regulate their emotions, we found that students primarily used emotion regulation to enhance their performance. In other words, these strategies were employed predominantly for instrumental reasons, as students believed that managing their emotions would improve their performance on the group assignment. Additionally, students reported using emotion regulation for hedonic reasons, aiming to mitigate the effects of negative emotions and maintain positive emotional state. Thus, it is evident that students regulate their emotions for both instrumental and hedonic reasons. In the educational context, Taxer and Gross (2018) found that teachers also regulate emotions for both instrumental and hedonic reasons. In this study, the instrumental motive was particularly prominent as students regulated their negative emotions while working on a project assignment because they believed that negative emotions would negatively affect their performance. By regulating their negative emotions, they could maintain a focus on completing the project efficiently and effectively. Ultimately, our findings highlight that students' use of emotion regulation strategies is driven by a combination of instrumental and hedonic motives. Understanding the role of these two motives is crucial for educators aiming to support students in regulating their emotions to achieve academic success.

Contextual factors and individual differences can also impact the effectiveness of emotion regulation strategies. In this study, we measured students' emotions and emotion regulation strategies they used only in the context of their group project. However, past research indicates that while emotions experienced during homework and those experienced in the classroom are related, in fact they are distinct and should be measured separately (Goetz et al., 2012). Moreover, while the majority of the sample consisted of female students in the Turkish higher education context, and revealing the gender, individual, and cultural differences in emotional processes was not one of the purposes of the study, past research shows that there are differences in experiencing emotions and employing emotion regulation strategies across genders, individuals, and cultures (Goetz et al., 2012; Kwon et al., 2013). These considerations suggest that future research should account for the influence of various contexts, as well as gender, individual, and cultural differences, to gain a more comprehensive understanding of emotions and emotion regulation in academic settings.

Limitations and Recommendations for Future Research

In the context of educational research, where diverse factors and individual differences play a crucial role, this study acknowledges several limitations that arise from its specific context and methodological choices:

1. The study's sample size is limited to 20 undergraduate students, which may not be representative of the broader student population. Future studies should include a larger and more diverse sample to enhance the generalizability of the findings.
2. The study has a gender imbalance with 17 female and 3 male participants. This disproportion can influence the results, as gender may play a role in emotion generation, emotion regulation strategies, and motives for emotion regulation. Ensuring a more balanced gender representation can provide a comprehensive understanding of how different genders regulate emotions in academic settings.
3. The study was conducted at a single state university in Turkey, which may limit the applicability of the findings to other educational contexts, such as different countries, cultures, or types of institutions. Expanding the study to multiple institutions or different cultures can help generalize the results across different educational contexts and cultures.
4. The study relies on self-reported data from students about their emotions and emotion regulation strategies. Self-reporting can be biased due to social desirability, memory recall issues, or personal interpretations of the questions. Combining self-reported data with other data sources such as interviews, focus groups, and observations can provide a richer and more accurate depiction of students' emotional experiences.
5. Data collection occurred over a short period (Weeks 7 to 14 of the semester), focusing on a specific course and project. This limited timeframe might not capture the full range of emotional experiences and regulation strategies students may use throughout the entire semester. A longitudinal approach can capture changes and developments in emotion generation and emotion regulation strategies over time.
6. The study focuses on emotions and emotion regulation in the context of a group project. Emotions and strategies might differ in other academic activities, such as exams, individual assignments, or different types of projects. Examining emotions and regulation strategies across different academic activities can offer a broader perspective on students' emotional experiences.
7. While students worked in groups, the study only considered individual emotional experiences and excluded group-level dynamics. Group interactions and dynamics can significantly influence emotions and emotion regulation strategies.

Considering group dynamics and interactions can provide insights into how collaborative environments influence emotions and regulation strategies.

Implications for Practice

The study has several practical implications for different aspects of education. These implications include:

1. Instructors can integrate instruction on emotion regulation strategies into their curriculum to help students manage their emotions effectively. This process can lead to improved academic performance and psychological well-being.
2. Learning environments should be designed to provide social support, allowing students to seek help from peers and instructors when needed. This support network can help students manage stress and other negative emotions.
3. Classrooms and other learning spaces should accommodate different emotion regulation strategies, such as areas for quiet reflection or group collaboration.
4. Administrators should provide professional development opportunities focused on emotion regulation. This training can help instructors understand the emotional processes of students and equip them with strategies to support students' emotional needs.
5. Educational policies should encourage reflective practices where students can document and reflect on their emotional experiences during learning activities. This can help them develop self-awareness and emotion regulation skills.
6. Policymakers should allocate resources for counselors and programs that teach emotion regulation skills.

CONCLUSION

This study underscores the significance of emotions and emotion regulation strategies in higher education. Students are expected to possess a diverse array of emotion regulation strategies for academic success and psychological well-being. Our study found that students experienced multiple emotions and employed various strategies while regulating their emotions. The primary motive driving their emotion regulation was often instrumental, aimed at improving performance. These findings emphasize the need for comprehensive training programs that prioritize the development of effective emotion regulation skills to enhance both learning outcomes and psychological well-being.

REFERENCES

Aldao, A., & Nolen-Hoeksema, S. (2012). When are adaptive strategies most predictive of psychopathology? *Journal of Abnormal Psychology*, 121(1), 276–281. DOI: 10.1037/a0023598 PMID: 21553934

Aldao, A., Nolen-Hoeksema, S., & Schweizer, S. (2010). Emotion-regulation strategies across psychopathology: A meta-analytic review. *Clinical Psychology Review*, 30(2), 217–237. DOI: 10.1016/j.cpr.2009.11.004 PMID: 20015584

Alonso-Tapia, J., Abello, D. M., & Panadero, E. (2020). Regulating emotions and learning motivation in higher education students. *The International Journal of Emotional Education*, 12(2), 73–89. https://www.um.edu.mt/library/oar/handle/123456789/65093

Artino, A. R.Jr, & Jones, K. D.II. (2012). Exploring the complex relations between achievement emotions and self-regulated learning behaviors in online learning. *The Internet and Higher Education*, 15(3), 170–175. DOI: 10.1016/j.iheduc.2012.01.006

Bakır-Yalçın, E., & Usluel, K. Y. (2024). Investigating the antecedents of engagement in online learning: Do achievement emotions matter? *Education and Information Technologies*, 29(4), 3759–3791. DOI: 10.1007/s10639-023-11995-z

Burić, I., Sorić, I., & Penezić, Z. (2016). Emotion regulation in academic domain: Development and validation of the Academic Emotion Regulation Questionnaire (AERQ). *Personality and Individual Differences*, 96, 138–147. DOI: 10.1016/j.paid.2016.02.074

Cavicchioli, M., Scalabrini, A., Northoff, G., Mucci, C., Ogliari, A., & Maffei, C. (2021). Dissociation and emotion regulation stratgies: A meta-analytic review. *Journal of Psychiatric Research*, 143, 370–387. DOI: 10.1016/j.jpsychires.2021.09.011 PMID: 34592484

Crowe, S., Cresswell, K., Robertson, A., Huby, G., Avery, A., & Sheikh, A. (2011). The case study approach. *BMC Medical Research Methodology*, 11(1), 1–9. DOI: 10.1186/1471-2288-11-100 PMID: 21707982

D'Mello, S., & Graesser, A. (2012). Dynamics of affective states during complex learning. *Learning and Instruction*, 22(2), 145–157. DOI: 10.1016/j.learninstruc.2011.10.001

Dever, D. A., Wiedbusch, M. D., Cloude, E. B., Lester, J., & Azevedo, R. (2022). Emotions and the comprehension of single versus multiple texts during game-based learning. *Discourse Processes*, 59(1-2), 94–115. DOI: 10.1080/0163853X.2021.1950450

Ganotice, F. A.Jr, Datu, J. A. D., & King, R. B. (2016). Which emotional profiles exhibit the best learning outcomes? A person-centered analysis of students' academic emotions. *School Psychology International*, 37(5), 498–518. DOI: 10.1177/0143034316660147

Garnefski, N., & Kraaij, V. (2006). Cognitive emotion regulation questionnaire–development of a short 18-item version (CERQ-short). *Personality and Individual Differences*, 41(6), 1045–1053. DOI: 10.1016/j.paid.2006.04.010

Glaser, B. G., & Strauss, A. L. (1967). *The discovery of grounded theory: Strategies for qualitative research*. Aldine Transaction.

Goetz, T., Nett, U. E., Martiny, S. E., Hall, N. C., Pekrun, R., Dettmers, S., & Trautwein, U. (2012). Students' emotions during homework: Structures, self-concept antecedents, and achievement outcomes. *Learning and Individual Differences*, 22(2), 225–234. DOI: 10.1016/j.lindif.2011.04.006

Gross, J. J. (1998a). Antecedent-and response-focused emotion regulation: Divergent consequences for experience, expression, and physiology. *Journal of Personality and Social Psychology*, 74(1), 224–237. DOI: 10.1037/0022-3514.74.1.224 PMID: 9457784

Gross, J. J. (1998b). The emerging field of emotion regulation: An integrative review. *Review of General Psychology*, 2(3), 271–299. DOI: 10.1037/1089-2680.2.3.271

Gross, J. J. (2015a). Emotion regulation: Current status and future prospects. *Psychological Inquiry*, 26(1), 1–26. DOI: 10.1080/1047840X.2014.940781

Gross, J. J. (2015b). The extended process model of emotion regulation: Elaborations, applications, and future directions. *Psychological Inquiry*, 26(1), 130–137. DOI: 10.1080/1047840X.2015.989751

Gross, J. J., & Feldman Barrett, L. (2011). Emotion generation and emotion regulation: One or two depends on your point of view. *Emotion Review*, 3(1), 8–16. DOI: 10.1177/1754073910380974 PMID: 21479078

Harley, J. M., Pekrun, R., Taxer, J. L., & Gross, J. J. (2019). Emotion regulation in achievement situations: An integrated model. *Educational Psychologist*, 54(2), 106–126. DOI: 10.1080/00461520.2019.1587297

Hoffmann, J. D., Brackett, M. A., Bailey, C. S., & Willner, C. J. (2020). Teaching emotion regulation in schools: Translating research into practice with the RULER approach to social and emotional learning. *Emotion (Washington, D.C.)*, 20(1), 105–109. DOI: 10.1037/emo0000649 PMID: 31961187

Jarrell, A., & Lajoie, S. P. (2017). The regulation of achievements emotions: Implications for research and practice. *Canadian Psychology*, 58(3), 276–287. https://doi.org/doi.org/10.1037/cap0000119. DOI: 10.1037/cap0000119

Jarrell, A., Lajoie, S. P., Hall, N. C., & Horrocks, P. T. M. (2022). Antecedents and Consequences of Emotion Regulation in STEM Degree Programs. *Innovative Higher Education*, 47(3), 493–514. DOI: 10.1007/s10755-021-09587-1

Kahu, E., Stephens, C., Leach, L., & Zepke, N. (2015). Linking academic emotions and student engagement: Mature-aged distance students' transition to university. *Journal of Further and Higher Education*, 39(4), 481–497. DOI: 10.1080/0309877X.2014.895305

Kappas, A. (2011). Emotion and regulation are one! *Emotion Review*, 3(1), 17–25. DOI: 10.1177/1754073910380971 PMID: 21479078

Karamarkovich, S. M., & Rutherford, T. (2021). Mixed feelings: Profiles of emotions among elementary mathematics students and how they function within a control-value framework. *Contemporary Educational Psychology*, 66, 101996. DOI: 10.1016/j.cedpsych.2021.101996

Kobylińska, D., & Kusev, P. (2019). Flexible emotion regulation: How situational demands and individual differences influence the effectiveness of regulatory strategies. *Frontiers in Psychology*, 10, 72. DOI: 10.3389/fpsyg.2019.00072 PMID: 30774610

Koole, S. L. (2009). The psychology of emotion regulation: An integrative review. *Cognition and Emotion*, 23(1), 4–41. DOI: 10.1080/02699930802619031

Kwon, H., Yoon, K. L., Joormann, J., & Kwon, J.-H. (2013). Cultural and gender differences in emotion regulation: Relation to depression. *Cognition and Emotion*, 27(5), 769–782. DOI: 10.1080/02699931.2013.792244 PMID: 23805826

Lee, J.-Y., & Chei, M. J. (2020). Latent profile analysis of Korean undergraduates' academic emotions in e-learning environment. *Educational Technology Research and Development*, 68(3), 1521–1546. DOI: 10.1007/s11423-019-09715-x

Naragon-Gainey, K., McMahon, T. P., & Chacko, T. P. (2017). The structure of common emotion regulation strategies: A meta-analytic examination. *Psychological Bulletin*, 143(4), 384–427. DOI: 10.1037/bul0000093 PMID: 28301202

Pekrun, R. (2006). The control-value theory of achievement emotions: Assumptions, corollaries, and implications for educational research and practice. *Educational Psychology Review*, 18(4), 315–341. DOI: 10.1007/s10648-006-9029-9

Pekrun, R. (2014). *Emotions and learning* (Vol. 24). International Academy of Education (IAE). http://staging.iaoed.org/downloads/edu-practices_24_eng.pdf

Pekrun, R., Goetz, T., Titz, W., & Perry, R. P. (2002). Academic emotions in students' self-regulated learning and achievement: A program of qualitative and quantitative research. *Educational Psychologist*, 37(2), 91–105. DOI: 10.1207/S15326985EP3702_4

Pekrun, R., & Stephens, E. J. (2010). Achievement emotions: A control-value approach. *Social and Personality Psychology Compass*, 4(4), 238–255. DOI: 10.1111/j.1751-9004.2010.00259.x

Rottweiler, A.-L., Stockinger, K., & Nett, U. E. (2022). *Students' Regulation of Anxiety and Hope – A Multilevel Latent Profile Analysis.* https://psyarxiv.com/mbrbj/download/?format=pdf DOI: 10.31234/osf.io/m6rbj

Schmidt, S., Tinti, C., Levine, L. J., & Testa, S. (2010). Appraisals, emotions and emotion regulation: An integrative approach. *Motivation and Emotion*, 34(1), 63–72. DOI: 10.1007/s11031-010-9155-z PMID: 20376165

Smith, C. A., & Lazarus, R. S. (1990). Emotion and adaptation. In Pervin, L. A. (Ed.), *Handbook of personality: Theory and research* (pp. 609–637). Guilford Press.

Sorić, I., Penezić, Z., & Burić, I. (2013). Big five personality traits, cognitive appraisals and emotion regulation strategies as predictors of achievement emotions. *Psihologijske Teme*, 22(2), 325–349. https://hrcak.srce.hr/clanak/159885

Sutton, R. E., & Wheatley, K. F. (2003). Teachers' emotions and teaching: A review of the literature and directions for future research. *Educational Psychology Review*, 15(4), 327–358. DOI: 10.1023/A:1026131715856

Tamir, M. (2016). Why do people regulate their emotions? A taxonomy of motives in emotion regulation. *Personality and Social Psychology Review*, 20(3), 199–222. DOI: 10.1177/1088868315586325 PMID: 26015392

Taxer, J. L., & Gross, J. J. (2018). Emotion regulation in teachers: The "why" and "how". *Teaching and Teacher Education*, 74, 180–189. DOI: 10.1016/j.tate.2018.05.008

Thompson, R. A. (1994). Emotion regulation: A theme in search of definition. *Monographs of the Society for Research in Child Development*, 59(2-3), 25–52. DOI: 10.1111/j.1540-5834.1994.tb01276.x PMID: 7984164

Titsworth, S., McKenna, T. P., Mazer, J. P., & Quinlan, M. M. (2013). The bright side of emotion in the classroom: Do teachers' behaviors predict students' enjoyment, hope, and pride? *Communication Education*, 62(2), 191–209. DOI: 10.1080/03634523.2013.763997

Vuorela, M., & Nummenmaa, L. (2004). Experienced emotions, emotion regulation and student activity in a web-based learning environment. *European Journal of Psychology of Education*, 19(4), 423–436. DOI: 10.1007/BF03173219

Xu, J., Du, J., Liu, F., & Huang, B. (2019). Emotion regulation, homework completion, and math achievement: Testing models of reciprocal effects. *Contemporary Educational Psychology*, 59, 101810. DOI: 10.1016/j.cedpsych.2019.101810

Yin, R. K. (2003). *Applications of case study research* (Vol. 34). SAGE Publications.

Zhoc, K. C. H., Cai, Y., Yeung, S. S., & Shan, J. (2022). Subjective wellbeing and emotion regulation strategies: How are they associated with student engagement in online learning during Covid-19? *The British Journal of Educational Psychology*, 00(4), 1–13. DOI: 10.1111/bjep.12513 PMID: 35567326

Chapter 13
Underlying Workplace Emotional Impacts upon a Professor's Experiential Approach

Caroline M. Crawford
University of Houston-Clear Lake, USA

ABSTRACT

This autoethnographic case study focuses upon a university professor's experiences within a workplace environment, that impacted learning design approaches and practices. The strengths, weaknesses, opportunities, and threats within the workplace environment supported the creatively engaging and critically analytic approach to embracing areas of control and positive impact within the work environment. Through the storytelling narrative approach that progresses through a Currere Method of engagement, complex conversations may occur. Through these complex and difficult conversations, recognitions and outcomes that the case study participant would not have proactively engaged in learning design practices that were ultimately positive, impactful, and deeply meaningful to the learning outcomes of students progressing through degree-focused coursework. The sense of "becoming" within this case study is strengthened and on display throughout the Currere Method's journey.

INTRODUCTION

The focus of this discussion is the instructional facilitator's cognitive-emotional experience through the Currere Method of engagement. The Currere Method offers a psychoanalytic technique that is qualitative in nature, offering the opportunity for

DOI: 10.4018/979-8-3693-2663-3.ch013

an autoethnographic methodological understanding focused upon a framework for analytic reflection that is embedded within self-understanding. The higher education workspace experiential environment can significantly impact the learning design of courses, including the instructional facilitator's engagement with learners within learning environments.

The university professor's work environment, reflected as an organizational work environment, can directly impact the instructor due to the mix of artistic, creative, and scientific nuances associated with the teaching and learning process. Some universities within higher education have issues retaining quality faculty, staff, and administration. The toxic organizational culture has been under study for several decades, with a strengthening focus upon research within the environment. This is specifically relevant within an academic organization, wherein a toxic culture has an opportunity to develop, be nurtured and enriched, and spread within an environment that is naturally competitive, with rivalries and opposition a natural juxtaposition to the nurturing focus upon student learning. A recent Google Scholar search for the keyword trail *toxic academic organizational culture academia* from 2023-August 2024 resulted in about 17,200 results. The relationship between toxic organizational cultures in academia and impacts upon instructional faculty is clear (Alkhodary, 2023; Bokek-Cohen et al., 2023; Choudhary et al., 2024; Cidlinska et al., 2023; Cidlinska et al., 2023; De Welde & Stepnick, 2023; Dolan, 2023; Heffernan & Bosetti, 2023; Hooven, 2023; Jagsi et al., 2023; Klahn Acuña & Male, 2024; Malik, 2023; Mandalaki, 2023; Mhaka-Mutepfa & Rampa, 2024; Soythong, 2023; Vem et al., 2023).

Learning design practices have been ever developing as the decades progress. With the dawning of the digital age, practices within the online learning environment have equally kept pace. The instructional designer is, many times, the course instructor (Bass, 2023; Bean, 2023; Blanchard & Thacker, 2023; Müller et al., 2023; Gros & García-Peñalvo, 2016; Salendab, 2023). Much as in a traditional face-to-face learning environment, the instructor of record is expected to develop an online course experience without any training or support on how to think about designing and developing a meaningful and engaging experience for learners (Alam, 2023; Blaschke, 2023, Børte et al, 2023, Bozkurt & Sharma, 2023; Clark & Mayer, 2023; Khasawneh et al., 2023; Patiño et al., 2023). Faculty and administrators, who are not associated with engaging in online instruction, assume that it's simple, because everything is occurring within the digital realm, without face-to-face instructional engagement. Yet the reality is that the previously three hours per week of instructional engagement, along with expectations of office hours, shifts into a twenty-four hour a day, seven day a week experience. This is exhausting for the online instructor who is facilitating the instructional experience and attempting to deeply engage the learners in a strongly positive learning experience (Beck et al., 2023; Lomer & Palmer, 2023; Wu et al., 2023).

To understand the depth of experience of one instructional facilitator who has successfully established herself as a viable professor within a university environment with over twenty-five years of professional experience, the Currere Method, as viewed through Pinar's (1994) frame of understanding as a "regressive-progressive-analytical-synthetical" (p. 19) method of developmental understanding, will offer a self-study approach that supports the focus upon the instructional designer and instructional facilitator's experience towards utilizing the professor's emotional experience within the professional work environment of a university structure that directly impacts the contractual expectations that are focused upon the holistic understanding of teaching practices.

This self-study, autoethnographic style of a qualitative methodological approach interweaves the prior work of the professor – including instructional design models, learning theory development, instructional-focused interactive activities recognitions, course theoretical constructs, as well as the synchronicity associated with learning design practices – throughout the self-study narrative that is the embodiment of the Currere approach. This emphasis upon complicated conversations (Pinar, 2012) is well described as "an ethical, political, and intellectual undertaking, as well as a form of curriculum that 'enables educational experience'" (O'Neil, 2014, p 1). This is an appropriate approach to this discussion around the utilization of emotional experiences in the design of learning practices and approaches, based within a recognition that course design reflects the person who designs the course, the course subject matter, and the philosophical belief systems held by the instructional designer and developer of the course experience. Equally impactful is the recognition that the design is just one aspect of the course, while the course instructor implements that course design as an interwoven facilitator and presence with the ability to engage the learners more fully within the course experience. The learning design practices that result in a course design may be outstanding and brilliant; however, the implementation of the course is dependent upon the skill, the quality, and the philosophical beliefs of the course instructor. This directly impacts the strength of the course experience and associated learner experience, as well as attainment of learning objective competencies and capabilities.

Through the implementation of an autoethnographic approach, specifically the Currere Method that emphasizes the ability to engage in complicated conversations (Pinar, 2012) that are deeply nuanced and complex, a narrative can be woven that suggests the influence and impact of the course design, the course development, and the implementation of the course experience by the instructor of record. As this specific narrative embeds the self-study approach with a professor who acts as their own course instructional designer, developing the course within the appropriate course environment no matter whether this is face-to-face, online, or even hybrid, the course instructor is also this professor who proactively has implemented the Currere Method self-study approach to a deeper understanding. The professor shares well-documented experiences and evaluations of learning design practices, while equally reflecting upon the impact of the workplace emotional impacts and associated experiential choices that occur within the course's learning design and associated instructional practices. Specifically, Pinar's (1994) Currere framework may be well described through his own description:

It is regressive-progressive-analytical-synthetical. It is therefore temporal and conceptual in nature, and it aims for the cultivation of a developmental point of view that hints at the transtemporal and transconceptual. From another perspective, the method is the self-conscious conceptualization of the temporal, and from another, it is the viewing of what is conceptualized through time. So it is that we hope to explore the complex relation between the temporal and conceptual. In doing so we might disclose their relation to the Self and its evolution and education. (p. 19)

This is an opportunity to reflect upon over a quarter-century of developing learning design practices that utilize emotional experience to embrace the cognitive-constructivist approach to learning within landscapes of practice (Wenger-Trayner, et al., 2014; Wenger-Trayner & Wenger-Trayner, 2015, Wenger-Trayner & Wenger-Trayner, 2020) that reflect:

…an understanding around value creation within the bounds of more socialized elearning spaces that are inherent within the hyperconnected world of the Internet, or the Web of Things (WoT) that has been embedded within the Digital Age's immediacy of information and the socialization that occurs as inherent within the learning process. (Crawford et al., 2022, p. 1)

Through each of the Currere progressive steps that are articulated as the regressive step, the progressive step, the analytical step, and the synthetical step, an acknowledgement of this professor's journey through a recognition of utilizing the professor's emotional experience towards the design of strong learning practices will parallel the professor's learner-focused, developing understanding and utilization of learner-embedded emotional experiences to design strongly viable and positively impactful practices within the learning environment. A recognition associated with a focused approach to distance learning design practices and online environments also viably undergirds the focus of this chapter's progressive self-study approach.

BACKGROUND

Complicated conversations are intriguing opportunities to consider where I've been, what I'm doing, and where I may be heading on my multifaceted, interwoven journey. The primary focus of this self-study is how I've worked through different experiences and attempted to develop superior learning design practices. This is my take on an experiential approach to my learning journey, attempting to continuously learn from course instructional experiences and quality learners in my courses, while working through workplace emotional impacts and maneuvering into a place and a space wherein I can positively support the students whom I happily and honestly tout as the best part of the university. As such, I recognize that my cognitive-emotional experience within the workplace environment potentially impacts the course design as well as facilitative instructional engagement efforts throughout the course experience. This self-study is implemented from a very personal, very vulnerable space. The reflective critical analysis that occurs throughout the Currere approach supports a larger journey that is individual yet equally impactful as a collective community journey.

As a professional academic, my philosophical stance is focused upon being of service to others. Equally, I desire to *pay forward* the quality of instructional engagement and experience that I've received from the best of the professors with whom I've had the honor to work. The quality of the instructional experience, the joys of significant and positive impacts upon the learners who pass through my courses, watching and supporting the learners succeed far beyond their most secret of wishes and dreams, are how I tithe my time of service within the academic world as well as the larger societal community.

The world in which I live, the academic world of teaching, research, and service, revolves as well as evolves through my focused approach to teaching. My efforts and attempts over the past quarter-century have emphasized high-quality course design, development, and implementation, no matter whether in traditional face-to-face courses, in blended course experiences, or through fully online course experiences. Strong course design, high quality assessment opportunities, deep and rich guiding feedback that is personalized towards individual competencies as well as capabilities, as well as a depth of carefully critically analytic approaches all inform the deep quality of the courses that I instruct. More importantly, the efforts towards redesigning courses that embrace an emphasis upon learner experience and associated course feedback is something that I deeply welcome as impactful and of utmost importance.

Without the quality of feedback that I can obtain from course learners, I would be at a loss not only as to how to move forward with my teaching, but equally with my research and service responsibilities. Interwoven, as a mixed amalgamation approach to my views of professional quality, are the encompassing aspects of teaching, research, and service, that interlace understandings of cognitive and motivational approaches to course design and the creativity associated with recognizing the quality of the learner experience throughout my instructional efforts. But equally important is my interest in the learner's program of study ease of progression, with deeply meaningful and learned understandings that equally entwine service efforts and responsibilities. My approach to my professorial experience is grounded within the underlying workplace emotional impacts. The joys, the concerns, the horrors, and the opportunities that I conceive as impactful within the university environment offer a lens through which I view my efforts towards the creation of learning design practices that engage, support, and enhance the learners who flow through my courses. Yet more fully impactful are the underlying emotional work impacts. How do my emotional experiences and understandings throughout the university environment in which I work, how do my emotional experiences and understandings within the larger academy that are beyond the campus experience, support and enhance my learning design practices? The Currere approach guides this complex conversation around this impactful journey of recognition and discovery.

REGRESSIVE STEP

The Currere Method, as framed by Pinar (1994), suggests that the regressive step is an approach wherein, "One returns to the past, to capture it as it was, and as it hovers over the present" (p. 21). A succinct understanding of the regressive step is useful to frame one's understanding, while a more well-developed understanding of the regressive step may be offered as:

That is the point of this phase of the method: to observe functioning in the past. Since the focus of the method is educational experience, one takes special notice of one's past life-in-schools, with one's past life-with-schoolteachers and one's past life-with-books and other school-related artifacts. Observe and record. Include present responses to what is observed. (Pinar, 1994, p. 23)

I have continuously conceived of myself as an analytic creative, who soaks up interesting ideas and information while molding ideas and conceptions into useful and forward-leaning outcomes. This is an analytic strength that I consider to be a creative talent, and I have enjoyed the style of puzzle that I conceive as valuably deft and malleably impactful when implemented within my learning design practices. The positivity associated with the analytically creative process is deeply personal while equally profound. The formative evaluations of course designs and learner experiences are continuous, not only from my own perception of the learner experience and learner-embedded outcomes, but equally as a form of 360-degree evaluative approach wherein I carefully listen and learn from my own analysis, learner analyses, colleague comments, and narratives around what their students share about my courses and course experiences, as well as other opportunities through which I have an opportunity to obtain formative feedback and evaluations of my learning design efforts.

High School Student, University Student

More specifically, I began developing my understanding of the teaching and learning process while I was a middle-school student. I was amazed by the poor quality teachers whom I experienced, the mind-numbing boredom that I experienced. I continuously wondered at how a potentially interesting topic could become so dry, so boring, and without the sense of life and living that seemed to have been torn out of the learning experience. Not only was the student experience a painful journey for me, but I wondered at the ability of the teachers to go through the motions hour after hour, day after day, without running out of the school screaming in anguish. If there was passion around the subject matter, I never viewed this in my teachers. If there was a curiosity around the course experience, the learner engagement, and sparks of interest in the subject matter, I never noticed the teacher's flicker of interest. How horrible to live their lives of quiet desperation, missing the spark of passion that fulfills a life's ambition. I experienced similar quality of the teaching-learning process throughout high school, in all courses except two; curiously, one course was a typing course with a controlling teacher who had a clear passion for the quality of her student's typing prowess, while the other course was the outstanding technical theater teacher who displayed boundless energy and always had a spark of the creative troublemaker behind his professional demeanor. The passion for their subjects, their interest in creating the most positive and engaged hands-on experience for every student in their classes, renewed my potential faith in the teaching profession.

Graduating from high school during my junior year, I felt as if I'd escaped from the controlled world of high school as well as the controlled world of my family home. Heading to university, I felt like I was finally beginning my life and spreading my wings with a sense of freedom and abounding opportunity. After the first week of my first semester in university, my hopes were crushed. The quality of instructors was equally questionable, with the primary difference being the strange sense of prowess and heightened perception of self that I observed in every instructor from adjunct instructor to department chair professor. These people were teaching how they had been taught, with the lack of creativity, the lack of interest in the success of their students, and the seeming self-centered hubris equated with academic boredom that was on display throughout my innumerable semesters and higher education institutions that I attended on my way to earning a bachelor's degree, engaging me in critically analytic concerns associated with whether I really wanted to earn my teacher licensure and move into what was perceived as a safe job of teaching in the K-12 secondary schools. The only reason that I continued on this journey was because I had an internal mettle and desire to successfully finish what I started. This was a horrible choice, as I then had the opportunity to learn more about the classroom teacher experience.

High School Classroom Teacher

The high school classroom teaching experience was truly mind-numbing, while the strange quirks and proclivities that were rampant throughout the high school were shocking to me. My daily classroom teacher experience consisted of teaching exactly the same thing, every hour on the hour, five days a week, four weeks a month, for several months each school year. My attempts to develop a sense of passion in the subject matter, my efforts to engage the students, were deemed *too loud* and *too unusual* and *troublesome* to the school administrators. I was an unusual classroom teacher, it seems, who wanted the students to enjoy the subject matter. Engaging the students in discussions, in different ways to consider the course information, was not a welcome effort by this school administration. My classroom must remain quiet, and my students could not engage in curriculum enhancements beyond the mandatory lock-step curriculum and handouts that the grade-level coordinator mandated that we follow. It seems that I was a problem, and the upper administration were going to teach me a lesson.

I was consistently called into the principal's office or assistant principal's office, mandated to explain why my student roll sheets designated that students were attending my classes while they were not attending any of their other classes. How could I explain this, other than I was not doing my job? Now, how could I possible answer why the students showed up for my class but they didn't attend any of their other courses throughout the day? They were in my class and I marked them as present because they were present in class. The students who were absent were marked as absent. I didn't understand the continual discussions around student roll sheets. The school administration would literally bound into my classroom during different classes, on different days, expecting to find that my student roll sheets were incorrect. The administrators would waste ten minutes of a fifty-minute class, calling out the student roll sheet that I'd already completed, attempting to find errors in my accounting of students' *butts in the seats*. After one such display, the principal and vice principal scolded one of my students for not attending their other classes but showing up for my class. This occurred in front of the whole classroom filled with students, in front of me. After they left, the classroom was quiet for a moment because we were all bemused by what had occurred. I finally snapped back into *teacher mode* and began refocusing the students into that day's lesson, acting as if nothing was amiss.

After class, the student who showed up to my class but seemed to skip the other assigned classes left, but returned during my class lunch break and apologized for what had occurred during class. The student shared that he just enjoyed our class so he showed up for it, but the other courses weren't the same experience. I tried to do the right thing by modeling my concern that he might impact his future career opportunities by these choices, and that he was a smart young man that had the potential to do great things. He had a puzzled look on his face and laughed a bit, saying that I was the only teacher who had ever said that to him. My heart was broken for this young man. He was almost eighteen years old, in my freshman English class, and had never had any teacher model that they believed in his quality and his potential. How could I make a positive difference in student lives when I was bored by the curriculum? How could I develop a passion for the curriculum, when it was without any culturally or socially relevant energy that engaged in an understanding that something as simplistic as Shakespeare could be perceived as a soap opera from a few hundred years ago? That our curriculum spent six weeks on Shakespeare's Romeo and Juliet, while in reality the play covered merely a few days in Romeo's and Juliet's lives? That the curriculum focused upon Martin Luther King Jr.'s *I Have a Dream* speech, but we did not wrap in the historical understanding or societal discontent associated with the importance and impact of the speech during this time period? That we focused upon Martin Luther King Jr.'s speech, but did not also study Malcom X or other equally impactful personages from that same period? Memorization, regurgitation, and disconnected facts reflected the state of information within the course curriculum.

I was frustrated. Frustrated for my students, frustrated for myself, and frustrated by the state of education. Towards the middle of my third year of classroom teaching, I finished my master's degree. With a bit of additional time on my hands, I began to ruminate over my current life trajectory and career path. This was not what I had in mind for the rest of my life. After careful consideration, I decided to conclude my classroom teaching job, happily walking away at the end of the school year. What was I going to do? I had no idea. But what I did know is that my future did not include another year as a high school classroom teacher.

Years of Doctoral Studies

I began my doctoral studies at the age of 24. I adored every moment of my doctoral school experience, from the creativity of the professors, to the collaborative nature of the doctoral students, to the joys of my hard work being not only recognized but appreciated. These were golden years that I did not want to end. But end they did, as my faculty advisor sat me down at the end of my fourth year in doctoral studies and informed me that I could only hold a graduate assistantship position for five years. Recognizing this, I had better become serious about my dissertation's progression forward. My faculty advisor concluded that conversation with a clear statement that I would have my dissertation proposal in his hands within two weeks. The dissertation proposal was written and in my faculty advisor's hands before the end of the two-week period. Within two more weeks, I was experiencing my dissertation proposal defense. The following spring I completed my final dissertation defense, made a few revisions, submitted it to ProQuest, was officially graduated, and needed to decide on a job.

Jumping from the Frying Pan into the Fire

A doctoral friend called me up one day, as I was beginning to wonder what I was going to do about a job, and asked if I would be interested in a lecturer position at a university just down the road from where I had earned my doctorate. I went down there for a few hours and was hired for a year-by-year lecturer position starting that fall semester, a few weeks after completing my degree and as I was concluding y graduate assistantship. By the following January, I was sitting in a tenure-track faculty position.

During my initial semester in this university, I had several strange experiences. One of the first experiences was taking a prior faculty's course syllabi and enhancing the courses in ways that I thought would be viably impactful to the students. One specific course that I found to be curious was focused upon developing a manuscript that would be viable for submission to an academic journal. My thought was, if the students were doing all the work to develop a viable manuscript, why not encourage them to submit their manuscripts to a double-blind peer-reviewed academic journal, if they desired to stretch their interests a bit more fully? Was the journal submission a mandatory part of the course experience? No. However, they would learn about developing a manuscript based upon a journal's author guidelines as a course enhancement, and have the option to submit their manuscript for a journal's peer review process if they desired. This was quite a lot of work for me, as I had approximately thirty students in a graduate course and, as an former English teacher, I took editorial feedback and associated guidance as the course instructor a bit more seriously than the students may have previously experienced. A few weeks into the semester, I was called into the Associate Dean's office for a conversation. It seems that several of the students were upset at the level of feedback and not earning an "A" grade on their initial coursework. Further, I was admonished for mandating that the students develop a manuscript that could be a viable journal submission. I sat there gobsmacked. Why were my course curriculum enhancements an issue? The course was closely aligned to the prior faculty's curriculum, with the small addition of alignment with an academic journal's author guideline expectations. When the Associate Dean concluded her tirade, I pulled out the course syllabus that I was given and emphasized that I was told that I had to follow that course syllabus and offered it for review. Then I pulled out my current course syllabus, that was almost exactly the same as the prior course syllabus, and requested that the Associate Dean review both syllabi prior to continuing the conversation. The administrator was embarrassed, having believed the students before speaking with me about the complaints. She couldn't bring herself to apologize, but at least she left me alone from that point forward.

I'd asked a few students with whom I was working about the course and why the prior faculty member had designed it in a rather unusual manner. The responses that I received were shocking to me. It seemed that the prior faculty member used this course as a way for the students to write manuscripts that could be tweaked, so the faculty member could submit the manuscripts under his own name, without including the students as first authors or co-authors. I didn't trust that the students were sharing correct information, so I began doing a bit of research on the prior faculty member. Indeed, knowing the course syllabus and seeing the quality of the majority of student products in the course, the published work did appear to be curiously aligned. Towards the end of this course experience, several of the students were readying their manuscripts for journal submission, so I was excited that some of the stronger students had decided to advance their manuscripts for double-blind peer review and potential publication in an academic journal. Yet again, I was unhappily surprised as they asked if I would submit their manuscripts. I did not understand what they were asking. Upon deeper discussion, the students misunderstood that I was first author on the manuscripts and they felt lucky to have second authorship. This had been their experience; this is how they had been trained. The outcome was an extensive discussion, explaining that this was their work, that I had not earned an author position, and that they should never allow anyone to supersede their authorship line if they were the primary author, especially if a course instructor wanted to include themselves as a co-author on the student's work. No, this was their work; they were proactively submitting their manuscript. I would help guide and support them through the process, but my name would not be included on the manuscript. At best, a lovely *shout out* in an acknowledgements section was the most that I would accept.

This was the first of many experiences of designing higher education courses. Several years after that initial semester at the university, one of the outstanding students in the course did publish their manuscript in an international, double-blind, peer-reviewed academic journal. I was so pleased for him. Unfortunately, he passed away too soon. I was invited to the memorial service and was so happily surprised to see that his journal publication was on display for all his loved ones and friends to see. One of his co-workers, whom I also knew as a prior student, introduced me to his wife, who swiftly threw her arms around me and shared that I was his favorite professor and that one of the most significant events of his life was the publication of his manuscript based on our course experience. His dream was to be a published author, and he achieved his dream through a prestigious academic journal publication. She thanked me profusely, and I was deeply touched as well as honored, because he had never shared this dream with me. He was an impressive student and of course his manuscript would be published because it was so impressive and added to the body of literature in the field, but I had never learned of his dream to be a published author. Through this experience, I expanded my understanding of the impact that course experiences may have upon course student colleagues. After that, I metaphorically opened the courses that I designed a bit more, attempting to learn more about students' secret dreams and allowing me a potential opportunity to guide them through their professional journeys. The personalization of the course experience, the potential for course enhancements to personalize the experience for each learner, were important and impactful take-aways that I retain to this day.

As I developed a more nuanced understanding of the student learners, I was able to more fully design courses that not only supported competency development but equally embraced the concept of capability supports. My experiences in the course flow helped guide my course design approach as well as redesign privileges. Initially I informally requested feedback of students enrolled in my courses as well as past students, to better understand what was working well and what required reconsideration. What I found to be most intriguing is that the students in the course, whom I labeled as learning colleagues or collegial learners, wanted to share their opinions about the course flow and the overarching course experience. There was no reason for me to be sensitive about requesting feedback; they wanted to share ideas and approaches with me. From this understanding, I integrated end-of-course reflective manuscripts that focused upon questions related to strengths of the course, weaknesses, what the student would change in the course, and the overarching take-aways from the course experience.

The course take-aways became one of the most intriguing responses to review, given my surprise while reading the personalized impacts and changes to their own teaching, learning, and instructional design approaches. All were based upon our course experiences. The weaknesses and suggested course redesign efforts provided my next most fascinating insights, as I began to realize that there is a depth of emotional impact upon the learners, dependent upon the course design that I implemented. Equally, I began to realize that the students appreciated my personalized engagement with each individual learner in the course, but equally desired the more public, holistic engagement as a cognitive apprentice style of mentorship support as well as facilitative guide through the course experience. The stress and anxiety-laden emotional impacts upon the learners were primarily based upon the learners overthinking the course expectations and associated course assignments. As I came to realize, the students had developed an expectation for a *guess what I'm thinking* approach by their course instructors, so the learners created stress and anxiety around course expectations, even when the course design emphasized a transparent approach to assignment expectations and aligned assessment rubrics. I had moved through formal education efforts with a learned response to the *guess what I'm thinking* approach by teachers and professors, and it was such a negative experience that I focused my learning design practices towards removing this sense of unknowing from courses that I instructed.

When students requested meetings with me, it was primarily to discuss course expectations and course assignments; recognizing this, I would pull up our current course assignments, ask them to explain to me what they read in the assignment description, and then pulled up the assessment rubric and asked them to articulate the more specific assignment expectations. They knew exactly what was the assignment and what was articulated in the associated assessment rubric. So what was the problem, why was there anxiety around accomplishing the assignment? When I've asked these questions, the response was always the same. The learners knew that there was more to the assignment than what I'd articulated, because it was too transparent. How many pages do I expect in a manuscript, for example? My response is always that I don't care how long it is; what I care about is that the learner has fully addressed each of the mandated components of the manuscript as articulated in the assignment description and assignment rubric. It can be two pages long, if the author is succinct and fully addresses all requirements; or, the manuscript can be ten, fifteen, or twenty pages, depending upon the writing style and an appropriate assurance of all competencies and expectation attained. The task is the task, there is no minimum page designation, there is no file naming structure, and there is no guessing associated with the assignment. I have communicated the assignment expectations, so whatever else the learner desires to add to the assignment or additional parameters that they desire to overlay onto the assignment is their own choice.

With this level of assurance, and the whispered gossip amongst the students, I'd learned that the comfort around the trust, the vulnerability, and the professional expectations associated with my course learning design practices were touted as highly desirable and appreciated by learners who had developed a sense of comfort and emotional stability within my courses. I also learned that many students sought out my course offerings, due to the opportunity for creativity, emphasis upon their own professional learning experience, and personalization of the course efforts. As the students enrolled in more of my courses, I enjoyed watching the learners' blossoming self-efficacy, emphasis upon learning communities, supporting and networking newer course learner colleagues by *taking newer students under their wing*, and full embraced control of their own learning experience throughout the course journey.

Related to my own workplace experience, as my course learning design practices evolved and the course evaluations reflected a superior course experience, I recognized that a level of envy began to develop amongst work colleagues. The envy, the comparative differentiation in student evaluations, the evolving reputations of different faculty, all became a situation within which the envy other faculty developed the opinion that I needed to learn my place in the organization. The envy was inherent and underlying every aspect of the workplace effort and engagement. Envy became bullying, which became academic mobbing (Andrews et al., 2021; Crawford, 2019a, 2019b, 2023; Crawford & White, 2021; Khoo, 2010; Newsum et al., 2023; Seguin, 2026):

> *Davenport et al. describes "mobbing" as a form of organizational pathology in which co-workers essentially "ganged up" and engaged in an ongoing rituals of humiliation, exclusion, unjustified accusations, emotional abuse and general harassment in their malicious attempt to force a targeted worker out of the workplace. It usually begins with one person who decides that he or she is threatened by a colleague and thus begins a desperate campaign that spreads through the workplace like a disease, infecting person after person with the desire to eliminate a target. (Khoo, 2010, p. 62)*

The general degradation into academic mobbing directly impacted every aspect of the workplace experience and I had to learn how to deal with the egregious undermining, lies, and personal and professional attacks, as well as proactive efforts to grow the bullying group into a full-blown academic mobbing situation that included everyone from unknowing students, to faculty colleagues, to all levels of mid-management and administrative leadership. Seguin (2016) described the development of an academic mobbing focus upon the unsuspecting target:

The process begins when a small group of instigators decides to cast someone out on the pretext that he or she is threatening their interests. This concept covers a variety of cases; perhaps the target is not behaving the way they would like, does not share their view of the organization, earns more than they do or challenges questionable practices. Mobbers use negative communication as their powerful weapon of elimination. (para. 5)

Further, Seguin shared that:

Workplace mobbing is a concerted process to get rid of an employee, who is better referred to as a "target" than a "victim" to emphasize the strategic nature of the process. The dynamic is reminiscent of Stalin's Moscow Trials: the targets are first convicted and evidence is later fabricated to justify the conviction. As sociologist of science Brian Martin put it, everything they say, are, write and do will be systematically used against them. (2016, para. 3)

The shocking aspect to this growing threat was that I was busy living my life and enjoying attempts to create a personal life and a professional life that was growing in comfort as well as a level of reputation that enhanced my opportunities to support other academics as well as my students. The faculty and administration within my workplace were so envious that attacks grew beyond childish yet nasty gossip, and into professional work attacks and creatively ridiculous lies. As described by Khoo (2010):

Academic mobbing is a non-violent, sophisticated, 'ganging up' behaviour adopted by academicians to "wear and tear" a colleague down emotionally through unjustified accusation, humiliation, general harassment and emotional abuse. These are directed at the target under a veil of lies and justifications so that they are "hidden" to others and difficult to prove. Bullies use mobbing activities to hide their own weaknesses and incompetence. Targets selected are often intelligent, innovative high achievers, with good integrity and principles. Mobbing activities appear trivial and innocuous on its own but the frequency and pattern of their occurrence over long period of time indicates an aggressive manipulation to "eliminate" the target. (Khoo, 2010, p. 61)

The workplace within which I was embedded was a toxic culture, focused upon ruining my career and running me out. The underlying workplace emotional impacts directly and negatively impacted every aspect of my workplace contractual obligation.

The one element that I could attempt to control within this environment would be my approach to learning design. For this reason, I fully focused my own efforts towards more deeply understanding the reasons behind *why* my instructional design efforts resulted in superior learning design practices. I recognized that my response to learner feedback and associated course design discussions was transparent; many times prior students would reach out and share that they heard our course redesign ideas had found their way into my courses. My response was always "yes, of course," because I respected their course experiential feedback and their instructional design talents. Why would I not implement the strong learner colleague feedback that was directly embedded within their course experience? The courses slowly developed into powerful learning design environments, and my own embedded experiential approaches to the course design did result in powerful learning design practices and deeper learning. The underlying workplace emotional impacts resulting from the consistent and ever-expanding academic mobbing efforts resulted in my continuous and focused efforts towards better understanding the design of learning experiences, as well as continually enhancing courses based upon and embedded within the quality collegial learner feedback received.

PROGRESSIVE STEP

Progressing forward, the next phase of the Currere method is the Progressive step, which is purposefully focused on the present time, place, and space. Considered within the Progressive step is a present metaphoric snapshot of confluence between the past and the potential future through this focused journey. How do I consider my present state associated with efforts towards superior learning design practices, while equally recognizing the underlying workplace emotional impacts upon a professor's experiential approach? This is the guiding question within this Progressive step. To more fully describe the Progressive step, Pinar (1994) frames the following guiding understanding:

Progressive derives from pro meaning "before" and gradi meaning "to step, go." In this phase we look the other way. We look, in Sartre's language, at what is not yet the case, what is not yet the present. We have found that the future is present in the same sense that the past is present. It influences, in complicated ways, the present; it forms the present. (p. 24)

From a progressive perspective of understanding, I consider the prior learning experiences to be impactful as I perceive that this was a sense of *becoming* in my own understanding of myself as well as who I am in the larger world space. The student collegial learners have been an impressive group of colleagues from whom I have learned the potential depth and breadth of impact by the careful learning design practices and proclivities that have been shared with me, as well as those which I have stumbled upon through careful study, connected insights, and pure luck.

From a current understanding of the emotional impacts upon my experiential approach to course design, course redesign, and the modeling, mentorship, and cognitive apprenticeship facilitative instructional efforts that I imbue within my course experience, I consider that my sense of *becoming* has been deeply impacted by the toxic workplace culture. Through this academic mobbing lens, I have attempted to address the cognitive and experiential gaps in the degree plan as well as in the organizational culture, to meet the needs of the learners and heighten my own instructional efforts and attempt to address the lack of professionalism, lack of subject matter learning, and heightened concerns of quality that I continuously hear from student colleagues who leave the degree program without completing it, who sense discontent and discomfort in their course experiences and knowledge learned, as well as the discomfort and emotionally charged tension underlying the program of study, the college, and even the larger university experience.

I was meeting with a student colleague just a few days prior to sitting down to journey through this Currere approach to my journey in attempting to develop superior learning design practices. Delving into the underlying workplace emotional impacts that directly guided my experiential approaches throughout my course design and experiential implementation is a difficult expedition; however, this is a journey that I humbly suggest is worthy of sharing as an addition to the body of literature. Beginning the conversation with the student colleague, she shared that she didn't have any questions or concerns, and really didn't have an agenda for our meeting, but instead just wanted to better understand who I am as a course instructor and long-standing professor within the university. My curiosity was piqued and I wanted to learn more from her, as I recognized her exceptionally impressive talents and depth of understanding. She had an old soul in a young person's body. As she became more comfortable, she shared that this was her first semester in the graduate program and that she'd been networking with other coursework student colleagues in order to figure out the metaphoric *lay of the land* within the graduate program. An interesting comment that surprised me was that master's and doctoral students with whom she had developed collegial relationships were telling her to take as many courses from me as possible, specifically due to the quality of experience and knowledge attained; that I am a professor with high standards to attain, but that I'm engaged and interested in the success of my course student colleagues. I was surprised, honored, and humbled, and I shared how that made me feel.

In response, she further shared that many of the students in the program had plenty to say about the quality of the course experience, including curiosity about why so many core courses were taught by adjuncts whom the students deemed to be lacking in quality and understanding of the subject matter, as well as unflattering comments associated with the program faculty. I attempted to change the subject a few times, but she would not comfortably allow the shift in conversation. I finally communicated that I am unaware who instructs the courses, as that information is not shared with me, and that I had asked to teach the program courses she had mentioned, but my requests had been declined. I was surprised that the student colleague knew enough about academia to understand that I am the senior faculty in the program and that this is not acceptable. I smiled and changed the topic.

The student then shared that she'd recently met with her advisor, who had talked about all the adjuncts and other faculty who instructed courses in the program but did not mention me. In response, the student brought up my name and shared her opinion of me and her course experiences, then added what other student colleagues had said to her about me. The response she received was a cold stare and total change in demeanor, resulting in a negative shift in the advising session discussion. The student suggested to me that she would like to change advisors, to which I responded that she should reconsider and attempt to progress forward with her current advisor. The student planned to graduate no later than the end of the year, so a few more months shouldn't be a concern. I was saddened to realize, yet again, that the students were being impacted by the toxic work environment that embedded the academic mobbing relished by so many of the weaker personnel. The student recognized that she was a pawn in whatever was occurring within the program and didn't like it. Although I kept maneuvering the conversation to less volatile topics, I was listening to what the student shared.

The rest of my evening was spent ruminating, wondering at the pronounced depth of impact on students. My efforts to strengthen my own course design and integrate real-world experiential approaches throughout the course curriculum, as well as attempts to understand and integrate superior learning design practices, were undercut due to the inherently broken environment within which the students were attempting to attain their degrees. My heart hurt that the students were so deeply impacted by personnel issues. My soul was impacted, recognizing that these issues were not of my making and were out of my control to successfully address.

I saw that nothing would change, that the situation would not only *never get better* but seemingly was becoming worse. The questionable behaviors were no longer only focused upon mobbing me, as the target of vicious animosity and envy, but the students were experiencing a growing impact as well.

My angst deepened as I reflected upon another superior graduate student colleague. This student was exceptionally intelligent and socially a brilliant colleague who easily maneuvered and manipulated course colleagues in our course. This student was a natural leader, assertively supportive and transparently fair while also straightforward. I was continuously impressed by this student colleague and developed a growing respect as I had worked with her in additional courses. It was time in this student's program of study to complete her capstone experience. Unfortunately, this student became an unwilling pawn in the bullying and ineptitude of the faculty and administration. The student was blocked from her practicum experience due to the ineptitude of the mid-management and administrative leadership. I was attempting to guide her practicum experience forward, but was blocked and negatively impacted at every effort and approach. The ultimate yet egregiously unprofessional experience for this student was a video conference meeting with the student, me as her advisor, program coordinator, department chair, associate dean, and dean. It became a public attack to reflect that what had occurred with this student was actually due to an incompetent advisor.

The attack was shocking, cruelly unprofessional, and unwarranted. The student sat watching and listening to what was occurring, slowly becoming more upset and shocked by what was on display. I corrected the continuous misinformation and flawed points, as the people on the call became increasingly more animated and vicious. Recognizing that the meeting was being recorded, I was careful to control my emotions and respond in a succinct and technical fashion. I had years of experience learning this style of communicative engagement, due to the years upon years of academic mobbing attacks that I've journeyed through within this organization. The student, on the other hand, had not previously experienced what was occurring. She had been included in progressive, transparent communications that ensured that she maintained her own documentation of her practicum experience efforts. The student was very upset and corrected the statements made by each person on the call, who were all blaming me for their own incompetence and blocking her degree progression. She informed them that she had all the documentation that reflected none of what they were saying was correct and true, that in fact I was the only one on the phone call who was professionally supporting her efforts, and that I was blocked from doing my job due to misinformation, disinformation, and a refusal of personnel to actively participate in their job responsibilities.

I was impressed by the qualities that this student displayed throughout the onerous video conference experience, although she finally had an emotional breakdown towards the end of the meeting as she was bullied into accepting the only option that would allow her to finish her degree. The emotional impact upon the student was significant, to the point of overwhelming. As the student turned off her video camera and muted her audio, I waited for a few minutes and then said that the student did not need to make a decision while on this video conference, that she could take a bit of time to make her decision and then inform the administration as to how she would progress forward. The top administrator in the meeting began yelling that it was not my place to say such things. The student immediately returned to the meeting and corrected the administrator's behavior, stating that I was the only person on the phone call who was proactively supporting her, that the viciousness displayed during this meeting was unprofessional and unacceptable, and that she had retained a lawyer so would follow my guidance and consult with her attorney before making any decision. Oh my, I decided to remain silent while this played out, because this was all new information to me.

The meeting quickly concluded after the student shared that she had retained a lawyer. I waited a moment before calling her to make sure that she was okay and to ensure that she had an opportunity to decompress and talk about anything that she felt was important to address. She answered on the second ring, still very upset by what had occurred. I explained that none of what occurred actually had anything to do with her, in my opinion, that I was sorry and that I would support whatever decision she made as we moved forward, and that she should tell me what she wants to do so I could try to ensure that it occurred without interference.

Based upon these experiences, as well as so many other experiences with similar storylines, I have come consider the underlying workplace emotional impacts upon my job and associated responsibilities within the university. I recognize that my career has thrived beyond the bounds of the university within which I work, specifically due to the recognition that I am mobbed and under-evaluated each year on my performance, and I describe my experience within the university as being informally censured. The only service roles achieved are those roles that are beyond the control of the program, department, and college. My research efforts are beyond the control of the workplace personnel, so the only remaining aspect that can be impacted and within which I have the potential to be bullied is my teaching role.

ANALYTIC STEP

The Analytic step in the Currere process emphasizes the present, the here and now. Pinar (1994) offers a well-rounded understanding of the analytic step, succinctly articulating the focus of this endeavor:

Ana-up, throughout. Lysis-a loosening. Conceptualization is detachment from experience. Bracketing what is, what was, what can be, one is loosened from it, potentially more free of it, hence more free to freely choose the present, and the future. (p. 26)

As I am very transparent in my statements, I openly tout that the best part of the university are the students. Without question, I perceive that this is a true statement. I enjoy the teaching aspect of the contractual expectation and have specifically focused my interest upon a teaching university due to the opportunity to deeply engage and positively impact the professional and academic journeys of my student colleagues. As the other aspects of my contractual obligations have been quietly stripped from me, I have found other ways to meet them. Yet the impact upon the students, the best part of the university, directly hits at the heart of who I am. My life's mission is to be of service to others, which is why I so deeply enjoy and feel an importance for strong course experiences and engagingly positive course learning design practices. The one remaining area that the academic mobbing can impact is my courses and my student advising. This is the reality of the workplace within which I find myself. This is a fair and impartial snapshot of the Progressive step in the Currere journey.

The question that arises during this present situation within which I find myself is, *how much is too much? Is this really worth the continuous attacks, the continuous undermining?* And most importantly, *do I really want to negatively impact the students in this way?* While recognizing that the bullies have attempted at every single opportunity to ruin my career and actively remove me from the university, without success, the remaining area for attack must be my teaching and course learning design experiences. For years, the bullies have attempted to portray me as a negative impact upon the students and my courses as inferior in learning design. Yet, even the students who acted as metaphoric flying monkey minions and were willing to claim horrors that never actually occurred would revise their opinions of me as they progressed in their degree programs of study. This may either be due to the number of students who were generous in their perceptions of me, a recognition that I love what I do with a deep professional passion, or perhaps it's merely that they recognized the error of their ways.

There is a student, known to a professional colleague, who initiated a brutal attack on my professional reputation and attempted to initiate censure procedures. So I am told. The effort was soon abandoned. The professional colleague did not share the student's name, nor did I request to know who it was. A few semesters later, I was writing a letter of recommendation for a student when this same professional colleague called for something. I asked if she could wait a moment because I was finishing up a letter of recommendation for a student in her program and needed to send it off before I lost my train of thought. My colleague patiently waited and after I'd finished and emailed the student, my colleague shared that this was the same student who had previously made outrageous claims and attempted to start censure proceedings against me. I responded that I didn't know who that student was nor what had been written in the letter that the administration claimed that they'd received, so I couldn't really speak to any of that. My colleague then shared a bit more information, knowing that the student had graduated and I wouldn't negatively impact the student's professional nor academic career. Indeed, she was correct; I don't recall the student's name and don't have any intention to hurt a student who was naïve and easily manipulated into being used for someone else's nefarious ends.

My colleague then shared that she had known that the student was in my classes because the student had informed her; however, the colleague hadn't told me at the time because she knew it would upset me and that I wouldn't want a potentially negative perception of a student to taint the course experience. My colleague also shared that the student had loved my classes and claimed that she highly respected me and my efforts, indeed had wished that she'd had the opportunity to take more classes with me. I laughed, asking if this was really the same student who had been trying to get me censured in the hopes of getting me fired? I then became a bit more serious, and thanked my colleague for not sharing any of that information until the student was gone. I suggested that the student was manipulated into doing what had occurred, and I imagined that she did not realize the seriousness of the claims made, the lies and overblown claims that hadn't actually occurred, also considering that the letter did not reflect the same style of communication as what the student had displayed throughout the course experience. I humbly suggested that someone else had edited whatever the student had actually written during a moment of over-indulgent hubris.

These types of experiences have become normal in my workplace. Egregious untruths, ridiculous claims, and sadly manipulative maneuvers directly impact my daily workplace efforts, focused upon attempts to undermine the quality of student experience. I find this intriguing, as its akin to an old saying about *shooting oneself in the foot*. Why create such a horrible narrative about faculty working in a degree program, knowing that it's all untruths, when the reputation of the degree may be impacted? I'm blessed in many ways, primarily that my reputation precedes most attempts to attack me within academia. It's unfortunate that the academic mobbing within the workplace is negatively impactful, and the underlying workplace emotional impacts upon my experiential approach to the teaching and learning process cause a struggle. Yet I continuously attempt to refocus upon the quality of the students and the quality of my courses and associated service to the students by heightening my efforts to develop and implement superior learning design practices.

SYNTHETICAL STEP

The Currere method's final step in the process is the Synthetical step. At this point in the progressively reflective process, I take upon myself an opportunity to reflect back upon the prior steps. What is in the past, what is the bridge between the past and the present, and how has the present grown out of the reflections and ruminations of learned experiences? This step is focused upon an attempt to understand the topic in focus, to understand my perception of the experiences that have led to this point in the reflective ruminations. As Pinar (1994) suggests,

What conceptual gestalt is finally visible? That is, what is one's "point of view?" Can one bracket and thus escape from the conceptual, take it into one's hands as it were, examine it, and see its relation to one's psychological, physical, biographic condition? See its relation to "one's form of life?" This includes one's public and private lives, one's externally observable behavior and the contents of one's stream-of-consciousness. (p. 27).

Recognizing my difficult journey within this toxic organization, and the underlying workplace emotional impacts upon my experiential approach to superior learning design practices, what are my take-aways? After this convoluted approach to reflecting on what has occurred, what do I ultimately believe and leave understanding? These are deeply impactful questions that are worthy of consideration.

I walk away understanding my talents and my worth within this space. I am a curious instructional designer and talented course instructor with deep-seated respect for student colleagues and a desire to enhance their learning experiences. The competencies and associated capabilities ensconced within my course design reflect my desire to make a positive difference in student colleagues' professional lives. Equally important and impactful are my more personalized efforts towards enhancing the course experience as a reflection of Wenger-Trayner's social learning work, including communities of learning and landscapes of practice (Wenger, 1998; Wenger-Trayner et al., 2014; Wenger-Trayner & Wenger-Trayner, 2015, Wenger-Trayner & Wenger-Trayner, 2020).

As one example, throughout the course design, I implemented a team approach within the course. Students worked in small teams to allow for different learning experiences and learning objectives that were specifically dependent upon the subject matter and desired achievements. One example of team implementation was within a production course experience, wherein the learners joined their team video conference as an opportunity to present their products to their teammates, analyzing the design choices and aspects of development efforts; equally, the teammates acted as formative evaluation opportunists, analyzing the products, asking questions, and offering feedback to enhance the product, as well as recording the video conference Teams meeting that would then be shared with the larger group of course learners and instructor for review and analytic feedback commentary. The public, real world venue within which peer review occurred was reflective of the professional work environment the learners would experience.

As a second example, one course design mandated that the learners present their course assignment to their *collegial community* which consisted of friends, family, work colleagues, work supervisors, university students in other courses, and university professors from other courses. This was a dual approach, supporting the learners in developing self-efficacy related to the course subject matter, while also acting as a subtle opportunity for other university professors to comfortably review and consider ways through which the learner assignments easily integrated fresh course design and subject-specific enhancements that were intended as mini-professional development opportunities for the professors. I was surprised by the speed with which the other professors began working with the course learners, as they recognized the resourcefulness and impressive ideas generated by the learners. To enhance this level of professorial engagement, my extensive feedback to each learner included suggestions related to sharing assignments with their advisors and their program faculty, as well as insights for program and degree enhancements. The outcomes were normally unknown to me as a course instructor, but I did hear back from several learners that different projects were implemented, such as program-specific podcasts implemented and owned by the students, learner assignments that were integrated into their program's coursework, and course enhancements that supported the learning process.

As a third and final example, one course experience was focused upon distance learning analysis at the program level, the course level, and the instructor level of engagement. Each learner within my course decided what program they desired to analyze, with the majority of learners focusing upon their own work environment's distance learning program. This was intended as a real-world implementation of their experiences, specifically approved and supported by their workplace supervisors. One learner, however, was a full-time graduate student who was taking my course as a fun elective. As such, she didn't have a workplace environment within which to analyze a distance learning program. Instead, I suggested that she focus upon her own graduate program experience, which also included a distance learning component. This learner dove into the assignments, qualitatively interviewing instructional faculty and graduate students throughout her program of study experience. The result of the analysis was an acknowledgement of the lack of support and informational transparency for the students in that program of study. Realizing this, the learner and I worked together to analyze potential ways to address this gap analysis. The learner met with the program director and suggested the creation of an online course environment within which all program students and program faculty would be housed. This course environment would act as a communication hub, ensuring advisor support for all program students and providing a system within which the students could easily communicate and feel deeply connected with their peers as well as program faculty. My course learner received a graduate assistantship, not only to create the distance learning course environment for the program of study, but to maintain the assistantship throughout her degree program of study. The faculty within her program actively reached out to me, emphasizing the positive impact that my course experience had had upon the quality of my learner, as well as the positive impact of the learner's efforts and outcomes upon the program of study.

Through the horrors of this toxic organization and academic mobbing situation, I have understood the importance and impact of a comfortably engaging, collegial, and vulnerably welcoming learning environment that I have labeled as the Implicit Cognitive Vulnerability theory (Crawford, 2015, 2016; Crawford & Smith, 2015). As suggested by Crawford, "The role of the instructor is to define the course culture and appropriate behaviors, not only through modeling and facilitating throughout the course experience, but also towards ensuring the instructor's immediacy and authenticity engage in understandings revolving around cognitive vulnerability as an instructional experience" (2016, p. 25). Yet, what is the concept of vulnerability? Bennett (2007) suggests that:

Vulnerability is not good or bad, it is simply real. Some kinds of vulnerability feel awesome and some feel terrifying. All vulnerability is profoundly experiential and memorable. The more we learn how to nurture our vulnerability, the more intimacy we can experience and the safer and happier we are likely to be in the world.

But live in a culture where vulnerability is ridiculed, abused, medicated, and repressed. Because of this, many reading this article do not even know about their vulnerability – consciously. Some literally have been abused out of a connection to their vulnerability. In these people, vulnerability seems bad and the need to "escape it" drives much of what they do. (para. 7-8)

Vulnerability within a course design is nuanced, with not only the course design impacting a sense of vulnerability and comfort offering the opportunity to grow and enhance within a course experience, but also the course instructor's personality and style of engaging with the learners which equally supports the sense of vulnerability within a learning environment. One example is the implementation of a team video conference assignment within which each learner must create their own *elevator speech* and present it to their teammates. An elevator speech is a thirty-second "this is me" verbal presentation, such as how one might introduce themself to their company president if they found themself walking onto an elevator and needing to explain who they are and their value to the organization. A person has about thirty seconds to make an impression; the elevator speech is a worthwhile assignment in-course that is equally impactful in the learner's real-world environment. The video conference is recorded and shared with all course learners, acting as an introduction for each learner within the course environment. Yet the enhanced element is the assigned team's peer review, during which teammates highlight the strengths of the elevator speech presentation as well as areas of potential enhancement. The course instructor has the opportunity to evaluate and offer formative feedback on this elevator speech prior to the team meeting, during which the instructor encourages the learner to emphasize their value, with specific examples and quantitative numbers associated with achievements. Although the learners initially considered the assignment to be simple, the instructor's emphasis upon their professional value and achievements shifted the assignment into a deep quality experience for each learner. The learners proactively supported each other early in our course, analyzing each elevator speech and highlighting the value of each learner that should be brought forward, as initially modeled by the course instructor in a gently professional yet significantly focused manner. This assignment set the stage for the remainder of the course experience, shifting from merely finishing each assignment to engaging with every opportunity to represent the learner's quality and professional value.

A second example of vulnerability within a course environment is the nuanced style of communication that the course instructor implements with each learner. As a personal effort, I attempt to refer to learners in my courses as "colleagues" and "course colleagues." This label shifts the power structure within a learning environment; although I am the instructor of record and do offer detailed assessments of the learners throughout the course experience, I am also continuously learning as an aspect of our course experience. One active aspect in which I attempt to engage is highlighting at least one learner who reaches out and asks a question about the course experience. I respond to the learner and then create a public communication that I share with all course learners, in which I emphasize one of our *brilliant colleagues* has a great question which I restate and then offer a fully developed response for everyone to review. Highlighting the *brilliant colleague* not only supports the implementation of the term *colleague* that I then implement throughout the rest of the course experience, but the positivity associated with the proactive engagement with the course instructor is viewed as a desirable effort. Sharing information and supportive considerations is viewed as a desirable effort in the course, which aligns a sense of comfort as the learners figure out how to work with me as the course instructor.

By the end of the first week or into the second week of a course experience, the learners are implementing my *colleague* label because they're parroting what they believe is acceptable in the course environment; by midpoint in the course, the shift in attitude is perceptible. Acting as a colleague within the course ignites a sense of comfort. The levels of engagement and transparency that I as the course instructor display are equally impactful, supporting the ease of engagement necessary for a respectful environment within which learners develop vulnerability and learning is emphasized over always having the correct answer or the perfect assignment. The vulnerability to move through a learning space is important and impactful, through developing bonds with course learners as well as the course instructor.

Many learners lament the end of our course experience, because the bonding, the comfort, the vulnerability achieved during the course enhances the learning experience but also engages the learners in a mutually supportive effort wherein the concept of individual success is equally important to everyone. Enrollment in my courses normally stabilizes after the first week of the add and drop enrollment period. Students rarely withdraw from my courses because the motivation associated with the learning experience is enhanced, and transparency and vulnerability support the *all for one and one for all* assurance of course completion and associated course success. Vulnerability within my courses is an expectation, although not a mandate; learners can be as vulnerable as they are comfortable within my courses. My expectation as the course instructor is that we are here to be successful and professionally supportive; this is the only acceptable demeanor to display throughout the course experience.

This sense of vulnerability is useful to consider, as prior efforts to articulate superior learning design practices also led me to a stronger understanding of the holistic interactive activities that engage within a learning environment, with a focus upon not only the learner's efforts, but the instructor's interactive activities and engagements as well. A well-rounded list of interactive activities that others initiated and which I have expanded upon, include:

- Learner-content (Moore, 1989)
- Learner-interface (Hillman et al., 1994)
- Learner-instructor (Moore, 1989)
- Learner-learner (Moore, 1989)
- Learner-self (Crawford, 2001)
- Learner-community (Burnham & Walden, 1997)
- Instructor-community (Crawford, 2001)
- Instructor-content (Crawford, 2001)
- Instructor-interface (Crawford, 2001)
- Instructor-self (Crawford, 2001, 2003)
- Learner-Web of Things (Crawford et al, 2021)
- Instructor-Web of Things (Crawford et al, 2021)
- Instructor-instructor colleagues (Crawford et al, 2021)

What is my point of view, as I conclude this Currere approach, to better understanding the underlying workplace emotional impacts upon a professor's experiential approach, with specific consideration towards designing, developing, and implementing superior learning design practices? Simply stated, I choose to perceive that the horrors of a toxic work environment, one that supports academic mobbing and egregious bullying behaviors as a natural way of being, offers me the opportunity to expand and enhance my professional and academic journey. Without finding myself in this type of workplace culture, with my experiential understandings of academia and academics gone awry, I would not have been nearly as productive or creative. My efforts to overcome, to save myself through controlling and enjoying my own work and life mission to be of positive service to others, have expanded my opportunities while equally expanding the quality of my curriculum vita and reputation. If I had found myself in a comfortably supportive organization, I may not have achieved as much as I have done, nor appreciated the professional warmth and quality of honorable and ethical colleagues who emphasize integrity above all else within the academic landscape. I have sought out these professionals and welcomed them into my professional life, as a balance to my workplace experiences.

SOLUTIONS AND RECOMMENDATIONS

The desirable solution begs the query, whether the chicken or the egg came first. One is a part of the other, so how can there be an adequate solution, an adequate response? This is my reflective stance on the underlying workplace emotional impacts upon a professor's experiential approach to advancing superior learning design practices. If I had not journeyed through such difficult levels of drama, intrigue, and nefarious situations, if I had not continuously dealt with bullying persons lacking integrity and honor, then I may not have journeyed into this exciting space and place of opportunity and excellence. If I had not attempted to find a place of respite within chaotic toxicity, perhaps I would not have focused significant attention upon the quality of the course design and design practices that strengthen the course experience while enhancing the talents and creative understanding of the learning colleagues.

Is there a solution? Yes, absolutely. There is always the ability to strengthen and overcome a toxic work environment that not only enables but enhances academic mobbing as its core featured experience. Strong leadership at all levels of the organization would directly impact and overcome such egregiously undermining realities. Yet as the university remains in chaos and questions associated with the implosion of higher education on a national scale move closer to reality, the recognition that the university has moved so far away from its mission, vision, and values that no longer align with the vast majority of the citizenry, one must critically question the viability of continuing the current higher education organizational structure. Until teaching returns as the central mission and vision, until teaching is reflected in every facet of the organization's values, the internal rot within academia will continue.

FUTURE RESEARCH DIRECTIONS

The impact of the organization's culture, strength of leadership, and focus upon its customers, along with an understanding of the organization's place and space within society, are all timely and impactful areas to seriously consider. The underlying workplace emotional impacts of toxic work environments, of academic bullying and mobbing that impacts the organization's reputation as well as the customer experience, are aspects of higher education that are whispered within and throughout the hallowed hallways of the ivory tower but are not directly addressed. Aspects of *somebody else's problem* and *stay in your lane* have become natural states of being within some higher education institutions.

A more direct approach to addressing toxic work environments is necessary. Equally important and impactful is the potential correlation between toxic organizations that negatively impact workplace personnel with the organization's reputation as well as the customer base experience. No matter how superior the course experience may be for student colleagues, the students must also deal with the administrative offices that dole out policies and procedures. Equally concerning are administrative personnel who ignore or make up their own policies and procedures in order to attack employees and, in some cases, the student customers. Superior learning design practices are important and impactful, and they may extend the higher education organization's timeline; however, the organization must recognize that the student customer is impacted by the toxicity of the workplace. Even while attempting to concede that the personnel issues are strange and curious personality issues, the reality is that the student customers are affected and the negative impact is deeply impressed upon the student's psyche, never to be forgotten. Are these the experiences that an institution of higher education desires for their students to remember?

CONCLUSION

The underlying workplace emotional impacts upon the professor's approach to superior learning design practices are highlighted as an experiential journey, through the implementation of the Currere Method. The complicated conversation through which this author has journeyed, and through which she has welcomed the immersion of the reader, is meant to reflect the difficulty of workplace issues, and equally the ability of people journeying through difficult spaces and places to find strength, creative results, and resources that may sustain a sense of positivity. The quality of a difficult workplace cannot be ignored, due to the professional and personal impacts that forever change persons who find themselves in the midst of egregious environments; yet an emphasis upon creative strengths and overcoming must be recognized as vital to the professional and personal welfare of personnel in the midst of these situations. The sense of *becoming* through the Currere analytic journey may foster a respect for the creative ways through which professionals continue to find outlets of worthy work and ways through which to serve.

REFERENCES

Alam, A. (2023, May). Improving Learning Outcomes through Predictive Analytics: Enhancing Teaching and Learning with Educational Data Mining. In *2023 7th International Conference on Intelligent Computing and Control Systems (ICICCS)* (pp. 249-257). IEEE Xplore. DOI: DOI: 10.1109/ICICCS56967.2023.10142392

Alkhodary, D. A. (2023). Exploring the relationship between organizational culture and well-being of educational institutions in Jordan. *Administrative Sciences*, 13(3), 92. DOI: 10.3390/admsci13030092

Andrews, S., Newsum, J. M., Crawford, C. M., & Moffett, N. L. (2021). Sisyphus Leans Into the Professoriate: Faculty Discuss Careers and the Academic Landscape. In N. L. Moffett's (Ed.) *Navigating Post-Doctoral Career Placement, Research, and Professionalism* (pp. 185-226). IGI Global. DOI: DOI: 10.4018/978-1-7998-5065-6.ch009

Bass, R. (2023). Social pedagogies in ePortfolio practices: Principles for design and impact. In *High-Impact ePortfolio Practice* (pp. 65–73). Routledge. DOI: 10.4324/9781003445098-7

Bean, C. (2023). *The accidental instructional designer: Learning design for the digital age*. Association for Talent Development.

Beck, D., Morgado, L., & O'Shea, P. (2023). Educational practices and strategies with immersive learning environments: Mapping of reviews for using the metaverse. *IEEE Transactions on Learning Technologies*, 17, 319–341. DOI: 10.1109/TLT.2023.3243946

Bennett, J. (2007). Great actors access vulnerability. The Jason Bennett Actor's Workshop. Retrieved from https://www.jbactors.com/actingreading/actorsaccessvulnerability.html

Blanchard, P. N., & Thacker, J. W. (2023). *Effective training: Systems, strategies, and practices*. SAGE Publications.

Blaschke, L. M. (2023). Self-determined learning: Designing for heutagogic learning environments. In Spector, J. M., Lockee, B. B., & Childress, M. D. (Eds.), *Learning, Design, and Technology: An International Compendium of Theory, Research, Practice, and Policy* (pp. 245–266). Springer International Publishing. DOI: 10.1007/978-3-319-17461-7_62

Bokek-Cohen, Y. A., Shkoler, O., & Meiri, E. (2023). The unique practices of workplace bullying in academe: An exploratory study. *Current Psychology (New Brunswick, N.J.)*, 42(23), 19466–19485. DOI: 10.1007/s12144-022-03090-2

Børte, K., Nesje, K., & Lillejord, S. (2023). Barriers to student active learning in higher education. *Teaching in Higher Education*, 28(3), 597–615. DOI: 10.1080/13562517.2020.1839746

Bozkurt, A., & Sharma, R. C. (2023). Challenging the status quo and exploring the new boundaries in the age of algorithms: Reimagining the role of generative AI in distance education and online learning. *Asian Journal of Distance Education*, 18(1), i–viii. DOI: 10.5281/zenodo.7755273

Burnham, B., & Walden, B. (1997). Interactions in distance education: A report from the other side. In *Proceedings of the Adult Education Research Conference*. Oklahoma State University. http://www.edst.educ.ubc.ca/aerc/1997/97burnham.html

Choudhary, A., Jena, B. P., & Patre, S. (2024). Unveiling the veil of workplace Loneliness: A Theory-Concept-Methodology (TCM) framework. *Psychology Hub*, 41(1), 79–90.

Cidlinska, K., Nyklova, B., Machovcova, K., Mudrak, J., & Zabrodska, K. (2023). "Why I don't want to be an academic anymore?" When academic identity contributes to academic career attrition. *Higher Education*, 85(1), 141–156. DOI: 10.1007/s10734-022-00826-8

Clark, R. C., & Mayer, R. E. (2023). *E-learning and the science of instruction: Proven guidelines for consumers and designers of multimedia learning*. John Wiley & Sons.

Crawford, C. (2015). Vulnerability in learning. In J. Spector (Ed.), The SAGE Encyclopedia of Educational Technology (pp. 832–835). Thousand Oaks, CA: SAGE Publications, Inc.; . n338DOI: 10.4135/9781483346397

Crawford, C. M. (2001). Developing webs of significance through communications: Appropriate interactive activities for distributed learning environments. *Campus-Wide Information Systems*, 18(2), 68–72. DOI: 10.1108/10650740110386675

Crawford, C. M. (2003). Emerging learning environments: Enhancing the online community. *Academic Exchange Quarterly*, 7(4), 131–135.

Crawford, C. M. (2016). Instructor immediacy and authenticity: engaging in cognitive vulnerability within the online instructional environment. In S. D'Augustino (Ed.) *Creating Teacher Immediacy in Online Learning Environments* (pp. 15-36). Hershey, PA: IGI Global. DOI: 10.4018/978-1-4666-9995-3.ch002

Crawford, C. M. (Ed.). (2019a). *Confronting academic mobbing in higher education: Personal accounts and administrative action*. IGI Global.

Crawford, C. M. (2019b). In the midst of the maelstrom: Struggling through the revulsions of academic mobbing while maintaining one's ethical compass. In C. M. Crawford's (Ed.) *Confronting Academic Mobbing in Higher Education: Personal Accounts and Administrative Action* (pp. 241-266). Hershey, PA: IGI Global.

Crawford, C. M. (2023). Now what?: A case study on the impact of nefarious Queen Bees. In K. L. Clarke & N. L. Moffett's (Eds.) *Addressing the Queen Bee Syndrome in Academia,* p. 1-25. IGI Global. DOI: DOI: 10.4018/978-1-6684-7717-5.ch001

Crawford, C. M., Andrews, S., & Wallace, J. K. Y. (2021). Co-creative collegial communities of instructional engagement. [IJHIoT]. *International Journal of Hyperconnectivity and the Internet of Things*, 5(2), 38–56. DOI: 10.4018/IJHIoT.2021070103

Crawford, C. M., Andrews, S., & Young Wallace, J. K. (2022). Implicit cognitive vulnerability through nudges, boosts, and bounces. *International Journal of Hyperconnectivity and the Internet of Things*, 6(1), 1–14. DOI: 10.4018/IJHIoT.285588

Crawford, C. M., & Smith, M. S. (2015). Rethinking Bloom's Taxonomy: Implicit Cognitive Vulnerability as an impetus towards higher order thinking skills. In Jin, Z. (Ed.), *Exploring Implicit Cognition: Learning, Memory, and Social Cognitive Processes* (pp. 86–103). Information Science Reference. DOI: 10.4018/978-1-4666-6599-6.ch004

Crawford, C. M., & White, S. A. (2021). Adventures on the Golden Road: A Promenade Through the Roadwork. In N. L. Moffett's (Ed.) *Navigating Post-Doctoral Career Placement, Research, and Professionalism* (pp. 28-52). IGI Global. DOI: 10.4018/978-1-7998-5065-6.ch002

De Welde, K., & Stepnick, A. (Eds.). (2023). *Disrupting the culture of silence: Confronting gender inequality and making change in higher education*. Taylor & Francis.

Dolan, V. L. (2023). '… but if you tell anyone, I'll deny we ever met:' the experiences of academics with invisible disabilities in the neoliberal university. *International Journal of Qualitative Studies in Education : QSE*, 36(4), 689–706. DOI: 10.1080/09518398.2021.1885075

Gros, B., & García-Peñalvo, F. J. (2016). Future trends in the design strategies and technological affordances of e-learning. In Spector, M., Lockee, B. B., & Childress, M. D. (Eds.), *Learning, Design, and Technology. An International Compendium of Theory, Research, Practice, and Policy* (pp. 1–23). Springer International Publishing., DOI: 10.1007/978-3-319-17727-4_67-1

Heffernan, T., & Bosetti, L. (2023). University bullying and incivility towards faculty deans. *International Journal of Leadership in Education*, 26(4), 604–623. DOI: 10.1080/13603124.2020.1850870

Hillman, D., Willis, D. J., & Gunawardena, C. (1994). Learner-interface interaction in distance education: An extension of contemporary models and strategies for practitioners. *American Journal of Distance Education*, 8(2), 30–42. DOI: 10.1080/08923649409526853

Hooven, C. K. (2023). Academic freedom is social justice: Sex, gender, and cancel culture on campus. *Archives of Sexual Behavior*, 52(1), 35–41. DOI: 10.1007/s10508-022-02467-5 PMID: 36344790

Jagsi, R., Griffith, K., Krenz, C., Jones, R. D., Cutter, C., Feldman, E. L., Jacobson, C., Kerr, E., Paradis, K., Singer, K., Spector, N., Stewart, A., Telem, D., Ubel, P., & Settles, I. (2023). Workplace harassment, cyber incivility, and climate in academic medicine. *Journal of the American Medical Association*, 329(21), 1848–1858. DOI: 10.1001/jama.2023.7232 PMID: 37278814

Khasawneh, Y. J. A., Alsarayreh, R., Al Ajlouni, A. A., Eyadat, H. M., Ayasrah, M. N., & Khasawneh, M. A. S. (2023). An Examination of Teacher Collaboration in Professional Learning Communities and Collaborative Teaching Practices. *Journal of Education and e-learning Research*, 10(3), 446–452. DOI: 10.20448/jeelr.v10i3.4841

Khoo, S. B. (2010). Academic mobbing: Hidden health hazard at workplace. *Malaysian Family Physician : the Official Journal of the Academy of Family Physicians of Malaysia*, 5(2), 61–67. https://www.ncbi.nlm.nih.gov/pmc/articles/PMC4170397/ PMID: 25606190

Klahn Acuña, B., & Male, T. (2024). Toxic leadership and academics' work engagement in higher education: A cross-sectional study from Chile. *Educational Management Administration & Leadership*, 52(3), 757–773. DOI: 10.1177/17411432221084474

Lomer, S., & Palmer, E. (2023). 'I didn't know this was actually stuff that could help us, with actually learning': Student perceptions of Active Blended Learning. *Teaching in Higher Education*, 28(4), 679–698. DOI: 10.1080/13562517.2020.1852202

Malik, A. (2023). An investigation on turnover intention antecedents amongst the academician in universities. *Problems and Perspectives in Management*, 21(1), 373–383. DOI: 10.21511/ppm.21(1).2023.32

Mandalaki, E., & Pérezts, M. (2023). Abjection overruled! Time to dismantle sexist cyberbullying in academia. *Organization*, 30(1), 168–180. DOI: 10.1177/13505084211041711

Mhaka-Mutepfa, M., & Rampa, S. (2024). Workplace bullying and mobbing: Autoethnography and meaning-making in the face of adversity in academia. *International Journal of Qualitative Studies in Education : QSE*, 37(1), 1–18. DOI: 10.1080/09518398.2021.1991028

Moore, M. (1989). Three types of interaction. *American Journal of Distance Education*, 3(2), 1–7. DOI: 10.1080/08923648909526659

Müller, C., Mildenberger, T., & Steingruber, D. (2023). Learning effectiveness of a flexible learning study programme in a blended learning design: Why are some courses more effective than others? *International Journal of Educational Technology in Higher Education*, 20(1), 10. DOI: 10.1186/s41239-022-00379-x PMID: 36811132

Newsum, J., Thomas, M., Crawford, C. M., & Moffett, N. (2023). The invisible incivility archetype that is imploding higher education from within: The Queen Bee Syndrome's canary in the coal mine. In K. L. Clarke & N. L. Moffett's (Eds.) *Addressing the Queen Bee Syndrome in Academia,* p. 68-94. IGI Global. DOI: DOI: 10.4018/978-1-6684-7717-5.ch004

O'Neill, S. A. (2014). Complicated conversation: Creating opportunities for T\transformative practice in higher education music performance research and pedagogy. In Harrison, S. (Ed.), *Research and Research Education in Music Performance and Pedagogy. Landscapes: the Arts, Aesthetics, and Education* (Vol. 11). Springer., DOI: 10.1007/978-94-007-7435-3_12

Patiño, A., Ramírez-Montoya, M. S., & Buenestado-Fernández, M. (2023). Active learning and education 4.0 for complex thinking training: Analysis of two case studies in open education. *Smart Learning Environments*, 10(1), 8. DOI: 10.1186/s40561-023-00229-x

Pinar, W. (2012). *What is curriculum theory?* (2nd ed.). Routledge.

Pinar, W. F. (1994). *The method of Currere (1975). Autobiography, Politics and Sexuality: Essays in Curriculum Theory 1972-1992*. Peter Lang., https://www.currereexchange.com/uploads/9/5/8/7/9587563/pinar_the_currere_method.pdf

Salendab, F. (2023). Proposed instructional scheme in the new normal education: Basis for pedagogical strategies/practices. *Psychology and Education: A Multidisciplinary Journal, 6*(8), 712-719.

Seguin, E. (2016, September 19). Academic mobbing, or how to become campus tormentors. *University Affairs*. Retrieved from https://www.universityaffairs.ca/opinion/in-my-opinion/academic-mobbing-become-campus-tormentors/

Soythong, K. (2023). The Effect of Quality of Work Life and Organizational Commitment to Employee Performance: A Case Study of Transportation Business in Nakhon Phanom Province of Thailand. *Journal of Roi Kaensarn Academi*, 8(5), 414–433.

Vem, L. J., Cheah, J. H., Ng, S. I., & Ho, J. A. (2023). Unethical pro-organizational behavior: How employee ethical ideology and unethical organizational culture contribute. *International Journal of Manpower*, 44(4), 577–598. DOI: 10.1108/IJM-11-2021-0635

Wenger, E. (1998). *Communities of practice: Learning, meaning, and identity*. Cambridge University Press., DOI: 10.1017/CBO9780511803932

Wenger-Trayner, E., Fenton-O'Creevy, M., Hutchison, S., Kubiak, C., & Wenger-Trayner, B. (2014). *Learning in Landscapes of Practice: Boundaries, Identity, and Knowledgeability in Practice-Based Learning*. Routledge., DOI: 10.4324/9781315777122

Wenger-Trayner, E., & Wenger-Trayner, B. (2015). Communities of practice: A brief introduction. Wenger-Taylor. https://wenger-trayner.com/introduction-to-communities-of-practice/

Wenger-Trayner, E., & Wenger-Trayner, B. (2020). *Learning to Make a Difference: Value Creation in Social Learning Spaces*. Cambridge University Press., DOI: 10.1017/9781108677431

Wu, J. G., Zhang, D., & Lee, S. M. (2023). Into the brave new metaverse: Envisaging future language teaching and learning. *IEEE Transactions on Learning Technologies*, 17, 44–53. DOI: 10.1109/TLT.2023.3259470

KEY TERMS AND DEFINITIONS

Currere Method: A framework of self-study within which the progressive analysis of regressive, progressive, analytical, and synthetical occurs.

Emotional Impacts: The psychological and mental ways through which positive, neutral, and negative emotions support the worker's, and also the learner's, ability to engage with subject matter material within a space and a place.

Experiential Approach: A learning design practice that implements an embedded instructional effort with a focus upon the learner's experience with real world understandings around the subject matter..

Higher Education Institution: A name for post-secondary educational institutions that may refer to a technical college, community college, a college, or a university.

Instructional Design: This is a field of practice, wherein learning design practices are implemented and may focus upon workshops, training events, or more developed and extensive course experiences, such as what occur within higher education institutions, business and industry, military education, or medical educational departments.

Learning Design: This is the design of learning environments and learning processes, with an understanding around instructional design and user experience.

Professor: An instructor within an educational institution. Within higher education, the term can describe any course instructor, or it can be the title of a full time teacher, designated as an assistant professor, an associate professor, or a professor.

Section 4
Focus on Educator Preparation

Chapter 14
Educator Preparation Design Practices That Encourage Candidate Social–Emotional and Affective Competencies as Needed Dispositions for Teaching

Billi L. Bromer
https://orcid.org/0000-0003-2168-4555
Independent Researcher, USA

ABSTRACT

University based educator preparation practices within onsite and online formats provide the practical knowledge and skills required for effective teaching but do not adequately provide a self-discovery experience where the needed social emotional growth of teacher candidates and the affective aspects of teaching are nurtured and encouraged. Enhanced self-awareness of the emotions experienced by teachers in daily encounters with students can be a component of educator preparation and its inclusion may minimize the stressors that lead to compassion fatigue and teacher burnout.

INTRODUCTION

The core purpose of educator preparation is to support the development of an effective teacher with the knowledge, skills, and dispositions to successfully educate K-12 students in the 21st century. To ensure that teachers are prepared for rapid change, educator preparation programs provide candidates timely information and the most innovative teaching strategies. Staying current can be challenging because the education of K-12 students must be responsive to the fast pace at which knowledge, technology, societal issues, and many other factors arise that affect education.

The social and emotional elements of teacher dispositions are critical in the development of teachers who can evolve and adapt to societal and cultural changes. Students benefit from teachers who can appropriately manage their own emotions to respond helpfully to the emotions of their students. Teacher dispositions are as vital in teaching as knowledge and skills, but the development of candidate dispositions in educator preparation may be lacking adequate attention to the social-emotional and affective competencies within a profession so impacted by societal events, such as an unexpected health crisis.

The profession of education learned most profoundly from the pandemic that the social-emotional well-being of both students and the teachers who support student needs falls within the purview of an effective teacher. Teachers as well as students experienced the intense effects of the pandemic in extensive and extraordinary ways that still reverberate with unanticipated repercussions such as student mental health issues and significant learning loss in students of all ages (Beard et al., 2021; Bromer & Deeb, 2022; Katz et al., 2020). The pandemic brought to the fore the role of emotions in education as a fundamental factor for not only K-12 students but also for the teachers who provide their education (Osika et al., 2022; Tysbulsky & Muchnik-Rozanov, 2021). Teachers faced with the stressors of the pandemic may not have had adequate preparation within their educator programs to manage their own individual and personal situations. During and following the pandemic, we learned that the social-emotional well-being of a teacher is vital and can be helpful toward developing overall teacher candidate competence (D'emidio-Caston, 2019; Donahue-Keegan et al., 2019; Katz et al., 2020; Koludrovic & Mrsic, 2022; McCarthy, 2021; Nenonee et al., 2019; Schonert Reichl, 2017; Soutter, 2023; Waajid et al., 2013). The chapter suggests that inclusion of affective competencies as a component of effective teaching is feasible. The author suggests that in a post-pandemic environment, it is also urgent.

MAIN FOCUS OF THE CHAPTER

This chapter emerges from a research-backed theoretical framework regarding the importance of including social-emotional competencies in educator preparation. There exists an equally grounded practical framework gleaned from the author's experience in and familiarity with both teaching and the preparation of teachers. It is suggested within this chapter that teachers who have applied the affective elements of learning and acquired social-emotional competencies during their preparation may be better equipped to address their own needs within a stressful profession and avoid challenges such as teacher burnout. They may also be better able to effectively address the social-emotional needs of the students for whom they are responsible. The importance of the social-emotional well-being of a teacher as a successful and effective professional cannot be minimized. It is also dependent upon appropriate opportunities during teacher preparation to acquire the dispositions needed to meet the social-emotional needs of future students (D'emidio-Kaston, 2019; Katz et al., 2020; McCarthy, 2021; Schonert Reichl, 2017; Soutter, 2023; Waajid et al., 2013).

The Collaborative for Academic, Social, and Emotional Learning (n.d.) supports the inclusion of SEL principles and strategies in educator preparation. The CASEL framework, often identified as the "CASEL wheel" consists of five core social-emotional competencies that include self-awareness, self-management, social awareness, relationship skills, and responsible decision making. Although the focus of CASEL's work is to support the social-emotional development of K-12 students, the competencies can be relevant to individuals of any age.

There are multiple ways in which the affective aspects of teaching can be provided within educator preparation programs and they will be discussed in the chapter. Educator preparation faculty *buy-in* regarding the value of affective competencies (Nenonene et al., 2019) is a first step. Faculty must perceive the importance of social-emotional competencies and perhaps consider including them within their program framework. Other ways to provide opportunities for candidates to acquire the competencies include embedded self-reflection across all elements of the curriculum (Bleakley et al., 2020), careful attention to social-emotional factors during clinical field experiences (McCarthy, 2021), and the creation of communities of support to candidates throughout their educator preparation program and within the induction phase of teaching during which an educator preparation program may collaborate with schools in which their graduates become teachers (Flushman et al., 2021).

BACKGROUND

Importance of Emotions

Managing emotions is necessary in all types of employment but, perhaps, most important in caring professions in which individuals interact with others as part of their responsibilities. The field of neuroscience has attempted to explain the relationship between emotions and feelings. Researchers have approached emotions from a physiological perspective, such as in the explanation of a "gut feeling." Some have examined the connection between emotions and gut microbiome diversity and found that both emotions and abilities to regulate emotions may be related to microbial differences (Ke et al., 2023). The concept of *knowing oneself* as awareness that individuals can have a physiological response to specific situations is also a useful element to understanding the role of emotions in an overall sense of well-being. Dan Goleman (2005) describes emotions within the context of emotional intelligence. Simply stated, he suggests that an individual can "know thyself" by attaining self-awareness. However, an element of Goleman's approach to emotional intelligence is also a recognition of the importance of a "gut feeling" (p.52). Individuals may have a sense of something not being right and an inclination to avoid a situation because of that. There may be no logical explanation, but there is a perceivable internal sense.

Emotional awareness can drive behavior and performance. Marc Brackett, Director of the Yale Center for Emotional Intelligence, suggests that we can all become "emotional scientists" by acquiring the skills of recognizing, understanding, labeling, expressing, and finally regulating our emotions (2019). The elements are easy to remember because Brackett titles them collectively as RULER (Brackett, p.55). **R**ecognizing an emotion requires an individual to become aware of subtle or significant differences in one's thoughts or even body language or voice. **U**nderstanding an emotion may also be explained as becoming aware of the reason the emotion may be affecting thoughts or body language. **L**abeling the emotion involves determining a precise word for it. **E**xpressing the emotion refers to the behavior a person may exhibit in the context of others (Brackett, 2019). For example, one might express excitement differently when in a professional setting than at home with family members. And finally an ability to **r**egulate the emotion, by acquiring the skills to manage any emotion in a reasonable way, can encompass both positive and negative emotions. For example, you might shout a *WooHoo* when you learn good news while with your family, but just smile widely when you receive the same news while with colleagues.

Well-being and Flourishing

Emotions can directly affect well-being across many parameters including learning (Carroll et al., 2022b; 2021). When learning a new skill, one may feel excited, nervous, or self-conscious. Flutters with tightness or other similar sensations could be a reflection of the emotions being experienced. The sensations could begin one way and perhaps change as the physical activity continues. Success in attaining a skill may produce calmer and happier feelings, while lack of success may induce self-conscious feelings. Emotions may either play a large part in a sense of well-being or be an obstacle to a sense of well-being (Osika et al., 2022).

The concept of flourishing is very much related to a sense of well-being. The Human Flourishing Project at Harvard University's Institute for Quantitative Social Science was begun in 2016 and "…promotes human flourishing" (Human Flourishing Project, n.d.). The project cuts across many disciplines but focuses on the elements of human well-being. Factors contributing to overall well-being are inclusive of both personal qualities and diverse experiences in which individuals participate as they relate to family interactions, professional responsibilities, or educational or religious involvement. In a keynote address at the Emotional Well-Being Annual Investigator Meeting, the Director of the Human Flourishing Project explained the way in which emotional well-being fits within the concept of flourishing (VanderWeele, 2023). Flourishing refers to the broadest aspects in which an individual perceives that his or her life is good within an individual context. Well-being is a subset of flourishing. Emotional well-being is a subset within mental or psychological well-being in which a person perceives that his or her emotional state is positive.

Well-being of Teacher Candidates

Teacher candidates enrolled in higher education programs are bombarded with the new content (knowledge) of the curriculum they must master to become effective teachers and the ways in which they must teach the curriculum to their future students (skills), as well as numerous additional abilities teachers must acquire, such as classroom management, knowledge of human development, knowledge of the law as it applies to teaching, and many other professional development topics. Teacher candidates may flourish in the context of career preparation that satisfies their professional goals and may experience well-being within their total higher educational environment when they perceive it as satisfying.

However, psychological and/or emotional well-being may become more challenging as one progresses from a student who is learning to becoming a professional who must demonstrate the knowledge and skills that have been acquired. Emotions, therefore, can be a key variable within the development of teacher candidates as they progress to greater expectations of their ability to demonstrate competence in managing the needs of their students. If teacher candidates and teachers are supported in maintenance of emotional well-being, they will be more likely to provide effective teaching, manage student behavior, and attain positive student learning outcomes as well. Those outcomes, in turn, provide positive feedback to the candidate regarding their sense of overall teaching competency (Donahue-Keegan et al., 2019; Hagenhauer et al., 2015; Stafford-Brizard, 2024)

EMOTIONS AND LEARNING

Brain physiology can be involved in social, emotional, and academic development (Immordino-Yang et al., 2018). For college students and adult learners, a sense of competence is a major factor in their ability to manage the demands of a course. When new learners of any skill perceive that they know what is required and how to do it, their emotions appear calm. As a higher education professor, the author has observed that when college students make an error in understanding an assignment or the creation of a course work product, their calmness lessens. They verbalize frustration and seek immediate relief. If there is opportunity for corrective behavior for an error made while learning, a sense of control can be restored and the student can reestablish emotional calmness. When there is no opportunity for correction, feelings of panic may arise. Teacher candidates, like all college students, are more likely to persist in their education if they perceive continued success. Less success at first may elicit less desire to continue.

Feelings of Competence and Motivation

For teacher candidates, motivation can be intrinsic, such as a lifelong desire to become an educator. It can also be extrinsic, such as interest in an extended summer vacation. Motivation can be what drives continued learning but when the learning occurs over an extended time, such as in educator preparation, there can be variability in levels of motivation. Teacher candidates become aware that teachers who are responsible for a large group of students should exhibit emotional calmness in the face of challenging situations. In addition to knowledge and skills acquired during educator preparation, teacher competence is attained through confidence in navigating emotional challenges faced in the classroom. Specifically addressing the development of social-emotional and affective dispositions during educator preparation better assures that the teacher candidate will develop the emotional regulation required as a teacher (Carroll et al., 2022b; 2021; Osika et al., 2022).

Importance of the Social Context in Adult Learning Environments

A critical part of influencing a learner's sense of control within a learning situation may also lie within the context of the social environment. Although online learning is available across all disciplines and in multiple degree programs, the importance of the social environment cannot be underestimated. Even fully online higher education in any discipline is affected by the context of learning with others in what may be suggested as a learning community. The Learner Centered Principles Work Group of the American Psychological Association's Board of Educational Affairs (1997, November) suggested that "learning is influenced by social interactions, interpersonal relations, and communication with others" (p.50). It is important to note that interpersonal involvement with others and the resulting sense of belonging is facilitative of learning. A sense of belonging within the learning community can inspire learning and the absence of a feeling of belonging can become a detriment to learning. Multiple authors have addressed the importance of creating a social environment in learning and the emotional consequences for students if they experience a lack of belonging (Bickle et al., 2019; Bromer, 2021; Buelow et al., 2018; Carlisle et al., 2018; Czerkawski, 2014; Dixson, 2010; Dunlap & Lowenthal, 2014; Fetzner, 2013; Kilis & Yildirim, 2019; Ladyshewsky, 2013; Pacansky-Brock et al., 2020; Peacock & Cowan, 2019; Richardson & Lowenthal, 2017).

TEACHERS' EMOTIONS AND EMOTIONAL CHALLENGES

Teacher dispositions have been described as personal qualities or characteristics such as care, empathy, respect, and similar affective qualities as well as attitudes and beliefs. These qualities form the basis for personal behavior and relationships with others (Bradley, et al., 2020; Notar et al., 2009). As a teacher and teacher educator for decades, the author suggests that dispositions might be identified as social-emotional readiness for personal interactions with others. The author further suggests that dispositions are not a set of characteristics that can be isolated and labeled but rather a more holistic approach to human interaction. The approach can be developed and nurtured over time within an educator preparation program through experiences and crafted circumstances that encourage candidates to examine their own emotions and how they may impact social encounters with their students.

In the State of the American Teacher Survey (Doan et al., 2023), feedback on multiple parameters of teaching were provided by licensed teachers. The responses were examined, including reports of well-being as well as overall working conditions. The working conditions included salary, hours worked, and administrative support.

The five elements of teacher well-being were identified from data in the survey as job-related stress, coping with the stress, symptoms of depression, burnout, and lack of resilience. Stress is inherent in many professions, but teaching is especially vulnerable to feelings of stress and burnout. A recent Pew Research survey conducted in November 2023 (Lin et al., 2024) found that a large percentage of the 2531 K-12 public school teachers who responded to the survey expressed concerns regarding gun violence within their own schools and classrooms. 41% said they were somewhat worried; 11% indicated that they were very worried; and 4% reported being very concerned. This data suggests that current teachers are experiencing a lack of emotional calmness within their professional situations.

Classroom Management Challenges

One of the most challenging aspects of becoming a teacher is classroom management (Greenberg et al., 2014). Teacher candidates frequently report classroom management as not only their largest concern regarding their competency as a teacher, but also the area in which they feel the least experienced and capable. Although teacher candidates feel and express warm and loving feelings toward their students, they are often challenged by disruptive student behavior. The affection, kindness, and patience that new teachers report having toward their students may give way during episodes of student behavior challenges to feelings of frustration. Effective classroom management is implemented when both student and teacher can remain calm. A student who may become agitated needs a teacher who doesn't. The key to a teacher remaining calm is knowing he or she perceives negative or intense emotions and has the social-emotional skill to manage his or her own emotions in the face of challenging student behavior (Hagenhaur et al., 2015; Kanbur & Kirikkaleli, 2023)

Compassion Fatigue

In a caring profession similar to mental health providers, teachers can experience a reduced ability to respond empathetically to students. When encounters with students become emotionally intense and exhausting, a teacher may experience what is identified as compassion fatigue (Oberg et al., 2023; Woolcot et al., 2023). Secondary stress can emerge when a teacher experiences in his or her way the stress observed in students (Smith, 2021). What can evolve from the secondary stress is teacher fatigue in managing not only the students' emotions but their own emotions as well. It can be felt when teachers become aware of some expression of stress exhibited by students (Cieslak et al., 2014). Students who themselves may be stressed need a teacher who can provide stability and an ongoing alternative environment to the stress they are experiencing (Post et al., 2020), yet educator preparation does not traditionally include any guidance or instruction on managing the needs of students who may have experienced or are experiencing acute or chronic trauma.

Teacher Burnout

Burnout can occur when teachers experience ongoing stress over time and want to leave the profession (Carroll et al., 2022; 2021; Christian-Brandt et al., 2020). The State of the American Teacher Survey (Doan et al., 2023) also addressed teacher decisions to leave the profession. A teacher candidate exits a preparation program with eagerness to engage with students, along with expressions of fondness for both the profession and for students, but also reflects feelings of stress and burnout. The 2nd Annual Merrimack Teacher Survey (2023) reported that 35% of survey respondents indicated that they are fairly or very likely to leave the profession within the next two years. Although this data suggests improvement in teacher attrition since immediately after the pandemic, it is still troubling.

Figure 1. Absence of social emotional competencies

CURRENT DESIGN PRACTICES IN TEACHER PREPARATION

Similar to the preparation of nurses, physicians, social workers, or other caring professions in which direct interaction with individuals and/or families is a component, a teacher candidate's ability to interact effectively with others is a required competency. A physician's ability to interact with patients is sometimes identified as bedside manner. A teacher's ability to interact with colleagues as well as their students and their students' families is identified as dispositions.

Knowledge, Skills, and Dispositions

The development of a teacher candidate's knowledge, skills, and dispositions to work closely with children and their families is the focus and goal of educator preparation. Knowledge of curriculum that will be taught to future K-12 students as well as topics such as child development, legal issues regarding teaching, and other topics can be acquired through specific coursework. Skill in teaching students can be developed through opportunities to model and practice the skills when placed in a K-12 classroom with an experienced mentor teacher and provided opportunities to "practice" the teaching skills that have first been observed.

Dispositions are a less tangible and more challenging component to even identify, much less evaluate in teacher candidates. The Interstate New Teacher Assessment and Support Consortium (INTASC) Model Core Teaching Standards is a guide for educator preparation providers (Council of Chief State Officers, April 2013). Within its framework is a description of dispositions as… *"the habits of professional action and moral commitments that underlie an educator's performance…"* The INTASC standards undergird educator preparation programs and notable within the category of the learner and learning Standard #3, Learner Environment, a need for teacher candidates is to develop the ability to "…*work[s] with others to create environments that support individual and collaborative learning, and that encourage positive social interaction, active engagement in learning, and self motivation…"*

The National Board for Professional Teaching Standards (NBPTS, n.d.), developed to recognize accomplished educators and revised in 2016, also includes teacher dispositions as a component of skilled teachers. The core propositions within the NBPTS include a statement that teachers know how to motivate students and engage them in learning, and further notes that *"accomplished teachers maintain an open mind and a balanced perspective…"* In educator preparation, these affective skills should be included as teacher dispositions.

DESIGN PRACTICES TO SUPPORT THE EMOTIONAL WELL-BEING OF TEACHERS DURING EDUCATOR PREPARATION

Attaining more desirable social-emotional characteristics such as adaptability, resilience, and regulation can be a strategy for improved teacher well-being in managing the daily stressors of teaching and the acute stressors caused by unique circumstances such as the pandemic. Teacher candidates may enter a program with minimal evidence of adaptability and resilience because the need to maintain them has not been experienced. When an expectation of these characteristics is built into educator preparation, with strategies embedded that provide opportunities for understanding and experiencing adaptability and resilience, candidates may acquire enhanced social-emotional and affective competencies (Ayguin & Alemdar, 2022; Bleakley et.al, 2020; Bradley et al., 2020; Woolcott et.al., 2023).

It is understandable that there may be limited time to provide opportunities to acquire the social-emotional, affective elements of dispositions during educator preparation, but there are also obstacles beyond time limitations. In a study conducted by Koludrovic & Mrsic (2022), the researchers found that teacher candidates are aware of the importance of the need for social-emotional and affective competencies but are uncertain that they adequately have developed those dispositions. Candidates are further cognizant that those competencies may not simply exist upon completion of an educator preparation program because they were not addressed in that program (Blad, 2017). Researchers have suggested that systematic program design practices addressing the development of social-emotional and affective competencies is both feasible and needed within educator preparation (Brackett & Cipriano, 2020).

Emotional Literacy

There is a variety of literacies to be attained by teacher candidates, such as technological literacy, information literacy, digital literacy, and others. Emotional literacy is often not addressed. It can be challenging to provide a specific description of emotions, but emotional literacy has been described as the ability to understand one's own emotions both in the moment and predictively in the future. It is a vital teacher disposition as it can directly relate to a teacher's effectiveness in managing student behavior (Bellochi, 2018; Bleakley et al, 2020; Buric et. al., 2020; Woolcott et al., 2023). The usefulness of a teacher's skill in not only identifying but also understanding his or her own emotions has not been well supported in educator preparation, yet it is a skill that can directly affect not only the well-being of students but also the teacher's ability to perceive success and satisfaction as a professional.

Emotional Literacy Coupled with Reflective Practice

The concept of emotional literacy as a desired teacher competency is gaining favor (Ayguin & Alemdar, 2022; Woolcott et al.,2023) and blends well with an established practice of reflection as a useful teacher practice. Reflection, or the ongoing process of retrospective thinking about one's teaching, is a way to enhance instructional effectiveness with students. Encouraging teacher candidates to become reflective practitioners is often a cornerstone of an education preparation program's conceptual framework and a practice encouraged throughout. When teachers can reflect on teaching or other situations they have experienced with students, they can refine the ability toidentify their own behaviors. Reflective practice can become a key element in the development of emotional literacy (Ayguin & Alemdar, 2020; Bleakley at al., 2020; Woolcott et al., 2023). An ability to attune to one's own emotional states during the experience becomes a vital element in developing emotional regulation and resilience, very much in sync with the concept of emotional intelligence suggested by Goleman (2005). A teacher candidate in the author's program shared this insight during one of the courses taught by the author that included content related to the importance of social-emotional learning within K-12 teaching.

- *Because every student comes to school with a different background, culture, and home life, we need to model healthy leadership and emotional regulation ourselves.*

Affective and Social-emotional Competencies

Social-emotional competencies are described by the Collaborative for Academic, Social, and Emotional Learning (CASEL) as consisting of five areas, the CASEL "wheel" puts social and emotional learning at the center surrounded by five areas of competence with self-awareness, self-management, social awareness, relationship skills, and responsible decision making (CASEL, n.d.). The skills emerge in childhood and extend through adult years. Although the focus of this chapter is on adult teacher candidates, the linkage between social-emotional competencies within teachers and child well-being is vividly apparent.

To be effective in teaching students, one must exhibit all five elements of social-emotional competence, not only to model the characteristics but also to maintain the personal equilibrium needed to manage the stressors inherent within the daily demands of teaching and the surprise events that can arise. The clearest example of unanticipated stressors within the profession of teaching was seen during the pandemic. Teachers were required to quickly learn how to provide online learning as well as manage their own personal needs related to the pandemic. The data reflected in the recent survey of teachers (Doan et al., 2023; Merrimack College, 2023) suggest that stressors remain present within the profession of teaching.

SOLUTIONS AND RECOMMENDATIONS

A solution to the issue of teacher burnout and the desire to leave the profession of teaching reported within recent surveys may lie within a modification of educator preparation design practices. The fundamentals of educator preparation identified as knowledge, skills, and dispositions are vital to the creation of an effective teacher candidate. However, it's not a curriculum that is too challenging to teach or the skills with which to teach it that causes a teacher to leave the profession; it is the emotional feelings teachers acquire that they cannot manage once in the classroom and experiencing the challenges of student behavior (Doan et al., 2023; Lin et al., 2024).

Mitigating Future Burnout

We have learned that a sense of overall well-being can be acquired and can also be a mitigating element for situations that can lead to burnout (Carroll et al, 2022a; 2021; Ormiston, 2022), yet educator preparation programs have been slow to include more understanding of and experience with social-emotional learning. The Center on the Developing Child (n.d.) is highly focused on the role of Adverse Childhood Experiences (ACES) and the toxic stress that can affect K-12 students' behavior. Embedding social-emotional learning in the face of experiences that might be displayed by students suggests a need for improved educator preparation design practices.

Improving Design Practices in Educator Preparation

The characteristics reported as required for effective teaching that don't result in teacher burnout include social-emotional, affective dispositions. Most educator preparation programs lack opportunities for candidates to become aware of emotions that may arise during classroom encounters. It is time for educator preparation programs to acknowledge their responsibility in guiding teacher candidates in acquiring the emotional regulation to manage student behavior and develop the emotional resilience to address challenging student behavior that may occur within any classroom. It can be described as building teacher resilience (Mansfield et al., 2016) or creating social-emotional competencies (Carroll et al.,2022; Demedio-Caston, 2019; Jennings, 2011), but it must be built into a program's framework. It is important to recognize the importance of social-emotional factors in learning and to embed the affective aspects of teaching in educator preparation courses and other experiences in person or online.

Figure 2. Presence of social emotional competencies

[Figure: Central circle "presence of social emotional competencies" with four surrounding circles: "effective classroom management" (top), "emotional co-regulation" (right), "emotional well-being" (bottom), "more emotional resilience" (left)]

Hesitancy within Educator Preparation Programs to Include Social-Emotional Competencies as Dispositions

Why might an educator preparation program not adequately embed greater emphasis on social-emotional competencies? There are processes within teacher education that can impact change. Programs emerge from a theoretical framework developed by the College of Education; alterations to that framework would take a great deal of effort and time. In addition, state licensure agencies affect what programs can or must do to maintain their ability to assure candidate licensure within the state. There are also multiple stakeholders who impact the nature of an educator preparation program.

Teacher educators who are included as faculty often bring their own perspectives regarding educator preparation based on their experiences. School-based stakeholders such as supervising teachers, in whose classroom candidates are placed for field experiences, play a large role in the preparation of candidates and bring their own perspectives to the supervisor-candidate relationship. Candidates themselves, especially non-traditional students who comprise a large component of educator preparation programs, can bring their own expectations to their anticipated preparation. Programs may exhibit hesitancy to change programmatic features for any of the above factors. However, hesitancy should not remain immutable. Having been a teacher educator for 18 years, the author provides multiple suggestions for changes in design practices.

Suggestion 1: Start With a Positive Emotional Environment in Coursework

An instructor can set the stage for enhancing teacher self-efficacy through an awareness of the emotional components discussed earlier regarding feelings of competence within educator preparation courses. By creating a less harsh and punitive approach to course management and also modeling a more understanding approach to student confusions, submission delays, or other issues that may interfere with student success, teacher educators can create the emotional environment desirable in a K-12 classroom. Onsite courses can readily provide a positive emotional environment because of the personal interaction among all participants.

Creating a positive emotional environment can be more challenging in an online program in which courses may be asynchronously provided. Bromer (2022) provided several guiding principles for creating a caring online course environment. These principles can help maintain student emotional equilibrium:

- Create and maintain an organized and engaging learning environment to encourage student independence and feelings of competence
- Provide clear course expectations that can be easily understood by students
- Maintain online courtesy among all participants to encourage a sense of belonging
- Assure instructor attention to student concerns by answering all questions promptly and as often as it takes for understanding by students
- Communicate often through the use of ice-breakers in a course, instructor participation in discussions, and visibility and availability within a course
- Include back-channel communication, such as texts, emails, and phone calls outside of the course, if the instructor is willing

The most important tip is to create at the start and maintain a personal overview that kindness and compassion matter. It has been reported that an environment that reflects kindness can encourage feelings of belonging (Childers, n.d.; Kilis & Yildirim, 2019; Revak, 2020).

There are additional suggestions for university teachers provided by Nugent et al. (2019) that include similar approaches to students within a course. They include helpful feedback that can move a lack of success on a body of work to a successful achievement and flexibility in assignments and assessments by recognizing learning misunderstandings and providing an opportunity to correct them. Most importantly, it is suggested that a conversation with students regarding their own competencies and the variability of their learning can enhance a student's emotional resilience.

A growth mindset stance in which there is a belief that ability is not fixed and improvements can be acquired through further learning and efforts can be helpful in avoiding emotional stress by encouraging the student to believe that learning may not have occurred "yet" but it doesn't mean it won't occur at all (Armstrong, 2019; Carroll, 2022b). A recent study reinforced the role of an instructor's own belief in a growth mindset as a factor in a student's emotional well-being (Canning et al., 2024).

Beyond assuring that a supportive learning environment is created and maintained in all educator preparation program courses, there are also core practices that undergird the skills needed to effectively support learner needs (Grossman & Fraefel, 2024). The approach to the preparation of teachers is practice-based and can consist of high-impact core practices included within college programs across all disciplines that are recognized as effective strategies for learning (Rodriguez, 2019). Some practices such as internships are already incorporated in educator preparation and others such as the creation of learning communities can be readily included.

Suggestion 2: Create a Framework of SEL

Educator preparation programs must include social-emotional learning (Stoltzfus, 2017). Some teacher educators in Massachusetts have gathered to develop an approach to integrate SEL and culturally responsive teaching (CRT) into their program frameworks (Donahue-Keegan et al., 2019). The inclusion of SEL is based on a perceived absence of adequate focus on the needs of teacher candidates for emotional preparedness for the stressors of teaching – broadly in the development of emotional resilience and specifically in the ability to provide effective classroom management. The authors of the study refer to emotional agility as a teacher's ability to avoid emotional exhaustion and be able to oversee and sustain engaging yet challenging student learning.

The Center for Reaching and Teaching the Whole Child (n.d.) provides resources for teachers to include the social and emotional aspects of teaching into their professional practices (Markowitz & Bufford, 2020). The Center provides a framework that includes adult social-emotional competencies and teaching practices. Students within the author's program have noted the importance of the social and emotional aspects of teaching while discussing the topic within a course focused on social-emotional learning.

- *The social and emotional needs of teachers and students is a critical issue because a lot of teachers aren't qualified to help students navigate through their social and emotional needs. Teachers are dealing with so much now that they themselves are struggling emotionally. Just as students need teachers to help them with their social and emotional needs, teachers need the same.*
- *Teachers and students are in need of SEL and positive psychology training. Especially teachers because our job can be mentally challenging. By having this training it can allow teachers to better understand how to properly manage their classroom.*

Suggestion 3: Incorporate SEL Into Courses and Field Experiences

A study was completed with online students in an educator preparation program within a course described as focused on SEL (Lapidot-Lefler, 2022). The course specifically addressed the needs of a K-12 learner as they relate to the five components of social-emotional learning: self-awareness, self-management, social awareness, managing relationships, and responsible decision making (Lapidot-Lefler, 2022).

Students were encouraged to plan and apply practices that reflect SEL components. The study suggested overall positive teacher candidate responses and the author of the study confirmed the importance of social presence in online instruction as a way to enhance an online learner's sense of well-being.

Systematic integration of social-emotional learning within field experiences is a simple and natural way to incorporate a focus on social-emotional and affective competencies (Lapidot-Lefler, 2022; McCarthy, 2021). Curriculum methods courses often are completed at the same time as teacher candidate placement in a K-12 classroom for direct classroom experience with students of the same ages as they will be teaching in the future. In a study completed by McCarthy (2021) with onsite college students, teacher candidates in curriculum methods courses were instructed to complete assignments related to social-emotional learning (SEL) competencies in conjunction with their classroom placement. Candidates completed a questionnaire at the end of the course and classroom placement, and rated the SEL assignments as useful and beneficial.

Suggestion 4: Include Applied Psychology Courses

Positive or applied psychology is a desirable component of educator preparation should be an element of educator preparation; a focus on well-being of teacher candidates can better prepare them to oversee the well-being of their future students (Seligman, et al., 2018; White, 2016). The educator preparation program in which the author taught includes a course in Psychology at both undergraduate and graduate levels of initial certification as a desirable component of educator preparation. The undergraduate Bachelor of Science degree program includes a required course in Developmental Psychology. The graduate Master of Arts in Teaching degree program includes a course in Applied Educational Psychology. Each course embeds a focus on knowing, understanding, and applying the principles of positive psychology to teaching. Students completing an Applied Psychology course noted its usefulness in educator preparation.

- *I am thankful and appreciative of what I have learned in regards to the psychology component of education. We set the tone for our students and our behavior should model and reflect commitment, consistency, and kindness.*
- *Students and teachers are both in need of SEL and positive psychology training.*

Suggestion 5: Create New Teacher Communities Focused on SEL

The creation of learning communities within the profession of teaching is not a new concept. Bromer (2022) noted the importance of a community of inquiry within which members share common ideas and a sense of belonging is developed. Collaboration between educator preparation programs and the schools into which their graduates are placed is also a common practice. Educator preparation programs are often called upon to support the needs of new teachers through an induction process. A community for new teachers with a specific focus of addressing social-emotional learning is both feasible and desirable (Flushman et al., 2021). Continuing to apply SEL practices within educator preparation through both coursework and field experiences into the initial first-year teacher experience can be a natural process.

Figure 3. Design practices framework

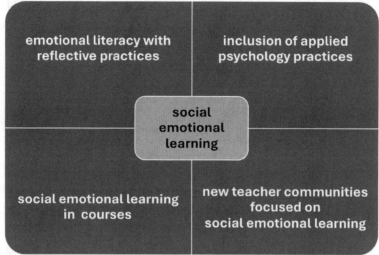

FUTURE DIRECTIONS

Teachers may face many of the same challenges as those in the field of mental health. Teachers are in a caring profession, as are psychologists and therapists. The pandemic brought many emotional stressors to families and children that may still be evident today. The American Psychological Association reported in its 2023 Trends Report that child mental health is in a crisis (Abrams, 2023). Beyond the pandemic, there still exist other stressors affecting children such as bullying, social media, school violence, and other situations and events that can affect their behavior, yet educator preparation programs are not focused on this element of preparation. Principles of positive psychology have given way to the concept of positive education, explained as education for both traditional skills and broader well-being (Seligman et al., 2009). Future research to improve educator preparation programs through design practices inclusive of candidate social-emotional competencies might include positive education strategies that could be helpful to teacher candidates.

Address Teacher Self-care

A focus on self-care as a vital practice for teachers should be a priority, just as reflection is at the core of educator preparation. Bromer (2022) noted that "teachers need to be aware of their own needs for self care…". Examples of self-care can be as simple as discussions in introductory Education Foundations courses as or as unique as the inclusion of a mindfulness program (Carroll, 2022b). Realistic educator preparation must include discussions of teacher burnout with an equal focus on mitigating the stressors that precede burnout. The following comment from a teacher candidate was made during an online discussion on teacher burnout.

- *What I need in teaching is to remember to have self-compassion. To put my best foot forward each day, focusing my attention on my student's needs as well as staying in tune with my own, I find being more mindful of moments no matter how small they are brings me more joy and that joy helps relieve stress.*

Teach Trauma-informed practices

Educator preparation courses do not include instruction or guidance in trauma-informed practices. Candidates may feel that it is their role to support students experiencing stressful environments, whether inside school such as bullying, or outside school such as abuse at home, but they don't feel adequately prepared to do so. New teachers report that explanations of trauma and how it can affect children and ways to intervene are not a significant component of educator preparation (L'Estrange & Howard, 2022). Teacher candidates who have developed social-emotional affective competencies can better understand their own emotional responses to student behavior and respond to students' emotions that are reflected in the student's behavior but whose etiology may lie in trauma (L'Estrange & Howard et al.; Koslouski, 2022).

Being a trauma-informed and prepared teacher is a desirable characteristic in the current post-pandemic environment. In addition to mitigating compassion fatigue and reducing burnout, it can enhance teacher candidates' sense of competence and well-being (Bailey, 2022; Deaton et al, 2022; L'Estrange & Howard, 2022; Katz, et al.,2020; Koslouski, 2022; Stokes et al., 2023). The Center on the Developing Child (n.d.) is highly focused on the role of Adverse Childhood Experiences (ACES) and toxic stress that can exhibit itself in K-12 students' behavior. Teacher candidates need to become aware of the brain connection to trauma and how they can properly intervene. As already suggested, teacher candidates' own social-emotional development can prepare them more fully to understand and address their students' behavior.

The concept of emotional co-regulation, or simply the ability of a teacher to identify a child's distress, and through their own social-emotional strength, not acquire the child's level of stress while intervening, is vital for teachers in creating a positive classroom environment. For children experiencing ACES or toxic stress, the proper intervention is crucial (Desautels, 2019). The concept of emotional co-regulation can be included in educator preparation courses and may actually enhance a teacher candidate's self-efficacy regarding classroom climate and behavior management. Bailey (2022) suggests a simple strategy identified as CHILL, an acronym for **C**alm down, **H**ear yourself breathe, **I**nvestigate your condition, **L**et yourself know your condition, and **L**et others know your condition. Stokes et al.(2023) notes that... *innovation must build upon findings well established in the trauma-informed literatures.*

CONCLUSION

Educator preparation has traditionally focused on knowledge, skills, and dispositions. Teacher candidates must be prepared with knowledge of the curriculum and curriculum standards related to the students they will teach. Teacher candidates must also be well-equipped with a range of skills to teach the curriculum they have been assigned to teach. It is impossible to teach effectively without knowledge and skills. It is equally impossible to teach effectively without the appropriate teacher dispositions, as have been described in the chapter.

Traditionally, dispositions have not focused on social and more importantly emotional competencies. Educator preparation programs address the topic of effective classroom management without fully exploring the emotional feelings they may arouse in a new teacher. The pandemic, although a few years ago, highlights how both students and teachers can be emotionally affected by sudden and acute environmental changes.

It is time to recognize that the affective aspects of dispositions are vital to not only intentional and successful teaching, but also to the maintenance of a teaching force that does not become overwhelmed by the stressors of a classroom. Suggestions have been included to provide ways to encourage more social and emotional self-awareness in teacher candidates. With enhanced self-awareness, growth of social-emotional skills and affective dispositions desirable for teaching can be both encouraged and increased. The outcome can be a reduction in the teacher burnout that currently creates a challenge in maintaining a consistent and gratified K-12 teaching force.

REFERENCES

Abrams, Z. (2023, January 1). Kids' mental health is in crisis: Here's what psychologists are doing to help. *American Psychological Association, 54*(1). https://www.apa.org/monitor/2023/01/trends-improving-youth-mental-health

Armstrong, K. (2019, October 29). Carol Dweck on how growth mindset can bear fruit in the classroom. *Association for Psychological Science.* https://www.psychologicalscience.org/observer/dweck-growth-mindsets

Ayguin, H. E., & Alemdar, M. (2022). Examining the social-emotional skills of pre-service teachers in the context of emotional literacy skills and social-emotional competency. *International Innovative Education Researcher, 2*(2), 206–240.

Bailey, S. (2022). Teacher-preparation programs and trauma-informed teaching practices: Getting students to CHILL. *Current Issues in Education (Tempe, Ariz.), 23*(2). Advance online publication. DOI: 10.14507/cie.vol23.iss3.2057

Beard, K. S., Vakil, J. B., Chao, T., & Hilty, C. D. (2021). Time for change: Understanding teacher social-emotional learning supports for anti-racism and student well-being during COVID-19, and beyond. *Education and Urban Society*, 1–19. DOI: 10.1177/00131245211062527

Bellocchi, A. (2018). Early career science teachers' experiences of social bonds and emotion management. *Journal of Research in Science Teaching, 56*(3), 322–347. DOI: 10.1002/tea.21520

Bickle, M. C., Rucker, R. D., & Burnsed, K. A. (2019). Online learning: Examination of attributes that promote student satisfaction. *Online Journal of Distance Learning Administration, 22*(1). https://www.westga.edu/~distance/ojdla/spring221/bickle_rucker_burnsed221.html

Blad, E. (2017, April 4). Teacher prep slow to embrace social-emotional learning. *Education Week.* https://www.edweek.org/leadership/teacher-prep-slow-to-embrace-social-emotional-learning/2017/04

Bleakley, J., Woolcott, G., Yeigh, T., & Whannell, R. (2020). Reflecting on emotions during teaching: Developing affective-reflective skills in novice teachers using a novel critical moments protocol. *The Australian Journal of Teacher Education, 45*(10), 55–72. Advance online publication. DOI: 10.14221/ajte.2020v45n10.4

Brackett, M. (2019). *Permission to Feel: The Power of Emotional Intelligence to Achieve Well-Being and Success.* Celadon Books.

Brackett, M., & Cipriano, C. (2020, April 7). Teachers are anxious and overwhelmed. They need SEL now more than ever. *EdSurge*. https://www.edsurge.com/news/2020-04-07-teachers-are-anxious-and-overwhelmed-they-need-sel-now-more-than-ever

Bradley, E., Isaac, P., & King, J. (2020). Assessment of pre-service teacher dispositions. *Excelsior (Oneonta, N.Y.)*, 13(1), 50–62. DOI: 10.14305/jn.19440413.2020.13.1.03

Bromer, B. L. (2021). Social presence in an online learning environment. In Crawford, C. M., & Simons, M. A. (Eds.), *eLearning engagement in a transformative social learning environment*. IGI Global., DOI: 10.4018/978-1-7998-6956-6.ch001

Bromer, B. L., & Deeb, A. M. D. (2022). Transformations in K-12 teaching: Using what was learned during the pandemic. In Bromer, B. L., & Crawford, C. M. (Eds.), *Handbook of research on learner-centered approaches to teaching in an age of transformational change*. IGI Global., DOI: 10.4018/978-1-6684-4240-1.ch004

Buelow, J. R., Barry, T., & Rich, L. E. (2018). Supporting learning engagement with online students. *Online Learning : the Official Journal of the Online Learning Consortium*, 22(4), 313–240. DOI: 10.24059/olj.v22i4.1384

Buric, I., Sliskovic, A., & Soric, I. (2020). Teachers' emotions and self-efficacy: A test of reciprocal relations. *Frontiers in Psychology*, 11, 1650. Advance online publication. DOI: 10.3389/fpsyg.2020.01650 PMID: 32982815

Canning, E.A., White, M. & Davis, W.B. (2024) Growth mindset messages from instructors improve academic performance among first-generation college students. *Life Sciences Education, 23* (2).

Carlisle, K. L., Carlisle, R., Ricks, S. A., & Mylroie, R. (2018). Is my instructor a robot? Creative Methods for creating social presence in online human service education. *Journal of Human Services*, 38(1), 61–73.

Carroll, A., Flynn, L., O'Connor, E. S., Forrest, K., Bower, J., Fynes-Clinton, S., York, A., & Ziaea, M. (2021). In their words: Listening to teachers' perceptions about stress in the workplace and how to address it. *Asia-Pacific Journal of Teacher Education*, 49(4), 420–434. Advance online publication. DOI: 10.1080/1359866X.2020.1789914

Carroll, A., Forrest, K., Sanders-O'Connor, E., Flynn, L., Bower, J. M., Fynes-Clinton, S., York, A., & Ziael, M. (2022a). Teacher stress and burnout in Australia: Examining the role of intrapersonal and environmental factors. *Social Psychology of Education*, 25(2-3), 441–469. Advance online publication. DOI: 10.1007/s11218-022-09686-7 PMID: 35233183

Carroll, A., Hepburn, S., & Bower, J. (2022b). Mindful practices for teachers: Relieving stress and enhancing positive mindsets. *Frontiers in Education*, 7, 954098. Advance online publication. DOI: 10.3389/feduc.2022.954098

Center for Reaching and Teaching the Whole Child. (n.d.) *Anchor competencies framework*. https://crtwc.org/

Center on the Developing Child. (n.d.). *Toxic stress*. https://developingchild.harvard.edu/science/key-concepts/toxic-stress/

Childers, E. (n.d.). *7 ways to show presence and compassion in online spaces.* https://todayslearner.cengage.com/7-ways-to-show-presence-and-compassion-in-online-spaces/

Christian-Brandt, A. S., Santacrose, D. E., & Barnett, M. L. (2020). In the trauma-informed care trenches: Teacher compassion satisfaction, secondary traumatic stress, burnout, and intent to leave education within underserved elementary schools. *Child Abuse & Neglect*, 110, 110. DOI: 10.1016/j.chiabu.2020.104437 PMID: 32151429

Cieslak, R., Shoji, K., Douglas, A., Melville, E., Luszczynska, A., & Benight, C. C. (2014). A meta-analysis of the relationship between job burnout and secondary traumatic stress among workers with indirect exposure to trauma. *Psychological Services*, 11(1), 75–86. DOI: 10.1037/a0033798 PMID: 23937082

Collaborative for Academic, Social, and Emotional Learning (n.d.). *What is the CASEL framework?* https://casel.org/fundamentals-of-sel/what-is-the-casel-framework/

Council of Chief State Officers. (2013, April). *INTASC model core teaching standards and learning progressions for teachers*. https://ccsso.org/sites/default/files/2017-12/2013_INTASC_Learning_Progressions_for_Teachers.pdf

Czercawski, B. C. (2014). Designing deeper learning experiences for online instruction. *Journal of Interactive Online Learning*, 13(2), 29–40.

Deaton, J. D., Ohrt, J. H., Linich, K., Wymer, B., Toomey, M., Lewis, O., Guest, J. D., & Newton, T. (2022). Teachers' experience with K-12 students' mental health. *Psychology in the Schools*, 59(5), 932–949. DOI: 10.1002/pits.22658

Demidio-Caston, M. (2019). Addressing social, emotional development, and resilience at the heart of teacher education. *Teacher Education Quarterly*.

Desaultels, L. (2019, October 15). The role of emotion co-regulation in discipline. *Edutopia*.

https://www.edutopia.org/article/role-emotion-co-regulation-discipline/#:~:text=If%20I'm%20the%20teacher,I%20act%20on%20that%20discipline

Dixson, M. D. (2010). Creating effective student engagement in online courses: What do students find engaging? *The Journal of Scholarship of Teaching and Learning*, 10(2), 1–13.

Doan, S., Steiner, E. D., & Woo, A. (2023). *State of the American teacher survey*. RAND Corporation., DOI: 10.7249/RRA1108-7

Donahue-Keegan, D., Villegas-Reimers, E., & Cressey, J. M. (2019). Integrating social-emotional learning and culturally responsive teaching in teacher education preparation programs: The Massachusetts experience so far. *Teacher Education Quarterly*, 46(4), 150–168.

Dunlap, J. C., & Lowenthal, P. R. (2014). The power of presence: Our quest for the right mix of social presence in online courses. In Pina, A. A., & Mizell, A. P. (Eds.), *Real life distance education: Case studies in practice*.

Fetzner, M. (2013). What do unsuccessful online students want us to know? *Online Learning : the Official Journal of the Online Learning Consortium*, 17(1), 1–27. DOI: 10.24059/olj.v17i1.319

Flushman, T., Guise, M., & Hegg, S. (2021). Partnership to support the social and emotional learning of teachers: A new teacher learning community. *Teacher Education Quarterly*, 48(3), 87–105.

Gendron, B. (2019). Emotional capital, positive psychology, and active learning and mindful teaching. *New Directions for Teaching and Learning*, 2019(160), 63–76. Advance online publication. DOI: 10.1002/tl.20365

Goleman, D. (2005). *Emotional intelligence: Why it can matter more than IQ*. Bantam Dell.

Greenburg, J., Putman, H., & Walsh, K. (2014). *Training our future teachers: Classroom management, Revised 2014*. National Council on Teacher Quality.

Grossman, P., & Fraefel, U. (2024). *Core practices in teacher education: A global perspective*. Harvard Education Press.

Hagenhauer, G. (2015). Teacher emotions in the classroom: Associations with students' engagement, classroom discipline and the interpersonal teacher-student relationship. *European Journal of Psychology of Education*, 30(4), 385–403. DOI: 10.1007/s10212-015-0250-0

Immordino Yang, M. H., Darling-Hammond, L., & Krone, C. (2018). *The brain basis for integrating social, emotional, and academic development: How emotions and social development drive learning*. Aspen Institute.

Jennings, P. A. (2011). Promoting teachers' social and emotional competencies to support performance and reduce burnout. In Cohan, A., & Honigsfield, A. (Eds.), *Breaking the Mold of Preservice and Inservice Teacher Education: Innovative and Successful Practices for the Twenty-first Century*. Rowman & Littlefield.

Kanbur, O., & Kirikkaleli, N. O. (2023). Interaction between teachers' emotional intelligence and classroom management. *Perspectives in Education*, 41(2), 3–15. Advance online publication. DOI: 10.38140/pie.v41i2.6847

Katz, D., Mahfouz, J., & Romas, S. (2020). Creating a foundation of well-being for teachers and students starts with SEL curriculum in teacher education programs. *Northwest Journal of Teacher Education*, 15(2), 1–12. DOI: 10.15760/nwjte.2020.15.2.5

Ke, S., Guimond, A., Tworoger, S. S., Chan, A. T., Liu, Y., & Kunzansky, L. D. (2023). Gut feelings: Associations of emotions and emotional regulation with the gut microbiome in women. *Psychological Medicine*, 53(15), 7151–7160. Advance online publication. DOI: 10.1017/S0033291723000612 PMID: 36942524

Kilis, S., & Yildirim, Z. (2019). Posting patterns of students' social presence, cognitive presence and teaching presence in online learning. *Online Learning : the Official Journal of the Online Learning Consortium*, 23(2), 179–195. DOI: 10.24059/olj.v23i2.1460

Koludrovic, M. K., & Mrsic, A. (2022). The attitudes of initial teacher education students toward teacher social emotional competence. *Ekonomska Istrazivanja*, 33(1), 4113–4127. DOI: 10.1080/1331677X.2021.2010114

Koslouski, J. B., & Chafouleas, S. M. (2022). Key consideration in delivering trauma-informed professional learning for educators. *Frontiers in Education*, 7, 853020. Advance online publication. DOI: 10.3389/feduc.2022.853020

L'Estrange, L., & Howard, J. (2022). Trauma-informed initial teacher education training: A necessary step in a system-wide response to addressing childhood trauma. *Frontiers in Education*, 7, 929582. Advance online publication. DOI: 10.3389/feduc.2022.929582

Ladyshewsky, R. K. (2013). Instructor presence in online courses and student satisfaction. *International Journal for the Scholarship of Teaching and Learning*, 7(1), 1–23. DOI: 10.20429/ijsotl.2013.070113

Lapidot-Lefler, N. (2022). Promoting the use of social-emotional learning in online teaching. *The International Journal of Emotional Education*, 14(2), 19–35. DOI: 10.56300/HSZP5315

Learner Centered Principles Work Group of the American Psychological Association's Board of Educational Affairs. (1997, November). *Learner-centered psychological principles: A framework for school reform and redesign*. Washington, DC: American Psychological Association.

Lin, L., Parker, K., & Horowitz, M. (2024, April 4). *What's it like to be a teacher in America today?* Pew Research Center. https://www.pewresearch.org/social-trends/2024/04/04/whats-it-like-to-be-a-teacher-in-america-today/

Mansfield, C., Beltman, S., Broadley, T., & Weatherby-Fell, N. (2016). Building resilience in teacher education: An evidence informed framework. *Teaching and Teacher Education*, 54, 77–87. Advance online publication. DOI: 10.1016/j.tate.2015.11.016

Markowitz, N. L., & Bouffard, S. M. (2020). *Teaching with a social, emotional, and cultural lens: A framework for educators and teacher educators*. Harvard Education Press.

McCarthy, D. (2021). Adding social-emotional awareness to teacher education field experiences. *Teacher Educator*, 56(3), 287–304. DOI: 10.1080/08878730.2021.1890291

Merrimack College: EdWeek Research Center (2023). *2nd annual Merrimack College teacher survey: Is teacher morale on the rise?* https://www.merrimack.edu/academics/education-and-social-policy/about/merrimack-college-teacher-survey/

National Board for Professional Teaching Standards. (n.d.). *National board certification overview*. https://www.nbpts.org/certification/overview/

Nenonene, R. L., Gallagher, C. E., Kelly, M. K., & Collopy, R. M. B. (2019). Challenges and opportunities of infusing social, emotional, and cultural competencies into teacher preparation: One program's story. *Teacher Education Quarterly*, 46(4), 92–115.

Notar, C. E., Riley, G. W., Taylor, P. W., Thornberg, R. A., & Cargille, R. L. (2009). Dispositions: Ability and assessment. *International Journal of Education*, 1(1). Advance online publication. DOI: 10.5296/ije.v1i1.133

Nugent, A., Lodge, J. M., Carroll, A., Bagraith, R., MacMahon, S., Matthews, K. E., & Sah, P. (2019). *Higher Education Learning Framework: An evidence-informed model for university learning*. The University of Queensland.

Oberg, G., Carroll, A., & Macmahon, S. (2023). Compassion fatigue and secondary traumatic stress in teachers: How they contribute to burnout and how they are related to trauma-awareness. *Frontiers in Education*, 8, 1128618. Advance online publication. DOI: 10.3389/feduc.2023.1128618

Ormiston, H. E., Nygaard, M. A., & Apgar, S. (2022). A systematic review of secondary traumatic stress and compassion fatigue in teachers. *School Mental Health*, 14(4), 802–817. Advance online publication. DOI: 10.1007/s12310-022-09525-2 PMID: 35694002

Osika, A., MacMahon, S., Lodge, J. M., & Carroll, A. (2022, March 18). Emotions and learning: What role do emotions play in how and why students learn. *Times Higher Education.* https://www.timeshighereducation.com/campus/emotions-and-learning-what-role-do-emotions-play-how-and-why-students-learn

Pacansky-Brock, M., Smedshammer, M., & Vincent-Layton, K. (2020). Humanizing online teaching to equitize higher education. *Current Issues in Education (Tempe, Ariz.)*, 21(2), 1–21. https://brocansky.com/wpcontent/uploads/2020/02/HumanizingOnlineTeachingToEquitizePrePrint.pdf

Peacock, S., & Cowan, J. (2019). Promoting sense of belonging in online learning communities of inquiry at accredited courses. *Online Learning : the Official Journal of the Online Learning Consortium*, 23(2), 67–81. DOI: 10.24059/olj.v23i2.1488

Post, P. B., Grybush, A. L., Elmadani, A., & Lockhart, C. E. (2020). Fostering resilience in classrooms through child–teacher relationship training. *International Journal of Play Therapy*, 29(1), 9–19. DOI: 10.1037/pla0000107

Revak, M. A. (2020, March 30). When the tide goes out: Identifying and supporting struggling students in online courses. *Faculty Focus*. https://www.facultyfocus.com/articles/online-education/identifyingand-

Richardson, J. C., & Lowenthal, P. (2017). *Instructor social presence: A neglected component of the community of inquiry framework* [Conference session]. The 13th International Scientific Conference eLearning and Software for Education. DOI: 10.12753/2066-026X-17-160

Rodriguez, R. J., & Koubek, E. (2019). Unpacking high-impact instructional practices and student engagement in a teacher preparation program. *International Journal for the Scholarship of Teaching and Learning*, 17(3). Advance online publication. DOI: 10.20429/ijsotl.2019.130311

Schonert Rechl, K. A. (2017). Social and emotional learning and teachers. *The Future of Children*, 27(1), 137–155. Advance online publication. DOI: 10.1353/foc.2017.0007

Seligman, M. E. P., & Adler, A. (2018). Positive education. *Global happiness policy report*, 52-73.

Seligman, M. E. P., Ernst, R. M., Gillham, J., Reivich, K., & Linkins, M. (2009). Positive education: Positive psychology and classroom interventions. *Oxford Review of Education*, 35(3), 293–311. Advance online publication. DOI: 10.1080/03054980902934563

Smith, T. D. (2021). Teaching through trauma: Compassion fatigue, burnout, or secondary traumatic stress? In Bradley, D., & Hess, J. (Eds.), *Trauma and Resilience in Music Education*. DOI: 10.4324/9781003124207-3

Soutter, M. (2023). Transformative social emotional learning for teachers; Critical and holistic well-being as a marker for success. *Journal of Teaching and Learning*, 17(1), 7–30. Advance online publication. DOI: 10.22329/jtl.v17i1.7001

Stafford- Brizard. B. (2024, March 1). *The power of educator EQ*. ASCD. https://www.ascd.org/el/articles/the-power-of-educator-eq

Stokes, H. E., Brunzell, T., & Howard, J. (2023). Editorial: Trauma-informed education. *Frontiers in Education*, 8, 1264629. Advance online publication. DOI: 10.3389/feduc.2023.1264629

Stoltzfus, K. (2017, June 7). How teacher prep programs can embrace social-emotional learning. *Education Week*. https://www.edweek.org/education/how-teacher-prep-programs-can-embrace-social-emotional-learning/2017/06

Tsybulsky, D., & Muchnik-Rozanov, Y. (2021). Project-based learning in science-teacher pedagogical practicum: The role of emotional experiences in building preservice teachers' competencies. *Disciplinary and Interdisciplinary Science Education Research*, 3(1), 9.

VanderWeele, T. J. (2023). Emotional well-being annual investigator keynote: Flourishing and emotional well-being. https://hfh.fas.harvard.edu/news/flourishing-and-emotional-well-being-keynote-address-emotional-well-being-annual

Waajid, B., Garner, P. W., & Owen, J. E. (2013). Infusing social emotional learning into the teacher education curriculum. *The International Journal of Emotional Education*, 5(2), 31–48.

White, M. A. (2016). Why won't it stick? Positive psychology and positive education. *Psychology of Well-Being*, 6(2), 2. DOI: 10.1186/s13612-016-0039-1 PMID: 26900547

Woolcott, G., Whannell, R., Marshman, M., Galligan, L., Yeigh, T., & Axelsen, T. (2023, July 7). Exploring pre-service teachers' affective-reflective skills: The effect of variations of a novel self-evaluation protocol. *Asia-Pacific Journal of Teacher Education*. Advance online publication. DOI: 10.1080/1359866X.2023.2227942

# Chapter 15
Promoting Pre-Service ESOL Teachers' Understanding of English Learners' Social-Emotional Learning

Brian Hibbs
https://orcid.org/0009-0005-0894-1555
Dalton State College, USA

ABSTRACT

This chapter explores a research study intended to document and understand ESOL (English to Speakers of Other Languages) teacher candidates' experiences regarding a course unit on social-emotional learning for English learners. The chapter begins with an overview of social-emotional learning and its relevancy for multilingual learners of English. Next, the chapter reviews several studies that have investigated the role of the approach in (language) teacher education. The chapter then outlines the logistics of multimodule course unit on social-emotional learning embedded within a language teaching methodology course. Finally, the chapter summarizes the results of an exploratory study designed to document and understand teacher candidates' perspectives regarding the strengths and weaknesses of the course unit.

INTRODUCTION

For more than two centuries, the American educational system has traditionally focused on the development of students' academic achievement in various content areas; more recently, however, educators and scholars have increasingly emphasized the need for schools to also address their mental, physical, and psychological health as well (Brackett et al., 2012); such goals are essential to simultaneously advance learners' intrapersonal and interpersonal skills and also promote their intellectual skills. Schonert-Reichl et al. (2015) agree with this perspective and contend that "students' academic and life successes, as well as their social-emotional well-being, are bolstered when attention is given to the social and emotional dimensions of teaching and learning" (p. 406). This is especially true for multilingual learners of English, who are not only expected to acclimate to a new language and culture but who are often dealing with some level of mental and psychological trauma due to conflict, economic conditions, displacement, political strife, etc.

Leonard and Woodland (2023) define social-emotional learning (SEL) as "the process through which people learn to understand and manage emotions, set goals, feel empathy for others, establish positive relationships, and make responsible decisions" (p. 270). Beecher at al. (2022) explain that SEL encompasses "knowledge, skills, and attitudes that assist in managing emotions, establishing and maintaining relationships, and making responsible decisions" (p. 155). These definitions highlight the fact that social-emotional learning includes not only understanding the importance of negotiating social relationships in healthy ways but also doing so successfully and effectively. More specifically, with respect to school-age students, Jones and Doolittle (2014) describe SEL as "children's ability to learn about and manage their own emotions and interactions in ways that benefit themselves and others, and that help [them] succeed in schooling, the workplace, relationships, and citizenship" (p. 4). This interpretation of social-emotional learning centers on the ideas that the healthiness of students' interpersonal and intrapersonal abilities benefits both others as well as themselves and that SEL equips them with the skills and strategies necessary to mediate their world both within and beyond school. Additionally, Katz et al. (2020) contend that "SEL…represents a part of learning that is inextricably tied to school success and positive student performance" (p. 3), suggesting that developing students' social-emotional competency not only helps them to become more well-adjusted citizens but promotes the advancement of their academic skills as well.

The Collaborative for Academic, Social, and Emotional Learning (CASEL, n.d.) identifies five components of social-emotional learning that are essential for students' success: relationship skills (one's capacity to initiate and sustain interpersonal associations in a variety of contexts), responsible decision-making (one's aptitude in conscientiously and deliberately selecting and demonstrating effective comportment and demeanor across conditions), self-awareness (one's appreciation of their psychological and sentimental state and the capacity to recognize its effect on their interactions with others), self-management (one's capability to govern their conduct in multiple settings), and social awareness (one's dexterity in perceiving reality from their interlocutor's perspective). Additionally, these facets of SEL should be explored and practiced consistently and coherently throughout different environments, including classrooms, schools, households, neighborhoods, and beyond. Although each of these elements focuses on a particular aspect of students' relational and affectional well-being, an interdependent and symbiotic relationship clearly exists among them all, and they equally play an integral part in the development of students' ability to navigate their internal and external worlds. Moreover, Bailey et al. (2019) outlines several principles that educators should keep in mind when designing and implementing SEL curricula in their respective situations. These programs should be tailored to and address the particular social and emotional needs of students that are suitable and age-appropriate, move beyond the strict and scripted fulfillment of outlined goals and objectives and instead be adaptable and user-friendly, addressing the specific interpersonal and psychological challenges and issues that students are currently facing.

Literature Review

Numerous scholars have investigated the practicalities of familiarizing K-12 students with the social-emotional learning approach and its contributions to their awareness and understanding of themselves and their interactions with others. Although these researchers have explored the effectiveness of such projects in a variety of elementary, secondary, and post-secondary contexts (e.g., Allbright et al., 2019; Elmi, 2020; Green at al., 2021; Wallender et al., 2020), less research has been conducted on similar efforts in the field of teacher education. Nevertheless, several studies have explored the integration of the approach into educator preparation. This section outlines previous research that has been conducted in teacher education writ large and in English for Speakers of Other Languages (ESOL) teacher education more specifically.

SEL in Teacher Education

Donahue-Keegan et al. (2019) describe the logistics of a program designed to incorporate social-emotional learning and culturally responsive teaching into educator preparation programs in Massachusetts. The program structure was guided by three essential principles: teacher candidates should be equipped with the skills and strategies necessary to understand and process their emotions as educators, particularly when they begin their teaching careers and need to learn to adjust to the multiple demands placed on them; advancing their own social-emotional learning will ultimately encourage the development of the same for their students since these educators not only see and understand the importance and relevancy of the approach for learning but can also serve as role models for their students as balanced individuals socially and emotionally; and teachers who are socially and emotionally proficient are often able to effectively instruct students from different cultural and linguistic backgrounds since they understand the importance of social and emotional well-being for these learners.

In furtherance of these goals, the Massachusetts Consortium for Social-Emotional Learning in Teacher Education (MA SEL-Ted) was created to identify and work with stakeholders to more intentionally embed social-emotional learning into teacher preparation programs. The consortium has focused its efforts on advocating for the inclusion of SEL in educator preparation programs across the state, conducting research on teachers' and administrators' perspectives regarding the importance of SEL in their respective contexts, and implementing professional development across the state to familiarize stakeholders with the tenets of the approach and its relevancy for instruction. While the consortium to date has indeed made important strides in endorsing social-emotional learning in schools and teacher education programs in Massachusetts, members of the consortium have also learned several important lessons along the way.

First, participation of faculty members in educator preparation programs is essential and should include buy-in from all stakeholders in the programs; efforts by only one or two sole faculty will likely not be sufficient to sustain such efforts. Second, teacher candidates should be paired with mentor teachers that deliberately embed SEL into their instruction so that these pre-service teachers are intentionally exposed to a variety of ways that the approach can be integrated into instruction. Third, including SEL in educator preparation requires a revision of multiple aspects of the program and not simply altering the logistics of a few courses within the program. Lastly, SEL should be ingrained into state certification standards to accentuate the importance of the concept in teacher preparation. The authors conclude by affirming that "there is a dearth of attention cultivating socio-emotional competence in teacher preparation programs in the United States" (p. 153) and that the consortium's efforts constitute one possible avenue for addressing this concern.

Goegan et al. (2017) investigated pre-service and in-service teachers' views concerning the SEL approach along with their beliefs regarding their support of and dedication to students' social-emotional competence (SEC) as well as their own. 137 teacher candidates attending a teacher education program at a large university in western Canada completed an online survey and 276 in-service teachers completed a face-to-face questionnaire to document their opinions regarding the approach and its relevancy to their instruction. Statistical analysis of participants' responses yielded several interesting findings. First, the in-service teachers ranked their feelings about their own social-emotional competence and their ease of implementing SEL into their classrooms at a higher level, whereas the pre-service teachers demonstrated a stronger commitment to the approach. Second, participants who believed they were more competent socially and emotionally were consequently more likely to report that they felt more at ease with implementing the approach in their instruction. Additionally, participants who indicated that their social-emotional levels were higher also reported that they felt more involved with students and that their teaching was inherently more effective. In conclusion, the authors note that few educator preparation programs specifically incorporate the SEL approach and that "teacher education programs need to support pre-service teachers in their development of comfort with SEL and in developing their own SEC" (p. 280).

To that end, Katz et al. (2020) propose a multicomponent program for addressing this curricular gap consisting of dedicated attention to several key areas. First, educator preparation faculty should develop teacher candidates' knowledge of what social-emotional learning is and the elements that constitute such learning, how SEL helps students deal effectively with various types of mental and psychological trauma, and how the approach advances equity, cultural understanding, and social justice in the classroom. Second, teacher educators should support pre-service teachers in learning to manage their own social-emotional state, not only to help them cope with the daily stressors of teaching but also to serve as role models for their students in this area. Third, educator preparation faculty should familiarize teacher candidates with the variety of SEL programs currently in existence so that they are aware of the structure and content of such programs and are able to critically evaluate the feasibility and efficacy of such programs. Lastly, teachers should continually review the SEL programmatic offerings at their schools to ensure the effectiveness and relevancy of these programs. The authors assert that "it is time that teacher education programs provide more formal training in SEL…to support the next generation of educators" (p. 9), and the model they propose strives to do just that. In a similar vein, Markowitz et al. (2018) present a model for social-emotional learning (the Anchor Competencies Framework) for use by/with both pre-service and in-service teachers that consists of seven core components: establishing supportive relationships, promoting reflection, adopting a growth mindset, advancing one's ability to persevere, instituting a classroom community, developing one's cooperative learning abilities, and handling conflict in effective and culturally responsive ways. The authors confirm that this framework may not only be utilized by teachers in their own classrooms but can also be successfully integrated into teacher preparation programs.

Additionally, Schonert-Reichl et al. (2015) conducted a study in which they examined the website of each state's educator preparation accrediting body and documented the extent to which social-emotional learning was an essential component of teacher education in that state with respect to the social-emotional competency (SEC) of teachers, the SEL of students, and various components of the learning context. Results indicated that developing teachers' SEC was given scant attention by the accrediting bodies and that few states explicitly address the development of students' SEL abilities. The authors argue that "little attention is given currently to the cultivation and promotion of pre-service teachers' own social competence and well-being" (p. 416) and that few states focus on developing students' social-emotional competencies; they consequently advocate for the inclusion of teacher certifications standards that address these gaps.

SEL in ESOL Teacher Education

Several studies have also addressed the role of social-emotional learning specifically in ESOL teacher education. For instance, Melani et al. (2020) outline the crucial and fundamental role of social-emotional learning in learning English as a foreign/second language. In contrast to previous approaches that viewed language learning as merely a cognitive process, scholars in applied linguistics now believe language acquisition to be more inherently social in nature in the sense that proficiency develops as a result of communicative interactions with others. Such interactions establish a Zone of Proximal Development (ZPD) (Vygotsky, 1978) in which learners connect with more proficient users of the target language in a variety of contexts who provide linguistic scaffolding and support via comprehensible input while also creating opportunities for students to expand their productive skills through language output. The authors argue that, despite the essential role of interaction in language acquisition, "the social context [of language learning] is often underestimated and overlooked" (p. 5). Additionally, a number of affective factors can have a consequential impact on the advancement of learners' communicative proficiency, including motivation (the desire or willingness to complete a given task), attitude (a feeling or way of thinking that affects a person's behavior), and anxiety (worry, nervousness, and/or uneasiness about a given task). For example, students may be integratively motivated to learn the language (for example, to become part of the community of target language users), instrumentally (for instance, to obtain a better professional position), internally (for example, to satisfy personal interests), and/or externally (for instance, to accomplish goals established by others). Learners' perspectives regarding the target language/culture may considerably influence their initial interest in acquiring and subsequent efforts to learn the target language. Additionally, emotions can directly influence language learning. According to the

Affective Filter Hypothesis (Krashen, 1982; 1985), if their affective state is high (e.g., being concerned, distressed, fearful), students tend to dedicate more attention to alleviating and resolving their sentimental challenges and attend less to linguistic input, thus leading ultimately to less successful language learning; conversely, if their affective state is low (e.g., being content, happy, satisfied), learners are likely to devote less attention to their emotional state and focus more on linguistic input, thereby leading to more successful language learning. The authors maintain that SEL is thus critical for the successful development of students' linguistic (and cultural) competencies and that, as a result, "teachers and educators…are first responders to language proficiency challenges in L2 classrooms" (p. 8) as well as other emotional and social difficulties learners may encounter.

Martínez-Alba et al. (2023) explore the role of social and emotional well-being among English as a Foreign/Second Language (EFL/ESL) educators and the vital role that it plays in both pre-service and in-service teachers' lives. Similar to Melani et al. (2020), the authors begin by noting that teacher preparation has tended to focus more on the pedagogical aspects of language instruction and less on the development of prospective teachers' social and emotional learning and well-being despite the fact that, in their view, "[language] teaching is, inevitably, an emotionally laden profession" (p. 31), particularly when dealing with students, who are often struggling with their own emotional challenges, and more especially with multilingual learners of English, who must also navigate additional psychological trauma due to a variety of political and social factors. Thus, many educators find themselves unprepared and unequipped to navigate such issues since "practitioners are rarely trained to consider their own well-being in their practice and beyond" (p. 32). In addition, scholarly endeavors in the field have focused more on the development of learners' social and emotional well-being to the exclusion of similar efforts on the part of educators, with the subsequent result of "placing language teachers on the periphery" (p. 37). Consequently, the authors advocate for investigative work that focuses on the advancement of ELT [English Language Teaching] professionals' social and emotional well-being with the ultimate aim of "placing teachers at the heart of ELT, where they belong" (p. 38).

Pentón Herrera (2020) contends that SEL should be an essential component of the education of multilingual learners of English since, in addition to adjusting to a new language, "our ELs [English learners] also have to discover…how to navigate the unwritten rules of the social and emotional landscape of American society" (p. 3). In other words, these students must learn how to adapt to the conventions, norms, and standards of a new culture while also managing the effects of psychological trauma they may have previously experienced prior to their arrival in the United States. Consequently, instruction for these pupils should not only focus on the development of their linguistic competencies but also include the exploration of strategies and techniques to advance and promote their social and emotional well-being: "our ESOL classrooms need to become a space that transcends traditional English instruction for academic purposes and relies on language as a tool for the restoration, support, and healing of our ELs" (p. 6). The author also examines a variety of methods and approaches that can be used with this student population to address their social and emotional needs, including bibliotherapy, mindfulness techniques, peace education, and restorative practices. In the end, Pentón Herrera (2020) affirms that, rather than seeing SEL as a separate and distinct component, such learning can in fact work symbiotically with content learning in reciprocally beneficial ways: "SEL and academic learning *can* and *do* work in synergy; they do not have to be mutually independent of one another" (p. 11; emphasis in original).

Furthermore, Megawati et al. (2022) conducted a study in which fifteen prospective English teachers attending several different educator preparation programs in Indonesia participated in a semi-structured interview about the implementation of SEL principles in their practicum experiences along with the social and emotional connections they established and maintained with both students and mentor teachers. Questions included in the interview protocol were organized according to the five components of the CASEL framework referenced above (CASEL, n.d.). Data for the study were analyzed using thematic analysis. Findings from the study revealed that teacher candidates possessed a certain level of self-awareness as educators with respect to their pedagogical role and views of themselves as teachers, intentionally and somewhat successfully created and sustained social and emotional connections with others, effectively handled and controlled their own social-emotional states when interacting with others, constructed relationships with others with relative success, and demonstrated responsibility for supporting student learning. The authors contend that such efforts can contribute positively to the development of pre-service teachers' professional identity in substantial ways but that "SEL must be recognized and promoted at the university and college level as a necessary part of teacher training efforts" (p. 80), thus highlighting the pivotal role that social-emotional learning should play in educator preparation.

As previously mentioned, research on social-emotional learning has tended to focus on interventions to develop K-12 students' competencies in this area; less attention has been focused on doing likewise for pre-service teachers, particularly with respect to teaching multilingual learners of English. Nevertheless, this is a particularly important participant population since teacher candidates must be prepared for the increasingly culturally and linguistically-diverse classrooms in which they will find themselves; they must be equipped with the techniques and procedures for effectively guiding and supporting these students as they work to acquire English, navigate the complexity of the American educational system, determine and establish their place in a new culture, and resolve previous psychological trauma as well.

Donahue-Keegan et al. (2019) contend that one large problem in this area is that "there is currently a dearth of attention cultivating social-emotional competence in teacher preparation programs in the United States (p. 153), particularly in the field of ESOL. More specifically, little research has been conducted that examines teacher candidates' views about the contributions of social-emotional learning to their own instructional practice. This chapter thus intends to address these scholarly gaps in the literature by outlining a research study designed to document and understand the relevancy of a course unit on social-emotional learning for multilingual learners of English. The next section highlights the setting for the investigation and the logistics of both the course unit and the study.

Research Context

The current study was conducted during the fall semester of 2023 and involved 53 students enrolled in one of two sections of a ESOL methodology course for which the author was the instructor. The course was implemented with undergraduate elementary-education teacher candidates attending a small four-year college in the southeastern United States designated as a minority-serving institution. Tables 1-3 below describe the demographic information of the participants of the study.

Table 1. Participants' ages

Class #1 (N = 26)		Class #2 (N = 27)	
20	1	20	2
21	7	21	5
22	7	22	11
23	4	23	3
24	2	24	1
		25	2
26	1		
27	1		
		28	1
30	1	30	1
31	1		
32	1	32	1

Table 2. Participants' self-identified gender

Class #1 (N = 26)		Class #2 (N = 27)	
Female	22	Female	24
Male	4	Male	3

Table 3. Participants' self-identified ethnicity

Class #1 (N = 26)		Class #2 (N = 27)	
		African-American	1
Caucasian/White	19	Caucasian/White	22
Hispanic/Latinx	6	Hispanic/Latinx	3
Hispanic/USA	1	Other	1

The goal of the course is to familiarize pre-service teachers with a variety of methods and approaches for effectively teaching multilingual learners of English; the social-emotional approach was reviewed as part of a multi-day unit embedded within the course.

Social-Emotional Learning Course Unit

This course unit consisted of the following three modules as illustrated in Table 4 below.

Table 4. Social-emotional learning course unit modules

Module	Description of the Module
1	The SEL Approach (Introduction)
2	The Social-Emotional Learning Approach (Theory)
3	The Social-Emotional Learning Approach (Practice)

Each module lasted approximately 2.5 hours. Modules 2 and 3 employed a multi-step jigsaw reading activity with respect to blog posts/articles. In the first phase of the activity, students were assembled into "vertical" (home) groups in which they explored their understandings and interpretations of the article with other students who had completed the same reading (i.e., S1, S5, S9, and S13 in Table 5 below). Next, students were arranged into "horizontal" (expert) groups in which they met with three other students who had each completed a different reading and discussed important details from their respective blog post/article with their groupmates (i.e., S1, S2, S3, and S4 in Table 6 below). In the third and final phase of the activity, students returned to their seats and, on a blank index card, noted several points of information they individually gained from the discussions that occurred in the home and expert groups, which they then shared with their classmates.

Table 5. Jigsaw reading activity groupings

Group A	Group B	Group C	Group D
S1	S2	S3	S4
S5	S6	S7	S8
S9	S10	S11	S12
S13	S14	S15	S16

* "S" = "Student"

Module 1: The SEL Approach (Introduction).

The first module of the course unit consisted of an introduction to the social-emotional learning approach via an instructor-led in-person presentation. The presentation began with a discussion that asked teacher candidates to consider what SEL meant to them, why they believed it was an important concept for all students more generally and for English language learners more specifically, and which strategies/techniques they utilized to promote their students' social-emotional well-being as well as their own. Then, the presentation provided an overview of the CASEL social-emotional learning framework (CASEL, n.d.) and engaged participants in a discussion of their perspectives of the framework.

Module 2: The SEL Approach (Theory).

The second module of the course unit was comprised of an exploration of the theoretical principles undergirding the social-emotional learning approach and its relevancy for multilingual learners of English. In this module, students were randomly assembled into groups with each group reading a different blog post that reviewed the major tenets of the SEL approach (see Table 6 below).

Table 6. Jigsaw group blog posts (Module 2)

Group	Blog Post
A	Breiseth (2022)
B	Breiseth (2023)

continued on following page

Table 6. Continued

Group	Blog Post
C	Kinsella (2022)
D	Scott (2015)

These readings were selected because they provide a concise summary of the SEL approach and its significance for English language learners. Breiseth (2022) highlights ten specific ways to intentionally embed social-emotional learning into instruction for multilingual learners of English. Breiseth (2023) reviews the CASEL framework for social-emotional learning and provides suggestions and examples of how to strategically integrate each of the five components of the framework into instruction for English learners. Kinsella (2022) outlines a variety of strategies to promote these students' social and academic learning through scaffolding, social interaction, and class discussions. Finally, Scott (2015) describes four techniques for creating a safe and welcoming space for English language learners via empathy, first language maintenance, art as a demonstration of culture, and visual scaffolding.

Module 3: The SEL Approach (Practice).

In the third and final module of the course unit, teacher candidates engaged in a second round of the jigsaw reading activity concerning articles which explored the tangible implementation of social-emotional learning into instruction for multilingual learners of English in a variety of contexts (see Table 7 below).

Table 7. Jigsaw group articles (Module 3)

Group	Article
A	Dresser (2012)
B	Lucido (2022)
C	Nall (2020)
D	Nanquil (2021)

As with the blog posts in the second module of the course unit, the articles in this module were intentionally selected to develop teacher candidates' awareness of and familiarity with a variety of approaches for integrating social-emotional learning into their current and future teaching. Dresser (2012) describes ways to utilize oral reading practices with English learners to promote their interest in reading, develop their academic language, and establish a supportive classroom atmosphere. Lucido (2022) reviews a variety of mindfulness and growth mindset activities that can be used to advance emergent bilinguals' linguistic and social-emotional competencies. Nall (2020) highlights several avenues for encouraging multilingual learners' exploratory play to facilitate both their language development and social-emotional learning. Finally, Nanquil (2021) outlines a research study designed to better understand language teachers' efforts to create a supportive classroom environment focused on the advancement of students' social-emotional well-being. Five Filipino ESL language teachers participated in the study, which utilized interviews and online discussions to gather information about strategies they used to establish and maintain this environment. Results of the study demonstrate that the teachers employed a variety of activities to support students' well-being in a variety of ways, including asking personalized questions, demonstrating appreciation, encouraging and motivating them, monitoring students' behaviors, and prayer.

RESEARCH STUDY

Data Collection

At the conclusion of the course unit, participants completed a post-course-unit questionnaire consisting of ten Likert-scale statements and five open-ended questions to document and explore their perspectives regarding the strengths and weaknesses of the activities that constituted the course unit along with suggestions for improving the course unit moving forward (see Appendix A).

Data Analysis

Quantitative data obtained during the study were analyzed using descriptive statistics, while qualitative data were analyzed using thematic analysis. According to Dörnyei (2007), the goal of descriptive statistics is to provide a summary of findings and describe general tendencies occurring in the data in order to provide a global picture of the behavior of the participants; this methodological approach is often used to "describe" data collected from a given sample of participants (Borg and Gall, 1989, p. 336). Additionally, Fisher and Marshall (2009) specify that descriptive statistics consist of various "…numerical and graphical techniques used to organise, present and analyse data" (p. 95). Four types of descriptive statistics were calculated in regards to the Likert-scale statements: the mean (the average of students' ratings for the statement), the median (the middle rating between the highest and lowest ratings for the statement), the mode (the rating occurring most often for the statement), and the range (the difference between the largest rating and the smallest rating for the statement). The mean for each statement was calculated by determining the average of participants' ratings for the statement. The median for each statement was computed by identifying the highest and lowest ratings for the statement and establishing the average score between these two ratings. The mode for each statement was calculated by selecting the rating that occurred most frequently among students' responses to the statement. Finally, the range for each statement was computed by finding the numerical difference between the highest and lowest ratings for the statement. The results of this analysis can be found in Appendix B.

In addition, thematic analysis was utilized to study participants' responses to the open-ended questions. Braun and Clarke (2006) define thematic analysis as "a method for identifying, analyzing and reporting patterns (themes) within data" (p. 79). Dawadi (2020) contends that the procedure involves "a search for themes that can capture the narratives available in the account of data sets" (p. 62). Moreover, Maguire and Delahunt (2017) state that the ultimate aim of thematic analysis is to "identify themes [or] patterns in the data that are important or interesting, and [then] use these themes to address the research [question(s)]" (p. 3353). Thus, thematic analysis helps investigators initially determine codes, or "the most basic segment, or element, of the raw data or information that can be assessed in a meaningful way regarding the phenomenon" (Boyatzis, 1998, p. 63), which are subsequently developed into themes, or "pattern[s] found in the information that at the minimum describes and organizes possible observations or at the maximum interprets aspects of the phenomenon" (Boyatzis, 1998, p. vi). The current study employed inductive coding (Braun & Clark, 2006) in the sense that, rather than utilizing *a priori* codes/themes established by previous theoreticians/researchers (deductive coding), the codes and themes emerged from a deep examination of the data themselves (in this case, participants' responses to the open-ended questions). Within the context of this study, the coding procedure involved a multi-step process. First, the author read through participants' responses to the open-ended questions and separated the data into distinct sections through which a series of codes was initially established (open coding). Then, the data sources were consulted for a second time, and codes that were related to one another were grouped together into themes (axial coding) (Strauss & Corbin, 1990). Finally, the system of codes and themes was "defined and refined" (Braun & Clarke, 2006, p. 92) in order to create a cohesive and coherent narrative.

Findings

This section highlights overall trends emerging from the analysis of both the quantitative and qualitative data collected during the study by examining similarities and differences among participants' responses across both classes. Due to the utilization of descriptive statistics to analyze the quantitative data collected during the study, the purpose of this section is to describe general tendencies that emerged from the analysis rather than establishing the statistical significance of these trends.

Quantitative Results

One important trend that surfaced from students' feedback on Part A of the questionnaire is that, participants in Class #1 tended to view the course unit overall less positively (a mean score of 3.61 out of 5 across the ten statements) than those in Class #2 (a mean score of 3.98 out of 5 across the ten statements) despite the fact that the course unit was implemented virtually identically in both sections of the course. This initial finding provides context for the subsequent results described below.

Other differences between both classes also emerged from analysis of the quantitative data which were notable but are not necessarily significant statistically. For instance, the statement that was ranked lowest amongst participants in Class #1 was Statement #10 ("The jigsaw activity of the article helped me understand how to use a social-emotional approach for teaching English learners in my own teaching.") with a mean score of 2.8 out of 5, while participants in Class #2 rated the statement much more highly (a mean score of 4.15 out of 5), intimating that teacher candidates in Class #2 believed that the jigsaw activity in Module 3 was significantly more successful in advancing their understanding about implementing the approach in their own teaching versus those in Class #1. Although there are a number of possible explanations for this result, it is conceivable that the jigsaw activity worked more efficaciously in Class #2 due to, among other factors, the level of preparedness of the teacher candidates and/or the degree of thoroughness of the group discussions during the activity, which will be discussed later.

Another dissimilarity between the classes exists with respect to Statement #4 ("The blog posts helped me understand how to use a social-emotional approach to teaching English learners in my own teaching."), with participants in Class #1 assigning the statement a mean score of 3.32 out of 5 and participants in Class #2 assigning the statement a mean score of 3.81 out of 5. Although perhaps not a large difference, this finding nevertheless appears to indicate that, in their view, teacher candidates in Class #1 considered the blog posts to be less effective in supporting their understanding of how to integrate the approach in their work with multilingual learners of English compared with those in Class #2. Among other possibilities, it is plausible that, while the blog posts did contribute somewhat to their awareness of the theory of the approach, the postings did not necessarily advance their understanding of how to integrate the approach into their instruction in concrete and practical terms.

Yet another divergence of opinion appears in regard to Statement #5 ("The jigsaw activity of the blog posts helped me understand the social-emotional approach to teaching English learners."), with participants in Class #1 assigning the statement a mean score of 3.32 out of 5 and participants in Class #2 assigning the statement a mean score of 4.07 out of 5. Thus, it seems that teacher candidates in Class #2 felt that the jigsaw activity in Module 2 was considerably more effective in developing their awareness and understanding of the relevancy of the approach for English language learners than did those in Class #1. This result may be due to, among other factors, their preparedness for the activity and/or the content of the readings; in other words, it is possible that teacher candidates in Class #1 may not have been as prepared to participate in the activity, or they may have believed that the content of the readings did not necessarily advance their understanding of the approach, which will also be explored later.

Similarly, participants in Class #1 rated Statement #6 ("The jigsaw activity of the blog posts helped me understand how to use a social-emotional approach to teaching English learners in my own teaching.") at a lower level (a mean score of 3.48 out of 5) than did those in Class #2 (a mean score of 3.96 out of 5), insinuating that, from their perspective, teacher candidates in Class #1 considered the blog posts to be less effective in promoting their awareness of how to integrate the approach into their teaching than those in Class #2. It is possible, amid other explanations, that the blog posts may not have adequately addressed the specific implementation of the approach, particularly with respect to English language learners.

Likewise, yet another difference between both classes surfaced from the analysis of the quantitative data with respect to Statement #3 ("The blog posts helped me understand the social-emotional approach to teaching English learners."), with the statement receiving a mean score of 3.44 out of 5 by participants in Class #1 and a mean score of 3.89 out of 5 by participants in Class #2. This finding suggests that teacher candidates in Class #2 believed that the blog posts contributed more positively to their knowledge of the overarching principles of the approach in comparison with those in Class #1; it is thus conceivable that the content of the blog posts may not have been appropriate for these students or that they may have needed more contextual information to make sense of the ideas expressed in the readings.

Despite the differences highlighted above, there were nevertheless several commonalities across both classes. For instance, the statement that was ranked highest amongst participants in both classes was Statement #2 ("I understand the importance of using a social-emotional approach to teaching English learners.") with a mean score of 4.33 out of 5 by participants in Class #1 and a mean score of 4.19 out of 5 by participants in Class #2. This finding suggests that the readings and corresponding discussions seemed to have contributed positively to teacher candidates' understanding of the approach and its specific relevancy for multilingual learners of English. Since this was the overarching goal of the course unit, it appears that the unit was successful in achieving its intended objective.

Another statement that received relatively similar ratings was Statement #1 ("I understand what a social-emotional approach to teaching English learners is."), receiving a mean score of 3.96 out of 5 by participants in Class #1 and a mean score of 3.82 out of 5 by participants in Class #2. This finding indicates that teacher candidates in both classes supported the view that, from their perspective, the unit modules contributed positively to their awareness and knowledge of the theoretical principles underlying the approach. Similarly, both classes rated Statement #9 ("The jigsaw activity of the articles helped me understand the social emotional approach to teaching English learners.") at a comparable level, with the statement receiving a mean score of 3.84 out of 5 by participants in Class #1 and a mean score of 3.91 out of 5 by participants in Class #2. This result suggests that the logistics of the activity played a relatively important role in shaping teacher candidates' awareness of the value of the approach and its specific relevancy for multilingual learners of English.

Qualitative Results

Analysis of the qualitative data collected during the study not only affirmed many of the findings obtained from the quantitative data but also add some explanatory evidence for these results. For example, with respect to the positive aspects of the course unit, numerous participants commented that the jigsaw activity supported their emergent understanding of the importance of social-emotional learning for multilingual learners of English, not only by exposing them to information on the topic with which they were previously unfamiliar but also by providing them with opportunities to share their own views on the readings while allowing them to consider different perspectives on the content. This may have encouraged them to empathize with the plight of their learners and familiarize them with a variety of strategies and techniques they could potentially integrate into their own instruction to advance their own students' social-emotional learning and well-being. Some participants also mentioned that the readings solidified their knowledge about the relevancy of SEL in education by acquainting them with ways to identify and determine learners' affective state along with the potential consequences and implications of the impact of students' mental and psychological states on their learning. Concerning the negative aspects of the unit, a number of participants remarked that, in some cases, the jigsaw activity was less effective in cases where their classmates either forgot or were unable to complete the readings before class, which obviously limited the richness of their group discussions. Various participants also indicated that, while they did contribute to their knowledge of SEL and its critical role in ESOL instruction, some of the readings were (1) academically dense, (2) challenging, complicated, and difficult to read, and (3) did not concretely or explicitly address the relationship between the content and their own instruction. To improve the unit moving forward, several participants mentioned that they would like to have been provided with additional resources not only to increase their evolving expertise on social emotional learning and its pivotal role in ESOL education but also enlighten them about additional ways to incorporate SEL into their teaching in tangible and explicit ways. Other participants noted that they would have preferred to have an opportunity to apply their learning through the creation and implementation of activities and lessons designed to broaden their own students' understanding of social emotional learning and facilitate the development of learners' mental and psychological well-being. These observations will certainly be taken into consideration when planning future iterations of the course unit.

Based on these findings, I plan to implement the following changes in subsequent iterations of the course unit. First, I aim to review the blog posts and articles that currently constitute the course unit to verify that they successfully advance teacher candidates' awareness and understanding of the approach and effectively familiarize them with concrete ways to implement the approach in their own instruction. Second, I propose inserting additional modules to deepen students' awareness and understanding of the approach; more specifically, I intend to supplement the unit with additional resources that explore multiple facets of the approach while also familiarizing them with other ways to integrate the approach into their own instruction. Third, I am considering the inclusion of an additional module focused on providing students with an opportunity to explore their own social-emotional competencies, reflect on the importance of their well-being both socially and emotionally, and consider avenues for further developing their abilities in this area. Lastly, I plan to increase the applicability of the course unit to their teaching by adding a module during which teacher candidates determine how they might strategically embed social-emotional learning into their instruction to support the development of their students' SEL at their current placements.

DISCUSSION

The higher mean scores on the Likert-scale items by participants in Class #2 when compared to Class #1 may be due to a variety of factors, including (but not limited to) their attitudes towards social and emotional learning, their interest in and desire to learn about the topic, their individual and collective personalities, their willingness to engage and explore their opinions with other classmates, and even their previous experiences with SEL. In order to more clearly elucidate possible reasons for these discrepancies, I plan to conduct more sophisticated statistical analyses on participants' responses to the statements and also intend to replicate the study with additional data points in order to get a more complete picture of the impact of the course unit on teacher candidates' attitudes towards the course unit while also triangulating the findings across these sources. While numerous participants commented on the positive contribution of the jigsaw activity to their emergent understandings concerning SEL, other participants mentioned that the activity was less than effective when their classmates did not complete the readings. Thus, the author proposes to add a supplementary activity prior to each jigsaw discussion in which students will be asked to complete, for example, an online discussion post in which they share their reactions and perspectives on each reading. A number of participants stated that some of the readings were too complex and obscure to understand, and so I plan to identify other readings that are less dense and complicated along with other sources of information that present similar information in alternative formats with additional examples of ways that ESOL educators have successfully integrated SEL into their instructional practice. Additionally, several participants commented that they would have preferred to have been given a chance to implement their learning with their own students; thus, the author aims to provide future students with multiple opportunities to consolidate their knowledge by devising and executing SEL lessons and activities in their own pedagogical contexts.

As mentioned previously, despite the fact that social and emotional learning has been gaining increased attention and prominence in K-12 education over the last two decades, this trend has not considerably altered ESOL teacher education; as of this date, few TESOL educator preparation programs specifically integrate social-emotional learning into their courses and/or curricula. To remedy this trend, it is essential to intentionally and strategically embed SEL into these programs in a holistic and integrative manner, not only to familiarize prospective teachers with this topic and its relevancy to student learning but also to acquaint them with the skills and dispositions necessary to effectively manage their own emotional and social health and well-being. It is important, however, to be cognizant of various logistical barriers that may come into play during the implementation of such efforts, such as departmental/institutional resistance and/or a lack of expertise, interest, or resources for integrating SEL into such programs. It is thus recommended that teacher educators ponder these ideas when creating and realizing such programming in their respective settings.

Additionally, due to the paucity of research on social-emotional learning and educator preparation writ large and in ESOL teacher education more specifically, future investigations should explore the contributions of such learning on teacher candidates' understanding of SEL and its importance in language education, their ability to successfully develop their own students' knowledge on the topic, and their expertise in supporting students' capacity to manage their affective and interpersonal skills and well-being as well as their own. Moreover, such endeavors should also strive to identify those strategies and techniques which are most effective in advancing both students' and educators' social-emotional health.

CONCLUSION

This chapter provided an overview of the components of a course unit on social-emotional learning embedded within a TESOL methodology course. The chapter began with an exploration of the approach more generally and its relevancy for multilingual learners of English more specifically. Next, the chapter reviewed several studies which have examined the role of social-emotional learning in teacher education and preparation. The chapter then reviewed the logistics of a multimodule unit on social-emotional learning integrated into a TESOL methods course for elementary-education pre-service teachers and summarized the results of an exploratory study designed to collect information about study participants' views concerning the strengths and weaknesses of the course unit on social-emotional learning. Preliminary findings suggest that participants benefitted in substantial ways from becoming educated about social-emotional learning and its relevancy for English learners. Furthermore, participants consistently remarked that, although the course unit was effective and practical in numerous ways, they would also have liked to spend more time developing their knowledge and expertise concerning SEL and to have seen additional examples of ways in which social-emotional learning could be more clearly operationalized and implemented in the classroom. In the end, Katz et al. (2020) observe that "despite the demands for teachers to have SEL competencies, our colleges and universities are behind the curve in providing coursework to develop these skills" (p. 3). It is my hope that this chapter not only begins to address this curricular gap but also inspires teacher educators to do likewise in their own settings.

REFERENCES

Allbright, T. N., Marsh, J. A., Kennedy, K. E., Hough, H. J., & McKibben, S. (2019). Social-emotional learning practices: Insights from outlier schools. *Journal of Research in Innovative Teaching & Learning*, 12(1), 35–52. DOI: 10.1108/JRIT-02-2019-0020

Bailey, R., Stickle, L., Brion-Meisels, G., & Jones, S. M. (2019). Reimagining social-emotional learning: Findings from a strategy-based approach. *Phi Delta Kappan*, 100(5), 53–58. DOI: 10.1177/0031721719827549

Beecher, S., Peterson, K. A., Peterson-Ahmad, M. B., & Luther, V. L. (2022). Social-emotional learning, awareness, and strategies for teachers: Collaborative approaches. In Peterson-Ahmad, M., & Luther, V. L. (Eds.), *Collaborative approaches to recruiting, preparing, and retaining teachers for the field* (pp. 136–155). IGI Global. DOI: 10.4018/978-1-7998-9047-8.ch008

Borg, W., & Gall, M. (1989). *Education research: An introduction* (5th ed.). Longman.

Brackett, M. A., Reyes, M. R., Rivers, S. E., Elbertson, N. A., & Salovey, P. (2012). Assessing teachers' beliefs about social and emotional learning. *Journal of Psychoeducational Assessment*, 30(3), 219–236. DOI: 10.1177/0734282911424879

Brackett, M. A., Rivers, S. E., Shiffman, S., Lerner, N., & Salovey, P. (2006). Relating emotional abilities to social functioning: A comparison of self-report and performance measures of emotional intelligence. *Journal of Personality and Social Psychology*, 91(4), 780–795. DOI: 10.1037/0022-3514.91.4.780 PMID: 17014299

Braun, V., & Clarke, V. (2006). Using thematic analysis in psychology. *Qualitative Research in Psychology*, 3(2), 77–101. DOI: 10.1191/1478088706qp063oa

Breiseth, L. (2022). *10 Strategies for supporting SEL for ELLs: "Grow as you go"*. Retrieved from https://www.colorincolorado.org/article/sel-ell-salina

Breiseth, L. (2023). *SEL for English language learners: What educators need to know*. https://www.colorincolorado.org/article/sel-english-language-learners-what-educators-need-know

Collaborative for Academic, Social, and Emotional Learning (CASEL) (n.d.). *What is the CASEL framework?* https://casel.org/fundamentals-of-sel/what-is-the-casel-framework

Dawadi, S. (2020). Thematic analysis approach: A step by step guide for ELT research practitioners. *Journal of the Nepal English Language Teachers' [NELTA]. Association*, 25(1-2), 62–71.

Donahue-Keegan, D., Villegas-Reimers, E., & Cressey, J. M. (2019). Integrating social-emotional learning and culturally responsive teaching in teacher education programs: The Massachusetts experience so far. *Teacher Education Quarterly*, 46(4), 150–168.

Dörnyei, Z. (2007). *Research methods in applied linguistics: Quantitative, qualitative, and mixed methodologies*. Oxford University Press.

Dresser, R. (2012). Reviving oral reading practices with English learners by integrating social-emotional learning. *Multicultural Education*, 20(1), 45–50.

Elmi, C. (2020). Integrating social emotional learning strategies in higher education. *European Journal of Investigation in Health, Psychology and Education*, 10(3), 848–858. DOI: 10.3390/ejihpe10030061 PMID: 34542515

Fisher, M. J., & Marshall, A. P. (2009). Understanding descriptive statistics. *Australian Critical Care*, 22(2), 93–97. DOI: 10.1016/j.aucc.2008.11.003 PMID: 19150245

Goegan, L. D., Wagner, A. K., & Daniels, L. M. (2017). Pre-service and practicing teachers' commitment to and comfort with social emotional learning. *The Alberta Journal of Educational Research*, 63(3), 267–285. DOI: 10.55016/ojs/ajer.v63i3.56284

Green, A. L., Ferrante, S., Boaz, T. L., Kutash, K., & Wheeldon-Reece, B. (2021). Social and emotional learning during early adolescence: Effectiveness of a classroom-based SEL program for middle school students. *Psychology in the Schools*, 58(6), 1056–1069. DOI: 10.1002/pits.22487

Jones, S. M., & Doolittle, E. J. (2017). Social and emotional learning: Introducing the issue. *The Future of Children*, 27(1), 3–11. DOI: 10.1353/foc.2017.0000

Katz, D., Mahfouz, J., & Romas, S. (2020). Creating a foundation of well-being for teachers and students starts with SEL curriculum in teacher education programs. *Northwest Journal of Teacher Education, 15*(2), Article 5.

Kinsella, K. (2022, March 29). *Creating a supportive SEL forum for English learner lesson contributions*. https://www.languagemagazine.com/2022/03/29/creating-a-supportive-sel-forum-for-english-learner-lesson-contributions

Krashen, S. D. (1982). *Principles and practices in second language acquisition*. Pergamon Press.

Krashen, S. D. (1985). *The input hypothesis: Issues and implications*. Longman.

Leonard, A. M., & Woodland, R. H. (2023). Teacher PLCs and the advancement of SEL. In Liston, D. (Ed.), *Exploring social emotional learning in diverse academic settings* (pp. 251–270). IGI Global. DOI: 10.4018/978-1-6684-7227-9.ch013

Lucido, F. (2022). Mindfulness and growth mindset in the bilingual/ESL classroom. *Journal of Education and Social Development*, 6(1), 1–6.

Maguire, M., & Delahunt, B. (2017). Doing a thematic analysis: A practical, step-by-step guide for learning and teaching scholars. *All Ireland Journal of Higher Education*, 9(3), 3351–33514.

Markowitz, N., Thowdis, W., & Gallagher, M. (2018). Sowing seeds of SEL: University-district partnership builds social and emotional learning across the teacher pipeline. *The Learning Professional*, 39(4), 30–34.

Martínez-Alba, G., Pentón Herrera, L. J., & Trinh, E. (2023). Situating teacher well-being in English language teaching. In Pentón Herrera, L. J., Martínez-Alba, G., & Trinh, E. (Eds.), *Teacher well-being in English language teaching: An ecological pathway* (pp. 29–42). Routledge.

Megawati, F., Iswahyuni, I., & Mukminatien, N. (2022). Social and emotional learning (SEL): How does it develop and contribute to pre-service English teachers' identity? *Pegem Journal of Education and Instruction*, 13(1), 75–83.

Melani, B. Z., Roberts, S., & Taylor, J. (2020). Social emotional learning practices in learning English as a second language. *Journal of English Learner Education*, 10(1), 3.

Murano, D., Way, J. D., Martin, J. E., Walton, K. E., Anguiano-Carrasco, C., & Burrus, J. (2019). The need for high-quality pre-service and inservice teacher training in social and emotional learning. *Journal of Research in Innovative Teaching & Learning*, 12(2), 111–113. DOI: 10.1108/JRIT-02-2019-0028

Nall, M. (2020). Supporting social and emotional learning in the EFL/ESL classroom: How the new science of child development can inform second language acquisition theory and practice. *Journal of English Learner Education*, 10(1), 1–11.

Nanquil, L. M. (2021). Promoting social and emotional well-being of ESL students through engaging and inclusive environment. *Linguistic Forum-A Journal of Linguistics*, 3(2), 15–19.

Pentón Herrera, L. J. (2020). Social-emotional learning in TESOL: What, why, and how. *Journal of English Learner Education*, 10(1), 1.

Schonert-Reichl, K. A., Hanson-Peterson, J. L., & Hymel, S. (2015). SEL and pre-service teacher education. In Durlak, J. A., Weissberg, R. P., Domitrovich, C. E., & Gullotta, T. P. (Eds.), *Handbook of social and emotional learning: Research and practice* (pp. 406–421).

Scott, R. (2015, May 26). *Practices to welcome and support ELLs*. https://www.edutopia.org/blog/practices-to-welcome-and-support-ells-robyn-scott

Strauss, A. L., & Corbin, J. M. (1990). *Basics of qualitative research: Grounded theory procedures and techniques*. SAGE Publications.

Vygotsky, L. S. (1978). *Mind in society: The development of higher psychological processes*. Harvard University Press.

Wallender, J., Hiebel, A. L., PeQueen, C. V., & Kain, M. A. (2020). Effects of an explicit curriculum on social-emotional competency in elementary and middle school students. The Delta Kappa Gamma Bulletin: International Journal for Professional Educators, 32–43.

KEY TERMS AND DEFINITIONS

Educator Preparation: A sequenced program of courses and corresponding experiences that ultimately lead to teacher licensure

English Learners: Students who are non-native speakers of English but who are developing their grammatical competence and linguistic proficiency in English

ESOL: English to Speakers of Other Languages

Social-Emotional Learning: The process by which children discover how to successfully manage their feelings and effectively negotiate interpersonal relationships

Teacher Education: A system of coursework and experiences designed to equip students with the knowledge and skills necessary to become effective teachers

APPENDIX I

Social-Emotional Learning Course Unit Post-Questionnaire

Part A. Please indicate the level of your agreement with the following statements by writing the number to the left of each statement that matches your level of agreement with the statement.

Table 8. Course unit post-questionnaire

"1" = "Strongly Disagree" "2" = "Moderately Disagree" "3" = "Neither Disagree Nor Agree" "4" = "Moderately Agree" "5" = Strongly Agree"	
Rating	**Statement**
	1. I understand what a social-emotional approach to teaching English learners is.
	2. I understand the importance of using a social-emotional approach to teaching English learners.
	3. The blog posts helped me understand the social-emotional approach to teaching English learners.
	4. The blog posts helped me understand how to use a social-emotional approach to teaching English learners in my own teaching.
	5. The jigsaw activity of the blog posts helped me understand the social-emotional approach to teaching English learners.
	6. The jigsaw activity of the blog posts helped me understand how to use a social-emotional approach to teaching English learners in my own teaching.
	7. The articles helped me understand the social-emotional approach to teaching English learners.
	8. The articles helped me understand how to use a social-emotional approach to teaching English learners in my own teaching.
	9. The jigsaw activity of the articles helped me understand the social-emotional approach to teaching English learners.
	10. The jigsaw activity of the articles helped me understand how to use a social-emotional approach to teaching English learners in my own teaching.

Part B. Please answer each question below by writing your response in the box under each question.

1. Which aspects of the course unit on social-emotional learning and English learners did you enjoy the MOST? Why?
2. Which aspects of the course unit on social-emotional learning and English learners did you enjoy the LEAST? Why?
3. Which aspects of the course unit on social-emotional learning and English learners did you find MOST helpful? Why?

4. Which aspects of the course unit on social-emotional learning and English learners did you find LEAST helpful? Why?

5. What suggestions do you have for improving the course unit on social-emotional learning and English learners?

APPENDIX II

Descriptive Statistics for the Social-Emotional Learning Course Unit Post-Questionnaire

Table 9. Course unit post-questionnaire

Statement #	Category	Class #1*	Class #2**
1	Mean	3.96	3.82
	Median	4	3
	Mode	4	4
	Range	2	4
2	Mean	4.33	4.19
	Median	4	3.5
	Mode	4	4
	Range	2	2
3	Mean	3.44	3.89
	Median	3.5	4
	Mode	3	4***/5***
	Range	3	4
4	Mean	3.32	3.81
	Median	3.5	4
	Mode	3	4
	Range	3	4
5	Mean	3.32	4.07
	Median	3	4
	Mode	3	4
	Range	4	4
6	Mean	3.48	3.96
	Median	3	4
	Mode	3	5
	Range	4	4

continued on following page

Table 9. Continued

Statement #	Category	Class #1*	Class #2**
7	Mean	3.76	4.00
	Median	3	4
	Mode	4	4
	Range	4	4
8	Mean	3.84	4.00
	Median	3	4
	Mode	4	4
	Range	4	4
9	Mean	3.84	3.91
	Median	4	4
	Mode	3	4***/5***
	Range	2	4
10	Mean	2.84	4.15
	Median	4	4
	Mode	3	4***/5***
	Range	2	4

* n = 26
** n = 27
*** There were an equal number of ratings for this statement.

Section 5
Learner Perspectives

Chapter 16
Arcie Mallari

Arcie Mallari
Silid Aralan, Inc., Philippines

ABSTRACT

Arcie shares his insights into empowerment and resilience through self-directed learning. He is currently exploring the benefits and applications of project-based learning. He wishes to become proficient in using these methodologies and tools to create curricula for students of Silid Aralan, the non-governmental organization he founded in 2007 to help low-performing, underprivileged learners in the Philippines and Indonesia. Arcie advocates that the classroom is the world. We cannot contain learning in a box; learning is everywhere.

INTRODUCTION

I have an ultimate goal. My personal purpose is to empower and educate. That's who I am and who I am to the world. Because of that, every year I always make it a point to plan ahead all I want to achieve. Every year I make sure that I learn something new but it's always intentional; it's purposeful in the sense that I can use these tools, this learning, in order for me to create projects to support my passion, which is education for kids, and now even for adults.

For this year what I really hope to learn about is project-based learning, and possibly later the design thinking approach. These are tools that I've read a lot about. I want to become proficient in using these methodologies and tools to create curricula for students, develop my skills as a business process consultant, and use for my personal benefit.

Eventually, I want to learn about these approaches in the United States because I know of a university can provide me with a classroom learning experience. But for now, because of the pandemic and my current situation, I'm just relying on internet research and attending some pocket seminars.

But the intention is really to learn a bit about project-based learning and design thinking, and then try to contextualize these methodologies. They are foreign approaches but I want to contextualize them in such a way that I can use them to develop curricula or learning frameworks for our learners here in the Philippines, children as well as adults.

So, that's why I chose these goals for this year. I will have a paper plan, which I will put together, but for now I'm just focusing on those pieces and trying to figure out how to navigate them, do some pilot testing, and then eventually launch them for our learners.

I started a non-governmental organization, Silid Aralan, in 2007. We help low-performing, underprivileged kids here in the Philippines, and I also established one in Jakarta Indonesia, as well. The reason behind it is that I believe that everyone is intelligent. Everyone has a different learning style and we have to acknowledge that. And we have to create a design and an environment in which these learners will flourish based on using their innate talent, innate intelligence, and by us as co-learners creating that space for them. So, we don't teach academics, like reading or math or science. We create the learning space in order for them to see who they are. And as they discover who they are, they increase their self-esteem, and as they increase their self-esteem, they become more responsible. The improvement in their grades at school – academic grades – are just a by-product of who they are, but that's not really the goal of the organization. So that's what I've been doing for the foundation that I created.

Silid Aralan means 'classroom' but it's not a classroom that is within the four corners of a space or a room, because my intention is to advocate that the classroom is really the world, that we cannot box learning, but learning is everywhere. And eventually that's what I hope to do, to create the world as the classroom.

To achieve my goals, I have to be very self-directed and intentional in choosing what I need to learn and why. I think that ability is rooted in my family experiences. I come from a family that struggled with many different issues. My parents really had problems with each other; they were so young. My parents have told me that they were planning to abort me, because they were just teenagers at the time. My mother drank something, a medicine, but it didn't work and I was resilient in just hanging on until they decided to just tell their parents. Their parents supported them and then I was born. I know it's unconscious, but I think there is a factor of resilience and how I was able to overcome these things, even if I was only just conceived.

Second is a time when they were building a family. Again, my parents were young. They had so many quarrels and in fact I at the time I didn't know what domestic violence was but I was exposed to domestic violence and it got to a point that me and my mom had to run out from our house and go somewhere else, without shoes. I can still remember that. And we stayed in different places. They were separated for a long time, for nine years. I was nine years old when we left, and then 18 when they got back together.

But I'm also the reason why they got back together. I was growing up on my own, living with my grandmother but without parents. I had to figure out how to overcome all these things. Maybe I'm a dreamer. I had these big dreams of mine, and I didn't just want to be defeated by the circumstances decided by other people. I wanted to choose the life that I wanted, but at the time, I don't know. I don't know the terminologies for that, but the drive, the spirit that I have, is still the same. I had to live on my own and really have a dream and pursue that dream. And that's what I did.

So, that's the past that I had. I still had good friends, but I was so focused on what I wanted to achieve. I kept talking to myself and really documenting what I was going through, to try to make sense of what was happening. I was so young and so hopeful. I prayed a lot for the day my parents would be together. But at the same time, I was hurt also by all of this, and also because of the stigma. I kept it as a secret that my parents were separated. I was in a Catholic private school and at the time, it was not normal that our family wasn't together and so I kept to myself what I had been through during those years.

But later on, I realized that the fate that I want to have has nothing to do with my parents. I mean, I can create another future that I want. They might affect me, but at the end of the day I can choose what I want for myself. And that's what happened. I became independent and at the age when I went to university, I just started to talk to both of my parents. At the time, they were in a rocky stage of their relationship. I asked them, why not try to be together, just try again.

And then they did. Instantly, I got a sister. We built a family. And then another sister. And that's it. But I guess I always look at who I am now because of those things. It was not easy at the time but when I look back, the resilience – how I see things, who I am, how passionate I am for education, also for not being a victim and just to choose what I want to do be and have – is something that is not instant but it is something that happened but I just processed it and now, bit by bit, I'm reaping the harvest and the product of those circumstances of my life.

That's how I believe it is. It was a sad story before, when I was young, but now I can publicly tell it. Although now when I'm asked to speak by youth organizations here, I don't tell the kids whose parents are separated to be hopeful that their parents will get back together, like mine did. Before, that was my script. Because as I've gotten older, I've realized that it just because your parents are separated, that doesn't mean that in your life, you have to be a victim of those circumstances. But it's just so happened by their parents' choice but not their choice. You can still choose the life that you want.

My script, from the time I was a teenager to now, as I'm getting older, has shifted because I realize and also appreciate the past that I had. So, that's who I am, because of those circumstances.

Coming back to the specific goal of learning about project-based learning, I have done my own reading in the area as well as completing one course consisting of three online sessions of two hours each. In the course, they taught us first the basics of the project-based learning approach, and then after that went through cases from different countries that are using it, most particularly in the States. Then they shared some forms, or templates, that they are using, that we can also use if we want.

So, after every session, all three sessions, I worked to figure out how I could apply what I learned about each part of the approach. I would look inward, and look at Silid Aralan, and think about how I could build a curriculum by applying this learning. And I think that's my learning style. Right after class, I would always write about it and apply it, so that I will retain what we covered.

I'm also a risk-taker, in the sense that after each learning, I always want to apply it, whether it will be effective or not, whether I got it or not. But from there I learn. That's why maybe the project-based learning approach that I have right now is already contextualized, because from basic theory I applied it, and when some parts of it don't work, then I tweak some it and now it's kind of working with the youth I'm testing it with.

The sessions were public seminars facilitated by one person and delivered by Zoom to a huge number of people, and there was very little engagement. That person talked throughout the sessions and our only option was to type in chat things like G for 'great' or Y for 'yes.' That was the only interaction for us.

There was no space for us to share. I would love to share because I would also like to consult, but it's not part of the program. It's up to us to download all the stuff and internalize it. Maybe because it's more of a marketing approach, like if you want then you can enrol in other classes. And I want to enrol, but with the minimum amount that I paid, I just want to maximize it, by applying it somehow. But I'm sure I want to have classroom-based learning as well, so I can interact with and learn from others.

I do feel half-fulfilled by this particular learning experience. Prior to starting, I was excited to take the problem-based learning course. And I was excited during the experience as well, but I also felt frustrated because there was no engagement. I always want to share. I also want to listen to hear the stories of others, not just from the teacher, one source of information. Maybe because of my learning style,

I want to learn from other people as well, and then synthesize all of it to create my own understanding.

The timing was frustrating for me. It was two hours, which is a long time to set aside at a time. There was also the challenge of different time zones, which is a factor for me.

I spent a total of six hours participating in the sessions, and then weeks applying and tweaking what I learned. First, I sat to write about what I learned, then I met with my team, the learning management team, and shared with them what I got about the project-based learning approach. So, in a way, that's also a strategy for me to retain my learning and to validate it, because after each session I would share with my teammates, and then after that we would brainstorm, and I would ask them what they think and how we could use this approach and tools. And we would put it all together on the wall. I've always done that, even just for myself, so I can contextualize what is in my brain.

And then every week, we continued to meet, and it all grew until it became a curriculum. Our goal is always to help learners develop their self-esteem. We decided to use the project-based learning approach to create a curriculum for our students in which they create their own projects. In this curriculum, they would also brainstorm, starting with a particular problem, and use the project-based framework to put their ideas together. Then they would build the project and launch it. So, that's what we did.

Here's an example of a problem that the kids have worked on so far. One of the groups chose to work on how to help the learners in their work who are deaf and mute. These kids are in the mainstream school system, together with them, and they are having troubles. When our students asked these kids why they are having difficulty, they said it's because they cannot understand the teachers. For them, the teachers are just opening their mouths, talking about math for example, and they cannot hear anything. These kids have to process the learning on their own, to make sense of all the drawings on the board and try to learn from them. And that creates frustrations for these hearing-impaired learners.

So, that's the problem this one group discovered and wanted to focus on. From there, they created a simulation to understand what this experience would really feel like. For instance, they sat in a class with a teacher who wasn't actually speaking but just opening and closing his mouth while teaching them a complicated subject, just for them to feel for themselves what the hearing-impaired learners in their class are feeling.

What the kids then did was brainstorm different solutions and they conceptualized a prototype of a special kind of eyeglasses. When you wear the eyeglasses, you will see at the side a teacher, beside the real teacher, who is doing sign language, along with subtitles that you can read. The eyeglasses would work in a way like a VR (virtual reality) gadget, translating the teachers' words into sign language and text, so the hearing-impaired students can both see the signs and read what the teacher is saying. That's the kind of work that they're doing right now.

I have not yet achieved my goal. My learning is intentional and I am passionate about it. Most of the time it is not easy to complete it, but if you know the value of having it, those hardships will be replaced by inspirations and motivations. I always start with the end in mind, my dream. Sometimes I feel discouraged, because of past experiences that it did not materialize. But once I catch myself caught up in the past, I immediately shift and find inspirations in the future.

Ultimately, I want to be certified in problem-based learning. Right now I just have the basics. And I'm still just testing the approach. To be able to teach others, I need to really become an expert in this methodology, but I want to become an expert and certified so I can bring this approach to the Philippines and share it with organizations like ours, so that they can also use it. From my research, there's no one who's teaching the project-based learning approach here. For me, I get the value of it and I want to share it with them.

Chapter 17
Linda Alexanian

Linda Alexanian
Organic Weave, Canada

ABSTRACT

Linda describes her approach to personal and professional growth as both an entrepreneur and a mother of entrepreneurs. She learns for understanding and discovery, rather than mastery. When she first started her business five years ago, she made mistakes. Now not only is she learning from them, but she has taken a whole new approach to gaining the skills and knowledge she needs to become successful. She's moving beyond previous experiences and assumptions, asking the right questions, and exploring many paths to find answers.

INTRODUCTION

In general, I learn to understand and discover rather than master a subject. My goal is to learn as much as possible about a single subject within a short time period, generally one month. This is important to me because studying any subject keeps my mind engaged and opens me to new ideas.

When it comes to personal learning, each day I give myself one hour to go down any kind of rabbit hole. Recently I've been following Tyler Cohen. He's an economist who sends out daily links on whatever has captured his attention. It could relate to the economy, politics, media – a wide range of topics that are of interest to him. Very often I'll click on one his links because I have no idea what it relates to. He provides access to so much valuable information. Cohen also runs the online Marginal Revolution University and I'd be interested in taking some of those courses.

Through Cohen's links, I spend a lot of time learning about things that I didn't even know existed, like the BRICS Alliance. Then I make notes about what I'm learning, so it's not in one ear and out the other. And although most days I may spend

DOI: 10.4018/979-8-3693-2663-3.ch017

about an hour exploring the subject, sometimes I end up following that rabbit hole further and further in, especially if it's a topic of real interest to me.

I'm also completing 'The 21 Day Essentialist' online course by Greg McKeown. I watch one 2-minute video every day. It's so doable; a story and a lesson, that's it. I think it's a beautiful formula. The idea is that from start to finish, you will learn something in twenty-one days, breaking a habit or starting a habit. In each video, McKeown shares an experience of something that went wrong and then explains how he was able to fix it. Learners are also encouraged to exchange insights and commitments with an accountability partner, starting from Day 1, to reinforce the new habits, although this part doesn't necessarily feel natural to me. But overall, I love this approach of regular, ongoing brief nuggets for learning.

That's how I've been approaching learning from a personal perspective. When it comes to business, I'm taking courses through Y Combinator (YC), a start-up accelerator company that offers a complete curriculum for launching new businesses. I also consult books and podcasts by entrepreneur and investor Tim Ferriss. These are the two core sources of content I consume.

YC offers a full curriculum of key topics for entrepreneurs, including start-up culture, the attributes of successful founders, and the factors that make a business successful. Ultimately, ten percent of what I'm learning is for me. The other 90 percent is for following the journey of my children who are currently preparing to launch a company. They're completing the live version of the program, interacting with experts in real time and getting feedback every step of the way, while I'm going through related online course materials in the form of recorded video interviews available to everyone.

Right now, in this three-month period, my children's focus is on how to fundraise. I review their fundraising documents and add my input. I correct the spelling. I try to look at the documents through the lens of an investor. I don't know quite how valuable my input is, because I'm certainly not an expert, and they do have access to experts. But I'm able to follow their journey and offer support along the way.

In the meantime, everything I'm learning is applicable to my own business, so it's of value. Whether I'm integrating it into how I operate my business though, that's another question. Over the past six weeks, I have consumed about 100 hours of educational content. I'm thinking about things differently, but it's still early on. In the practical terms of how I approach my business, I have yet to integrate and apply the learnings.

When it comes to starting a business, most people have an idea and think the world needs it and then they push it forward. Anybody who is selling anything is an entrepreneur or a business owner, and that requires an entrepreneurial spirit. But lacking the proper framework for starting a business – the fundamental structures and concepts – is probably the reason why 90% of start-ups or businesses fail. Just because I have a really good idea, and I think the market wants it or needs it, that doesn't mean that the market wants it or needs it, or that I'm going to be able to get my product, no matter how good it is, in front of customers.

When I first started my business five years ago, I knew a lot about my product and believed that the market needed it, without considering product-market fit, without considering launching a minimal viable product. I made a lot of mistakes. I needed my product to be perfect before I would present it. I've learned many things now through YC and one of them is, if you aren't embarrassed by what you're launching, you're launching too late. You just have to get your product out there. The only way we can know if we're on the right track is through our users. So, talk to users, talk to users, talk to users. ABC: always be curious, curious about your users. Not about you, not about your problem, not about whatever it is you think you're trying to solve, but how users are interacting with your product.

I would have benefitted from going through a program like YC instead of approaching my business the way I have so far. I think I wasted a good five years as a result of not knowing a lot of the basic concepts and truths of business. I didn't understand the whole premise of what separates those who are super successful from those who are just successful, or not really successful. I didn't know some of the most basic keys to success like, Act first think later. Pick up the phone. Get out there in front of people with your product or service and talk to them about it.

I was asking a lot of questions but didn't realize I wasn't asking the right ones. As Henry Ford said, 'If I had asked people what they wanted, they would have said a faster horse.' So even though I was talking to people, I didn't know the right questions to ask. Now I'm getting a real framework to work with, an established formula for determining product-market fit for example, based in part by asking the right questions.

My family ran a business. What I learned from my family is how to treat customers. The customer is always right; it doesn't matter how much it costs to make the situation right, just make the situation right. That I really believe in. The reputation of your business will carry you forward. I learned that.

Through my years of working in my family's business, I learned about product. But I never learned how to operate a business, how to launch a business and then launch new products, which is like starting whole new businesses. Most businesses are family businesses or owner-operator businesses, and I think there's an assumption that because you know your product, you know how to sell it. That's just not true; in fact, there's no correlation, in my opinion.

I thought things would go very differently when I launched my own business five years ago. I tried to focus on what I knew best, where I felt most comfortable, which was product development: getting the product, spending money on photography and website graphics, that kind of thing – having a pretty marketplace. But you can have the most beautiful anything, and if there are no customers, there's no business.

For example, I have a high-end product. In the beginning, I was reaching a lot of people who, as it turned out, couldn't afford my product. But I was getting a lot of traffic at the time and thinking, 'Oh wow, it's resonating.' I miscalculated even these basic metrics, thinking that I was doing well and it was just a matter of time before the business would grow, while in fact I wasn't even reaching my target market.

What would have been really valuable to me at the beginning would have been to join a group of other entrepreneurs, to hear about their experiences, what different approaches they were considering, how much time they focused here and there. Having a coach or taking online courses would also have been so valuable for me. I should have done this kind of learning when I launched my business, but I'm starting to do it now and the YC courses are helping me see my business in a very different way.

Most often, the YC courses are in the form of video interviews. Some may feature a high-level entrepreneur like Mark Zuckerberg, but usually it's two experts discussing a particular topic. One person may be asking questions while the other answers, but they are both experts with specific and relevant experience in the topic they're discussing.

The experts share real stories about what they've been through. It's almost like you're sitting in someone's living room, watching a discussion between two people who both happen to be successful geniuses. The content is fun and easy to consume. You can tell that none of the talking is rehearsed and I appreciate that aspect of it. It's a natural, casual discussion; it doesn't feel static or formal, but more like you're eavesdropping on a conversation between two people, one asking the other, 'Hey, what worked for you?'

If I were ever in a teaching position, I would use the storytelling approach because I find it so compelling. I would tell a story and then ask the audience to think of a story that they can relate to my story, which is what people naturally do anyway. They're constantly scanning their experience for something that resonates. I would pause and give them a chance to consider in real time what stories comes to mind. That's a very effective way of forming connections with people.

The YC interviews can last anywhere from ten minutes to about an hour; the majority are under 30 minutes. In the last two months, I have really consumed a lot of material, and I appreciate being able to complete it online because I can easily stop and start as I need to. The browser stays open so even if I want to come back to the content in a day or two, it's always accessible. I find that really convenient. But ideally, I prefer learning chunks of 20 minutes in total. I can be attentive for 20 minutes, and after that my attention can get pulled in other directions.

As I reflect on how these learning experiences today, I realize that my approach to learning as an adult is totally different from how I felt about education as a younger person. I don't think that I was a great student during my formal education. The setup didn't work for me, having one person standing at the front of a room – the teacher – delivering what he or she knew, and I didn't know. That approach is based on one all-knowing person transmitting information to the other person who knows nothing. There's nothing collaborative about that. No stories were injected, certainly no humour. One thing I know for sure is that I learned things for the test; that's it. I did not think what I was learning was going to be important for life and a lot of it wasn't, sadly.

One of the things I value most about learning through stories is when people share their mistakes. We learn from others' mistakes. I don't recall a single experience growing up, during my formal education, when a single teacher shared a mistake. Sharing and learning from mistakes really resonates with me; we're all human. So, as I'm learning things now that I didn't know before, it's within a supportive accepting environment. I appreciate my progress and don't beat myself up just because I didn't know a lot of these things before.

Arthur Ashe said, 'Start where you are, use what you have, do what you can.' That's excellent advice for accomplishing anything. The point is to start; nothing has to be perfect. I've let go of that idea of trying to be perfect. As long as it's acceptable and there are no typos, I can publish a post on Instagram, for instance, or publish a blog post to my website.

Initially I did feel stupid when I realized there were so many basic truths and rules that I didn't know or ignored in my own business, business frameworks that could have provided the structure and guidance I needed. I felt like an imposter. That lasted a moment, like a slap in the face. I'm not even sure what got me through that period. But I accepted that I needed to start from where I was, and now I'm grateful to have the opportunity to learn all these fundamentals. I'm delighted to be thinking about things in a new way and be able to use tools that I didn't have before.

And now I recognize how much I benefit from learning, how much it contributes to my confidence. Having a base knowledge about what's going on in the world, hearing about any given subject and maybe having some knowledge of it, certainly not being blindsided by something as basic as BRICS. There's so much to know about. There's geography, there's finances – we could spend months just studying Bitcoin, for instance. But knowing that Bitcoin is at its highest valuation right now, this kind of knowledge and understanding gives me confidence as an adult in a way that it didn't when I was younger. I did not feel empowered when I had more knowledge as a student; I do now as an adult. I also find it more fun to learn.

I think maybe the shift happened for me when I started raising children. I watched their progress and the process in elementary school and thought, this is a totally different world than I was educated in. Then as they became older and were in middle school and high school, it was cool to be a nerd. We had that word 'nerd' when we were growing up and it was not cool to be a nerd. But the most popular kids at my children's school were those with straight As. It was cool to be smart and attentive in class, instead of messing around and throwing things and passing notes like it was when I was in school.

So that's where the shift started for me. And then as a parent, one of my motivations for all of this is wondering how I may have failed my children, what I may have forgotten to teach them. But one of the great ways to stay connected with and support other people, including our own children, is to learn about them and talk about what interests them. Luckily there is this alignment between me and my children, who are starting businesses. I love thinking about business and entrepreneurship, and taking courses through Y Combinator is an excellent way to connect with my kids and talk their language. As I continue to take courses and support them, I am encouraged and proud of myself for learning so many new concepts and ideas that will help me with my business and with understanding the journey my children are on.

Chapter 18
Mary Ann Becker

Mary Ann Becker
Independent Researcher, USA

ABSTRACT

Mary Ann is pursuing ongoing creative development as a photographer, walking the streets of Paris and forests beyond the city. She hopes that she can provide others with social and historical information regarding what she has experienced, the places and the people she has visited and photographed. In this chapter, she strives to make others feel that they are not alone in the ways they process information, perceive the world, and learn. Every learner is unique and has something special to offer.

INTRODUCTION

At my age, writing about learning goals makes me feel like I am writing a bucket list related to what I want to accomplish before death or making out a business plan with specific outcomes for success. My goals are hopefully to live and maintain good health and state of mind so that I can continue to travel, walk, photograph, observe, read, think, write, research my family tree, and learn for my own personal benefit, to ultimately be remembered.

Maybe the collected images, descriptions, and writing from my journals, etc. will provide others with social and historical information regarding the time I have lived in, the places and people I have visited and photographed. If I had been asked about my goals when I was in my twenties, I would have said that I wanted to be a famous artist, but my life and personal choices changed as I aged.

On a universal level maybe, my contribution to this book will make others feel like they are not alone in the way that they process information, perceive the world, and learn. Everyone is unique learning in different ways (visual, auditory, performing, or reading) and has something special to offer to the world despite a

DOI: 10.4018/979-8-3693-2663-3.ch018

learning disability, insecurities, anxiety, or fear. Some of us are more balanced in the different ways of learning while others lean heavily on one of them. The inner child can be healed.

I am retired from the life of, "metro, boulot, dodo," (the grind) to bring home a paycheck each week, but definitely not from my artistic endeavors. My real learning began after graduate school when there was no longer any need to please someone else, or bend in someone else's direction to receive a grade or be accepted. I could truly pursue my own artistic interests without any anxiety. I made and continue to produce art because I had a need to express myself that took on different forms and materials over the years, whether a sculpture, an installation, an idea, or photographing a tree, examining it from all perspectives, circling, evaluating, and reflecting. I seek to know all aspects of the subject as if it is the topic of a debate where one needs to know all the sides, examining it at a distance and then zooming in on a detail to better understand it.

As a child at a young age my mother taught me that I should walk a mile in another's shoes to experience what they do before judging them. In high school I learned to look at both sides of a topic and to be able to defend it even if I didn't personally believe in it. Visually this is something that I also learned from accompanying a group of students under the tutelage of another professor, putting the tripod in the place that Eugene Atget did when he took photographs of the Pantheon a hundred and twenty years ago, which informed me of Atget's photographic approach and helped me to develop my own.

As an artist/photographer, my motivation to create is both personal and professional. Since receiving my MFA I have been the one orchestrating my creative life. As an artist I don't ever see myself retiring from making images or objects. Things may shift over time for me due to physical and space limitations or how ideas grow and change. I admire Robert Rauschenberg for his ability to move between mediums and change courses during his artistic growth without losing his audience.

Galleries often want to control the direction of an artist's output based on the buyer's market and what they can sell. I may have limited myself by not following this path and choosing to support myself financially by other means. Stradling a life in two countries (France and the USA) with two languages has also created its own compromises and challenges.

It is difficult for me to address just one example of a recent learning experience. There are many projects within the last several years that are significant from which I have learned different things which continue to incubate.

Walking the city of Paris and the forests outside of Paris and photographing what I encounter is a process of collection. Among the collections are: the forest, streets of Paris (people on the street and unknown portraits), sunograms (shadows on ground, pavement, trees, etc.), poubelles (trash cans complete with garbage or flower arrangements or offerings left on their edge), electric boxes (altars containing signs of human interaction), writings about the pandemic walk in Paris in November 2020, poems and descriptions, and the refurbishment of metro station Marx Dormoy that revealed decades of peeling advertisements and posters once hidden now exposed during a renovation.

I will concentrate here on my photographic projects that I have pursued while traversing the city of Paris photographing urban spaces and the forest of Fontainebleau. They have been a part of my art practice and have been important to my learning and creative experiences. You might ask yourself how an urban setting and a forest landscape can be related? Both are related to the culture and history of France, and both are marked with roads, trails, and markings that have existed for centuries.

The streets of Paris hold poetry waiting to unfold. They are full of people, noisy at times, and contain a certain bustling energy, while the forest generally has an opposing calmness where you can hear yourself think, nature singing, and with only a few interruptions of traffic, voices, airplanes, and other sounds. In Paris, one doesn't greet individuals passing on the street unless you know them or are asking for directions but in the forest, it would be highly irregular and against protocol if one didn't say, "bonjour," and make eye contact with an individual or group passing by.

The slower and relaxed pace of the forest walk allows me to stop, look, listen, and photograph. I find myself examining a subject from all sides and angles as well as closeup as a detail or further back at a distance or circling around an object or place as the photographer Eugene Atget did when he photographed the Pantheon in Paris.

After beginning the series of forest pictures during the pandemic, I became interested in the phenomena of pareidolia, the perception of anthropomorphic or biomorphic images hidden in boulders, trees, on the ground, and in the landscape. This is my most recent and growing body of photographic work.

For me the forest is magical and full of hidden treasures where I can fall back in time and history or face wild boars crossing the road with gunfire in the distance or witness deer running at full speed amidst the trees next to the path, or it can be quiet observing beetles or spider webs. Depending on the season the cuckoo bird or crow can be heard. If the wind is very boisterous trees creak and limbs fall. The forest changes with the seasons, weather, and time of day. Rain washes the air clean and makes dimples and gullies in the trail, snow blankets it in silence, rain makes mud and the rocks become slippery. These changes contribute to a sense of discovery.

Upon encountering a dolmen (ancient burial site) hidden in a circle of trees, I am transported back to neolithic times. One remarkable oak tree in the forest has a girth of five-and-a-half times that of my outstretched arms. Two granite tax tables reside in different areas of the Fontainebleau Forest, a date of 1723 carved in their legs placing them in the reign of King Louis XV. Here I imagine the taxes collected at these tables are equivalent to the taxes filed today on paper or internet.

In summer ferns rise higher than my head, hiding the ground below, and make me feel as if a dinosaur might raise its head up at any moment. On the ground fungi abound, the devil's claw appeared one time in fall, red mushrooms with white spots like the ones illustrated in Fairy tale books can be found (I always thought they were an artistic invention and not real), and other mushrooms of all colors and varieties peek through dead leaves at certain times of the year.

Several areas of the ancient forest are defined by "bornes," thigh-high stone boundary markers, each engraved with a number, marking the edge of the forest. Sometimes one is lucky enough to find polissoirs (neolithic marks engraved on a rock made by sharpening stone blades) or other marks hidden in a cave.

On some excursions in the Fontainebleau Forest, I saw modeled boulders that made me think about the figural sculptures of Henry Moore. I wondered if he had ever visited this forest and if he had been influenced by what he had seen there or in another forest. Thus far I haven't found any evidence that Moore visited the Fontainebleau Forest, only that he walked in the forest near his hometown and collected objects from nature during those walks that inspired him. At another time I came upon the impression of a figure washed into the earth by nature that made me think about the outline of a body from the "Silueta Series" that Ana Mendietta preserved in photographs.

Observation is a great part of my learning process. The mysteries held within the forest fascinate me. It took me a year or so to discover what my main photographic interests there were about. I continue to learn about nature and how to physically push myself beyond the fear and anxiety of crawling and climbing over boulders, standing near the edge of an overlook, looking down, and grappling with vertigo.

To summarize, I am normally stimulated by something that I have seen and that then usually causes me to want to learn more about the subject by researching it with whatever resources are available to me.

Travel nourishes me, feeding my curiosity. The forests around Paris and the city of Paris became my own private classroom for visual exploration. Since my first visit to Paris and later in the nearby forests I have been passionate about exploring and photographing them on foot. In the city I walk daily for an hour or more whether doing errands or just exploring various neighborhoods and streets. The walks in the forest are longer, six to eight hours a day depending on the time of year, once or twice a week.

I have been photographing the forest of Fontainebleau since the pandemic (2020 to currently) and the city of Paris since my first visit in 1984, first as a tourist and later as an artist. The subject matter has evolved and matured over the years, and I continue to be excited by the city, still not having experienced or seen all that it has to offer. It changes daily, yearly, and from one minute to the next.

In fact, I don't limit the possibilities of subject matter that I photograph or write about because I never know where an idea will come from, or an image will lead me. The camera is my constant companion for framing the world. I don't start one project and follow it through to completion before starting the next and have never worked that way. I have always had several projects in process, moving back and forth between them. Sometimes they are completed in tandem. I work intuitively and am not always clear about where a project begins, where it is going, or when and where it will end. I try to leave myself open to possibilities and allow time for the ideas to incubate and develop. The end may not come until years later. As an undergraduate and graduate student, semesters were the defining end point for completing work, whereas at this stage of my life I have a lot of latitude regarding the completion of a project.-

Walking is the common thread between the city of Paris and the forest of Fontainebleau, two very different environments, two different forms of intrigue, and excitement, both holding a potential for serendipity. Both can be claustrophobic. I am intrigued by these two different temperaments.

The city has an intensity of crowds, noise, and visual overload. In its energy I lose myself photographing people, children, signs, etc. The forest breathes life into me. In it I find serenity and tranquility, a stillness that soothes. It can be spiritual, the forest path with its tree columns rising straight up on both sides arching far overhead forming a canopy akin to a gothic cathedral. I think about how many centuries people have passed through this place as I listen to the changing voices of the wind rushing through the trees. I think about how the forest changes from season to season, how living things depend upon each other existing symbiotically in the forest, the cycle of life to death that transpires, how trees fall with others catching them, and how plants and trees grow in places that seem improbable for their survival.

I have stressed over agreeing to contribute my story to this book. I feel like I have walked into the unknown and it is challenging me to take risks. I must trust others to read and offer suggestions regarding my ideas and writing. This is a challenge because I have always felt inadequate regarding my writing and language skills. In my art making process I am the lone wolf with total control. My success or failure is my own.

When I have a camera in my hand on a visual pursuit, whether in Paris or a forest near Paris, I am at play and there is no specific goal to attain, to shoot a certain number of images or address a theme, nothing other than the discovery of whatever comes my way. Each walk is an adventure, a quest, to see what the city or forest will present to me.

This notion of play was born in me in childhood, and I have tried to access it throughout my artistic practice. Walking has become part of that practice. It clears my head and opens me up to possibilities, a meditation of sorts. It allows me to play unrestrictedly with the camera, without boundaries or rules. There are no penalties, no time restraints, and no win or lose situations, only a dependency on the light which changes throughout the day and seasons.

My choices vary as where and when to walk. I have had a habit of carrying the camera with me wherever I go for many years. When I am walking and looking, I forget about myself and feel as if I am invisible. Sometimes I am lost in reverie or composing descriptions or poems in my head that a photograph can't capture. I get so involved in the act of looking and photographing that I often forget that others may be watching me, what they may be thinking, or that I may be making a spectacle of myself.

Walking has historically been embedded in writings about Paris and continues into this century through other contemporary writers such as Lauren Elken and Eric Hazan. In the nineteenth century Baudelaire wrote about the Flaneur. The cretinizing voyage was practiced by surrealist writers such as Andre Breton, Louis Aragon, and others. Guy Debord who played a part in the situationist movement evolved walking into the "Derive" (urban drift). As a visual artist I have used aspects of the Derive as a starting point, a strategy which allows me to navigate the city of Paris freely and independently using my intuition and impulses to discover streets or neighborhoods of the city that I may not have traversed before. With my trusty "Plan de Paris" in tow I have no fear of not finding my way home. I can be a rat walking an unending maze. When I complete the walk all I need to do is look for the plaque on the corner of the building that contains the street's name and arrondissement. This becomes the locator for where I am and how to get home.

In the forest, if one can read a compass and follow a topographical map, navigation is easy even without a GPS app on your phone and without worry of the phone battery going dead. Most paths and trails are marked with numbers on trees relating to the topo map, or there are "les bandes de randonnée," colored stripes demarcating different trails.

I share these hikes with my spouse who is the navigator. We found that my body deflects the compass needle from its time reading so it is of limited use to me. We complement each other in that we walk at a similar pace and both of us participate in the act of photographing on these excursions. Sometimes there is silence and other times conversation.

These "forest baths" began for me during the pandemic when one was required to wear a mask in the city of Paris but in the forest, one could abandon the mask and breathe freely. On several occasions it was scary for me when we got separated for various reasons because I didn't have a map, compass, or GPS app but ultimately, we worked out a system where we no longer lost each other, we didn't need to walk in tandem, and we could each have moments alone to photograph our individual interests using our phones as the last resort for communication.

Since the pandemic ended, I have continued this love affair with the forest. For me there is a sense of magic and mystery in the forest that takes me back to my childhood spent on my maternal Grandfather's farm exploring the small, wooded area near the creek that ran through his property and reading Grimm's fairy tales which further fed my imagination.

At the end of these photographic excursions, whether alone on the streets of Paris or in the forest with my spouse, I often find myself tired from the day's activities of walking, looking, and photographing. In the days afterwards when I begin editing the photos, I become excited about some of the images and disappointed with others when what I thought I saw with my eyes wasn't realized in the photograph.

This reflection has been a good point of departure allowing me to examine my life regarding my learning disability, fears, anxiety, success, satisfaction, and enjoyment, to understand how what could have been used by me as an excuse early in life was only a stumbling block, a challenge, something to overcome, and understand more fully. Some teachers helped me along the way and others had the power to sting with their words. When one is born with a learning disability, others don't necessarily realize it since the affliction is invisible. It's not like having a visual physical deformity. I just tried harder to succeed.

In my artistic life, I have learned over time that I am the master of the puppet strings thus I am ultimately in control of the process of what I choose to learn and produce. I have always worked intuitively, and I don't see that changing. It feels like it is part of my genetic make-up. I work quickly shooting many images, taking risks, and this is very different from my methodical approach to other aspects of my life.

It has been suggested by friends that to further my growth as an artist, I should find a way to share my photos with others in book form, an exhibition, or other format to achieve closure and to gain feedback. For many years now I have been more interested and excited about producing photographs than attending to the business aspects of updating my website, seeking an exhibition, grant funding, or fame, or attaining an art career. Maybe I would have been more proactive in exhibiting, for example, if I had been dependent on art for my livelihood but my personality preferred receiving a regular paycheck and not the stress of living on credit, not knowing where or when the next paycheck would arrive. It seems to me artists often live a life of drinking, drugs, and sexual freedom in order to create a personal mythology of hype surrounding their art and life that makes it exciting and saleable. This was contrary to how I was raised to be humble, not bragging concerning my accomplishments or who I knew or what I had or didn't have.

I have always liked and enjoyed the challenges of learning. I don't think all learning in life can be controlled by the teacher in the classroom; emotional learning begins from birth. My parents played an important role in how I was raised. My father worked long hours at his job supporting his family. My mother was a devoted housewife. Both of my parents were raised Catholic. At an early age in the home my mother taught me empathy and tolerance by not passing judgement on others until after, "walking a mile in someone else's shoes, "and trying to understand their perspective. This greatly influenced how I looked at the world.

At the age of three my parents purchased their first house and suddenly I had a room to myself with a big bed. The fear of sleeping alone in a bed in a room by myself for the first time without my parents in the same room was unsettling. My father would lie in bed with me until I went to sleep then returned to his bedroom joining my mom already in bed with my little brother asleep in the baby bed. I remember waking up in the middle of the night and being alone. To soothe my fears in the darkness of night my mom taught me her version of the prayer, "Now I lay me down to sleep." Over the years I outgrew the fear of sleeping or being alone.

I realized as a young girl, if you weren't born a classical beauty then you had better have brains to make up for not having an idealized body type. I was a pudgy kid who ate for comfort. Being the oldest of seven children saddled me with many responsibilities. I took them seriously and emotionally carried the weight of the world on my shoulders. I knew that physically I wasn't in the body that my thin parents felt comfortable with, who wondered where this kid got her genes. This influenced the way that I felt about my body and the mirror cracked. My art has utilized this pain. The title of my MFA Thesis Exhibition was, "The Ugly Duckling is really a Swan."

Learning began at home watching my mother sew, cook, bake, and clean. What I know about cars I learned from my father holding a flashlight, being quiet, listening, and watching. Responsibility was learned at home, first babysitting my younger siblings and later others. I ran errands to the corner store, returning home with the correct change and in my teens chauffeuring my younger siblings to the dentist, etc. I was burdened with responsibility and blamed for acts committed by my younger siblings as the oldest child in some miraculous way I was supposed to control their actions and set a good example. They watched over their children with a critical eye. I learned through osmosis.

My parents each had an eighth-grade education. They were hard workers descended from farm families having a great amount of common sense and were both gifted with their hands. I observed them reading sections of the local newspaper but never a book other than one for their children. They were content with raising a family and rarely left us in the care of others. They believed in education and sacrificed a lot to send all seven of their children to private Catholic school. They lived simply and never went out to a movie after marriage. There was always food on the table and never a sense that their children were a burden or there wasn't enough money for the necessities of life. I was secure in feeling that I was loved by them.

I always knew that I was intelligent and could think but I couldn't always find the words and the tone to express myself. I learned that words have power and was often frustrated by what came out of my mouth as garbled speech which didn't match what flowed through the pen onto paper where I had more than one chance to correct my writing. In speech I had only one chance to express myself eloquently and not sound stupid and uneducated. My brain could receive information that I processed and understood but my retrieval system didn't always jump quickly and succinctly over the axons and dendrites. My eyes moved slowly across the page. I felt that my brain was slow like the movement of a turtle, but I was determined like it to keep prodding along. I also knew that with my level of education if I had had better language skills that I would have been more employable at a higher salary.

I was always a photographer looking at the world from the outside, framing it, and feeling as if I didn't quite belong. I didn't feel comfortable being photographed and felt the photos didn't capture the essence of my inner nature, and I didn't like looking at myself in many of the family photographs standing next to my younger skinny siblings. Later I discovered that being behind the camera gave me the power to control the compositions. I was present as the composer and the author of the images. I started photographing my younger siblings playing in the backyard when I was 14 years old. I rejected the portrait tradition of lining them up in rows. I was interested in catching and freezing them in movement. I used my father's camera to photograph my siblings, a simple one with bellows whose view finder wasn't a one-to-one match to what I saw or was caught on the film. I think this limitation allowed me in later years to have the confidence to work intuitively without always looking through the view finder or camera's back screen to see what is framed at the moment of exposure and then editing the results later. I never studied photography in the classroom but my formal drawing classes as an undergraduate taught me about chiaroscuro and composition which clearly applied to photography.

As a child I possessed a visual curiosity running my eyes across a room, soaking up and penetrating it while memorizing the placement of objects. Years later I could describe an interior I had visited only once in my childhood. My mother didn't appreciate that my roving eyes memorized spaces and that I seemed to see more than I was supposed to, which made her uncomfortable. I feel that my ability to observe is a gift that has served me well as an artist but as a child it made me feel as if I had committed a crime.

Teachers throughout my education left their wounds and scars on me as much as my parents, but there were also moments of caring. I did well in school in math, science, spelling, and art. English was my most challenging subject from an early age. When I started school they didn't have a test to detect learning disabilities and to form an educational plan of action. I knew that I didn't see the world the way others did, but I was also lucky not to have been burdened by a label. I had no excuses for not excelling.

I got my first pair of glasses in second grade. I was fortunate that I had a very dedicated teacher in second grade who was astute and noticed that I had trouble reading, seeing, and hearing, and who reached out to my parents to get me the help that I needed.

When reading a book or singing from a hymnal my eyes would skip lines or words would disappear off the page. I didn't learn until much later that the prisms in my eyes were turned, not lining up correctly, and this was the cause for the above symptoms as well as my sometime seeing double halos. In elementary school I was a slow reader, but I had a high comprehension level. Memorizing and then reciting poems, for example, was challenging. I also had a difficult time reading out loud in class. I stumbled through the words on the page. As far back as I can remember I would leave words out and others completed my sentences. I felt less than confident in my reading, speaking, and writing skills, and as an adult I still feel that way.

For me retrieval of information was often problematic. It was filed alphabetically in my brain. If the word didn't immediately roll off my tongue, I knew the first letter of the word or concept; otherwise, I would see an image of the object or scene before the word(s) emerged. Timed tests were especially stressful and frustrating because often time expired before I was finished. I felt limited.

I remember being humiliated in fourth grade by my teacher after each row in the classroom was to select a student to read a poem, the rows being in competition with each other. I was selected by the students in my row and the teacher said to me in front of the class, "Why did you pick her?" This did nothing to boost my confidence.

However, I liked poetry and checked out poetry books geared towards young readership at the local library during the summer. I learned that one could express themselves through words and that through poetry one could create word pictures and explore feelings without following the rules of formal grammar.

In 5th or 6th grade I suffered a concussion on the way to school. I was walking backwards against the cold winter wind and tripped backward on an uneven edge of the sidewalk, landing flat on my back, hitting my head, and receiving a golf-ball-sized lump to the back of my head. Spinning followed almost immediately, and vomiting later.

The first hour of class that day I completed my exam, through all the spinning and text moving off the page. There were no MRIs at that time to determine any damage to my brain. I didn't tell the school nurse that I had fallen, and she was very upset later to learn I had suffered a concussion. My father drove me to the doctor, I was given a shot to end the dry heaves, and then sent home to rest. I have never known if this fall had exacerbated my learning disability.

In high school my freshman or sophomore English teacher gave me my first letter grade of a "C" which made me feel humiliated and inadequate, so you can imagine that I liked English class the least. I knew I could think but my speaking, grammar, and language skills were limiting me. Grammar didn't make sense to me, and I felt something was missing in my brain.

I took Latin as a foreign language in high school because it was a dead language that was written and not spoken. It helped to expand my vocabulary and to decipher the meaning of unknown words on the ACT test for college entrance. Later, as an undergraduate art student there was no language requirement for graduation, and for over thirty years I have struggled to learn fundamental French while living abroad.

My first three years at a private all-girls' Catholic high school were formative. My teachers and role models during those years were all women who had dedicated their lives to teaching and whose leadership, expectations, and examples instilled in me feminist values even though they never uttered the word "feminism." I felt confident competing academically with other girls and I didn't have to dumb myself down or worry about my appearance. I felt empowered.

My senior year, the girls' and boys' schools joined hands to become coed. Due to their own prejudices, the male teachers sometimes had different expectations for the two genders. One teacher gave different projects to the boys and girls in the same class, the boys learning to draw up electrical and plumbing plans in the interior design class while the girls built model homes complete with furniture, to be entered in the model home contest sponsored at the local Home Show. Both genders learned to draw floor and elevation plans.

I procrastinated taking typing class until the first semester of my senior year in high school. This was when I realized that the coordination between my eyes and brain also affected my hands while typing. Letters would be reversed within words and my right hand would often leave extra spaces between words. This was frustrating, causing more mistakes and slowing down my speed.

As an undergraduate in the 1970's men outnumbered the female professors in the art faculty at the university I attended. The ceramics area had only one full-time male professor teaching upper classes. One semester the professor gave everyone in the class I was taking was a "C." How can you fight a professor over what felt like an unjust grade when art is so subjective and there are no objective criteria of exams or papers on which to base the grade? You're in a double-bind situation considering that in order to complete your degree you have more classes to complete with this professor in your area of major.

I disliked the thought of public speaking so much that I procrastinated until the last year of college before completing this requirement and chose to take Interpersonal Communication instead of Speech Class because I didn't want to compose speeches and cope with the anxiety of presenting them in front of the class. That stress hasn't left me, but I have nevertheless given presentations to students regarding my artwork and been interviewed for a podcast.

In graduate school a male professor in an independent study class at the end of the semester suggested that if I wanted an "A, B, or C" it would cost me a certain amount of money. At least he wasn't asking for sexual favors, a possibility I had been warned about by another female student. As a result, I took an incomplete passing and never completed the course because I refused to submit to this power play.

At a meeting, the chair of my MFA thesis committee implied that someone else had written my thesis because I had used some language that was more sophisticated than my regular speech pattern when conversing. I had to explain that I understood the terms, had used a thesaurus, and that no one else had written or edited the material. As a woman I was humiliated at having my ethics called into question.

Marcia Tucker (the founder and director of the New Museum of Contemporary Art in New York City) was a visiting artist when I was in graduate school. During her lecture or studio visit she spoke of how we all have baggage that we carry around with us wherever we go, something I could relate to strongly. This was her way of talking about the wounds of the inner child (feelings). I think artists carry these positive and negative feelings from childhood into adulthood. They nourish our imagination and creativity. I know I have pulled from this interior baggage. Working through and resolving issues, the baggage can lighten, or it can become heavier and cumbersome.

My real education began after graduate school when I first traveled to New York City, then to Europe, exploring the art and architecture that I had studied in art and art history classes and that I had known up to then only as images projected on a wall or printed in books or magazines further instilled in me my passion for art.

As a woman competing in a man's world, I always felt like I had to be better than my male counterparts. Sometimes I succeeded beyond my own expectations and other times I failed. I continue to evolve and grow through visiting museums, galleries, reading, watching films, videos, and attending lectures.

In an art museum looking at an art object I enjoy testing my knowledge by guessing who the artist is, when and where it was made, etc., before looking at the identifying label. Since learning about WORDLE and ARTLE I have been playing them daily. From time to time, I also play "Melie Melo," the French version of "Word Find." I find all these enjoyable, stimulating, and challenging.

Reading the essays from the book "Funny Weather: Art in an Emergency" by Olivia Laing was a voyage of ideas and sensations like wandering through the streets of Paris or the forest where the journey isn't always revealed at the beginning but makes itself known along the way. She weaves the personal and works of artists into a patchwork of ideas which is tied into a glorious bow at the end. Her writing is truly a gift of empathy.

"Empathy is not something that happens to us when we read Dickens. It's work. What art does is provide material with which to think: new registers, new spaces. After that, friend, it's up to you."

—— Olivia Laing, Funny Weather: Art in an Emergency

In the process of writing and researching the cretinizing voyage of the surrealists I came across the website of Ellen Mueller: https://teaching.ellenmueller.com/walking/category/surrealism/

She mentions surrealist books that employ déambulations (wanderings) as in the novels of Andre Breton, Louis Aragon, Philippe Soupault, and Roger Caillois's "Guide to the 15th arrondissement" in Paris. I had never heard of Caillois but was intrigued and curious because I live between France and the USA. I was interested in this book which caused me to research him further and discovered that his 1958 book, "Man, Play and Games," was about the activity of play. This resonated with the role of "child's play" in my own process of working. I was totally unaware of the work of Caillois before this chance event and this deserves further investigation on my part.

On a flight returning to the USA from France I saw the movie, "Barbie," released in 2023 and found the sense of play relating to childhood with dolls and motherhood and the breaking of stereotypes to be of interest, recalling my mother saying to me, "That I could do whatever I put my mind to." I wondered if every woman of my age had been fortunate enough to hear those words as a young girl.

I recently saw the film, "Apartment for Peggy," originally released in 1948. It was made just after WWII when soldiers returned home to their wives and entered colleges. The newlywed wives were threatened that their husbands would intellectually outgrow them. When one woman found lipstick on her husband's collar, a group of them formed a study group headed by a philosophy professor and began the journey to enriching their intellectual lives through lectures, studying various subjects, reading recommended books, and raising challenging questions to be better able to converse with their husbands at home and maintain their marital relationships, while at the same time raising babies. In the movie, Peggy, a pregnant wife, expresses herself eloquently regarding what she wants for her unborn child. The film reveals the power and intelligence of women at a time when after the war they were supposed to reproduce and stay at home. It was released over 75 years ago but bears the struggles that women still face in marriage, pregnancy, and motherhood.

Reading the book, "Visual Thinking," by Temple Grandin made me realize that as a detail-oriented person I am part of a neurodiverse group. Her book gave me some credence knowing that I wasn't alone, but also showed how Visual thinkers are needed even though Verbal thinkers are often more highly prized and rewarded in society.

Suddenly, the other day while I was writing about my own creative and learning process, the title of the film, "Why Man Creates," by Saul Bass released in 1968 serendipitously came to mind. I saw this film many times in high school and at least once as an undergraduate, most likely in an English class. It made a huge impression on me. This memory caused me to look for it online to view it once again. https://www.youtube.com/watch?v=ONVZ8AH4yKc

It is a short animated film about the creative process through history and addresses how time unfolds within the process, whether you are a writer, visual artist, or scientist, sometimes involving years, sometimes leading to a dead end and starting over due to failure. The summation at the end of the film is, "To look into oneself and say I am unique." Many years ago, as an undergraduate studying art, I concluded that each person sees and conceives differently, and makes marks in another way no matter what the media. As a result, I needed to acknowledge that what makes one person as an artist different from others is a gift. We are not all from the same mold and don't share the same experiences. We each delve into ourselves tapping into our emotional past lying beneath our own edifice and why we create.

Chapter 19
Xuan-Vinh Nguyen

Xuan-Vinh Nguyen
 https://orcid.org/0009-0008-4236-6699
Independent Researcher, Canada

ABSTRACT

Xuan-Vinh solves business problems by continuing to develop as a curious generalist who is able to apply methodologies and tools acquired through past experiences to each new situation. He currently works as a project manager in the Information Technology space, which continues to evolve at a fast pace. He believes training can be pursued for several different reasons: to improve performance, to explore what we're curious about, and to understand more about the broader context in which we work. He is especially passionate about the Why. Why are we doing this as an organization? Why is this important?

Introduction

I work as a project manager in the Information Technology space, which evolves at a fast pace.

Purpose of training

I believe that training can have different purposes that depend on context.

First, it may be for performance. For example, when you are new to a role you focus on what you need to be able to perform the requirements of your job, because you're not yet able to meet those requirements. When you are comfortable with your job requirements, you then may want to improve your performance within the job.

DOI: 10.4018/979-8-3693-2663-3.ch019

Second, it may be out of curiosity; there's something specific to your job you find interesting that you want to learn more about.

Third, it may be as part of wanting to know more about the wider space you work in, how you fit in the organisation or how your field will evolve. An example of learning in the context of IT could be to get a better understanding of how IT fits within the broader organisation and focus on the business value of IT. Or you might want to learn about different technologies, like aspects of Cloud computing and its implications.

On my end, I've gone through each of these three approaches.

Specialist versus Generalist

A second aspect of training that may differ from person to person is whether a person is looking to grow as a specialist or a generalist, and that is in any field, not just IT.

Specialists typically look to develop their expertise in a very specific subject. But I consider myself more of a generalist. What I appreciate about the generalist mindset is that I feel you are there to recognize patterns. Once you start to recognize patterns, you realise that problems ultimately reflect similar patterns in any of the work you do. In my case, as an IT project manager, at the root it's usually either a human problem or a technical problem.

When I was being interviewed for project manager roles in IT, I was often asked why I like project management, because at its essence, project management is boring; it's really just about coordinating work. What makes it an exciting field are the problems that come up. Through time I've learned that the source of most project problems, even in IT, is people.

Sometimes it's a question of technology, and then the answer is usually a simple yes or no. First you need to determine if the solution is technically feasible or not. If it is, then you can figure out what combination of money, time, and expertise is needed to build the solution. These are straightforward questions to answer. But ultimately, achieving a successful solution comes down to influencing stakeholders to agree to the investments needed to resolve the issue.

Whether the issue is mainly technological or human, and although every scenario is unique and requires a unique combination of tools to resolve it, as a generalist I'm able to apply tools I've gathered through past experiences to each new situation.

Types of Learners

Another aspect of training that I have observed is that there are two different types of learners.

There are the people who like to be told what to do to be successful in their jobs, that want to take direction on what they should be learning.

Then there are the people who want to figure things out in their own way, who recognize that there's no one size fits all, that every scenario is unique, and they want to figure out what they need to learn to work through each individual situation.

I believe I fall in the latter group, and I'm certainly not saying that this is the best approach. In either case, you may end up learning the wrong thing, whether it's what someone told you to do or something you chose for yourself. There are risks on both sides, pros and cons to both.

I believe it's more a question of personality: are you the kind of person who prefers to take direction, or someone who tries to figure things out independently? It doesn't make you a better person, or learner, if you're more self-directed. In fact, the downside is that you may tend to be more short-sighted and focus on one way of doing things, as opposed to listening to somebody with more experience or expertise. You do need to find a way to balance these things out.

What Directs my Learning

What drives me to learn may not be to address today's needs; it may be to achieve a milestone that will enable me to develop in a topic that could interest me later, even if I don't see an immediate practical application at the moment.

As I go through work, I see different problems that come and go. If I see something consistently happening, this is what I delve into and choose to learn more about. I'm very self-directed in that way.

I'm motivated to solve business problems that I encounter; that's where the real learning opportunities are within the scope of my role as a project manager. I learn a lot when there's a business problem that I need to resolve and I don't have all the tools or frameworks to address it, or I want to look beyond the standard approaches and identify a better way to resolve the issue.

Ultimately, I believe I'm driven by the Why. If you ask me what my motivation is, it's the Why. Why are we doing this? Why is this important? If I don't feel that it's important, then I'm not interested, curious, or motivated. Other people are more motivated by the What; that's what they need to know to want to move forward. That's not me.

I'm always asking myself, Why are we doing this as an organization? Why does this specific problem happen? Why does this specific domain work in this way?

When I think about this distinction between being a generalist and being a specialist, I wonder if it's about what that Why looks like. Specialists are interested in the Why, but from a narrower perspective. As a generalist, I'm interested in a much broader, more holistic perspective and taking inputs from sources other people may not think of accessing. We all have our own Whys, but we differ in terms of what type of Why is most meaningful to us.

The Why is what gets me engaged. I was not a high performer in school. Back when you're in school, you don't know why you're learning things. So, I wasn't interested. I did whatever I needed to do to get to the next stage, just to get it done. If I'd had the Why, then I would've been more interested.

Now, as an adult, I have the opportunity to have the Why and learn things that are very much applicable to the work I'm interested in doing. As soon as I have the Why, I want to go deep into learning about it. That's what motivates me. I knew at a very young age – I think every child knows this – that if I wasn't interested in something, I wasn't going to spend much time on it. I learned to find the Why.

How I Learn

In terms of approach, when I learn it's important for me to be hands-on. I have to be able to discuss, debate, and test ideas to be engaged and interested. It's active learning that matters to me.

Completing lab work – experimenting – is very important. When I'm learning something related to IT, I really enjoy when I have the opportunity to practise using the tools in a dummy system that simulates the real-life environment, being given an objective and asked to follow the steps in the system to achieve it.

I always prefer to complete these kinds of learning exercises individually, rather than in a group. I have a very linear way of approaching problems and I need to be able to follow that process, walking through and mastering one step at a time. I can't skip steps. Some people can but I can't. So, it can be frustrating for them to work through learning activities with me, just as it can be frustrating for me to try and follow the flow of the group. It can really interfere with my ability to understand and learn as I complete the activities.

The same applies to other types of activities, such as open discussions. I tend to approach each discussion methodically. I identify the premises of the argument and then work through the implications of each one, one at a time. I want to conclude each one and put it aside before moving forward to the next topic. That's how my brain works.

Something I have noticed is that making mistakes helps me tremendously. If I follow the steps and everything works as it's supposed to, then I'm not learning as much as I could. I know that when I try to accomplish the same tasks in real life, I'll make mistakes and I won't be prepared; I won't be able to backtrack and figure out what I've done wrong. I won't understand why I made the mistake. When you make a mistake, that's when you're really testing the scope of what you've understood.

Lectures or people talking to me for long periods of time has never been a good way for me to learn. A 1-hour class of someone "shooting information at my face" will not work. Recently, what has worked best for me, whether the material is delivered through video or face-to-face, is to learn in short snippets, 5–10-minute increments. What I like about online learning is that I can stop the moment I lose interest. So, for example, I may watch two 5-minute videos and then decide I've had enough for the day, knowing I can continue when I'm more motivated or more generally in the right state of mind.

While I very much appreciate an online learning environment for lab work and videos, for example, it is poor when it comes to opportunities for open discussions. But then again, open discussions can also be challenging in a classroom environment. When people attend class, the benefit is an interesting range of diverse opinions, but it also brings together different personality types; not everyone is open-minded or comfortable speaking in public.

The most effective way for me to learn through conversation is to organise these kinds of discussions on my own. I identify people I know, who are not associated with the class but do have some kind of connection to the topic, and then talk through the topic with them. I hand-select the right people, the ones I know will engage in an open discussion rather than throwing their opinions around.

In general, as I reflect on my preference for more independent, self-directed learning and career development, I know how important it is for me to always be able to take a step back when I get stuck and ask myself if the issue really matters. For example, suppose I'm completing a curriculum with fifty different topics. If topics aren't sequential and I miss one, I might decide that I understand 90% of what I need to understand and that's good enough.

On the other hand, if the topics are sequential and I do get stuck and can't progress from there, that's what the internet is for. I feel competent to find the answer on my own. Whether I find it in the course, online, or in the scope of my work, it doesn't really change anything. No course is perfect, every course has its flaws, and we all have different ways of learning. We just have to figure out what we need to do to mitigate these imperfections.

Another opportunity for learning I really benefit from is putting my hand up when I see projects that people don't want to take on due to the complexity at work. Because when people don't want to do something, that's usually where there's the most opportunity to learn, and to prove you can apply concepts and tools you've learned elsewhere to resolve the current problem.

Timing is also important to my learning. It's like how we know that teenagers need to sleep later into the day, but most schools are still scheduled to start early in the morning. It's the same for me; there is a prime time for me to learn. Accomplishing things first thing in the morning works best for me, because it's usually when I'm most focused, least distractible. Ideally, I do focused work in the mornings and have my conversations in the afternoon.

My Own Questions about Learning

I wonder about the role of the educator in ensuring learning is meaningful and relevant for learners. For a student like me, what would happen if an educator asked questions to find out what kind of learner I am, to discover that I am someone who needs to take time on his own to figure things out? Because if I don't understand something in the moment, I'm most likely to walk away, work through it, and then come back once I've figured it out.

For people like me, maybe a different learning approach is required. Maybe I need more time; maybe I need the material ahead of time so I can work through it, see what I understand and where the gaps are, and then use the class time to ask the teacher questions that are particularly relevant for me.

It would be different with a different kind of student, such as someone who needs to have the teacher walk through the content step by step to learn most effectively. Then that's how the face time would be used, with the teacher telling that person what he or she needs to learn and going through the slides together, for example.

It would be great if a course syllabus identified the content, described how it will be covered, and then also included different strategies reflecting different learning preferences. Then each of us would know how we can be proactive and best prepare for class. I would go through the material and plan my questions in advance, for example, while another student would wait to cover the content as a group during class.

The more proactive we can be, as teachers and students, the better. Teaching, assessing, and strategizing all at the same time is a lot for the teacher to be managing, and I think it would help a lot for all of us to plan for and contribute to the process as best we can. To really personalize the learning experience, we need to get better at uncovering what we need and want.

It's a question of ownership. Who's in charge of learning? Is it the teacher's job or is it the student's job?

Conclusion

Through the contributions of many authors, a diverse range of topics and approaches have been explored with respect to the impact of emotions on learning. Several themes wove naturally among them, such as:

- Transformation through learning
- Self-directed learning and motivation
- Mindfulness and meditation
- Reflection and journaling
- Narrative and storytelling
- Uncertainty and the benefits of making mistakes
- Chunked learning/breaks
- Measurement/analytics

The question I'm left with, in view of the evidence and arguments supporting the impact of emotions during the learning process, is why isn't this considered more often in practice? Why aren't we, as learning professionals, doing a better job of taking emotions into account in our daily work?

Our own transformation lies at the heart of this question. What must we think, feel, and do differently to ensure learners are properly supported in their growth and development?

cedars are terribly sensitive to change of time and light – sometimes they are bluish cold-green, then they turn yellow warm-green – sometimes their boughs flop heavy and sometimes float, then they are fairy as ferns and then they droop, heavy as heartaches

- Emily Carr, in an undated letter to Ira Dilworth

Compilation of References

Abbott, H. P. (2008). *The Cambridge introduction to narrative* (2nd ed.). Cambridge University Press. DOI: 10.1017/CBO9780511816932

Abedini, A., Abedin, B., & Zowghi, D. (2023). A framework of environmental, personal, and behavioral factors of adult learning in online communities of practice. *Information Systems Frontiers*. Advance online publication. DOI: 10.1007/s10796-023-10417-2

Abrams, Z. (2023, January 1). Kids' mental health is in crisis: Here's what psychologists are doing to help. *American Psychological Association, 54*(1). https://www.apa.org/monitor/2023/01/trends-improving-youth-mental-health

AbuHamda, E., Islam, A. I., & Bsharat, T. (2021). Understanding quantitative and qualitative research methods: A theoretical perspective for young researchers. *International Journal of Research*, 8(2), 71–79.

Achen, K., & Rutledge, D. (2023). The transition from emergency remote teaching to quality online course design: Instructor perspectives of surprise, awakening, closing loops, and changing engagement. *Community College Journal of Research and Practice*, 47(6), 428–442. DOI: 10.1080/10668926.2022.2046207

Acosta-Gonzaga, E., & Ramirez-Arellano, A. (2021). The influence of motivation, emotions, cognition, and metacognition on students' learning performance: A comparative study in higher education in blended and traditional contexts. *SAGE Open*, 11(2), 215824402110275. DOI: 10.1177/21582440211027561

Adogwa, O., Elsamadicy, A. A., Sergesketter, A. R., Black, C., Tarnasky, A., Ongele, M. O., & Karikari, I. O. (2017). Relationship Among Koenig Depression Scale and Postoperative Outcomes, Ambulation, and Perception of Pain in Elderly Patients (≥ 65 Years) Undergoing Elective Spinal Surgery for Adult Scoliosis. *World Neurosurgery*, 107, 471–476. DOI: 10.1016/j.wneu.2017.07.165 PMID: 28826716

Ajjawi, R., Dracup, M., Zacharias, N., Bennett, S., & Boud, D. (2020). Persisting students' explanations of and emotional responses to academic failure. *Higher Education Research & Development*, 39(2), 185–199. DOI: 10.1080/07294360.2019.1664999

Alam, A. (2023, May). Improving Learning Outcomes through Predictive Analytics: Enhancing Teaching and Learning with Educational Data Mining. In *2023 7th International Conference on Intelligent Computing and Control Systems (ICICCS)* (pp. 249-257). IEEE Xplore. DOI: DOI: 10.1109/ICICCS56967.2023.10142392

Alam, A., & Ahmad, M. (2018). The role of teachers' emotional intelligence in enhancing student achievement. *Journal of Asia Business Studies*, 12(1), 31–43. DOI: 10.1108/JABS-08-2015-0134

Alamri, H., Lowell, V., Watson, W., & Watson, S. L. (2020). Using personalized learning as an instructional approach to motivate learners in online higher education: Learner self-determination and intrinsic motivation. *Journal of Research on Technology in Education*, 52(3), 322–352. DOI: 10.1080/15391523.2020.1728449

Aldao, A., & Nolen-Hoeksema, S. (2012). When are adaptive strategies most predictive of psychopathology? *Journal of Abnormal Psychology*, 121(1), 276–281. DOI: 10.1037/a0023598 PMID: 21553934

Aldao, A., Nolen-Hoeksema, S., & Schweizer, S. (2010). Emotion-regulation strategies across psychopathology: A meta-analytic review. *Clinical Psychology Review*, 30(2), 217–237. DOI: 10.1016/j.cpr.2009.11.004 PMID: 20015584

Alderman, M. K. (2007). *Motivation for Achievement: Possibilities for Teaching and Learning* (3rd ed.). Routledge., DOI: 10.4324/9780203823132

Aldowah, H., Al-Samarraie, H., & Fauzy, W. M. (2019). Educational data mining and learning analytics for 21st century higher education: A review and synthesis. *Telematics and Informatics*, 37, 13–49. DOI: 10.1016/j.tele.2019.01.007

Alfrobel Inc. (2020). *We Live Here* [VR experience]. Meta. https://www.meta.com/experiences/2537261906377373/

Aliasgari, M. A. J. I. D., & Farzadnia, F. (2012). The relationship between emotional intelligence and conflict management styles among teachers. *Interdisciplinary Journal of Contemporary Research in Business*, 4(8), 555–562.

Alkhatlan, A., & Kalita, J. (2019). Intelligent Tutoring Systems: A Comprehensive Historical Survey with Recent Developments. *International Journal of Computer Applications*, 181(43), 1–20. DOI: 10.5120/ijca2019918451

Alkhodary, D. A. (2023). Exploring the relationship between organizational culture and well-being of educational institutions in Jordan. *Administrative Sciences*, 13(3), 92. DOI: 10.3390/admsci13030092

Allbright, T. N., Marsh, J. A., Kennedy, K. E., Hough, H. J., & McKibben, S. (2019). Social-emotional learning practices: Insights from outlier schools. *Journal of Research in Innovative Teaching & Learning*, 12(1), 35–52. DOI: 10.1108/JRIT-02-2019-0020

Alonso-Tapia, J., Abello, D. M., & Panadero, E. (2020). Regulating emotions and learning motivation in higher education students. *The International Journal of Emotional Education*, 12(2), 73–89. https://www.um.edu.mt/library/oar/handle/123456789/65093

Alqurashi, E. (2019). Predicting student satisfaction and perceived learning within online learning environments. *Distance Education*, 40(1), 133–148. DOI: 10.1080/01587919.2018.1553562

Alves, P., Miranda, L., & Morais, C. (2017). The Influence of Virtual Learning Environments in Students' Performance. *Universal Journal of Educational Research*, 5(3), 517–527. DOI: 10.13189/ujer.2017.050325

Amabile, T. M. (1996). *Creativity in context: Update to The Social Psychology of Creativity*. Westview Press.

Ambrose, S. A., Bridges, M. W., DiPietro, M., Lovett, M. C., & Norman, M. K. (2010). *How learning works: Seven research-based principles for smart teaching*. John Wiley & Sons.

Anand, S., & Kerketta, E. (2016). Teaching emotional intelligence: A foundation for better living. *International Journal of Applied Research*, 2(5), 967–969.

Andreev, A. (2022, Jul 26). *Learning* Outcomes. https://www.valamis.com/hub/learning-outcomes

Andrews, S., Newsum, J. M., Crawford, C. M., & Moffett, N. L. (2021). Sisyphus Leans Into the Professoriate: Faculty Discuss Careers and the Academic Landscape. In N. L. Moffett's (Ed.) *Navigating Post-Doctoral Career Placement, Research, and Professionalism* (pp. 185-226). IGI Global. DOI: DOI: 10.4018/978-1-7998-5065-6.ch009

Antoniou, P., Arfaras, G., Pandria, N., Ntakakis, G., Bambatsikos, E., & Athanasiou, A. (2020). Real-Time Affective Measurements in Medical Education, Using Virtual and Mixed Reality. In *Lecture Notes in Computer Science (including subseries Lecture Notes in Artificial Intelligence and Lecture Notes in Bioinformatics)* (pp. 87–95). DOI: 10.1007/978-3-030-60735-7_9

Antoniou, P. E., Arfaras, G., Pandria, N., Athanasiou, A., Ntakakis, G., Babatsikos, E., Nigdelis, V., & Bamidis, P. (2020). Biosensor Real-Time Affective Analytics in Virtual and Mixed Reality Medical Education Serious Games: Cohort Study. *JMIR Serious Games*, 8(3), e17823. DOI: 10.2196/17823 PMID: 32876575

Arghode, V. (2013). Emotional and social intelligence competence: Implications for instruction. *International Journal of Peagogies and Learning*, 8(2), 66–77. DOI: 10.5172/ijpl.2013.8.2.66

Argyris, C. (1991). Teaching smart people how to learn. *Harvard Business Review*, 69(3), 99–109.

Argyris, C., & Schön, D. A. (1996). *Organizational learning II: Theory, method, and practice*. Addison-Wesley.

Arif, I., Umer, A., Kazmi, S. W., & Khalique, M. (2019). Exploring the relationship among university teachers' emotional intelligence, emotional labor strategies, and teaching satisfaction. *Abasyn Journal of Social Sciences*, 12(1). Advance online publication. DOI: 10.34091/AJSS.12.1.03

Aristovnik, A., Keržič, D., Ravšelj, D., Tomaževič, N., & Umek, L. (2020). Impacts of the COVID-19 Pandemic on Life of Higher Education Students: A Global Perspective. *Sustainability (Basel)*, 12(20), 8438. DOI: 10.3390/su12208438

Armstrong, K. (2019, October 29). Carol Dweck on how growth mindset can bear fruit in the classroom. *Association for Psychological Science*. https://www.psychologicalscience.org/observer/dweck-growth-mindsets

Arroyo, I., Cooper, D. G., Burleson, W., Woolf, B. P., Muldner, K., & Christopherson, R. (2009). Emotion sensors go to school. *Frontiers in Artificial Intelligence and Applications*, 17–24. DOI: 10.3233/978-1-60750-028-5-17

Artino, A. R.Jr. (2010). Online or face-to-face learning? Exploring the personal factors that predict students' choice of instructional format. *The Internet and Higher Education*, 13(4), 272–276. DOI: 10.1016/j.iheduc.2010.07.005

Artino, A. R.Jr, & Jones, K. D.II. (2012). Exploring the complex relations between achievement emotions and self-regulated learning behaviors in online learning. *The Internet and Higher Education*, 15(3), 170–175. DOI: 10.1016/j.iheduc.2012.01.006

Artino, A. R. Jr., & Stephens, J. M. (2009). Academic motivation and self-regulation: A comparative analysis of undergraduate and graduate students learning online. *The Internet and Higher Education*, 12(3), 146–151. DOI: 10.1016/j.iheduc.2009.02.001

Asfahani, A., El-Farra, S. A., & Iqbal, K. (2023). International Benchmarking of Teacher Training Programs: Lessons Learned from Diverse Education Systems. *EDUJAVARE: International Journal of Educational Research*, 1(2), 141–152.

Aspin, D. N., & Chapman, J. D. (Eds.). (2007). *Values education and lifelong learning: Principles, policies, programmes* (Vol. 10). Springer Science & Business Media. DOI: 10.1007/978-1-4020-6184-4_1

Asrar-ul-Haq, M., Anwar, S., & Hassan, M. (2017). Impact of emotional intelligence on teacher s performance in higher education institutions of Pakistan. *Future Business Journal*, 3(2), 87–97. DOI: 10.1016/j.fbj.2017.05.003

Atkisson, M., & Wiley, D. (2011). Learning analytics as interpretive practice. *Proceedings of the 1st International Conference on Learning Analytics and Knowledge*, 117–121. New York, NY, USA: ACM. DOI: 10.1145/2090116.2090133

Attributed to Einstein. A. (n.d.). Learning is experience. Everything else is just information. [Quote]. Retrieved from https://www.brainyquote.com/authors/albert-einstein-quotes

Axelsen, M., Redmond, P., Heinrich, E., & Henderson, M. (2020). The evolving field of learning analytics research in higher education. *Australasian Journal of Educational Technology*, 36(2), 1–7. DOI: 10.14742/ajet.6266

Ayguin, H. E., & Alemdar, M. (2022). Examining the social-emotional skills of pre-service teachers in the context of emotional literacy skills and social-emotional competency. *International Innovative Education Researcher*, 2(2), 206–240.

Bada, S. O., & Olusegun, S. (2015). Constructivism learning theory: A paradigm for teaching and learning. *Journal of Research & Method in Education*, 5(6), 66–70.

Bailey, R., Stickle, L., Brion-Meisels, G., & Jones, S. M. (2019). Reimagining social-emotional learning: Findings from a strategy-based approach. *Phi Delta Kappan*, 100(5), 53–58. DOI: 10.1177/0031721719827549

Bailey, S. (2022). Teacher-preparation programs and trauma-informed teaching practices: Getting students to CHILL. *Current Issues in Education (Tempe, Ariz.)*, 23(2). Advance online publication. DOI: 10.14507/cie.vol23.iss3.2057

Bakhshinategh, B., Zaiane, O. R., ElAtia, S., & Ipperciel, D. (2018). Educational data mining applications and tasks: A survey of the last 10 years. *Education and Information Technologies*, 23(1), 537–553. DOI: 10.1007/s10639-017-9616-z

Bakır-Yalçın, E., & Usluel, K. Y. (2024). Investigating the antecedents of engagement in online learning: Do achievement emotions matter? *Education and Information Technologies*, 29(4), 3759–3791. DOI: 10.1007/s10639-023-11995-z

Balkaya, S., & Akkucuk, U. (2021). Adoption and use of learning management systems in education: The role of playfulness and self-management. *Sustainability (Basel)*, 13(3), 1127. DOI: 10.3390/su13031127

Bal, M. (2017). *Narratology: Introduction to the theory of narrative* (4th ed.). University of Toronto Press.

Bandura, A. (1977). Self-efficacy: Toward a unifying theory of behavioral change. *Psychological Review*, 84(2), 191–215. DOI: 10.1037/0033-295X.84.2.191 PMID: 847061

Bandura, A. (1993). Perceived self-efficacy in cognitive development and functioning. *Educational Psychologist*, 28(2), 117–148. DOI: 10.1207/s15326985ep2802_3

Bandura, A. (1997). *Self-Efficacy: The Exercise of Control*. W.H. Freeman and Company.

Banihashem, S. K., Aliabadi, K., Pourroostaei Ardakani, S., Delaver, A., & Nili Ahmadabadi, M. (2018). Learning Analytics: A Systematic Literature Review. *Interdisciplinary Journal of Virtual Learning in Medical Sciences*, 9(2). Advance online publication. DOI: 10.5812/ijvlms.63024

Bannert, M., Molenaar, I., Azevedo, R., Järvelä, S., & Gašević, D. (2017). Relevance of learning analytics to measure and support students' learning in adaptive educational technologies. *Proceedings of the Seventh International Learning Analytics & Knowledge Conference*, 568–569. New York, NY, USA: ACM. DOI: 10.1145/3027385.3029463

Barahona Mora, A. (2020). Gamification for Classroom Management: An Implementation Using ClassDojo. *Sustainability (Basel)*, 12(22), 9371. DOI: 10.3390/su12229371

Barbalet, J. (1998). *Emotion, social theory and social structure*. Cambridge University Press. DOI: 10.1017/CBO9780511488740

Barkley, A. P. (2020). *Student engagement techniques: A handbook for college faculty*. John Wiley & Sons.

Bar-On, R. (1985). The development of an operational concept of psychological wellbeing. Unpublished doctoral dissertation, Rhodes University, South Africa.

Bar-On, R., Tranel, D., Denburg, N. L., & Bechara, A. (2003). Exploring the neurological substrate of emotional and social intelligence. *Brain*, 126(8), 1790–1800. DOI: 10.1093/brain/awg177 PMID: 12805102

Barsade, S. (2002). The ripple effect: Emotional contagion and its influence on group behavior. *Administrative Science Quarterly*, 47(4), 644–675. DOI: 10.2307/3094912

Bass, R. (2023). Social pedagogies in ePortfolio practices: Principles for design and impact. In *High-Impact ePortfolio Practice* (pp. 65–73). Routledge. DOI: 10.4324/9781003445098-7

Basu, A., & Mermillod, M. (2011). Emotional intelligence and social-emotional learning: An overview. *Online Submission*, 1(3), 182–185.

Baumeister, R. F., DeWall, C. N., & Zhang, L. (2007). Do emotions improve or hinder the decision-making process? In K. D. Vohs, R. F. Baumeister, R. F. & G. Loewenstein (Eds.), *Do emotions help or hurt decision making? A hedgefoxian perspective* (pp. 11–31). New York: Russell Sage.

Bean, C. (2023). *The accidental instructional designer: Learning design for the digital age*. Association for Talent Development.

Beard, C., Clegg, S., & Smith, K. (2007). Acknowledging the affective in higher education. *British Educational Research Journal*, 33(2), 235–252. DOI: 10.1080/01411920701208415

Beard, K. S., Vakil, J. B., Chao, T., & Hilty, C. D. (2021). Time for change: Understanding teacher social-emotional learning supports for anti-racism and student well-being during COVID-19, and beyond. *Education and Urban Society*, •••, 1–19. DOI: 10.1177/00131245211062527

Beck, D., Morgado, L., & O'Shea, P. (2023). Educational practices and strategies with immersive learning environments: Mapping of reviews for using the metaverse. *IEEE Transactions on Learning Technologies*, 17, 319–341. DOI: 10.1109/TLT.2023.3243946

Becker, E. S., Goetz, T., Morger, V., & Ranellucci, J. (2014). The importance of teachers' emotions and instructional behavior for their students' emotions – An experience sampling analysis. *Teaching and Teacher Education*, 43, 15–26. DOI: 10.1016/j.tate.2014.05.002

Beecher, S., Peterson, K. A., Peterson-Ahmad, M. B., & Luther, V. L. (2022). Social-emotional learning, awareness, and strategies for teachers: Collaborative approaches. In Peterson-Ahmad, M., & Luther, V. L. (Eds.), *Collaborative approaches to recruiting, preparing, and retaining teachers for the field* (pp. 136–155). IGI Global. DOI: 10.4018/978-1-7998-9047-8.ch008

Bellocchi, A. (2018). Early career science teachers' experiences of social bonds and emotion management. *Journal of Research in Science Teaching*, 56(3), 322–347. DOI: 10.1002/tea.21520

Bennett, J. (2007). Great actors access vulnerability. The Jason Bennett Actor's Workshop. Retrieved from https://www.jbactors.com/actingreading/actorsaccessvulnerability.html

Berehil, M., Roubi, S., & Arrhioui, K. (2020). Towards a model for an emotionally intelligent learning environment using NLP tools. *Proceedings of the European Conference on E-Learning, ECEL*. https://doi.org/DOI: 10.34190/EEL.20.096

Berlyne, D. E. (1960). Conflict, arousal, and curiosity.

Berman, N. B., & Artino, A. R.Jr. (2018). Development and initial validation of an online engagement metric using virtual patients. *BMC Medical Education*, 18(1), 213. DOI: 10.1186/s12909-018-1322-z PMID: 30223825

Bernstein, P. (2013, December 13). The 3 rules of transmedia storytelling from transmedia guru Jeff Gomez. *IndieWire*.https://www.indiewire.com/2013/12/the-3-rules-of-transmedia-storytelling-from-transmedia-guru-jeff-gomez-32325

Berry, S. (2019). Teaching to connect: Community-building strategies for the virtual classroom. *Online Learning : the Official Journal of the Online Learning Consortium*, 23(1), 164–183. DOI: 10.24059/olj.v23i1.1425

Bickle, M. C., Rucker, R. D., & Burnsed, K. A. (2019). Online learning: Examination of attributes that promote student satisfaction. *Online Journal of Distance Learning Administration*, 22(1). https://www.westga.edu/~distance/ojdla/spring221/bickle_rucker_burnsed221.html

Bieg, M., Goetz, T., Sticca, F., Brunner, E., Becker, E., Morger, V., & Hubbard, K. (2017). Teaching methods and their impact on students' emotions in mathematics: An experience-sampling approach. *ZDM Mathematics Education*, 49(3), 411–422. DOI: 10.1007/s11858-017-0840-1

Birmingham, W. C., Wadsworth, L. L., Lassetter, J. H., Graff, T. C., Lauren, E., & Hung, M. (2023). COVID-19 lockdown: Impact on college students' lives. *Journal of American College Health*, 71(3), 879–893. DOI: 10.1080/07448481.2021.1909041 PMID: 34292141

Bishop, D. T., Karageorghis, C. I., & Kinrade, N. P. (2009). Effects of musically-induced emotions on choice reaction time performance. *The Sport Psychologist*, 23(1), 59–76. DOI: 10.1123/tsp.23.1.59

Bishop, D. T., Karageorghis, C. I., & Loizou, G. (2007). A grounded theory of young tennis players' use of music to manipulate emotional state. *Journal of Sport & Exercise Psychology*, 29(5), 584–607. DOI: 10.1123/jsep.29.5.584 PMID: 18089894

Bittencourt, I. I., Chalco, G., Santos, J., Fernandes, S., Silva, J., Batista, N., Hutz, C., & Isotani, S. (2023). Positive Artificial Intelligence in Education (P-AIED): A Roadmap. *International Journal of Artificial Intelligence in Education*. Advance online publication. DOI: 10.1007/s40593-023-00357-y

Blad, E. (2017, April 4). Teacher prep slow to embrace social-emotional learning. *Education Week*. https://www.edweek.org/leadership/teacher-prep-slow-to-embrace-social-emotional-learning/2017/04

Blanchard, P. N., & Thacker, J. W. (2023). *Effective training: Systems, strategies, and practices*. SAGE Publications.

Blaschke, L. M., & Hase, S. (2016). Heutagogy: A holistic framework for creating twenty-first-century self-determined learners. In B. Gros, Kinshuk, & M. Maina (Eds.), *The future of ubiquitous learning: Learning designs for emerging pedagogies* (pp. 25-40). Springer. https://doi.org/DOI: 10.1007/978-3-662-47724-3_2

Blaschke, L. M. (2012). Heutagogy and lifelong learning: A review of heutagogical practice and self-determined learning. *International Review of Research in Open and Distance Learning*, 13(1), 56–71. DOI: 10.19173/irrodl.v13i1.1076

Blaschke, L. M. (2023). Self-determined learning: Designing for heutagogic learning environments. In Spector, J. M., Lockee, B. B., & Childress, M. D. (Eds.), *Learning, Design, and Technology: An International Compendium of Theory, Research, Practice, and Policy* (pp. 245–266). Springer International Publishing. DOI: 10.1007/978-3-319-17461-7_62

Bleakley, J., Woolcott, G., Yeigh, T., & Whannell, R. (2020). Reflecting on emotions during teaching: Developing affective-reflective skills in novice teachers using a novel critical moments protocol. *The Australian Journal of Teacher Education*, 45(10), 55–72. Advance online publication. DOI: 10.14221/ajte.2020v45n10.4

Bloom's taxonomy. (2024, Apr 10). In *Wikipedia*. https://en.wikipedia.org/w/index.php?title=Bloom%27s_taxonomy&oldid=1218203352

Bodily, R., Kay, J., Aleven, V., Jivet, I., Davis, D., Xhakaj, F., & Verbert, K. (2018). Open learner models and learning analytics dashboards. *Proceedings of the 8th International Conference on Learning Analytics and Knowledge*, 41–50. New York, NY, USA: ACM. DOI: 10.1145/3170358.3170409

Boehrer, J., & Linsky, M. (1990). Teaching with cases: Learning to question. *New Directions for Teaching and Learning*, 1990(42), 41–57. DOI: 10.1002/tl.37219904206

Boekaerts, M. (2016). Engagement as an inherent aspect of the learning process. *Learning and Instruction*, 43, 76–83. DOI: 10.1016/j.learninstruc.2016.02.001

Bokek-Cohen, Y. A., Shkoler, O., & Meiri, E. (2023). The unique practices of workplace bullying in academe: An exploratory study. *Current Psychology (New Brunswick, N.J.)*, 42(23), 19466–19485. DOI: 10.1007/s12144-022-03090-2

Bond, L. (2023). Unlocking the Potential of Educational Escape Rooms in Higher Education: Theoretical Frameworks and Pathways Ahead. p. 27. *In Fostering Pedagogy Through Micro and Adaptive Learning in Higher Education: Trends, Tools, and Applications*. DOI: DOI: 10.4018/978-1-6684-8656-6.ch007

Bonesso, S., Bruni, E., Gerli, F., Bonesso, S., Bruni, E., & Gerli, F. (2020). Emotional and social intelligence competencies in the digital era. *Behavioral competencies of digital professionals: Understanding the role of emotional intelligence*, 41-62.

Borg, W., & Gall, M. (1989). *Education research: An introduction* (5th ed.). Longman.

Børte, K., Nesje, K., & Lillejord, S. (2023). Barriers to student active learning in higher education. *Teaching in Higher Education*, 28(3), 597–615. DOI: 10.1080/13562517.2020.1839746

Bosch, N., & D'Mello, S. (2017). The Affective Experience of Novice Computer Programmers. *International Journal of Artificial Intelligence in Education*, 27(1), 181–206. DOI: 10.1007/s40593-015-0069-5

Bosch, N., D'Mello, S. K., Baker, R. S., Ocumpaugh, J., Shute, V., Ventura, M., & Zhao, W. (2016). Detecting student emotions in computer-enabled classrooms. *IJCAI International Joint Conference on Artificial Intelligence*, 4125–4129.

Bostock, J. R. (2018). A model of flexible learning: Exploring interdependent relationships between students, lecturers, resources and contexts in virtual spaces. *Journal of Perspectives in Applied Academic Practice*, 6(1), 12–18. DOI: 10.14297/jpaap.v6i1.298

Bowlby, J. (1969). *Attachment and loss* (Vol. I). Basic Books.

Boyatzis, R. (2021). Learning life skills of emotional and social intelligence competencies. In M. London (Ed.), *The Oxford handbook of lifelong learning* (2nd ed., pp. 131–145). Oxford University Press.

Boyatzis, R. E., Gaskin, J., & Wei, H. (2015). Emotional and social intelligence and behavior. Handbook of intelligence: Evolutionary theory, historical perspective, and current concepts, 243-262. DOI: 10.1007/978-1-4939-1562-0_17

Boyatzis, R. E. (1982). *The competent manager: A model for effective performance.* John Wiley & Sons.

Boyatzis, R. E., Goleman, D., Gerli, F., Bonesso, S., & Cortellazzo, L. (2019). Emotional and social intelligence competencies and the intentional change process. In *Cognitive Readiness in Project Teams* (pp. 147–169). Productivity Press. DOI: 10.4324/9780429490057-7

Boyatzis, R., Goleman, D., & Rhee, K. (2000). Clustering competence in emotional intelligence: Insights from the emotional competence inventory (ECI). In Bar-On, R., & Parker, J. D. A. (Eds.), *Handbook of emotional intelligence.* Jossey-Bass.

Bozkurt, A., & Sharma, R. C. (2023). Challenging the status quo and exploring the new boundaries in the age of algorithms: Reimagining the role of generative AI in distance education and online learning. *Asian Journal of Distance Education*, 18(1), i–viii. DOI: 10.5281/zenodo.7755273

Bozkurt, T., & Ozden, M. S. (2010). The relationship between empathetic classroom climate and students' success. *Procedia: Social and Behavioral Sciences*, 5, 231–234. DOI: 10.1016/j.sbspro.2010.07.078

Brackett, M. A., & Caruso, D. R. (2007) Emotional literacy for educators. Cary, NC: SELMedia.

Brackett, M., & Cipriano, C. (2020, April 7). Teachers are anxious and overwhelmed. They need SEL now more than ever. *EdSurge*. https://www.edsurge.com/news/2020-04-07-teachers-are-anxious-and-overwhelmed-they-need-sel-now-more-than-ever

Brackett, M. (2019). *Permission to Feel: The Power of Emotional Intelligence to Achieve Well-Being and Success.* Celadon Books.

Brackett, M. (2019). *Permission to feel: Unlocking the power of emotions to help our kids, ourselves, and our society thrive.* Celadon Books.

Brackett, M. (2019). *Permission to feel: Unlocking the power of emotions to help ourselves, our kids, and our society thrive.* Celadon Books.

Brackett, M. A., Bailey, C. S., Hoffmann, J. D., & Simmons, D. N. (2019). RULER: A theory-driven, systemic approach to social, emotional, and academic learning. *Educational Psychologist*, 54(3), 144–161. DOI: 10.1080/00461520.2019.1614447

Brackett, M. A., & Katulak, N. A. (2013). Emotional intelligence in the classroom: Skill-based training for teachers and students. In *Applying emotional intelligence* (pp. 1–27). Psychology Press.

Brackett, M. A., Reyes, M. R., Rivers, S. E., Elbertson, N. A., & Salovey, P. (2012). Assessing teachers' beliefs about social and emotional learning. *Journal of Psychoeducational Assessment*, 30(3), 219–236. DOI: 10.1177/0734282911424879

Brackett, M. A., Rivers, S. E., Shiffman, S., Lerner, N., & Salovey, P. (2006). Relating emotional abilities to social functioning: A comparison of self-report and performance measures of emotional intelligence. *Journal of Personality and Social Psychology*, 91(4), 780–795. DOI: 10.1037/0022-3514.91.4.780 PMID: 17014299

Bradley, E., Isaac, P., & King, J. (2020). Assessment of pre-service teacher dispositions. *Excelsior (Oneonta, N.Y.)*, 13(1), 50–62. DOI: 10.14305/jn.19440413.2020.13.1.03

Brame, C. (2013). *Flipping the classroom*. Vanderbilt University Center for Teaching.

Braun, V., & Clarke, V. (2006). Using thematic analysis in psychology. *Qualitative Research in Psychology*, 3(2), 77–101. DOI: 10.1191/1478088706qp063oa

Breiseth, L. (2022). *10 Strategies for supporting SEL for ELLs: "Grow as you go"*. Retrieved from https://www.colorincolorado.org/article/sel-ell-salina

Breiseth, L. (2023). *SEL for English language learners: What educators need to know*. https://www.colorincolorado.org/article/sel-english-language-learners-what-educators-need-know

Bresler, D. (2005). Physiological consequences of guided imagery. *Practical Pain Management*, 5(6).

Brewster, B. (1882). Theory and practice. [Retrieved from Google Books.]. *The Yale Literary Magazine*, 47(5), 202.

Bromer, B. L. (2021). Social presence in an online learning environment. In Crawford, C. M., & Simons, M. A. (Eds.), *eLearning engagement in a transformative social learning environment*. IGI Global., DOI: 10.4018/978-1-7998-6956-6.ch001

Bromer, B. L., & Deeb, A. M. D. (2022). Transformations in K-12 teaching: Using what was learned during the pandemic. In Bromer, B. L., & Crawford, C. M. (Eds.), *Handbook of research on learner-centered approaches to teaching in an age of transformational change*. IGI Global., DOI: 10.4018/978-1-6684-4240-1.ch004

Brookfield, S. D. (1987). *Developing critical thinkers: Challenging adults to explore alternative ways of thinking and acting*. Jossey-Bass.

Bruner, J. (1991). The narrative construction of reality. *Critical Inquiry*, 18(1), 1–21. DOI: 10.1086/448619

Buelow, J. R., Barry, T., & Rich, L. E. (2018). Supporting learning engagement with online students. *Online Learning : the Official Journal of the Online Learning Consortium*, 22(4), 313–240. DOI: 10.24059/olj.v22i4.1384

Burgess, H. & Wellington, J. (2010) "Exploring the impact of the professional doctorate on students' professional practice and personal development: early indications" in Work Based Learning E-journal Vol.1, No.1, pp. 160-176.

Burić, I. (2019). The role of emotional labor in explaining teachers' enthusiasm and students' outcomes: A multilevel mediational analysis. *Learning and Individual Differences*, 70, 12–20. DOI: 10.1016/j.lindif.2019.01.002

Burić, I., & Frenzel, A. C. (2021). Teacher emotional labour, instructional strategies, and students' academic engagement: A multilevel analysis. *Teachers and Teaching*, 27(5), 335–352. DOI: 10.1080/13540602.2020.1740194

Burić, I., Slišković, A., & Penezić, Z. (2019). A two-wave panel study on teachers' emotions and emotional-labour strategies. *Stress and Health*, 35(1), 27–38. DOI: 10.1002/smi.2836 PMID: 30194896

Buric, I., Sliskovic, A., & Soric, I. (2020). Teachers' emotions and self-efficacy: A test of reciprocal relations. *Frontiers in Psychology*, 11, 1650. Advance online publication. DOI: 10.3389/fpsyg.2020.01650 PMID: 32982815

Burić, I., Sorić, I., & Penezić, Z. (2016). Emotion regulation in academic domain: Development and validation of the Academic Emotion Regulation Questionnaire (AERQ). *Personality and Individual Differences*, 96, 138–147. DOI: 10.1016/j.paid.2016.02.074

Burnham, B., & Walden, B. (1997). Interactions in distance education: A report from the other side. In *Proceedings of the Adult Education Research Conference*. Oklahoma State University. http://www.edst.educ.ubc.ca/aerc/1997/97burnham.html

Calavia, M. B., Blanco, T., Casas, R., & Dieste, B. (2023). Making design thinking for education sustainable: Training preservice teachers to address practice challenges. *Thinking Skills and Creativity*, 47, 101199. DOI: 10.1016/j.tsc.2022.101199

Campbell, J. (2004). *Pathways to bliss: Mythology and personal transformation* (Vol. 16). New World Library.

Campbell, J. (2008). *The hero with a thousand faces* (Vol. 17). New World Library.

Campbell, J. P., DeBlois, P. B., & Oblinger, D. G. (2007). Academic Analytics: A New Tool for a New Era. *EDUCAUSE Review*, 42(4), 40.

Candy, P. C. (1991). *Self-Direction for Lifelong Learning*. Jossey-Bass.

Canning, E.A., White, M. & Davis, W.B. (2024) Growth mindset messages from instructors improve academic performance among first-generation college students. *Life Sciences Education, 23* (2).

Cantabella, M., Martínez-España, R., Ayuso, B., Yáñez, J. A., & Muñoz, A. (2019). Analysis of student behavior in learning management systems through a Big Data framework. *Future Generation Computer Systems*, 90, 262–272. DOI: 10.1016/j.future.2018.08.003

Cao, W., & Yu, Z. (2023). Exploring learning outcomes, communication, anxiety, and motivation in learning communities: A systematic review. *Humanities & Social Sciences Communications*, 10(1), 866. DOI: 10.1057/s41599-023-02325-2

Carliner, S. (2021). *Training design in the corporate world*. Routledge.

Carlisle, K. L., Carlisle, R., Ricks, S. A., & Mylroie, R. (2018). Is my instructor a robot? Creative Methodsfor creating social presence in online human service education. *Journal of Human Services*, 38(1), 61–73.

Carroll, A., Flynn, L., O'Connor, E. S., Forrest, K., Bower, J., Fynes-Clinton, S., York, A., & Ziaea, M. (2021). In their words: Listening to teachers' perceptions about stress in the workplace and how to address it. *Asia-Pacific Journal of Teacher Education*, 49(4), 420–434. Advance online publication. DOI: 10.1080/1359866X.2020.1789914

Carroll, A., Forrest, K., Sanders-O'Connor, E., Flynn, L., Bower, J. M., Fynes-Clinton, S., York, A., & Ziael, M. (2022a). Teacher stress and burnout in Australia: Examining the role of intrapersonal and environmental factors. *Social Psychology of Education*, 25(2-3), 441–469. Advance online publication. DOI: 10.1007/s11218-022-09686-7 PMID: 35233183

Carroll, A., Hepburn, S., & Bower, J. (2022b). Mindful practices for teachers: Relieving stress and enhancing positive mindsets. *Frontiers in Education*, 7, 954098. Advance online publication. DOI: 10.3389/feduc.2022.954098

Casalino, G., Castellano, G., Di Mitri, D., Kaczmarek-Majer, K., & Zaza, G. (2024). A Human-centric Approach to Explain Evolving Data: A Case Study on Education. *2024 IEEE International Conference on Evolving and Adaptive Intelligent Systems (EAIS)*, 1–8. IEEE. DOI: 10.1109/EAIS58494.2024.10569098

CASEL. (2023, March 3). What is the Casel Framework? CASEL. https://casel.org/fundamentals-of-sel/what-is-the-casel-framework/

Castillo, R., Salguero, J. M., Fernández-Berrocal, P., & Balluerka, N. (2013). Effects of an emotional intelligence intervention on aggression and empathy among adolescents. *Journal of Adolescence*, 36(5), 883–892. DOI: 10.1016/j.adolescence.2013.07.001 PMID: 24011104

Castro, M. D. B., & Tumibay, G. M. (2021). A literature review: Efficacy of online learning courses for higher education institutions using meta-analysis. *Education and Information Technologies*, 26(2), 1367–1385. DOI: 10.1007/s10639-019-10027-z

Cavicchioli, M., Scalabrini, A., Northoff, G., Mucci, C., Ogliari, A., & Maffei, C. (2021). Dissociation and emotion regulation stratgies: A meta-analytic review. *Journal of Psychiatric Research*, 143, 370–387. DOI: 10.1016/j.jpsychires.2021.09.011 PMID: 34592484

CBC News. (2023, June 16). Montreal Children's Hospital uses VR tool for pediatric trauma. *CBC News*. https://www.cbc.ca/player/play/1.7138766

Cebral-Loureda, M., & Torres-Huitzil, C. (2021). Neural Deep Learning Models for Learning Analytics in a Digital Humanities Laboratory. *2021 Machine Learning-Driven Digital Technologies for Educational Innovation Workshop*, 1–8. IEEE. DOI: 10.1109/IEEECONF53024.2021.9733775

Center for Reaching and Teaching the Whole Child. (n.d.) *Anchor competencies framework*. https://crtwc.org/

Center on the Developing Child. (n.d.). *Toxic stress*. https://developingchild.harvard.edu/science/key-concepts/toxic-stress/

Cercone, K. (2008). Characteristics of adult learners with implications for online learning design. AACE review (formerly. *AACE Journal*, 16(2), 137–159.

Chamo, N., Biberman-Shalev, L., & Broza, O. (2023). 'Nice to Meet You Again': When Heutagogy Met Blended Learning in Teacher Education, Post-Pandemic Era. *Education Sciences*, 13(6), 536. DOI: 10.3390/educsci13060536

Charitopoulos, A., Rangoussi, M., & Koulouriotis, D. (2020). On the Use of Soft Computing Methods in Educational Data Mining and Learning Analytics Research: A Review of Years 2010–2018. *International Journal of Artificial Intelligence in Education*, 30(3), 371–430. DOI: 10.1007/s40593-020-00200-8

Charmaz, K. (2003). *Grounded theory. Qualitative psychology: A practical guide to research methods*. Sage.

Charmaz, K. (2014). Constructing grounded theory. *Sage (Atlanta, Ga.)*.

Chatti, M. A., & Muslim, A. (2019). The PERLA Framework: Blending Personalization and Learning Analytics. *International Review of Research in Open and Distance Learning*, 20(1). Advance online publication. DOI: 10.19173/irrodl.v20i1.3936

Chaucer, G. (1835). *The Pardoner's Tale*. Clarendon Press.

Chaudhry, S., Tandon, A., Shinde, S., & Bhattacharya, A. (2024). Student psychological well-being in higher education: The role of internal team environment, institutional, friends and family support and academic engagement. *PLoS One*, 19(1), e0297508. DOI: 10.1371/journal.pone.0297508 PMID: 38271390

Chechi, K. V. (2012). Emotional intelligence and teaching. *International Journal of Research in Economics & Social Sciences*, 2(2), 297–304.

Chen, J. (2019). Exploring the impact of teacher emotions on their approaches to teaching: A structural equation modelling approach. *The British Journal of Educational Psychology*, 89(1), 57–74. DOI: 10.1111/bjep.12220 PMID: 29603123

Chen, J. (2020). Teacher emotions in their professional lives: Implications for teacher development. *Asia-Pacific Journal of Teacher Education*, 48(5), 491–507. DOI: 10.1080/1359866X.2019.1669139

Cherry, C., Hopfe, C., MacGillivray, B., & Pidgeon, N. (2015). Media discourses of low carbon housing: The marginalisation of social and behavioural dimensions within the British broadsheet press. *Public Understanding of Science (Bristol, England)*, 24(3), 302–310. DOI: 10.1177/0963662513512442 PMID: 24336448

Childers, E. (n.d.). *7 ways to show presence and compassion in online spaces.* https://todayslearner. cengage.com/7-ways-to-show-presence-and-compassion-in-online- spaces/

Chi, M. T. H., & Wylie, R. (2014). The ICAP Framework: Linking cognitive engagement to active learning outcomes. *Educational Psychologist*, 49(4), 219–243. DOI: 10.1080/00461520.2014.965823

Chng, E., Tan, A. L., & Tan, S. C. (2023). Examining the Use of Emerging Technologies in Schools: A Review of Artificial Intelligence and Immersive Technologies in STEM Education. *Journal for STEM Education Research*, 6(3), 385–407. DOI: 10.1007/s41979-023-00092-y

Cho, M. H., & Heron, M. L. (2015). Self-regulated learning: The role of motivation, emotion, and use of learning strategies in students' learning experiences in a self-paced online mathematics course. *Distance Education*, 36(1), 80–99. DOI: 10.1080/01587919.2015.1019963

Choudhary, A., Jena, B. P., & Patre, S. (2024). Unveiling the veil of workplace Loneliness: A Theory-Concept-Methodology (TCM) framework. *Psychology Hub*, 41(1), 79–90.

Christakou, A., Vasileiadis, G., & Kapreli, E. (2021). Motor imagery as a method of maintaining performance in pianists during forced non-practice: A single case study. *Physiotherapy Theory and Practice*, 37(4), 540–548. DOI: 10.1080/09593985.2019.1636917 PMID: 31267825

Christian-Brandt, A. S., Santacrose, D. E., & Barnett, M. L. (2020). In the trauma-informed care trenches: Teacher compassion satisfaction, secondary traumatic stress, burnout, and intent to leave education within underserved elementary schools. *Child Abuse & Neglect*, 110, 110. DOI: 10.1016/j.chiabu.2020.104437 PMID: 32151429

Christison, M., & Murray, D. E. (2023). THE IMPORTANCE OF EI COMPETENCE FOR TEACHERS AND LEADERS IN DIVERSE ELT CONTEXTS. *European Journal of Applied Linguistics & TEFL*, 12(2).

Cidlinska, K., Nyklova, B., Machovcova, K., Mudrak, J., & Zabrodska, K. (2023). "Why I don't want to be an academic anymore?" When academic identity contributes to academic career attrition. *Higher Education*, 85(1), 141–156. DOI: 10.1007/s10734-022-00826-8

Cieslak, R., Shoji, K., Douglas, A., Melville, E., Luszczynska, A., & Benight, C. C. (2014). A meta-analysis of the relationship between job burnout and secondary traumatic stress among workers with indirect exposure to trauma. *Psychological Services*, 11(1), 75–86. DOI: 10.1037/a0033798 PMID: 23937082

Clarke, A. (2005). Situational analysis: Grounded theory after the postmodern turn. *Sage (Atlanta, Ga.)*.

Clark, R. C., & Mayer, R. E. (2023). *E-learning and the science of instruction: Proven guidelines for consumers and designers of multimedia learning*. John Wiley & Sons.

Cleveland-Innes, M., & Campbell, P. (2006, November). *Understanding emotional presence in an online community of inquiry*. Paper presented at the 12th Annual SLOAN-C ALN Conference, Orlando, Florida.

Cleveland-Innes, M., & Campbell, P. (2012). Emotional presence, learning, and the online learning environment. *International Review of Research in Open and Distance Learning*, 13(4), 269. DOI: 10.19173/irrodl.v13i4.1234

Cleveland-Innes, M., Garrison, R., & Kinsel, E. (2007). Role adjustment for learners in an online community of inquiry: Identifying the needs of novice online learners. *International Journal of Web-Based Learning and Teaching Technologies*, 2(1), 1–16. DOI: 10.4018/jwltt.2007010101

Cloninger, C. R., Cloninger, K. M., Zwir, I., & Keltikangas-Järvinen, L. (2019). The complex genetics and biology of human temperament: A review of traditional concepts in relation to new molecular findings. *Translational Psychiatry*, 9(1), 290. DOI: 10.1038/s41398-019-0621-4 PMID: 31712636

Close, M., Killingly, C., Gaumer-Erickson, A. S., & Noonan, P. M. (2023). SEL and Its Origins. Inclusive Education for the 21st Century: Theory. *Policy & Practice*.

Clow, D. (2013). An overview of learning analytics. *Teaching in Higher Education*, 18(6), 683–695. DOI: 10.1080/13562517.2013.827653

Cohen, L., Manion, L., & Morrison, K. (2013). *Research methods in education*. Routledge. DOI: 10.4324/9780203720967

Collaborative for Academic, Social, and Emotional Learning (CASEL) (n.d.). *What is the CASEL framework?* https://casel.org/fundamentals-of-sel/what-is-the-casel-framework

Collaborative for Academic, Social, and Emotional Learning (n.d.). *What is the CASEL framework?* https://casel.org/fundamentals-of-sel/what-is-the-casel-framework/

Conver, S. (2020). Investing in Education: The Ideas Behind Venture Philanthropy and the Marketized Practice of Educational Improvement. *Proceedings of the 2020 AERA Annual Meeting*. Washington DC: AERA. DOI: 10.3102/1577229

Coombs, P. H., & Ahmed, M. (1974). *Attacking rural poverty: How non-formal education can help*. Johns Hopkins University Press.

Costley, J. (2020). Using cognitive strategies overcomes cognitive load in online learning environments. *Interactive Technology and Smart Education*, 17(2), 215–228. DOI: 10.1108/ITSE-09-2019-0053

Council of Chief State Officers. (2013, April). *INTASC model core teaching standards and learning progressions for teachers*. https://ccsso.org/sites/default/files/2017-12/2013_INTASC_Learning_Progressions_for_Teachers.pdf

Cranton, P. (2006). *Understanding and promoting transformative learning: A guide for educators of adults*. Jossey-Bass.

Craske, M., Liao, B., Brown, L., & Vervliet, B. (2012). Role of inhibition in exposure therapy. *Journal of Experimental Psychopathology*, 3(3), 322–345. DOI: 10.5127/jep.026511

Crawford, C. (2015). Vulnerability in learning. In J. Spector (Ed.), The SAGE Encyclopedia of Educational Technology (pp. 832–835). Thousand Oaks, CA: SAGE Publications, Inc.; . n338DOI: 10.4135/9781483346397

Crawford, C. M. (2016). Creating teacher immediacy in online learning environments. In S. D'Austino's (Ed.) *Teacher Immediacy in Online Learning Environments.* (pp. 15-36). IGI Global.

Crawford, C. M. (2016). Instructor immediacy and authenticity: engaging in cognitive vulnerability within the online instructional environment. In S. D'Augustino (Ed.) *Creating Teacher Immediacy in Online Learning Environments* (pp. 15-36). Hershey, PA: IGI Global. DOI: 10.4018/978-1-4666-9995-3.ch002

Crawford, C. M. (2019b). In the midst of the maelstrom: Struggling through the revulsions of academic mobbing while maintaining one's ethical compass. In C. M. Crawford's (Ed.) *Confronting Academic Mobbing in Higher Education: Personal Accounts and Administrative Action* (pp. 241-266). Hershey, PA: IGI Global.

Crawford, C. M. (2023). Now what?: A case study on the impact of nefarious Queen Bees. In K. L. Clarke & N. L. Moffett's (Eds.) *Addressing the Queen Bee Syndrome in Academia,* p. 1-25. IGI Global. DOI: DOI: 10.4018/978-1-6684-7717-5.ch001

Crawford, C. M., & White, S. A. (2021). Adventures on the Golden Road: A Promenade Through the Roadwork. In N. L. Moffett's (Ed.) *Navigating Post-Doctoral Career Placement, Research, and Professionalism* (pp. 28-52). IGI Global. DOI: 10.4018/978-1-7998-5065-6.ch002

Crawford, C. M. (2001). Developing webs of significance through communications: Appropriate interactive activities for distributed learning environments. *Campus-Wide Information Systems*, 18(2), 68–72. DOI: 10.1108/10650740110386675

Crawford, C. M. (2003). Emerging learning environments: Enhancing the online community. *Academic Exchange Quarterly*, 7(4), 131–135.

Crawford, C. M. (Ed.). (2019a). *Confronting academic mobbing in higher education: Personal accounts and administrative action*. IGI Global.

Crawford, C. M., Andrews, S., & Wallace, J. K. Y. (2021). Co-creative collegial communities of instructional engagement. [IJHIoT]. *International Journal of Hyperconnectivity and the Internet of Things*, 5(2), 38–56. DOI: 10.4018/IJHIoT.2021070103

Crawford, C. M., Andrews, S., & Young Wallace, J. K. (2022). Implicit cognitive vulnerability through nudges, boosts, and bounces. *International Journal of Hyperconnectivity and the Internet of Things*, 6(1), 1–14. DOI: 10.4018/IJHIoT.285588

Crawford, C. M., & Smith, M. S. (2015). Rethinking Bloom's Taxonomy: Implicit Cognitive Vulnerability as an impetus towards higher order thinking skills. In Jin, Z. (Ed.), *Exploring Implicit Cognition: Learning, Memory, and Social Cognitive Processes* (pp. 86–103). Information Science Reference. DOI: 10.4018/978-1-4666-6599-6.ch004

Crawford, C. M., White, S. A., & Young Wallace, J. (2019). Rethinking pedagogy, andragogy and heutagogy. *Academic Exchange Quarterly*, 23(1), 4–10.

Crescenzi-Lanna, L. (2020). Multimodal Learning Analytics research with young children: A systematic review. *British Journal of Educational Technology*, 51(5), 1485–1504. DOI: 10.1111/bjet.12959

Crick, R. (2017). Learning Analytics: Layers, Loops and Processes in a Virtual Learning Infrastructure. In *Handbook of Learning Analytics* (pp. 291–307). Society for Learning Analytics Research (SoLAR). DOI: 10.18608/hla17.025

Croft, N., Dalton, A., & Grant, M. (2010). Overcoming isolation in distance learning: Building a learning community through time and space. *The Journal for Education in the Built Environment*, 5(1), 27–64. DOI: 10.11120/jebe.2010.05010027

Crowe, S., Cresswell, K., Robertson, A., Huby, G., Avery, A., & Sheikh, A. (2011). The case study approach. *BMC Medical Research Methodology*, 11(1), 1–9. DOI: 10.1186/1471-2288-11-100 PMID: 21707982

Crow, S. (2006). What motivates a lifelong learner? *School Libraries Worldwide*, 12(1), 22–34.

Csikszentmihalyi, M. (1990). *Flow: The psychology of optimal experience*. Harper & Row.

Cuddy, A. J., Norton, M. I., & Fiske, S. T. (2016). Corrigendum to "This Old Stereotype: The Pervasiveness and Persistence of the Elderly Stereotype". *The Journal of Social Issues*, 72(3), 614–614. DOI: 10.1111/josi.12185

Cukurova, M., & Luckin, R. (2018). *Measuring the Impact of Emerging Technologies in Education: A Pragmatic Approach*. DOI: 10.1007/978-3-319-71054-9_81

Czercawski, B. C. (2014). Designing deeper learning experiences for online instruction. *Journal of Interactive Online Learning*, 13(2), 29–40.

D'Mello, S. K., & Jensen, E. (2022). Emotional Learning Analytics. In *The Handbook of Learning Analytics* (pp. 120–129). SOLAR., DOI: 10.18608/hla22.012

D'Mello, S., & Graesser, A. (2012). Dynamics of affective states during complex learning. *Learning and Instruction*, 22(2), 145–157. DOI: 10.1016/j.learninstruc.2011.10.001

Dafoulas, G. A., Maia, C. C., Clarke, J. S., Ali, A., & Augusto, J. (2018). Investigating the role of biometrics in education – The use of sensor data in collaborative learning. *MCCSIS 2018 - Multi Conference on Computer Science and Information Systems;Proceedings of the International Conferences on e-Learning 2018.*

Daineko, L. V., Goncharova, N. V., Zaitseva, E. V., Larionova, V. A., & Dyachkova, I. A. (2023). Gamification in Education: A Literature Review. In *Lecture Notes in Networks and Systems* (pp. 319–343). DOI: 10.1007/978-3-031-48020-1_25

Dallimore, E. J., Hertenstein, J. H., & Platt, M. B. (2004). Classroom participation and discussion effectiveness: Student-generated strategies. *Communication Education*, 53(1), 103–115. DOI: 10.1080/0363452032000135805

Daoudi, I. (2022). Learning analytics for enhancing the usability of serious games in formal education: A systematic literature review and research agenda. *Education and Information Technologies*, 27(8), 11237–11266. DOI: 10.1007/s10639-022-11087-4 PMID: 35528757

Dawadi, S. (2020). Thematic analysis approach: A step by step guide for ELT research practitioners. *Journal of the Nepal English Language Teachers'* [NELTA]. *Association*, 25(1-2), 62–71.

De Welde, K., & Stepnick, A. (Eds.). (2023). *Disrupting the culture of silence: Confronting gender inequality and making change in higher education.* Taylor & Francis.

Deaton, J. D., Ohrt, J. H., Linich, K., Wymer, B., Toomey, M., Lewis, O., Guest, J. D., & Newton, T. (2022). Teachers' experience with K-12 students' mental health. *Psychology in the Schools*, 59(5), 932–949. DOI: 10.1002/pits.22658

Deci, E. L., & Ryan, R. M. (2008). Self-determination theory: A macrotheory of human motivation, development, and health. *Canadian Psychology*, 49(3), 182–185. DOI: 10.1037/a0012801

Demetriou, H., Wilson, E., & Winterbottom, M. (2009). The role of emotion in teaching: Are there differences between male and female newly qualified teachers' approaches to teaching? *Educational Studies*, 35(4), 449–473. DOI: 10.1080/03055690902876552

Demidio-Caston, M. (2019). Addressing social, emotional development, and resilience at the heart of teacher education. *Teacher Education Quarterly*.

Denzin, N. (1984). *On understanding emotion*. Jossey-Bass.

Derakhshandeh, Z., Vora, V., Swaminathan, A., & Esmaeili, B. (2023, March). On the importance and facilitation of learner-learner interaction in online education: a review of the literature. In *Society for Information Technology & Teacher Education International Conference* (pp. 207-215). Association for the Advancement of Computing in Education (AACE).

D'Errico, F., Paciello, M. & Cerniglia, L. (2016). When emotions enhance students' engagement in e-learning processes. *Journal of e-Learning and Knowledge Society, 12*(4).

DeRue, D. S., & Ashford, S. J. (2010). Who will lead and who will follow? A social process of leadership identity construction in organizations. *Academy of Management Review*, 35(4), 627–647.

Desaultels, L. (2019, October 15). The role of emotion co-regulation in discipline. *Edutopia*.

Dever, D. A., Wiedbusch, M. D., Cloude, E. B., Lester, J., & Azevedo, R. (2022). Emotions and the comprehension of single versus multiple texts during game-based learning. *Discourse Processes*, 59(1-2), 94–115. DOI: 10.1080/0163853X.2021.1950450

Dewaele, J.-M., Gkonou, C., & Mercer, S. (2018). Do ESL/EFL teachers' emotional intelligence, teaching experience, proficiency and gender affect their classroom practice? In *Emotions in Second Language Teaching* (pp. 125–141). Springer International Publishing. DOI: 10.1007/978-3-319-75438-3_8

Diep, A. N., Zhu, C., Cocquyt, C., De Greef, M., Vo, M. H., & Vanwing, T. (2019). Adult learners' needs in online and blended learning. *Australian Journal of Adult Learning*, 59(2), 223–253. DOI: 10.22459/AJAL.2019.18

Dietz-Uhler, B., & Hurn, J. E. (2013). Using learning analytics to predict (and improve) student success: A faculty perspective. *Journal of Interactive Online Learning*, 12(1), 17–26.

Ding, C., Ramdas, M., & Mortillaro, M. (2024). Emotional intelligence in applied settings: Approaches to its theoretical model, measurement, and application. *Frontiers in Psychology*, 15, 1387152. DOI: 10.3389/fpsyg.2024.1387152 PMID: 38515968

Dirkx, J. M. (2001). The Power of feelings: Emotion, imagination, and the construction of meaning in adult learning. *New Directions for Adult and Continuing Education*, 2001(89), 63–72. DOI: 10.1002/ace.9

Dirkx, J. M. (2006). Engaging emotions in adult learning: A Jungian perspective on emotion and transformative learning. *New Directions for Adult and Continuing Education*, 2006(109), 15–26. DOI: 10.1002/ace.204

Dirkx, J. M. (2008). The meaning and role of emotions in adult learning. *New Directions for Adult and Continuing Education*, 2008(120), 7–18. DOI: 10.1002/ace.311

Diwakar, S., Kolil, V. K., Francis, S. P., & Achuthan, K. (2023). Intrinsic and extrinsic motivation among students for laboratory courses-Assessing the impact of virtual laboratories. *Computers & Education*, 198, 104758. DOI: 10.1016/j.compedu.2023.104758

Dixson, M. D. (2010). Creating effective student engagement in online courses: What do students find engaging? *The Journal of Scholarship of Teaching and Learning*, 10(2), 1–13.

Doan, S., Steiner, E. D., & Woo, A. (2023). *State of the American teacher survey*. RAND Corporation., DOI: 10.7249/RRA1108-7

Dolan, V. L. (2023). '… but if you tell anyone, I'll deny we ever met:' the experiences of academics with invisible disabilities in the neoliberal university. *International Journal of Qualitative Studies in Education : QSE*, 36(4), 689–706. DOI: 10.1080/09518398.2021.1885075

Donahue-Keegan, D., Villegas-Reimers, E., & Cressey, J. M. (2019). Integrating social-emotional learning and culturally responsive teaching in teacher education preparation programs: The Massachusetts experience so far. *Teacher Education Quarterly*, 46(4), 150–168.

Donahue-Keegan, D., Villegas-Reimers, E., & Cressey, J. M. (2019). Integrating social-emotional learning and culturally responsive teaching in teacher education programs: The Massachusetts experience so far. *Teacher Education Quarterly*, 46(4), 150–168.

Donker, M. H., van Gog, T., Goetz, T., Roos, A.-L., & Mainhard, T. (2020). Associations between teachers' interpersonal behavior, physiological arousal, and lesson-focused emotions. *Contemporary Educational Psychology*, 63(101906), 101906. https://doi.org/10.1016/j.cedpsych.2020.101906

Dörnyei, Z. (2007). *Research methods in applied linguistics: Quantitative, qualitative, and mixed methodologies*. Oxford University Press.

Drachsler, H., & Greller, W. (2016). Privacy and analytics. *Proceedings of the Sixth International Conference on Learning Analytics & Knowledge - LAK '16*, 89–98. New York, New York, USA: ACM Press. DOI: 10.1145/2883851.2883893

Dresser, R. (2012). Reviving oral reading practices with English learners by integrating social-emotional learning. *Multicultural Education*, 20(1), 45–50.

Driscoll, M. P. (2004). *Psychology of Learning for Instruction* (3rd ed.). Pearson Education.

Du Boulay, B., Avramides, K., Luckin, R., Martínez-Mirón, E., Méndez, G. R., & Carr, A. (2010). Towards systems that care: A Conceptual Framework based on motivation, metacognition and affect. *International Journal of Artificial Intelligence in Education*, 20(3), 1997–229. DOI: 10.3233/JAI-2010-0007

Du Toit-Brits, C. (2019). A focus on self-directed learning: The role that educators' expectations play in the enhancement of students' self-directedness. *South African Journal of Education*, 39(2), 1–11. DOI: 10.15700/saje.v39n2a1645

Duckworth, A. L., Peterson, C., Matthews, M. D., & Kelly, D. R. (2007). Grit: Perseverance and passion for long-term goals. *Journal of Personality and Social Psychology*, 92(6), 1087–1101. DOI: 10.1037/0022-3514.92.6.1087 PMID: 17547490

Duckworth, A. L., Quinn, P. D., & Seligman, M. E. (2009). Positive predictors of teacher effectiveness. *The Journal of Positive Psychology*, 4(6), 540–547. DOI: 10.1080/17439760903157232

Duff, P. A., & Anderson, T. (2015). Case-study Research. *The Cambridge Guide to Research in Language Teaching and Learning*, 112.

Duffy, M. C., Lajoie, S. P., Pekrun, R., & Lachapelle, K. (2018). Emotions in medical education: Examining the validity of the Medical Emotion Scale (MES) across authentic medical learning environments. *Learning and Instruction*.

Dunlap, J. C., & Lowenthal, P. R. (2014). The power of presence: Our quest for the right mix of social presence in online courses. In Pina, A. A., & Mizell, A. P. (Eds.), *Real life distance education: Case studies in practice*.

Dunn, T. J., & Kennedy, M. (2019). Technology-enhanced learning in higher education; motivations, engagement, and academic achievement. *Computers & Education*, 137, 104–113. DOI: 10.1016/j.compedu.2019.04.004

Durlak, J. A., Weissberg, R. P., Dymnicki, A. B., Taylor, R. D., & Schellinger, K. B. (2011). The impact of enhancing students' social and emotional learning: A meta-analysis of school-based universal interventions. *Child Development*, 82(1), 405–432. DOI: 10.1111/j.1467-8624.2010.01564.x PMID: 21291449

Dweck, C. S. (2006). *Mindset: The New Psychology of Success*. Ballantine Books.

Dweck, C. S. (2006). *Mindset: The new psychology of success*. Random House.

Dweck, C. S. (2010). Mind-sets. *Principal Leadership*, 10(5), 26–29.

Dwyer, K. K., Bingham, S. G., Carlson, R. E., Prisbell, M., Cruz, A. M., & Fus, D. A. (2004). Communication and connectedness in the classroom: Development of the connected classroom climate inventory. *Communication Research Reports*, 21(3), 264–272. DOI: 10.1080/08824090409359988

Dymond, D. (2014, August 14). Ideal performance state? How about ideal performance no matter what state? [LinkedIn post].

Dyulicheva, Y. Y., & Bilashova, E. A. (2022). Learning analytics of MOOCs based on natural language processing. *CEUR Workshop Proceedings*.

Eberle, J. (2013). Lifelong learning. In Hase, S., & Kenyon, C. (Eds.), *Self-determined learning: Heutagogy in action*. Bloomsbury Academic.

Eberle, J., & Childress, M. (2009). Using heutagogy to address the needs of online learners. In Rogers, P., Berg, G. A., Boettecher, J. V., & Justice, L. (Eds.), *Encyclopedia of distance learning* (2nd ed.). Idea Group Inc. DOI: 10.4018/978-1-60566-198-8.ch331

Edmondson, A. C., Kramer, R. M., & Cook, K. S. (2004). Psychological safety, trust, and learning in organizations: A group-level lens. Trust and distrust in organizations: Dilemmas and approaches, 12(2004), 239-272.

Edmondson, A. C., & Roloff, K. S. (2008). Overcoming barriers to collaboration: Psychological safety and learning in diverse teams. In *Team effectiveness in complex organizations* (pp. 217–242). Routledge.

Egan, K. (1997). *The educated mind: How cognitive tools shape our understanding*. University of Chicago Press. DOI: 10.7208/chicago/9780226190402.001.0001

Eisenhardt, K. M. (1989). Building theories from case study research. *Academy of Management Review*, 14(4), 532–550. DOI: 10.2307/258557

Elias, M., Zins, J. E., & Weissberg, R. P. (1997). *Promoting social and emotional learning: Guidelines for educators*. Ascd.

Elmi, C. (2020). Integrating social emotional learning strategies in higher education. *European Journal of Investigation in Health, Psychology and Education*, 10(3), 848–858. DOI: 10.3390/ejihpe10030061 PMID: 34542515

Endres, T., Weyreter, S., Renkl, A., & Eitel, A. (2020). When and why does emotional design foster learning? Evidence for situational interest as a mediator of increased persistence. *Journal of Computer Assisted Learning*, 36(4), 514–525. Advance online publication. DOI: 10.1111/jcal.12418

European Union Aviation Safety Agency. (2015). *Startle effect management* (Final report EASA_REP_RESEA_2015_3).

Fang, C. M., McMahon, K., Miller, M. L., & Rosenthal, M. Z. (2021). A pilot study investigating the efficacy of brief, phone-based behavioral interventions for burnout in graduate students. *Journal of Clinical Psychology*, 77(12), 2725–2745. DOI: 10.1002/jclp.23245 PMID: 34517431

Febriantoro, W., Gauthier, A., & Cukurova, M. (2023). The Promise of Physiological Data in Collaborative Learning: A Systematic Literature Review. In *Lecture Notes in Computer Science (including subseries Lecture Notes in Artificial Intelligence and Lecture Notes in Bioinformatics)* (pp. 75–88). DOI: 10.1007/978-3-031-42682-7_6

Feidakis, M., Daradoumis, T., Caballe, S., & Conesa, J. (2013). Measuring the Impact of Emotion Awareness on e-learning Situations. *2013 Seventh International Conference on Complex, Intelligent, and Software Intensive Systems*, 391–396. IEEE. DOI: 10.1109/CISIS.2013.71

Fensie, A. (2023). Toward a science of adult learning. https://doi.org/DOI: 10.13140/RG.2.2.13966.95043

Feraco, T., Resnati, D., Fregonese, D., Spoto, A., & Meneghetti, C. (2022). An integrated model of school students' academic achievement and life satisfaction linking soft skills, extracurricular activities, self-regulated learning, motivation, and emotions. *European Journal of Psychology of Education*, •••, 1–22. DOI: 10.1007/s10212-022-00601-4

Ferguson, R. (2012). Learning analytics: Drivers, developments and challenges. *International Journal of Technology Enhanced Learning*, 4(5/6), 304. DOI: 10.1504/IJTEL.2012.051816

Fernández-Berrocal, P., & Extremera, N. (2006). Emotional intelligence: A theoretical and empirical review of its first 15 years of history. *Psicothema*, 18, 7–12. PMID: 17295952

Ferrari, R. (2015). Writing narrative style literature reviews. *Medical Writing*, 24(4), 230–235. DOI: 10.1179/2047480615Z.000000000329

Fetzner, M. (2013). What do unsuccessful online students want us to know? *Online Learning : the Official Journal of the Online Learning Consortium*, 17(1), 1–27. DOI: 10.24059/olj.v17i1.319

Fink, C. K. (2013). Consciousness as Presence: An Exploration of the Illusion of Self. *Buddhist Studies Review*, 30(1), 113–128. DOI: 10.1558/bsrv.v30i1.113

Fisher, M. J., & Marshall, A. P. (2009). Understanding descriptive statistics. *Australian Critical Care*, 22(2), 93–97. DOI: 10.1016/j.aucc.2008.11.003 PMID: 19150245

Fitzpatrick, J. J. (2018). Teaching Through Storytelling: Narrative Nursing. *Nursing Education Perspectives*, 39(2), 60. DOI: 10.1097/01.NEP.0000000000000298 PMID: 29461432

Flushman, T., Guise, M., & Hegg, S. (2021). Partnership to support the social and emotional learning of teachers: A new teacher learning community. *Teacher Education Quarterly*, 48(3), 87–105.

Fong, C. J., & Schallert, D. L. (2023). Feedback to the future: Advancing motivational and emotional perspectives in feedback research. *Educational Psychologist*, 58(3), 146–161. DOI: 10.1080/00461520.2022.2134135

Forehand, M. (2010). Bloom's taxonomy. In Orey, M. (Ed.), *Emerging perspectives on learning, teaching, and technology* (pp. 41–47). Jacobs Foundation.

Frankl, V. E. (2006). *Man's Search for Meaning*. Beacon Press.

Fraser, B. J., & Treagust, D. F. (1986). Validity and use of an instrument for assessing classroom psychological environment in higher education. *Higher Education*, 15(1-2), 37–57. DOI: 10.1007/BF00138091

Fredrickson, B. L. (2001). The role of positive emotions in positive psychology: The broaden-and-build theory of positive emotions. *The American Psychologist*, 56(3), 218–226. DOI: 10.1037/0003-066X.56.3.218 PMID: 11315248

Fredrickson, B. L. (2013). Positive emotions broaden and build. In *Advances in experimental social psychology* (Vol. 47, pp. 1–53). Academic Press.

Freire, P. (1970). *Pedagogy of the Oppressed*. Penguin Books.

Frenzel, A. C., Daniels, L., & Burić, I. (2021). Teacher emotions in the classroom and their implications for students. *Educational Psychologist*, 56(4), 250–264. DOI: 10.1080/00461520.2021.1985501

Frey, T. K. (2019). Classroom emotions scale. In *Communication Research Measures III* (pp. 195–201). Routledge. DOI: 10.4324/9780203730188-16

Friedkin, N. E. (2004). Social cohesion. *Annual Review of Sociology*, 30(1), 409–425. DOI: 10.1146/annurev.soc.30.012703.110625

Frisby, B. N. (2019). The influence of emotional contagion on student perceptions of instructor rapport, emotional support, emotion work, valence, and cognitive learning. *Communication Studies*, 70(4), 492–506. DOI: 10.1080/10510974.2019.1622584

Frisby, B. N., Beck, A.-C., Smith Bachman, A., Byars, C., Lamberth, C., & Thompson, J. (2016). The influence of instructor-student rapport on instructors' professional and organizational outcomes. *Communication Research Reports*, 33(2), 103–110. DOI: 10.1080/08824096.2016.1154834

Frisby, B. N., & Martin, M. M. (2010). Instructor–student and student–student rapport in the classroom. *Communication Education*, 59(2), 146–164. DOI: 10.1080/03634520903564362

Frisby, B. N., & Myers, S. A. (2008). The Relationships among Perceived Instructor Rapport, Student Participation, and Student Learning Outcomes. *Texas Speech Communication Journal*, 33, 27–34.

Fuhrmann, B. S., & Grasha, A. F. (1983). *A practical handbook for college teachers*. No Title.

Futch, L. S., DeNoyelles, A., Thompson, K., & Howard, W. (2016). Comfort" as a Critical Success Factor in Blended Learning Courses. *Online Learning : the Official Journal of the Online Learning Consortium*, 20(3), 140–158. DOI: 10.24059/olj.v20i3.978

Ganotice, F. A.Jr, Datu, J. A. D., & King, R. B. (2016). Which emotional profiles exhibit the best learning outcomes? A person-centered analysis of students' academic emotions. *School Psychology International*, 37(5), 498–518. DOI: 10.1177/0143034316660147

Gardner, H. (1993). Multiple intelligences.

Gardner, A., Hase, S., Gardner, G., Dunn, S. V., & Carryer, J. (2008). From competence to capability: A study of nurse practitioners in clinical practice. *Journal of Clinical Nursing*, 17(2), 250–258. DOI: 10.1111/j.1365-2702.2006.01880.x PMID: 17419787

Garfield, C. A., & Bennett, H. Z. (1984). *Peak performance: Mental training techniques of the world's greatest athletes*. Tarcher.

Garnefski, N., & Kraaij, V. (2006). Cognitive emotion regulation questionnaire–development of a short 18-item version (CERQ-short). *Personality and Individual Differences*, 41(6), 1045–1053. DOI: 10.1016/j.paid.2006.04.010

Garrison, D. R., Anderson, T., & Archer, W. (2001). Critical thinking, cognitive presence, and computer conferencing in distance education. *American Journal of Distance Education*, 15(1), 7–23. DOI: 10.1080/08923640109527071

Gašević, D., Dawson, S., Rogers, T., & Gasevic, D. (2016). Learning analytics should not promote one size fits all: The effects of instructional conditions in predicting academic success. *The Internet and Higher Education*, 28, 68–84. DOI: 10.1016/j.iheduc.2015.10.002

Geertshuis, S. A. (2019). Slaves to our emotions: Examining the predictive relationship between emotional well-being and academic outcomes. *Active Learning in Higher Education*, 20(2), 153–166. DOI: 10.1177/1469787418808932

Gendron, B. (2019). Emotional capital, positive psychology, and active learning and mindful teaching. *New Directions for Teaching and Learning*, 2019(160), 63–76. Advance online publication. DOI: 10.1002/tl.20365

Genette, G. (1980). *Narrative Discourse: An Essay in Method* (Lewin, J. E., Trans.). Cornell University Press.

Giannakos, M., & Cukurova, M. (2023). The role of learning theory in multimodal learning analytics. *British Journal of Educational Technology*, 54(5), 1246–1267. DOI: 10.1111/bjet.13320

Gkontzis, A. F., Kotsiantis, S., Kalles, D., Panagiotakopoulos, C. T., & Verykios, V. S. (2020). Polarity, emotions and online activity of students and tutors as features in predicting grades. *Intelligent Decision Technologies*, 14(3), 409–436. DOI: 10.3233/IDT-190137

Glaser, B. G., & Strauss, A. L. (1967). *The discovery of grounded theory: Strategies for qualitative research*. Aldine Transaction.

Glaser, B., & Strauss, A. (1967). *The discovery of grounded theory: Strategies of qualitative research.* Wiedenfeld and Nicholson.

Goegan, L. D., Wagner, A. K., & Daniels, L. M. (2017). Pre-service and practicing teachers' commitment to and comfort with social emotional learning. *The Alberta Journal of Educational Research*, 63(3), 267–285. DOI: 10.55016/ojs/ajer.v63i3.56284

Goetz, T., Bieleke, M., Gogol, K., van Tartwijk, J., Mainhard, T., Lipnevich, A. A., & Pekrun, R. (2021). Getting along and feeling good: Reciprocal associations between student-teacher relationship quality and students' emotions. *Learning and Instruction*, 71(101349), 101349. DOI: 10.1016/j.learninstruc.2020.101349

Goetz, T., Keller, M. M., Lüdtke, O., Nett, U. E., & Lipnevich, A. A. (2020). The dynamics of real-time classroom emotions: Appraisals mediate the relation between students' perceptions of teaching and their emotions. *Journal of Educational Psychology*, 112(6), 1243–1260. DOI: 10.1037/edu0000415

Goetz, T., Nett, U. E., Martiny, S. E., Hall, N. C., Pekrun, R., Dettmers, S., & Trautwein, U. (2012). Students' emotions during homework: Structures, self-concept antecedents, and achievement outcomes. *Learning and Individual Differences*, 22(2), 225–234. DOI: 10.1016/j.lindif.2011.04.006

Golby, M. (1996). Teachers' Emotions: An illustrated discussion. *Cambridge Journal of Education*, 26(3), 423–434. DOI: 10.1080/0305764960260310

Goldman, Z. W., & Goodboy, A. K. (2014). Making students feel better: Examining the relationships between teacher confirmation and college students' emotional outcomes. *Communication Education*, 63(3), 259–277. DOI: 10.1080/03634523.2014.920091

Goldsworthy, R. (2000). Designing instruction for emotional intelligence. *Educational Technology*, 40(5), 43–58.

Goleman, D. (1995). *Emotional intelligence: Why it can matter more than IQ.* Bantam Books.

Goleman, D. (2000a). Emotional intelligence. In Sadock, B., & Sadock, V. (Eds.), *Comprehensive textbook of psychiatry* (7th ed.). Lippincott Williams & Wilkins.

Goleman, D. (2005). *Emotional intelligence.* Bantam.

Goleman, D. (2011). Emotional mastery. *Leadership Excellence*, 28(6), 12–13.

Goleman, D., Boyatzis, R. E., & McKee, A. (2002). *Reawakening your passion for work.* Harvard Business School Publishing Corporation.

Gomez, J. (2017a, February 6). Why is this happening? A new narrative model explains it. *Collective Journey* [blog]. https://blog.collectivejourney.com/why-is-this-happening-d1287d5ee4ee

Gomez, J. (2017b, February 7). The hero's journey is no longer serving us: classic storytelling models are faltering in the digital age. *Collective Journey* [blog]. https://blog.collectivejourney.com/the-heros-journey-is-no-longer-serving-us-85c6f8152a50#.psdwtk4kp

Gomez, J. (2017c, February 17). The collective journey comes to television: Game of Thrones, Walking Dead, Orange is the New Black & others are subverting the hero's journey. *Collective Journey* [blog]. https://blog.collectivejourney.com/the-collective-journey-story-model-comes-to-television-151bb4011ce2

Gomez, J. (2017d, March 8). Regenerative listening: Collective journey narratives require genuine engagement. *Collective Journey* [blog]. https://blog.collectivejourney.com/the-secret-to-new-storytelling-regenerative-listening-5250c65b6391

Gomez, J. (2017e, May 22). Superpositioning: each of us can now be in five places at once. *Collective Journey* [blog]. https://blog.collectivejourney.com/superpositioning-fef1e10ff24c

Gomez, J. (2017f, September 16). Social self-organization: story can take what we imagine and make it real. *Collective Journey* [blog]. https://blog.collectivejourney.com/social-self-organization-47a562cfb351

Gray, R. (Host). (2016, September 22). Applying music in sport [Audio podcast episode]. In *The Perception Action Podcast*. Retrieved from https://perceptionaction.com/36c/

Green, A. L., Ferrante, S., Boaz, T. L., Kutash, K., & Wheeldon-Reece, B. (2021). Social and emotional learning during early adolescence: Effectiveness of a classroom-based SEL program for middle school students. *Psychology in the Schools*, 58(6), 1056–1069. DOI: 10.1002/pits.22487

Greenburg, J., Putman, H., & Walsh, K. (2014). *Training our future teachers: Classroom management, Revised 2014*. National Council on Teacher Quality.

Gros, B., & García-Peñalvo, F. J. (2016). Future trends in the design strategies and technological affordances of e-learning. In Spector, M., Lockee, B. B., & Childress, M. D. (Eds.), *Learning, Design, and Technology. An International Compendium of Theory, Research, Practice, and Policy* (pp. 1–23). Springer International Publishing., DOI: 10.1007/978-3-319-17727-4_67-1

Gross, J. J. (1998a). Antecedent-and response-focused emotion regulation: Divergent consequences for experience, expression, and physiology. *Journal of Personality and Social Psychology*, 74(1), 224–237. DOI: 10.1037/0022-3514.74.1.224 PMID: 9457784

Gross, J. J. (1998b). The emerging field of emotion regulation: An integrative review. *Review of General Psychology*, 2(3), 271–299. DOI: 10.1037/1089-2680.2.3.271

Gross, J. J. (2015a). Emotion regulation: Current status and future prospects. *Psychological Inquiry*, 26(1), 1–26. DOI: 10.1080/1047840X.2014.940781

Gross, J. J. (2015b). The extended process model of emotion regulation: Elaborations, applications, and future directions. *Psychological Inquiry*, 26(1), 130–137. DOI: 10.1080/1047840X.2015.989751

Gross, J. J., & Feldman Barrett, L. (2011). Emotion generation and emotion regulation: One or two depends on your point of view. *Emotion Review*, 3(1), 8–16. DOI: 10.1177/1754073910380974 PMID: 21479078

Grossman, J. (2021). Social-emotional learning and educator implementation.

Grossman, P., & Fraefel, U. (2024). *Core practices in teacher education: A global perspective*. Harvard Education Press.

Guenaga, M., & Garaizar, P. (2016). From Analysis to Improvement: Challenges and Opportunities for Learning Analytics. *IEEE Revista Iberoamericana de Technologias del Aprendizaje*, 11(3), 146–147. DOI: 10.1109/RITA.2016.2589481

Gutsell, J. N., & Inzlicht, M. (2012). Intergroup differences in the sharing of emotive states: Neural evidence of an empathy gap. *Social Cognitive and Affective Neuroscience*, 7(5), 596–603. DOI: 10.1093/scan/nsr035 PMID: 21705345

Guzmán-Valenzuela, C., Gómez-González, C., Rojas-Murphy Tagle, A., & Lorca-Vyhmeister, A. (2021). Learning analytics in higher education: A preponderance of analytics but very little learning? *International Journal of Educational Technology in Higher Education*, 18(1), 23. DOI: 10.1186/s41239-021-00258-x PMID: 34778523

Hagelskamp, C., Brackett, M. A., Rivers, S. E., & Salovey, P. (2013). Improving classroom quality with the RULER approach to social and emotional learning. *School Psychology Review*, 42, 193–204. PMID: 23444004

Hagenauer, G., Gläser-Zikuda, M., & Volet, S. (2016). University teachers' perceptions of appropriate emotion display and high-quality teacher-student relationship: Similarities and differences across cultural-educational contexts. *Frontline Learning Research*, 4(3), 44–74. DOI: 10.14786/flr.v4i3.236

Hagenauer, G., Hascher, T., & Volet, S. E. (2015). Teacher emotions in the classroom: Associations with students' engagement, classroom discipline and the interpersonal teacher-student relationship. *European Journal of Psychology of Education*, 30(4), 385–403. https://doi.org/10.1007/s10212-015-0250-0

Hager, P., & Halliday, J. (2009). *Recovering informal learning: Wisdom, judgement and community*. Springer.

Hanin, Y. L. (2003). Performance related emotional states in sport: A qualitative analysis. *Forum Qualitative Sozialforschung / Forum: Qualitative. Social Research*, 4(1).

Hara, N., & Kling, R. (2003). Students' distress with a web-based distance education course: An ethnographic study of participants' experiences. *Turkish Online Journal of Distance Education*, 4(2).

Hardt, M. (2010). Militant life. *New Left Review*, 64, 151–160.

Harley, J. M., Pekrun, R., Taxer, J. L., & Gross, J. J. (2019). Emotion regulation in achievement situations: An integrated model. *Educational Psychologist*, 54(2), 106–126. DOI: 10.1080/00461520.2019.1587297

Harrington, C., & Thomas, M. (2023). *Designing a motivational syllabus: Creating a learning path for student engagement*. Taylor & Francis.

Hart, J. W. (2012). Adult learning in the workplace. In Kasworm, C. E., Rose, A. D., & Ross-Gordon, J. M. (Eds.), *Handbook of adult and continuing education* (2010 ed., pp. 371–380). Sage.

Hase, S., & Kenyon, C. (2000). From andragogy to heutagogy. *UltiBase*. Retrieved from http://ultibase.rmit.edu.au/Articles/dec00/hase2.htm

Hase, S. (2014). Capability and learning: Beyond competence. In Harteis, C., Rausch, A., & Seifried, J. (Eds.), *Discourses on professional learning: On the boundary between learning and working* (pp. 45–59). Springer., DOI: 10.1007/978-94-007-7012-6_4

Hase, S., & Kenyon, C. (2007). Heutagogy: A child of complexity theory. *Complicity: An International Journal of Complexity and Education*, 4(1), 111–119. DOI: 10.29173/cmplct8766

Hasnine, M. N., Nguyen, H. T., Tran, T. T. T., Bui, H. T. T., Akçapınar, G., & Ueda, H. (2023). A Real-Time Learning Analytics Dashboard for Automatic Detection of Online Learners' Affective States. *Sensors (Basel)*, 23(9), 4243. DOI: 10.3390/s23094243 PMID: 37177447

Hawk, T. F., & Shah, A. J. (2007). Using learning style instruments to enhance student learning. *Decision Sciences Journal of Innovative Education*, 5(1), 1–19. DOI: 10.1111/j.1540-4609.2007.00125.x

Headrick, J., Renshaw, I., Davids, K., Pinder, R., & Araújo, D. (2015). The dynamics of expertise acquisition in sport: The role of affective learning design. *Psychology of Sport and Exercise*, 16(1), 83–90. DOI: 10.1016/j.psychsport.2014.08.006

Heffernan, T., & Bosetti, L. (2023). University bullying and incivility towards faculty deans. *International Journal of Leadership in Education*, 26(4), 604–623. DOI: 10.1080/13603124.2020.1850870

Herbert, F. (1965). *Dune*. Chilton Books.

Hermans, E. J., Henckens, M. J., Joëls, M., & Fernández, G. (2014). Dynamic adaptation of large-scale brain networks in response to acute stressors. *Trends in Neurosciences*, 37(6), 304–314. DOI: 10.1016/j.tins.2014.03.006 PMID: 24766931

Hernández-de-Menéndez, M., Morales-Menendez, R., Escobar, C. A., & Ramírez Mendoza, R. A. (2022). Learning analytics: State of the art. [IJIDeM]. *International Journal on Interactive Design and Manufacturing*, 16(3), 1209–1230. DOI: 10.1007/s12008-022-00930-0

Hess, U. (2017). Emotion Categorization. In *Handbook of Categorization in Cognitive Science* (pp. 107–126). Elsevier., DOI: 10.1016/B978-0-08-101107-2.00005-1

Hilliard, J., Kear, K., Donelan, H., & Heaney, C. (2020). Students' experiences of anxiety in an assessed, online, collaborative project. *Computers & Education*, 143, 103675. DOI: 10.1016/j.compedu.2019.103675

Hill, J., Berlin, K., Choate, J., Cravens-Brown, L., McKendrick-Calder, L., & Smith, S. (2021). Exploring the emotional responses of undergraduate students to assessment feedback: Implications for instructors. *Teaching & Learning Inquiry*, 9(1), 294–316. DOI: 10.20343/teachlearninqu.9.1.20

Hillman, D., Willis, D. J., & Gunawardena, C. (1994). Learner-interface interaction in distance education: An extension of contemporary models and strategies for practitioners. *American Journal of Distance Education*, 8(2), 30–42. DOI: 10.1080/08923649409526853

Hmelo-Silver, C. E. (2004). Problem-based learning: What and how do students learn? *Educational Psychology Review*, 16(3), 235–266. DOI: 10.1023/B:EDPR.0000034022.16470.f3

Hoemann, K., Gendron, M., & Barrett, L. F. (2022). Assessing the Power of Words to Facilitate Emotion Category Learning. *Affective Science*, 3(1), 69–80. DOI: 10.1007/s42761-021-00084-4 PMID: 36046100

Hoffmann, J. D., Brackett, M. A., Bailey, C. S., & Willner, C. J. (2020). Teaching emotion regulation in schools: Translating research into practice with the RULER approach to social and emotional learning. *Emotion (Washington, D.C.)*, 20(1), 105–109. DOI: 10.1037/emo0000649 PMID: 31961187

Hökkä, P., Vähäsantanen, K., & Paloniemi, S. (2020). Emotions in learning at work: A Literature review. *Vocations and Learning*, 13(1), 1–25. DOI: 10.1007/s12186-019-09226-z

Hong, F.-Y., Shao-I., C., Huang, D.-H., & Chiu, S.-L. (2021). Correlations among classroom emotional climate, social self-efficacy, and psychological health of university students in Taiwan. *Education and Urban Society*, 53(4), 446–468. DOI: 10.1177/0013124520931458

Hooda, M. (2020). Learning Analytics Lens: Improving Quality of Higher Education. *International Journal of Emerging Trends in Engineering Research*, 8(5), 1626–1646. DOI: 10.30534/ijeter/2020/24852020

Hooven, C. K. (2023). Academic freedom is social justice: Sex, gender, and cancel culture on campus. *Archives of Sexual Behavior*, 52(1), 35–41. DOI: 10.1007/s10508-022-02467-5 PMID: 36344790

Horstmann, G. (2006). Latency and duration of the action interruption in surprise. *Cognition and Emotion*, 20(2), 242–273. DOI: 10.1080/02699930500262878

Hosek, A. M. (2021). Cognitive vs. Affective: Reconsidering Bloom's Taxonomy. *Psychology Teacher Network*, 31(3), 9–13.

Hsieh, Y.-Z., Lin, S.-S., Luo, Y.-C., Jeng, Y.-L., Tan, S.-W., Chen, C.-R., & Chiang, P.-Y. (2020). ARCS-Assisted Teaching Robots Based on Anticipatory Computing and Emotional Big Data for Improving Sustainable Learning Efficiency and Motivation. *Sustainability (Basel)*, 12(14), 5605. DOI: 10.3390/su12145605

https://www.edutopia.org/article/role-emotion-co-regulation-discipline/#:~:text=If%20I'm%20the%20teacher,I%20act%20on%20that%20discipline

Huang, T., & Wang, W. (2024). Relationship between fear of evaluation, ambivalence over emotional expression, and self-compassion among university students. *BMC Psychology*, 12(1), 128. DOI: 10.1186/s40359-024-01629-5 PMID: 38449046

Ifenthaler, D., & Yau, J. Y.-K. (2022). Higher Education Stakeholders' Views on Guiding the Implementation of Learning Analytics for Study Success. *ASCILITE Publications*, 453–457, 453–457. Advance online publication. DOI: 10.14742/apubs.2019.311

Immordino Yang, M. H., Darling-Hammond, L., & Krone, C. (2018). *The brain basis for integrating social, emotional, and academic development: How emotions and social development drive learning.* Aspen Institute.

Immordino-Yang, M. H. (2011). Implications of affective and social neuroscience for educational theory. *Educational Philosophy and Theory*, 43(1), 98–103. DOI: 10.1111/j.1469-5812.2010.00713.x

Immordino-Yang, M. H., & Damasio, A. (2007). We feel, therefore we learn: The relevance of affective and social neuroscience to education. *Mind, Brain and Education : the Official Journal of the International Mind, Brain, and Education Society*, 1(1), 3–10. DOI: 10.1111/j.1751-228X.2007.00004.x

Isen, A. M. (2003). Positive affect as a source of human strength. In *A psychology of human strengths: Fundamental questions and future directions for a positive psychology* (pp. 179–195). American Psychological Association., DOI: 10.1037/10566-013

Jagsi, R., Griffith, K., Krenz, C., Jones, R. D., Cutter, C., Feldman, E. L., Jacobson, C., Kerr, E., Paradis, K., Singer, K., Spector, N., Stewart, A., Telem, D., Ubel, P., & Settles, I. (2023). Workplace harassment, cyber incivility, and climate in academic medicine. *Journal of the American Medical Association*, 329(21), 1848–1858. DOI: 10.1001/jama.2023.7232 PMID: 37278814

James, W. (1952). *The principles of psychology.* Encyclopedia Britannica.

Jarrell, A., & Lajoie, S. P. (2017). The regulation of achievements emotions: Implications for research and practice. *Canadian Psychology*, 58(3), 276–287. https://doi.org/doi.org/10.1037/cap0000119. DOI: 10.1037/cap0000119

Jarrell, A., Lajoie, S. P., Hall, N. C., & Horrocks, P. T. M. (2022). Antecedents and Consequences of Emotion Regulation in STEM Degree Programs. *Innovative Higher Education*, 47(3), 493–514. DOI: 10.1007/s10755-021-09587-1

Jarvis, P. (2006). *Towards a comprehensive theory of human learning.* Routledge.

Jeannerod, M. (1994). The representing brain: Neural correlates of motor intention and imagery. *Behavioral and Brain Sciences*, 17(2), 187–202. DOI: 10.1017/S0140525X00034026

Jelińska, M., & Paradowski, M. B. (2021). Teachers' engagement in and coping with emergency remote instruction during COVID-19-induced school closures: A multinational contextual perspective. *Online Learning : the Official Journal of the Online Learning Consortium*, 25(1). Advance online publication. DOI: 10.24059/olj.v25i1.2492

Jennings, P., Frank, J., & Montgomery, M. (2020). Social and emotional learning for educators. *Rethinking learning: A review of social and emotional learning for education systems*, 127-153.

Jennings, P. A. (2011). Promoting teachers' social and emotional competencies to support performance and reduce burnout. In Cohan, A., & Honigsfield, A. (Eds.), *Breaking the Mold of Preservice and Inservice Teacher Education: Innovative and Successful Practices for the Twenty-first Century*. Rowman & Littlefield.

Jézégou, A. (2012). Towards a distance learning environment that supports learner self-direction: The model of presence. *International Journal of Self-Directed Learning*, 9(1), 11–23.

Jiang, J., Vauras, M., Volet, S., & Salo, A.-E. (2019). Teacher beliefs and emotion expression in light of support for student psychological needs: A qualitative study. *Education Sciences*, 9(2), 68. DOI: 10.3390/educsci9020068

Jiang, M., & Koo, K. (2020). Emotional presence in building an online learning community among non-traditional graduate students. *Online Learning : the Official Journal of the Online Learning Consortium*, 24(4), 93–111. DOI: 10.24059/olj.v24i4.2307

Johnson, D. W., & Johnson, R. T. (1999). *Learning together and alone: Cooperative, competitive, and individualistic learning*. Allyn & Bacon.

Joksimovic, S., Kovanovic, V., Joksimović, S., Kovanović, V., & Dawson, S. (2019). The Journey of Learning Analytics. In *HERDSA Review of Higher Education*.

Jomon, K. J., & Romate John Ph, D. (2017). Emotional competence and student engagement of the first year undergraduate students in Kerala. *International Journal of Indian Psychology*, 4(4). Advance online publication. DOI: 10.25215/0404.144

Jones, S. M., & Doolittle, E. J. (2017). Social and emotional learning: Introducing the issue. *The Future of Children*, 27(1), 3–11. DOI: 10.1353/foc.2017.0000

Joseph, D. L., & Newman, D. A. (2010). Emotional intelligence: An integrative meta-analysis and cascading model. *The Journal of Applied Psychology*, 95(1), 54–78. DOI: 10.1037/a0017286 PMID: 20085406

Joseph-Richard, P., Uhomoibhi, J., & Jaffrey, A. (2021). Predictive learning analytics and the creation of emotionally adaptive learning environments in higher education institutions: A study of students' affect responses. *The International Journal of Information and Learning Technology*, 38(2), 243–257. DOI: 10.1108/IJILT-05-2020-0077

Joukes, E., Cornet, R., de Bruijne, M. C., & de Keizer, N. F. (2016). Eliciting end-user expectations to guide the implementation process of a new electronic health record: A case study using concept mapping. *International Journal of Medical Informatics*, 87, 111–117. DOI: 10.1016/j.ijmedinf.2015.12.014 PMID: 26806718

Juslin, P. N. (2009). Emotion in music performance. In Hallam, S., Cross, I., & Thaut, M. (Eds.), *The Oxford handbook of music psychology* (pp. 377–389). Oxford University Press.

Kagan, S. H. (2017). 6 Ageism and the Helping Professions. *Ageism: Stereotyping and Prejudice against Older Persons*, 165.

Kahu, E., Stephens, C., Leach, L., & Zepke, N. (2015). Linking academic emotions and student engagement: Mature-aged distance students' transition to university. *Journal of Further and Higher Education*, 39(4), 481–497. DOI: 10.1080/0309877X.2014.895305

Kaiqi, S., & Kutuk, G. (2024). Exploring the impact of online teaching factors on international students' control-value appraisals and achievement emotions in a foreign language context. *The Asia-Pacific Education Researcher*, 33(4), 943–955. DOI: 10.1007/s40299-024-00831-8

Kalogiannakis, M., & Touvlatzis, S. (2015). Emotions experienced by learners and their development through communication with the tutor-counsellor. *European Journal of Open Distance and E-Learning*, 18(2), 36–48. DOI: 10.1515/eurodl-2015-0012

Kanbur, O., & Kirikkaleli, N. O. (2023). Interaction between teachers' emotional intelligence and classroom management. *Perspectives in Education*, 41(2), 3–15. Advance online publication. DOI: 10.38140/pie.v41i2.6847

Kang, C., & Wu, J. (2022). A theoretical review on the role of positive emotional classroom rapport in preventing EFL students' shame: A control-value theory perspective. *Frontiers in Psychology*, 13, 977240. Advance online publication. DOI: 10.3389/fpsyg.2022.977240 PMID: 36532974

Kang, M., Kim, S., & Park, S. (2007). Developing emotional presence scale for measuring students' involvement during e-Learning process. In Montgomerie, C., & Seale, J. (Eds.), *Proceedings of World Conference on Educational Multimedia, Hypermedia and Telecommunications 2007* (pp. 2829–2832). Chesapeake, VA: AACE.

Kappas, A. (2011). Emotion and regulation are one! *Emotion Review*, 3(1), 17–25. DOI: 10.1177/1754073910380971 PMID: 21479078

Karamarkovich, S. M., & Rutherford, T. (2021). Mixed feelings: Profiles of emotions among elementary mathematics students and how they function within a control-value framework. *Contemporary Educational Psychology*, 66, 101996. DOI: 10.1016/j.cedpsych.2021.101996

Kashdan, T. B., Gallagher, M. W., Silvia, P. J., Winterstein, B. P., Breen, W. E., Terhar, D., & Steger, M. F. (2009). The curiosity and exploration inventory-II: Development, factor structure, and psychometrics. *Journal of Research in Personality*, 43(6), 987–998. DOI: 10.1016/j.jrp.2009.04.011 PMID: 20160913

Kasliwal, P. S., Gunjan, R., & Shete, V. (2023). Computation of E-learners Textual Emotion to Enhance learning Experience. *International Journal of Intelligent Systems and Applications in Engineering*, 11(10s), 849–858.

Katsarou, E., & Chatzipanagiotou, P. (2021). A critical review of selected literature on learner-centered interactions in online learning. *Electronic Journal of e-Learning*, 19(5), 349–362. DOI: 10.34190/ejel.19.5.2469

Katz, D., Mahfouz, J., & Romas, S. (2020). Creating a foundation of well-being for teachers and students starts with SEL curriculum in teacher education programs. *Northwest Journal of Teacher Education, 15*(2), Article 5.

Katz, D., Mahfouz, J., & Romas, S. (2020). Creating a foundation of well-being for teachers and students starts with SEL curriculum in teacher education programs. *Northwest Journal of Teacher Education*, 15(2), 1–12. DOI: 10.15760/nwjte.2020.15.2.5

Kaur, I., Shri, C., & Mital, K. M. (2019). The role of emotional intelligence competencies in effective teaching and teacher's performance in higher education. *Higher Education for the Future*, 6(2), 188–206. DOI: 10.1177/2347631119840542

Kazanidis, I., Pellas, N., & Christopoulos, A. (2021). A Learning Analytics Conceptual Framework for Augmented Reality-Supported Educational Case Studies. *Multimodal Technologies and Interaction*, 5(3), 9. DOI: 10.3390/mti5030009

Ke, F. (2010). Examining online teaching, cognitive, and social presence for adult students. *Computers & Education*, 55(2), 808–820. DOI: 10.1016/j.compedu.2010.03.013

Keller, M. M., & Becker, E. S. (2021). Teachers' emotions and emotional authenticity: Do they matter to students' emotional responses in the classroom? *Teachers and Teaching*, 27(5), 404–422. DOI: 10.1080/13540602.2020.1834380

Kelly, G. (2016). Methodological considerations for the study of epistemic cognition in practice. *Handbook of Epistemic Cognition*, 393-408.

Kelly, D. M. (2017). Teaching for social justice. *Revista Intercambio*, (3), 26.

Kemp, C. L., Ball, M. M., Morgan, J. C., Doyle, P. J., Burgess, E. O., & Perkins, M. M. (2018). Maneuvering Together, Apart, and at Odds: Residents' Care Convoys in Assisted Living. *The Journals of Gerontology: Series B*.

Kennedy, M., Billett, S., Gherardi, S., & Grealish, L. (2015). Practice-based learning in higher education: jostling cultures. In *Practice-based Learning in Higher Education* (pp. 1–13). Springer. DOI: 10.1007/978-94-017-9502-9_1

Ke, S., Guimond, A., Tworoger, S. S., Chan, A. T., Liu, Y., & Kunzansky, L. D. (2023). Gut feelings: Associations of emotions and emotional regulation with the gut microbiome in women. *Psychological Medicine*, 53(15), 7151–7160. Advance online publication. DOI: 10.1017/S0033291723000612 PMID: 36942524

Khasawneh, Y. J. A., Alsarayreh, R., Al Ajlouni, A. A., Eyadat, H. M., Ayasrah, M. N., & Khasawneh, M. A. S. (2023). An Examination of Teacher Collaboration in Professional Learning Communities and Collaborative Teaching Practices. *Journal of Education and e-learning Research*, 10(3), 446–452. DOI: 10.20448/jeelr.v10i3.4841

Khoo, S. B. (2010). Academic mobbing: Hidden health hazard at workplace. *Malaysian Family Physician : the Official Journal of the Academy of Family Physicians of Malaysia*, 5(2), 61–67. https://www.ncbi.nlm.nih.gov/pmc/articles/PMC4170397/ PMID: 25606190

Kihlstrom, J. F., & Cantor, N. (2000). Social intelligence. Handbook of intelligence, 2, 359-379.King, A. (1993). From sage on the stage to guide on the side. *College Teaching*, 41(1), 30–35.

Kilag, O. K., Marquita, J., & Laurente, J. (2023). Teacher-led curriculum development: Fostering innovation in education. *Excellencia: International Multi-disciplinary Journal of Education (2994-9521)*, 1(4), 223-237.

Kilis, S., & Yildirim, Z. (2019). Posting patterns of students' social presence, cognitive presence and teaching presence in online learning. *Online Learning : the Official Journal of the Online Learning Consortium*, 23(2), 179–195. DOI: 10.24059/olj.v23i2.1460

Kim, M. K., Lee, I. H., & Kim, S. M. (2021). A longitudinal examination of temporal and iterative relationships among learner engagement dimensions during online discussion. *Journal of Computers in Education*, 8(1), 63–86. DOI: 10.1007/s40692-020-00171-8

Kinsella, K. (2022, March 29). *Creating a supportive SEL forum for English learner lesson contributions.* https://www.languagemagazine.com/2022/03/29/creating-a-supportive-sel-forum-for-english-learner-lesson-contributions

Kirkpatrick, J. D., & Kirkpatrick, W. K. (2016). *Kirkpatrick's four levels of training evaluation.* ATD Press.

Kitchenham, B. (2004). Procedures for performing systematic reviews. In *UK, Keele University*. UK, Keele University: Keele. https://doi.org/DOI: 10.1.1.122.3308

Kivimäki, V., Ketonen, E. E., & Lindblom-Ylänne, S. (2023). Engineering students' justifications for their selections in structured learning diaries. *Frontiers in Education*, 8, 1223732. Advance online publication. DOI: 10.3389/feduc.2023.1223732

Klahn Acuña, B., & Male, T. (2024). Toxic leadership and academics' work engagement in higher education: A cross-sectional study from Chile. *Educational Management Administration & Leadership*, 52(3), 757–773. DOI: 10.1177/17411432221084474

Knight, S., & Buckingham Shum, S. (2017). Theory and Learning Analytics. In *Handbook of Learning Analytics* (pp. 17–22). Society for Learning Analytics Research (SoLAR). DOI: 10.18608/hla17.001

Knobe, J., & Samuels, R. (2013). Thinking like a scientist: Innateness as a case study. *Cognition*, 126(1), 72–86. DOI: 10.1016/j.cognition.2012.09.003 PMID: 23063235

Knowles, M. S. (1984). Andragogy in action.

Knowles, M. S. (1980). From pedagogy to andragogy. *Religious Education (Chicago, Ill.).*

Knowles, M. S. (1984). *Andragogy in Action*. Jossey-Bass.

Knowles, M. S., Holton, E. F.III, & Swanson, R. A. (2005). *The adult learner* (6th ed.). Routledge. DOI: 10.4324/9780080481913

Knowles, M. S., Holton, E. F., & Swanson, R. A. (2015). *The adult learner: The definitive classic in adult education and human resource development* (8th ed.). Routledge.

Kobylińska, D., & Kusev, P. (2019). Flexible emotion regulation: How situational demands and individual differences influence the effectiveness of regulatory strategies. *Frontiers in Psychology*, 10, 72. DOI: 10.3389/fpsyg.2019.00072 PMID: 30774610

Kochan, J., Breiter, E., & Jentsch, F. (2005). Surprise and unexpectedness in flying: Factors and features. *13th International Symposium on Aviation Psychology*, 398-403.

Koch, M. (1999). The neurobiology of startle. *Progress in Neurobiology*, 59(2), 107–128. DOI: 10.1016/S0301-0082(98)00098-7 PMID: 10463792

Kolb, D. A. (1984). *Experiential learning: Experience as the source of learning and development*. Prentice-Hall.

Kolb, D. A. (1984). *Experiential Learning: Experiences as a source of learning and development*. Prentice-Hall.

Koludrovic, M. K., & Mrsic, A. (2022). The attitudes of initial teacher education students toward teacher social emotional competence. *Ekonomska Istrazivanja*, 33(1), 4113–4127. DOI: 10.1080/1331677X.2021.2010114

Komarraju, M., & Nadler, D. (2013). Self-efficacy and academic achievement: Why do implicit beliefs, goals, and effort regulation matter? *Learning and Individual Differences*, 25, 67–72. DOI: 10.1016/j.lindif.2013.01.005

Koole, S. L. (2009). The psychology of emotion regulation: An integrative review. *Cognition and Emotion*, 23(1), 4–41. DOI: 10.1080/02699930802619031

Kordts-Freudinger, R. (2017). Feel, think, teach – Emotional Underpinnings of Approaches to Teaching in Higher Education. *International Journal of Higher Education*, 6(1), 217. https://doi.org/doi:10.5430/ijhe.v6n1p217

Korn, M. (2022). Stanford course for entrepreneurs puts passion before business plans. Wall Street Journal. https://www.wsj.com/articles/stanford-course-for-entrepreneurs-puts-passion-before-business-plans-11641263201

Koslouski, J. B., & Chafouleas, S. M. (2022). Key consideration in delivering trauma-informed professional learning for educators. *Frontiers in Education*, 7, 853020. Advance online publication. DOI: 10.3389/feduc.2022.853020

Krashen, S. D. (1982). *Principles and practices in second language acquisition*. Pergamon Press.

Krashen, S. D. (1985). *The input hypothesis: Issues and implications*. Longman.

Krathwohl, D. R., Bloom, B. S., & Masia, B. B. (1964). *Taxonomy of educational objectives, the classification of educational goals.* Handbook II: Affective domain. David McKay Company.

Kryshko, O., Fleischer, J., Waldeyer, J., Wirth, J., & Leutner, D. (2020). Do motivational regulation strategies contribute to university students' academic success? *Learning and Individual Differences*, 82, 101912. DOI: 10.1016/j.lindif.2020.101912

Kumar, N., Rose, R. C., & Subramaniam, . (2008). The bond between intelligences: Cultural, emotional, and social. *Performance Improvement*, 47(10), 42–48. DOI: 10.1002/pfi.20039

Kwon, H., Yoon, K. L., Joormann, J., & Kwon, J.-H. (2013). Cultural and gender differences in emotion regulation: Relation to depression. *Cognition and Emotion*, 27(5), 769–782. DOI: 10.1080/02699931.2013.792244 PMID: 23805826

Kyndt, E., Dochy, F., Michielsen, M., & Moeyaert, B. (2009). Employee retention: Organisational and personal perspectives. *Vocations and Learning*, 2(3), 195–215. DOI: 10.1007/s12186-009-9024-7

L'Estrange, L., & Howard, J. (2022). Trauma-informed initial teacher education training: A necessary step in a system-wide response to addressing childhood trauma. *Frontiers in Education*, 7, 929582. Advance online publication. DOI: 10.3389/feduc.2022.929582

Ladyshewsky, R. K. (2013). Instructor presence in online courses and student satisfaction. *International Journal for the Scholarship of Teaching and Learning*, 7(1), 1–23. DOI: 10.20429/ijsotl.2013.070113

Lakoff, G., & Johnson, M. (1999). *Philosophy in the flesh: The embodied mind and its challenge to western thought.* Basic books.

Lampropoulos, G., Keramopoulos, E., Diamantaras, K., & Evangelidis, G. (2022). Augmented Reality and Virtual Reality in Education: Public Perspectives, Sentiments, Attitudes, and Discourses. *Education Sciences*, 12(11), 798. DOI: 10.3390/educsci12110798

Landis, C., & Hunt, W. A. (1939). *The Startle Pattern.* Farrar & Rinehart.

Lang, P. J., Bradley, M. M., & Cuthbert, B. N. (1990). Emotion, attention, and the startle reflex. *Psychological Review*, 97(3), 377–395. DOI: 10.1037/0033-295X.97.3.377 PMID: 2200076

Lapidot-Lefler, N. (2022). Promoting the use of social-emotional learning in online teaching. *The International Journal of Emotional Education*, 14(2), 19–35. DOI: 10.56300/HSZP5315

Larradet, F., Niewiadomski, R., Barresi, G., Caldwell, D. G., & Mattos, L. S. (2020). Toward Emotion Recognition From Physiological Signals in the Wild: Approaching the Methodological Issues in Real-Life Data Collection. *Frontiers in Psychology*, 11, 1111. Advance online publication. DOI: 10.3389/fpsyg.2020.01111 PMID: 32760305

Learner Centered Principles Work Group of the American Psychological Association's Board of Educational Affairs. (1997, November). *Learner-centered psychological principles: A framework for school reform and redesign*. Washington, DC: American Psychological Association.

LeDoux, J. (1997). Emotion, memory and the brain. *Scientific American*, 7(1), 68–75. PMID: 8023118

LeDoux, J. (1999). *The emotional brain: The mysterious underpinnings of emotional life*. Phoenix.

Lee, J. J., & Hammer, J. (2011). Gamification in education: What, how, why bother? *Academic Exchange Quarterly*, 15(2), 1–5.

Lee, J. Y., & Chei, M. J. (2020). Latent profile analysis of Korean undergraduates' academic emotions in e-learning environment. *Educational Technology Research and Development*, 68(3), 1521–1546. DOI: 10.1007/s11423-019-09715-x

Lee, K. (2021). Embracing authenticity and vulnerability in online PhD studies: The self and a community. In Fawns, T., Aitken, G., & Jones, D. (Eds.), *Online Postgraduate Education in a Postdigital World. Postdigital Science and Education*. Springer., DOI: 10.1007/978-3-030-77673-2_4

Lee, M., & van Vlack, S. (2018). Teachers' emotional labour, discrete emotions, and classroom management self-efficacy. *Educational Psychology*, 38(5), 669–686. DOI: 10.1080/01443410.2017.1399199

Lee, T.-Y., Chang, C.-W., & Chen, G.-D. (2007). Building an Interactive Caring Agent for Students in Computer-based Learning Environments. *Seventh IEEE International Conference on Advanced Learning Technologies (ICALT 2007)*, 300–304. IEEE. DOI: 10.1109/ICALT.2007.87

Lehman, B., Matthews, M., D'Mello, S., & Person, N. (2008). What are you feeling? Investigating student affective states during expert human tutoring sessions. In *Intelligent Tutoring Systems* (pp. 50–59). Springer Berlin Heidelberg. DOI: 10.1007/978-3-540-69132-7_10

Lehman, R. (2006). The role of emotion in creating instructor and learner presence in the distance education experience. *Journal of Cognitive Affective Learning*, 2(2), 12–26.

Leonard, A. M., & Woodland, R. H. (2023). Teacher PLCs and the advancement of SEL. In Liston, D. (Ed.), *Exploring social emotional learning in diverse academic settings* (pp. 251–270). IGI Global. DOI: 10.4018/978-1-6684-7227-9.ch013

Leony, D., Muñoz-Merino, P. J., Pardo, A., & Delgado Kloos, C. (2013). Provision of awareness of learners' emotions through visualizations in a computer interaction-based environment. *Expert Systems with Applications*, 40(13), 5093–5100. DOI: 10.1016/j.eswa.2013.03.030

Lerner, J., & Keltner, D. (2000). Beyond valence: Toward a model of emotion-specific influences on judgment and choice. *Cognition and Emotion*, 14(4), 473–503. DOI: 10.1080/026999300402763

Letteri, C. A. (1980). Cognitive Profile: Basic Determinant of Academic Achievement. *The Journal of Educational Research*, 73(4), 195–199. DOI: 10.1080/00220671.1980.10885234

Levy, D., Duffey, T., Yumiko, A., Cohen, S., Frye, A., & Weissman, G. (2019). The effect of mindfulness meditation training on medical student well-being, empathy, and suicidality. *Medical Science Educator*, 29(3), 905–911.

Lewis, C. (2002). *Lesson study: A handbook of teacher-led instructional change*. Research for Better Schools.

Lewis, N., & Bryan, V. (2021). Andragogy and teaching techniques to enhance adult learners' experience. *Journal of Nursing Education and Practice*, 11(11), 31–40. DOI: 10.5430/jnep.v11n11p31

Li, L., & Yao, D. (2023). Emotion Recognition in Complex Classroom Scenes Based on Improved Convolutional Block Attention Module Algorithm. *IEEE Access : Practical Innovations, Open Solutions*, 11, 143050–143059. DOI: 10.1109/ACCESS.2023.3340510

Lin, L., Parker, K., & Horowitz, M. (2024, April 4). *What's it like to be a teacher in America today?* Pew Research Center. https://www.pewresearch.org/social-trends/2024/04/04/whats-it-like-to-be-a-teacher-in-america-today/

Lindgren, R., & Johnson-Glenberg, M. (2013). Emboldened by embodiment: Six precepts for research on embodied learning and mixed reality. *Educational Researcher*, 42(8), 445–452. DOI: 10.3102/0013189X13511661

Lin, S., & Muenks, K. (2022). Perfectionism profiles among college students: A person-centered approach to motivation, behavior, and emotion. *Contemporary Educational Psychology*, 71, 102110. Advance online publication. DOI: 10.1016/j.cedpsych.2022.102110

Lin, T. J., Liang, J. C., Tsai, C. C., & Chang, H. W. (2012). Science learning outcomes in alignment with learning environment preferences. *Journal of Science Education and Technology*, 21(6), 643–650.

Litman, J. (2005). Curiosity and the pleasures of learning: Wanting and liking new information. *Cognition and Emotion*, 19(6), 793–814. DOI: 10.1080/02699930541000101

Liu, B., Xing, W., Zeng, Y., & Wu, Y. (2021). Quantifying the influence of achievement emotions for student learning in MOOCs. *Journal of Educational Computing Research*, 59(3), 429–452. DOI: 10.1177/0735633120967318

Liu, Z., Zhang, W., Sun, J., Cheng, H. N. H., Peng, X., & Liu, S. (2016). Emotion and Associated Topic Detection for Course Comments in a MOOC Platform. *2016 International Conference on Educational Innovation through Technology (EITT)*, 15–19. IEEE. DOI: 10.1109/EITT.2016.11

Livingstone, D. W. (2001). Adults' informal learning: Definitions, findings, gaps and future research. *NALL Working Paper No. 21*. Retrieved from https://nall.oise.utoronto.ca/res/21adultsifnormal.htm

Loehr, J. E. (1983). The ideal performance state. *Science Periodical on Research and Technology in Sport*, 1, 1–7.

Loeng, S. "Self-Directed Learning: A Core Concept in Adult Education", Education Research International, vol. 2020, Article ID 3816132, 12 pages, 2020. https://doi.org/DOI: 10.1155/2020/3816132

Loewenstein, G. (1994). The psychology of curiosity: A review and reinterpretation. *Psychological Bulletin*, 116(1), 75–98. DOI: 10.1037/0033-2909.116.1.75

Lomer, S., & Palmer, E. (2023). 'I didn't know this was actually stuff that could help us, with actually learning': Student perceptions of Active Blended Learning. *Teaching in Higher Education*, 28(4), 679–698. DOI: 10.1080/13562517.2020.1852202

Lopes, P. N., Brackett, M. A., Nezlek, J. B., Schütz, A., Sellin, I., & Salovey, P. (2004). Emotional intelligence and social interaction. *Personality and Social Psychology Bulletin*, 30(8), 1018–1034. DOI: 10.1177/0146167204264762 PMID: 15257786

Lopes, P. N., Salovey, P., & Straus, R. (2003). Emotional intelligence, personality, and the perceived quality of social relationships. *Personality and Individual Differences*, 35(3), 641–658. DOI: 10.1016/S0191-8869(02)00242-8

Lorenz, E. (1963). The predictability of hydrodynamic flow. Transactions of the N.Y 387 Academy of Science, 25, 409 – 432.

Lorenz, E. (1994). *The essence of chaos*. University of Washington Press.

Lorenz, E. N. (1972). Predictability: does the flap of a butterfly's wings in Brazil set off a tornado in Texas? *139th Annual Meeting of the American Association for the Advancement of Science*.

Lowenthal, P. R., Horan, A., DeArmond, M. C., Lomellini, A., Egan, D., Johnson, M., Moeller, K. N., Keldgord, F., Kuohn, J., Jensen, S., Stamm, A., & Pounds, D. (2023). Classroom Community and Online Learning: A Synthesis of Alfred Rovai's Research. *TechTrends*, 67(6), 931–944. DOI: 10.1007/s11528-023-00904-3

Lucardie, D. (2014). The impact of fun and enjoyment on adult's learning. *Procedia: Social and Behavioral Sciences*, 142, 439–446. DOI: 10.1016/j.sbspro.2014.07.696

Lucido, F. (2022). Mindfulness and growth mindset in the bilingual/ESL classroom. *Journal of Education and Social Development*, 6(1), 1–6.

Luo, Z., & Luo, W. (2022). Discrete achievement emotions as mediators between achievement goals and academic engagement of Singapore students. *Educational Psychology*, 44(6), 749–766. DOI: 10.1080/01443410.2022.2048795

Lupton, D. (1998). *The emotional self: A socio-cultural exploration*. Sage. DOI: 10.4135/9781446217719

Lu, Y., Hong, X., & Xiao, L. (2022). Toward high-quality adult online learning: A systematic review of empirical studies. *Sustainability (Basel)*, 14(4), 2257. DOI: 10.3390/su14042257

Lyn, A. E., Broderick, M., & Spranger, E. (2023). Student well-being and empowerment: SEL in online graduate education. In *Exploring Social Emotional Learning in Diverse Academic Settings* (pp. 312–336). IGI Global. DOI: 10.4018/978-1-6684-7227-9.ch016

Lytras, M. D., Aljohani, N. R., Visvizi, A., Ordonez De Pablos, P., & Gasevic, D. (2018). Advanced decision-making in higher education: Learning analytics research and key performance indicators. *Behaviour & Information Technology*, 37(10–11), 937–940. DOI: 10.1080/0144929X.2018.1512940

Maddox, T., Sparks, C. Y., Oldstone, L., Chibbaro, M., Sackman, J., Judge, E., Maddox, R., Bonakdar, R., & Darnall, B. D. (2024). Perspective: The promise of virtual reality as an immersive therapeutic. *Journal of Medical Extended Reality*, 1(1), 27–34. DOI: 10.1089/jmxr.2023.0003

Maguire, M., & Delahunt, B. (2017). Doing a thematic analysis: A practical, step-by-step guide for learning and teaching scholars. *All Ireland Journal of Higher Education*, 9(3), 3351–33514.

Mainhard, T., Oudman, S., Hornstra, L., Bosker, R. J., & Goetz, T. (2018). Student emotions in class: The relative importance of teachers and their interpersonal relations with students. *Learning and Instruction*, 53, 109–119. DOI: 10.1016/j.learninstruc.2017.07.011

Majeski, R. A., Stover, M., & Valais, T. (2018). The community of inquiry and emotional presence. *Adult Learning*, 29(2), 53–61. DOI: 10.1177/1045159518758696

Majeski, R. A., Stover, M., Valais, T., & Ronch, J. (2017). Fostering emotional intelligence in online higher education courses. *Adult Learning*, 28(4), 135–143. DOI: 10.1177/1045159517726873

Majid, A., & Mohammad, R. (2021). The impact of music on sports activities: A scoping review. *Journal of New Studies in Sport Management*, 2(4), 274–285.

Malik, A. (2023). An investigation on turnover intention antecedents amongst the academician in universities. *Problems and Perspectives in Management*, 21(1), 373–383. DOI: 10.21511/ppm.21(1).2023.32

Mallarangan, A. D. D., Rahman, A., Nur, S., Lathifah, Z. K., & Lubis, F. M. (2024). Analysis Of The Influence Of Continuous Training Development And Education On Professional Competence Of Teachers In Public Schools. *Journal of Education*, 6(2), 13449–13456.

Mamat, N. H., & Ismail, N. A. H. (2021). Integration of emotional intelligence in teaching practice among university teachers in higher education. *Malaysian Journal of Learning and Instruction*, 18(2), 69–102.

Mandalaki, E., & Pérezts, M. (2023). Abjection overruled! Time to dismantle sexist cyberbullying in academia. *Organization*, 30(1), 168–180. DOI: 10.1177/13505084211041711

Mandermach, B. J., Gonzales, R. M., & Garrett, A. L. (2006). An examination of online instructor presence via threaded discussion participation. *Journal of Online Learning and Teaching*, 2, 248–260.

Mansfield, C., Beltman, S., Broadley, T., & Weatherby-Fell, N. (2016). Building resilience in teacher education: An evidence informed framework. *Teaching and Teacher Education*, 54, 77–87. Advance online publication. DOI: 10.1016/j.tate.2015.11.016

Marchand, G. C., & Gutierrez, A. P. (2012). The role of emotion in the learning process: Comparisons between online and face-to-face learning settings. *The Internet and Higher Education*, 15(3), 150–160. DOI: 10.1016/j.iheduc.2011.10.001

Marginson, S., & Rhoades, G. (2002). Beyond national states, markets, and systems of higher education: A glonacal agency heuristic. *Higher Education*, 43(3), 281–309. DOI: 10.1023/A:1014699605875

Markowitz, N. L., & Bouffard, S. M. (2020). *Teaching with a social, emotional, and cultural lens: A framework for educators and teacher educators*. Harvard Education Press.

Markowitz, N., Thowdis, W., & Gallagher, M. (2018). Sowing seeds of SEL: University-district partnership builds social and emotional learning across the teacher pipeline. *The Learning Professional*, 39(4), 30–34.

Martin, A. J., & Rubin, R. S. (1995). A new model of career success: A longitudinal study of U.S. Army officers. *Personnel Psychology*, 48(2), 397–421.

Martínez-Alba, G., Pentón Herrera, L. J., & Trinh, E. (2023). Situating teacher well-being in English language teaching. In Pentón Herrera, L. J., Martínez-Alba, G., & Trinh, E. (Eds.), *Teacher well-being in English language teaching: An ecological pathway* (pp. 29–42). Routledge.

Martin, F., Kumar, S., Ritzhaupt, A. D., & Polly, D. (2023). Bichronous online learning: Award-winning online instructor practices of blending asynchronous and synchronous online modalities. *The Internet and Higher Education*, 56, 100879. DOI: 10.1016/j.iheduc.2022.100879

Marzouk, Z., Rakovic, M., Liaqat, A., Vytasek, J., Samadi, D., Stewart-Alonso, J., Ram, I., Woloshen, S., Winne, P. H., & Nesbit, J. C. (2016). What if learning analytics were based on learning science? *Australasian Journal of Educational Technology*, 32(6). Advance online publication. DOI: 10.14742/ajet.3058

MasterClass. (2021, September 3). *Writing 101: What is the Hero's Journey? 2 Hero's Journey Examples in Film*. Masterclass. https://www.masterclass.com/articles/writing-101-what-is-the-heros-journey

Mayer, J. D., Salovey, P., & Caruso, D. R. (2008). Emotional intelligence: New ability or eclectic traits? *The American Psychologist*, 63(6), 503–517. DOI: 10.1037/0003-066X.63.6.503 PMID: 18793038

Mayer, J. D., Salovey, P., Caruso, D. R., & Sitarenios, G. (2001). Emotional intelligence as a standard intelligence. *Emotion (Washington, D.C.)*, 1(3), 232–242. DOI: 10.1037/1528-3542.1.3.232 PMID: 12934682

Mayer, R. E. (2020). Searching for the role of emotions in e-learning. *Learning and Instruction*, 7, 1–3. DOI: 10.1016/j.learninstruc.2019.05.010

McCarthy, D. (2021). Adding social-emotional awareness to teacher education field experiences. *Teacher Educator*, 56(3), 287–304. DOI: 10.1080/08878730.2021.1890291

McClelland, D. C. (1973). Testing for competence rather than for" intelligence. *The American Psychologist*, 28(1), 1–14. DOI: 10.1037/h0034092 PMID: 4684069

McCombs, B. L. (1997). Self-assessment and reflection: Tools for promoting teacher changes toward learner-centered practices. *NASSP Bulletin*, 81(587), 1–14. DOI: 10.1177/019263659708158702

McGarry, A. (2015). Sample evaluation of caseload complexity in a community health-care NHS trust. *British Journal of Community Nursing*, 20(4), 174–180. DOI: 10.12968/bjcn.2015.20.4.174 PMID: 25839875

McGowan, H. E., & Shipley, C. (2020). *The adaptation advantage: Let go, learn fast, and thrive in the future of work*. John Wiley & Sons.

McLean, S., & Attardi, S. M. (2023). Sage or guide? Student perceptions of the role of the instructor in a flipped classroom. *Active Learning in Higher Education*, 24(1), 49–61. DOI: 10.1177/1469787418793725

Mega, C., Ronconi, L., & De Beni, R. (2014). What makes a good student? How emotions, self-regulated learning, and motivation contribute to academic achievement. *Journal of Educational Psychology*, 106(1), 121–131. DOI: 10.1037/a0033546

Megawati, F., Iswahyuni, I., & Mukminatien, N. (2022). Social and emotional learning (SEL): How does it develop and contribute to pre-service English teachers' identity? *Pegem Journal of Education and Instruction*, 13(1), 75–83.

Melani, B. Z., Roberts, S., & Taylor, J. (2020). Social emotional learning practices in learning English as a second language. *Journal of English Learner Education*, 10(1), 3.

Menz, H. B. (2016). Chronic foot pain in older people. *Maturitas*, 91, 110–114. DOI: 10.1016/j.maturitas.2016.06.011 PMID: 27451329

Merriam, S. B. (2001). Andragogy and self-directed learning: Pillars of adult learning theory. *New Directions for Adult and Continuing Education*, 2001(89), 3–14. DOI: 10.1002/ace.3

Merriam, S. B., & Caffarella, R. S. (1999). *Learning in Adulthood* (2nd ed.). Jossey-Bass.

Merriam, S. B., Cafferella, R. C., & Baumgartner, L. M. (2007). *Learning in adulthood* (3rd ed.). Jossey-Bass.

Merrimack College: EdWeek Research Center (2023). *2nd annual Merrimack College teacher survey: Is teacher morale on the rise?* https://www.merrimack.edu/academics/education-and-social-policy/about/merrimack-college-teacher-survey/

Mesagno, C., Marchant, D., & Morris, T. (2009). Alleviating choking: The sounds of distraction. *Journal of Applied Sport Psychology*, 21(2), 131–147. DOI: 10.1080/10413200902795091

Mesaros, H. (2008). *Bravo Fortissimo Glenn Gould: The Mind of a Canadian Virtuoso*. American Literary Press.

Mezirow, J. (1991). Transformative dimensions of adult learning. Jossey-Bass, 350 Sansome Street, San Francisco, CA 94104-1310.

Mezirow, J. (1993). A transformation theory of adult learning. In *Adult Education Research Annual Conference Proceedings* (Vol. 31, pp. 141-146).

Mezirow, J. (1997). Transformative learning. *New Directions for Adult and Continuing Education*, 74(74), 5–12. DOI: 10.1002/ace.7401

Mezirow, J. (2000). Learning to think like an adult: Core concepts of transformation theory. In Mezirow, J. (Eds.), *Learning as transformation: Critical perspectives on a theory in progress* (pp. 3–34). Jossey Bass.

Mezirow, J. (2003). Transformative learning as discourse. *Journal of Transformative Education*, 1(1), 58–63. DOI: 10.1177/1541344603252172

Mhaka-Mutepfa, M., & Rampa, S. (2024). Workplace bullying and mobbing: Autoethnography and meaning-making in the face of adversity in academia. *International Journal of Qualitative Studies in Education : QSE*, 37(1), 1–18. DOI: 10.1080/09518398.2021.1991028

Miles, M. B., & Huberman, A. M. (1994). *Qualitative data analysis: An expanded sourcebook*. Sage.

Milk, C. (2015, March). How virtual reality can create the ultimate empathy machine [Video]. TED Conferences. https://www.ted.com/talks/chris_milk_how_virtual_reality_can_create_the_ultimate_empathy_machine/transcript?language=en

Minkley, N., Schröder, T. P., Wolf, O. T., & Kirchner, W. H. (2014). The socially evaluated cold-pressor test (SECPT) for groups: Effects of repeated administration of a combined physiological and psychological stressor. *Psychoneuroendocrinology*, 45, 119–127. DOI: 10.1016/j.psyneuen.2014.03.022 PMID: 24845183

Mohammad, S. (2019). Investigation of EFL student teachers' emotional responses to affective situations during practicum. *European Journal of Educational Research*, 8(4), 1201–1215. DOI: 10.12973/eu-jer.8.4.1201

Moon, J. A. (1999). *Reflection in learning and professional development: Theory and practice*. Routledge.

Moon, J. A. (2004). *A handbook of reflective and experiential learning: Theory and practice*. Routledge.

Moore, G. F., Audrey, S., Barker, M., Bond, L., Bonell, C., Hardeman, W., & Baird, J. (2015). Process evaluation of complex interventions: Medical Research Council guidance. *BMJ (Clinical Research Ed.)*, 350(mar19 6), h1258. DOI: 10.1136/bmj.h1258 PMID: 25791983

Moore, M. (1989). Three types of interaction. *American Journal of Distance Education*, 3(2), 1–7. DOI: 10.1080/08923648909526659

Moore, R. L. (2020). Developing lifelong learning with heutagogy: Contexts, critiques, and challenges. *Distance Education*, 41(3), 381–401. DOI: 10.1080/01587919.2020.1766949

Moos, R. H. (1987). Person-environment congruence in work, school, and health care settings. *Journal of Vocational Behavior*, 31(3), 231–247. DOI: 10.1016/0001-8791(87)90041-8

Moreno-Marcos, P. M., Alario-Hoyos, C., Munoz-Merino, P. J., Estevez-Ayres, I., & Kloos, C. D. (2018). Sentiment analysis in MOOCs: A case study. *2018 IEEE Global Engineering Education Conference (EDUCON)*, 1489–1496. IEEE. DOI: 10.1109/EDUCON.2018.8363409

Mortiboys, A. (2013). *Teaching with emotional intelligence: A step-by-step guide for higher and further education professionals*. Routledge. DOI: 10.4324/9780203806463

Müller, C., Mildenberger, T., & Steingruber, D. (2023). Learning effectiveness of a flexible learning study programme in a blended learning design: Why are some courses more effective than others? *International Journal of Educational Technology in Higher Education*, 20(1), 10. DOI: 10.1186/s41239-022-00379-x PMID: 36811132

Muller, K. E. (2008). Self-directed learning and emotional intelligence: Interrelationships between the two constructs, change, and problem solving. *International Journal of Self-Directed Learning*, 5(2), 11–22.

Munezero, M., Montero, C. S., Mozgovoy, M., & Sutinen, E. (2013). Exploiting sentiment analysis to track emotions in students' learning diaries. *Proceedings of the 13th Koli Calling International Conference on Computing Education Research*, 145–152. New York, NY, USA: ACM. DOI: 10.1145/2526968.2526984

Murano, D., Way, J. D., Martin, J. E., Walton, K. E., Anguiano-Carrasco, C., & Burrus, J. (2019). The need for high-quality pre-service and inservice teacher training in social and emotional learning. *Journal of Research in Innovative Teaching & Learning*, 12(2), 111–113. DOI: 10.1108/JRIT-02-2019-0028

Murphy, E., & Rodriguez, A. M. (2012). Rapport in distance education. *International Review of Research in Open and Distance Learning*, 13(1), 167–190. DOI: 10.19173/irrodl.v13i1.1057

Murty, V. P., LaBar, K. S., & Adcock, R. A. (2016). Threat of punishment motivates memory encoding via amygdala, not midbrain, interactions with the medial temporal lobe. *The Journal of Neuroscience : The Official Journal of the Society for Neuroscience*, 36(26), 6969–6976. PMID: 22745496

Mu, S., Cui, M., & Huang, X. (2020). Multimodal Data Fusion in Learning Analytics: A Systematic Review. *Sensors (Basel)*, 20(23), 6856. DOI: 10.3390/s20236856 PMID: 33266131

Mustika, R., Yo, E.C., Faruqi, M., & Zhuhra, R.T. (2021). Evaluating the Relationship Between Online Learning Environment and Medical Students' Wellbeing During COVID-19 Pandemic.

Nafukho, F. M., Irby, B. J., Pashmforoosh, R., Lara-Alecio, R., Tong, F., Lockhart, M. E., El Mansour, W., Tang, S., Etchells, M., & Wang, Z. (2023). Training design in mediating the relationship of participants' motivation, work environment, and transfer of learning. *European Journal of Training and Development*, 47(10), 112–132. DOI: 10.1108/EJTD-06-2022-0070

Nall, M. (2020). Supporting social and emotional learning in the EFL/ESL classroom: How the new science of child development can inform second language acquisition theory and practice. *Journal of English Learner Education*, 10(1), 1–11.

Namoun, A., & Alshanqiti, A. (2020). Predicting Student Performance Using Data Mining and Learning Analytics Techniques: A Systematic Literature Review. *Applied Sciences (Basel, Switzerland)*, 11(1), 237. DOI: 10.3390/app11010237

Nancarrow, S., & Borthwick, A. (2016). Interprofessional working for the health professions. *The Routledge companion to the professions and professionalism*, 343.

Nanquil, L. M. (2021). Promoting social and emotional well-being of ESL students through engaging and inclusive environment. *Linguistic Forum-A Journal of Linguistics*, 3(2), 15–19.

Naragon-Gainey, K., McMahon, T. P., & Chacko, T. P. (2017). The structure of common emotion regulation strategies: A meta-analytic examination. *Psychological Bulletin*, 143(4), 384–427. DOI: 10.1037/bul0000093 PMID: 28301202

Nashine, M. A., Becker, B. W., & Ranalli, L. A.. (2019). Impact of a Longitudinal Empathy Curriculum on Medical Students' Attitudes Towards Physician-Patient Communication. *Journal of General Internal Medicine*, 34, 2595. DOI: 10.1007/s11606-019-05395-6

National Aeronautics and Space Administration. (2024). *Aviation Safety Reporting System (ASRS)*. NASA. https://asrs.arc.nasa.gov/

National Board for Professional Teaching Standards. (n.d.). *National board certification overview*. https://www.nbpts.org/certification/overview/

Neelen, M., & Kirschner, P. A. (2020). *Evidence-informed learning design: Creating training to improve performance*. Kogan Page Publishers.

Nenonene, R. L., Gallagher, C. E., Kelly, M. K., & Collopy, R. M. B. (2019). Challenges and opportunities of infusing social, emotional, and cultural competencies into teacher preparation: One program's story. *Teacher Education Quarterly*, 46(4), 92–115.

Newsum, J., Thomas, M., Crawford, C. M., & Moffett, N. (2023). The invisible incivility archetype that is imploding higher education from within: The Queen Bee Syndrome's canary in the coal mine. In K. L. Clarke & N. L. Moffett's (Eds.) *Addressing the Queen Bee Syndrome in Academia,* p. 68-94. IGI Global. DOI: DOI: 10.4018/978-1-6684-7717-5.ch004

Nguyen, H. (2023). TikTok as Learning Analytics Data: Framing Climate Change and Data Practices. *LAK23: 13th International Learning Analytics and Knowledge Conference*, 33–43. New York, NY, USA: ACM. DOI: 10.1145/3576050.3576055

Nideffer, R. M. (2002). *Getting into the optimal performance state*. Enhanced Performance Systems.

Nkomo, L. M., Daniel, B. K., & Butson, R. J. (2021). Synthesis of student engagement with digital technologies: A systematic review of the literature. *International Journal of Educational Technology in Higher Education*, 18, 1–26. PMID: 34778529

Noddings, N. (2005). *The challenge to care in schools: An alternative approach to education*. Teachers College Press.

Noddings, N. (2013). *Caring: A relational approach to ethics and moral education*. University of California Press.

Noroozi, O., Alikhani, I., Järvelä, S., Kirschner, P. A., Juuso, I., & Seppänen, T. (2019). Multimodal data to design visual learning analytics for understanding regulation of learning. *Computers in Human Behavior*, 100, 298–304. DOI: 10.1016/j.chb.2018.12.019

North, A. C., & Hargreaves, D. J. (2008). Music and taste. In North, A. C., & Hargreaves, D. J. (Eds.), *The social and applied psychology of music* (pp. 75–142). Oxford University Press. DOI: 10.1093/acprof:oso/9780198567424.003.0003

North, M. S., & Fiske, S. T. (2015). Modern attitudes toward older adults in the ageing world: A cross-cultural meta-analysis. *Psychological Bulletin*, 141(5), 993–1021. DOI: 10.1037/a0039469 PMID: 26191955

Notar, C. E., Riley, G. W., Taylor, P. W., Thornberg, R. A., & Cargille, R. L. (2009). Dispositions: Ability and assessment. *International Journal of Education*, 1(1). Advance online publication. DOI: 10.5296/ije.v1i1.133

Nugent, A., Lodge, J. M., Carroll, A., Bagraith, R., MacMahon, S., Matthews, K. E., & Sah, P. (2019). *Higher Education Learning Framework: An evidence-informed model for university learning*. The University of Queensland.

Nunn, S., Avella, J. T., Kanai, T., & Kebritchi, M. (2016). Learning Analytics Methods, Benefits, and Challenges in Higher Education: A Systematic Literature Review. *Online Learning : the Official Journal of the Online Learning Consortium*, 20(2). Advance online publication. DOI: 10.24059/olj.v20i2.790

O'Neill, S. A. (2014). Complicated conversation: Creating opportunities for T\transformative practice in higher education music performance research and pedagogy. In Harrison, S. (Ed.), *Research and Research Education in Music Performance and Pedagogy. Landscapes: the Arts, Aesthetics, and Education* (Vol. 11). Springer., DOI: 10.1007/978-94-007-7435-3_12

O'Regan, K. (2003). Emotion and e-learning. *JALN*, 7(3), 78–92.

Oaster, B. D., Peck, G. D., Scott, R. A., & Feith, G. A. (2022). The E-Factor—The importance of self-efficacy and adaptive skills surrounding startle & surprise events in the cockpits of modern jet airliners. Unpublished manuscript, London, United Kingdom.

Oatley, K. (2016). Fiction: Simulation of social worlds. *Trends in Cognitive Sciences*, 20(8), 618–628. DOI: 10.1016/j.tics.2016.06.002 PMID: 27449184

Oberg, G., Carroll, A., & Macmahon, S. (2023). Compassion fatigue and secondary traumatic stress in teachers: How they contribute to burnout and how they are related to trauma-awareness. *Frontiers in Education*, 8, 1128618. Advance online publication. DOI: 10.3389/feduc.2023.1128618

Öhman, A., & Soares, J. J. F. (1994). "Unconscious anxiety": Phobic responses to masked stimuli. *Journal of Abnormal Psychology*, 103(2), 231–240. DOI: 10.1037/0021-843X.103.2.231 PMID: 8040492

Olson, R. E., McKenzie, J., Mills, K. A., Patulny, R., Bellocchi, A., & Caristo, F. (2019). Gendered emotion management and teacher outcomes in secondary school teaching: A review. *Teaching and Teacher Education*, 80, 128–144. DOI: 10.1016/j.tate.2019.01.010

Onwuegbuzie, A. J. (2004). Academic procrastination and statistics anxiety. *Assessment & Evaluation in Higher Education*, 29(1), 3–19. DOI: 10.1080/0260293042000160384

Opengart, R. (2005). Emotional intelligence and emotion work: Examining constructs from an interdisciplinary framework. *Human Resource Development Review*, 4(1), 49–62. DOI: 10.1177/1534484304273817

Oplatka, I. (2007). Managing emotions in teaching: Toward an understanding of emotion displays and caring as nonprescribed role elements. *Teachers College Record (1970)*, 109(6), 1374–1400. DOI: 10.1177/016146810710900603

Ordóñez de Pablos, P., Lytras, M. D., Zhang, X., & Chui, K. T. (2019). *Opening Up Education for Inclusivity Across Digital Economies and Societies (Patricia Ordóñez de Pablos* (Lytras, M. D., Zhang, X., & Chui, K. T., Eds.). IGI Global., DOI: 10.4018/978-1-5225-7473-6

Ormiston, H. E., Nygaard, M. A., & Apgar, S. (2022). A systematic review of secondary traumatic stress and compassion fatigue in teachers. *School Mental Health*, 14(4), 802–817. Advance online publication. DOI: 10.1007/s12310-022-09525-2 PMID: 35694002

Osika, A., MacMahon, S., Lodge, J. M., & Carroll, A. (2022, March 18). Emotions and learning: What role do emotions play in how and why students learn. *Times Higher Education*. https://www.timeshighereducation.com/campus/emotions-and-learning-what-role-do-emotions-play-how-and-why-students-learn

Paas, F., Tuovinen, J. E., Van Merrienboer, J. J., & Aubteen Darabi, A. (2005). A motivational perspective on the relation between mental effort and performance: Optimizing learner involvement in instruction. *Educational Technology Research and Development*, 53(3), 25–34. DOI: 10.1007/BF02504795

Pacansky-Brock, M., Smedshammer, M., & Vincent-Layton, K. (2020). Humanizing online teaching to equitize higher education. *Current Issues in Education (Tempe, Ariz.)*, 21(2), 1–21. https://brocansky.com/wpcontent/uploads/2020/02/HumanizingOnlineTeachingToEquitizePrePrint.pdf

Pajares, F. (1996). Self-efficacy beliefs in academic settings. *Review of Educational Research*, 66(4), 543–578. DOI: 10.3102/00346543066004543

Palloff, R. M., & Pratt, K. (2007). *Building online learning communities: Effective strategies for the virtual classroom.* John Wiley Sons.

Pan, X., Hu, B., Zhou, Z., & Feng, X. (2022). Are students happier the more they learn? Research on the influence of course progress on academic emotion in online learning. *Interactive Learning Environments*, •••, 1–21. DOI: 10.1080/10494820.2022.2052110

Paolini, A. C. (2020). Social Emotional Learning: Key to Career Readiness. *Anatolian Journal of Education*, 5(1), 125–134. DOI: 10.29333/aje.2020.5112a

Park, H., & Lee, J. (2017). The influence of media, positive perception, and identification on survey-based measures of corruption. *Business Ethics (Oxford, England)*, 26(3), 312–320. DOI: 10.1111/beer.12143

Park, S., & Yun, H. (2017). Relationships between motivational strategies and cognitive learning in distance education courses. *Distance Education*, 38(3), 302–320. DOI: 10.1080/01587919.2017.1369007

Parsons, T., Bales, R. F., & Family, S. (1955). *Interaction Process*.

Parveen, H., & Bano, M. (2019). Relationship between teachers' stress and job satisfaction: Moderating role of teachers' emotions. *Pakistan Journal of Psychological Research*, 34(2), 353–366. DOI: 10.33824/PJPR.2019.34.2.19

Patiño, A., Ramírez-Montoya, M. S., & Buenestado-Fernández, M. (2023). Active learning and education 4.0 for complex thinking training: Analysis of two case studies in open education. *Smart Learning Environments*, 10(1), 8. DOI: 10.1186/s40561-023-00229-x

Paudel, P. (2021). Online education: Benefits, challenges and strategies during and after COVID-19 in higher education. *International Journal on Studies in Education*, 3(2), 70–85. DOI: 10.46328/ijonse.32

Peacock, S., & Cowan, J. (2019). Promoting sense of belonging in online learning communities of inquiry at accredited courses. *Online Learning: the Official Journal of the Online Learning Consortium*, 23(2), 67–81. DOI: 10.24059/olj.v23i2.1488

Pekrun, R. (2014). *Emotions and learning* (Vol. 24). International Academy of Education (IAE). http://staging.iaoed.org/downloads/edu-practices_24_eng.pdf

Pekrun, R. (2006). The control-value theory of achievement emotions: Assumptions, corollaries, and implications for educational research and practice. *Educational Psychology Review*, 18(4), 315–341. DOI: 10.1007/s10648-006-9029-9

Pekrun, R., Goetz, T., Frenzel, A. C., Barchfeld, P., & Perry, R. P. (2011). Measuring emotions in students' learning and performance: The Achievement Emotions Questionnaire (AEQ). *Contemporary Educational Psychology*, 36(1), 36–48. DOI: 10.1016/j.cedpsych.2010.10.002

Pekrun, R., Goetz, T., Titz, W., & Perry, R. P. (2002). Academic emotions in students' self-regulated learning and achievement: A program of qualitative and quantitative research. *Educational Psychologist*, 37(2), 91–105. DOI: 10.1207/S15326985EP3702_4

Pekrun, R., & Linnenbrink-Garcia, L. (Eds.). (2014). *International handbook of emotions in education*. Routledge. DOI: 10.4324/9780203148211

Pekrun, R., & Stephens, E. J. (2010). Achievement emotions: A control-value approach. *Social and Personality Psychology Compass*, 4(4), 238–255. DOI: 10.1111/j.1751-9004.2010.00259.x

Pekrun, R., & Stephens, E. J. (2012). Academic emotions. In Harris, K. R., Graham, S., Urdan, T., Graham, S., Royer, J. M., & Zeidner, M. (Eds.), APA educational psychology handbook: Vol. 2. *Individual differences and cultural and contextual factors* (pp. 3–31). American Psychological Association.

Pentón Herrera, L. J. (2020). Social-emotional learning in TESOL: What, why, and how. *Journal of English Learner Education*, 10(1), 1.

Pereira, H. A., De Souza, A. F., & De Menezes, C. S. (2016). A Computational Architecture for Learning Analytics in Game-Based Learning. *2016 IEEE 16th International Conference on Advanced Learning Technologies (ICALT)*, 191–193. IEEE. DOI: 10.1109/ICALT.2016.3

Pereira, H. A., De Souza, A. F., & De Menezes, C. S. (2018). Obtaining evidence of learning in digital games through a deep learning neural network to classify facial expressions of the players. *2018 IEEE Frontiers in Education Conference (FIE)*, 1–8. IEEE. DOI: 10.1109/FIE.2018.8659216

Perry, B., & Edwards, M. (2005). Exemplary online educators: Creating a community of inquiry. *Turkish Online Journal of Distance Education*, 6(2), 46–54.

Pham, P., & Wang, J. (2018). Predicting Learners' Emotions in Mobile MOOC Learning via a Multimodal Intelligent Tutor. In *Lecture Notes in Computer Science (including subseries Lecture Notes in Artificial Intelligence and Lecture Notes in Bioinformatics)* (pp. 150–159). DOI: 10.1007/978-3-319-91464-0_15

Phillips, R., & Waugh, F. (2018). Emancipatory social work with older people: challenging students to overcome the limitations of ageism and institutional oppression. *Social Work and Policy Studies: Social Justice, Practice and Theory, 1*(001).

Pinar, W. (2012). *What is curriculum theory?* (2nd ed.). Routledge.

Pinar, W. F. (1994). *The method of Currere (1975). Autobiography, Politics and Sexuality: Essays in Curriculum Theory 1972-1992*. Peter Lang., https://www.currereexchange.com/uploads/9/5/8/7/9587563/pinar_the_currere_method.pdf

Piniel, K., & Albert, Á. (2018). Advanced learners' foreign language-related emotions across the four skills. *Studies in Second Language Learning and Teaching*, 8(1), 127–147. DOI: 10.14746/ssllt.2018.8.1.6

Pintrich, P. R. (2003). A motivational science perspective on the role of student motivation in learning and teaching contexts. *Journal of Educational Psychology*, 95(4), 667–686. DOI: 10.1037/0022-0663.95.4.667

Pintrich, P. R., & De Groot, E. V. (1990). Motivational and self-regulated learning components of classroom academic performance. *Journal of Educational Psychology*, 82(1), 33–40. DOI: 10.1037/0022-0663.82.1.33

Plass, J. L., & Kaplan, U. (2016). Emotional design in digital media for learning. In *Emotions, technology, design, and learning* (pp. 131–161). Academic Press. DOI: 10.1016/B978-0-12-801856-9.00007-4

Plintz, N., & Ifenthaler, D. (2023). LEVERAGING EMOTIONS TO ENHANCE LEARNING SUCCESS IN ONLINE EDUCATION: A SYSTEMATIC REVIEW. *20th International Conference on Cognition and Exploratory Learning in Digital Age, CELDA 2023.*

Plutchik, R. (2001). The nature of emotions. *American Scientist*, 89(4), 344–350. DOI: 10.1511/2001.28.344

PMI (Project Management Institute). (2013). 5th ed.). Guide to the Project Management Body of Knowledge/PMBOK.

Postareff, L., & Lindblom-Ylänne, S. (2011). Emotions and confidence within teaching in higher education. *Studies in Higher Education*, 36(7), 799–813. DOI: 10.1080/03075079.2010.483279

Post, P. B., Grybush, A. L., Elmadani, A., & Lockhart, C. E. (2020). Fostering resilience in classrooms through child–teacher relationship training. *International Journal of Play Therapy*, 29(1), 9–19. DOI: 10.1037/pla0000107

Poulou, M. S., Reddy, L. A., & Dudek, C. M. (2019). Relation of teacher self-efficacy and classroom practices: A preliminary investigation. *School Psychology International*, 40(1), 25–48. DOI: 10.1177/0143034318798045

PraveenKumar., T., Manorselvi, A., & Soundarapandiyan, K. (2020). Exploring the students feelings and emotion towards online teaching: sentimental analysis approach. In Re-imagining Diffusion and Adoption of Information Technology and Systems: A Continuing Conversation: IFIP WG 8.6 International Conference on Transfer and Diffusion of IT, TDIT 2020, Tiruchirappalli, India, December 18–19, 2020, Proceedings, Part I (pp. 137-146). Springer International Publishing.

Putwain, D. W., Wood, P., & Pekrun, R. (2022). Achievement emotions and academic achievement: Reciprocal relations and the moderating influence of academic buoyancy. *Journal of Educational Psychology*, 114(1), 108–126. DOI: 10.1037/edu0000637

Quinlan, K. M. (2016). How emotion matters in four key relationships in teaching and learning in higher education. *College Teaching*, 64(3), 101–111. DOI: 10.1080/87567555.2015.1088818

Rabha, B., & Saikia, P. (2019). Emotional intelligence and academic performance of higher secondary school students: A study in Kamrup district, India. *The Clarion- International Multidisciplinary Journal*, 8(1), 34. DOI: 10.5958/2277-937X.2019.00005.4

Rager, K. B. (2009). I feel, therefore, I learn: The role of emotion in self-directed learning. *New Horizons in Adult Education and Human Resource Development*, 23(2), 22–33. DOI: 10.1002/nha3.10336

Rakow, K. E., Upsher, R. J., Foster, J. L., Byrom, N. C., & Dommett, E. J. (2023). "It Ain't What You Use, It's the Way That You Use It": How Virtual Learning Environments May Impact Student Mental Wellbeing. *Education Sciences*, 13(7), 749. DOI: 10.3390/educsci13070749

Ramana, T. V. (2013). Emotional intelligence and teacher effectiveness: An analysis. Voice of research, 2(2), 18-22.

Rania, N., Siri, A., Bagnasco, A., Aleo, G., & Sasso, L. (2014). Academic climate, well-being and academic performance in a university degree course. *Journal of Nursing Management*, 22(6), 751–760. DOI: 10.1111/j.1365-2834.2012.01471.x PMID: 23617787

Ranjeeth, S., Latchoumi, T. P., & Paul, P. V. (2020). A Survey on Predictive Models of Learning Analytics. *Procedia Computer Science*, 167, 37–46. DOI: 10.1016/j.procs.2020.03.180

RelievERx Inc. (2022). *RelievERx* [Virtual reality tool for pain management]. https://www.relieveRx.com

Rennie Center. (2015). Stanford research shows promoting a growth mindset improves student grades. Rennie Center. https://www.renniecenter.org/news/stanford-research-shows-promoting-growth-mindset-improves-student-grades

Revak, M. A. (2020, March 30). When the tide goes out: Identifying and supporting struggling students in online courses. *Faculty Focus*. https://www.facultyfocus.com/articles/online-education/identifyingand-

Reyes, M. R., Brackett, M. A., Rivers, S. E., White, M., & Salovey, P. (2012). Classroom emotional climate, student engagement, and academic achievement. *Journal of Educational Psychology*, 104(3), 700–712. DOI: 10.1037/a0027268

Richardson, J. C., & Lowenthal, P. (2017). *Instructor social presence: A neglected component of the community of inquiry framework* [Conference session]. The 13th International Scientific Conference eLearning and Software for Education. DOI: 10.12753/2066-026X-17-160

Riches, S., Iannelli, H., Reynolds, L., & Hamilton, L. (2022). Virtual reality-based training for mental health staff: A novel approach to increase empathy, compassion, and subjective understanding of service user experience. *Advances in Simulation (London, England)*, 7(1), 19. DOI: 10.1186/s41077-022-00217-0 PMID: 35854343

Rinchen, S., Ritchie, S. M., & Bellocchi, A. (2016). Emotional climate of a pre-service science teacher education class in Bhutan. *Cultural Studies of Science Education*, 11(3), 603–628. https://doi.org/10.1007/s11422-014-9658-0

Rincon-Flores, E. G., & Santos-Guevara, B. N. (2021). Gamification during Covid-19: Promoting active learning and motivation in higher education. *Australasian Journal of Educational Technology*, 37(5), 43–60. DOI: 10.14742/ajet.7157

Ritchie, J., & Spencer, L. (2002). Qualitative data analysis for applied policy research. *The qualitative researcher's companion, 573*, 305-329.

Ritter, F. E., & Schooler, L. J. (2001). The learning curve. International encyclopedia of the social and behavioral sciences, 13, 8602-8605.

Robin, B. R. (2008). Digital storytelling: A powerful technology tool for the 21st century classroom. *Theory into Practice*, 47(3), 220–228. DOI: 10.1080/00405840802153916

Rodríguez, A. O. R., Riaño, M. A., García, P. A. G., Marín, C. E. M., Crespo, R. G., & Wu, X. (2020). Emotional characterization of children through a learning environment using learning analytics and AR-Sandbox. *Journal of Ambient Intelligence and Humanized Computing*, 11(11), 5353–5367. DOI: 10.1007/s12652-020-01887-2

Rodriguez, R. J., & Koubek, E. (2019). Unpacking high-impact instructional practices and student engagement in a teacher preparation program. *International Journal for the Scholarship of Teaching and Learning*, 17(3). Advance online publication. DOI: 10.20429/ijsotl.2019.130311

Roeser, R. W., Skinner, E., Beers, J., & Jennings, P. A. (2012). Mindfulness training and teachers' professional development: An emerging area of research and practice. *Child Development Perspectives*, 6(2), 167–173. DOI: 10.1111/j.1750-8606.2012.00238.x

Romero, C., & Ventura, S. (2013). Data mining in education. *Wiley Interdisciplinary Reviews. Data Mining and Knowledge Discovery*, 3(1), 12–27. DOI: 10.1002/widm.1075

Rosanbalm, K. (2021). *Social and Emotional Learning during COVID-19 and Beyond: Why It Matters and How to Support It*. Hunt Institute.

Rosier, R. H. (Ed.), *(1994-1997). The competency model handbook* (Vol. 1-4). Linkage.

Rottweiler, A.-L., Stockinger, K., & Nett, U. E. (2022). *Students' Regulation of Anxiety and Hope – A Multilevel Latent Profile Analysis*. https://psyarxiv.com/mbrbj/download/?format=pdf DOI: 10.31234/osf.io/m6rbj

Rovai, A. (2002). Building Sense of Community at a Distance. *International Review of Research in Open and Distance Learning*, 3(1), 1–16. DOI: 10.19173/irrodl.v3i1.79

Rovai, A. (2007). Facilitating online discussions effectively. *The Internet and Higher Education*, 1(1), 77–88. DOI: 10.1016/j.iheduc.2006.10.001

Rovai, A., & Wighting, M. (2005). Feelings of alienation and community among higher education students in a virtual classroom. *The Internet and Higher Education*, 8(2), 97–110. DOI: 10.1016/j.iheduc.2005.03.001

Rowe, A. D., & Fitness, J. (2018). Understanding the role of negative emotions in adult learning and achievement: A social functional perspective. *Behavioral Sciences (Basel, Switzerland)*, 8(2), 27. DOI: 10.3390/bs8020027 PMID: 29461487

Roy, M. (2022). A study on emotional intelligence and job satisfaction level among male and female teachers of elementary level in Kolkata. Towards Excellence, 1138–1144. https://doi.org/DOI: 10.37867/te1404103

Rubin, H. (2009). *Collaborative leadership: Developing effective partnerships for communities and schools*. Corwin Press.

Ruiz, S., Charleer, S., Urretavizcaya, M., Klerkx, J., Fernández-Castro, I., & Duval, E. (2016). Supporting learning by considering emotions: Tracking and visualization a case study. *Proceedings of the Sixth International Conference on Learning Analytics & Knowledge - LAK '16*. DOI: 10.1145/2883851.2883888

Russell, J.-E., Smith, A., & Larsen, R. (2020). Elements of Success: Supporting at-risk student resilience through learning analytics. *Computers & Education*, 152, 103890. DOI: 10.1016/j.compedu.2020.103890

Rus, V., D'Mello, S., Hu, X., & Graesser, A. C. (2013). Recent Advances in Conversational Intelligent Tutoring Systems. *AI Magazine*, 34(3), 42–54. DOI: 10.1609/aimag.v34i3.2485

Ruus, V. R., Veisson, M., Leino, M., Ots, L., Pallas, L., Sarv, E. S., & Veisson, A. (2007). STUDENTS WELL-BEING, COPING, ACADEMIC SUCCESS, AND SCHOOL CLIMATE. *Social Behavior and Personality*, 35(7), 919–936. DOI: 10.2224/sbp.2007.35.7.919

Ryan, R. M., & Deci, E. L. (2000). Intrinsic and extrinsic motivations: Classic definitions and new directions. *Contemporary Educational Psychology*, 25(1), 54–67. DOI: 10.1006/ceps.1999.1020 PMID: 10620381

Ryan, R. M., & Deci, E. L. (2000). Self-determination theory and the facilitation of intrinsic motivation, social development, and well-being. *The American Psychologist*, 55(1), 68–78. DOI: 10.1037/0003-066X.55.1.68 PMID: 11392867

Sakiz, G. (2012). Perceived instructor affective support in relation to academic emotions and motivation in college. *Educational Psychology*, 32(1), 63–79. DOI: 10.1080/01443410.2011.625611

Saldaña, J. (2015). The coding manual for qualitative researchers. *Sage (Atlanta, Ga.)*.

Salendab, F. (2023). Proposed instructional scheme in the new normal education: Basis for pedagogical strategies/practices. *Psychology and Education: A Multidisciplinary Journal, 6*(8), 712-719.

Salovey, P., & Mayer, J. D. (1990). Emotional intelligence. *Imagination, Cognition and Personality*, 9(3), 185–211. DOI: 10.2190/DUGG-P24E-52WK-6CDG

Salovey, P., & Mayer, J. D. (1995). Emotional intelligence and the construction and regulation of feelings. *Applied & Preventive Psychology*, 4(3), 197–208. DOI: 10.1016/S0962-1849(05)80058-7

San Pedro, M. O. Z., Baker, R. S., & Heffernan, N. T. (2017). An Integrated Look at Middle School Engagement and Learning in Digital Environments as Precursors to College Attendance. *Technology. Knowledge and Learning*, 22(3), 243–270. DOI: 10.1007/s10758-017-9318-z

Say, R., Visentin, D., Saunders, A., Atherton, I., Carr, A., & King, C. (2024). Where less is more: Limited feedback in formative online multiple-choice tests improves student self-regulation. *Journal of Computer Assisted Learning*, 40(1), 89–103. DOI: 10.1111/jcal.12868

Scherer, K. R. (2009). The dynamic architecture of emotion: Evidence for the component process model. *Cognition and Emotion*, 23(7), 1307–1351. DOI: 10.1080/02699930902928969

Schmidt, S., Tinti, C., Levine, L. J., & Testa, S. (2010). Appraisals, emotions and emotion regulation: An integrative approach. *Motivation and Emotion*, 34(1), 63–72. DOI: 10.1007/s11031-010-9155-z PMID: 20376165

Schmitz, B., & Hanke, K. (2023). Engage me: Learners' expectancies and teachers' efforts in designing effective online classes. *Journal of Computer Assisted Learning*, 39(4), 1132–1140. DOI: 10.1111/jcal.12636

Schön, D. A. (1983). *The reflective practitioner: How professionals think in action*. Basic Books.

Schonert Rechl, K. A. (2017). Social and emotional learning and teachers. *The Future of Children*, 27(1), 137–155. Advance online publication. DOI: 10.1353/foc.2017.0007

Schonert-Reichl, K. A., Hanson-Peterson, J. L., & Hymel, S. (2015). SEL and pre-service teacher education. In Durlak, J. A., Weissberg, R. P., Domitrovich, C. E., & Gullotta, T. P. (Eds.), *Handbook of social and emotional learning: Research and practice* (pp. 406–421).

Schonert-Reichl, K. A., Oberle, E., Lawlor, M. S., Abbott, D., Thomson, K., Oberlander, T. F., & Diamond, A. (2015). Enhancing cognitive and social–emotional development through a simple-to-administer mindfulness-based school program for elementary school children: A randomized controlled trial. *Developmental Psychology*, 51(1), 52–66. DOI: 10.1037/a0038454 PMID: 25546595

SchoolSims. (2024, May 28). Simulations for school leaders & teachers. https://schoolsims.com/

Schutz, P. A. (2014). Inquiry on teachers' emotion. *Educational Psychologist*, 49(1), 1–12. DOI: 10.1080/00461520.2013.864955

Schwabe, L., Hermans, E. J., Joëls, M., & Roozendaal, B. (2022). Mechanisms of memory under stress. *Neuron*, 110(9), 1450–1467. DOI: 10.1016/j.neuron.2022.02.020 PMID: 35316661

Scott, R. (2015, May 26). *Practices to welcome and support ELLs*. https://www.edutopia.org/blog/practices-to-welcome-and-support-ells-robyn-scott

Seal, C. R., Boyatzis, R. E., & Bailey, J. R. (2006). Fostering emotional and social intelligence in organizations. *Organizational Management Journal*, 3(3), 190–209. DOI: 10.1057/omj.2006.19

Sedrakyan, G., Leony, D., Muñoz-Merino, P. J., Kloos, C. D., & Verbert, K. (2017). Evaluating Student-Facing Learning Dashboards of Affective States. In *Lecture Notes in Computer Science (including subseries Lecture Notes in Artificial Intelligence and Lecture Notes in Bioinformatics)* (pp. 224–237). DOI: 10.1007/978-3-319-66610-5_17

Seema, G. (2012). *Emotional intelligence in classroom*. Advances in Management.

Seery, M. D., Leo, R. J., Lupien, S. P., Kondrak, C. L., & Almonte, J. L. (2013). An upside to adversity? Moderate cumulative lifetime adversity is associated with resilient responses in the face of controlled stressors. *Psychological Science*, 24(7), 1181–1189. DOI: 10.1177/0956797612469210 PMID: 23673992

Seguin, E. (2016, September 19). Academic mobbing, or how to become campus tormentors. *University Affairs*. Retrieved from https://www.universityaffairs.ca/opinion/in-my-opinion/academic-mobbing-become-campus-tormentors/

Seligman, M. E. P., & Adler, A. (2018). Positive education. *Global happiness policy report*, 52-73.

Seligman, M. E. (2011). *Flourish: A visionary new understanding of happiness and well-being*. Simon and Schuster.

Seligman, M. E. P., Ernst, R. M., Gillham, J., Reivich, K., & Linkins, M. (2009). Positive education: Positive psychology and classroom interventions. *Oxford Review of Education*, 35(3), 293–311. Advance online publication. DOI: 10.1080/03054980902934563

Seow, A. N., Lam, S. Y., Choong, Y. O., & Choong, C. K. (2024). Online learning effectiveness in private higher education institutions: The mediating roles of emotions and students' learning behaviour. *Quality Assurance in Education*, 32(2), 180–196. DOI: 10.1108/QAE-07-2022-0128

Shabani, K., Khatib, M., & Ebadi, S. (2010). Vygotsky's zone of proximal development: Instructional implications and teachers' professional development. *English Language Teaching*, 3(4), 237–248. DOI: 10.5539/elt.v3n4p237

Sharma, P., Mangal, S., & Nagar, P. (2016). To study the impact of Emotional Intelligence on Academic Achievement of teacher trainees. *IRA International Journal of Education and Multidisciplinary Studies*, 4(1). Advance online publication. DOI: 10.21013/jems.v4.n1.p6

Sharma, S., & Arora, S. (2012). Teaching with emotional intelligence in higher education. Opinion. *International Journal of Management*, 2(1), 52–58.

Shea, P., Li, C. S., Swan, K., & Pickett, A. (2005). Developing learning community in online asynchronous college courses: The role of teaching presence. *Journal of Asynchronous Learning Networks*, 9(4), 59–82.

Shen, S., Mostafavi, B., Barnes, T., & Chi, M. (2018). Exploring Induced Pedagogical Strategies Through a Markov Decision Process Frame-work: Lessons Learned. *Journal of Educational Data Mining*, 10(3).

Shlisky, J., Bloom, D. E., Beaudreault, A. R., Tucker, K. L., Keller, H. H., Freund-Levi, Y., Fielding, R. A., Cheng, F. W., Jensen, G. L., Wu, D., & Meydani, S. N. (2017). Nutritional Considerations for Healthy Ageing and Reduction in Age-Related Chronic Disease. *Advances in Nutrition*, 8(1), 17–26. DOI: 10.3945/an.116.013474 PMID: 28096124

Shuck, B., Albornoz, C., & Winberg, M. (2013). *Emotions and their effect on adult learning: A constructivist perspective.* https://digitalcommons.fiu.edu/sferc/2007/2007_suie/4/

Shu, F., Zhao, C., Liu, Q., Li, H., & Huang, Y. (2022). Enhancing Adults' Online Course Learning Behavior Performance through Live Class in Distance and Open Education. *Proceedings of the 6th International Conference on Education and Multimedia Technology*, 65–69. New York, NY, USA: ACM. DOI: 10.1145/3551708.3556205

Shukla, P., & Garg, A. (2022). Sentiment Analysis of Online Learners in Higher Education: A Learning Perspective through Unstructured Data. In *Intelligent System Algorithms and Applications in Science and Technology* (pp. 157–170). Apple Academic Press., DOI: 10.1201/9781003187059-15

Siemens, G. (2013). Learning analytics: The emergence of a discipline. *The American Behavioral Scientist*, 57(10), 1380–1400. DOI: 10.1177/0002764213498851

Simons, H. (2009). *Case study research in practice.* SAGE publications. DOI: 10.4135/9781446268322

Sinek, S. (2011). *Start with why: How great leaders inspire everyone to take action.* Penguin.

Singh Gill, G. (2017). An exploration of emotional intelligence in teaching: Comparison between practitioners from the United Kingdom & India. *Journal of Psychology & Clinical Psychiatry*, 7(2). Advance online publication. DOI: 10.15406/jpcpy.2017.07.00430

SINGH., M., BANGAY, S., & SAJJANHAR, A. (2022). An Architecture for Capturing and Presenting Learning Outcomes using Augmented Reality Enhanced Analytics. *2022 IEEE International Symposium on Mixed and Augmented Reality Adjunct (ISMAR-Adjunct)*, 611–612. IEEE. DOI: 10.1109/ISMAR-Adjunct57072.2022.00126

Singh, M., Bangay, S., & Sajjanhar, A. (2022). Augmented Reality Enhanced Analytics to Measure and Mitigate Disengagement in Teaching Young Children. *2022 IEEE International Symposium on Mixed and Augmented Reality Adjunct (ISMAR-Adjunct)*, 782–785. IEEE. DOI: 10.1109/ISMAR-Adjunct57072.2022.00166

Sitzman, K. L. (2007). Teaching-learning professional caring based on Jean Watson's theory of human caring. *International Journal for Human Caring*, 11(4), 8–15. DOI: 10.20467/1091-5710.11.4.8

Small, A. C. (1982). The effect of emotional state on student ratings of instructors. *Teaching of Psychology*, 9(4), 205–211. DOI: 10.1207/s15328023top0904_3

Smith, C. A., & Lazarus, R. S. (1990). Emotion and adaptation. In Pervin, L. A. (Ed.), *Handbook of personality: Theory and research* (pp. 609–637). Guilford Press.

Smith, L. B., & Thelen, E. (2003). Development as a dynamic system. *Trends in Cognitive Sciences*, 7(8), 343–348. DOI: 10.1016/S1364-6613(03)00156-6 PMID: 12907229

Smith, T. D. (2021). Teaching through trauma: Compassion fatigue, burnout, or secondary traumatic stress? In Bradley, D., & Hess, J. (Eds.), *Trauma and Resilience in Music Education*. DOI: 10.4324/9781003124207-3

Sniderman, S. (n.d.). Learning through Vulnerability: Applying the Principle of Prospect-Refuge to Create Emotionally Resonant Learning Experiences.

Soanes, D. G., & Sungoh, S. M. (2019). Influence of emotional intelligence on teacher effectiveness of science teachers. *Psychology (Irvine, Calif.)*, 10(13), 1819–1831. DOI: 10.4236/psych.2019.1013118

Sogunro, O. A. (2015). Motivating factors for adult learners in higher education. *International Journal of Higher Education*, 4(1), 22–37.

Song, L. (2005). Adult learners' self-directed learning in online environments: Process, personal attribute, and context. Unpublished Dissertation, The University of Georgia, Athens, GA.

Song, D., & Bonk, C. J. (2016). Motivational factors in self-directed informal learning from online learning resources. *Cogent Education*, 3(1), 1205838. DOI: 10.1080/2331186X.2016.1205838

Song, L., & Hill, J. R. (2007). A conceptual model for understanding self-directed learning in online environments. *Journal of Interactive Online Learning*, 6(1), 27–42.

Sorić, I., Penezić, Z., & Burić, I. (2013). Big five personality traits, cognitive appraisals and emotion regulation strategies as predictors of achievement emotions. *Psihologijske Teme*, 22(2), 325–349. https://hrcak.srce.hr/clanak/159885

Soutter, M. (2023). Transformative social emotional learning for teachers; Critical and holistic well-being as a marker for success. *Journal of Teaching and Learning*, 17(1), 7–30. Advance online publication. DOI: 10.22329/jtl.v17i1.7001

Soythong, K. (2023). The Effect of Quality of Work Life and Organizational Commitment to Employee Performance: A Case Study of Transportation Business in Nakhon Phanom Province of Thailand. *Journal of Roi Kaensarn Academi*, 8(5), 414–433.

Spikol, D., Prieto, L. P., Rodríguez-Triana, M. J., Worsley, M., Ochoa, X., Cukurova, M., & Ringtved, U. L. (2017). Current and future multimodal learning analytics data challenges. *Proceedings of the Seventh International Learning Analytics & Knowledge Conference*, 518–519. New York, NY, USA: ACM. DOI: 10.1145/3027385.3029437

Spitzer, D. R. (2001). Don't forget the high touch with the high tech in distance learning. *Educational Technology*, 41(2), 51–55.

Spooner, M., Duane, C., Uygur, J., Smyth, E., Marron, B., Murphy, P. J., & Pawlikowska, T. (2022). Self-regulatory learning theory as a lens on how undergraduate and postgraduate learners respond to feedback: A BEME scoping review: BEME Guide No. 66. *Medical Teacher*, 44(1), 3–18. DOI: 10.1080/0142159X.2021.1970732 PMID: 34666584

Srimadhaven, T., Chris Junni, A., & Naga Harshith, J. (2020). Learning Analytics: Virtual Reality for Programming Course in Higher Education. *Procedia Computer Science*, 172, 433–437. DOI: 10.1016/j.procs.2020.05.095

Stafford- Brizard. B. (2024, March 1). *The power of educator EQ*. ASCD. https://www.ascd.org/el/articles/the-power-of-educator-eq

Stake, R. E. (1995). The art of case study research. *Sage (Atlanta, Ga.)*.

Stake, R. E. (2013). *Multiple case study analysis*. Guilford Press.

Staudt, K., Grushetskaya, Y., Rangelov, G., Domanska, M., & Pinkwart, N. (2018). Heart rate, electrodermal activity and skin conductance as new sources for Learning Analytics. *CEUR Workshop Proceedings*.

Stephanou, G., & Oikonomou, A. (2018). Teacher emotions in primary and secondary education: Effects of self-efficacy and collective-efficacy, and problem-solving appraisal as a moderating mechanism. *Psychology (Irvine, Calif.)*, 09(04), 820–875. DOI: 10.4236/psych.2018.94053

Stokes, H. E., Brunzell, T., & Howard, J. (2023). Editorial: Trauma-informed education. *Frontiers in Education*, 8, 1264629. Advance online publication. DOI: 10.3389/feduc.2023.1264629

Stoltzfus, K. (2017, June 7). How teacher prep programs can embrace social-emotional learning. *Education Week*. https://www.edweek.org/education/how-teacher-prep-programs-can-embrace-social-emotional-learning/2017/06

Stough, T., Ceulemans, K., Lambrechts, W., & Cappuyns, V. (2018). Assessing sustainability in higher education curricula: A critical reflection on validity issues. *Journal of Cleaner Production*, 172, 4456–4466. DOI: 10.1016/j.jclepro.2017.02.017

Strauss, A. L., & Corbin, J. M. (1990). *Basics of qualitative research: Grounded theory procedures and techniques*. SAGE Publications.

Studies, C. University of Northern BC (n.d.). *OH&S - Occupational Health & Safety Online Certificate*. https://www2.unbc.ca/continuing-studies/courses/ohs-occupational-health-safety-online-certificate

Suero Montero, C., & Suhonen, J. (2014). Emotion analysis meets learning analytics. *Proceedings of the 14th Koli Calling International Conference on Computing Education Research*, 165–169. New York, NY, USA: ACM. DOI: 10.1145/2674683.2674699

Suleman, Q., Hussain, I., Syed, M. A., Parveen, R., Lodhi, I. S., & Mahmood, Z. (2019). Association between emotional intelligence and academic success among undergraduates: A cross-sectional study in KUST, Pakistan. *PLoS One*, 14(7), e0219468. DOI: 10.1371/journal.pone.0219468 PMID: 31291333

Sultana, J., Fontana, A., Giorgianni, F., Basile, G., Patorno, E., Pilotto, A., Molokhia, M., Stewart, R., Sturkenboom, M., & Trifirò, G. (2018). Can information on functional and cognitive status improve short-term mortality risk prediction among community-dwelling older people? A cohort study using a UK primary care database. *Clinical Epidemiology*, 10, 31–39. DOI: 10.2147/CLEP.S145530 PMID: 29296099

Sun, D., Ouyang, F., Li, Y., & Chen, H. (2020). Exploring creativity, emotion and collaborative behavior in programming for two contrasting groups. *Proceedings of International Conference on Computational Thinking Education*, 36–37.

Sutton, R. E., & Wheatley, K. F. (2003). Teachers' emotions and teaching: A review of the literature and directions for future research. *Educational Psychology Review*, 15(4), 327–358. DOI: 10.1023/A:1026131715856

Syiem, I. (2012). Emotional intelligence: Why it matters in teaching. IOSR Journal of Humanities and Social Science [Internet]. *IOSR Journals*, 2(2), 42–43.

Tajfel, H., & Turner, J. C. (2004). The social identity theory of intergroup behavior. In *Political psychology* (pp. 276–293). Psychology Press. DOI: 10.4324/9780203505984-16

Tamir, M. (2016). Why do people regulate their emotions? A taxonomy of motives in emotion regulation. *Personality and Social Psychology Review*, 20(3), 199–222. DOI: 10.1177/1088868315586325 PMID: 26015392

Tam, M. (2000). Constructivism, instructional design, and technology: Implications for transforming distance learning. *Journal of Educational Technology & Society*, 3(2), 50–60.

Tamura, Y., & Murakami, K. (2015). Heartbeat feedback for learners' emotional self control. *Workshop Proceedings of the 23rd International Conference on Computers in Education, ICCE 2015.*

Tang, D., Fan, W., Zou, Y., George, R. A., Arbona, C., & Olvera, N. E. (2021). Self-efficacy and achievement emotions as mediators between learning climate and learning persistence in college calculus: A sequential mediation analysis. *Learning and Individual Differences*, 92, 102094. DOI: 10.1016/j.lindif.2021.102094

Tao, W. (2022). Understanding the relationships between teacher mindfulness, work engagement, and classroom emotions. *Frontiers in Psychology*, 13, 993857. Advance online publication. DOI: 10.3389/fpsyg.2022.993857 PMID: 36248498

Tareen, H., & Haand, M. T. (2020). A case study of UiTM post-graduate students' perceptions on online learning: Benefits challenges. *International Journal of Advanced Research and Publications*, 4(6), 86–94.

Taşçı, G., & Titrek, O. (2019). Evaluation of lifelong learning centers in higher education: A sustainable leadership perspective. *Sustainability (Basel)*, 12(1), 22. DOI: 10.3390/su12010022

Taxer, J. L., Becker-Kurz, B., & Frenzel, A. C. (2019). Do quality teacher–student relationships protect teachers from emotional exhaustion? The mediating role of enjoyment and anger. *Social Psychology of Education*, 22(1), 209–226. DOI: 10.1007/s11218-018-9468-4

Taxer, J. L., & Gross, J. J. (2018). Emotion regulation in teachers: The "why" and "how". *Teaching and Teacher Education*, 74, 180–189. DOI: 10.1016/j.tate.2018.05.008

Taylor, E. W. (2017). Transformative learning theory. In *Transformative learning meets Bildung* (pp. 17–29). Brill Sense. DOI: 10.1007/978-94-6300-797-9_2

Telles, S., Sharma, S. K., Gupta, R. K., Pal, D. K., Gandharva, K., & Balkrishna, A. (2019). The impact of yoga on teachers' self-rated emotions. *BMC Research Notes*, 12(1), 680. Advance online publication. DOI: 10.1186/s13104-019-4737-7 PMID: 31640779

Tempelaar, D. T., Rienties, B., & Nguyen, Q. (2017). Towards Actionable Learning Analytics Using Dispositions. *IEEE Transactions on Learning Technologies*, 10(1), 6–16. DOI: 10.1109/TLT.2017.2662679

Tempelaar, D., Rienties, B., & Nguyen, Q. (2020). Subjective data, objective data and the role of bias in predictive modelling: Lessons from a dispositional learning analytics application. *PLoS One*, 15(6), e0233977. DOI: 10.1371/journal.pone.0233977 PMID: 32530954

Terry, P. C., Karageorghis, C. I., Mecozzi Saha, A., & D'Auria, S. (2012). Effects of synchronous music on treadmill running among elite triathletes. *Journal of Science and Medicine in Sport*, 15(1), 52–57. DOI: 10.1016/j.jsams.2011.06.003 PMID: 21803652

Thakur, S. (2016). Comparative study of emotional competence among teacher trainees in relation to gender. *International Journal of Science and Research (Raipur, India)*, 5(1), 956–959. DOI: 10.21275/v5i1.NOV152874

Thomas, L., Herbert, J., & Teras, M. (2014). A sense of belonging to enhance participation, success and retention in online programs. The International Journal of the First Year Thorndike, E. L. (1920). Intelligence and its use. Harper's Magazine, 140, 227-235.

Thompson, R. A. (1994). Emotion regulation: A theme in search of definition. *Monographs of the Society for Research in Child Development*, 59(2-3), 25–52. DOI: 10.1111/j.1540-5834.1994.tb01276.x PMID: 7984164

Thulasingam, M., Sen, A., Olickal, J., Sen, A., Kalaiselvy, A., & Kandasamy, P. (2020). Emotional intelligence and perceived stress among undergraduate students of arts and science colleges in Puducherry, India: A cross-sectional study. *Journal of Family Medicine and Primary Care*, 9(9), 4942. DOI: 10.4103/jfmpc.jfmpc_823_20 PMID: 33209826

Timoštšuk, I., Kikas, E., & Normak, M. (2016). Student teachers' emotional teaching experiences in relation to different teaching methods. *Educational Studies*, 42(3), 269–286. DOI: 10.1080/03055698.2016.1167674

Timoštšuk, I., & Ugaste, A.Timoštšuk. (2012). The role of emotions in student teachers' professional identity. *European Journal of Teacher Education*, 35(4), 421–433. DOI: 10.1080/02619768.2012.662637

Titsworth, S., McKenna, T. P., Mazer, J. P., & Quinlan, M. M. (2013). The bright side of emotion in the classroom: Do teachers' behaviors predict students' enjoyment, hope, and pride? *Communication Education*, 62(2), 191–209. DOI: 10.1080/03634523.2013.763997

Tokuhama-Espinosa, T. (2011). *Mind, brain, and education science: A comprehensive guide to the new brain-based teaching*. WW Norton & Company.

Toney, S., Light, J., & Urbaczewski, A. (2021). Fighting Zoom fatigue: Keeping the zoombies at bay. *Communications of the Association for Information Systems*, 48(1), 10. DOI: 10.17705/1CAIS.04806

Travis, J., Kaszycki, A., Geden, M., & Bunde, J. (2020). Some stress is good stress: The challenge-hindrance framework, academic self-efficacy, and academic outcomes. *Journal of Educational Psychology*, 112(8), 1632–1643. DOI: 10.1037/edu0000478

Trespalacios, J., & Uribe-Florez, L. J. (2020). Developing online sense of community: Graduate students' experiences and perceptions. *Turkish Online Journal of Distance Education*, 21(1), 57–72. DOI: 10.17718/tojde.690340

Trigwell, K. (2012). Relations between teachers' emotions in teaching and their approaches to teaching in higher education. *Instructional Science*, 40(3), 607–621. DOI: 10.1007/s11251-011-9192-3

Trigwell, K., Ellis, R. A., & Han, F. (2012). Relations between students' approaches to learning, experienced emotions and outcomes of learning. *Studies in Higher Education*, 37(7), 811–824. DOI: 10.1080/03075079.2010.549220

Tsai, Y.-S., Rates, D., Moreno-Marcos, P. M., Muñoz-Merino, P. J., Jivet, I., Scheffel, M., Drachsler, H., Delgado Kloos, C., & Gašević, D. (2020). Learning analytics in European higher education—Trends and barriers. *Computers & Education*, 155, 103933. DOI: 10.1016/j.compedu.2020.103933

Tsybulsky, D., & Muchnik-Rozanov, Y. (2021). Project-based learning in science-teacher pedagogical practicum: The role of emotional experiences in building preservice teachers' competencies. *Disciplinary and Interdisciplinary Science Education Research*, 3(1), 9.

Tucker, R. B. (2002). *Driving growth through innovation: How leading firms are transforming their futures*. Berrett-Koehler Publishers.

Tyng, C. M., Amin, H. U., Saad, M. N., & Malik, A. S. (2017). The influences of emotion on learning and memory. *Frontiers in Psychology*, 8, 1454. DOI: 10.3389/fpsyg.2017.01454 PMID: 28883804

Tzafilkou, K., Perifanou, M., & Economides, A. A. (2021). Negative emotions, cognitive load, acceptance, and self-perceived learning outcome in emergency remote education during COVID-19. *Journal of Educational Technology & Society*, 26(4), 7497–7521. DOI: 10.1007/s10639-021-10604-1 PMID: 34149299

Uiboleht, K., Karm, M., & Postareff, L. (2018). The interplay between teachers' approaches to teaching, students' approaches to learning and learning outcomes: A qualitative multi-case study. *Learning Environments Research*, 21(3), 321–347. DOI: 10.1007/s10984-018-9257-1

Ulutaş, N. K. (2023). *Rethinking Learning Engagement Through Emotional Learning Analytics in K-12 Classrooms Through Social-Emotional Learning and Mindfulness*. DOI: 10.4018/979-8-3693-0066-4.ch009

Usher, E. L., & Pajares, F. (2008). Self-efficacy for self-regulated learning: A validation study. *Educational and Psychological Measurement*, 68(3), 443–463. DOI: 10.1177/0013164407308475

Valente, S., Veiga-Branco, A., Rebelo, H., Lourenço, A. A., & Cristóvão, A. M. (2020). The relationship between emotional intelligence ability and teacher efficacy.

Valente, S., & Lourenço, A. A. (2020, February). Conflict in the classroom: How teachers' emotional intelligence influences conflict management. [). Frontiers Media SA.]. *Frontiers in Education*, 5, 5. DOI: 10.3389/feduc.2020.00005

Valente, S., Veiga-Branco, A., Rebelo, H., Lourenço, A. A., & Cristóvão, A. M. (2020). The relationship between emotional intelligence ability and teacher efficacy. *Universal Journal of Educational Research*, 8(3), 916–923. DOI: 10.13189/ujer.2020.080324

Van Maanen, J. (2011). *Tales of the field: On writing ethnography*. University of Chicago Press. DOI: 10.7208/chicago/9780226849638.001.0001

VanderWeele, T. J. (2023). Emotional well-being annual investigator keynote: Flourishing and emotional well-being. https://hfh.fas.harvard.edu/news/flourishing-and-emotional-well-being-keynote-address-emotional-well-being-annual

Vem, L. J., Cheah, J. H., Ng, S. I., & Ho, J. A. (2023). Unethical pro-organizational behavior: How employee ethical ideology and unethical organizational culture contribute. *International Journal of Manpower*, 44(4), 577–598. DOI: 10.1108/IJM-11-2021-0635

Vidal, J. (2023). Emerging Technologies: The Birth of Artificial Intelligence (AI) in Education. SSRN *Electronic Journal*. DOI: 10.2139/ssrn.4512063

Vidhya, R., & Vadivu, G. (2019). Smart Way to Inspect Student Performance using Emotional State on Learning Analytics. [IJRTE]. *International Journal of Recent Technology and Engineering*, 8(3), 5352–5357. DOI: 10.35940/ijrte.C6882.098319

Voigt, C., Kieslinger, B., & Schäfer, T. (2017). User Experiences Around Sentiment Analyses, Facilitating Workplace Learning. In *Lecture Notes in Computer Science (including subseries Lecture Notes in Artificial Intelligence and Lecture Notes in Bioinformatics)* (pp. 312–324). DOI: 10.1007/978-3-319-58562-8_24

Vuorela, M., & Nummenmaa, L. (2004). Experienced emotions, emotion regulation and student activity in a web-based learning environment. *European Journal of Psychology of Education*, 19(4), 423–436. DOI: 10.1007/BF03173219

Vygotsky, L. S. (1934/1987). Thinking and speech. In R.W. Rieber & A.S. Carton (Eds.), *The collected works of L.S. Vygotsky, Volume 1: Problems of general psychology (pp. 39–285)*. Plenum Press.

Vygotsky, L. S. (1933/1966). Play and its role in the mental development of the child. *Social Psychology*, 12(6), 62–76.

Vygotsky, L. S. (1935). *Mental development of children during education*. Uchpedgiz.

Vygotsky, L. S. (1962). *Thought and language*. MIT Press. DOI: 10.1037/11193-000

Vygotsky, L. S. (1978). *Mind in society: The development of higher psychological processes*. Harvard University Press.

Vygotsky, L. S. (1981). The genesis of higher mental functions. In Wertsch, J. V. (Ed.), *The concept of activity in Soviet psychology*. Sharpe.

Waajid, B., Garner, P. W., & Owen, J. E. (2013). Infusing social emotional learning into the teacher education curriculum. *The International Journal of Emotional Education*, 5(2), 31–48.

Wadsworth, B. J. (1996). *Piaget's theory of cognitive and affective development: Foundations of constructivism*. Longman Publishing.

Wallender, J., Hiebel, A. L., PeQueen, C. V., & Kain, M. A. (2020). Effects of an explicit curriculum on social-emotional competency in elementary and middle school students. The Delta Kappa Gamma Bulletin: International Journal for Professional Educators, 32–43.

Wang, L. (2022). Exploring the relationship among teacher emotional intelligence, work engagement, teacher self-efficacy, and student academic achievement: A moderated mediation model. *Frontiers in Psychology*, 12, 810559. Advance online publication. DOI: 10.3389/fpsyg.2021.810559 PMID: 35046879

Wang, M. T., Degol, J. L., Amemiya, J., Parr, A., & Guo, J. (2020). Classroom climate and children's academic and psychological well being: A systematic review and meta-analysis. *Developmental Review*, 57, 100912. DOI: 10.1016/j.dr.2020.100912

Wang, Z., Ho, S.-B., & Cambria, E. (2020). A review of emotion sensing: Categorization models and algorithms. *Multimedia Tools and Applications*, 79(47–48), 35553–35582. DOI: 10.1007/s11042-019-08328-z

Wang, Zuowei, Miller, K., & Cortina, K. (2013). Using the LENA in teacher training: Promoting student involvement through automated feedback. *Unterrichtswissenschaft*, •••, 4.

Wara, E., Aloka, P. J. O., & Odongo, B. C. (2018). Relationship between emotional engagement and academic achievement among Kenyan secondary school students. *Academic Journal of Interdisciplinary Studies*, 7(1), 107–118. DOI: 10.2478/ajis-2018-0011

Webster, L. (2020). Marvel, Star Wars and the risk of being a hero: Social responsibilities for transmedia storytellers in the age of collective journey. *Cultural Science Journal*, 12(1), 59–67. DOI: 10.5334/csci.138

Weissberg, R. P., Durlak, J. A., Domitrovich, C. E., & Gullotta, T. P. (2015). Social and emotional learning: Past, present, and future.

Wenger, E. (1998). *Communities of practice: Learning, meaning, and identity.* Cambridge University Press., DOI: 10.1017/CBO9780511803932

Wenger-Trayner, E., & Wenger-Trayner, B. (2015). Communities of practice: A brief introduction. Wemger-Taylor. https://wenger-trayner.com/introduction-to-communities-of-practice/

Wenger-Trayner, E., & Wenger-Trayner, B. (2015). Communities of practice: A brief introduction. Wenger-Taylor. https://wenger-trayner.com/introduction-to-communities-of-practice/

Wenger-Trayner, E., Fenton-O'Creevy, M., Hutchison, S., Kubiak, C., & Wenger-Trayner, B. (2014). *Learning in Landscapes of Practice: Boundaries, Identity, and Knowledgeability in Practice-Based Learning*. Routledge., DOI: 10.4324/9781315777122

Wenger-Trayner, E., & Wenger-Trayner, B. (2020). *Learning to Make a Difference: Value Creation in Social Learning Spaces*. Cambridge University Press., DOI: 10.1017/9781108677431

Wesch, N. (2022). Identify Your IPS. Special Olympics. https://soctraining.ca/sites/default/files/2022-10/Ideal-Performance-State_WORKSHEET_EN.pdf

West, D., Heath, D., & Huijser, H. (2015). Let's Talk Learning Analytics: A Framework for Implementation in Relation to Student Retention. *Online Learning : the Official Journal of the Online Learning Consortium*, 20(2). Advance online publication. DOI: 10.24059/olj.v20i2.792

Westera, W., van der Vegt, W., Bahreini, K., Dascalu, M., & van Lankveld, G. (2016). Software components for serious game development. *Proceedings of the European Conference on Games-Based Learning*.

White, M. A. (2016). Why won't it stick? Positive psychology and positive education. *Psychology of Well-Being*, 6(2), 2. DOI: 10.1186/s13612-016-0039-1 PMID: 26900547

Whiteside, A. L., Dikkers, A. G., & Swan, K. (Eds.). (2023). *Social presence in online learning: Multiple perspectives on practice and research*. Taylor & Francis.

Wickens, C. D. (2001). Keynote address: Attention to safety and the psychology of surprise. In *11th International Symposium on Aviation Psychology* (pp. 1-11). The Ohio State University.

Williamson, B. (2017). Decoding ClassDojo: Psycho-policy, social-emotional learning and persuasive educational technologies. *Learning, Media and Technology*, 42(4), 440–453. DOI: 10.1080/17439884.2017.1278020

Williamson, B. (2021). Psychodata: Disassembling the psychological, economic, and statistical infrastructure of 'social-emotional learning.'. *Journal of Education Policy*, 36(1), 129–154. DOI: 10.1080/02680939.2019.1672895

Wilson, J. H. (2008). Instructor attitudes toward students: Job satisfaction and student outcomes. *College Teaching*, 56(4), 225–229. DOI: 10.3200/CTCH.56.4.225-229

Winkleman, P., & Harmon-Jones, E. (2006). *Social neuroscience*. Oxford University Press.

Winne, P. H. (2021). Cognition, Metacognition, and Self-Regulated Learning. In *Oxford Research Encyclopedia of Education*. Oxford University Press., DOI: 10.1093/acrefore/9780190264093.013.1528

Wintrup, J. (2017). Higher Education's Panopticon? Learning Analytics, Ethics and Student Engagement. *Higher Education Policy*, 30(1), 87–103. DOI: 10.1057/s41307-016-0030-8

Wlodkowski, R. (1999). *Enhancing adult motivation to learn*. Jossey-Bass.

Wlodkowski, R. J., & Ginsberg, M. B. (2017). *Enhancing adult motivation to learn: A comprehensive guide for teaching all adults*. John Wiley & Sons.

Wolfe, P. (2006). The role of meaning and emotion in learning. *New Directions for Adult and Continuing Education*, 110(110), 35–41. DOI: 10.1002/ace.217

Wolgemuth, J. R., Erdil-Moody, Z., Opsal, T., Cross, J. E., Kaanta, T., Dickmann, E. M., & Colomer, S. (2015). Participants' experiences of the qualitative interview: Considering the importance of research paradigms. *Qualitative Research*, 15(3), 351–372. DOI: 10.1177/1468794114524222

Wong, J., Baars, M., He, M., de Koning, B. B., & Paas, F. (2021). Facilitating goal setting and planning to enhance online self-regulation of learning. *Computers in Human Behavior*, 124, 106913. Advance online publication. DOI: 10.1016/j.chb.2021.106913

Woolcott, G., Whannell, R., Marshman, M., Galligan, L., Yeigh, T., & Axelsen, T. (2023, July 7). Exploring pre-service teachers' affective-reflective skills: The effect of variations of a novel self-evaluation protocol. *Asia-Pacific Journal of Teacher Education*. Advance online publication. DOI: 10.1080/1359866X.2023.2227942

Woolf, B. P. (2010). *Building intelligent interactive tutors: Student-centered strategies for revolutionizing e-learning*. Morgan Kaufmann.

Wosnitza, M., & Volet, S. (2005). Origin, direction and impact of emotions in social online learning. *Learning and Instruction*, 15(5), 449–464. DOI: 10.1016/j.learninstruc.2005.07.009

Wu, C., Gong, X., Luo, L., Zhao, Q., Hu, S., Mou, Y., & Jing, B. (2021). Applying control-value theory and unified theory of acceptance and use of technology to explore pre-service teachers' academic emotions and learning satisfaction. *Frontiers in Psychology*, 12, 738959. DOI: 10.3389/fpsyg.2021.738959 PMID: 34819895

Wu, C., Jing, B., Gong, X., Mou, Y., & Li, J. (2021b). Student's learning strategies and academic emotions: Their influence on learning satisfaction during the COVID-19 pandemic. *Frontiers in Psychology*, 12, 717683. DOI: 10.3389/fpsyg.2021.717683 PMID: 34630228

Wu, J. G., Zhang, D., & Lee, S. M. (2023). Into the brave new metaverse: Envisaging future language teaching and learning. *IEEE Transactions on Learning Technologies*, 17, 44–53. DOI: 10.1109/TLT.2023.3259470

Wu, R., & Yu, Z. (2022). Exploring the effects of achievement emotions on online learning outcomes: A systematic review. *Frontiers in Psychology*, 13, 977931. DOI: 10.3389/fpsyg.2022.977931 PMID: 36160514

Xu, J., Du, J., Liu, F., & Huang, B. (2019). Emotion regulation, homework completion, and math achievement: Testing models of reciprocal effects. *Contemporary Educational Psychology*, 59, 101810. DOI: 10.1016/j.cedpsych.2019.101810

Xu, W., Wu, Y., & Ouyang, F. (2023). Multimodal learning analytics of collaborative patterns during pair programming in higher education. *International Journal of Educational Technology in Higher Education*, 20(1), 8. DOI: 10.1186/s41239-022-00377-z

Yan, E. M., Evans, I. M., & Harvey, S. T. (2011). Observing emotional interactions between teachers and students in elementary school classrooms. *Journal of Research in Childhood Education*, 25(1), 82–97. DOI: 10.1080/02568543.2011.533115

Yang, Y. D., Zhou, C. L., & Wang, Z. Q. (2024). The relationship between self-control and learning engagement among Chinese college students: The chain mediating roles of resilience and positive emotions. *Frontiers in Psychology*, 15, 1331691. DOI: 10.3389/fpsyg.2024.1331691 PMID: 38445063

Yen, Y. C. G., Dow, S. P., Gerber, E., & Bailey, B. P. (2017, June). Listen to others, listen to yourself: Combining feedback review and reflection to improve iterative design. In *Proceedings of the 2017 ACM SIGCHI Conference on Creativity and Cognition* (pp. 158-170). DOI: 10.1145/3059454.3059468

Yerkes, R. M., & Dodson, J. D. (1908). The relation of strength of stimulus to rapidity of habit-formation. *The Journal of Comparative Neurology and Psychology*, 18(5), 459–482. DOI: 10.1002/cne.920180503

Yin, H. (2015). The effect of teachers' emotional labour on teaching satisfaction: Moderation of emotional intelligence. *Teachers and Teaching*, 21(7), 789–810. DOI: 10.1080/13540602.2014.995482

Yin, H.-B., Lee, J. C. K., Zhang, Z.-H., & Jin, Y.-L. (2013). Exploring the relationship among teachers' emotional intelligence, emotional labor strategies and teaching satisfaction. *Teaching and Teacher Education*, 35, 137–145. DOI: 10.1016/j.tate.2013.06.006

Yin, H., Huang, S., & Lee, J. C. K. (2017). Choose your strategy wisely: Examining the relationships between emotional labor in teaching and teacher efficacy in Hong Kong primary schools. *Teaching and Teacher Education*, 66, 127–136. DOI: 10.1016/j.tate.2017.04.006

Yin, R. K. (2011). *Applications of case study research*. Sage.

Yin, R. K. (2013). *Case study research: Design and methods*. Sage.

Ylänne, V. (2015). Representations of ageing in the media. *Routledge handbook of cultural gerontology*, 369-376.

Yun, H., & Park, S. (2020). Building a structural model of motivational regulation and learning engagement for undergraduate and graduate students in higher education. *Studies in Higher Education*, 45(2), 271–285. DOI: 10.1080/03075079.2018.1510910

Zaki, N. A. A., Zain, N. Z. M., Noor, N. A. Z. M., & Hashim, H. (2020). Developing a Conceptual Model of Learning Analytics in Serious Games for STEM Education. *Jurnal Pendidikan IPA Indonesia*, 9(3), 330–339. DOI: 10.15294/jpii.v9i3.24466

Zebrowitz, L. A., and Montepare, J. M. (2000). Too young, too old: Stigmatizing adolescents and elders. *The social psychology of stigma*, 334-373.

Zembylas, M. (2008). Adult learners' emotions in online learning. *Distance Education*, 29(1), 71–87. DOI: 10.1080/01587910802004852

Zembylas, M., Theodorou, M., & Pavlakis, A. (2008). The role of emotions in the experience of online learning: Challenges and opportunities. *Educational Media International*, 45(2), 107–117. DOI: 10.1080/09523980802107237

Zhang, L.-F., Fu, M., Li, D. T., & He, Y. (2019). Emotions and teaching styles among academics: The mediating role of research and teaching efficacy. *Educational Psychology*, 39(3), 370–394. DOI: 10.1080/01443410.2018.1520970

Zheng, J., Huang, L., Li, S., Lajoie, S. P., Chen, Y., & Hmelo-Silver, C. E. (2021). Self-regulation and emotion matter: A case study of instructor interactions with a learning analytics dashboard. *Computers & Education*, 161, 104061. DOI: 10.1016/j.compedu.2020.104061

Zheng, L., Zhong, L., & Niu, J. (2022). Effects of personalised feedback approach on knowledge building, emotions, co-regulated behavioural patterns and cognitive load in online collaborative learning. *Assessment & Evaluation in Higher Education*, 47(1), 109–125. DOI: 10.1080/02602938.2021.1883549

Zhoc, K. C. H., Cai, Y., Yeung, S. S., & Shan, J. (2022). Subjective wellbeing and emotion regulation strategies: How are they associated with student engagement in online learning during Covid-19? *The British Journal of Educational Psychology*, 00(4), 1–13. DOI: 10.1111/bjep.12513 PMID: 35567326

Zhoc, K. C., King, R. B., Chung, T. S., & Chen, J. (2020). Emotionally intelligent students are more engaged and successful: Examining the role of emotional intelligence in higher education. *European Journal of Psychology of Education*, 35(4), 839–863. DOI: 10.1007/s10212-019-00458-0

Zhoc, K. C., Li, J. C., & Webster, B. J. (2017). New reliability and validity evidence of the Emotional Intelligence Scale. *Journal of Psychoeducational Assessment*, 35(6), 599–614. DOI: 10.1177/0734282916653901

Zhu, M., Bonk, C. J., & Doo, M. Y. (2020). Self-directed learning in MOOCs: Exploring the relationships among motivation, self-monitoring, and self-management. *Educational Technology Research and Development*, 68(5), 2073–2093. DOI: 10.1007/s11423-020-09747-8

Zimmerman, B. J. (2000). Self-efficacy: An essential motive to learn. *Contemporary Educational Psychology*, 25(1), 82–91. DOI: 10.1006/ceps.1999.1016 PMID: 10620383

Zins, J. E., Weissberg, R. P., Wang, M. C., & Walberg, H. J. (Eds.). (2004). *Building academic success on social and emotional learning: What does the research say?* Teachers College Press.

About the Contributors

Sarah Sniderman is a senior learning strategist with over 25 years of experience creating instructional programs that meet the performance needs of global organizations. She is an independent consultant, team player, and reflective practitioner with strong communication skills, always adapting to deliver high-quality learning experiences that fulfill client expectations, engage participants, and deliver on opportunities. As founder and host of the Vulnerability in life and art podcast, she speaks with artists and other creatives about their experiences of vulnerability, what it means to take risks, and the ways in which they reveal themselves through the works they create. Sarah presents, writes, and facilitates on a range of topics including interactivity, fundamentals of learning design and development, and the emotional experience of learning.

***

Vishnu Achutha Menon is an independent journalist, writer, researcher, and an Indian percussionist. He is a recipient of the Junior Scholarship the Ministry of Culture awarded. His research interests are film studies, verbal & nonverbal communication, south Asian performances, Natyasastra, media studies, media analysis techniques, Laban Movement Analysis, and Ethnomusicology.

Linda Alexanian is the Founder of Organic Weave, the world's only organic rug company. She is passionate about fair trade labour and has worked to eradicate child labour in India's textile industry since 1990. When not traveling, Linda can be found walking the streets of Montreal with her Bernese Mountain Dog. She holds a B.A from McGill University. As a lifelong learner, and a Mother of 3, she has spent countless hours considering how individuals learn. Of particular interest is the intersection between the material being delivered, and the state of mind of the teacher and the learner at the time of delivery.

Fahad Aljabr is an associate professor in the English department at the University of Ha'il, Saudi Arabia. Dr. Aljabr has a masters degree in Applied Linguistics from the University of Adelaide 2011 and a PhD in Applied Linguistics from the University of Birmingham, 2018. His research interests include: (written) discourse analysis, evaluative language, ESL/EFL teaching and learning.

Eda Bakır-Yalçın is a research assistant at the Department of Computer Education and Instructional Technology at Recep Tayyip Erdoğan University, Turkey. She has a Ph.D. in Computer Education and Instructional Technology from Hacettepe University. Previously, she worked as an Information Technologies teacher at the Ministry of National Education. She currently teaches various undergraduate and graduate level courses in Information Technologies, Media Literacy, and Contemporary Approaches in Education. She is interested in conducting research on learner engagement in online learning environments and online learners' emotions and behaviors.

Mary Ann Becker Currently I divide my time between the United States and Paris, France. Travel brings me face to face with the unknown and allows my curiosity to be nourished. I obtained my BFA from Wichita State University in 1977 and my MFA in 1979 from the University of Colorado at Boulder. My current photographic work explores the ambiance of Parisian spaces and forests near Paris on foot. Walking has become an important part of my artistic practice. I am interested in pareidolia found in nature, etc. and in developing a personal urban iconography. The camera is the tool I use as a memory catcher and my images bear witness to the poetry of these ordinary moments. I am fascinated by the relationship between writing and images, the ways they can complement each other or fill a void that one or the other lacks. Both can emit powerful responses carrying the viewer or reader along with the experience. For more information see: https://maryannbecker.com

Billi L. Bromer, is a retired Professor of Education, having been at Brenau University in Gainesville, Georgia for 18 years. She taught a range of undergraduate and graduate courses in Brenau's online educator preparation program. She has presented numerous papers at state, national, and international educational conferences as well as authored multiple chapters on a variety of topics related to educator preparation, online teaching, and issues related to PK-6 education. She is especially interested in social-emotional development and the importance of the social elements of online learning for students of all ages.

Caroline M. Crawford, Ed.D., is a Professor of Instructional Design and Technology at the University of Houston-Clear Lake in Houston, Texas, United States of America. She earned her doctoral degree from the University of Houston in Houston, Texas, United States of America, in 1998, with specialization areas in Instructional Technology and Curriculum Theory, and began her tenure at the University of Houston-Clear Lake (UHCL) the same year. At this point in Dr. Crawford's professional career, her main areas of interest focus upon communities of learning and the appropriate and successful integration of technologies into the learning environment; the learning environment may be envisioned as face-to-face, blended and online (virtual or text-driven) environments, as well as microlearning and micro-assist deliverables. Dr. Crawford may be contacted through her e-mail address, crawford@uhcl.edu.

James L. Dillard, II, Ed.D., is a medically-retired Coast Guard Public Affairs specialist 2nd class. He is currently in a Military Security and Strategic Studies program at the University of Calgary in Canada. He entered academia and discovered that he truly enjoyed not only learning, but helping others learn, as well. His goals moving forward are to try to make the world a better place by helping anyone he can learn everything they wish.

Ian Gaither A graduate of the Concordia Educational Technology Masters' program, Ian has designed simulation and game-based training for astronauts, airline pilots, environmental engineers, soldiers, ophthalmologists, mass transit specialists and grocery clerks.

Carrie Grimes is an Assistant Professor of the Practice in the Department of Leadership, Policy and Organizations and also serves as the Director of the Independent School Leadership Master's program at Vanderbilt University.

Catherine Hayes is Professor of Health Professions Pedagogy and Scholarship at the University of Sunderland, UK. She is a UK National Teaching Fellow and Principal Fellow of the UK Higher Education Academy. As a graduate of Podiatric Medicine in 1992, Catherine was a Founding Fellow of the Faculty of Podiatric Medicine at the Royal College of Physicians and Surgeons (Glasgow) in 2012 and was awarded Fellowship of the Royal College of Podiatry (London) in 2010. She is currently Programme Leader of the University of Sunderland's Professional Doctorate pathways for the DBA, EdD, DPM and DProf.

Brian Hibbs, Ph.D., is a professor of education/ESOL at Dalton State College, USA. He teaches courses in applied linguistics, language teaching methodology, and culture and education to prepare pre-service elementary education teachers to work with multilingual learners in their own instructional contexts. His scholarly interests include applied linguistics, faculty development, intercultural competence, language teaching methodology, second language acquisition, study abroad, and teacher research.

Islam A. Ismail, from Palestine, holds a Ph.D. in English Language Education. Ismail does research on using AI in education and works as a proofreader in the academic English field. He aims to find innovative and effective ways to facilitate language acquisition and proficiency.

Jerine Jain Mathew is a PhD scholar from Bengaluru, India, and has completed her MBA with a specialization in Human resources. She works in the field of learning and development and content creation. She is passionate about creating and designing content for leadership development and organizational learning, fostering effective growth opportunities for leaders and employees.

Arcie Mallari A champion of social development and a visionary of a beyond-classroom approach to personal growth and consequent scholastic transformation, Arcie G. Mallari is a prime mover in children, youth and community empowerment anchored on igniting the love of learning that transcends textbook knowledge. He obtained his Master's degree in Educational Management and Leadership at McGill University in Montreal, Quebec in Canada as a Sauveì Scholar by the Jeanne Sauveì Foundation. His work was published in 2012 entitled Human Rights Voices of World's Young Activists. This impressive educational background is enriched by his experience in social and personal development: Kuya Arcie is a certified international goal-attainment coach, total quality management specialist, and behavioral consultant in various private and government agencies. He has been a coach, facilitator, and resource speaker on the aforementioned in various conferences and seminars here and abroad since 2009. His concerted efforts with the community earned him special citations in Ashoka Foundation, TAYO Awards, Department of Education Stakeholder of the Year, Civic Movers of the Year by news network Rappler, and recently cited as the National Grand Awardee for the CSR Youth Awards Philippines 2016.

Urmila R. Menon is an Assistant Professor at LEAD College of Management, Palakkad, Kerala, India. With over three years of experience in academia, she specializes in educational research, behavioral finance, and faculty engagement. Urmila has a strong background in data analysis using SPSS and has developed excellent skills in teamwork, team management, interpersonal communication, and adaptability. Throughout her career, Urmila has been actively involved in research and has presented several papers at national and international conferences. Some of her notable presentations include topics on investors' attitudes towards financial derivatives, behavioral intentions towards adopting innovative teaching aids, and the impact of caravan tourism in Kerala during the COVID-19 pandemic. She has also explored various facets of faculty engagement, such as its role in creating organizational citizenship behavior and the influence of personal factors on engagement levels.

Sridevi Nair is an academic and mentor at Christ University, deeply committed to advancing innovative teaching approaches and promoting holistic education. My research spans diverse fields, including social-emotional learning (SEL) for adult learners, sustainable development, and gamification, with a particular focus on learning and development. In addition to my research, I have published teaching cases and remain actively involved in creating and refining innovative tools for teaching and learning.

Xuan-Vinh Nguyen has been working in the fields of information technology and project management for over 10 years. He is passionate about learning and growth, both for his career and his own personal development, and pursues every opportunity to challenge himself and what he can contribute to organizations, colleagues, and his family.

JB Oleet is a scholar interested in the post-pandemic digital divide, which concerns access gaps to emerging technologies like blockchain and artificial intelligence. Their research examines how these innovations shape students' emotional and social dynamics in learning environments, particularly within urban and inner-city populations.

George A. Papakostas received the diploma in Electrical and Computer Engineering in 1999 and M.Sc. and Ph.D. in Electrical and Computer Engineering in 2002 and 2007, respectively, from the Democritus University of Thrace (DUTH), Greece. He is a Tenured Full Professor in the Department of Computer Science International Hellenic University, Greece. He is the Head of the Machine Learning and Vision (MLV) Research Group. Prof. Papakostas has (co)authored more than 200 publications, his publications have over 4000 citations with an h-index 36 (Google Scholar). His research interests include machine learning, computer/machine vision, pattern recognition, and computational intelligence.

Corrie Pitzer is a specialist in safety transformation, leadership and strategic safety management. He consults in this field throughout USA, Canada, South America, Australia and South Africa. He has developed many 'new' concepts in safety: Risk Competency, Latent Safety Metrics, Deep Safety and Readiness-To-Respond to risk as a definition of 'safe'. His company, SAFEmap International, is based in the USA and Canada and is today regarded as the leading consultancy in this field, with several international corporations utilizing his expertise.

Kyriaki Tychola received the Diploma Degrees from the Department of Geoinformation and Surveying from the Technological Educational Institute, Serres, Greece and in Landscape Architecture from the Technological Educational Institute of Kavala, Greece in 2005 and 2013 respectively and M.Sc Degree from the Department of Geography and applied Geoinformatics in 2022 specializing in GIS and Photogrammetry. She has publications in international scientific journals in computer vision field. As a researcher, she is a member of the Machine Learning and Vision (MLV) Research Group, where she participates in research projects.

Eleni Vrochidou received the Diploma, the M.Sc and Ph.D. Degrees from the Department of Electrical & Computer Engineering, Democritus University of Thrace (DUTH), Greece, in 2004, 2007, and 2016, respectively. She is currently a part-time lecturer in the Department of Computer Science (IHU) at the International Hellenic University. Her research interests are intelligent systems, signal processing, pattern recognition, and embedded systems. She has several publications in international scientific conferences, journals, and book chapters in these areas. As a researcher, she is a member of the Machine Learning and Vision (MLV) Research Group, where she participates in research projects.

Lynda Williams has worked in instructional design, and associated management roles, for over two decades. She ran the development lab for online courses at UNBC in the 1990s and 2000s and served as functional lead for Simon Fraser University's learning management system migration spanning 2012 to 2015. Lynda has taught and developed curriculum for introductory computing courses since the 1990s, and holds two masters degrees (M.Sc. Computation and Masters of Library Science) as well as a B.A. in Liberal Studies.

Yasin Yalçın is an assistant professor of Computer Engineering at Recep Tayyip Erdoğan University, Turkey. Dr. Yalçın has a Ph.D. in Instructional Systems and Learning Technologies from Florida State University where he earned a number of awards for his scholarship including the Outstanding Doctoral Student Award and Outstanding International Student Award. He has over 10 years of professional experience in the field of Instructional Design and Technology (IDT) as a researcher, instructor, and instructional designer. Dr. Yalçın has published in a number of top-tier journals including the British Journal of Educational Technology and Educational Technology Research & Development. He is interested in conducting research on the development and measurement of competencies in instructional design and teaching, learner competencies in online learning environments, and online learners' motivations and behaviors.

Chien Yu is a Professor in Mississippi State University. She has published numerous articles and book chapters in a variety of national refereed journals and books, and made many presentations at national/international conferences in the areas of distance learning, multimedia instruction, instructional design and technology, and educational leadership.

Index

A

Academic Mobbing 392, 393, 394, 395, 396, 397, 399, 400, 403, 406, 411, 412, 413
Administration 131, 140, 183, 248, 380, 386, 393, 397, 398, 399, 412, 440
adult learning 17, 18, 19, 20, 21, 22, 25, 33, 36, 37, 42, 43, 52, 119, 120, 126, 131, 137, 138, 139, 142, 148, 149, 156, 163, 166, 172, 194, 195, 196, 198, 200, 205, 208, 210, 213, 214, 217, 218, 220, 425
Adult Online Learning 120, 128, 132, 134, 135, 137, 139, 142, 156, 157, 160, 163, 164, 165, 166, 167, 168, 169, 171, 172, 173, 174, 178, 182, 185, 198
Affective 1, 2, 7, 8, 9, 10, 11, 12, 13, 17, 18, 19, 20, 21, 22, 23, 26, 27, 30, 31, 33, 34, 35, 36, 37, 40, 41, 42, 43, 57, 69, 75, 80, 81, 82, 83, 87, 89, 90, 92, 93, 103, 104, 108, 113, 156, 158, 160, 164, 198, 212, 224, 228, 231, 233, 244, 247, 253, 255, 261, 262, 264, 265, 266, 267, 270, 271, 277, 278, 281, 286, 287, 292, 293, 299, 311, 312, 359, 374, 419, 420, 421, 424, 425, 428, 429, 430, 431, 432, 435, 438, 439, 440, 447, 454, 455, 465, 467
Affective learning 19, 198, 231, 247, 253
Ageism 255, 256, 258, 259, 260, 262, 263, 264, 265, 266, 267, 270, 272, 280, 281, 282, 284, 285, 286, 287
Andragogy 37, 46, 49, 50, 51, 52, 53, 61, 68, 69, 126, 127, 137, 147, 149, 210, 213, 220, 317, 318, 322, 338, 339, 340, 345, 350
Auditory 281, 491
Authenticity 11, 198, 276, 287, 295, 298, 311, 403, 410

B

Back to School 289, 290
Becoming 9, 69, 180, 323, 331, 379, 394, 395, 396, 397, 408, 422, 423, 426, 468

C

CASEL 206, 207, 208, 213, 215, 217, 219, 421, 430, 442, 450, 456, 459, 460, 469
Classroom Emotions 289, 297, 309, 310, 313
Cognitive Dissonance 12, 234, 317, 318, 321, 322, 334, 338, 339, 341, 342, 345
Communities of Practice 48, 194, 317, 318, 320, 322, 338, 339, 340, 341, 345, 353, 414
community building 161, 169, 170, 171, 191
compassion fatigue 419, 426, 438, 445, 446, 447
Complex Conversation 384
Constructivism 143, 152, 263, 266, 267, 286, 287
Continuing Studies 2
Corrie PItzer 1, 4, 9, 11, 12
Course 2, 3, 9, 10, 12, 26, 27, 31, 37, 72, 79, 86, 88, 89, 90, 92, 95, 97, 100, 101, 110, 113, 127, 128, 131, 132, 133, 136, 138, 140, 141, 145, 150, 158, 159, 163, 165, 166, 167, 169, 181, 182, 183, 184, 185, 186, 188, 189, 190, 192, 196, 199, 203, 226, 236, 238, 256, 261, 317, 318, 319, 320, 321, 322, 323, 324, 325, 326, 327, 328, 329, 330, 331, 332, 333, 334, 335, 336, 337, 338, 339, 340, 341, 342, 343, 344, 345, 346, 347, 348, 349, 353, 354, 355, 362, 363, 367, 369, 372, 380, 381, 382, 383, 384, 385, 386, 387, 388, 389, 390, 391, 392, 394, 395, 396, 397, 399, 400, 401, 402, 403, 404, 405, 406, 407, 415, 424, 433, 434, 435, 436, 449, 457, 458, 459, 460, 461, 463, 464, 465, 466, 468, 473, 474, 475, 482, 486, 502, 509, 510

Critical Analysis 303, 305, 346, 383
Critical Reflection 126, 133, 262, 263, 265, 266, 279, 285, 287
Currere 379, 381, 382, 383, 384, 394, 395, 398, 399, 400, 405, 407, 408, 413, 414

D

Data Science 98
Design Thinking 349, 479, 480
distance education 69, 145, 146, 149, 196, 198, 199, 201, 202, 349, 351, 352, 410, 412, 413, 443

E

Education 9, 12, 14, 17, 18, 19, 21, 22, 25, 26, 28, 29, 33, 34, 35, 36, 37, 38, 39, 40, 41, 42, 43, 46, 47, 48, 49, 50, 51, 53, 54, 55, 56, 57, 61, 63, 64, 65, 67, 68, 69, 71, 72, 74, 75, 76, 80, 81, 83, 87, 88, 90, 94, 98, 101, 103, 104, 105, 106, 107, 108, 109, 110, 111, 112, 113, 114, 115, 116, 119, 121, 123, 124, 125, 126, 127, 128, 129, 142, 143, 145, 146, 147, 148, 149, 150, 151, 152, 153, 161, 162, 167, 168, 172, 192, 194, 195, 196, 197, 198, 199, 200, 201, 202, 208, 210, 216, 217, 219, 220, 221, 226, 243, 253, 255, 258, 259, 264, 265, 266, 270, 278, 280, 281, 282, 283, 284, 285, 286, 287, 290, 291, 300, 308, 309, 310, 311, 312, 313, 314, 315, 329, 330, 337, 344, 347, 349, 350, 351, 352, 356, 362, 371, 373, 374, 376, 377, 378, 380, 382, 386, 387, 390, 391, 406, 407, 410, 411, 412, 413, 414, 415, 420, 423, 424, 425, 430, 432, 436, 437, 438, 440, 441, 442, 443, 444, 445, 446, 447, 449, 451, 452, 453, 454, 455, 456, 457, 465, 467, 468, 469, 470, 471, 472, 479, 481, 489, 498, 499, 502
Educational Data Mining 75, 78, 79, 103, 104, 105, 113, 409
educator preparation 419, 420, 421, 424, 425, 426, 428, 429, 431, 432, 433, 434, 435, 436, 437, 438, 439, 451, 452, 453, 454, 456, 467, 472
Embodied cognition 19, 41
Embodied emotions 19
emotion 8, 17, 18, 19, 20, 23, 25, 26, 29, 30, 33, 34, 36, 38, 39, 40, 42, 43, 80, 81, 82, 86, 87, 88, 90, 91, 92, 93, 101, 103, 107, 108, 109, 110, 112, 114, 115, 116, 124, 145, 150, 151, 155, 156, 158, 163, 164, 167, 177, 179, 193, 194, 195, 196, 198, 199, 201, 202, 220, 234, 236, 247, 248, 289, 290, 291, 299, 300, 301, 302, 304, 305, 306, 309, 310, 311, 312, 314, 355, 356, 357, 358, 359, 360, 361, 362, 363, 364, 365, 366, 367, 368, 369, 370, 371, 372, 373, 374, 375, 376, 377, 378, 422, 440, 442
Emotional design 28, 39, 41, 43, 196
emotional engagement 19, 25, 28, 42, 43, 45, 46, 49, 57, 60, 62, 63, 64, 65, 162, 167, 171, 180, 181, 182, 183, 186, 190, 203, 244, 296, 299, 314, 317, 345
Emotional Learning Analytics 71, 73, 79, 80, 106, 114
emotional literacy 63, 144, 206, 429, 430, 440
Emotional Regulation 21, 31, 43, 83, 122, 123, 165, 175, 176, 214, 217, 241, 245, 424, 430, 431, 444
Emotional Social Intelligence 119, 121, 123, 124, 129, 130, 142
Emotional Social Intelligence Competencies 130
emotion regulation strategies 355, 356, 358, 359, 360, 361, 362, 364, 366, 367, 369, 370, 371, 372, 373, 376, 377, 378
emotions 10, 11, 17, 18, 19, 20, 21, 22, 23, 24, 25, 26, 27, 28, 29, 30, 31, 32, 33, 34, 35, 36, 38, 39, 40, 41, 42, 43, 46, 47, 57, 58, 59, 60, 61, 62, 70, 73, 75, 76, 79, 80, 81, 82, 83, 84, 85, 86, 87, 88, 89, 90, 91, 92, 93, 94, 100, 101, 105, 107, 109, 110, 111, 112, 116, 120, 121, 125, 128, 134, 144, 148, 150, 155, 156, 157, 158, 159, 160,

161, 162, 163, 164, 165, 166, 167,
168, 169, 170, 171, 172, 173, 175,
176, 177, 178, 179, 180, 181, 182,
183, 184, 185, 193, 194, 195, 196,
197, 198, 199, 200, 201, 202, 203,
205, 206, 207, 208, 212, 214, 223,
224, 228, 233, 235, 240, 241, 243,
244, 246, 289, 291, 292, 293, 294,
295, 296, 297, 298, 299, 300, 304,
306, 308, 309, 310, 311, 312, 313,
314, 315, 355, 356, 357, 358, 359,
360, 361, 362, 363, 364, 365, 366,
367, 368, 369, 370, 371, 372, 373,
374, 375, 376, 377, 378, 397, 414,
419, 420, 422, 423, 424, 425, 426,
429, 431, 438, 440, 441, 443, 444,
446, 450, 452, 454

English Learners 449, 455, 460, 463, 464, 465, 468, 470, 472, 473, 474

Epistemic Knowledge 261, 287

Experience 1, 2, 5, 8, 10, 12, 18, 19, 20, 21, 22, 24, 34, 45, 46, 53, 54, 55, 56, 57, 58, 59, 61, 62, 63, 65, 72, 78, 81, 82, 86, 94, 101, 104, 109, 120, 124, 127, 130, 134, 136, 137, 138, 139, 140, 141, 142, 147, 156, 157, 158, 159, 160, 163, 166, 167, 168, 169, 170, 173, 174, 179, 182, 184, 187, 188, 190, 191, 193, 198, 202, 212, 214, 220, 224, 226, 228, 230, 233, 236, 238, 239, 240, 241, 242, 243, 244, 246, 247, 249, 256, 260, 262, 263, 265, 267, 277, 281, 282, 292, 294, 297, 300, 305, 308, 309, 317, 318, 319, 320, 321, 322, 323, 324, 325, 326, 327, 328, 329, 330, 331, 332, 334, 335, 337, 338, 340, 341, 342, 343, 344, 345, 346, 347, 348, 353, 356, 357, 361, 362, 369, 375, 379, 380, 381, 382, 383, 384, 385, 386, 387, 388, 389, 390, 391, 392, 394, 395, 396, 397, 398, 400, 401, 402, 403, 404, 405, 406, 407, 414, 415, 419, 421, 423, 425, 426, 427, 430, 431, 435, 436, 442, 443, 470, 480, 482, 483, 486, 488, 489, 492, 507, 510

I

Ideal Performance State 224, 225, 226, 228, 230, 232, 233, 236, 238, 244, 245, 247, 248

Immersive Technologies 105, 223, 224

Implicit Cognitive Vulnerability 403, 411

Instructional Design 1, 4, 13, 17, 19, 20, 24, 27, 30, 40, 42, 128, 131, 140, 141, 142, 152, 157, 160, 174, 224, 318, 345, 381, 391, 394, 415

Instructional Practices 18, 120, 123, 124, 125, 129, 130, 131, 141, 382, 446

Instructor Immediacy 410

Instructor-Student Rapport 289, 290, 291, 299, 300, 301, 302, 303, 304, 305, 306, 309

Interactive Activities 62, 134, 203, 317, 318, 321, 322, 331, 334, 339, 342, 343, 345, 349, 381, 405, 410

K

Kerala 289, 290, 291, 301, 302, 306, 310

Kudumbashree 289, 290, 291, 292, 301, 302, 303, 304, 305, 306, 307

L

Landscapes of Practice 317, 318, 322, 338, 339, 340, 341, 345, 353, 382, 401, 414

Learner Engagement 43, 53, 109, 136, 166, 187, 317, 318, 320, 321, 322, 334, 338, 339, 345, 385

Learning 2, 4, 8, 10, 11, 14, 17, 18, 19, 20, 21, 22, 23, 24, 25, 26, 27, 28, 29, 30, 31, 32, 33, 34, 35, 36, 37, 38, 39, 40, 41, 42, 43, 45, 46, 47, 48, 49, 50, 51, 52, 53, 54, 55, 56, 57, 58, 59, 60, 61, 62, 63, 64, 65, 66, 67, 68, 69, 70, 71, 72, 73, 74, 75, 76, 77, 78, 79, 80, 81, 82, 83, 84, 85, 86, 87, 88, 89, 90, 91, 92, 93, 94, 95, 96, 97, 98, 99, 100, 101, 103, 104, 105, 106, 107, 108, 109, 110, 111, 112, 113, 114, 115, 116, 119, 120, 123, 124, 125, 126, 127, 128, 129, 130, 131, 132, 133,

134, 135, 136, 137, 138, 139, 140, 141, 142, 143, 144, 145, 146, 147, 148, 149, 150, 151, 152, 153, 155, 156, 157, 158, 159, 160, 161, 162, 163, 164, 165, 166, 167, 168, 169, 170, 171, 172, 173, 174, 175, 176, 177, 178, 179, 180, 181, 182, 183, 184, 185, 186, 187, 188, 189, 190, 191, 192, 193, 194, 195, 196, 197, 198, 199, 200, 201, 202, 203, 205, 206, 207, 208, 209, 210, 211, 212, 213, 214, 215, 216, 217, 218, 219, 220, 221, 223, 224, 226, 227, 231, 232, 233, 238, 240, 241, 244, 245, 246, 247, 249, 253, 255, 258, 260, 261, 262, 263, 264, 265, 266, 267, 270, 271, 272, 277, 278, 279, 280, 281, 282, 283, 284, 286, 287, 289, 291, 292, 293, 294, 296, 297, 299, 300, 304, 306, 307, 308, 309, 310, 311, 312, 314, 317, 318, 319, 320, 321, 322, 323, 324, 325, 326, 327, 328, 329, 330, 331, 332, 333, 334, 335, 336, 337, 338, 339, 340, 341, 342, 343, 344, 345, 346, 347, 348, 349, 350, 351, 352, 353, 354, 356, 358, 360, 361, 370, 373, 374, 375, 376, 377, 378, 379, 380, 381, 382, 383, 384, 385, 390, 391, 392, 394, 395, 396, 397, 399, 400, 401, 402, 403, 404, 405, 406, 407, 409, 410, 411, 412, 413, 414, 415, 420, 421, 423, 424, 425, 428, 430, 431, 433, 434, 435, 436, 440, 441, 442, 443, 444, 445, 446, 447, 449, 450, 451, 452, 453, 454, 455, 456, 457, 458, 459, 460, 461, 465, 466, 467, 468, 469, 470, 471, 472, 473, 474, 475, 479, 480, 482, 483, 484, 485, 486, 488, 489, 490, 491, 492, 493, 494, 497, 498, 499, 500, 501, 502, 504, 506, 507, 508, 509, 510

Learning Analytics 70, 71, 72, 73, 74, 76, 77, 79, 80, 87, 88, 89, 90, 91, 92, 93, 103, 104, 105, 106, 107, 108, 109, 110, 111, 112, 113, 114, 115, 116, 312

Learning Design 17, 25, 26, 29, 30, 33, 42, 43, 45, 46, 47, 49, 60, 61, 62, 63, 64, 65, 95, 101, 145, 247, 289, 352, 379, 380, 381, 382, 383, 384, 385, 391, 392, 394, 395, 396, 399, 400, 401, 405, 406, 407, 409, 413, 414, 415

Learning Domains 270, 287

M

Metacognition 26, 30, 35, 52, 58, 75, 86, 106, 115, 133, 259, 287

Meta-cognitive Strategies 237

motives for emotion regulation 355, 360, 368, 369, 372

N

Narratives 60, 61, 62, 267, 343, 350, 385, 462

negative emotions 20, 23, 24, 29, 33, 58, 61, 83, 94, 128, 155, 159, 160, 161, 165, 166, 167, 168, 169, 170, 171, 172, 173, 175, 176, 179, 183, 193, 200, 201, 202, 292, 294, 295, 296, 298, 356, 367, 368, 370, 371, 373, 414, 422

O

Occupational Health and Safety 1, 2, 9

online 1, 14, 22, 24, 35, 40, 43, 48, 49, 51, 54, 55, 56, 63, 68, 75, 81, 83, 87, 88, 89, 91, 92, 93, 104, 105, 106, 107, 108, 109, 110, 111, 112, 113, 115, 116, 119, 120, 125, 126, 127, 128, 129, 130, 131, 132, 133, 134, 135, 136, 137, 138, 139, 140, 141, 142, 143, 145, 146, 147, 148, 149, 150, 151, 152, 155, 156, 157, 158, 159, 160, 161, 162, 163, 164, 165, 166, 167, 168, 169, 170, 171, 172, 173, 174, 175, 176, 177, 178, 180, 181, 182, 185, 186, 188, 189, 190, 191, 192, 193, 194, 195, 196, 197, 198, 199, 200, 201, 202, 203, 255, 261, 300, 308, 310, 311, 312, 313, 314, 317, 318, 319, 320, 321, 322, 323, 324, 325, 326, 327, 331, 332, 334,

335, 336, 337, 338, 340, 342, 343, 344, 345, 346, 347, 348, 349, 350, 351, 352, 353, 354, 361, 363, 374, 378, 380, 382, 383, 402, 410, 419, 425, 430, 432, 433, 435, 438, 440, 441, 442, 443, 444, 445, 446, 447, 452, 461, 467, 482, 485, 486, 488, 504, 509

Online Learning 24, 40, 43, 49, 55, 63, 75, 81, 83, 87, 91, 93, 105, 106, 111, 115, 119, 120, 125, 126, 127, 128, 129, 130, 131, 132, 134, 135, 136, 137, 139, 140, 142, 143, 145, 146, 147, 148, 149, 151, 152, 155, 156, 157, 158, 159, 160, 161, 162, 163, 164, 165, 166, 167, 168, 169, 171, 172, 173, 174, 175, 176, 177, 178, 181, 182, 185, 186, 190, 191, 193, 194, 195, 197, 198, 199, 200, 201, 202, 310, 318, 320, 321, 322, 323, 336, 337, 342, 346, 347, 349, 350, 351, 353, 374, 378, 380, 410, 425, 430, 440, 441, 442, 443, 444, 446, 509

Outcomes 1, 2, 7, 8, 9, 10, 11, 12, 13, 14, 19, 21, 22, 23, 24, 26, 27, 31, 32, 33, 34, 35, 37, 41, 42, 43, 46, 51, 56, 57, 58, 61, 63, 64, 65, 73, 76, 77, 79, 80, 88, 94, 95, 96, 98, 100, 113, 119, 121, 122, 123, 124, 125, 128, 129, 133, 135, 141, 152, 156, 158, 160, 162, 163, 165, 167, 168, 170, 171, 172, 173, 174, 175, 177, 178, 180, 182, 183, 185, 190, 193, 195, 201, 202, 226, 228, 243, 278, 283, 291, 292, 293, 294, 295, 296, 297, 298, 299, 302, 303, 305, 306, 307, 308, 309, 310, 311, 314, 331, 344, 358, 361, 370, 375, 379, 384, 385, 402, 403, 409, 424, 491

P

Pedagogy 14, 46, 49, 51, 52, 68, 97, 210, 220, 258, 279, 317, 318, 322, 338, 339, 340, 345, 350, 413

Performing 109, 135, 226, 235, 479, 480, 491

Personnel 97, 142, 220, 337, 396, 397, 398, 407, 408

positive education 437, 446, 447

positive emotions 20, 23, 24, 27, 29, 33, 36, 57, 58, 61, 92, 125, 157, 159, 160, 161, 162, 163, 164, 165, 166, 167, 169, 170, 171, 172, 173, 175, 178, 179, 182, 185, 196, 202, 292, 293, 294, 295, 296, 297, 298, 356, 370, 371

positive psychology 87, 108, 196, 219, 435, 436, 437, 443, 447

Prejudice 254, 281, 284, 287, 365, 368

preservice teachers 349, 447

Project-based Learning 48, 54, 56, 62, 447, 479, 480, 482, 483, 484

R

reflection 5, 10, 27, 31, 33, 48, 51, 52, 53, 58, 60, 94, 101, 126, 133, 137, 148, 153, 179, 180, 184, 185, 189, 190, 203, 210, 212, 214, 220, 244, 245, 258, 261, 262, 263, 265, 266, 267, 270, 278, 279, 280, 281, 282, 285, 287, 373, 380, 401, 421, 423, 430, 437, 453, 497

Reflexivity 259, 262, 263, 266, 267, 270, 278, 279, 280, 282, 287

Relationship Skills 26, 206, 207, 208, 213, 214, 217, 218, 421, 430, 450

Resilience 25, 32, 49, 90, 112, 123, 161, 163, 164, 165, 168, 173, 174, 175, 176, 179, 180, 188, 189, 191, 202, 211, 223, 228, 231, 236, 239, 304, 330, 426, 429, 430, 431, 434, 442, 445, 446, 447, 479, 480, 481

Responsible Decision Making 421, 430, 435

S

SafeMap 1, 4

SEL 25, 26, 57, 63, 148, 205, 206, 207, 208, 209, 213, 214, 216, 217, 218, 219, 421, 434, 435, 436, 441, 442, 444, 450, 451, 452, 453, 454, 455, 456, 458, 459, 460, 465, 466, 467, 468, 469, 470, 471, 472

Self-Awareness 26, 28, 30, 31, 34, 41, 57, 58, 60, 94, 120, 121, 123, 131, 132, 133, 134, 138, 141, 181, 206, 207, 208, 212, 213, 214, 217, 218, 295, 297, 373, 419, 421, 422, 430, 435, 439, 451, 456

self-efficacy 17, 21, 22, 23, 25, 26, 30, 35, 37, 38, 39, 42, 46, 49, 128, 139, 142, 147, 150, 161, 168, 175, 188, 191, 194, 201, 203, 223, 226, 227, 232, 233, 236, 238, 245, 246, 249, 292, 293, 294, 295, 298, 304, 311, 313, 314, 323, 324, 327, 329, 340, 353, 392, 402, 433, 439, 441

Self-Management 136, 137, 138, 141, 143, 153, 156, 165, 206, 208, 213, 214, 218, 421, 430, 435, 451

self-regulation 30, 31, 32, 35, 56, 92, 116, 120, 125, 155, 161, 164, 165, 171, 172, 174, 181, 190, 201, 203, 208, 282

Signature Pedagogies 288

Situational Awareness 223, 235, 245

Sjuzhet 59, 60, 61, 62, 63, 65

Social Awareness 134, 135, 138, 141, 206, 207, 208, 213, 214, 217, 218, 421, 430, 435, 451

Social-emotional development 421, 438

Social-Emotional Learning 28, 57, 63, 87, 114, 115, 143, 205, 206, 207, 208, 216, 217, 218, 219, 430, 431, 434, 435, 436, 440, 443, 444, 447, 449, 450, 451, 452, 453, 454, 456, 457, 458, 459, 460, 461, 465, 466, 467, 468, 469, 470, 471, 472, 473, 474, 475

social presence 129, 132, 133, 134, 152, 161, 169, 172, 186, 187, 191, 197, 435, 441, 443, 444, 446

T

teacher burnout 419, 421, 427, 431, 438, 439

Teacher Education 67, 145, 308, 311, 312, 314, 315, 377, 432, 440, 441, 442, 443, 444, 445, 447, 449, 451, 452, 453, 454, 467, 468, 470, 472

teacher preparation 421, 428, 445, 446, 452, 453, 455, 457

Teaching and Learning 28, 35, 51, 67, 69, 72, 74, 75, 78, 83, 94, 99, 100, 123, 143, 155, 162, 163, 278, 282, 283, 286, 312, 331, 345, 353, 380, 385, 400, 409, 414, 443, 444, 446, 447, 450

Training 1, 18, 22, 23, 25, 26, 28, 33, 34, 36, 37, 43, 48, 51, 55, 60, 64, 95, 97, 99, 100, 101, 115, 125, 135, 142, 144, 183, 188, 215, 216, 217, 221, 223, 224, 228, 230, 232, 233, 236, 237, 238, 239, 240, 241, 243, 244, 247, 249, 253, 255, 290, 295, 296, 298, 299, 306, 332, 333, 337, 341, 348, 349, 351, 352, 363, 373, 380, 409, 413, 415, 435, 436, 443, 444, 446, 453, 456, 471, 505, 506, 507

Transformative education 18, 29, 38

Tyler Cohen 485

V

Virtual Reality 62, 63, 109, 113, 223, 241, 243, 248, 249, 483

Visual 111, 261, 278, 281, 338, 363, 460, 491, 494, 495, 496, 497, 499, 503, 504